Which MBA?

16th edition

Making the right choice of executive education

George Bickerstaffe

PEARSON
Education

Pearson Education Limited

Edinburgh Gate, Harlow, Essex CM20 0JE

Website: http://www.pearsoned.co.uk

The Economist Intelligence Unit

The Economist Intelligence Unit is a specialist publisher serving companies establishing and managing operations across national borders. For over 50 years it has been a source of information on business developments, economic and political trends, government regulations and corporate practice worldwide.

The EIU delivers its information in four ways: through our digital portfolio, where our latest analysis is updated daily; through printed subscription products ranging from newsletters to annual reference works; through research reports; and by organising conferences and roundtables. The firm is a member of The Economist Group.

London	**New York**	**Hong Kong**
The Economist Intelligence Unit	The Economist Intelligence Unit	The Economist Intelligence Unit
15 Regent Street	The Economist Building	60/F, Central Plaza
London	111 West 57th Street	18 Harbour Road
SW1Y 4LR	New York	Wanchai
United Kingdom	NY 10019, US	Hong Kong
Tel: (44.20) 7830 1000	Tel: (1.212) 554 0600	Tel: (852) 2585 3888
Fax: (44.20) 7499 9767	Fax: (1.212) 586 1181/2	Fax: (852) 2802 7638
E-mail: london@eiu.com	E-mail: newyork@eiu.com	E-mail: hongkong@eiu.com

Website: http://www.eiu.com

Electronic delivery

This publication can be viewed by subscribing online at http://store.eiu.com

Copyright

ISBN 0273 69536 3

British Library Cataloguing in Publication Data.
A catalogue of this publication is available from the British Library.

Library of Congress Cataloging in Publication Data applied for.

The authors of EIU Research Reports are drawn from a wide range of professional and academic disciplines. All the information in the reports is verified to the best of the authors' and the publisher's ability, but neither can accept responsibility for loss arising from decisions based on these reports. Where opinion is expressed, it is that of the authors, which does not necessarily coincide with the editorial views of the Economist Intelligence Unit Limited or of The Economist Newspaper Limited.

10 9 8 7 6 5 4 3 2 1

08 07 06 05 04

Printed and bound in Great Britain by Ashford Colour Press Ltd., Gosport.

Contents

List of tables

Which MBA? © The Economist Intelligence Unit Limited 2004

The Lancaster MBA
"A life-changing experience"

Gill Hall, IBM

Join an elite group of high calibre international managers on a unique programme

One of only two UK Business Schools to be rated a 6-star (6*) centre of world class research in business and management.

An internationally acclaimed MBA - ranked in the Global Top 100 (Financial Times and the Economist). Ranked 1st in the world by the FT for the best mix of participants, and 17th in the world for value for money.

Our MBA develops longer-lasting benefits than conventional MBAs. We challenge conventional thinking. We integrate 'action learning', through consultancy and corporate placements. We focus on the skills needed for strong and effective leadership.

Opportunities for exchanges with other top international business schools

Full-time and Executive part-time modes

Scholarships available

Lancaster University
MANAGEMENT SCHOOL

Contact: +44 (0) 1524 594068
email: mba@lancaster.ac.uk

www.lums.lancs.ac.uk

EQUIS
ACCREDITED

"An extremely valuable and unforgettable experience"
Julia Fedoruchenko, DS&A Ltd

"The all-round skills are of real value"
Randall Zindler, CEO, Medair

"A major turning point in my career"
Amina Oyagbola Head, HR Strategy, Shell plc

K73053

Acknowledgements

We would like to thank all the business schools that filled in our lengthy questionnaire and encouraged their students and graduates to complete the separate questionnaire designed for them. Thanks, too, to those schools that made available for interviews their faculty, administrators and students during our editorial visits or took the time to visit the Economist Intelligence Unit offices in London. Lastly, we are grateful to all the students and graduates who contributed valuable comments on schools and programmes.

Preface

As well as its regular Economist Intelligence Unit rankings and descriptions of MBA programmes and business schools around the world, the 2004 edition of *Which MBA?* contains some innovative additions that greatly expand its coverage and usefulness to prospective students and anyone interested in business and management education. The first addition is essays from current and recent business school students and graduates describing their own experiences in taking various MBA programmes and executive education courses.

The second is information about executive education. For the first time we have included details of the executive education offerings of business schools (included in each school's directory entry from page 107), and Chapter 6 explores the executive education market, the types of courses offered, their utility, and present and future trends. As this chapter makes clear, there is a good reason for this innovation. The "shelf-life" of even the best MBA is necessarily limited, perhaps to as little as five years. Although the basic elements remain valid and the habits of thinking gained from an MBA will always be useful, the latest thinking and research can be digested only through continuing business education.

The last and perhaps most important addition is Chapter 1, which is based on an exclusive Economist Intelligence Unit online survey of senior executives around the world carried out during May and June 2004. The executives were asked for their views on what the managers of the future would need in terms of professional development, and the role management education can play in equipping them with the skills they will need. The results give a vivid insight into the future of management education from the manager's viewpoint as well as the skills that MBA students should be seeking to acquire during their time at business school. This chapter was written by Matthew Bishop, business editor of *The Economist*.

As always, as well as a comparative ranking of the 100 best full-time MBA programmes offered by business schools around the world, *Which MBA?* 2004 provides comprehensive descriptions of the business schools offering them. Each school entry contains essential data (faculty size, student intake and facilities, admission requirements and deadlines, tuition fees and likely accommodation costs) as well as comments on the school's history, present philosophy and future plans. In the directory section, schools are listed alphabetically by parent university (if applicable). For an interactive version of the rankings, visit www.which-mba.com.

The introductory chapters include the survey of senior executives, pointers on choosing a school, types of MBA and executive education programmes, the admissions process, taking the GMAT, financing your MBA, finding a job after graduation and a description of the methodology used to compile the ranking. Additional data on schools and programmes run throughout this guide.

We hope the information in the following pages and on the website will help you choose the business school and programme that will fulfil your ambitions.

George Bickerstaffe
July 2004

Part 1
Choosing a programme

Chapter 1

Which skills will tomorrow's leader need?

For the consumer of management education, this is the very best of times. Today's aspiring corporate big cheeses can choose from a greater variety of courses and programmes than ever, from the traditional full-time MBA to a wide variety of part-time and executive MBAs and other executive programmes, to in-house training provided by an employer. And with applications to business school currently going through one of their periodic downturns, at least in the US where an abundance of jobs has reduced the appeal of taking time out to study, educational institutions are doing all they can to attract customers, including upgrading the quality of their courses and thinking more creatively about what they teach.

But with so many options, how do you make the right choice? For those whose main objective is to network with other future corporate titans, there remains only one right decision: do a full-time MBA at one of the handful of global elite schools, such as Harvard, Stanford, Kellogg and Tuck in the US, or London Business School or INSEAD in Europe. For most people, however, making the right choice can be a demanding process, requiring extensive investigation into what different management courses provide and what new skills are most likely to help achieve those career ambitions.

What variety of management education works best has long been a matter on which opinions differ. But in recent years it has turned into a fierce debate, including among even the elite business schools, some of which have been embarrassed by the leading roles played by some of their alumni in the high-profile corporate failures and scandals of recent years. Did what was taught, or not taught, at business school to the likes of Enron's ex-chief executive Jeffrey Skilling (a Harvard MBA) or its chief financial officer, Andrew Fastow (Kellogg MBA), somehow contribute to that firm's spectacular collapse? Some business school academics fear so.

Certainly, there is evidence that, in more modest ways, business schools have helped to change the values of their students in a direction that is not unambiguously positive. In 2002, the Aspen Institute surveyed 2,000 MBA students and found that their values altered during the course. By the end, they cared less about customer needs and product quality and more about shareholder value. Increasingly, business schools think they ought to have a more clearly positive effect on their students.

But some critics are increasingly sceptical. In 2003, Booz Allen Hamilton, a consultancy, published an article deriding "cookie-cutter" MBAs that leave a big gap between what graduates offer and firms need. In a new book, *Managers not MBAs*, Henry Mintzberg, a professor at McGill University in Canada and a veteran management guru, complains that traditional MBA courses provide "specialised training in the functions of business, not general education in the practice of management". Students on these courses are typically too young and inexperienced, and they would do better learning the skills they need to be effective managers in the workplace than at school. And, he says, conventional MBA programmes ignore the fact that management is a craft, requiring energy and the use of intuition, not just an ability to analyse data and invent strategies.

Chapter 1
Which skills will tomorrow's leader need?

To put all this in perspective, and help you to make the right choice about management education, the Economist Intelligence Unit recently surveyed over 100 senior executives from
around the world, spanning medium to very large businesses. One clear message emerged:
for all the criticisms described above, the executives still value management education. Of
those surveyed, only 10% thought that managers could develop all the skills needed
through experience, and that training only had value as an employee benefit; 34% said that
management education is critical in building the knowledge and skills of managers; and the
rest thought it had at least some useful role to play in complementing what managers
learned through experience.

Table 1.1
What role does management education and training play in developing your company's best talent?
(%)

A manager can develop all of the skills he or she needs through experience, and management education and training is useful only because staff perceive it as a benefit	10
A manager can develop most of the skills he or she needs through experience, and the gaps can be plugged through education and training	28
A manager can develop some of the skills he or she needs through experience, and the rest can be developed through education and training	27
Management education and training is critical in building the knowledge and skills of managers	34

Over the next five years, 35% of the executives expected to make more use of management
education to train their best employees, and only 5% expected to make less use of it. Moreover, for all the increased debate about the usefulness of an MBA, 35% of the executives
said that business schools have the most important role to play in developing their executives, compared with 29% who said that it would be an in-house trainer.

Table 1.2
**Over the next five years, do you expect your company will rely less or more on executive education
(including MBAs) to train its best employees?**
(%)

Less	5
No change	59
More	35

Table 1.3
**Which type of provider do you believe has the most important role to play in developing executives at
your company?**
(%)

Business school	35
In-house trainer	29
Corporate university	14
Independent provider/consultant	22

For many people, the purpose of management education is to help them get a better—and,
ideally, better paying—job. Helpfully, as well as giving their vote of confidence in management education, the executives also identified the skills they are most looking for in their

Which MBA? © The Economist Intelligence Unit Limited 2004

future top managers. Incidentally, although most of the executives thought that the firm and the manager were equally responsible for equipping the manager with the necessary skills, only 7% thought that it was more the responsibility of the company, whereas 22% said it was primarily a matter to be dealt with by the manager himself or herself. If in doubt, then, it is best get the skills for yourself

What is top of the list of critical skills? The majority of executives said that honesty and integrity are critical, giving this category an importance rating of 86%, more than any other. Perhaps they would have said the same before the scandals at Enron and several other big firms, but it seems more likely that there is a new appreciation of such virtues in an era when senior executives are increasingly held responsible for the wrongdoing of their staff, and can find themselves facing costly lawsuits or even a long spell in jail.

Next on the list of critical qualities are excellent people skills, rated at 81% by executives, and communication skills, rated at 80%. Increasingly, firms want their talent to have the soft skills of leadership. A few years ago, during the technology boom when a bright idea was everything, a grasp of technology or financial engineering could take someone a long way. Now, a good understanding of technology is given just a 60% importance rating by the executives surveyed, and—perhaps surprisingly, given the corporate financial scandals of recent years—financial knowledge is rated at only 58%. Even less critical are previous managerial experience (57%) or management education (50%), no doubt because the executives expect their firms to provide plenty of both.

Table 1.4
Who is more responsible for equipping a manager with necessary skills?
(%)

The company	7
The manager himself or herself	22
Equal responsibility	71

Table 1.5
Which characteristics does your company currently look for in its most talented young managers?
(importance rating, %)

Honesty and integrity	86
Excellent people skills	81
Communication skills	80
Innovativeness/openness to new ideas	78
Strategic vision	75
Deep knowledge of market needs and operations	71
Dealmaking ability	63
International knowledge/the ability to manage across cultures	63
A good understanding of technology	60
Functional knowledge of various parts of the business	59
Financial knowledge	58
Management experience	57
Management education	50

Chapter 1
Which skills will tomorrow's leader need?

Table 1.6
In five years' time, do you believe these characteristics will have gained or decreased in importance as the qualities required of potential company leaders?
(%)

	Decreased	No change	Increased
Honesty and integrity	3	57	41
Excellent people skills	2	41	57
Communication skills	0	51	49
Innovativeness/openness to new ideas	1	29	70
Strategic vision	3	32	66
Deep knowledge of market needs and operations	2	52	46
Dealmaking ability	5	58	37
International knowledge/the ability to manage across cultures	2	36	62
A good understanding of technology	3	54	43
Functional knowledge of various parts of the business	6	68	26
Financial knowledge	3	70	28
Management experience	5	71	24
Management education	6	69	25

This emphasis on the softer skills is unlikely to be a short-lived overreaction to the lack of such skills revealed by the recent corporate scandals. On the contrary, looking ahead five years, the executives surveyed mostly expect the skills they value now to become even more important: 57% think that people skills will matter even more than they do today; 49% think so about good communication; and 41% think so about honesty and integrity. (In each case, fewer than 3% think they will become less important.)

Perhaps because they are already considered so important, an even higher proportion of the executives predict growing importance for certain currently undervalued qualities. As memories of the recession and corporate rebuilding efforts of the early years of this decade (hopefully) become ever more distant, firms will increasingly be seeking to exploit fresh opportunities, just as they were in the go-go late 1990s. Thus 70% of the executives say that innovativeness and openness to new ideas will matter more in five years than they do now.

There were two other high scorers: 66% of the executives reckon that strategic vision will become increasingly important, and 62% international knowledge and the ability to manage across cultures. Both predictions are consistent with some underlying trends. The process of globalisation shows no sign of slowing; indeed, it may well accelerate. The political backlash against moving rich-country jobs offshore to places such as India seems to be running out of steam. And rather than operate separate businesses in lots of countries, global firms are increasingly seeking to integrate their many operations around the world seamlessly: hence the need for international knowledge and the ability to cross cultures. As for strategic insight, this is currently finding its way back into the executive toolkit after a period in which it seemed obsolete as firms concentrated on their core businesses, often doing nothing more imaginative than trying to squeeze costs. Now, as the title of one recent management book puts it, firms are looking to move *Beyond the core*, and this will require managers with strategic insight.

If knowing the likely demand for different skills is helpful in deciding which management education option to choose, knowing their supply-side forecast may be even more so. The skills most worth acquiring are those likely to be in shortest supply. Asked to identify the main skills shortages among their current crop of up-and-coming talent, executives cited strategic vision as being most rare, followed by international knowledge and the ability to manage across cultures.

Table 1.7
Which of the following skills are most prevalent and which most lacking among your company's up-and-coming talent?
(0 – extremely rare, 100 = extremely prevalent)

Honesty and integrity	64
A good understanding of technology	56
Functional knowledge of various parts of the business	54
Communication skills	54
Excellent people skills	54
Innovativeness/openness to new ideas	52
Deep knowledge of market needs and operations	50
Management experience	50
Dealmaking ability	49
Financial knowledge	48
International knowledge/the ability to manage across cultures	42
Strategic vision	36

Table 1.8
In which functional areas do you see the greatest shortfalls in managerial talent over the next five years?
(%)

Strategic vision	57
Excellent people skills	41
International knowledge/the ability to manage across cultures	28
Deep knowledge of market needs and operations	26
Innovativeness/openness to new ideas	25
Communication skills	24
A good understanding of technology	19
Honesty and integrity	17
Management experience	16
Functional knowledge of various parts of the business	16
Dealmaking ability	16
Financial knowledge	16

Chapter 1
Which skills will tomorrow's leader need?

Still, for the most part, executives expect the supply of critical skills to rise to meet the growing demand for them over the next five years. But there are some notable exceptions. Some 57% of the executives surveyed expect that over the next five years there will be a significant shortfall of managers with strategic insight; 41% think there will be a significant lack of people with excellent people skills; and 28% expect a shortage of people with international knowledge and the ability to manage across cultures. More encouragingly—or, perhaps, wishfully—only 17% of the executives think there will be a shortfall of managers with honesty and integrity.

Strategy has long been one of the core subjects taught by business schools, particularly on MBA programmes. It is something they are good at. Indeed, it is somewhat curious that the executives surveyed expect a shortage of future managers with strategic insight, given that this is, on the face of it, fairly easy to fix by sending up-and-coming managers on an MBA or executive MBA. Such programmes are likely to be increasingly useful in providing international knowledge and teaching students about cross-cultural management. Business schools are rapidly hiring more faculty from abroad and forming partnerships with foreign schools so that students can spend at least some of their course actually living and studying in another culture.

Table 1.9
Which kind of management education is best at delivering the following benefits, in your view?
(%)

	MBA/EMBA	Executive education	In-house training
Analytical skills	62	30	8
Leadership skills	29	50	21
Interpersonal skills	24	44	32
Motivated employees	18	35	47
Operational knowledge	18	15	68
Compliance awareness	16	30	54
Awareness of cultural values of the firm	7	9	84

The executives surveyed reckon that MBA and executive MBA programmes do just one thing outstandingly well: 62% said they were far better than the alternatives in teaching analytical skills. Next come teaching leadership skills (29%) and interpersonal skills (24%), in each case a lower score than that given to other sorts of executive programmes (50% and 44% respectively). How interesting, then, that business schools are increasingly putting leadership and other soft, unanalytical subjects such as social responsibility and ethics at the heart of their MBA programmes. Will they be able to improve their ratings in these areas, or—in the process of trying to do so—simply sacrifice some of the edge they currently have in teaching analytical skills?

Courses in leadership—a subject until recently largely left to schools like Harvard and Wharton—have become ubiquitous at business schools, even though it is quite possible that good leaders are simply born that way and use skills that cannot be taught. At some schools, students can receive executive coaching to help them hone their people and other soft skills. Many new courses have been launched in which students are required to work in teams in order to learn to collaborate with each other. In at least one business school, MBA students are even taught stand-up comedy in order to improve how they communicate.

About the survey

During May and June 2004 the Economist Intelligence Unit conducted an online survey of senior executives asking them their views on what they thought the manager of the future would look like and the role management education would play in equipping future managers with the skills they need. Some 117 senior executives participated in the survey, including C-level executives (CEO, CFO, etc), senior vice-presidents and directors in a variety of functional areas. There was a wide industry spread, including manufacturing, professional services and tourism. The annual revenue of the companies involved ranged from under US$500,000 to more than US$8bn.

But nothing is booming in business schools as much as the teaching of ethics, and in no subject is it less clear whether anything of value is being imparted to the student. Most business schools include an ethics course as a core subject in their MBA, although Columbia Business School in New York aspires to discuss ethics in every course rather than teach the subject separately. The University of Maryland's business school even takes students to visit white-collar criminals in prison. Whether any of this will mean that business-school graduates, faced with enormous temptations, will be more likely to resist, remains to be seen. Tellingly, though, some 54% of the executives surveyed reckon that the form of management education best able to teach compliance awareness (a fairly practical aspect of ethics) is in-house training, compared with just 16% who reckon that business school is best.

One last point arises from the survey. Asked which forms of management education have delivered good value for their firm in developing talent, in-house training came out top, with the MBA following. But the executives were much less upbeat about executive courses, especially "open" ones where students from many firms mix together. This lack of enthusiasm may have little to do with the quality of education on such courses, and everything to do with the fact that open courses have acquired a reputation for providing an excellent opportunity for a firm's up-and-coming managers to network themselves into a better job elsewhere. So what is the moral? In choosing what sort of management education to pursue, it is certainly useful to know what senior executives are looking for: they are potential customers for your skills, after all. But, even so, it is important to remember that their interests are not necessarily your interests.

Table 1.10
Which of the following courses deliver good value in developing talent at your firm?
(0 = very little value, 100 = excellent value)

In-house training	67
Executive programmes (tailored)	59
MBA	59
EMBA	52
Executive programmes (open)	50
Executive programmes (consortium)	44

This chapter was written by Matthew Bishop, business editor of *The Economist*.

D V RSITY

Without Instituto de Empresa many concepts would not make sense

-**International MBA**
-Full-time programme (thirteen months)
-82% International students
 (over 65 nationalities on campus)
-1 annual intake in November

-**International Executive MBA**
-Part-time programme (thirteen months)
-Three intensive two week periods
 (Madrid - Miami - Madrid) and two
 online periods of six months each
-90% International Students
-2 annual intakes (June and November)

Diversity, a single word that defines the IE learning environment. Maximising synergies by adeptly managing multicultural work groups - a skill that is found at the very heart of IE's MBA programmes.

Based in the heart of Madrid, IE programmes are taught in a truly international environment - skillfully integrating academic excellence with practical business application. This excellence enables IE to shed new light on many of the most important issues currently faced in the business world.

Chapter 2

Full-time MBAs

An MBA can be studied full-time or part-time (including executive MBA programmes and other variations) or by distance learning. All have advantages and drawbacks. This chapter concentrates on full-time programmes. Chapter 3 looks at part-time programmes, Chapter 4 at distance learning, Chapter 5 at executive MBAs and Chapter 6 at shorter executive education programmes.

Advantages and drawbacks

Full-time programmes offer a "total immersion" in the "MBA experience". There are few distractions from the learning process and the atmosphere is stimulating. Access to teaching faculty is usually good and, as the accepted cliché is that you learn at least as much from fellow students as from professors, having easy and frequent opportunities to meet and talk with classmates is a big advantage.

There are drawbacks to a two-year programme in terms of forgone salary (see below) and time out of the job market, but the attractions are considerable. Many students say that two years allow more time for reflection about the future and more opportunity for in-depth study. There is also less stress than on a shorter programme because more time is available, especially for job searching.

It is worth noting that full-time programmes form the basis of the Economist Intelligence Unit ranking and they represent the only programme type that delivers all four elements in the ranking: career opportunities; increased salary; networking; and personal development/education experience. Part-time and executive MBA students are mainly sponsored so the career/salary issues are less important, and distance-learning students, by definition, find networking difficult.

This is an important point. Networking is one of the key benefits students look for in an MBA programme (see Table 2.1). This is much easier on a full-time programme. As one of our student diarists points out (see the student's perspective on page 28), full-time students, particularly at a campus-based school, generally work and play together and often form life-long friendships.

Of course, networks exist on other types of programme. Part-time students, for example, spend large amounts of time together and establish friendships as do EMBA students. But the experience is on a slightly lesser scale: less intensive and perhaps less long-lasting.

Chapter 2
Full-time MBAs

Table 2.1
Why did you decide to study for an MBA degree?

Full-time students (%)[a]	
To open new career opportunities	37
Personal development	22
To increase salary	14
To further current career	12
Educational experience	9
Potential to network	6
Company advice or requirement	1

[a] Importance accorded by students to each factor.

Full-time options (one-year, two-year)

Although they all carry the label "full-time", such programmes last for an astonishing variety of periods: two years, one year or less, or something in between. Two-year full-time programmes, which are the norm in the US, are run over four semesters (or sometimes eight mini-semesters) of about 13–14 weeks each in the winter and spring of each year. (Which means they do not actually last two years in total teaching time, just two calendar years overall.) Variations on the semester system include three periods, variously known as trimesters, terms or quarters, in each of the two years.

There is much greater variety outside the US. Some leading schools, such as London Business School and IESE in Barcelona, follow a two-year style programme. At INSEAD in France and IMD in Switzerland programmes last for less than a year. At Bocconi in Milan, the full-time programme lasts 13 months; at HEC in Paris it takes 16 months; and at Hong Kong University of Science and Technology it takes 18 months.

Even in the US there has been some tinkering with programmes to reduce the time taken to gain an MBA. A number of US business schools, such as Notre Dame (Mendoza), Florida (Warrington) and Emory (Goizueta), offer accelerated one-year tracks for students who have studied business or related degrees at undergraduate level. Students take a short top-up course in business fundamentals during the summer and then go straight into the second year. However, there are no signs yet that any of the top-ranked American schools, with the exception of Pittsburg (Katz), are about to switch to one-year programmes. Indeed, Katz has introduced a much more traditional two-year programme alongside its long-running one-year European-style MBA.

The classic two-year programme

Generally "core" courses (the fundamentals of business, typically including finance, financial and managerial accounting, human resources management, information management, macroeconomics and microeconomics, marketing, organisational behaviour, production and operations management, and quantitative analysis) are taught during the first year of a two-year programme, although increasingly schools like to offer one or two electives in the first year to allow earlier specialisation. The second year often begins with a compulsory integrative (or "capstone") course, often based on business strategy, designed to pull together the first year's work. But generally students pursue their own interests or career objectives through taking optional subjects, or electives. The longer the course, the more time students have to devote to these. Most programmes also include in-company project work and softer elements such as leadership, interpersonal skills and general personal development, either as courses in their own right or as parallel workshops and seminars. Such two-year programmes, however, only occasionally include the project-based thesis that is a feature of many one-year programmes, particularly in the UK.

This mixture of a required core and a range of electives (which is typical of virtually all MBA programmes) allows students considerable freedom to design an MBA closely tailored to their personal interests and career objectives. The long summer vacation, modelled on university practice, is traditionally the time for summer jobs, or internships, which are a means of gaining company experience. In theory this is not compulsory (although some schools now make internships a required and assessed part of their programme) and students can just go on holiday; in any case few jobs last the whole vacation.

However, internships are now a crucial element in a two-year programme, particularly for a student's career search. Many recruiters expect students to have served an internship with them if they want to be offered a job on graduation. As a result, most schools, especially in North America, put almost as much effort into helping students find internships as helping them find a full-time job after graduation. This is one development that has discouraged US schools from shortening their programmes through continuous teaching during the summer months.

A 2003 survey by the Graduate Management Admissions Council (GMAC) found that 74% of recruiters offered full-time posts to MBA interns before interviewing other job candidates.

The one-year-plus programme

Although so-called one-year programmes vary considerably in length, there is no doubt that they are extremely intensive. They follow the same core/elective framework, but because of time constraints the range of electives offered is frequently limited. (Some schools, such as Cranfield in the UK and others highlighted in the directory, do offer an extensive range of electives, however.) In addition, some schools, especially in the UK, include a lengthy in-company or research project that also restricts the time allocated to teaching; in many, Edinburgh and Leeds for example, the final quarter of the year is taken up by off-campus research and thesis writing. The intense pressure of a one-year course is a good preparation for business life, where time management and setting priorities are essential skills, although the first year of a two-year programme can be just as gruelling.

Proponents of one-year programmes argue that the time spent face-to-face with teaching staff differs little from two-year programmes, but their opponents respond that one year is not long enough for issues to be covered comprehensively or in depth.

What should be in an MBA programme

Although the fundamentals of MBA programmes have remained remarkably constant over the years, business schools and MBA programme directors are far from immune from fads and fashions. At the end of the 20th century, for example, they reacted speedily to the dotcom boom, hastily assembling courses on e-business and entrepreneurship and spending a great deal of money to create incubators that would help students develop and market their own companies.

However, there are certain elements that must be present to make an MBA. They include initial functional or core courses (such as finance, marketing and economics) and specialist analytical techniques (mainly statistics), followed by more advanced courses or electives in one or more of the core areas. Soft skills may be part of the core courses or taught in supplementary seminars and workshops. This is essentially an American model (dating from the 1950s and earlier), aimed at enabling a general manager to understand the work of functional specialists and how the various activities fit into the business as a whole. Elective courses can produce specialists, but they will be specialists who can understand the other functions of management.

There are wide variations on this theme and experiments with new approaches are widespread. The list below is a checklist of what an MBA programme should ideally contain. Although developed by the Economist Intelligence Unit, this is not dissimilar from the criteria used by accreditation bodies such as AACSB International, the Association of MBAs (AMBA) and the European Foundation for Management Development (EQUIS).

Checklist for an MBA programme

The programme should ideally contain the following:
- Pre-programme courses on quantitative methods, computing and mathematics, for students not already skilled in these areas.
- An orientation programme at the start of the first term to meet other students and members of the faculty, and for team-building exercises.
- Solid grounding in core courses for general management.
- Waivers for existing skills (these are opposed by some schools).
- A wide choice of electives, but they should allow in-depth specialisation. Some courses outside the business school (for example, in university departments) should be allowed and encouraged.
- Good international content, for example: course material, the number of foreign students and teachers, visits to foreign companies, the opportunity for language tuition and exchanges with foreign schools.
- Reasonable emphasis on soft skills.
- A good range of company projects.

The school should also provide the following:
- Good teaching skills and research and library facilities.
- A satisfactory programme of senior executives as guest speakers, "executives in residence" and others.
- Open doors to members of faculty.
- An administration willing to respond to student concerns.
- Formal help with finding accommodation.
- Excellent careers services, including training in interview skills.
- A good and active network of alumni.

Cost

Counting the cost

Studying for an MBA is expensive; and studying full time is most expensive of all. The full-time two-year MBA programme at Dartmouth College (Tuck) in the US, for example, costs US$36,390 per year, the 16-month full-time programme at HEC in Paris costs €35,000 (US$39,772), and the 13-month programme at IE in Spain costs €36,900 (US$41,932). These figures are just what the schools charge for tuition. You will also have to find the cash for rent, books and food—all without the comfort of a regular salary cheque.

There are some general points about the cost of an MBA that are worth considering. For example, in the US, business schools that are part of state universities can be considerably cheaper than private institutions, with little effect on quality. Canadian schools also generally have lower than average tuition fees and offer good value for money. Most schools in Europe are cheaper than their North American counterparts (largely because they have shorter programmes), although there are exceptions. Even so, any good programme will be expensive and will represent a significant investment in personal terms. Schools with less prestige, but often excellent programmes, can be cheaper. Furthermore, different ways of taking an MBA can significantly affect the total price; for example, distance learning is generally cheaper than part-time, which, in turn, is usually cheaper than full-time.

At many schools charges vary according to the origins of students. Foreign and (in North America) out-of-state students can expect to pay more. In Europe, the differentiation is often between residents and non-residents of the EU. The rationale is borrowed from the undergraduate system, where the argument is that if taxpayers are being called upon to subsidise studies, the benefit should be focused on local students, not all-comers. This is an odd argument since in most countries postgraduate study is rarely subsidised. However, it should be noted that in the US state residence may be awarded after one year to American nationals and that the EU now includes 25 countries.

Costs for full-time students break down into three areas: tuition; living expenses; and forgone earnings. Note that tuition may not always include other business school expenses such as textbooks, fees for the use of a gym and so on.

Tuition

Tuition costs can vary greatly between schools. At Northwestern University (Kellogg), for example, tuition fees per year are currently US$34,314. Canada is traditionally cheaper than the US and at McGill University in Montreal, tuition for foreign students is C$20,000 (US$14,286) per year. McGill charges residents of Quebec state just C$1,668 (US$1,191) per year and other Canadians C$4,173 (US$2,980) per year. The Ohio State University (Fisher) charges in-state residents US$13,365 and others US$24,846.

Although tuition in Europe has traditionally been somewhat cheaper, the current weakness of the US dollar means that the comparative cost has risen. This means that, at the top schools, the cost of a one-year European MBA can approach that of two-year US one. At INSEAD in France, for example, total tuition is €43,500 (US$49,432) and at IMD in Lausanne Swfr75,000 (US$55,556). The total tuition cost for the two-year London Business School programme is currently £41,970 (US$68,803), matching schools such as Pennsylvania (Wharton) and Chicago.

Elsewhere, the National University of Singapore's business school charges non-residents S$24,000 (US$13,793) for its MBA, and the cost for the total MBA programme at Melbourne in Australia is A$48,000 (US$31,169).

Living expenses

For full-time students, tuition costs are only the beginning. They also have to find accommodation and fund their living expenses, and some may have their families with them. Accommodation costs vary according to location. For example, the University of California at Berkeley (Haas) estimates (for a nine-month period) housing and utilities US$8,570, food/subsistence US$4,396, books and supplies US$2,500, personal US$2,762 and transport US$1,274. Health insurance for students and any family members will be in addition to this.

In the UK, Lancaster University Management School, which is not based in the most expensive part of the country, estimates that students should add as much as £7,350 (US$12,049) to tuition fees, which breaks down as: accommodation £2,700 (US$4,426) on-campus or £3,400 (US$5,574) off-campus; food/ subsistence £2,500 (US$4,098); books, stationery, clothes, local travel, entertainment £1,500 (US$2,459).

Other expenses that need to be considered include networking (going for meals or drinks with other students or contacts), exchanges, which may include spending time in expensive European cities or the US, and simple things such as photocopying and printing, which are often charged to students as additional costs.

Table 2.2
Accommodation costs around the world,[a] 2004

City	Three-room furnished apartment (per month)	Four-room furnished apartment (per month)
Europe		
Amsterdam	€1,100 (US$1,250)	€1,400 (US$1,591)
Barcelona	€840 (US$955)	€962 (US$1,093)
Brussels	€900 (US$1,023)	€1095 (US$1,244)
Dublin	€1,100 (US$1,250)	€1,300 (US$1,477)
Geneva	Swfr2,500 (US$1,852)	Swfr2,800 (US$2,074)
Helsinki	€650 (US$739)	€945 (US$1,074)
London	£1,176 (US$1,928)	£1,900 (US$3,115)
Lyon	€575 (US$653)	€680 (US$773)
Madrid	€826 (US$939)	€1,245 (US$1,415)
Manchester	£650 (US$1,066)	£895 (US$1,467)
Milan	€1,096 (US$1,245)	€1,300 (US$1,477)
Oslo	Nkr7,600 (US$1,073)	Nkr9,500 (US$1,342)
Paris	€1,900 (US$2,159)	€2,300 (US$2,614)
North America		
Atlanta	US$1,000	US$1,200
Boston	US$2,225	US$2,500
Chicago	US$1,550	US$2,225
Cleveland	US$750	US$1,110
Detroit	US$1,250	US$1,450
Houston	US$2,000	US$2,400
Los Angeles	US$1,810	US$2,300
Minneapolis	US$1,300	US$1,800
Montreal	C$1,200 (US$857)	C$1,700 (US$1,214)
New York	US$5,000	US$5,500
Pittsburgh	US$700	US$1,000
San Francisco	US$2,400	US$3,000
Toronto	C$1,400 (US$1,000)	C$2,400 (US$1,714)
Vancouver	C$1,325 (US$946)	C$2,500 (US$1,786)
Washington, DC	US$1,700	US$1,850
Asia and Australasia		
Hong Kong	HK$38,000 (US$4,878)	HK$60,000 (US$7,702)
Melbourne	A$1,700 (US$1,104)	A$2,300 (US$1,494)
Perth	A$1,325 (US$860)	A$1,550 (US$1,006)
Shanghai	Rmb12,000 (US$1,449)	Rmb24,000 (US$2,899)
Singapore	S$2,900 (US$1,667)	S$5,100 (US$2,931)
Sydney	A$1,700 (US$1,214)	A$3,250 (US$2,321)

[a] Moderate cost accommodation taken from the *Worldwide Cost of Living Survey*, June 2004, The Economist Intelligence Unit.

Most schools go to considerable lengths to ensure students are aware of the financial burden they face, although they say the real problem for many students is not so much the expense of an MBA but living on a tight budget after a number of years in well-paid jobs. And because many assume that their earnings will increase considerably after graduation, there is a temptation to spend money. The cost of forgone earnings should not be underestimated. These can add up to well over the equivalent of US$50,000 a year. It is no surprise, therefore, that a typical MBA student on a full-time, two-year programme can end up with debts of more than US$100,000 by the end of the programme.

Chapter 2
Full-time MBAs

The financial rewards

Business schools say that they make little money out of MBA students. They argue that in many ways MBA programmes, particularly full-time programmes, are "loss leaders", essential to the reputation of a school; the real revenue comes from premium-priced executive education programmes and courses. In the end, though, business schools charge what the market will bear, and there is little indication that high costs deter students. Applications are much more likely to be affected by more general issues such as the state of the economy. MBA students are also quite capable of working out that an MBA is an investment and that the return, in terms of increased salary after graduation, is good enough to justify the outlay.

For example, Table 2.3 shows the average starting salaries for MBA graduates reported by a number of schools. (Further details can be found in the comparative tables in the Appendix.) Given the state of the world economy in the first years of the 21st century, these do not show huge rises compared with previous years. Even so, they are not insignificant. Graduates from leading North American schools, for example, can expect to earn well over US$90,000 a year plus bonuses (though these, too, have declined). Indeed, the top three schools report six-figure base salaries. In Europe, the overall figures are slightly lower, but the top three schools report higher six-figure base salaries (in US$).

In its 2003 annual Global MBA Graduate Survey of MBA students the Graduate Management Admissions Council found that the typical MBA graduate was expecting a mean salary on graduation of US$75,000 (exactly the same as in 2002). The typical mean undergraduate starting salary of US$50,000 is higher than the 2002 survey figure of US$41,000, representing a decrease on the premium offered by an MBA degree from US$34,000 to US$25,000.

Table 2.3
Average starting salaries of recent graduates from selected schools[a]

Europe	Salary (US$)	North America	Salary (US$)	Asia & Australasia	Salary (US$)
Ashridge	177,049	Stanford	96,000	Macquarie	85,416
Henley	127,869	Harvard	94,308	Australian GSM	78,064
IMD	123,000	Virginia (Darden)	90,180	Melbourne	66,883
Warwick	109,977	Columbia	89,091	International University of Japan	60,366
Oxford (Saïd)	103,279	MIT (Sloan)	88,217	Queensland	54,256
Strathclyde	98,361	Northwestern (Kellogg)	88,000	Hong Kong UST	45,154
IESE	97,492	Dartmouth (Tuck)	86,736	Singapore	39,714
City (Cass)	95,007	Chicago	85,000	Nanyang	37,632
HEC, Paris	93,436	UCLA (Anderson)	85,000	Indian Institute (Ahmedabad)	33,439
London	92,566	Duke (Fuqua)	85,000	Chinese University of Hong Kong	25,475
NIMBAS	92,500	Michigan	85,000		
Cranfield	91,803	Pennsylvania (Wharton)	85,000		
Dublin (Trinity)	90,909	Penn State (Smeal)	84,857		
Theseus	90,909	California at Berkeley (Haas)	84,345		
Aston	90,164	New York (Stern)	83,439		

Note: Local currencies converted using average exchange rates for 2003: US$1 = A$1.54, €0.88, HK$7.79, £0.61, S$1.74, Y115.96.
[a] Data supplied by schools; not available for all schools.

Choosing a school

The most important factors when choosing a business school, according to the Economist Intelligence Unit's survey of students and graduates for *Which MBA?* 2004 are reputation, programme content, location, the quality of the teaching faculty and a school's published ranking position. There are many other criteria, too, and naturally the importance of factors varies from student to student; for example, location is weighted with less importance in North America than it is in Europe, where there are more language and cultural hurdles.

Table 2.4
How did you choose the school where you are taking or took your MBA?
(full-time students, %)[a]

	World	Europe	North America	Asia & Australasia
Reputation of school	35	35	35	36
Content of programme	16	16	16	12
Location	11	13	10	12
Quality of teaching faculty	11	10	11	13
Published ranking position	11	10	11	9
Tuition and living costs	5	4	4	6
Teaching methods	4	4	4	2
Friend's recommendation	3	3	3	2
Careers services record	2	1	2	2
Starting salary of graduates	2	2	2	3
Published guides	1	1	1	0

[a] Importance accorded by students to each factor.

The results in Table 2.4 show the overwhelming importance of a school's reputation. Careers services and starting salaries, according to our survey, play a remarkably small part in attracting students. Why this should be so is unclear, since MBA students complain vociferously if they feel that these areas are underperforming. It may reflect a growing acceptance that even the best careers office cannot promise, let alone guarantee, a job.

Based on our research, we have selected a number of criteria that are frequently considered by students. Of course, other factors not mentioned here might be more significant to some individuals.

Programme

The elements that need to be included in a good MBA programme, including the distinction between core and elective subjects, projects and so on, are discussed in the box on page 14. You can usually get this information from schools' websites and brochures. But it is important to look carefully at the precise details of the programme you are interested in. Students' views on their programmes, according to our survey, are set out in Table 2.5. The results are based on questions covering areas such as the content and structure of the programme, the range of electives, the teaching quality and practical relevance.

Chapter 2
Full-time MBAs

Table 2.5
Student and graduate ratings of programme content

School	%	School	%
Chicago	96	HEC, Paris	91
Pennsylvania (Wharton)	96	Cornell (Johnson)	90
Northwestern (Kellogg)	94	Indian Institute (Ahmedabad)	90
Glasgow	93	London	90
Michigan	93	Washington St Louis (Olin)	90
MIT (Sloan)	93	York (Schulich)	90
Cranfield	92	New York (Stern)	89
Harvard	92	Virginia (Darden)	89
Stanford	92	Yale	89
Carnegie Mellon (Tepper)	91	Vanderbilt (Owen)	88

Note. These figures are derived from our survey of students and alumni; caution should be used when interpreting them.

Faculty

The quality of a school's faculty—teachers and research staff—is the foundation of its reputation. Their abilities and qualifications are one of the best indicators of a school's standing. Faculty are also prime marketing tools and are crucial in attracting good students and corporate support.

Table 2.6
What students think of the faculty: student rating by region
(full-time students, %)[a]

	World	Europe	North America	Asia & Australasia
Teaching ability	85	81	87	80
Attitude and receptiveness/approachability	90	84	92	84
Leading-edge research/capability/knowledge	84	80	87	78

[a] Importance accorded by students to each factor.

Really good academic staff who can combine original and innovative thinking, a realistic grasp of corporate issues, and the skill to impart their knowledge and enthusiasm to their students are hard to come by. A shortage of good young business faculty is currently causing problems for a number of schools eager to recruit them and is driving up academic salaries.

As well as their own faculty members, many schools also play host to visiting lecturers from other schools (sometimes as a prelude to poaching them), practising executives and others, normally known as visiting and adjunct faculty, who bring fresh knowledge and perspectives into the classroom.

Table 2.7
Student and graduate ratings of faculty

School	%	School	%
Harvard	97	Dartmouth (Tuck)	92
Stanford	95	New York (Stern)	92
Pennsylvania (Wharton)	94	Virginia (Darden)	92
Yale	94	California at Berkeley (Haas)	91
Carnegie Mellon (Tepper)	93	Ohio (Fisher)	91
Chicago	93	Washington St Louis (Olin)	91
Cornell (Johnson)	93	Glasgow	90
Indiana (Kelley)	93	Maryland (Smith)	90
Michigan	93	North Carolina (Kenan-Flagler)	90
Northwestern (Kellogg)	93	Queen's	90

Note. These figures are derived from our survey of students and alumni; caution should be used when interpreting them.

Culture

Differences between MBA programmes and schools boil down to what can be called their culture. The experiences offered by, say, China Europe International Business School (CEIBS) in Shanghai and the University of Virginia (Darden) in the US differ much more than simple geography. They reflect the schools' culture, that all-pervading quality that stems from a stated purpose, history, staff, students, business environment and so on. A school's prevailing culture may not be easy to assess, but students consistently point out how important it can be to the overall MBA experience. The editorial comments in the directory indicate the more important cultural highlights.

Nationality has a powerful, but not always simple, bearing on a school's culture, and it is discussed fully below. There are many other significant factors. For example, all business schools encourage teamwork and most either suggest or require that some (often a great deal of) work is done in small groups. But schools generally divide into two groups: the competitive, where students actively compete with each other to get good grades; and the co-operative, where students encourage and help each other. Both kinds exist in all countries, although there is a strong trend towards trying to establish a co-operative culture. (At least, most schools now find it hard to describe themselves as "competitive".) Of course, a vital ingredient of the culture is the students themselves. In our survey we asked students to assess their own classmates. The highest scores are listed in Table 2.8, and a breakdown by question and by region is given in Table 2.9.

Chapter 2
Full-time MBAs

Table 2.8
Student and graduate ratings of quality of student body

School	%	School	%
Stanford	98	Columbia	93
Dartmouth (Tuck)	96	Cranfield	93
Harvard	96	Duke (Fuqua)	93
IMD	96	INSEAD	93
Northwestern (Kellogg)	96	UCLA (Anderson)	93
Pennsylvania (Wharton)	96	Virginia (Darden)	93
Michigan	94	Emory (Goizueta)	91
MIT (Sloan)	94	London	91
Yale	94	Oxford (Saïd)	91
California at Berkeley (Haas)	93	Queen's	91

Note. These figures are derived from our survey of students and alumni; caution should be used when interpreting them.

Table 2.9
What students think of the quality of the student body

(%)[a]

	World	Europe	North America	Asia & Australasia
Esprit de corps	89	87	91	82
Quality of fellow students	86	82	87	80
Work experience	84	82	86	76

[a] Importance accorded by students to each factor.

Size

Like culture, size is often overlooked when prospective students are weighing up different business schools. But it can have a huge influence on the experience of taking an MBA. As with culture, school size varies enormously. Many schools deliberately restrict the size of the full-time intake, sometimes to fewer than 30, arguing that this small size improves the quality of the teaching and learning experience. Harvard, however, which hardly falls short on either criterion, has one of the largest annual intakes at around 900.

The full-time average intake per year at North American schools in the directory this year is 231, compared with 114 in Europe and 96 in Asia and Australasia. The directory entries show the number of students enrolled in the most recent incoming programme and the size of the faculty.

You can apply some basic assumptions. Smaller schools probably allow more involvement but may lack the resources to provide an extensive choice of other elements, such as electives. Bigger schools running two-year courses can have more than 1,000 students on campus. They may have the resources but they may also be anonymous, offering minimal contact with the faculty. It is worth noting that a school running a small full-time course that also has a large part-time programme or a lot of executive education may offer more choice. Also relevant is the number of recruiting employers attracted to a school. Although bigger schools may attract more recruiters, the ratio of recruiters to students may be more favourable at a smaller school. However, such variations mean that on-campus visits and conversations with current students are often better indicators.

Facilities

The physical facilities at most business schools are excellent. The directory entries give an indication of what is available. Although the content matters more than the packaging, the need to attract good students and staff and to introduce new technology, which is easier in a modern building, has stimulated a major and continuing business school building boom. For example, in the UK, Imperial College London has spent £25m on its new Tanaka building and City University a more modest £5m on Cass Business School. In the US, Chicago Graduate School of Business has spent US$125m, more than four times the total spent by the two UK schools, on its new business school building (scheduled to open in November 2004).

The competition for students means that a once low-cost, high-return business now requires considerable investment not only in facilities and staff, but also in research, technology, marketing, administration and careers services. This has been good for students. North American schools, with their large endowments and ability to call on wealthy alumni, have created some superb facilities. Table 2.10 shows the results produced when we surveyed students and recent graduates on schools' facilities and the back-up they received from schools' administrations. This is a summation of ratings for such things as the quality and accessibility of libraries, computers, databases and other facilities and services; the range and suitability of teaching methods; the attitude and receptiveness of faculty, the attitude of programme and school administrators; and the extent and usefulness of the alumni network.

Table 2.10
Student and graduate ratings of back-up and facilities

School	%	School	%
Emory (Goizueta)	96	Lancaster	91
Cornell (Johnson)	95	Ohio (Fisher)	91
Dartmouth (Tuck)	95	Northwestern (Kellogg)	91
Harvard	95	Wake Forest (Babcock)	91
Queen's	94	Washington St Louis (Olin)	91
Iowa (Tippie)	93	Florida (Warrington)	90
Bath	92	Indiana (Kelley)	90
Duke (Fuqua)	92	Stanford	90
Glasgow	92	Vanderbilt (Owen)	90
Nanyang	92	Virginia (Darden)	90

Note. These figures are derived from our survey of students and alumni; caution should be used when interpreting them.

The ability to raise large sums to pay for modern facilities has become a critical competitive factor for business schools. High-quality facilities can make a big difference to the MBA experience and should not be ignored. Many MBA students have recently left modern, well-equipped offices, and it can be frustrating to have to settle for less.

Minimum requirements include a good library of management and business books, preferably reserved for MBA students, and access to national and international databases and communication systems, CD-ROM files and, especially, the Internet. Easy laptop access (either via lots of jacks or wireless) to a school's own intranet is becoming essential. Many schools now require or advise students to have their own laptop computer (where this is so it is indicated in the directory entry), although computer centres with plenty of PCs remain important. Sports and recreation facilities are also highly desirable.

If schools provide on-campus accommodation, whether to live on or off campus becomes yet another decision point. On-campus living allows easy access to facilities (most libraries and computer centres are open for long hours, often permanently) and makes group-study evenings more practicable. It promotes camaraderie and a sense of community, but it can also become oppressive. A haven of peace when the going gets tough may be more attractive, but the penalty is less easy access to the facilities and to fellow students.

Careers services

Whether your chosen school can help you find the kind of job you want at graduation is a prime measure of its success and reputation. How students view careers services and the salaries they achieve after graduation are important elements in the ranking of schools by the Economist Intelligence Unit. In general terms, North American schools devote more resources to these services, which are often better organised and staffed than is normal in Europe, where many university-based schools merely direct their MBA graduates to the central careers office. This is a cause of many complaints

Apart from reference to this guide, the success of schools in the job market can, to some degree, be assessed from the annual tables of the types of jobs their graduates have found, the types of companies that recruit from them and the range of starting salaries (usually published on websites and in brochures). Current students and graduates can also provide useful information. However, you should be aware that business schools are not there solely to find you a job. You need to take some responsibility yourself.

Internationalism

You will find that every business school claims to be international in its outlook as well as in its student body, faculty and teaching material. Indeed, many are going out of their way to prove it. This is reflected in two developments. The first is the growing number of overseas satellite campuses. INSEAD, for example, has a full-time campus in Singapore, and Chicago has outposts in Barcelona and Singapore. As well as attracting foreign students who might not otherwise come to these schools, perhaps even more importantly they allow faculty much greater exposure to other cultures and business environments.

But even though internationalism may generally be seen as a good thing, it has its critics. Some schools are accused of neglecting their home market. Some students point out that foreign students can limit a programme because they lack linguistic skills, their background is too alien, or they have a cultural aversion to participation. Native speakers of the teaching language may be held back and feel obliged, for example, to help with grammar and proofreading essays.

Table 2.11
Schools by percentage of foreign students

School	%	School	%
Monaco	100	Bradford	89
Hult	98	INSEAD	89
IMD	98	Leeds	88
Birmingham	97	Oxford (Saïd)	87
Rotterdam (Erasmus)	97	London	87
Newcastle	96	Nanyang	84
Sheffield	93	Cambridge (Judge)	83
Concordia (Molson)	91	IE	83
ESCP–EAP	90	Glasgow	82
Hong Kong FBE	90	Hong Kong UST	82
		Nottingham	82

Table 2.12
Foreign students by region

Europe	%	North America	%	Asia & Australasia	%
Monaco	100	Hult	98	Hong Kong FBE	90
IMD	98	Concordia (Molson)	91	Nanyang	84
Birmingham	97	York (Schulich)	70	Hong Kong UST	82
Rotterdam (Erasmus)	97	Brandeis	64	International University of Japan	80
Newcastle	96	McGill	63	Melbourne	80
Sheffield	93	British Columbia (Sauder)	58	Singapore	80
ESCP–EAP	90	Thunderbird (Garvin)	58	Chinese University of Hong Kong	62
Bradford	89	Illinois	56	Australian GSM	52
INSEAD	89	Southern California (Marshall)	50	Macquarie	46
Leeds	88	Texas (McCombs)	50	China Europe International Business School	12

Table 2.13
Student and graduate ratings of internationalism

School	%	School	%
Thunderbird	97	Pennsylvania (Wharton)	87
Brandeis	92	International University of Japan	87
INSEAD	92	Monaco	87
Georgetown (McDonough)	91	China Europe International Business School	86
London	91	ENPC	86
South Carolina (Moore)	91	ESADE	86
HEC, Paris	89	New York (Stern)	86
Helsinki	89	Southern California (Marshall)	86
Michigan	88	Lancaster	85
IESE	87	Rotterdam (Erasmus)	85

Note. These figures are derived from our survey of students and alumni; caution should be used when interpreting them.

Given the issues surrounding internationalism, you will find that some schools argue that what matters more than numbers of foreign students or faculty is the way teaching and case-work are done. Unfortunately, this is hard for would-be students to assess. There are no simple answers. Is an American professor more "international" in Paris than in Boston? Is an

Chapter 2
Full-time MBAs

American student seeking international exposure better off in a European school or in Hong Kong, or with 30% of foreigners or 70%? Business schools like to assign students to study groups based on diversity, but how normal is it in the workplace to find a team composed of five or six different nationalities? Undoubtedly, a good mix of nationalities in the student body fosters cross-cultural awareness. Ultimately it is for you to decide.

As mentioned above, the most common method of assessing internationalism is simply to measure the percentage of non-national students and faculty studying and teaching at schools. Tables 2.14 and 2.15, derived from our 2004 survey, provide these figures.

Table 2.14
Schools by percentage of foreign faculty

School	%	School	%
IMD	98	Solvay	51
McGill	95	Hong Kong FBE	50
NIMBAS	91	Australian GSM	49
Hong Kong UST	88	Chinese University of Hong Kong	49
Helsinki	83	International University of Japan	49
Monaco	73	York (Schulich)	48
Concordia (Molson)	65	Singapore	42
INSEAD	62	Calgary (Haskayne)	41
Nanyang	56	Queen's	40
London	55	Cambridge (Judge)	39

Table 2.15
Foreign faculty by region

European	%	North America	%	Asia & Australasia	%
IMD	98	McGill	95	Hong Kong UST	88
Helsinki	83	Concordia (Molson)	65	Nanyang	56
Monaco	73	York (Schulich)	48	Hong Kong FBE	50
INSEAD	62	Calgary (Haskayne)	41	Australian GSM	49
London	55	Queen's	40	Chinese University of Hong Kong	49
Solvay	51	Case Western (Weatherhead)	37	International University of Japan	49
Cambridge (Judge)	39	Washington St Louis (Olin)	37	Singapore	42
Dublin (Trinity)	33	Harvard	35	China Europe International Business School	36
Warwick	31	Duke (Fuqua)	32	Melbourne	25
ESSEC	28	Columbia	28	Macquarie	21
Institut d'Etudes Politiques	28				

It should also be possible to spend a term in another country (or continent) during an MBA programme, at least on the longer ones. Generally there is no additional tuition cost for students involved in these, although there may be extra expense. Schools simply balance the numbers leaving them and the numbers they accept. Normally, exchanges are used to study elective courses, which receive full credit from their home institution.

English may be the international business language, and international courses are almost invariably given in English, but the more internationally-minded schools place a strong emphasis on linguistic ability. MBA programmes at IESE in Barcelona and Bocconi in Milan are bilingual. INSEAD expects students to be fluent in French and English when they arrive and to have picked up a third language by the time they leave, and London Business School requires foreign-language skills for graduation. Schools' directory entries indicate whether language training is available and in some cases in which languages.

Location

Talking to students, you often find that many choose where they would like to study for their MBA first, and then look round for a suitable school. This is not as whimsical as it might first appear. In the US, for example, an MBA programme can be a good way to find a job in a particular region. Schools in favoured locations such as California or the south-eastern sun belt attract many out-of-state students who settle in the area after graduation. In other parts of the world, students may be attracted across national borders because they have an interest in working in a particular country. Students often have existing links with, or an interest in, their chosen country of study; they may already know the language and may plan to work there, at least for a time, after graduation. In any event, most students find that, although it may add to the pressures, working for an MBA in a new location adds to the development potential of any programme.

Accreditation

Accreditation is a system of ensuring the quality of MBA programmes. Normally, it is undertaken by an independent outside body (often set up by the schools themselves), which will visit individual schools and ensure they are meeting prescribed criteria for such things as quality of faculty, teaching skills, teacher/student ratios and facilities.

The main argument against accreditation is that it measures inputs, such as the number of faculty with a PhD, rather than outputs, such as the number of successful managers produced, and that it inevitably favours "poorer" schools by promulgating the doctrine of the lowest common denominator. In other words, any school that attains accreditation, however marginally, will inevitably compare itself with the best school in the same accreditation scheme.

Which MBA? includes the accreditation of a business school or MBA programme, but you should continue to follow the recommendations set out in this chapter and elsewhere in this guide. Above all, ensure you choose a business school and a programme that suit your needs and do not be swayed by any outside factors. Not every school in this guide has accreditation from one of the three main bodies (AACSB International, AMBA and EQUIS) and you should not be too swayed by that. A particular school may have decided to opt out of the accreditation system. Accreditation is an indicator of a minimum standard achieved not a hallmark of particular quality.

The student's perspective: full-time one-year MBA

Cathrin Pfeiffer, MBA 2003, Cranfield School of Management, UK. Direct marketing manager, Willtek Communications GmbH, Ismaning, Germany.

Before I studied for the MBA I had my own successful small company as a simultaneous translator, working in German, Spanish and English. I wanted a career change and therefore decided on an intensive one-year programme in order to be able to re-enter professional life within the shortest possible time.

I went to Cranfield because of the school's good position in the rankings (11th in the world in the 2003 Economist Intelligence Unit ranking), its academic track record, its professional organisation of the programme and its case-study-based way of teaching, which is so different from how things are taught at German universities.

I graduated in September 2003, and what I had come for in the first place in September 2002 (an excellent course of business administration at a top school) differs completely from what I consider to be the most important things I've taken away.

There seems to be little difference in what is taught during the core courses at most reputable business schools. However, everything beyond the core courses gives each business school its unique character.

Of course I have left Cranfield knowing how to calculate net present value and the weighted average cost of capital, but I am convinced I could have gained similar knowledge (albeit maybe not from such eminent teachers) doing a distance-learning course. There are three factors that contributed to my experience at Cranfield: its location; its focus on personal development; and, most of all, the people.

The fact that Cranfield is a campus university creates a unique atmosphere. As MBA students, we not only studied together but also shared our lives, played sports and partied together. And by doing all this, we became more than just fellow students—we became friends for life.

The work in international learning teams, the leadership course and a host of different opportunities for personal development have made me more aware of myself and of what is going on in my work environment. At events like the International Business Schools' Regatta, which Cranfield organises on the Isle of Wight, it was interesting to see that every business school leaves its mark on its students. Or is it the schools' selection process that brings together a group of students who are incredibly diverse and yet united from the beginning by an intangible bond, be it ambition, common goals, attitudes or motivations? Even across different years, it seems that Cranfield students are not only extremely well educated and bright, but typically they are also open, internationally-minded team players.

The year was what we made of it and it was no doubt one of the most intense years I will ever experience. Periods of concentrated studying were followed by great parties: our Christmas party; a 70s party after term two with our MBA band, called 23G (a reference to the Cranfield tuition fees); and our end-of-year ball.

The two events that I would consider were my personal highlights of the year were rugby—the fact that we beat the London Business School girls on our sports day was the peak of my short MBA rugby career—and sailing, where we were a little less successful but had just as much fun seeing so many like-minded people from different business schools in one place.

I am now back in work life and while the Cranfield network is, of course, a formal network with website and alumni book, more importantly it is a social network, uniting students across years and across continents.

Chapter 3

Part-time MBAs

Part-time is one of the most popular ways of taking an MBA and a large percentage of MBA degrees awarded around the world are studied this way. Data are hard to come by, but according to a 2001–02 survey (the most recent available) by AACSB International, a US accrediting body, 45% of students enrolled in US and Canadian business schools were studying on evening and weekend part-time programmes. This compares with 22.8% taking traditional two-year full-time programmes. Around the world probably even more MBAs are studied via distance-learning programmes (see Chapter 4), but part-time programmes remain the bedrock of the MBA.

Part-time classes are usually held on weekday evenings, at weekends, or both (though there are many different types of part-time programmes—see below). Many programmes also require students to spend short periods of time, typically a week, in residence together on campus or at other locations. Occasionally, part-time and full-time students study together, the only difference being the time in which the degree is completed (ENPC School of International Management in Paris is one example of this), but more commonly, part-time students may find themselves studying only elective courses with full-time students. Increasingly, though, business schools are realising the benefits of mixing full-timers and part-timers.

Typically, part-time students are slightly older and with more work experience than their full-time counterparts. At the University of Michigan Business School, for example, the average age of students in the part-time Evening MBA is 30; in the full-time cohort it is 28. The motivation for taking an MBA may also be different. Although it is hard to generalise, our survey of students shows that more part-timers are seeking to advance their existing careers, compared with full-time students who are more likely to be attempting to use an MBA to change their career entirely. Equally, the majority of part-time students try to persuade their existing employers to sponsor (or at least partially fund) their degree. This is rarely the case with full-timers.

Table 3.1
Why did you decide to study for an MBA degree?
(%)[a]

Part-time students	
To open new career opportunities	33
Personal development	21
To further current career	20
To increase salary	14
Educational experience	6
Potential to network	5
Company advice or requirement	1

[a] Importance accorded by students to each factor.

Table 3.2
Part-time students sponsored by their company
(%)

World	Europe	North America	Asia & Australasia
57	61	61	38

Table 3.3
Length of time part-time sponsored students agreed to stay with their company
(%)

	World	Europe	North America	Asia & Australasia
Up to two years	33	34	33	33
3–5 years	8	14	6	5
Longer than 5 years	0	0	0	0
No agreement required	59	52	61	61

The curriculum of part-time MBA programmes is usually identical or very similar to the full-time version offered by a school. The degree is generally exactly the same as that earned through the full-time programme and has equal standing. Differences may be that the range of electives available to part-timers is smaller and some of the less academic elements of a full-time programme, such as foreign trips, project work and outdoor management development, may not be offered (although the trend is towards including them).

You can expect to take 2–4 years to complete a part-time programme, but many offer considerable flexibility within a time limit of 5–7 years in which the degree must be completed. Generally, the time taken to complete a part-time programme reflects the span of the full-time version. In Europe, where one-year programmes are common, a part-time programme may take 2–3 years to complete; in the US, where two-year full-time programmes predominate, the part-time version may take 3–4 years. However, in most cases the emphasis is on flexibility.

Advantages and drawbacks

The whole point of a part-time MBA is to combine it with your working life, and this has advantages and disadvantages. Not having to forgo your salary and spreading the cost of an MBA over a longer period is a strong incentive to study part-time. Another is being able to apply academic principles immediately to real business life. Picking up an interesting theoretical model in class on a Tuesday evening, then putting it to work and seeing it succeed in your own organisation by the end of the week is both a powerful aid to work and study and a highly satisfying personal experience.

But combining an MBA programme with a full-time job is not to be undertaken lightly and there are downsides. It is not just a case of spending one or two long and demanding evenings a week in class. You also have to allow additional time (perhaps 15 hours a week) for individual study, preparation and group work. To do this you will have to balance study, work and sometimes family. This can be difficult, especially if you do not have an understanding employer.

The total immersion or involvement that is characteristic of a full-time programme is also often missing from part-time programmes and some (but by no means all) may lack camaraderie. As with full-time programmes, it is useful to visit the school and meet the faculty and students. Most business schools arrange "open days" for their part-time programmes. The Tanaka School at Imperial College in London is fairly typical. It runs information sessions approximately once a month in the evening and less frequently on Saturday mornings. Prospective students attend a presentation about the programme and then have a chance to talk to faculty, alumni and current students at a drinks reception.

Many schools like students' employers to know they are studying for an MBA, to appreciate the work involved and to be prepared to support them. However, involving companies can raise the delicate issue of careers services for part-time students. Many part-timers are studying because they want to improve their prospects in their current career (unlike full-time students, who are usually more interested in changing career) and the majority are being sponsored by their company. Some schools may restrict part-time students' access to the careers service—or even ban it completely—out of a concern that employers might stop sponsoring students if the schools are seen to be helping them change jobs. Other schools, though, adopt an opposite approach, believing that because part-time students often have extensive experience, they are an attractive proposition to employers, and so allow them the same access to career services as their full-time counterparts.

There are also geographical limitations. Part-time programmes are, almost by definition, local. There are stories in the US of students flying hundreds of miles to attend classes (and some American schools, such as Chicago, deliberately cater for this by offering weekend rather than evening classes—see Student's perspective below), but generally students have to take what is available within easy reach. Similarly, there are likely to be few foreign students on a part-time programme.

However, because their part-time programmes are financially important to them, schools are starting to address this issue. Kellogg School of Management in the US, for example, has established the post of assistant dean and director of student affairs for its part-time programme. The aim is to help strengthen the connection between part-time students and the school, encouraging greater involvement in extracurricular activities and a sense of community for students.

Options

The modular MBA

The modular MBA is a variant of the part-time MBA. Modular students alternate periods, or modules, of traditional MBA on-campus education, usually lasting one or two months, with periods back in their own company undertaking projects based on the theory they have learned. Although the training may be full-time, the programme design and student experiences are different from traditional full-time programmes.

The modular delivery method is common in consortium, company and executive MBAs (see below) and is increasingly linked to distance-learning elements (see Chapter 4). On most modular programmes, schools insist on keeping in close contact with students during their time back in their companies, often via Internet-based technologies. Many involve the company directly in the programme by asking it to appoint an executive, usually a fairly senior manager, as a contact for the school and a mentor for the student. There are regular meetings of the people concerned.

One of the best examples of a modular programme is the one at Warwick Business School in the UK (page 498). Emory University's Goizueta Business School in the US also runs a modular executive MBA (page 224); students study over 20 months via a mix of distance learning and eight one-week on-campus modules plus a ten-day international module.

The consortium MBA

Consortium MBAs are specially designed programmes aimed at the employees of a small group of companies (usually between three and six but sometimes more). They provide an educational experience for these employees that is relevant to their own company but wide enough to allow the networking and broadening process that is a major advantage of traditional programmes. Increasingly, as with modular programmes, distance-learning elements are being introduced into such programmes.

An interesting example is the International Masters Programme in Practising Management (see box), which is run by a consortium of schools around the world for a consortium of companies, including British Telecom, Lufthansa and Motorola. It is held in various locations and includes some distance-learning elements.

The IMPM (www.impm.org) is a part-time management development programme for middle to senior managers aged from 35 upwards. Participants are sponsored by their companies to attend the 18-month programme, which, if successfully completed, can be extended for a further six months to achieve a master's degree in management. Companies send small groups of participants to the IMPM so that they can work together on company issues during the programme.

The five modules are based on mindsets, which are derived from managers' work. These are:
● the reflective mindset: managing self;
● the analytic mindset: managing the organisation;
● the worldly mindset: managing the context;
● the collaborative mindset: managing relationships;
● the action mindset: managing continuity and change.

The programme is run by a partnership of schools: Lancaster University in the UK; McGill University in Canada; Indian Institute of Management in Bangalore, India; INSEAD in France; and academics from a consortium of Japanese universities.

Some business schools have been unwilling to become involved in consortium programmes. They argue that academic content will be influenced too much by the wishes of the consortium companies, that they will be able to teach only what is regarded as best practice (rather than pass on research) and that the range of cultures involved will be small (most consortium programmes are national and, unless the consortium is skilfully put together, may represent only a narrow industry sector). Because of this, they say, even the best consortium programme will lack the elements that make the traditional MBA so effective: academic rigour, teaching based on sound research and exposure to a wide range of individuals with diverse backgrounds and experience. This attitude is changing, however, and many leading schools now offer consortium programmes that lead to the same degree as that awarded on full-time or part-time programmes.

In contrast, companies have generally been solid supporters, largely because of differences between them and business schools about what an MBA degree is supposed to achieve. In the corporate view, the aim of an MBA programme should be to make existing managers more effective in their current (or future) job; it should not be a way to help young individuals improve their job prospects or change their careers. The real test of an MBA programme, companies say, is its output (does it produce better managers?), not its input (does it have academic rigour, good research and cultural diversity?).

The company MBA

Company MBA programmes are tailored by a business school for the employees of a single company. They are most common in the UK but are not unknown elsewhere. Michigan, for example, offers company programmes via its Global MBA. Company MBAs usually consist of a mix of courses taught by the partner business school or university (often drawn from the regular MBA output) and modules produced by the company and usually taught by company staff. The school gives credits for each part.

Like consortium MBAs, company MBAs are criticised for lacking the independent, general management outlook of a regular MBA and the stimulation that can come from a classroom of students from diverse backgrounds. It is also argued that company programmes stray over the ill-defined border between education and training, between what is in the student's and what is in the company's interest.

Well, yes but. The content of a company MBA is likely to be no less rigorous than that of any other type of MBA programme, and it is certainly not in the interests of any company to accept a low-grade programme for the undoubtedly substantial amounts of money it will be paying. The extent to which a company can interfere with such a programme is in any case small. The amount of tailoring involved to meet specific needs, according to academics involved in this type of programme, is normally confined to less than 10% of the total.

However, the future of company MBAs may be problematic. They lack some of the benefits of consortium programmes, and they are expensive compared with the mass development that companies can offer their employees via distance-learning MBAs.

Again, the degree awarded is the same as that offered by other delivery methods. The Global MBA offered by Michigan is a good example. Although it is developed in conjunction with individual companies, it has virtually the same course work as Michigan's regular programme; and although the companies nominate candidates for the programme, the candidates must submit applications individually, and the admission requirements and procedures are the same as those of the regular MBA.

Cost

Generally, tuition fees for part-time programmes are lower than those for the full-time version. For example, at Edinburgh University tuition for the full-time programme costs £21,400 (US$35,082) and for the part-time programme £13,000 (US$21,311); at Wisconsin-Madison it costs US$49,004 (for the two-year programme) and US$41,000. Add to this the lack of accommodation costs and, above all, forgone salary, and part-time programmes start to make a lot of financial sense. Part-time students will finish their degree with a considerably lower level of debt than their full-time counterparts.

Chapter 3
Part-time MBAs

Table 3.4
Part-time tuition fees at selected schools

School	Total tuition fees
Ashridge	£33,900 (US$55,573)
Aston	£12,860 (US$21,082)
Bath	£20,250 (US$33,197)
Bradford	£13,500 (US$22,131)
California at Davis	US$39,840
Chinese University of Hong Kong	US$25,730
British Columbia (Sauder)	C$36,000 (US$25,714)
Curtin	A$32,000 (US$20,779)
Edinburgh Management School	£13,000 (US$21,311)
ENPC	€34,000 (US$38,636)
Florida (Warrington)	US$25,666
Helsinki	€23,000 (US$26,136)
E.M. Lyon	€28,000 (US$31,818)
Macquarie	A$42,400 (US$27,532)
Manchester	£20,600 (US$33,770)
Nanyang	S$28,000 (US$16,092)
Pittsburgh (Katz)	US$63,000
Southern California (Marshall)	US$32,175
Wisconsin-Madison	US$41,000

Choosing a school

As mentioned earlier, the choice of school for a part-time MBA is often constrained by simple geography. Lengthy journey times after work when classes may be scheduled twice a week are simply not an option. This may be one of the most critical issues involved and is one reason many decide to opt for a full-time or distance-learning programme—the quality of programme or school they are looking for may simply not be available locally.

Table 3.5
How did you choose the school where you are taking or took your MBA?
(part-time students, %)[a]

	World	Europe	North America	Asia & Australasia
Reputation of school	39	33	40	42
Location	16	13	18	11
Quality of teaching faculty	13	11	14	14
Content of programme	13	19	11	16
Published ranking position	9	5	10	7
Teaching methods	4	10	3	4
Friend's recommendation	2	5	1	3
Tuition and living costs	1	2	1	2
Starting salary of graduates	1	1	1	0
Careers services record	1	0	1	0
Published guides	0	1	0	0
Advertising	0	1	0	0

[a] Importance accorded by students to each factor.

If you happen to live in a major city such as New York, London or Hong Kong, you may have as many as three top-ranked business schools on your doorstep, all offering excellent part-time programmes. In this case, the advice has to be to research the school and the programme as you would the full-time version. And do visit the school and talk to the students.

The student's perspective: part-time MBA

Rob Bryant, currently a Weekend MBA student, Chicago Graduate School of Business, US. Entrepreneur.

I choose to attend the University of Chicago for my MBA despite living about 500 miles away. I fly every Saturday morning to Chicago and ride the bus with my fellow students to the university's Gleacher Center in downtown Chicago. I take a three-hour course in the morning followed by an hour for lunch, and then go back for my second three-hour course in the afternoon. The bus leaves school at 4.10 pm, gets to O'Hare airport at about 5 pm and my flight takes off at 6.15 pm, which if things are on schedule has me pulling into my driveway at 8 pm.

As an undergrad at the University of Nebraska I read a book by Milton Friedman. His theories on free-market economics made a big impression on me. As I looked around for an MBA programme the University of Chicago kept popping up on the shortlist of top-ranked schools. As my business career advanced (I've owned my own business for eight years) and my family grew (my wife and I have five young children) over the ten years following my undergrad degree, the dream of pursuing an MBA seemed to be slipping away.

As I started investigating my options I decided that unless my MBA was from a top school I would probably not gain enough from the experience to offset the sacrifice my wife and I would be making. Once I heard about the weekend programme at the University of Chicago it sounded like a dream come true. I am able to attend a school I dreamed of attending without having to relocate and with a relatively small amount of disruption to my family or my business.

I have really enjoyed my courses at the University of Chicago. As I had been promised, all the courses are taught by the same professors that teach during the week. Also the opportunity to get to know people from all over the country has been an invaluable experience.

Chapter 4

Distance-learning MBAs

Distance-learning students work in their own time at home or even while travelling, and programmes can take three years or sometimes much longer to complete. Distance-learning programmes have been revitalised and given increased credibility by the increased application of new information technology, particularly the Internet and e-mail.

Most distance-learning programmes involve using a mix of study materials. At the UK's Open University Business School (OUBS), a pioneer in interactive distance-learning technology, the material supplied (which the school says is everything you need) includes course books, a study guide (which basically helps you to work through the material), CD-ROMs, videotapes, audiotapes and access to a website. Some other programmes, notably in Canada, make use of online lectures delivered by videoconference technology, allowing live interaction between students and lecturer.

Distance-learning programmes are not all isolation and high-tech, however. Many schools insist that students get together, either on campus for occasional residential weeks and weekends or in local study groups. Henley Management College's distance-learning MBA, for example, has two-day residential modules approximately every three months, optional overseas study tours and a monthly Saturday Club at the college where tutors and administrative staff are available.

Similarly, the OUDS offers local face-to-face tutorials with over 750 tutors at centres throughout the UK and in parts of western Europe. These provide day schools and residential sessions of between two and five days. For students who cannot attend these sessions, the school has an online conference system called "First Class". It also allocates every student to a personal tutor (each tutor may have around 10–20 students at any time), who can be contacted by phone, e-mail or post. As well as providing feedback (by marking assignments, for example), tutors also organise the residential sessions for students in the locality.

Distance-learning programmes are concentrated in the US and the UK, both countries having a well-established tradition of "correspondence courses", the precursors of distance learning. Some leading US business schools are beginning to become involved in distance learning. For example, Columbia, Stanford, Carnegie Mellon (Tepper) and Chicago (as well as the UK's London School of Economics) are partners of UNext, a distance-learning provider with its own university, Cardean. The schools provide a lot of the academic input.

In 2003, UNext and the New York Institute of Technology also formed a strategic alliance to launch Ellis College of NYIT, a new online school created to deliver accelerated graduate degree programmes for working adults. Again, many courses were developed in association with the schools mentioned above. Students at Ellis can complete a generalist MBA in 18 months or less. Over a slightly longer period, they can earn an MBA with a specialisation in one of 14 areas.

One of the biggest US-based providers is the University of Phoenix, founded in 1976. It was one of the first accredited universities to provide college degree programmes via the Internet, starting in 1989. Carnegie Mellon offers a part-time distance-learning MBA that is also a consortium programme (see Chapter 3). This three-year FlexMode MBA is designed for employees of United Technologies Corporation, Lockheed Martin Company and General Electric Company. Rather than being Internet-based, it uses interactive, televised lectures.

Useful web links	
Unext	www.unext.com
Cardean	www.cardean.edu
NYIT	ellis.nyit.edu
University of Phoenix	www.phoenix.edu

Thunderbird follows a similar approach with its Global MBA for Latin American Managers, which is offered via a combination of live satellite broadcasts, local classes and virtual interaction at a number of Tecnológico de Monterrey campuses in Mexico and sites in Bolivia, El Salvador, Panama and Peru. Other countries are expected to be added to the network in the future.

Another mainstream US school, Warrington College of Business at the University of Florida, claims to have one of the first online MBA degrees to be offered by a fully accredited business school. The degree earned via its Internet (Flexible) MBA programme is equivalent to any other MBA offered by the school. The programme has a 27-month curriculum in which students meet for one weekend (Saturday and Sunday) at the end of each term (eight times). As well as time on campus, course work is offered electronically through Internet communications such as e-mail, web browsers, bulletin boards, synchronous group discussion software, asynchronous class presentation software, video and audio streaming, and interactive CD-ROM technology. A one-year Internet MBA for students with an undergraduate business degree within the last seven years and 2–7 years' work experience is also available.

The two UK market leaders are long established. The OUBS and Henley, each of which has several thousand distance-learning students spread around the world, have been operating for many years. The OUBS is an offshoot of the Open University, a pioneering political initiative in distance learning of the 1960s, which as well as written material uses radio and television programmes via the BBC.

Both programmes comprise a similar mix of modular, multimedia distance learning and local tutorials, short residential blocks, local student self-help groups and electronic conferencing. Other leading UK providers include Durham Business School, Edinburgh Business School at Heriot-Watt University, Strathclyde Graduate Business School and Warwick Business School.

The Warwick programme is typical of the increasingly professional approach to distance-learning programmes and the way they are integrated into schools' activities. At Warwick students take seven core courses throughout the three-part programme, five electives in parts two and three and a project and dissertation in part three. Each part begins with an induction seminar (held at Warwick and other sites). There is a required eight-day seminar each September at Warwick as well as optional weekend seminars. The school encourages students to form local study groups and to stay in touch via e-mail.

Advantages and drawbacks

The distance-learning MBA is a reasonably inexpensive route to an MBA (see Costs) compared with other methods. It also offers independence and convenience of study, although it can cause disruption in students' personal lives. It is not for the faint-hearted: if you can attain an MBA by distance learning, you can attain it by any route.

Distance-learning programmes are also becoming increasingly popular among employers. Companies are more likely to provide support for such programmes than for other delivery methods. They are significantly cheaper, and, since students study in their own time, the disruption to an employee's work commitments is minimal. Many companies believe that distance-learning programmes are more practical than some of the alternatives, especially the full-time options. They also allow students to be involved in projects within their own organisations, which are of direct benefit to the employer.

Table 4.1
Why did you decide to study for an MBA degree?
(distance-learning students, %)[a]

To open new career opportunities	30
Personal development	28
To further current career	21
To increase salary	10
Educational experience	7
Company advice or requirement	1
Friend's recommendation	1
Potential to network	1

[a] Importance accorded by students to each factor.

Although the introduction of IT has allowed distance-learning students to have much more contact with faculty at their business school and with other students, and many schools make provision for personal interaction, lack of face-to-face contact and support from teachers and peers is one of the perennial problems with distance-learning programmes. Nevertheless, some students like this hands-off approach and opt for distance-learning programmes that specifically do not require on-campus attendance or other contact.

Unsurprisingly, perhaps, given the difficulties of studying by distance learning the "drop-out" rate is higher than in other types of programme. Of the schools that are included in *Which MBA?* the percentage enrolled students that go on to complete their programme ranges from 55% at the OUBS, to 98% at Carnegie Mellon.

Despite the efforts schools make to involve students, the potential for networking and learning from other students (an issue that many students identify as a key aspect of full-time programmes) is inevitably limited. However, if you are fortunate enough to be in an area where a reasonable number of other students are following the same distance-learning programme, this can be alleviated. Many schools make great efforts to put students in touch with each other, and, as with the OUBS approach mentioned earlier, tutors can organise sessions that differ little from classroom teaching. Students are also frequently encouraged to set up their own small study groups.

Some students do worry about the quality of distance-learning programmes. There is no real accreditation system for them, although the DETC (formerly the National Home Study Council) in the US, which has been accrediting distance-learning programmes since it was set up in 1926, is now moving into the MBA market, and AACSB International, which accredits leading business schools around the world, is taking an increasing interest in the subject. However, with more and more leading schools becoming involved in distance learning, these concerns are starting to fade. No leading school is going to risk its reputation by delivering a poor programme, and, as noted earlier, distance-learning programmes at such institutions almost always offer exactly the same degree as that earned via any other delivery method. This is an important element of "quality control", and if you are interested in a distance-learning programme you must ensure that the degree offered is properly accredited.

One important point about distance-learning programmes is the "public service" element involved. You may not be able to take a full-time programme at a leading school because you lack the academic qualifications or the finance. But you can join a good distance-learning programme wherever you are in the world. Many programmes are "open access", which means you do not require a first degree (although you will have to complete some sort of preliminary course), and the cost, though significant, does not compare with full-time programmes.

Distance-learning students are also much less constrained by geography. Our survey shows that only 3% viewed location as a major determining factor when choosing a school. This can be particularly important in areas such as Africa and the Middle East, which are not well supplied with top-level business schools. The OUBS, for example, operates in 44 different countries.

Table 4.2
How did you choose the school where you are taking or took your MBA?
(distance-learning students, %)[a]

Reputation of school	28
Teaching methods	22
Content of programme	22
Quality of teaching faculty	7
Friend's recommendation	5
Tuition and living costs	5
Published ranking position	4
Location	3
Published guides	2
Advertising	1

[a] Importance accorded by students to each factor.

Cost

The cost of a distance-learning programme can vary considerably. Henley's programme, for example, costs £13,700 (US$22,459), whereas the OUBS charges £2,500 (US$4,098) per year (average completion time is two and a half years) and Warwick charges £4,100 (US$6,721) a year. The most expensive programme, at US$34,500, is offered by Warrington, but it includes provision of a (required) laptop computer and specialised software.

Choosing a school

Choosing a distance-learning programme is just as difficult and just as important a decision as choosing any other type of MBA. Try to avoid the temptation to opt for a programme that looks "easy" in terms of workload just because you will be (or think you will be) working relatively unsupervised and at your own pace. To be worth anything, a distance-learning programme should be as rigorous and demanding as any other MBA. You will only get out of it proportionately what you put in.

Also be wary of cost. As Table 4.3 shows these vary widely and, although all the programmes listed are of high repute, cost is not an indicator of quality. You should ensure that a reputable business school backs any distance-learning MBA you sign up for, just as you would for a full-time or part-time programme.

Lastly, make sure you choose a programme that suits you. Many distance-learning MBA programmes make a big issue out of providing local seminars or group working or traditional classroom sessions. If you like that, fine. But many people deliberately opt for distance learning because they like working on their own and are not looking for contact and feedback from fellow students. Make sure that a distance-learning programme matches your personality.

Chapter 4
Distance-learning MBAs

Table 4.3
Selected distance-learning programmes

School	Programme	Intakes per year	Students per intake	Total enrolled students	Completion rate (%)a
Aston	MBA	3	15	120	97
Bradford	Distance Learning MBA	6	40	292	n/a
Carnegie Mellon (Tepper)	Flex Mode MBA	1	45	136	98
Curtin	MBA	3	150	110	92
Durham	Durham Distance Learning MBA	2	95	912	n/a
Florida (Warrington)	Internet MBA (1-year & 2-year options)	2	48	230	95
Henley	Henley Distance Learning MBA	3	80	4,713	65
Heriot-Watt (Edinburgh)	MBA	Continuous	1,700	7,940	74
Manchester Business School	Distance Learning MBA	2	172	1,807	65
Open University	MBA	2	3,900	12,000	55
Warwick	The Warwick MBA by Distance Learning	2	150	1,416	73

a % of enrolled students that complete the programme.

The student's perspective: distance-learning MBA

Arif Zaman, distance-learning MBA 2003, Henley Management College. Global market and industry analyst, British Airways.

With hindsight, for me the MBA was only partly about the content, crucial and central though this often seems, especially before exams. It was much more about the process in which the learning takes place, the impact this has on where you feel you can add value through changed perspectives, the relationships you cultivate with a diverse group and, of course, timing. Henley scored highly on all counts.

Timing matters because Enron and the September 11th 2001 terrorist attacks in the US happened towards the end of my MBA but not too late for Henley to be one of the first business schools to provide people with the space in which to reflect on how business practice (not theory) might change as a result. Moreover, Henley is the only business school to provide a mandatory course on corporate reputation and, what it sees as a subset of this, corporate social responsibility and governance.

I was fortunate in being one of the last people to be sponsored by my company, British Airways, in my case for the distance-learning MBA. The structure of the MBA, with foundation courses and an early emphasis on managing people, enables deeper understanding in later courses. A wide-ranging elective programme from "competitor intelligence" to "corporate governance" in the final stage is strengthened by the international nature of the student community.

Applicants: places	Women (%)	Average age	Average GMAT score	Average work experience (years)	Duration of programme (in months)	Programme fees
2:1	20	32	n/a	10	27	£12,860 (US$21,082)
6:1	27	32	n/a	8	48	£9,500 (US$15,574)
2:1	15	27	643	4	36	US$407 per unit
1:1	35	33	610	9	12	A$24,000 (US$15,584)
n/a	24	34	n/a	13	n/a	£8,800 (US$14,426)
2:1	23	29	610	6	27	US$34,500
2:1	32	34	n/a	10	36	£13,700 (US$22,459)
n/a	32	35	n/a	12	n/a	£900 (US$1,475) per course
n/a	33	36	n/a	10	36	£12,600 (US$20,656)
1:1	40	36	n/a	12	30	£2,500 (US$4,098) per year
2:1	25	33	n/a	6	36	£4,100 (US$6,721) per year

This means that e-learning groups can be particularly stimulating. On my e-business elective (Henley's first), capturing perspectives from Africa and various parts of Asia provided a much more realistic sense of the global potential of the Internet at a time when the hype machine from the business—and academic—press was in overdrive.

In addition, action-learning networks in areas such as future work trends, leadership and intrapreneurship, the Henley Learning Network (which shares best practice among member organisations) and active alumni networks with both a regional and a sectoral focus (in which students are encouraged to participate from an early stage) all provide plenty of opportunities to set theory against practice. They also help to develop social capital and networks.

Henley has a collegiate atmosphere with a friendly and approachable faculty prepared to engage in discussion rather than rote learning, which is surprisingly common even at well-known business schools. The workload can be demanding but the college is flexible in accommodating life changes—in relationships, work and much else—which are highly likely during a period of study invariably undertaken at crucial life stages.

Added to this is the spectacular picture-postcard setting, less than an hour's drive from Heathrow, which I challenge anyone not to be inspired by to think and learn.

Chapter 5

Executive MBAs

The executive MBA (EMBA) is not a huge part of the MBA market. According to AACSB International, for example, around 7% of students enrolled in MBA programmes in 2001–02 were studying for EMBAs. Another survey in October 2003 by the Graduate Management Admissions Council, which administers the GMAT, found that only around 6–8% of the people registered on its prospective students website (www.mba.com) were potential EMBA students.

However, the EMBA is an interesting and potentially growing element in the MBA scene. It was first introduced at Chicago's Graduate School of Business in 1943 and spread quickly. Because the people studying for EMBAs are generally working professional managers with considerable experience (many schools demand at least ten years), and because employers are generally closely involved (not least by paying the fees), the degree meets many of the criticisms made about management education via the MBA route.

Although most EMBA programmes lead to the same degree offered on full-time and part-time "traditional" MBA programmes, the content and scheduling are often quite different, being geared to the needs of senior working managers. EMBA programmes are a cross between part-time and modular programmes. Classes are typically held on Fridays and Saturdays, and there are often large modules of residential work and foreign field trips.

EMBAs are essentially career enhancing rather than career changing, particularly as employers frequently foot the bill. The impetus for studying an EMBA varies. Often the participant will initiate the idea, persuading his or her company of the value to be gained. Sometimes it may be part of corporate strategy. In the past, employers often considered participation in an EMBA programme as reward for good service and/or a potential retention tool. Now the approach is likely to be more hard-headed, with such programmes seen as part of a company's overall executive education strategy. This has led many business schools to include the EMBA in their executive education portfolio, even though the degree awarded is the same as the general MBA.

Table 5.1
Why did you decide to study for an MBA degree?
(executive MBA students, %)[a]

To open new career opportunities	27
Personal development	26
To further current career	22
Educational experience	8
To increase salary	7
Potential to network	6
Company advice or requirement	2

[a] Importance accorded by students to each factor.

There are signs of further change. Some schools are reporting increased numbers of EMBA students who are self-sponsored (or at least making some contribution). It is difficult to say what this reflects. It might be that such students are older, more experienced and more senior than "regular" MBA students and so feel more comfortable with an EMBA programme, or that companies are starting to balk at the high price of an EMBA.

The EMBA is also the area where business schools (particularly in the US) have experimented most boldly and successfully with integrating IT into management teaching. Many EMBA programmes now combine elements of modular programmes with lengthy residential sessions and distance learning. They are increasingly global in scope with classes held in various locations around the world and intervening periods spent in online learning and group work.

The Duke MBA–Global Executive at Duke University's Fuqua School of Business was the first example of this. This 19-month programme involves two- to three-week residencies in North America, Europe, Asia and South America. Between these sessions, students work via distance-learning technology that complements and extends the classroom experience.

This approach has found favour. The 15-month Global Executive MBA at IESE in Barcelona, for example, centres on seven two-week residential learning modules: five at IESE, one at the China Europe International Business School (CEIBS) in Shanghai and one in Silicon Valley. Each module is separated by an eight-week period during which participants continue to learn and maintain contact with each other via IESE's "Global Campus", an interactive Internet system developed by IESE in collaboration with Duke Corporate Education (a for-profit spin-off from Duke).

This globalisation is reflected in the student mix. As the student's perspective on page 50 makes clear, an Icelandic manager apparently has no problem with studying an MBA at a Spanish business school that includes residential sessions in China and the US.

Schools have also used the EMBA (and technology) to strengthen alliances among themselves. The EMBA–Global offered jointly by London Business School (LBS) and Columbia Business School in New York, for example, mixes campus-based lectures, case studies, projects, teamwork, field trips and online learning. In the first year, a once-a-month class schedule alternates between LBS and Columbia. The second year consists of a company project and electives at either or both schools. It also includes a one-week international study tour.

Advantages and drawbacks

EMBAs are expensive (see below), but in return for high fees the programmes are usually innovative and closely related to experience rather than classroom speculation. Participants say that the opportunity to share classes with highly experienced and (usually) senior managers is one of the principal attractions of such programmes; and despite the high costs, many companies are enthusiastic sponsors of participants. All sides seem to win. Business schools gain valuable income, individuals obtain a prestigious MBA, often at no cost, and organisations have a useful recruitment and retention tool.

The EMBA does attract criticism, however. Some argue that because it can differ significantly from mainstream MBA programmes it is really a form of intensive executive education (see Chapter 6), with the letters MBA added on as an incentive. Nevertheless, at their best, EMBAs offer an opportunity for highly motivated and experienced executives to come into contact with leading business academics.

Table 5.2
Executive MBA students sponsored by their company
(%)

World	Europe	North America	Asia & Australasia
70	67	70	71

Table 5.3
Length of time executive MBA sponsored students agreed to stay with their company
(%)

	World	Europe	North America	Asia & Australasia
Up to two years	34	35	52	27
3–5 years	17	14	27	31
Longer than 5 years	1	1	2	6
No agreement required	49	50	20	37

Cost

EMBAs are not cheap. However, this is not a problem for most students as their fees are paid by their employer. For example, LBS's Global Executive Programme costs US$115,000, Columbia's Executive MBA US$112,200, Chicago's traditional North American Program US$96,000 and IESE's Global Executive MBA €79,500 (US$90,341). It should be noted, though, that these fees generally include accommodation costs.

Choosing a school

Because most students are sponsored, the choice of school and programme is often a joint decision by students and their employers. It is often the case, though, that it is the student who does the initial research and decides on the school and programme. It then becomes a question of persuading the employer to agree.

If a student has any say in choosing an EMBA programme, there are certain things to look for.

- **The quality of the participants.** The experience and seniority of other students are key factors. These should match, or if possible slightly exceed, your own.

- **Faculty.** Make sure the programme is taught by the school's best faculty. Your company (or you) will be paying a lot of money.

- **Globalisation.** Some element of internationalism, even if the programme does not span continents is important. There should be at least one international study trip.

- **Commitment**. Be sure you can handle the workload. EMBAs are not a cushy option. You will have to do the studying and hold down your job at the same time.

Chapter 5
Executive MBAs

Table 5.4
Selected executive MBA programmes

School	Name of programme	Annual intake	Applicants: places	Women (%)
Australian GSM	MBA (Executive)	1,548	n/a	30
Bath	MBA Executive	25	2:1	8
Chicago	Executive MBA North American	77	n/a	21
Columbia/Berkeley (Haas)	Berkeley–Columbia Executive MBA	60	n/a	27
Florida (Warrington)	Executive MBA	26	2:1	24
HEC, Paris	Executive MBA	317	8:1	8
IESE	Global Executive MBA	30	3:1	15
IMD	Executive MBA	65	n/a	8
London	EMBA–Global	69	2:1	25
Melbourne	Executive MBA	35	1:1	18
New York (Stern)	Executive MBA	91	5:1	28
Newcastle	Executive MBA	10	2:1	40
NIMBAS	Executive MBA	24	3:1	4
Northwestern (Kellogg)/Hong Kong UST	Kellogg–HKUST Executive MBA	48	n/a	29
Oxford	Executive MBA	31	1:1	10
Pennsylvania (Wharton)	MBA for Executives	204	5:1	16
Rice (Jones)	MBA for Executives	84	n/a	0
Singapore	Asia-Pacific Executive MBA	55	3:1	6

The student's perspective: executive MBA

Erna Gisladottir, current EMBA student, IESE. Managing director, car importing company, Iceland.

I am from Iceland, where I have been working for one of the country's main automobile importers for the last 13 years, first as general manager and now as managing director.

An economist by training, I realised in my early 30s that I needed to widen my skills and knowledge base. After exploring the available qualifications, and taking into account my need to hold down my current job, I chose IESE. I had spoken to MBA graduates and others who had studied the Global Executive MBA and was impressed by their reports. The school also has an excellent reputation and the design of the course seems specifically suited to executives such as myself; it offers the maximum flexibility through its short but intensive periods in Spain coupled with the most up-to-date and effective web-based learning techniques.

I am currently in the middle of my fifth distance-learning stint, with two more modules to go before the course finishes in October 2004. In these I will travel to Shanghai and lastly to Barcelona.

What has impressed me most throughout the course has been the immediacy and relevance of the course to my career. At the end of each module, I have been able to apply the studies directly to my work, particularly the entrepreneurial and negotiation components, which I have used in drafting a business plan and talking

Average age	Programme fees	Duration of programme (months)	Average GMAT score	Average work experience (years)
34	A$45,260 (US$29,390)	48	n/a	7
35	£20,000 (US$32,787)	24	n/a	12
37	US$96,000	20	n/a	14
35	US$118,750	19	n/a	10
36	US$32,000	20	636	11
39	€30,500 (US$34,659)	15	n/a	14
34	€79,500 (US$90,341)	16	670	10
38	Swfr115,000 (US$85,185)	0	580	13
33	US$115,000	20	n/a	10
40	A$ 88,000 (US$57,143)	14	n/a	15
32	US$111,300	22	621	8.7
35	£14,200 (US$23,279)	24	n/a	15
38	€18,250 (US$20,739)	24	670	13
37	US$70,500	15	n/a	14
37	£37,000 (US$60,656)	21	620	14
33	US$122,000	24	700	10
n/a	US$77,000	22	n/a	n/a
40	S$48,000 (US$27,586)	18	n/a	15

to our suppliers in mainland Europe.

Entering the final phase of the Global Executive MBA, I can say my approach to work has been transformed by the fresh ideas and energy I have acquired at IESE. And although the up-to-30 hours a week required outside my working time can be demanding, we receive excellent guidance and all subjects are constantly being put into applicable contexts. I find the exposure to new techniques and the teaching methods at IESE keep me more than motivated. Our interaction with professors during and after the modules has been particularly helpful to those of us seeking guidance both in our careers and with the daily problems that come up at the office.

My class is small, although they are from all over the world. I have found it beneficial to get so many different perspectives on the issues we have discussed. We have worked closely during the last months, and I can now say that I have friends around the world to help me in the future.

It is precisely this international aspect that has opened my eyes to new ways of dealing with problems and overcoming communication barriers through the imaginative use of technology coupled with human interaction to solve problems.

Chapter 6

Executive programmes at business schools

For the first time, the Economist Intelligence Unit's *Which MBA?* includes a chapter on executive education. This comprises the short and not-so-short courses for practising managers that do not involve them leaving their jobs (as does a full-time MBA), trekking across continents and oceans, piling up debt and then desperately trying to get themselves re-hired by the corporate world they left.

There is good reason for this innovation. If a dog is for life and not just for Christmas, then an MBA is in some ways the reverse. The "shelf-life" of an MBA—the time it takes for those cutting-edge ideas of your favourite professor to become outdated—is comparatively short, just five years by most estimates. Of course, the basic elements remain valid and the habits of thinking inculcated by, say, the case method will always be useful. But for really new thinking you will probably have to go back to business school (or, indeed, somewhere else, as we discuss below); and because you will probably not want to take another MBA, you will need executive education.

The profile of a participant on an executive education course is likely to be very different from that of an MBA student. After several years of training less-experienced managers for senior positions, the top schools are once again attracting a greying crowd. The average age of participants in Columbia University's leadership courses, for example, is back to being in the 45- to 49-year-old range, following an influx of 30-somethings during the dotcom boom of the late 1990s.

What companies expect from executive education is also changing. Although there is still a demand for business schools to teach hard, practical skills, such as finance and marketing, there seems to be an increasing market for softer skills, such as leadership. A touchy-feely element pervades many of the most popular leadership courses. At Northwestern (Kellogg), for instance, the Soul of Leadership programme, taught by Deepak Chopra, a mind/body guru, examines how leaders can harness their emotional intelligence, intuition and creativity. Soft skills are also in evidence in Harvard's High Potentials Leadership Program, where actors, for example, teach public-speaking techniques.

Another important factor is whether executive education actually delivers any return on the investment. The search to measure (let alone prove) a real return on investment for executive education is referred to by many business academics as "the Holy Grail". Lots of providers are looking, but so far none has discovered it. Unfortunately, that is not good enough. As one US academic told the Economist Intelligence Unit: "Companies are now no longer happy to hear you say "well, it's really difficult to measure the return". They just say: "Well go and figure out a way to measure it."

The observation that companies spend on executive education like drunken sailors when the economy is doing well and like parsimonious bean counters at the first sign of a downturn has been made so often that it deserves a place in some book of world clichés. But like most clichés it is true. Put simply, when the economics of a company are hit, the urge to cut back on management development training is often irresistible; it has an immediate effect on

Chapter 6
Executive programmes at business schools

costs but no immediate impact on revenue.

Currently, companies appear to be hovering somewhere between parsimony and, although certainly not drunken, at least a marginally convivial mode. In many parts of the world the situation is improving, but participation, particularly on "open" programmes (see below), is still lagging behind historical highs. In any case, 2003 was such a disastrous year for the executive education market, with the state of the world economy and SARS resulting in half-empty classrooms across the globe, that some recovery in 2004 was inevitable.

Advantages and disadvantages

The overarching issue in executive education is the growth of customised programmes— those developed for specific companies—at the expense of open-enrolment offerings. Both, however, have their advantages and drawbacks.

"Open" executive education programmes have traditionally been business schools' bread and butter. Every year they could offer more or less the same programmes and confidently expect their lecture rooms to be filled with high-paying executives. This is no longer the case. The market for open programmes has been overtaken by the growth in company-specific, or "customised", programmes.

Customised programmes

A study of leading European business schools by the Economist Intelligence Unit showed that customised programmes now represent on average 57% of their executive education business. At some schools, such as Manchester Business School, the figure is 95%.

Table 6.1
Customised programmes at leading European schools

School	Executive education revenue (€m)[a]	Customised programmes (%)
INSEAD	54.0	50
IMD	50.0[b]	50
London	28.9	60
IESE	28.0	30
Cranfield	21.6	47
Henley	21.5[b]	70[b]
Ashridge	21.4	66
Bocconi	14.8[b]	65
HEC, Paris	13.2	55
ESADE	11.0	36
IE	10.5	45
Vlerick Leuven Gent	9.0	33
Rotterdam (Erasmus)	9.0[b]	80
ESCP–EAP	7.4	42
Manchester	5.8	95
E.M. Lyon	5.3	66
Warwick	3.0	75

[a] Income from non-degree executive education (latest available data as provided by schools). Revenues converted at 2003 average rates.
[b] Economist Intelligence Unit estimate.

Customised programmes are concerned with the education of individuals in the context of their organisation, and it is this involvement in the detail of corporate strategy and culture change that sets them apart. However, the increasing switch towards customised programmes has forced business schools to wrestle with their consciences. Until recently, because they felt such programmes to be too close to consulting, some of the leading schools, especially in the US, were opposed to offering them. However, the acceptance of market realities and the realisation that they themselves had much to learn in terms of in-depth research and faculty development have helped schools to change their minds.

From a company's perspective the increasing use of customised programmes is understandable—after all, if it is spending significant amounts of money on sending managers to business school, it is only natural that it would want to tailor courses as closely as possible to its own particular needs—but there is some concern about the benefit for the organisation. In particular, there is a worry that individuals on a single-company programme will not be exposed to the kind of diverse cultural experience that is gained when sitting in a classroom with executives from different companies. This is where business schools' expertise comes in. They will have plenty of experience in dealing with companies and executives from a wide range of industries, and they should ensure that faculty members are in position to give companies a diverse cultural input.

Most customised programmes begin with a diagnostic session, involving a business school faculty team and senior managers, to discuss the company issues to be addressed and the required outcome. On this basis the school will begin to put together a programme, listing objectives, content and design. This is then likely to be further refined. As many schools point out, a customised programme only makes sense if senior managers have established explicit, precise goals, and the business school should be closely involved in this goal-setting phase.

Open programmes

Despite the rise of customised programmes, there is still a reasonable and respectable place for open programmes. One of their principal advantages is the opportunity they offer for networking: not just meeting a senior manager from a competitor or supplier in the coffee break, but learning about their experiences in the classroom. Like all management education these days, open courses rely heavily on bringing working experiences into the classroom.

In the same way, open courses also offer the kind of diversity (managers from many different industries, functions and backgrounds) that may not be possible on a customised course devised for a single company.

However, many companies are wary of the time involved in allowing managers to attend courses lasting more than a few days. The pressures of work are now such that any lengthy absences can be disruptive. There is also the well-known syndrome of executives returning from a course that has inspired them and attempting to introduce wholesale changes that are wholly unsuitable given the ethos and culture of their organisation. (In this context, at least one senior manager of a telecoms company in Europe suggests that, despite the time involved, managers take a short vacation after a course, partly to digest and reflect on what they have experienced and partly to avoid such confusion.)

To lead or follow?

So much of business school output is impenetrable esoteric research, to be found only in the pages of academic journals. But is it a school's job to concentrate on cutting-edge research or on what its customers actually want, which is usually solidly taught, established business theory? The answer is both.

If you choose to spend US$51,000 sending a manager on an executive development programme like, say, Harvard Business School's four-week Program for Management Development, presumably you expect him or her to learn something. But what? Would you prefer "What the new dynamics of business ecosystems mean for strategy, innovation and sustainability", or something a little more relevant that would help him boost the bottom line when he gets back? In other words, should business schools be providing their executive customers with "cutting-edge" research or simply passing on what is sometimes disparagingly referred to as "best practice"?

In today's overcrowded market, and despite business school insiders believing that original research is their only competitive selling point, the answer is likely to be that companies will get whatever they ask for. Considering that providers of executive education earned over US$600m in 2002–03, according to Business Week, this may not be surprising.

Leave the cutting edge outside the classroom

Most academics agree that a reputation as a leading research institution attracts companies to business schools as customers; but there is a difference between that and what they want in the classroom. Jim Dean, associate dean for executive education at the University of North Carolina's Kenan-Flagler Business School, says: "If you went into a class and said here's some new research that says it's not a good thing to communicate with your employees then the response would be pretty frosty."

In any case, much of the business schools' (like other providers') output is aimed at middle managers rather than strategy-savvy CEOs and other senior managers. Often what companies need at this level is the transfer of solid information about what is already known. One way of doing this is simply recycling what the best companies are doing already, seeing what works in one and then applying it to others. Clark Callahan, executive director for executive education at Tuck School of Business at Dartmouth College in the US, says: "One of the real sources of value for business schools is in being a professional explainer of things; looking at things that happen in business then explaining them so you understand and learn from them."

For some, however, this betrays the real value that they believe business schools can add beyond, say, consultants, the educational media, training companies and others in the executive education market.

Conceptual knowledge

Steve LaCivita, associate dean for executive education at Chicago Graduate School of Business, for example, believes that only research-based schools can give companies what he calls the "conceptual knowledge" to

Non-business school offerings

How long the boom in customised programmes will continue is anyone's guess; many business schools believe that it will last indefinitely. But competition, particularly in the form of "corporate universities", has intensified in recent years. Estimates vary but there have been suggestions that there are already 4,000 such institutions in the US alone and that more are being created every day. The Brussels-based European Foundation for Management Development (EFMD), which set up a task-force to examine the issues raised by corporate universities, describes them as "a real phenomenon of the contemporary management development help them reinvent themselves through strategies that change the rules of the competitive game. "If your objective is how to improve the bottom line, then go to a consultancy," he says. This division of the market may well be the shape of things to come.

Many university business schools, especially in the US, invest a huge amount of money in "pure" academic research that usually appears only in the more rarefied academic journals and maybe the odd textbook. (More practical research is often published in practitioner-based journals such as the Harvard Business Review, where it is quickly picked up by consultants, senior managers and other academics.) Such schools rarely have the time or inclination to become experts in best practice in a particular subject in a particular industry (which consultants excel at).

Schools also argue that talking about an idea that is years old does not attract companies, and that business people do look to business school research to gain access to new knowledge, often in particular areas. For example, according to Santiago Iniguez, who took over as dean of IE in Madrid in September 2004, there is currently great interest in research into managing diversity, in terms of both culture and gender and (because of terrorism) managing security and risk.

Schools can also score when they have a faculty member with the status of a "thought leader" (someone whose research is timely and relevant) who is also capable of teaching a room full of executives. "When you find someone with the right blend it is incredible," says Mr Callahan.

Transatlantic divide

The approach to research varies on either side of the Atlantic, however. For example, Dan Evans of E.M. Lyon in France suggests that the close relationship between business schools and business in France (where most schools were set up by local chambers of commerce) inevitably means that French schools combine both intellectual research and relevance to business.

Another European academic argues that business school research in Europe and in North America is qualitatively different, with the European variety being more relevant to business. He argues that this is largely because North American, especially US, colleagues have the endowment resources to allow them to indulge in academic research that may lack immediate relevance to business. "European business schools are much more dependent on corporate partners," he says.

Whatever the case may be, schools and other providers—wherever they are in the world—are facing one burgeoning question from their corporate customers: is it worth spending a lot of money on executive training? Answering it may prove to be far more important for executive education as a whole in the future than debating the relative merits of esoteric research and dull best practice.

movement" and says that they challenge the domain of traditional business schools.

Indeed they do. Many, such as the Walt Disney Institute, set in the middle of the company's main theme park in Orlando, Florida, make a virtue out of making their expertise available to outsiders.

One of the oldest corporate universities is Motorola University, which began in 1981 as the Motorola Training and Education Center. During the 1980s, Motorola University's charter was to help the corporation build a quality culture. By the end of the decade, the university had expanded its operations both in the US and around the world. More recently it began offering new and more comprehensive services, particularly its own Six Sigma quality improvement methodology, via both open and customised programmes.

Other independent providers can be broken down as follows:

- offshoots of global management consultancies;
- general providers of management development and training across a wide range of issues and disciplines; this is by far the largest area and players range from very large to very small;
- niche players concentrating on a narrow area such as leadership or change management and increasingly offering technology-based solutions;
- large or small organisations offering specialised training and development based on "proprietary" management philosophies or research.

Somewhere between business schools and the rest is Duke Corporate Education, a spin-off from Duke University's Fuqua School of Business. It handles all the school's customised programmes and topped the Financial Times's 2004 ranking of customised programme providers.

Cost

Customised programmes vary according to circumstances and it is difficult to give indications of costs, not least because business schools and companies are unwilling to disclose them. However, because they involve considerable inputs from the company and the provider and take time to develop and deliver, they are usually not cheap. The price depends to some extent on the nature of the programme. For example, a high-level programme aimed at, say, members of the board and involving considerable pre-programme research may well run into six or seven figures; lunch-time seminars on a relatively simple topic, such as globalisation, will be considerably cheaper; and company-wide culture change programmes can be as expensive as the board-level variety, although they cover many more employees.

The cost of open programmes also varies considerably depending on the prestige of the provider, the length of time involved, accommodation and the number of people taking part. For example, the three-day Finance for Global Managers programme at Thunderbird costs US$4,850 including meals and accommodation; the four-week flagship Advanced Executive Program at Kellogg costs US$28,000. The fact that open programmes are currently somewhat in decline does not mean that prices will fall; management education does not follow such simple economic rules.

Choosing a provider

Choosing an executive education programme is similar to choosing an MBA, although the final choice is more often made by company executives (usually from the human resources function) than by the participants. Again, the main distinction is between open and customised programmes.

Open programmes

There are three main criteria to consider when choosing an open programme.

- **Subject matter**. Schools often have particular strengths in particular areas such as marketing, finance or strategy, so choose the one that is best in the area you are interested in.

- **Participants**. Follow Groucho Marx's maxim and make sure that the calibre of your fellow participants will be high. Most of the benefit from open programmes comes from interaction and networking with your classmates.

- **Feedback**. Make sure that the programme provider will give a least a minimum amount of feedback to ensure that you can justify the expense and time of the programme in terms of the likely return you will get in increased performance.

Customised programmes

Customised programmes are designed to tackle a particular problem within an organisation. Before setting one up, make sure that you understand the issue or issues you want it to address and that the providers you approach will be able to come up with a viable programme. Identify at an early stage the executives, usually senior, who will work with the academics on identifying issues and proposing solutions and make sure they are committed and have the time to see the project through. Lastly, make sure that senior management is in favour of the idea and will give it emotional, managerial and financial support.

The student's perspective: executive education, customised programme

Jim Bonevac, a senior vice-president of Wachovia Corporation, a US financial services group, attended the Executive Leadership Program, a customised programme designed for Wachovia Corporation by the University of North Carolina's Kenan-Flagler Business School.

The Executive Leadership Program (ELP) was fantastic. Wachovia has made a major financial investment in developing the programme with the University of North Carolina (UNC) Kenan-Flagler. It also represents a significant investment of time by the company for the executives who attend the programme as well as the senior managers who participate in its delivery.

The ELP was an intensive effort. We went to UNC the first week of each month for four consecutive months. In addition to the study and preparation time required by the programme, we needed to manage our day-to-day work. To participate, we did have to go above and beyond our typical workload but it was a privilege to do so in order to participate in the programme.

Our class of about 25 worked together closely and built strong relationships that continue today. This is very useful at Wachovia, which has undergone numerous mergers in the last decade and, consequently, has a mixture of cultures. Wachovia is using the ELP to develop its next group of leaders. Those of us who have been through it share a language as well as a common perspective about how to approach problems and opportunities. We use a systems thinking approach, and know that other senior leaders are "on the same page".

ELP helps you see the big picture. You develop contacts—allies and friends—throughout the company, which has about 80,000 employees. We shared our challenges, we developed new perspectives and we learned to understand the perspective of others. It was a mind-expanding experience that created alignment among the executives. The programme helped us to think about what's best for the bank and the shareholder, not just for the individual business unit.

We would typically arrive at UNC Kenan-Flagler the night before the programme started. Our only real "down time" was during meals and in the evenings. Although some participants knew a few of the other members of the class, most participants were unfamiliar with each other. In order to "break the ice", the programme began with a "ropes" course. This outdoor physically challenging class broke down barriers and acted as a catalyst for our team-building efforts.

Interaction with the programme faculty was important and abundantly available. We would spend each day in the classroom with the professors. They integrated themselves into our social structure and it felt like they were part of the team. The professors were already familiar with Wachovia so there was very little time spent on bringing them up to speed on the issues and opportunities the company is facing. The UNC facilities were wonderful and very conducive to learning and building team spirit in an intimate and comfortable setting.

The commitment of Wachovia's senior leadership is critical to the success of ELP. They are truly involved and spent significant time with us during the programme. They shared their issues, opportunities, experiences and perspectives with us. It's rare to have time discussing critical, strategic issues with top leadership and we valued and benefited tremendously from it. In fact, their active participation was the key to the programme's success. They were fully engaged and energised, and this was transferred to the programme's participants. That energy and engagement remains with me today, eight months after completing the programme.

Chapter 7

Other considerations

How to pay for your programme

The costs of an MBA are considerable. Part-time students, for example, can expect tuition fees of around US$3,500 per course at a leading business school such as Chicago or Kellogg and £33,900 (US$55,574) for the 27-month part-time programme at Ashridge in the UK. Executive MBAs, where the costs are most often borne by employers, can be even more costly. The EMBA at IMD in Switzerland, for example, which includes residential blocks and distance learning elements costs Swfr115,000 (US$85,185) plus accommodation costs. Even distance learning, often seen as the cheapest route to an MBA, can be expensive, costing £13,700 (US$22,459) at Henley in the UK, for example.

But it is full-time students who can expect to bear the highest costs. Full-time students at leading schools can expect to graduate with debts of at least US$100,000, assuming they have paid all their own costs (as most of them will have done). Since most full-time students will have given up their jobs before taking an MBA or be planning to change jobs once they graduate, few are sponsored by their employers.

Parental help or even a willing spouse can be useful, but most MBA programmes will have to be financed through savings and loans. Since a sizeable increase in salary can be expected following graduation, most banks are willing to lend the money. The various approaches to financing an MBA, based on the Economist Intelligence Unit's survey for *Which MBA?* 2004, are outlined in Table 7.1.

Table 7.1
How students finance their MBA programmes
Were you sponsored by your company?[a]

	Yes
All students	17
Full-time	7
Part-time	57
Executive	70
Distance-learning	44

If sponsored, for how long have you agreed not to leave your employment?[b]

	Up to two years	3–5 years	More than 5 years	No agreement required
All students	36	15	1	48
Full-time	48	26	2	25
Part-time	33	8	0	59
Executive	34	17	1	48
Distance-learning	21	8	0	71

If self-financed, how was the money raised?[c]

	Bank loan	Savings	Parents	Spouse	Redundancy/severance
World	34	40	17	8	1
Full-time	34	38	18	8	1
Part-time	32	51	8	8	2
Executive	31	56	5	6	1
Distance-learning	10	75	9	5	1

[a] % of respondents. [b] % of students sponsored by their company. [c] Importance accorded by all students to each factor.

Savings and loans

The most common way for students to fund their MBA, at least in part, is through savings, but the balance will almost certainly come from loans. Nearly all MBA students will be able to obtain loans in their own countries through either government schemes or private banks. Typically, these are soft loans with more favourable interest rates and repayment periods than the market offers. Schemes differ considerably from country to country. Many business schools are able to put students in touch with the appropriate organisations, and most list available loan schemes on their websites or in their brochures. Schemes are generally confined to nationals or full-time residents of the country concerned, but most will cover study in an overseas country.

The Graduate Management Admission Council (GMAC) sponsors the MBA Loans Program in the US. Would-be students in North America can visit www.salliemae.com/mbaloans. In the UK, the Association of MBAs (AMBA) organises soft loans (www.mba.org.uk).

Scholarships

Most schools offer some form of scholarship. However, the number and value vary enormously. Details of the amounts made available to students are contained in each school's directory entry. Most are linked to:

● merit (high scholastic achievement and potential that will reflect well on the school);

● need (high potential but few resources); or

● specific groups (for example, minorities or women).

Few scholarships cover all costs, although in exceptional cases they might. The Economist Intelligence Unit's 2004 survey of business schools (see Table 7.2) shows that total aid available for all students can range from several million dollars at some American schools to thousands of dollars per school in Europe and other parts of the world.

Scholarships are one of the many marketing tools that business schools employ. Some schools offer them to attract the best students to increase their ratings in GMAT scores, grade averages or salaries on graduation. Others use them to attract a particular type of student or even a single individual. Some trade-off might be involved in going to a second-choice school that offers help rather than a first-choice one that does not, but nothing can match the feeling of security of a debt-free MBA. Details of scholarships and bursaries can be found on schools' websites and in brochures, and these should be studied. You have nothing to lose by applying. It needs to be done early, well before arriving at the school, because by that time most of the available money will probably have been allocated.

There are also national scholarship schemes for management and business students. It is impractical to list these here, but national and local education authorities should have details.

Sponsorship

Many MBA students will try to get someone else to pay for their programme, but it is not easy, particularly for a full-time programme. Few employers will pay employees to be away from the office for one or two years, although there are exceptional cases. Full time students rarely receive sponsorship (with the exception of government-funded overseas students and employees of a few large consultancy firms or companies). However, employer support for part-time and distance-learning programmes is common among organisations with a management development focus. Around 57% of part-time and 44% of distance-learning students were sponsored, according to the Economist Intelligence Unit's 2004 survey of MBA students and recent alumni. Even so, an employer may agree to pay only under an arrangement that requires an employee to stay with the company for a specified time after graduation.

Earning and studying

Working while studying is becoming an accepted part of undergraduate education throughout the world and the same is true of MBA students. However, time constraints are much greater than for undergraduate courses and working is frowned on in short one-year programmes and the first year of two-year programmes. Schools say that this is not just because it may affect their studies, but also because students can miss out on extra-curricular activities and socialising. It is easier to work in the second year of longer programmes, where pressures are much less intense. Many students combine second-year study with part-time work, either with local companies or within the school itself, helping out in computer laboratories, admissions, careers services and as teaching assistants. Some schools try to help spouses accompanying an MBA student to find work, either with local companies or within the school itself.

Lastly, of course, you can always try to persuade your new employer after graduation to pay for the cost of your MBA. When times are good and employers are lining up to recruit MBA graduates, this is not such a bizarre idea as it seems, and it can be quite common. However, when the market is depressed, employers are hard to find and competition for jobs is fierce, such offers often dry up. In any case, warn business school careers officers, following this route can lead MBA graduates to choose the wrong job for the wrong reasons.

Chapter 7
Other considerations

Table 7.2
Financial aid available for MBA students, selected schools[a]

School	Aid in local currency and US$	Types of assistance	Criteria for granting aid
North America			
Stanford	US$46.5m	Fellowships, loans	Admission to the programme, qualifications, financial need
Virginia (Darden)	US$32.3m	Merit scholarships, needs-based grants	GMAT, merit, financial need
Duke (Fuqua)	US$24.8m	Merit scholarships, federal loans	Merit, financial need
Georgetown (McDonough)	US$14.8m	Loans, work-study, grants, scholarships	Merit, financial need
Emory (Goizueta)	US$11.7m	Scholarships, loans	Merit, financial need
Harvard	US$10.2m	Needs-based fellowships, loans	Merit
California at Berkeley (Haas)	US$9.8m	Scholarships, loans, grants, teaching & research assistants	Financial need
Notre Dame (Mendoza)	US$9.8m	Fellowships, private & federal loans	n/a
Vanderbilt (Owen)	US$8.9m	Scholarships, assistantships, loans	Merit, financial need
Case Western Reserve (Weatherhead)	US$8.5m	Scholarships, loans, assistantships	GMAT over 640, excellent academic record
Europe			
ESSEC	€3m (US$3.4m)	Grants, apprenticeships, assistantships	Outstanding application
Bocconi	€1.2m (US$1.3m)	Scholarships, loans	Formal scholarship application process, mainly merit-based
IMD	Swfr1.5m (US$1.1m)	Scholarships, loans	Merit, admission criteria
London	£400,000 (US$655,738)	Scholarships	Strong academic record, high GMAT & TOEFL scores, relevant work experience
Cranfield	£350,000 (US$573,770)	Scholarships	Merit
Rotterdam (Erasmus)	€500,000 (US$568,182)	Scholarships	Merit
Nottingham	£246,000 (US$403,279)	10 half-fee scholarships on full-time MBA for UK/EU applicants	Merit, candidate profile
IESE	€260,000 (US$295,455)	Scholarships, loans	Strong academic record, financial need
Strathclyde	£130,000 (US$213,115)	Scholarships, partial awards	Merit
HEC, Paris	€110,000 (US$125,000)	Scholarships, loans	Merit
Rest of the world			
Singapore	S$1.5m (US$885,057)	Loans	Background, test scores
International University of Japan	¥61.6m (US$530,838)	Scholarships	Merit, financial need
China Europe International Business School	US$444,434	Scholarships, loans, grants	Scholarships based on academic performance in MBA programme
Melbourne	A$370,000 (US$240,260)	Scholarships	n/a
Australian GSM	A$325,700 (US$211,494)	Scholarships	Merit, financial need
Nanyang	S$255,100 (US$146,609)	Scholarships	Merit
Monash	A$160,000 (US$103,896)	Scholarships, government loans for Australian students	n/a
Indian Institute (Ahmedabad)	Rs4.4m (US$94,891)	Scholarships	Academic & professional merit, financial need
Curtin	A$125,000 (US$81,169)	Scholarships	Merit, financial need
Wits	R500,000 (US$66,138)	Scholarships	Merit, financial need
Hong Kong BS	HK$64,000 (US$64,000)	Scholarships	Merit, financial need (justification letter required)

[a] Supplied by schools.

How to get into a school: admissions, interviews, GMAT

Although there are many business schools offering MBA degrees, we assume that people reading this guide want an MBA from a top-ranked business school, which narrows their choice to fewer than 150 schools around the world. Looking at the full-time intakes of the schools featured in *Which MBA?*, only around 20,000 students will achieve their ambition. Even a non-MBA graduate can work out the implications: when demand exceeds supply the price goes up. In MBA terms, this means the price of admission—not so much the financial cost (although that is high enough), but the hoops students must jump through to get in. Getting into a programme is probably one of the hardest parts of an MBA.

At times the top schools seem determined to keep people out. They are not. They just want the best. It is hardly surprising that they can afford to take a lot of time and trouble in selecting students. They are choosing from a well-stocked pool of talent. The result is that applying to a business school is a long and arduous process. This section looks at what the business schools are seeking through the different stages of admission, including application forms, interviews, the GMAT and other tests.

The GMAC reports that applications to business schools slowed in 2002 and 2003. It identifies three main reasons for the decline.

● The effects of a weak economy on income and jobs. According to the GMAC, faced with a weak economy prospective students initially believe that going back to school is a better alternative than job hunting in a tight market. But during an extended weak economy, prospective students are less able (or willing) to pay for an MBA programme because of salary freezes, depleted savings and cuts in company sponsorship. They are less likely to forgo the security of a steady income.

● A demographic decline in the US the numbers of 25–34 year-olds. According to the US Department of Education, overall graduate enrolment in the US for the age range 25–34 (the typical age range of students in graduate business schools) has been negative to flat from 1999 to 2004, but it will start to increase in 2005.

● Worldwide political and health issues. The war in Iraq, SARS and other political developments have affected prospective students both psychologically, through concerns about safety, and practically, through travel and visa restrictions. As a result, says the GMAC, individuals are applying to programmes in different regions.

In the Economist Intelligence Unit's 2004 survey for *Which MBA?*, students and graduates were asked to rate how difficult it was to get into their school. The results are given in Table 7.3.

Chapter 7
Other considerations

Table 7.3
How difficult was it to get into your school?[a]

School	Rating	School	Rating
American (Kogod)	3.0	International University of Japan	3.4
Arizona (Eller)	3.1	Lancaster	3.6
Ashridge	3.0	Leeds	2.8
Aston	2.9	London	4.2
Australian GSM	3.2	E.M. Lyon	3.7
Bath	3.9	Macquarie	3.0
Birmingham	3.3	Manchester	3.3
Bocconi	3.5	Maryland (Smith	3.8
Bradford	2.9	MIT (Sloan)	4.7
Brandeis	3.8	McGill	3.0
British Columbia (Sauder)	3.3	Melbourne	3.5
Calgary (Haskayne)	2.7	Michigan	4.4
California at Berkeley (Haas)	4.4	Minnesota (Carlson)	3.2
California at Davis	3.5	Monaco	2.9
Cambridge (Judge)	3.8	Nanyang	3.5
Carnegie Mellon (Tepper)	3.9	New York (Stern)	4.3
Case Western Reserve (Weatherhead)	3.2	Newcastle	3.3
Chicago	4.7	NIMBAS	3.6
China Europe International Business School	4.0	North Carolina (Kenan-Flagler)	4.1
Chinese University of Hong Kong	3.1	Northwestern (Kellogg)	4.7
City (Cass)	3.2	Norwegian BI	3.3
Columbia	4.6	Notre Dame (Mendoza)	3.5
Concordia (Molson)	3.5	Nottingham	2.9
Cornell (Johnson)	4.1	Nyenrode	3.5
Cranfield	3.7	Ohio (Fisher)	3.5
Dartmouth (Tuck)	4.6	Oxford (Saïd)	4.0
Dublin (Trinity)	3.0	Penn State (Smeal)	3.3
Duke (Fuqua)	4.2	Pennsylvania (Wharton)	4.8
Durham	2.9	Pittsburgh (Katz)	3.4
EADA	3.2	Purdue (Krannert)	3.5
Edinburgh	3.2	Queen's	3.8
Emory (Goizueta)	3.8	Rice (Jones)	3.5
ENPC	3.4	Rochester Simon)	3.6
ESADE	3.3	Rotterdam (Erasmus)	3.3
ESCP–EAP	3.6	Sheffield	3.0
ESSEC	4.4	Singapore	3.5
Florida (Warrington)	3.5	Solvay	3.0
Georgetown (McDonough)	4.0	South Carolina (Moore)	3.4
Georgia (Terry)	3.6	Southern California (Marshall)	3.8
Glasgow	3.5	Southern Methodist (Cox)	3.3
Harvard	4.7	Stanford	4.9

School	Rating	School	Rating
HEC, Paris	3.9	Strathclyde	2.7
Helsinki	3.0	Texas (McCombs)	3.7
Henley	3.1	Theseus	3.3
Hong Kong SB	3.5	Thunderbird (Garvin)	3.3
Hong Kong UST	3.1	UCLA (Anderson)	4.3
Hult	3.0	Vanderbilt (Owen)	3.7
IE	3.7	Virginia (Darden)	4.3
IESE	4.0	Vlerick Leuven Gent	3.5
Illinois	3.3	Wake Forest (Babcock)	3.5
IMD	4.7	Warwick	3.7
Imperial (Tanaka)	3.4	Washington St Louis (Olin)	3.7
Indian Institute (Ahmedabad)	5.0	Western Ontario (Ivey)	3.6
Indiana (Kelley)	3.7	William & Mary	3.3
INSEAD	4.4	Wisconsin-Madison	3.3
Institut d'Etudes Politiques	3.8	Yale	4.4
Iowa (Tippie)	3.2	York (Schulich)	3.3

a Rated on a scale of 1 to 5, where 1 means no difficulty or little effort required, 3 means reasonable effort required and 5 means extremely competitive, arduous entrance procedure. Schools are listed in alphabetical order.

Getting into the school of your choice

An application to a business school is rather like a first date. The business schools are woo-ing the best students and the students are wooing the best schools. Which MBA? is firmly on the side of prospective students, aiming to help you look beneath the surface. That outward-ly impressive business school may not be what you want for the long run. Be discriminating, and make sure that what you eventually sign up for is dependable, of high quality and suited to your needs.

Although getting in to a leading school is tough, admissions staff invariably present a smil-ing face. After all, you may be their ideal candidate. As a result, you can expect them to be efficient in answering queries and eventually making an offer of a place should you be suc-cessful. Anecdotal evidence suggests that a common reason for choosing a particular school is the helpfulness and efficiency of the admissions office. Schools also make an effort to get applicants on campus. Good candidates are much more easily persuaded to sign up when they are physically on campus and can meet the faculty members, sit in on classes and talk to students. Many admissions departments also telephone prospective students to continue the selling process. For those who fit the student profile the school is aiming for, consider-able help, in the form of scholarships and even living allowances, can be available.

What is the school looking for?

The friendly face of admissions is about attracting applications, however. Once the forms and online submissions start rolling in, the job of admissions changes. The concern then becomes how to select only the best candidates and to make sure that none of them defect to compet-ing schools. There are good commercial reasons for this. The best students attract the best recruiters and get the best jobs. Graduates who get the best, highest-paid jobs are great advertisements for the school and become (the school hopes) grateful and generous alumni.

At first sight, the qualities that admissions departments look for in candidates are fairly standard. They expect a good first degree (generally the subject is not important, although some schools offer fast tracks to applicants with undergraduate majors in areas such as business studies, economics or finance) and a good GMAT score, although this will vary from school to school. All schools that require the GMAT have an effective minimum score (whatever they say to the contrary), and it follows that the higher the average at the school, the higher is the minimum requirement. Also required are a solid work background, generally of at least three years; good interpersonal skills and leadership potential; a belief that you really want to come to their school; and a "wow" factor that somehow sets candidates apart (this might be an interesting former career such as ballerina or marine corps colonel or charitable work in developing countries).

Diversity is another issue. White males still predominate on MBA programmes and the schools would like more women and people from minority groups. They also like "international" students. Some European schools appear to be attracted to nationality almost for the sake of it. They like to claim that a class of 80 students, for example, contains 80 different nationalities. Admissions staff constantly monitor the balance of applicants offered a place so that they can achieve the required diversity. So even a brilliant Spanish auditor with high GMAT and TOEFL (Test of English as a Foreign Language) scores and an impressive business record might be turned down if the school already has enough Spanish auditors (or even just Spanish men) in the class. The best it can offer may be a place on the same programme the following year.

However, this emphasis on diversity can sometimes lead to half-whispered complaints among MBA students that women and people from minority groups have an easier time during the applications process and are more likely to be awarded finance-easing scholarships and the like. This is a sore point that schools discuss only off the record. But it does not take a genius to work out that if schools are looking for diversity in their classrooms, they must perforce operate some kind of informal quota system. If you are determined that no one national group will predominate in the classroom, you must restrict the numbers of that group that you admit.

The final decision on whether you get into a school is entirely in the hands of the admissions office and its director. They typically have long experience of selection and claim the ability to spot students who will and will not succeed. The reality is that for the majority of candidates the judgement is finely balanced and largely subjective. It may also be weighted by considerations that go well beyond the qualities of a particular candidate. For example, the school may want to boost the number of foreign students or increase the average number of years of work experience or GMAT scores.

Given the link between bright students, bright graduate recruits and grateful graduates, the admissions and careers services departments work closely together. If they decide after reviewing applications that certain candidates have unrealistic goals for their subsequent careers, they may not be prepared to risk their job record by taking them on. Even successful applicants will be encouraged to start the job search early on.

Apply early

An important factor that prospective students must be aware of is the need to apply early to their chosen school or schools. Business school websites, brochures and this guide give final dates for applications, but these really are final. Admissions offices usually work on a rolling basis and start to fill up their classes as soon as applications are received. Lists may therefore be full long before the deadline arrives.

Application forms, references, essays and interviews

Application forms

Application forms are long, complicated, hard to understand and even harder to complete. Traditionally, North American business schools produce the most fearsome forms but European schools and others are catching up. Why they should be such an obstacle course is hard to understand. After all, they are asking for fairly standard information:

- personal details;
- academic record, with grades obtained (you will have to organise official transcripts);
- a work and experience record;
- references, normally unseen by the applicant, from two or three individuals who know your academic and work experience;
- up to four short essays designed to give an insight into your personality and attitudes.

The application form is a, if not the, key element admissions offices use to select students. It is your chance to impress the admissions office by pulling together your undergraduate performance, GMAT score, work experience and anything else you can think of to impress them. But remember, however good the content is, a poorly completed application form will not get you very far.

Electronic applications

Increasingly, the applications procedure is being handled electronically, with a large number of schools including a facility to download and return an application form on their website. Many schools now insist on electronic application.

References

References (often called recommendations by North American schools) should be written by people who have relevant and detailed knowledge of your academic or work background and a good sense of your personality. Think carefully about who you ask to do this. Forget spouses, parents, aunts and uncles: the business schools expect referees to have been your direct business or academic supervisor at some time. Whoever you choose, make sure they know what an MBA is and the reasons you want to study one. You should also brief them as much as possible on the schools you are applying to, why you have chosen those schools and your subsequent career plans. Their support is vital, so a discussion with them before they complete their part of the application form is important. The applications office expects them to provide a rounded (and accurate) picture of you and your achievements.

Alumni of your targeted business schools are considered to be particularly useful as referees, so if you know any then don't be afraid to approach them. But the really important point to bear in mind is that whoever you choose must be someone you can trust to give a good reference in good time.

Essay questions

Writing application essays is probably the most difficult, and potentially dangerous, part of the process. Admissions staff say they read every essay submitted and regard them as important indicators, especially in borderline cases. They see essays as a way of getting to your real personality, tempting you either to brag outrageously or to be destructively self-critical. Don't be fooled. They are not really trying to trip you up. What most schools want to see is a middle course, an objective assessment of successes and failures, strengths and weaknesses.

Most essay questions are straightforward, although some are occasionally outlandish. However, they are all open-ended and require a good deal of thought if you are to take the right approach. Essays should be interesting and original, but not too out of the ordinary. The admissions staff look for something a little unusual with a bit more bite than the stock response, but nothing too extravagant.

Most of the essay questions posed by schools are broadly similar, and schools face the predictable problems of ready-prepared essays (not always written by the candidate) and the same essays being submitted to many schools. But for the majority of candidates, essays represent an opportunity for quality work and honesty. Admissions staff are experienced at spotting anything phoney and are ever alert to fraudulent work. They are also clear about what they want. Applicants should be equally clear and, within the bounds of honesty, legality and morality, present themselves as fitting the particular school's ideal model. Careful reading of brochures, contact with schools and guides such as this provide a good grounding in what they are looking for.

You can, of course, enter a few key words into an Internet search engine to reveal the many services available to help with essay writing of this kind. These may range from reviewing or editing your finished essay to effectively writing it for you. This is not something that should be encouraged, but it happens and cannot be ignored. No doubt some services genuinely help candidates.

The best advice, though, still has to be to do your own thing to the best of your own ability. After all, in the end you have to take the MBA yourself and no one has (as yet) developed a web-based service that will do that for you.

Interviews

Although not all top-rated schools require them, schools are putting greater emphasis on interviews as MBA programmes focus more on soft skills. Consequently, the personality of students has become a more important ingredient in their success on a programme, and schools need to gain a more rounded view of candidates in order to assess their personalities. So far, old-fashioned interviews are the best test they have come up with. Another factor is greater diversity. Standardised admission processes produce standardised classes. An interview is a good way of assessing students who may not quite match the academic ground rules but who have other desirable qualities. Interviews are designed to elicit an idea of your personality, but some schools structure them more formally and may have a checklist of questions to go through.

Generally, interviews take place after the application form has been reviewed. Most often they are conducted on campus by admissions staff, although sometimes, as at Kellogg, interviews are conducted by students. For foreign students or those living a significant distance away, schools must use outside interviewers (normally their own graduates). Business schools go to considerable lengths to ensure that these interviewers are well briefed and adopt a uniform approach, so interviewees should not be at a disadvantage. However, if you possibly can, do take an interview on campus. That way you get experienced admissions office staff rather than volunteer alumni, who, however well meaning and well briefed, are still not the real thing. Remember, too, that no interview is foolproof and that from the school's point of view the best selection, as for any job, is usually achieved by doing well at all elements in the admissions hurdle-course.

The GMAT and other admissions tests

The MBA is a conversion degree, taking any student with a good first degree in any subject and equipping them with the tools and knowledge required for a move into business management. You do not normally need to have previously studied a business subject. (In some "open" programmes, normally by distance learning, such as that offered by the Open University Business School in the UK, you do not even need a degree; entry to these programmes is via a series of preparatory courses.) Since an MBA is essentially a degree in general management, it is a generalised subject and hence no previous specialist knowledge is required to study it. However, MBA programmes are usually heavy on mathematics and statistics (not to mention such subjects as accounting). Anyone with limited mathematical skills may well struggle.

Don't be fooled by an increased emphasis on teaching so-called soft skills, such as interpersonal relations, negotiation, leadership and so on. This does not mean that top-ranked schools have relaxed their approach. Soft skills may be desirable, but academic business teaching remains underpinned by some hefty quantitative analysis. This is especially true in the US. Although some European schools may appear to place less emphasis on the quantitative approach and be more oriented towards soft skills, they do not offer a refuge for those who cannot add two and two. Many leading schools, again especially in the US, require students to have previously studied quantitative disciplines, notably calculus. But most schools also run pre-programme refresher or cramming courses in all the quantitative areas. Anyone in any doubt about their ability should definitely attend; indeed, some schools make it mandatory. This quantitative approach is one reason why the GMAT is such an important element in MBA applications.

The GMAT

Even before they get to their first business school class, MBA students will already feel like battle-hardened veterans if they have had to take ("write" in the jargon) the Graduate Management Admission Test (GMAT). Although some schools may not require it, usually substituting their own test or asking for the GMAT only for foreign students, this most feared and hated part of the business school admission process is something that most applicants will have to go through.

The GMAT is sponsored and directed by the Graduate Management Admissions Council (GMAC, www.gmac.com), a US-based international organisation of 139 graduate schools of management, although it is administered on the GMAC's behalf by the Educational Testing Service in New Jersey. Nearly 2,000 business schools around the world require GMAT scores from applicants, according to the GMAC.

The GMAT measures language, quantitative and writing skills and is designed to help predict a student's potential academic performance. Most schools find that it is a good predictor of likely success at graduate management school, particularly the quantitative aspects of a typical MBA programme. People who score poorly in this area of the GMAT may have trouble with subjects such as statistics, accounting and finance. Perhaps not surprisingly, a five-year study by the GMAC backs up the predictive ability of the GMAT. It claims that the correlation between GMAT scores and performance on the core component of a programme is extremely high across race, gender and age.

Although paper versions are still used in a few parts of the world, the GMAT is effectively fully computerised and is known as a computer-adaptive test (CAT). This means that the test adjusts itself to the respondent's ability as it progresses. Applicants sit in front of a computer screen and answer one question at a time, automatically displayed from a large pool of questions organised by content and level of difficulty (see box on page 78). The GMAC says the test requires minimal computer skills, and each test is preceded by a computer-based tutorial. The GMAT can take up to four hours to complete, with two five-minute breaks. Test conditions can be strenuous.

The number of GMAT-takers is currently declining. According to the GMAC, the number of GMAT tests (including people who took the test more than once) taken in the first three months of 2004 was, at 53,342, 9.68% lower compared with the same time period in 2003. The decrease was 4.29% in the US and 19.22% outside the US and reflects the decline in applicants mentioned above. This is a significant change from the record year of 2002, when, during the 12 months, the test was taken nearly 250,000 times, the highest number in its history.

Test scores

Official test scores are distributed automatically to the schools chosen by applicants (every business school has an official GMAT code number), usually within two weeks. Unofficial scores, which do not include essay marks, are available to applicants as soon as they have finished the test. Although many schools do not stipulate minimum GMAT scores, most will have a cut-off point in mind. At leading schools with high average GMAT scores this could be around 600–650; at other schools, or those with less commitment to GMAT scores, it could be as low as 500.

The maximum achievable GMAT score is 800, but in any given year an average of only around 50 candidates score maximum points. Those who score the maximum usually attribute it to a mixture of luck and practice. Tables 7.4 and 7.5 show the average scores of students for selected schools; the directory entries list the average for each school. Some, however, refuse to reveal their averages on the grounds that they are misleading, since a high average does not necessarily imply overall ability. GMAT scores reported by schools are also used as part of the Economist Intelligence Unit's 2004 ranking of business schools (see methodology, page 101).

Table 7.4
Average GMAT scores of students (world)[a]

School	GMAT score	School	GMAT score
Stanford	716	California at Berkeley (Haas)	700
Pennsylvania (Wharton)	713	New York (Stern)	700
MIT (Sloan)	710	Dartmouth (Tuck)	697
Columbia	709	Michigan	692
Harvard	707	Oxford (Saïd)	692
INSEAD	707	Chicago	690
Duke (Fuqua)	705	Southern California (Marshall)	689
UCLA (Anderson)	705	IESE	685
Northwestern (Kellogg)	703	London	684
Yale	703	Queen's	684

[a] As reported by schools. Not all schools require the GMAT or reveal GMAT scores.

Table 7.5
Average GMAT scores of students by region[a]

Europe	GMAT score	North America	GMAT score	Asia & Australasia	GMAT score
INSEAD	707	Stanford	716	China Europe International Business School	669
Oxford (Saïd)	692	Pennsylvania (Wharton)	713	Singapore	662
IESE	685	MIT (Sloan)	710	Australian GSM	654
London	684	Columbia	709	Nanyang	651
Cambridge (Judge)	680	Harvard	707	Hong Kong UST	633
IMD	680	Duke (Fuqua)	705	Melbourne	627
Bocconi	670	UCLA (Anderson)	705	Chinese University of Hong Kong	618
Cranfield	670	Northwestern (Kellogg)	703	Hong Kong SB	610
IE	670	Yale	703	International University of Japan	592
ESSEC	668	California at Berkeley (Haas)	700		
ESADE	660	New York (Stern)	700		
HEC, Paris	660	Dartmouth (Tuck)	697		
NIMBAS	640	Michigan	692		
Vlerick Leuven Gent	634	Chicago	690		

[a] As reported by schools. Not all schools require the GMAT or reveal GMAT scores.

GMAT scores are climbing higher and higher. A look at the historical data compiled by the Economist Intelligence Unit since 1994 confirms this. The highest average scores have risen consistently over the past ten years. No one is quite sure why this is happening. The GMAC attributes the rise to the increasing number of people taking the test, but some business schools express private concern and various theories are being touted, such as the computer version being easier, students taking more coaching or candidate impersonation, despite the strict security at GMAT centres.

Chapter 7
Other considerations

Figure 7.1
Average GMAT scores (top ten schools) 1994–2004

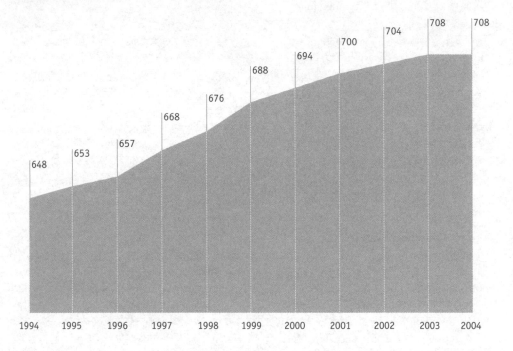

Even though it is extremely important, the GMAT is not the be-all and end-all. As the GMAC itself cautions, the GMAT is only one indicator, and by no means a perfect one. Academic records, references, interviews and all the other paraphernalia of the business school admissions process are equally important. In Europe and elsewhere, many schools run their own tests (usually only for local students) in addition to the GMAT because they believe that they are more accurate predictors.

Cultural bias

The GMAT sits firmly inside the US tradition of standardised testing for entry to academic institutions. All US undergraduate courses and postgraduate degrees, such as law, require them. It is therefore surprising that the GMAT has become such a global phenomenon. The test exists only in (American) English, and its multiple-choice approach is alien to some cultures. As a result, there are concerns about cultural bias, which is said to work particularly to the disadvantage of Japanese and other applicants from East Asia. Schools claim, however, that they are well aware of the bias and allow for it.

The GMAC says that it is working hard to remove any signs of cultural bias from the GMAT, and considerable changes have been made. Essay questions were added to the multiple-choice sections in 1994. Essays are difficult to prepare in advance and, it is hoped, tell schools more about candidates. According to the GMAC, both schools and employers asked for the test to include essay questions because they were interested in students' ability to write about complex issues. It claims the essays are not a test of writing skill but of thinking ability, like the multiple-choice questions but in a different format.

The GMAC also points out that students whose first language is not English may do less well than they are capable of in the verbal and essay sections of the test. It recommends that for such students schools should take account of their results in the TOEFL as well as the GMAT.

TOEFL

An English-language MBA programme is a daunting prospect for people whose first language is not English. Even native speakers have trouble in classes where a student is picked at random to lead a discussion on a case study, and where students are assessed on their participation in class.

Most schools teaching in English therefore demand some objective proof of fluency from non-native speakers. A few schools run their own tests or accept other qualifications, but the Test of English as a Foreign Language, or TOEFL (pronounced "toe-fell") is widely accepted as a standard measure. However, like the GMAT, the test has come under fire. Many feel that it does not give a good indication of language ability and that it is open to cheating.

There is, however, little alternative. English fluency is important, and people should not rely on polishing it up after they arrive since other pressures may be too great to allow this. Although English-speaking students will often help (by editing written assignments, for example), they, too, are generally under severe time pressure. Thus language lessons may be necessary before embarking on the programme. Details of the test can be obtained from the TOEFL website (www.toefl.org).

How to get a job

It used to be considered tactless to talk about getting a job until towards the end of an MBA programme, and many schools actively discouraged recruiters from approaching students until after most of their studies were completed. This is no longer the case. One of the biggest changes in business schools' careers services over recent years has been an increased emphasis on the job search, with careers issues being raised at orientation sessions that were traditionally designed to allow new students to meet and bond with each other in a relaxed atmosphere and throughout the MBA programme.

This increased emphasis reflects both demand from students, especially in a tough economic climate, and the growing influence of careers services departments. The careers office is one of the main determinants of a business school's success and has a corresponding influence on its policies. Indeed, it is one of the principal drivers of change in the MBA business, particularly the design of MBA programmes. A good example of this is the revamping of MBA programmes in the late 1980s and early 1990s, which stemmed from employers' criticism, filtered through careers offices, of MBA graduates' alleged lack of soft skills and ability to manage people.

The provision of careers services can be expensive, though, and standards vary among schools and regions. Generally, larger schools (with larger budgets) do it best, but you need to check this out before accepting an offer from a school. Look at job offers, starting salaries and placement statistics, which are usually displayed on a school's website and in its brochures. A rating of the careers service is also included in the *Which MBA?* ranking. The gold standard is undoubtedly set in the US, where careers services (once known more confidently as "placement") are part of a well-oiled machine that "processes" carefully chosen, high-quality students into well-paid graduates and, ultimately, wealthy and generous alum-

How the GMAT works

What does it involve?

Taking the GMAT is not for the faint-hearted. Candidates sit at a computer in one of a row of tiny cubicles in deathly silence. The screen displays one question at a time. The first is always of medium difficulty. The selection of each question after that depends on the answers given to all previous questions. In effect, the test adjusts to the respondent's ability level; there should be few questions that are either too easy or too difficult. However, this means that every question must be answered and there is no way of changing previous answers. So if you get into a series of easy questions it is hard to break out into more high-scoring ones.

The GMAT includes verbal, quantitative and analytical writing questions. Candidates have 75 minutes to complete 37 quantitative questions, 75 minutes for 41 verbal questions, and 30 minutes for each of the two analytical writing topics, which begin the test. The verbal and quantitative sections are computer adaptive, but the two analytical writing questions are not, although they are keyed into the computer.

When and where?

The GMAT is offered three weeks a month, six days a week throughout the year at over 400 computer-based testing centres in North America and in 98 countries around the world (though less frequently in some countries so you need to check). Security at test centres is intense. Concern about impersonation may be growing now, but it has been a perennial problem.

The minimum identification requirements are a passport and a driving licence. Tests are continually audiotaped and videotaped. Candidates are allowed to take nothing, not even food and drink, into their cubicle except a prominently displayed means of identification; all rough notes are collected afterwards. Failure to comply with regulations can mean scores are cancelled or candidates are even physically ejected. Special facilities are available for candidates with disabilities.

How?

Registration is via the GMAT Information Bulletin, which can be downloaded from the GMAC website (www.gmac.com*). This informative site gives details of the test, sample questions, test aids and other useful information, and allows online registration. Applicants can schedule or change a test appointment by mail, phone or online, and an appointment can be made with only a few days' notice. The test is changed once a month, which is why even those with a masochistic streak can take it only once in a calendar month.

Since January 2002 no one can take the test more than five times within a 12-month period without seeking written permission from the GMAC. According to the GMAC, around 20% of GMAT-takers repeat the test, usually taking it two or three times. On average, retakers can expect to add 30 points to their total score by taking the test a second time.

ni. Outside the US the approach can be more patchy. In Europe, for example, some of the leading schools such as London Business School, IMD and INSEAD have good reputations, but at other schools the reaction of students can be mixed. Often the problem is that business schools tied to universities rely on existing undergraduate careers offices, or that a tradition of executive education and/or sponsored students has resulted in a lack of investment in careers services.

The Economist Intelligence Unit's 2004 survey for *Which MBA?* of students' and graduates' experiences of their school's careers services shows, as in previous surveys, that satisfaction

Useful aids

Help and advice on the test can be found in The Official Guide for GMAT Review (US$29.95 plus shipping). This contains more than 1,400 GMAT questions, 200 analytical writing assessment topics, tips on taking the test, a maths review covering the kinds of topics tested in the GMAT (arithmetic, algebra, geometry and word problems) and a chapter summarising the content of the test tutorials.

Candidates can also take a mock test using POWERPREP, which can be downloaded free from the GMAC website (www.mba.com*). It features two timed computer-adaptive tests driven by the testing engine used for the actual exam, hundreds of practice questions, answers and explanations, as well as a maths review, real-time scoring, online help and computer based testing tutorials. POWERPREP replicates the actual testing experience and computes verbal and quantitative scores to gauge a candidate's readiness for the GMAT.

There are independent MBA and GMAT training and preparation centres in most countries. The training is useful, some say essential, since it is a peculiar test, particularly if maths is a problem. A number of comprehension questions are based on American business and economic journals, and it is worth becoming familiar with these.

Results

Unofficial verbal and quantitative scores can be obtained at testing centres as soon as the test is completed. Official score reports, including scores on the essay questions, usually arrive at your chosen school(s) in about two weeks. The basic test registration fee covers sending a score report to up to five schools (selected on the day of the test). Additional score reports can be sent for US$28 per school.

Cost

Registering for the test costs US$225 anywhere in the world, payable when an appointment for the test is made. It is advisable to use a credit card because the rules for other forms of payment are horribly complex and bureaucratic. Appointments made via the Internet or phone must be paid for with Visa, MasterCard or American Express. If your credit card is declined, your GMAT appointment will automatically be cancelled. Cheques, bank drafts, money orders, eurocheques payable in US dollars and so on must be drawn on banks located in the US. Payments in other major currencies must be made at the telegraphic transfer selling (TTS) exchange rate of the US dollar equivalent.

*Note that the GMAC has two websites:

- www.mba.com is strictly for test-takers. As well as being a comprehensive and vital starting point for advice and guidance, it has a store for buying GMAT-related materials, free downloads and allows online registration for the test.

- www.gmac.com is for business school professionals, although it also contains some fascinating information that would probably interest any would-be MBA student.

is high in North America, reflecting the highly professional approach there. However, six non-North American schools now feature among the top 20. In 1999, there were no schools outside North America at this level.

Chapter 7
Other considerations

Table 7.6
Student and graduate ratings of careers services

School	%	School	%
Chicago	89	New York (Stern)	82
Indian Institute (Ahmedabad)	88	Harvard	81
Michigan	88	IMD	80
Northwestern (Kellogg)	87	Imperial (Tanaka)	80
Cornell (Johnson)	86	Emory (Goizueta)	80
Stanford	84	Indiana (Kelley)	79
Dartmouth (Tuck)	83	ESSEC	79
Virginia (Darden)	83	Carnegie Mellon (Tepper)	78
Columbia	83	North Carolina (Kenan-Flagler)	78
IE	82	ESCP–EAP	78

Note. These figures are derived from our survey of students and alumni; caution should be used when interpreting them.

Campus visits

Traditionally, companies have visited business school campuses to make presentations about their organisations and to interview candidates whose details they liked. Some schools have impressive interview rooms for this purpose. Although many companies still do this, especially in the US, others are finding the costs prohibitive. It is now common either for students to have to go to the company, or for several schools to form a consortium so that companies can see students at one convenient location.

When recruiters do visit the campus they usually come in the second year of a two-year programme or the third term of a one-year programme. Most business schools also produce a profile (or résumé) book. This is a directory of all students about to graduate. It gives personal details, work experience, academic background and career interests, and normally includes a photograph. The directory, often now on a school's website, is circulated to all major recruiters, who use it to select candidates they would like to meet on the campus. Students can then decide whether they want to be interviewed.

Other ways to find a job

This traditional process is changing, however. Smaller companies and start-ups are not particularly interested in joining the traditional recruitment round and this is making the job-search process more informal and ad hoc. Increasingly, teleconferencing, long-distance interviewing and the Internet are featuring in recruitment. Many MBA students now have their own home pages, often linked to their school's website. Schools provide plenty of opportunities for meeting potential employers. Many faculty members do regular consultancy work and can provide contacts; guest speakers spend time with students; and the help of well-placed alumni of the business school is frequently enlisted.

Projects and internships have also become much more important in the job search. For example, investment bank Merrill Lynch, says on its careers website that although it does hire some second-year MBA students for full-time positions following graduation, its recruiting emphasis is on the summer associate programmes (that is, internships), "which are the pipelines for full-time offers". In the US, many companies only consider students who have served summer internships with them, and as a result these are now almost always administered by the careers service.

What companies want from MBA graduates

Most companies are looking for people with senior management potential. In their view, MBA graduates have an above-average chance of fulfilling this need, but they are careful not to raise students' expectations too high. They also want people who can quite rapidly be effective. The many MBA students wanting to change career direction can therefore have difficulties in the short term, whatever their long-term potential. An engineer trying to move over to finance may be successful, but may be restricted to a job as a financial analyst specialising in the engineering sector.

Employers' recruitment policies are becoming much more short-term in response to fast-changing markets and technologies. In the late 1990s and early 2000s, many traditional recruiters of MBA graduates, such as management consultants and investment banks, had trouble attracting the number of graduates they would have liked. The lure of high-tech start-ups in the dotcom boom was too strong. But as the bubble burst, students flocked back to them. Now, after a period of recession, even these workhorses of MBA recruitment are nowhere near the levels of offers and hires they used to make.

Employers seem to have lost much of their suspicion of MBA graduates, even in some non-traditional areas. A few years ago many human resources directors, especially in Europe, preferred not to employ MBA graduates on the grounds of their arrogance, their excessive expectations of career and salary potential, and the difficulty of fitting them into established teams and career systems. Managers saw MBA graduates as having been programmed to want to run things immediately, without taking time to gain the practical skills they needed or to learn how to manage other people. As organisations became flatter, destroying old-style career structures and putting heavy emphasis on teamwork among equals, such attitudes were even more alien.

Now the experience of most companies seems to be that much of the perceived arrogance has disappeared. Any that remains is blamed on the business schools for not properly managing the expectations of their students, which are still sometimes pumped artificially high. The schools claim that, as a group, most MBA students are well aware of trends in the job market and of the fact that they have to climb the ladder (such as it is) like anyone else. But they also argue that there is a fine dividing line between undesirable arrogance and the desirable ambition, confidence and intellect that an MBA is supposed to instil.

Many companies still complain that MBA graduates' excellent theoretical knowledge is not matched by sufficient interpersonal and, especially, supervisory skills, which are essential in a good manager. Graduates who are hired, therefore, have to be given the opportunity to learn these skills.

Some companies still consider that students are taking their MBAs at too young an age. The argument is that companies need young people in their 20s who are, to an extent, specialists, such as engineers and economists, but it is not until they reach their 30s that they are likely to need the kind of broadening into general management that the MBA experience can provide. It is also one of the main reasons so many companies favour part-time, consortium, executive and distance-learning programmes, which can better fit into a manager's career at the appropriate time. This view is particularly common in Europe (especially the UK) and in Asia, where MBA students are largely sponsored by companies and study part time.

Chapter 7
Other considerations

MBAs and management consultants: a cultural fit

The love affair between MBA graduates and management consultants, in the US at least, dates back to the 1970s. Back then, few companies were willing to invest in recruiting new graduates with a first degree, employing them for two years and then encouraging them to leave to go to business school with no guarantee of their return. The only people who did this were management consultants. First-degree graduates were recruited as research associates, encouraged to go to business school and then re-recruited as MBA graduates. Consequently, business schools found their applicant pools and recruitment base dominated by consulting. They also found that students with a consultancy background were more demanding, insisting, for example, on analytical "tool kits". The curriculum was therefore geared more towards consultancy with a strong emphasis on strategy.

Although recession and corporate scandals have severely reduced recruiting by management consultants, there remain good reasons why they are, and will probably remain, predominant in the MBA job market. They attract MBA graduates not just because of the high salaries they offer, but also because such graduates fit easily into the consultancy culture. Management consultancy executives (many of whom have an MBA themselves) know what MBA graduates can do and how to use them effectively. Graduates do not have to battle against antagonism or misunderstanding, and there are likely to be others with a similar background on the staff. Moreover, their academic training is suited to investigations in, for example, consultancy and mergers and acquisitions work.

Despite the good cultural fit, few of the MBA graduates that join consulting firms spend the rest of their lives there. Many are attracted by the high salaries, the lifestyle and the high-profile nature of the job, which allows them access to corporate life at the highest levels. Typically, many leave consulting for mainstream business after three or four years. But management consultants themselves know and almost expect this, and it is another reason why they are keen recruiters.

The way more traditional employers assimilate new MBA graduates is to place them in central staff positions, with roles such as strategic planning, where they are close to the levers of power and where their breadth of view can be put to good use. Special induction and training programmes are sometimes used, with a senior executive acting as a personal mentor. After a year or two they may be tested in line positions. Problems arise if the employer treats them like first-degree graduates. MBA graduates have more to offer and expectations based on this have to be met.

In this regard, traditional employers still have a lot to learn from investment banks and consultants (see box). Merrill Lynch, for example, has an orientation programme for MBA and other advanced degree graduates. New hires are brought together from around the world for two days in New York City (plus an extra day of required community service in the city), followed by a seven-day core training programme back in their home country, designed to address their business and technology development needs. MBA graduates are then placed in jobs, and they can continue to take development courses and programmes.

At consultants McKinsey & Co, which has been the number one choice for graduating MBAs for the past six years, according to research by Universum, an academic consulting firm, MBA graduates normally join as associates and are quickly involved in consultancy teams. Like Merrill Lynch, McKinsey also offers continuing management development through both formal programmes and on-the-job mentoring.

Which MBA? © The Economist Intelligence Unit Limited 2004

Part 2
Rankings and directory

Full-time rankings

Why rank?

For the third year, *Which MBA?* includes a comparative ranking of 100 of the world's best full-time MBA programmes. Business schools traditionally dislike rankings (after all, no one likes to be graded by outsiders) but now generally accept them as inevitable and, indeed, useful for their prospective students. The reality is that people pay attention to rankings because they are a simple and effective tool for prospective students to compare schools. Using a number of surveys together, students may gain a rounded picture. But no one pretends rankings are perfect. They need to be handled with care.

How is the Economist Intelligence Unit ranking different?

The Economist Intelligence Unit ranking differs from other leading surveys. For well over a decade the Economist Intelligence Unit has regularly surveyed MBA students about why they take an MBA. Four factors consistently emerge:

● to open new career opportunities and/or further current career;

● personal development and educational experience;

● to increase salary;

● the potential to network.

These factors are the basis of our ranking. The Economist Intelligence Unit ranks full-time MBA programmes on their ability to deliver these elements to students. It weights each element according to the average importance given to it by students surveyed over the past five years. The criteria used to measure each of these four factors are detailed in Table 8.8.

The ranking of full-time MBA programmes by the Economist Intelligence Unit is one of the "big five" rankings, alongside those produced by *Business Week*, the *Financial Times*, *US News and World Report* and the *Wall Street Journal* (see Other rankings). The Economist Intelligence Unit is among the best qualified to undertake a ranking given its long experience in collecting survey data for the many reports it produces, including 16 editions of *Which MBA?* (*Business Week* has published MBA rankings for 14 years and the *Financial Times* for six years).

Other rankings

Business Week's ranking is probably the most influential, especially in North America. It surveys MBA graduates and MBA recruiters on a wide range of issues. Perhaps mindful of the *Financial Times* (see below), it has introduced a measure of "intellectual capital", which it describes as "a school's influence and prominence in the realm of ideas". Intellectual capital makes up 10% of the overall rankings, with the remaining 90% split evenly between students and recruiters.

The *Financial Times* bases its ranking on three main criteria: the career progression obtained from the MBA (particularly its purchasing power in the marketplace); diversity of experience; and the school's research qualities. Although the largest component of the ranking pertains to salary, it is the third criterion that is perhaps the most controversial aspect of the *Financial Times*'s approach. It measures a school's performance in research, which accounts for 20% of the total weighting, and many believe this is too high. The research rating is based on the number of publications in 35 international and professional journals. For each publication, points are awarded to the school where the faculty member is currently employed.

US News and World Report bases its ranking on four criteria: reputation (surveys of business school deans and directors of accredited programmes and corporate recruiters); placement success (measured by mean starting salary and bonus and employment rates at graduation and three months after graduation); student selectivity (measured by mean GMAT, mean undergraduate GPA and the proportion of applicants accepted by the school); and speciality rankings (surveys of business school deans and programme heads asking which ten schools offer the best programmes in specialist areas such as finance or marketing).

The *Wall Street Journal* ranking is based purely on a survey of over 2,200 MBA recruiters. Each school is rated on 26 factors that "influence a recruiter's decision to visit a particular campus and hire a particular graduate", such as the careers services office, the core curriculum, and students' leadership potential and teamwork skills.

How is the Economist Intelligence Unit ranking different?

All MBA programme rankings depend on surveys of interested parties: the business schools; the students or graduates; and recruiters. The Economist Intelligence Unit ranking follows this pattern but differs from the rest in several important areas.

- **More student-centric** (continuing *Which MBA?*'s tradition of appealing to a student audience). It measures the way schools meet the demands students have of an MBA programme.
- **All-embracing.** It is based on detailed questionnaires completed by business schools and 21,616 current MBA students and graduates around the world. Key numerical data (such as average GMAT scores) are combined with subjective views from students and graduates (such as their assessment of a business school's faculty).
- **Global.** It allows direct comparison of MBA programmes around the world.
- **Regional.** It compares MBA programmes in three regions: North America, Europe, and Asia and Australasia.
- **Flexible.** Programmes may be ranked in many ways, producing, for example, tables of the top ten US or Asian and Australasian schools by GMAT score or the top ten US and European schools by percentage of foreign students.
- **Transparent.** All the data used to rank schools are published as part of the school's profile in the directory section of this book.

Other rankings have some, but not all, of the above features.

How did we choose which schools to rank?

The Economist Intelligence Unit ranking of full-time MBA programmes was based on an initial selection of 132 leading business schools around the world. All 132 schools were invited to take part in our two-stage survey, which requires input from schools and the students/alumni of each school. Of these, we were unable to rank 18 schools (see Table 8.1). The global top 100 schools were gleaned from the remaining 114. Schools outside the top 100 were given a regional ranking only.

Table 8.1
Why schools could not be ranked

Failed to respond/unable or unwilling to take part
Franklin W Olin Graduate School of Business—Babson College
University College Dublin—The Michael Smurfit Graduate School of Business
Kingston Business School
Middlesex University Business School
Norwegian School of Economics and Business Administration (NHH)
University of Toronto—Joseph L Rotman School of Management
Insufficient data[a]
Brunel Graduate Business School
University of Cape Town—Graduate School of Business
Curtin University Graduate School of Business
Heriot Watt University—Edinburgh Business School
University of London—Royal Holloway School of Management
Maastricht School of Management
Monash University—Faculty of Business and Economics
University of Otago—School of Business
University of Queensland Business School
University of Southampton—School of Management
University of Witwatersrand—Graduate School of Business Administration
No full-time programme
Open University Business School

Note: Details of schools with insufficient data or no full-time programme appear in the directory section of this book.

[a] Minimum threshold not met for school data or number of student/alumni responses. See methodology (page 101) for details.

Given that 420 schools in the US have AACSB International accreditation for an MBA programme and that probably at least that number are not accredited, it could be argued that, with 54 North American schools, the Economist Intelligence Unit ranking under-represents this important MBA market. However, one of the main objectives of the survey is to provide global comparisons and it was limited to leading schools throughout the world (so even schools at the bottom of our rankings are among the world's best).

In common with all other rankings, there was an element of selectivity before the ranking process began. The programmes we have chosen are taught either entirely in English or bilingually with English one of the languages. In addition we are looking at schools with genuine international content and standing. However, the absence of a particular programme implies nothing about that programme's quality.

Results

Rankings are little more than an indication of the MBA market at a particular time. They reflect the prevailing conditions such as salaries, jobs available and the situation at a school at the time the survey was carried out. Results of rankings can be notoriously volatile, so they should be treated with caution. However, the Economist Intelligence Unit survey looks at data over a three-year period, which helps provide a more rounded picture. Table 8.2 is a listing of schools in rank order.

Table 8.2
Global ranking, 2004

Rank (2003 position in brackets)		School	Country
1	(1)	Northwestern University—Kellogg School of Management	US
2	(3)	Stanford Graduate School of Business	US
3	(2)	Dartmouth College—Tuck School of Business	US
4	(n/a)	Harvard Business School	US
5	(9)	IMD—International Institute for Management Development	Switzerland
6	(5)	University of Chicago—Graduate School of Business	US
7	(6)	Columbia Business School	US
8	(n/a)	University of Pennsylvania—Wharton School	US
9	(28)	IESE Business School—University of Navarra	Spain
10	(15)	New York University—Leonard N Stern School of Business	US
11	(10)	University of Michigan Business School	US
12	(12)	University of Virginia—Darden Graduate School of Business Administration	US
13	(4)	Duke University—Fuqua School of Business	US
14	(7)	Yale School of Management	US
15	(47)	Vlerick Leuven Gent Management School	Belgium
16	(18)	Massachusetts Institute of Technology—MIT Sloan School of Management	US
17	(13)	Cornell University—Johnson Graduate School of Management	US
18	(14)	UCLA—The Anderson School	US
19	(16)	University of California at Berkeley—Haas School of Business	US
20	(19)	INSEAD	France/Singapore
21	(8)	IE—Instituto de Empresa	Spain
22	(22)	York University—Schulich School of Business	Canada
23	(36)	University of Southern California—Marshall School of Business	US
24	(25)	Ohio State University—Fisher College of Business	US
25	(38)	University of Birmingham—Birmingham Business School	UK
26	(17)	Henley Management College	UK
27	(24)	HEC School of Management, Paris	France
28	(11)	Cranfield School of Management	UK
29	(34)	Carnegie Mellon University—Tepper School of Business	US
30	(50)	Warwick Business School	UK
31	(23)	London Business School	UK

Rank (2003 position in brackets)	School	Country
32 (20)	University of Edinburgh Management School	UK
33 (30)	Emory University—Goizueta Business School	US
34 (31)	Washington University in St Louis—Olin School of Business	US
35 (58)	ESADE Business School	Spain
36 (21)	University of Illinois at Urbana-Champaign—College of Business	US
37 (35)	University of North Carolina at Chapel Hill—Kenan-Flagler Business School	US
38 (33)	University of Iowa—Henry B Tippie School of Management	US
39 (29)	University of Notre Dame—Mendoza College of Business	US
40 (57)	University of Oxford—Saïd Business School	UK
41 (27)	Georgetown University—Robert Emmet McDonough School of Business	US
42 (37)	Imperial College London—Tanaka Business School	UK
43 (86)	University of Bath School of Management	UK
44 (26)	Aston Business School	UK
45 (32)	University of Texas at Austin—McCombs School of Business	US
46 (39)	University of Minnesota—Carlson School of Management	US
47 (n/a)	University of California at Davis	US
48 (52)	University of Maryland—Robert H Smith School of Business	US
49 (44)	Pennsylvania State University—Smeal College of Business	US
50 (40)	Macquarie Graduate School of Management	Australia
51 (48)	Purdue University—Krannert Graduate School of Management	US
52 (71)	Lancaster University Management School	UK
53 (53)	E.M. Lyon	France
54 (51)	Indiana University—Kelley School of Business	US
55 (62)	Vanderbilt University—Owen Graduate School of Management	US
56 (81)	NIMBAS Graduate School of Management	Netherlands
57 (54)	Rice University—Jesse H Jones Graduate School of Management	US
58 (41)	Manchester Business School	UK
59 (43)	Hult International Business School	US
60 (n/a)	University of Newcastle upon Tyne Business School	UK
61 (46)	University of Rochester—William E Simon Graduate School of Business	US
62 (77)	University of Cambridge—Judge Institute of Management	UK
63 (n/a)	Wake Forest University—Babcock Graduate School of Management	US
64 (45)	Indian Institute of Management—Ahmedabad	India
65 (72)	University of Wisconsin-Madison—Graduate School of Business	US
66 (49)	Sheffield University Management School	UK
67 (87)	University of Strathclyde Graduate School of Business	UK
68 (79)	University of Hong Kong—School of Business	Hong Kong
69 (56)	Queen's University—Queen's School of Business	Canada
70 (60)	University of British Columbia—Sauder School of Business	Canada
71 (42)	Case Western Reserve University—Weatherhead School of Management	US
72 (83)	Ashridge	UK

Full-time rankings

Rank (2003 position in brackets)		School	Country
73	(66)	University of Pittsburgh—Joseph M Katz Graduate School of Business	US
74	(59)	Southern Methodist University—Cox School of Business	US
75	(64)	University of Western Ontario—Richard Ivey School of Business	Canada
76	(n/a)	ESSEC Business School	Spain
77	(84)	Australian Graduate School of Management	Australia
78	(61)	Durham Business School	UK
79	(63)	University of Glasgow—Business School	UK
80	(80)	Nottingham University Business School	UK
81	(90)	Leeds University Business School	UK
82	(92)	ESCP-EAP European School of Management	France
83	(67)	Thunderbird—The Garvin School of International Management	US
84	(82)	International University of Japan—Graduate School of International Management	Japan
85	(n/a)	College of William & Mary—School of Business Administration	US
86	(74)	Bocconi University—SDA Bocconi School of Management	Italy
87	(95)	University of Arizona—Eller College of Business and Public Administration	US
88	(69)	Rotterdam School of Management—Erasmus Graduate School of Business	Netherlands
89	(93)	University of Florida—Warrington College of Business	US
90	(98)	Solvay Business School—Université Libre de Bruxelles	Belgium
91	(68)	City University—Cass Business School	UK
92	(97)	University of Melbourne—Melbourne Business School	Australia
93	(n/a)	Nanyang Technological University—Nanyang Business School	Singapore
94	(n/a)	University of South Carolina—Moore School of Business	US
95	(65)	China Europe International Business School (CEIBS)	China
96	(n/a)	Bradford School of Management	UK
97	(85)	University of Georgia—Terry College of Business	US
98	(55)	Universiteit Nyenrode—The Netherlands Business School	Netherlands
99	(94)	International University of Monaco	Monaco
100	(76)	Institut d'Etudes Politiques de Paris—MBA Sciences Po	France

Once again, the Economist Intelligence Unit's 2004 ranking of full-time MBA programmes underlines the dominance of US schools. Sixteen of the top 20 are US schools, with Kellogg ranking number one for the third successive year, and Stanford, Tuck, Harvard, Chicago, Columbia, Wharton and Stern all featuring in the top ten. The only European schools to feature in the top ten are IMD in Switzerland, fifth, and IESE in Spain, ninth.

The main things that set these schools apart are a robust programme and excellent faculty. But what they often also possess is a strong collegiate sense. This manifests itself in the number of students who take part in our survey. Although the number of questionnaires returned does not have a direct impact on a school's ranking, as long as a minimum threshold is reached this *esprit de corps* obviously has a big effect on the way its students and graduates respond to the questionnaire. Once again, Kellogg had the highest number of student and graduate responses, at 893, and it is famous for its determination to involve students in all aspects of running the school. Michigan, Goizueta, Tuck and Cornell also had high numbers of student responses.

However, although the position of the top US schools seems entrenched, two European schools, IESE and Vlerick Leuven Gent, have put in stellar performances and have both moved significantly up the ranking. Vlerick's perhaps surprising rise has come in the wake of major efforts to improve both its careers services—which have impressed many students—and its alumni network.

To find the highest ranked school in Asia and Australasia (excluding INSEAD, which has campuses in both France and Singapore), it is necessary to look down to 50th place, which is filled by Australia's Macquarie Graduate School of Management. This highlights a clear regional pecking order when it comes to full-time MBA programmes: North America leads the way, followed by Europe, and then Asia and Australasia, which still has a lot of ground to make up (see regional round-up).

US schools generally do particularly well in the "open new career opportunities" category. This is partly because careers services in the US are often more lavishly funded, better organised and more professionally set up than in the rest of the world. At Stanford, for example, 86% of students find a job within three months of graduating, all via the school's careers services.

Table 8.3
Top ten schools by category

	Open new career opportunities	Personal development and educational experience	Increase salary	Potential to network
1	Indian Institute (Ahmedabad)	Pennsylvania (Wharton)	Ashridge	Henley
2	Dartmouth (Tuck)	Stanford	Henley	E.M. Lyon
3	Northwestern (Kellogg)	Macquarie	Aston	HEC, Paris
4	Chicago	Northwestern (Kellogg)	IMD	Queen's
5	Columbia	Dartmouth (Tuck)	Edinburgh	Vlerick Leuven Gent
6	Stanford	INSEAD	Warwick	IMD
7	Harvard	London	Northwestern (Kellogg)	Thunderbird (Garvin)
8	IESE	Vlerick Leuven Gent	Birmingham	Virginia (Darden)
9	China Europe International Business School	New York (Stern)	Stanford	South Carolina (Moore)
10	IE	Harvard	Oxford (Saïd)	IE

US schools also dominate the personal development and educational experience category. US institutions invest heavily in their faculty. It is not unusual to find that everyone teaching on a top US programme has a PhD; this is the case at Wharton and UCLA, for example. They are also choosy about the students they admit. Eleven US schools, including Stanford, Wharton, MIT (Sloan) and Columbia, have average GMAT scores over 700 (the maximum GMAT score is 800).

Where European schools do beat their US counterparts is, perhaps surprisingly, in the salaries of their graduates. At Ashridge in the UK, for example, graduates can expect to earn an average of US$177,000 per year; at Henley and IMD the figure is around US$125,000. In contrast, no US schools can boast average salaries in the six-figure bracket. Some of this can be explained by the strength of European currencies against the dollar, but it is also a reflection of the relatively weak job market in the US, particularly when compared with the UK.

European schools, which often have more international alumni, also do well in the networking category.

Regional round-up

North America

US business schools dominate the full time MBA world as the Economist Intelligence Unit's 2004 ranking makes clear. US-based schools take eight of the top ten and 31 of the top 50 slots. Within this dominant position there are few surprises. Kellogg, Stanford, Tuck, Harvard and Chicago stand out, as they do in many other rankings and surveys.

Table 8.4
North American schools by rank

Rank (2003 position in brackets)		School	Country
1	(1)	Northwestern (Kellogg)	US
2	(3)	Stanford	US
3	(2)	Dartmouth (Tuck)	US
4	(n/a)	Harvard	US
5	(5)	Chicago	US
6	(6)	Columbia	US
7	(n/a)	Pennsylvania (Wharton)	US
8	(12)	New York (Stern)	US
9	(8)	Michigan	US
10	(9)	Virginia (Darden)	US
11	(4)	Duke (Fuqua)	US
12	(7)	Yale	US
13	(14)	MIT (Sloan)	US
14	(10)	Cornell (Johnson)	US
15	(11)	UCLA (Anderson)	US
16	(13)	California at Berkeley (Haas)	US
17	(16)	York (Schulich)	Canada
18	(26)	Southern California (Marshall)	US
19	(17)	Ohio (Fisher)	US
20	(24)	Carnegie Mellon (Tepper)	US
21	(20)	Emory (Goizueta)	US
22	(21)	Washington St Louis (Olin)	US
23	(15)	Illinois	US
24	(25)	North Carolina (Kenan-Flagler)	US
25	(23)	Iowa (Tippie)	US

Rank (2003 position in brackets)		School	Country
26	(19)	Notre Dame (Mendoza)	US
27	(18)	Georgetown (McDonough)	US
28	(22)	Texas at Austin (McCombs)	US
29	(27)	Minnesota (Carlson)	US
30	(n/a)	California at Davis	US
31	(34)	Maryland (Smith)	US
32	(30)	Penn State (Smeal)	US
33	(32)	Purdue (Krannert)	US
34	(33)	Indiana (Kelley)	US
35	(39)	Vanderbilt (Owen)	US
36	(35)	Rice (Jones)	US
37	(29)	Hult	US
38	(31)	Rochester (Simon)	US
39	(n/a)	Wake Forest (Babcock)	US
40	(43)	Wisconsin-Madison	US
41	(36)	Queen's	Canada
42	(38)	British Columbia (Sauder)	Canada
43	(28)	Case Western Reserve (Weatherhead)	US
44	(41)	Pittsburgh (Katz)	US
45	(37)	Southern Methodist (Cox)	US
46	(40)	Western Ontario (Ivey)	Canada
47	(42)	Thunderbird (Garvin)	US
48	(n/a)	College of William & Mary	US
49	(46)	Arizona (Eller)	US
50	(45)	Florida (Warrington)	US
51	(n/a)	South Carolina (Moore)	US
52	(44)	Georgia (Terry)	US
53	(n/a)	McGill	Canada
54	(n/a)	Calgary (Haskayne)	Canada
55	(n/a)	Brandeis	US
56	(47)	Concordia (Molson)	Canada
57	(n/a)	American (Kogod)	US

The MBA scene in the US is going through one of its periodic bursts of self-examination. This is partly to do with capturing headlines through the announcement of new initiatives, but there are some significant underlying issues. The complaint (from employers) that MBA students are great at analysis but not much good at putting things into practice is almost as old as the degree itself, but it is resurfacing. In particular, the teaching of ethics (a popular subject in the late 1980s) is being touted again. Schools are trying to integrate this topic more fully into their curricula, not least because of the accounting scandals that have dogged the US in recent years and the business schools' shamefaced admission that they may have had something to do with teaching these techniques. At the same time, they are trying to teach MBA students such amorphous topics as leadership and global awareness.

So how is all this packed into already overflowing student schedules? In the future, the answer will increasingly be via online learning. Some of the basic material students must master will be available electronically without the need to attend a class, and they may even have to study some material before arriving on campus. Online delivery may also be used for a portion of the life-long learning materials after graduation.

This suggests that the volatile North American MBA scene is going through another upheaval as the MBA model is reworked (this happened in the 1950s and again in the early 1990s). What the new-style MBA programme will look like is not yet clear. But many are predicting that the two-year programme will become more of an introduction to business and business methods, with a much more practical orientation (almost an apprenticeship, some have suggested) than the current practice of attempting to pack in every business subject. Once students have mastered the basics, they will return regularly for short, top-up executive education programmes throughout their career. It is not exactly a new model (the thinking has been around for some time), but if it is put into operation it will change the North American MBA forever.

Europe

Studying in Europe offers first-hand experience of an economic trading bloc that rivals North America and Asia and the opportunity to mix with students and faculty who are cosmopolitan and outgoing. European schools are growing in stature and academic standards, and their credibility with employers is equal to anything in the world. Best estimates put the number of MBA programmes in the region at around 700. European business schools have been greatly strengthened by the development of the EU, which has given the continent a much greater sense of cohesion. Moreover, developments such as the single market and the single currency have greatly increased interest in business and management education.

In the Economist Intelligence Unit's 2004 ranking of full-time MBA programmes, IMD came top (it was second last year), with IESE and Vlerick rising sharply to take second and third spots. INSEAD is fourth, with last year's number one European school, IE, slipping to fifth.

Table 8.5
European schools by rank

Rank (2003 position in brackets)		School	Country
1	(2)	IMD	Switzerland
2	(10)	IESE	Spain
3	(14)	Vlerick Leuven Gent	Belgium
4	(5)	INSEAD	France/Singapore
5	(1)	IE	Spain
6	(12)	Birmingham	UK
7	(4)	Henley	UK
8	(8)	HEC, Paris	France
9	(3)	Cranfield	UK

Rank (2003 position in brackets)		School	Country
10	(16)	Warwick	UK
11	(7)	London	UK
12	(6)	Edinburgh	UK
13	(20)	ESADE	Spain
14	(19)	Oxford (Saïd)	UK
15	(11)	Imperial (Tanaka)	UK
16	(33)	Bath	UK
17	(9)	Aston	UK
18	(25)	Lancaster	UK
19	(17)	E.M. Lyon	France
20	(31)	NIMBAS	Netherlands
21	(13)	Manchester	UK
22	(n/a)	Newcastle	UK
23	(28)	Cambridge (Judge)	UK
24	(15)	Sheffield	UK
25	(34)	Strathclyde	UK
26	(32)	Ashridge	UK
27	(n/a)	ESSEC	France
28	(21)	Durham	UK
29	(22)	Glasgow	UK
30	(30)	Nottingham	UK
31	(37)	Leeds	UK
32	(38)	ESCP-EAP	France
33	(26)	SDA Bocconi	Italy
34	(24)	Rotterdam (Erasmus)	Netherlands
35	(40)	Solvay	Belgium
36	(23)	City (Cass)	UK
37	(n/a)	Bradford	UK
38	(18)	Nyenrode	Netherlands
39	(39)	Monaco	Monaco
40	(27)	Institut d'Etudes Politiques	France
41	(n/a)	Helsinki	Finland
42	(n/a)	Theseus	France
43	(n/a)	Norwegian School of Management BI	Norway
44	(41)	Dublin (Trinity)	Ireland
45	(n/a)	EADA	Spain
46	(n/a)	ENPC	France

The UK

MBA programmes in the UK, which is by far the biggest MBA market in the region with around 100 business schools and some 13,000 graduates a year, share many of the characteristics of programmes in the rest of Europe. They are generally short with an emphasis on hands-on project work. Although the first UK business schools—London Business School (LBS) and Manchester Business School—were set up in the 1960s (based largely on the US model), only LBS still adheres to a two-year programme. The typical full-time programme in the UK lasts for one calendar year, usually made up of three taught terms and a project or dissertation that takes up the summer. Part-time programmes generally last for 2–3 years but can be studied over longer periods. The content of both is often identical.

Schools in the UK also have the same strong links to industry and business as many of their European counterparts, although the involvement of local chambers of commerce (so common in France, for example) is rare. Most business schools are linked to a university, often being carved out of existing faculty structures such as accounting and economics, and many are subservient to university authorities in terms of what they can do. Ashridge and Henley Management College, which were set up by business people and companies, are exceptions. Ashridge is effectively a charitable trust and City University in London validates its degrees. Henley confers its own degrees.

The UK was also an early pioneer of practical education linked to business. It developed the idea of single-company MBA and consortium programmes, for example, and virtually invented modern distance learning (although it is being overtaken in this area by North America in terms of the application of technology if not in numbers of students). These types of programmes are probably of greater importance to UK schools than full-time MBA degrees. Many programmes have a high international content and a lot of overseas students, and provide extensive language training.

Continental Europe

Although European MBA programmes owe much to the US model, they have developed in quite different ways. Many US business schools gave a great deal of help in establishing European schools. For example, Harvard Business School played a significant role in helping to set up IESE; and Erasmus University's close links with the University of Michigan helped it create the Rotterdam School of Management in the 1970s. However, although IESE has continued with the US model (a two-year programme with heavy reliance on the case method), many European schools have gone in different directions, often encouraged by the involvement of local businesses or trade and municipal bodies.

One notable difference is the length of programmes, which varies considerably. Although IESE has stuck to the two-year model, most others, such as INSEAD, offer programmes lasting around 12 months. IMD has reduced its programme to a hectic ten months.

After the UK, the MBA is probably most developed in France, where a number of schools, including INSEAD, HEC and E.M. Lyon, compete on world terms. Spain is also an active market, with three world-class schools: IESE, IE and ESADE. The odd man out is Germany, which has no national MBA tradition (it has only 1,600 MBA graduates a year) and virtually no recognised business schools (largely because of its lengthy education system). However, as a visit to a business school campus virtually anywhere in the world will confirm, MBA students appear to be one of Germany's biggest exports.

There are two European models of internationalism, although both rely on a mixture of nationalities among students and faculty. IMD in Switzerland and INSEAD in France are the main examples of the first model. They have opted for a deliberately non-nationalist approach, creating campuses where no single nationality is allowed to dominate. The majority of students and faculty are foreign-born, and the fact that the schools are situated in a single country (although INSEAD now has a campus in Singapore) is seen as a geographic detail. The campuses could be anywhere in the world without much change in atmosphere or culture.

In the second model, schools have retained their national culture but created an international ambience around it. SDA Bocconi in Milan, IESE in Barcelona and HEC near Paris are examples. They attract large numbers of overseas students but also encourage their own nationals to apply. Many of the faculty are also local. The result is an atmosphere in which overseas students are encouraged to learn more about the local culture; for example, learning the language is often an important ingredient. Such schools are often viewed as an entry ticket into the national business scene.

Asia and Australasia

The Asia and Australasia region is a hotbed of MBA education and home to a large number of MBA programmes. Local businesses are enthusiastic sponsors of employees at business schools (which is why so many programmes are part-time or distance-learning). However, the MBA is not quite the barometer of business school prestige in this region as it is in North America and Europe—the MCom and Master of Management qualifications are equally highly regarded.

Many of the schools are, or at least are aspiring to be, of world-class quality, although few can hold their own with other leading schools around the world. Only 8 schools from this region made it into the top 100 of the Economist Intelligence Unit's ranking of full-time MBA programmes, and of these only one—Macquarie—reached the top 50. However, it may be worth noting that full-time MBA programmes (on which the rankings are based) are somewhat unusual in the region, which emphasises MBA education as a part-time or distance-learning activity.

Table 8.6
Asian and Australasian schools by rank

Rank (2003 position in brackets)		School	Country
1	(1)	Macquarie	Australia
2	(2)	Indian Institute (Ahmedabad)	India
3	(7)	Hong Kong BS	Hong Kong
4	(9)	Australian GSM	Australia
5	(8)	International University of Japan	Japan
6	(11)	Melbourne	Australia
7	(n/a)	Nanyang	Singapore
8	(3)	China Europe International Business School	China
9	(5)	Hong Kong UST	Hong Kong
10	(12)	Singapore	Singapore
11	(n/a)	Chinese University of Hong Kong	Hong Kong

Apart from its indigenous business schools, the region has proved a lure for both US and European interests and business schools. INSEAD and Chicago have set up fully fledged campuses in Singapore to teach their MBA programmes; the University of Western Ontario (Ivey) has a similar facility in Hong Kong; and many other schools offer their MBAs through partner institutes in the region or by distance learning.

Studying for an MBA in Asia involves a trade-off. Although matching the academic excellence and reputation of the top schools in North America and Europe is still a tough task, many Asian schools are closely involved in the complex web of businesses that operate in the region. Business contacts and networks are probably more significant in this region than anywhere else in the world. This is why a business school's links with its local community are so important. Anyone seriously interested in following a career in Asia should take this into account.

Although Australasian schools are increasingly seeking to portray themselves as "global" in outlook (by, for example, hiring visiting faculty from outside the region), their ability to understand and teach pan-Asian management is still crucial. Although foreigners may misguidedly view Asia as a homogeneous whole, cultural differences between countries that are quite close geographically can be at least as great as in, say, Europe. The experience of faculty in conducting research and consulting with companies in a variety of Asian countries is therefore an important asset.

Choosing a school in Asia depends very much on an individual's personal goals. Students wanting to work in a particular location will often find that a local school can open doors to local contacts and networks. Students who want to pursue a career in the region should choose institutions with a proven track record of cross-cultural research and consulting. Students who are contemplating an international career should consider the top schools in Australia and New Zealand.

Methodology

To qualify for inclusion in the Economist Intelligence Unit rankings, the schools with full-time MBA programmes that responded to our survey had to meet various thresholds of data provision, as well as attaining a minimum number of responses to a survey gauging the opinion of current students and alumni who graduated within the last three years. These were set as a proportion of the annual intake of students to the programme as shown in Table 8.7.

Table 8.7
Proportion of responses required from students and recent graduates

Student intake	Minimum responses required
Up to 43	10
44–200	25% of intake
More than 200	50

Data were collected during spring 2004 using two web-based questionnaires, one for business schools and one for students and recent graduates. Schools distributed the web address of the latter questionnaire to their own students and graduates. A total of 21,616 students and graduates participated: this is one of the largest responses to a survey of this kind. All data received from schools were subject to verification checks, including, where possible, comparison with historical data, peer schools and other published sources. Student and graduate questionnaires were audited for multiple or false entries.

This year some schools, most notably Harvard and Wharton, made a policy decision to refuse all ranking organisations, including the Economist Intelligence Unit, access to their students and alumni. For a student-centric ranking such as ours, the views of students and alumni are central to our methodology and thus the co-operation of schools in circulating questionnaires is essential. In order to include these schools in the ranking, we have drawn on our extensive database of past responses and included the opinions of students where they would still meet our criteria of having graduated within the last three years.

Memory has been built into the rankings by taking a weighted average of 2004 (50%), 2003 (30%) and 2002 (20%) data to provide a rounded picture of the school. Sudden movements in data, which might not produce an immediate increase in quality, are thus reflected gradually, much as the improvement would affect students.

Table 8.8 summarises the measures used to calculate the rankings together with their respective weightings. Student and alumni ratings make up 20% of the total ranking, and 80% is based on data provided by schools. The statistical methodology adopted for the ranking gives each business school a unique score (known to statisticians as a z-score). Unlike other rankings, the Economist Intelligence Unit does not include any "equal" schools (for example, four schools ranked equal sixth followed by one ranked tenth). However, it should be noted that differences between some schools might be very slight.

Methodology

Table 8.8
Summary of ranking criteria and weightings[a]

Measure	Indicators	Weighting as percentage of category
A. Open new career opportunities (35%)		
1. Diversity of recruiters	Number of industry sectors	25.00
2. Assessment of careers services	Percentage of graduates in jobs three months after graduation	25.00
3. Jobs found through the careers service	Percentage of graduates finding jobs through careers service	25.00
4. Student assessment	Meeting expectations and needs	25.00
B. Personal development/education experience (35%)		
1. Faculty quality	Ratio of faculty to students[b]	8.33
	Percentage of faculty with PhD (full-time only)	8.33
	Faculty rating by students	8.33
2. Student quality	Average GMAT score	12.50
	Average length of work experience	12.50
3. Student diversity	Percentage of foreign students	8.33
	Percentage of women students	8.33
	Student rating of culture and classmates	8.33
4. Education experience	Student rating of programme content and range of electives	6.25
	Range of overseas exchange programmes	6.25
	Number of languages on offer	6.25
	Student assessment of facilities and other services	6.25
C. Increase salary (20%)		
1. How much did your salary increase after graduating?	Salary change from pre-MBA to post-MBA (excluding bonuses)	25.00
2. Leaving salary	Post-MBA salary (excluding bonuses)	75.00
D. Potential to network (10%)		
1. Breadth of alumni network	Ratio of registered alumni to current students	33.33
2. Internationalism of alumni	Ratio of students to overseas alumni branches	33.33
3. Alumni effectiveness	Student assessment of alumni network	33.33

[a] A minimum threshold of data was required for each category. Weightings for schools meeting the category threshold but not providing all data were distributed evenly within the category. [b] Faculty were weighted as follows: full-time 100%; part-time 50%; visiting 25%.

It is essential that all rankings are open and transparent about data collection and the problems encountered. This ensures that students and business schools can interpret the results correctly and take account of the caveats that inevitably surround such undertakings. Below are some of the important considerations that should be observed in using the data and ranking numbers in each of the four main categories surveyed.

Open new career opportunities

To gauge the effectiveness with which a school was able to open new career opportunities for graduating students, this category measured the diversity of recruiters (by number of industry sectors—see box on opposite page); the percentage of graduates in jobs three months after graduation; the percentage of graduates finding jobs through the careers service; and students' reports on whether a school's careers services department met their needs and expectations.

Diversity of recruiters

For the diversity of recruiters category, schools were asked which of the following sectors recruited graduates from its most recent class.

- Banking, finance
- Consumer, retail
- Consulting, professional services
- Entertainment, publishing
- Industry, engineering, manufacturing
- Technology, media, telecoms
- Non-profit, public sector
- Pharmaceuticals, healthcare

Ideally, we would also have liked to include a measure of the volume of recruiters that visit a school. It has been difficult to come up with a suitable and acceptable measure for this. In particular, many of the business schools surveyed are members of the US-based MBA Career Services Council (CSC), a body founded in 1994 with the purpose, among other things, of developing and promoting standard and ethical operating procedures, including the reporting of salary and employment data. The CSC does not regard the number of companies either recruiting on campus or contacting a business school as a good indicator of careers services and advises against schools revealing such data. One business school in the US said that, according to the CSC:

- It should not be perceived as negative if a student is able to obtain a job with a company that does not come on campus.
- To be a good measurement, there should be a way to count recruiters accurately and compare schools fairly. Differentiating between companies and their various divisions, businesses or locations can be complicated. For example, should GE businesses be counted as one or more than one?
- Some careers services offices support undergraduate as well as MBA students and therefore may automatically have access to more companies.

Personal development and educational experience

This category measured factors such as the ratio of faculty to students, the percentage of faculty with a PhD, the percentage of foreign and women students, and students' perceptions of the quality of their programme and of their school's facilities and other services. Much of this information was simple to collect and analyse.

One factor included was average GMAT scores. Not every business school requires the GMAT (although most do), and where this was the case the GMAT score weighting was redistributed within the category.

Increase salary

The Economist Intelligence Unit does not assign as great an importance to salary as some other rankings do, but it is obviously an important indicator. Our survey attempts to measure the increase in remuneration delivered by an MBA as well as the absolute salary level at graduation. Schools were asked to provide both the average salary of incoming students and the average salary they received after graduation. A number of schools were unable to provide all this information, and in these cases the Economist Intelligence Unit has included an estimate based on our survey of students, our own research and other published data.

Potential to network

This category measures the extent to which students benefit from a business school's network of alumni. It does this by measuring the ratio of alumni to current students and the number of overseas alumni branches to students, and students' and graduates' own assessment of how their school performed in this area.

Data from North American schools were widely available. Some schools outside that region, however, had few or little-developed alumni branches, although almost all said they were actively working to develop their alumni network and many had set up additional branches since last year. Where there were no overseas alumni branches schools were rated at zero, which will have affected their ranking position.

Using the directory

The directory contains profiles of the most prominent MBA programmes (full-time, part-time, executive and distance learning) offered by the business schools that were invited to participate in the Economist Intelligence Unit's ranking. It is therefore not a comprehensive listing and the absence of a particular school or programme implies nothing about its quality. Details of the criteria used to select schools for the ranking are detailed in Chapter 8.

Schools are listed alphabetically by parent university (if applicable).

Ranking table

The EIU's global and regional rankings of a school's full-time programme are detailed in the ranking table at the beginning of the profile. Schools in the top 100 have been given a global rank. Schools outside the top 100 have been given only a regional rank.

The ranking is made up of four categories: open new career opportunities; personal development and educational experience; increase in salary; and potential to network. How a school ranks in each is given in the ranking table. Additionally, each of the categories is made up of individual criteria (such as student assessment of careers services, faculty quality and so on). Individual rankings for each criterion can also be found in the table.

Where a school is ranked outside the top 100 for a particular category or criterion it is shown as ">100". For a fuller explanation of the criteria see Chapter 8.

Other tables

In addition to the rankings, school profiles contain standard tables such as faculty, students, recruiters and costs. Where possible these give a matrix of information, allowing you to compare the different programmes offered by a school. For example, it is possible to compare the average number of months' work experience of students on full-time, part-time or executive programmes.

Where data in a table are ranking criteria, the ranking figure is shown in brackets.

Please note that the ranking is based on a three-year average, whereas the individual figures shown are the latest available. This will explain any apparent discrepancies whereby, for example, schools with the same GMAT score are ranked differently.

Strengths and weaknesses

Each school profile gives a list of a school's particular strengths and weaknesses. Strengths are those cited by the schools themselves as their areas of expertise. Weaknesses have been gleaned from the student survey undertaken for Which MBA? 2004. For this reason it is important to remember that weaknesses are only relative to a particular programme. For example, if students cite marketing classes as an area of weakness, this is because they believe these have fallen below the standards of other courses at the school. It does not mean that the school's marketing output will be poorer than at other schools.

Where we have cited limited elective choice as a weakness, again this is based on feedback from students and not on a quantitative measure of the number of electives offered. It is worth remembering that even if elective choice is limited, schools may still offer the electives that are of interest to you, and it is important to check schools' websites and brochures to make an objective assessment.

Executive education

Where a school offers short executive education courses, brief details are given in this section.

Student/alumni quotes

These have been selected from comments made by students when completing our questionnaire. We have tried to make them as representative as possible.

Note on tables

In this directory:

"–" means that data were not provided by the school

"n/a" means the data are not applicable

There is good, and then there is great.

MBA@Melbourne Business School

Melbourne Business School (MBS) is the leading provider of management education in the Asia Pacific.

We offered the first MBA degree in Australia in 1964 and since have become the largest business school in the region.

Our academic standing is grounded in the heritage and reputation of The University of Melbourne.

We are a proven performer in creative and innovative thinking with a focus on practical business application.

MBA – Full time

→ An intensive 16-month program focusing on cutting-edge business themes.

→ A truly international experience with about 70% of students coming from more than 30 countries across all continents.

→ International exchange opportunities with over 30 business schools around the globe.

→ We offer teaching excellence in a collaborative study environment.

→ Partial scholarships offered.

Executive MBA

→ Designed for senior executives with at least 10 years work experience seeking strategic capabilities.

→ Course completed through 4 x One-month residential modules (Oct 2005, Mar, Jul and Nov 2006).

→ One module undertaken internationally.

How can I find out more?

We invite you to visit **www.mbs.edu** for more details on our MBA programs and forthcoming information sessions. For brochures and enquiries contact **Timeke Plymin** on **+613 9349 8204** or email **enquiries@mbs.edu**

Opening minds.
Changing lives.

List of schools

Directory
List of schools

Directory
List of schools

Which MBA? © The Economist Intelligence Unit Limited 2004

American University—The Kogod School of Business

Address
4400 Massachusetts
Avenue, N.W.
Washington, DC
US
20016

Tel:
+1 202 885 1994

Fax:
+1 202 885 1030

E-mail:
KogodMBA@american.
edu

Website:
kogod.american.edu

Programme director:
Sondra Smith

Figures in brackets
represent rank

Ranking	Rank (out of 100) Full-time
Overall rank	n/a
Regional rank	53

Background

The Kogod School of Business, named after Robert and Arlene Kogod, dates from 1955 and says it was the first school of business in Washington, DC. The school teaches undergraduates and postgraduates and makes the most of its location in the US capital, stressing both its global perspective and technological focus. The Center for Information Technology and the Global Economy (CITGE) aims to link the two through research into business issues affected by both IT and globalisation.

The school says its focuses on private-sector management and applying theory to practical management. As well as access to Washington policymakers, the school has excellent links with business. The greater Washington area is a high-tech corridor and executives are a regular presence on campus, both as guest speakers and as executives in residence.

Facilities

Kogod has its own building at the centre of American University's 84-acre campus equipped with wireless network, web terminals, classrooms, student lounges and meeting rooms. There is no on-campus housing but the university has an apartment building for students and accommodation is generally fairly easy to obtain.

	Full-time MBA
Student assessment of facilities	3.7 (n/a)

Faculty

Number of faculty: 60 full-time, 24 part-time

	Full-time MBA	Part Time MBA
Number of faculty per student	0.9 (n/a)	2.1
Percentage of faculty with PhD	95 (n/a)	95
Student rating of faculty	4.1 (n/a)	–

Strengths and weaknesses

Strengths: finance; marketing; international business

Weakness: careers services

Programme highlights

Kogod's two-year MBA starts with a required orientation (four days for full-time students and one day for part-time students) followed by a fairly standard set of six core courses and five "advanced breadth" subjects, which cover wider issues of management. These are followed in the second year by electives, which can be grouped into up to two concentrations (accounting, entrepreneurship and management, finance, international finance, international management, international marketing, management of global information technology, marketing information and technology, marketing management, and real estate and urban development are offered). Students can also work with faculty to design their own programme of study. Waivers are available and some electives can be taken in other university departments. The programme concludes with an in-company team consultancy project.

The school has an exchange agreement with the University of Paris, Dauphine.

Kogod's part-time MBA is exactly the same as the full-time version and students can switch between the two. There is considerable flexibility but students usually take two courses at a time. Classes meet on Mondays and Wednesdays, or Tuesdays and Thursdays (5.30–8 pm). Some classes may meet

American University—The Kogod School of Business

8.10–10.40 pm or on Saturday morning. The programme is generally completed in 33 months.

In 2004 Kogod introduced a new Master of Science in Management (MSM) degree, a 15-month full-time programme with a concentration in management for individuals who do not have a business degree, have little or no business experience, or who want to learn core management fundamentals.

	Full-time MBA	Part Time MBA
Student rating of programme	3.9 (n/a)	–
Number of overseas exchange programmes	4 (n/a)	–
Number of languages on offer	0 (n/a)	–

Students

	Full-time MBA	Part Time MBA
Annual intake	78	40
Applicants:places	6:1	3:1
Percentage of women students	40 (n/a)	43
Percentage of foreign students	42 (n/a)	n/a
Average GMAT score	590 (n/a)	570
Average number of months' work experience	60 (n/a)	72
Age range of students	24-30	25-34
Average age	27	31
Student rating of culture and classmates	3.6 (n/a)	–

Student profile (full time)

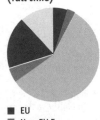

- ■ EU
- ■ Non-EU Europe
- ▨ North America
- ■ Other Americas
- ■ Asia/Australasia
- ▨ Middle East

Recruiters/careers service

	Full-time MBA	Part Time MBA
Number of industry sectors that recruited graduates	6 (n/a)	–
Percentage of graduates in jobs 3 months after graduation	60 (n/a)	–
Percentage of graduates finding jobs through careers services	n/a (n/a)	–
Student rating of careers service	2.3 (n/a)	–
Post-MBA salary, US$	62,403 (n/a)	–
Percentage increase in salary	46 (n/a)	–
Principal recruiters of graduates	United States Department of Commerce, World Bank, Johnson & Johnson	

Cost

	Full-time MBA	Part Time MBA
Application fees	US$60	US$60
Programme fees	US$25,766	US$930
Comments	Per year, tuition only	Per credit hour
Accommodation costs (on campus, per year)	US$9,676	–
Accommodation costs (off campus, per year)	n/a	–
Financial aid available	n/a	–
Type of aid available	Scholarships and loans	–
Criteria on which aid is granted	Merit, financial need	–

Accreditation

AACSB International

Application details

	Full-time MBA	Part Time MBA
Application deadline	August 1st	August 1st
Programme dates	Aug start, 21 months	Aug start, 36 months
Admission requirements	First degree; at least 2 years' work experience; TOEFL if first language not English (250 minimum); 2 references; essay; laptop; interview by request	First degree; at least 2 years' work experience; TOEFL if first language not English (250 minimum); 2 references; essay; laptop; interview by request

Executive education

All of Kogod's executive education output consists of customised in-company programmes. Recent subjects covered include entrepreneurship, global financial management, leadership, marketing management and e-business.

Student/alumni quotes

"My experience has been outstanding. I have learned a lot and I have had fun learning, which is also very important. There is room for improvement in some aspects, like careers services, but this happens at every school."

"At Kogod, being part of a smaller programme has afforded me the opportunity to receive the individual attention from faculty. This includes such things as career coaching, research opportunities and general mentoring by world-renowned faculty."

"I was worried that this was not a name school, and that would hurt my job prospects upon graduation. This was unfounded."

University of Arizona—Eller College of Management

Ranking	Rank (out of 100) Full-time
Overall rank	87
Regional rank	49

Criteria	Rank (out of 100) Full-time
Open new career opportunities	**55**
Diversity of recruiters	84
Number in jobs three months after graduation	51
Jobs found through the careers service	28
Student assessment of careers service	>100
Personal development and educational experience	**>100**
Faculty quality	12
Student quality	93
Student diversity	>100
Education experience	>100
Increase in salary	**85**
Increase in salary	48
Post-MBA salary	86
Potential to network	**98**
Breadth of alumni network	39
Internationalism of alumni	>100
Alumni effectiveness	>100

Address
McClelland Hall 210
PO Box 210108
Tucson, AZ
US
95721-0108

Tel:
+1 520 621 4962

Fax:
+1 520 621 2606

E-mail:
mbaadmissions@eller.
arizona.edu

Website:
www.ellermba.arizona.
edu

Programme director:
Dr E LaBrent Chrite

Figures in brackets
represent rank

Background

The College of Management at the University of Arizona was named after Karl Eller, an alumnus and Arizona businessman, in 1999. The university began offering a bachelor of commerce degree as early as 1913. Eller is a full-range college teaching more than 4,500 undergraduate and 600 graduate students and offering a range of executive education programmes. Eller Graduate School of Management teaches the MBA programme, which is not large by US standards, within the main College of Management. It has good links with the local business community.

Facilities

The college is based in McClelland Hall, a large building on the university campus. Facilities are excellent and reflect the laid-back Arizona lifestyle.

	Full-time MBA
Student assessment of facilities	3.8 (>100)

Faculty

Number of faculty: 106 Full-time, 26 part-time, 0 visiting

	Full-time MBA	Eller Working Professionals MBA Program
Number of faculty per student	1.9 (16)	2.3
Percentage of faculty with PhD	95 (46)	95
Student rating of faculty	4.2 (73)	–

Strengths and weaknesses

Strengths: management information systems; entrepreneurship; accounting

Weakness: elective choice

Programme highlights

Eller's two-year full-time MBA has a standard core with interesting additions such as required courses in leadership, communications and personal development as well as what the school calls an "experiential learning opportunity" (it is an in company project). The first semester is said to be particularly tough. The second year is given over to electives, which can be taken broadly or grouped into a concentration. A concentration involves a minimum of four elective courses. Many students opt to take two concentrations, which are offered in entrepreneurship, finance, management and policy, managing information systems, marketing and operations management.

The two-year part-time programme, the Working Professionals MBA, is similar to the full-time programme without the required personal development components (although these are covered in the programme) and concentrations. The second year involves a week's study tour to Mexico. The programme is offered in the evenings (classes meet every Wednesday evening during term 4–9.45 pm) or at weekends (alternate weekends, Fridays 1–5 pm and Saturdays 8 am–5 pm).

	Full-time MBA	Eller Working Professionals MBA Program
Student rating of programme	3.9 (>100)	–
Number of overseas exchange programmes	0 (93)	–
Number of languages on offer	0 (77)	–

Student profile (full time)

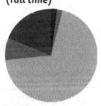

- ■ EU
- ■ Non-EU Europe
- ■ North America
- ■ Other Americas
- ■ Asia/Australasia
- ▫ Middle East

Students

	Full-time MBA	Eller Working Professionals MBA Program
Annual intake	64	58
Applicants:places	5:1	1:1
Percentage of women students	19 (>100)	24
Percentage of foreign students	30 (>100)	n/a
Average GMAT score	639 (64)	557
Average number of months' work experience	42 (>100)	60
Age range of students	24-30	26-34
Average age	27	29
Student rating of culture and classmates	3.9 (96)	–

Recruiters/careers service

	Full-time MBA	Eller Working Professionals MBA Program
Number of industry sectors that recruited graduates	6 (84)	–
Percentage of graduates in jobs 3 months after graduation	84 (51)	–
Percentage of graduates finding jobs through careers services	68 (28)	–
Student rating of careers service	3.3 (>100)	–
Post-MBA salary, US$	65,171 (86)	–
Percentage increase in salary	58 (48)	
Principal recruiters of graduates	Intel Corporation, Avery Dennison, Federal Express Corporation	

The directory
University of Arizona—Eller College of Management

Cost

	Full-time MBA	Eller Working Professionals MBA Program
Application fees	US$50	US$50
Programme fees	US$22,828	US$15,000
Comments	Per year. Fees for Arizona residents are US$13,848 per year	Per year
Accommodation costs (on campus, per year)	n/a	–
Accommodation costs (off campus, per year)	US$6,800	–
Financial aid available	US$700,000	–
Type of aid available	Scholarship, tuition waivers	–
Criteria on which aid is granted	Merit	–

Accreditation

AACSB International

Application details

	Full-time MBA	Eller Working Professionals MBA Program
Application deadline	end of April	June 15th
Programme dates	Aug start, 21 months	Aug start, 24 months
Admission requirements	First degree; at least 2 years' work experience; TOEFL if first language not English; 2 references; 3 essays; interview; laptop	First degree; at least 2 years' work experience; TOEFL if first language not English; 2 references; 3 essays

Executive education

Eller offers open-enrolment executive education programmes ranging from short seminars in areas such as marketing, IT, finance, communication and negotiation to longer programmes on more general business topics. It also offers customised in-company programmes.

Student/alumni quotes

"Small, intimate programme. Everyone knows everyone and you become close as a class. Teachers know everyone and are interested in learning about you as well as teaching you the things you need to learn."

"Class size is too small to create enough alumni."

"The atmosphere was very co-operative, and the quality of my classmates was outstanding. I had a great experience, and I now work with students from more prestigious schools and would rate myself very comparable with them in professional settings."

Ashridge

Address
Ashridge
Berkhamsted
Hertfordshire
UK
HP4 1NS

Tel:
+44 1442 841 289

Fax:
–

E-mail:
jane.tobin@ashridge.
org.uk

Website:
www.ashridge.com

Programme Director:
Dr James McCalman

Figures in brackets
represent rank

Ranking	Rank (out of 100) Full-time
Overall rank	72
Regional rank	26

Criteria	Rank (out of 100) Full-time
Open new career opportunities	**>100**
Diversity of recruiters	>100
Number in jobs three months after graduation	88
Jobs found through the careers service	n/a
Student assessment of careers service	>100
Personal development and educational experience	**>100**
Faculty quality	>100
Student quality	17
Student diversity	>100
Education experience	>100
Increase in salary	**1**
Increase in salary	80
Post-MBA salary	1
Potential to network	**78**
Breadth of alumni network	45
Internationalism of alumni	45
Alumni effectiveness	81

Background

Ashridge's main concern is executive education (it also has a consulting arm) and the MBA is at present a relatively small part of its output. However, the programme has a central role and in the past its somewhat unusual structure and approach has reflected Ashridge's development-driven, competency-based approach. Kai Peters (formerly head of Rotterdam School of Management) now leads the school, and some changes to propel Ashridge into a front-rank role can be expected. The one-year MBA for self-sponsored students has already undergone some changes (see below).

Facilities

	Full-time MBA
Student assessment of facilities	4.1 (48)

The 150 acre campus (mainly woodland) is centred on a 19th-century neo-Gothic stately home, although the original site dates back to the 13th century. The facilities are very good. The Learning Resource Centre is open 24 hours a day. There are excellent computer and video facilities (although participants are encouraged to bring their own computers) and a language laboratory. The Virtual Learning Resource Centre allows remote access to many of the learning materials, such as learning guides, summaries and reviews of books, and a series of software guides. There are links to other websites in some of the principal areas of business and management, and access to several online information sources.

On-campus accommodation is available in self-contained study/bedrooms, although many students opt for local flats or hotels. There is a good restaurant and bar, a fitness centre and ample sporting facilities.

The directory
Ashridge

Faculty

Number of faculty: 34 full-time, 7 part-time, 8 visiting

	Full-time MBA	Ashridge Part Time EMBA
Number of faculty per student	2.3 (6)	1.4
Percentage of faculty with PhD	35 (>100)	35
Student rating of faculty	3.5 (>100)	–

Strengths and weaknesses

Strengths: leadership; personal development; strategy

Weakness: low global profile

Programme highlights

Under the leadership of Kai Peters, Ashridge has reconfigured its full-time programme to be more in line with the European tradition. The programme starts in January and lasts a calendar year, divided into three stages: the fundamentals (people, performance, processes); integration (global environment, organisational life cycle, business in society, creating value, leading change); and electives (including finance, strategy, leadership, information systems, information technology, financial services, consulting). There is a lengthy in-company project before the elective stage and the programme is heavily influenced by Ashridge's expertise in leadership development.

The programme is extended by a series of "Masterclasses", usually led by outside experts. Topics are often selected by students and have included entrepreneurship, strategic sourcing, corporate social responsibility, and leading and directing change.

The two-year Executive MBA at Ashridge is designed for sponsored students (the full-time programme is aimed at students seeking a career change). The programme involves 14 residential modules (of about one week each) over two years and considerable project work.

Ashridge also administers a consortium MBA for Bosche, Deutsche Bank, Lufthansa and Merck. The syllabus is similar to the two-year programme.

	Full-time MBA	Ashridge Part Time EMBA
Student rating of programme	3.7 (>100)	–
Number of overseas exchange programmes	0 (93)	–
Number of languages on offer	0 (94)	–

Students

	Full-time MBA	Ashridge Part Time EMBA
Annual intake	17	36
Applicants:places	3:1	3:1
Percentage of women students	12 (>100)	14
Percentage of foreign students	47 (54)	n/a
Average GMAT score	580 (100)	580
Average number of months' work experience	120 (2)	108
Age range of students	29-41	30-35
Average age	32	33
Student rating of culture and classmates	3.8 (74)	–

**Student profile
(full time)**

- ■ EU
- ■ Non-EU Europe
- ▨ North America
- ■ Other Americas
- ■ Asia/Australasia
- ▨ Middle East

Recruiters/careers service

	Full-time MBA	Ashridge Part Time EMBA
Number of industry sectors that recruited graduates	4 (>100)	–
Percentage of graduates in jobs 3 months after graduation	84 (88)	–
Percentage of graduates finding jobs through careers services	n/a (n/a)	–
Student rating of careers service	2.4 (>100)	–
Post-MBA salary, US$	177,049 (1)	–
Percentage increase in salary	35 (80)	–
Principal recruiters of graduates	MacMaster, Pacific Link Creations, Windworks Energy Co	

Cost

	Full-time MBA	Ashridge Part Time EMBA
Application fees	None	None
Programme fees	£29,500 (US$48,361)	£33,900 (US$55,574)
Comments	–	–
Accommodation costs (on campus, per year)	n/a	–
Accommodation costs (off campus, per year)	£8,000 (US$13,115)	–
Financial aid available	£29,500 (US$48,361)	–
Type of aid available	Scholarship	–
Criteria on which aid is granted	Open to all	–

Accreditation

AACSB International, AMBA, EQUIS

Application details

	Full time MBA	Ashridge Part Time EMBA
Application deadline	October 31st	July 31st
Programme dates	Jan start, 12 months	Sep start, 27 months
Admission requirements	First degree; at least 3 years' work experience; GMAT; TOEFL if first language not English; 2 references; interview; laptop	First degree; at least 5 years' work experience; GMAT; TOEFL if first language not English; 2 references; interview

Executive education

Ashridge has a wide portfolio of open-enrolment executive education programmes in areas such as alliances, collaboration and acquisitions, consulting skills, corporate social responsibility, finance, general management, leadership, marketing and sales, people skills and strategic management. It has a strong reputation in delivering customised in-company programmes.

Student/alumni quotes

"Ashridge is really superb ... its only real problem is that it has steadfastly not pushed its main benefits in the media. It needs to be more marketing savvy in order for people to know about it. It really should be far higher up the rankings. It is an oddball and doesn't fit into the normal MBA ranking structures."

"The Ashridge experience is significantly different from large-classroom MBA factories very intense learning environment, very close interaction with fellow students and tutors, strong focus on 'real' management issues, not just a theoretical, academic approach."

"Being a small school it was expected that Ashridge wasn't going to be a target for companies doing the milk round and hoping to recruit high numbers of candidates. The school, however, excelled at coaching students on a one-to-one basis to work out their own desired futures. This to me seemed much more appropriate for a more mature and experienced group."

Aston Business School

Ranking	Rank (out of 100) Full-time
Overall rank	44
Regional rank	17

Criteria	Rank (out of 100) Full-time
Open new career opportunities	**78**
Diversity of recruiters	95
Number in jobs three months after graduation	15
Jobs found through the careers service	52
Student assessment of careers service	85
Personal development and educational experience	**55**
Faculty quality	34
Student quality	40
Student diversity	40
Education experience	98
Increase in salary	**3**
Increase in salary	1
Post-MBA salary	18
Potential to network	**94**
Breadth of alumni network	27
Internationalism of alumni	74
Alumni effectiveness	>100

Address
Aston Business School
Aston University
Aston Triangle
Birmingham
UK
B4 7ET

Tel:
+44 121 359 3611
ext 5321

Fax:
+44 121 359 5356

E-mail:
abspg@aston.ac.uk

Website:
www.astonmba.com

Programme director:
Dr Jim Rimmer

Figures in brackets
represent rank

Background

Aston Business School, just over 50 years old, is a large full-range school with 2,500 undergraduate, postgraduate and executive education students. It has strong contacts with business, particularly in the Midlands area of the UK (as well as internationally), and a good reputation for research. However, full-time students were surprised that a dedicated careers adviser for MBA students has only just been appointed (in 2004) and that no recruiters visited campus.

The university's 40-acre campus is based in the centre of Birmingham, the UK's third largest city, which offers a wide range of cultural and leisure activities. Accommodation is generally on campus.

Facilities

The business school has on-campus teaching facilities in the main university building and in the Nelson building. There is a purpose-built postgraduate suite, which, as well as teaching and syndicate rooms, contains 24-hour computer laboratories and a recreation lounge. Sports and leisure amenities are available on campus.

	Full-time MBA
Student assessment of facilities	3.5 (89)

Which MBA? © The Economist Intelligence Unit Limited 2004

Faculty

Number of faculty: 85 full-time, 2 part-time, 12 visiting

	Full-time MBA	MBA (part time off-campus)	MBA (part time on-campus)
Number of faculty per student	3.0 (5)	0.8	4.0
Percentage of faculty with PhD	79 (90)	79	79
Student rating of faculty	3.6 (91)	–	–

Strengths and weaknesses

Strengths: organisational studies; marketing and e-business; international business

Weakness: careers services

Programme highlights

Aston's one-year MBA has a traditional format of core and four electives followed by a project (which is essential to completing the degree). At the time of writing the programme was being revised to include new modules, a two-week pre-programme orientation and improved careers services, and to allow full-time students to complete the degree more quickly (by the end of July).

The content of the Aston MBA is identical whichever delivery route—full-time, part-time or distance learning—is chosen. The only difference is in timing. The part-time programme is extremely flexible. Students on the part-time programme generally study one or two modules each term and the project can take up to nine months. They can choose to attend classes for one day or one or two evenings a week and can study some modules by video.

Taking the degree by distance learning involves a minimum of 21 months' study as well as a nine-month project. There are also study weekends, e-mail, fax and telephone support, and local self-help groups. Part-time students can start the programme in October, January or April.

	Full-time MBA	MBA (part time off-campus)	MBA (part time on-campus)
Student rating of programme	3.8 (69)	–	–
Number of overseas exchange programmes	0 (88)	–	–
Number of languages on offer	0 (91)	–	–

Student profile (full time)

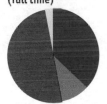

- ■ EU
- ■ Non-EU Europe
- ▨ North America
- ■ Other Americas
- ■ Asia/Australasia
- ▨ Middle East

Students

	Full-time MBA	MBA (part time off-campus)	MBA (part time on-campus)
Annual intake	30	45	25
Applicants:places	9:1	2.1	2:1
Percentage of women students	38 (39)	20	20
Percentage of foreign students	77 (29)	n/a	n/a
Average GMAT score	620 (73)	n/a	n/a
Average number of months' work experience	90 (14)	120	120
Age range of students	27-36	26-40	26-40
Average age	30	32	32
Student rating of culture and classmates	3.8 (90)	–	–

The directory
Aston Business School

Recruiters/careers service

	Full-time MBA	MBA (part time off-campus)	MBA (part time on-campus)
Number of industry sectors that recruited graduates	6 (95)	–	–
Percentage of graduates in jobs 3 months after graduation	89 (15)	–	–
Percentage of graduates finding jobs through careers services	48 (52)	–	–
Student rating of careers service	2.8 (85)	–	–
Post-MBA salary, US$	90,164 (18)	–	–
Percentage increase in salary	175 (1)		–
Principal recruiters of graduates	Ford, Healthgain Solutions		

Cost

	Full-time MBA	MBA (part time off-campus)	MBA (part time on-campus)
Application fees	None	None	None
Programme fees	£18,380 (US$30,131)	£12,860 (US$21,082)	£12,860 (US$21,082)
Comments	Fee is for total programme, including travel and accommodation cost for two one-week foreign study visits	Fee is for the total programme and can be paid in six instalments	Fee is for the total programme and can be paid in six instalments
Accommodation costs (on campus, per year)	£2,800 (US$4,590)	–	–
Accommodation costs (off campus, per year)	£3,000 (US$4,918)	–	–
Financial aid available	£60,000 (US$98,361)	–	–
Type of aid available	Bursaries	–	–
Criteria on which aid is granted	Outstanding applicants may be awarded bursaries giving them reduced price tuition	–	–

Accreditation

AACSB International, AMBA, EQUIS

Application details

	Full-time MBA	MBA (part time off-campus)	MBA (part time on-campus)
Application deadline	July 1st	Rolling admissions	Rolling admissions
Programme dates	Sep start, 10 months	Oct start, 27 months	Oct start, 27 months
Admission requirements	A good UK honours degree or an overseas degree which is recognised by Aston University, or a degree-equivalent professional qualification; at least 3 years' work experience; GMAT; TOEFL score of at least 650 (paper-based) or 280 (computer-based) or an IELTS score of 7.0 overall with no less than 6.5 in any section if first language not English; 2 references	First degree (applicants without a degree but with sufficient work experience may be considered for initial enrolment as Diploma candidates with the opportunity for conversion to Masters registration); at least 3 years' work experience; TOEFL score of at least 650 (paper-based) or 280 (computer-based) or an IELTS score of 7.0 overall with no less than 6.5 in any section if first language not English; 2 references	First degree (applicants without a degree but with sufficient work experience may be considered for initial enrolment as Diploma candidates with the opportunity for conversion to Masters registration); at least 3 years' work experience; TOEFL score of at least 650 (paper-based) or 280 (computer-based) or an IELTS score of 7.0 overall with no less than 6.5 in any section if first language not English; 2 references

Executive education

Aston's executive education courses are all customised and are based on the school's main study areas: strategic management, finance, accounting and law, marketing, operations and information management, work and organisational psychology, and public management and sociology. A number of courses are accredited and count towards diplomas, certificates and degrees. Training generally takes place at Aston's well-equipped on-campus Management Training Centre.

Student/alumni quotes

"I have to admire the present career guidance counsellor. Her recent appointment to this post, however, begs a question: how come there wasn't one before her? Nonetheless, she has put in a lot of effort ... She is probably the only bright 'spark' around. However, it might be too little too late as this does not compensate for the lack of any recruiters whatsoever coming on campus."

"Aston's distance-learning programme is excellent. It is run efficiently and effectively and gives access to high-quality teaching through video, weekend visits and communication with staff."

"On the whole I think that my time at Aston Business School has been worthwhile, although I did expect a bit more for the money that I was paying. I would recommend it to anyone thinking of embarking on the full-time programme who wants to specialise in marketing or HR."

Australian Graduate School of Management

Ranking	Rank (out of 100) Full-time
Overall rank	77
Regional rank	4

Criteria	Rank (out of 100) Full-time
Open new career opportunities	**65**
Diversity of recruiters	40
Number in jobs three months after graduation	92
Jobs found through the careers service	24
Student assessment of careers service	90
Personal development and educational experience	**91**
Faculty quality	77
Student quality	61
Student diversity	100
Education experience	90
Increase in salary	**54**
Increase in salary	86
Post-MBA salary	40
Potential to network	**83**
Breadth of alumni network	40
Internationalism of alumni	69
Alumni effectiveness	89

Address
Australian Graduate
School of
Management
University of New
South Wales
Sydney, NSW
Australia
2052

Tel:
+61 2 9931 9317

Fax:
+61 2 9931 9539

E-mail:
mba@agsm.edu.au

Website:
www.agsm.edu.au

Programme director:
Sue Bennett-Williams

Figures in brackets
represent rank

Background

The Australian Graduate School of Management (AGSM) is a faculty of both the University of New South Wales and the University of Sydney, following its merger with the latter's Graduate School of Business. The AGSM has always been regarded as one of the leading business schools in Australia and this remains true. The merger appears to have brought about some changes, in particular a more "Australian" style in terms of, for example, an increased emphasis on part-time programmes. The AGSM was somewhat American in style and this remains apparent in the full-time programme.

Facilities

The AGSM has additional campuses providing part-time programmes in Adelaide, Brisbane, Canberra, Melbourne, Perth and Sydney. It also has a campus in Hong Kong. The home campus in Kensington, Sydney, is well equipped and houses the Frank Lowy Library, the most comprehensive management education library in the region. Computer facilities are also good, as are the school and university facilities generally. For students on the full-time programme accommodation is available on campus, although not in the school. Off-campus housing is readily available and reasonably priced.

	Full-time MBA
Student assessment of facilities	4.0 (81)

Which MBA? © The Economist Intelligence Unit Limited 2004

Faculty

Number of faculty: 45 full-time, 0 part-time, 4 visiting

	Full-time MBA	MBA (Executive)
Number of faculty per student	0.5 (79)	n/a
Percentage of faculty with PhD	98 (25)	98
Student rating of faculty	4.0 (80)	–

Strengths and weaknesses

Strengths: strategy and general management; organisational behaviour; finance and accounting
Weaknesses: elective range; low profile

Programme highlights

The AGSM's full-time MBA starts in January and can be completed in 15 months of continuous study or 18 months including an internship. The programme is fairly traditional in outline with core and electives and compulsory integrative programmes (delivered in a three- or four-day intensive mode at the beginning of each term to address the complexity and inter-relatedness of business issues).

The part-time programme (called an Executive MBA) is based on a staged certificate–diploma–MBA system. The first two stages (certificate and diploma) are delivered in six cities (Adelaide, Brisbane, Canberra, Melbourne, Perth and Sydney) around Australia and take between one and a half and five years. The third stage, the "executive year", involves two sessions of 18 weeks.

The AGSM also offers a part-time MBA taught by its own faculty in Hong Kong. Classes are held at the Central Conference Centre in Hong Kong. The programme can be completed in a minimum of two years or a maximum of seven, including an option to complete the programme at the AGSM campus.

	Full-time MBA	MBA (Executive)
Student rating of programme	3.7 (100)	–
Number of overseas exchange programmes	50 (26)	–
Number of languages on offer	1 (83)	–

Students

Student profile (full time)

- EU
- Non-EU Europe
- North America
- Other Americas
- Asia/Australasia
- Middle East

	Full-time MBA	MBA (Executive)
Annual intake	89	1,548
Applicants:places	2:1	n/a
Percentage of women students	26 (92)	30
Percentage of foreign students	52 (55)	n/a
Average GMAT score	654 (55)	n/a
Average number of months' work experience	60 (52)	84
Age range of students	26-35	28-43
Average age	30	34
Student rating of culture and classmates	3.9 (89)	–

Recruiters/careers service

	Full-time MBA	MBA (Executive)
Number of industry sectors that recruited graduates	8 (40)	–
Percentage of graduates in jobs 3 months after graduation	75 (92)	–
Percentage of graduates finding jobs through careers services	85 (24)	–
Student rating of careers service	2.0 (90)	–
Post-MBA salary, US$	78,064 (40)	–
Percentage increase in salary	19 (86)	–
Principal recruiters of graduates	Boston Consulting Group, Blue Scope Steel, Australian Business	

The directory
Australian Graduate School of Management

Cost

	Full-time MBA	MBA (Executive)
Application fees	A$100 (US$65)	–
Programme fees	A$56,280 (US$36,545)	A$45,260 (US$29,390)
Comments	Total programme. Fee for Australian students is A$49,140	Total programme
Accommodation costs (on campus, per year)	n/a	–
Accommodation costs (off campus, per year)	A$11,100 (US$7,208)	–
Financial aid available	A$325,700 (US$211,494)	–
Type of aid available	Scholarships	–
Criteria on which aid is granted	Academic performance, financial need	–

Accreditation

AACSB International

Application details

	Full-time MBA	MBA (Executive)
Application deadline	September 30th	Rolling admissions
Programme dates	Jan start, 15 months	Jan start, 48 months
Admission requirements	Bachelors degree from a recognised university (exceptional career attainments may be considered in lieu of a degree); at least 2 years' work experience; GMAT; TOEFL or IELTS if first language not English; 2 references; 4 essays; interview; laptop; Undergraduate Grade Point Average (GPA) of at least 2; curriculum vitae	Undergraduate degree (candidates with at least 6 years' management or professional experience may be considered in lieu of a degree); at least 2 years' work experience; TOEFL or IELTS if first language not English; reference; essay; candidates must be currently employed in a management or professional capacity; Australian residence

Executive education

The AGSM offers open-enrolment executive education programmes in general management and leadership and short specialist programmes in areas such as strategy, finance, marketing and human resource management. The school's customised in-company programmes focus on leadership and management training to meet strategic goals.

Student/alumni quotes

"The tough selection process means that everyone on the course was really committed to working hard but in true Aussie style (soon learned by all of us international students) also to playing hard—a good experience."

"It is an excellent small school, which lacks the 'ego' of the larger and higher ranked schools. Excellent location and lifestyle."

"Not enough electives."

University of Bath School of Management

Address
The Bath MBA
School of
Management
University of Bath
Bath
UK
BA2 7AY

Tel:
+44 1225 386 741

Fax:
+44 1225 383 902

E-mail:
mba-admit@
management.bath.ac.
uk

Website:
www.bathmba.com

Programme director:
Peggy van Luyn

Figures in brackets
represent rank

Ranking	Rank (out of 100) Full-time
Overall rank	43
Regional rank	16

Criteria	Rank (out of 100) Full-time
Open new career opportunities	**58**
Diversity of recruiters	62
Number in jobs three months after graduation	25
Jobs found through the careers service	69
Student assessment of careers service	65
Personal development and educational experience	**28**
Faculty quality	60
Student quality	40
Student diversity	10
Education experience	52
Increase in salary	**39**
Increase in salary	66
Post-MBA salary	37
Potential to network	**42**
Breadth of alumni network	44
Internationalism of alumni	39
Alumni effectiveness	43

Background

The University of Bath's School of Management is among the longest-established and largest business schools in the UK. It offered its first MBA in 1968. There are more than 100 teaching and research staff, 50 administrative staff, around 450 MBA students, nearly 180 taught master's students, 133 full-time and part-time research students and over 750 undergraduates.

Facilities

The MBA programme is housed in the Centre for Executive Development, which has purpose-designed facilities including lecture and seminar rooms and common rooms. The library and learning centre are open 24-hours-a day in term time, and there are good computer labs (although students are encouraged to have their own laptops) and sporting facilities. On-campus accommodation is available.

	Full-time MBA
Student assessment of facilities	4.6 (34)

Faculty

Number of faculty: 53 full-time, 10 part-time, 9 visiting

	Full-time MBA	The Bath MBA Modular Programme	The Bath MBA Executive Programme
Number of faculty per student	1.2 (30)	1.8	2.9
Percentage of faculty with PhD	79 (80)	79	79
Student rating of faculty	4.4 (50)	–	–

The directory
University of Bath School of Management

Strengths and weaknesses

Strengths: strategic purchasing and supply; leadership and governance; information systems

Weakness: elective choice

Programme highlights

Bath offers a generalist MBA with a strong entrepreneurial content. The programme includes core courses; the mandatory Claverton Enterprise group project (an eight-month business start-up exercise); electives; strategy and change management; leadership and personal skills development; and an in-company project and thesis carried out in the summer.

The programme is also offered in a modular version, in which students study self-contained modules over a period of, typically, 3–4 years.

Bath's two-year Executive MBA is taught on Fridays and Saturdays (15 sessions a year). An EMBA is also offered (though in a different format) at the school's recently opened campus in Swindon. This has an engineering, science and technology orientation and students must first complete a specialised one-year engineering postgraduate certificate. Lastly, Bath faculty teach an EMBA as a part-time programme in Athens in co-operation with the Hellenic Management Association.

	Full-time MBA	The Bath MBA Modular Programme	The Bath MBA Executive Programme
Student rating of programme	4.3 (57)	–	–
Number of overseas exchange programmes	0 (93)	–	–
Number of languages on offer	>5 (44)	–	–

Students

	Full-time MBA	The Bath MBA Modular Programme	The Bath MBA Executive Programme
Annual intake	51	39	25
Applicants:places	5:1	2:1	2:1
Percentage of women students	48 (8)	28	8
Percentage of foreign students	69 (44)	n/a	n/a
Average GMAT score	580 (99)	n/a	n/a
Average number of months' work experience	96 (5)	120	144
Age range of students	25-36	26-46	28-48
Average age	30	34	35
Student rating of culture and classmates	4.3 (56)	–	–

Recruiters/careers service

	Full-time MBA	The Bath MBA Modular Programme	The Bath MBA Executive Programme
Number of industry sectors that recruited graduates	7 (62)	–	–
Percentage of graduates in jobs 3 months after graduation	100 (25)	–	–
Percentage of graduates finding jobs through careers services	43 (69)	–	–
Student rating of careers service	3.8 (65)	–	–
Post-MBA salary, US$	88,505 (37)	–	–
Percentage increase in salary	56 (66)	–	–
Principal recruiters of graduates	n/a		

Student profile (full time)

- ■ EU
- ■ Non-EU Europe
- North America
- ■ Other Americas
- ■ Asia/Australasia
- Middle East

Cost

	Full-time MBA	The Bath MBA Modular Programme	The Bath MBA Executive Programme
Application fees	£50 (US$82)	n/a	n/a
Programme fees	£20,000 (US$32,787)	£20,250 (US$33,197)	£20,000 (US$32,787)
Comments	Total fees	Based on three-year progression	
Accommodation costs (on campus, per year)	n/a	–	–
Accommodation costs (off campus, per year)	n/a	–	–
Financial aid available	£105,000 (US$172,131)	–	–
Type of aid available	scholarships	–	–
Criteria on which aid is granted	various; details available from school	–	–

Accreditation

AMBA

Application details

	Full-time MBA	The Bath MBA Modular Programme	The Bath MBA Executive Programme
Application deadline	June 1st	Six weeks prior to intended start date	September 1st
Programme dates	Sep start, 12 months	n/a	Oct start, 24 months
Admission requirements	Degree at first or second class honours level or equivalent classification/GPA awarded by an approved institution or final qualification of a professional body acceptable to the University (non-degree holders with considerable work experience also considered); at least 3 years' work experience; TOEFL 600 (paper) or 250 (computer) or IELTS 7.0 if first language not English; 2 references; 4 essays; interview; laptop	Degree at first or second class honours level or equivalent classification/GPA awarded by an approved institution or final qualification of a professional body acceptable to the University (non-degree holders with considerable work experience and GMAT score of 550 also considered); at least 3 years' work experience; TOEFL 600 (paper) or 250 (computer) or IELTS 7.0 if first language not English; 2 references; 4 essays; interview	Degree at first or second class honours level or equivalent classification/GPA awarded by an approved institution or final qualification of a professional body acceptable to the University (non-degree holders with considerable work experience and GMAT score of 550 also considered); at least 3 years' work experience; TOEFL 600 (paper) or 250 (computer) or IELTS 7.0 if first language not English; 2 references; 4 essays; interview

Executive education

Bath has offered customised executive courses in many areas, including strategy, leadership, change management and so on, for many years. It has recently started to offer open-enrolment courses in project management.

Student/alumni quotes

"An excellent course. I have learnt far more than I expected."

"My co-students come from a range of backgrounds and one of the primary benefits of this course has been the opportunity to learn from them."

"Most students are extremely tired because the course is very tough."

University of Birmingham Business School

Ranking	Rank (out of 100) Full-time
Overall rank	25
Regional rank	6

Criteria	Rank (out of 100) Full-time
Open new career opportunities	**42**
Diversity of recruiters	68
Number in jobs three months after graduation	30
Jobs found through the careers service	n/a
Student assessment of careers service	69
Personal development and educational experience	**45**
Faculty quality	>100
Student quality	13
Student diversity	3
Education experience	45
Increase in salary	**8**
Increase in salary	4
Post-MBA salary	26
Potential to network	**69**
Breadth of alumni network	90
Internationalism of alumni	21
Alumni effectiveness	67

Address
University House
Edgbaston Park Road
Birmingham
UK
B15 2TX

Tel:
+44 121 414 6249

Fax:
+44 121 414 3553

E-mail:
mba@bham.ac.uk

Website:
mba.bham.ac.uk

Programme director:
Dr Paul Forrester

Figures in brackets
represent rank

Background

Birmingham has been teaching business via the Faculty of Commerce since 1902. The business school was created in 1989, following the merger of the Commerce and Accounting and Finance departments of the university, and now offers a wide range of undergraduate and postgraduate programmes. The school has excellent links with local, national and international companies and strong Asian connections. It also has extensive international contacts, particularly in emerging economies, and is strong in languages.

Facilities

The school moved into a new home in 2004, the refurbished University House, which includes a new 3,000 sq m learning and teaching facility for postgraduate and continuing professional development students, as well as study and conference facilities and faculty offices. On-campus accommodation is available.

	Full-time MBA
Student assessment of facilities	4.4 (37)

Faculty

Number of faculty: 53 full-time, 3 part-time, 10 visiting

	Full-time MBA	MBA International Business (Executive)
Number of faculty per student	0.4 (72)	1.6
Percentage of faculty with PhD	60 (>100)	60
Student rating of faculty	4.1 (83)	–

Strengths and weaknesses

Strengths: strategy; organisational behaviour; finance

Weaknesses: may need to invest more in faculty

Programme highlights

The main Birmingham MBA programme focuses on international business and global markets. It is also taught in Singapore, Hong Kong and Mauritius as a part-time modular programme. Like all Birmingham's MBA programmes, it is based on a core of courses covering functional disciplines. Depending on the options taken, students can focus on a special field in marketing, finance, international trade and finance, and human resource management and organisational behaviour. As well as the assessed modules, there are modules covering areas such as computing, leadership, team dynamics and cross-cultural understanding.

As well as the main international MBA, the school offers specialised MBA programmes in International Banking and Finance (full-time) and Strategy and Procurement Management (part-time modular).

The Birmingham MBA is also offered in part-time and executive modular versions, which are broadly similar to the full-time version. The part-time programme is taught on two evenings a week during university semesters. The executive modular programme is taught in seven-day blocks offered five times a year during university vacations. Students may take whichever combination of evening or block modules suits them best. Entry is possible at any point at which a module is delivered. There are optional soft skills and communication courses, and the degree is completed by a dissertation.

Birmingham also runs bilingual joint MBA programmes with ESC Montpellier, France, and FUNDESEM, Alicante, Spain

	Full-time MBA	MBA International Business (Executive)
Student rating of programme	4.1 (78)	–
Number of overseas exchange programmes	15 (69)	–
Number of languages on offer	>5 (1)	–

Student profile (full time)

- ■ EU
- ■ Non-EU Europe
- ▨ North America
- ■ Other Americas
- ■ Asia/Australasia
- ▨ Middle East
- ■ Other

Students

	Full-time MBA	MBA International Business (Executive)
Annual intake	134	42
Applicants:places	8:1	2:1
Percentage of women students	43 (7)	25
Percentage of foreign students	97 (4)	n/a
Average GMAT score	n/a (n/a)	n/a
Average number of months' work experience	84 (24)	144
Age range of students	26-38	25-50
Average age	30	33
Student rating of culture and classmates	3.9 (92)	–

Recruiters/careers service

	Full-time MBA	MBA International Business (Executive)
Number of industry sectors that recruited graduates	7 (68)	–
Percentage of graduates in jobs 3 months after graduation	86 (30)	–
Percentage of graduates finding jobs through careers service	n/a (n/a)	–
Student rating of careers service	3.5 (69)	–
Post-MBA salary, US$	85,188 (26)	–
Percentage increase in salary	128 (4)	–
Principal recruiters of graduates	n/a	–

The directory
University of Birmingham Business School

Cost

	Full-time MBA	MBA International Business (Executive)
Application fees	None	None
Programme fees	£12,500 (US$20,492)	£12,500 (US$20,492)
Comments	Fee for EU students; fee for non-EU students is £13,800	May be paid by instalments as modules taken
Accommodation costs (on campus, per year)	£3,800 (US$6,230)	–
Accommodation costs (off campus, per year)	£2,500 (US$4,098)	–
Financial aid available	n/a	–
Type of aid available	n/a	–
Criteria on which aid is granted	n/a	–

Accreditation

AMBA

Application details

	Full-time MBA	MBA International Business (Executive)
Application deadline	July 1st	Rolling admissions
Programme dates	Sep start, 12 months	Sep start, 24 months
Admission requirements	First degree; at least 5 years' work experience; TOEFL 580 or IELTS 6.5 if first language not English; 2 references	First degree; at least 5 years' work experience; TOEFL 580 or IELTS 6.5 if first language not English; 2 references

Executive education

Birmingham does not currently offer open-enrolment or customised in-company executive education programmes.

Student/alumni quotes

"This programme has given me a lot. It was practical, international and diverse, but at the same time sufficiently deep."

"Some weak teaching staff."

"A friendly and homely atmosphere for international students."

Bocconi University—SDA Bocconi School of Management

Address
Via Bocconi, n.8
Milan
Italy
20136

Tel:
+39 02 5836 3281

Fax:
+39 02 5836 3293

E-mail:
rossana.camera@
sdabocconi.it

Website:
www.sdabocconi.it

Programme director:
Valter Lazzari

Figures in brackets
represent rank

Ranking	Rank (out of 100) Full-time
Overall rank	86
Regional rank	33

Criteria	Rank (out of 100) Full-time
Open new career opportunities	**69**
Diversity of recruiters	57
Number in jobs three months after graduation	100
Jobs found through the careers service	46
Student assessment of careers service	82
Personal development and educational experience	**>100**
Faculty quality	>100
Student quality	63
Student diversity	93
Education experience	>100
Increase in salary	**64**
Increase in salary	41
Post-MBA salary	65
Potential to network	**>100**
Breadth of alumni network	87
Internationalism of alumni	54
Alumni effectiveness	100

Background

Founded in 1971, SDA (Scuola di Direzione Aziendale) is the graduate school of management of Bocconi University, Italy's leading business university, which celebrated its centenary in 2002. The MBA class size is small and interaction with faculty is good. Nevertheless, Bocconi is a big school; it says that in a typical year it offers more than 1,000 courses to nearly 11,000 students and managers.

It has a strong academic faculty and good links with business and industry. However, some students say the atmosphere is too "Italian" and that the school is not as yet leveraging the Bocconi brand internationally.

Facilities

The MBA is run by the Masters Division of SDA Bocconi, which is housed in a pleasant building (once a convent school and chapel) a short distance from the main university. There are 11 classrooms with multimedia support and around 80 areas set aside for work groups.

Executive education is run in a separate building nearby, with 16 classrooms, work areas and dining facilities as well as offices.

	Full-time MBA
Student assessment of facilities	3.2 (>100)

The directory
Bocconi University—SDA Bocconi School of Management

Faculty

Number of faculty: 87 full-time, 42 part-time, 24 visiting	
	Full-time MBA
Number of faculty per student	0.8 (37)
Percentage of faculty with PhD	80 (85)
Student rating of faculty	3.6 (>100)

Strengths and weaknesses

Strengths: finance; marketing; entrepreneurship

Weakness: careers services for international students

Programme highlights

SDA Bocconi offers a somewhat unusual MBA that combines an international approach with Italian flair. The programme lasts a short and exceptionally tough 13 months (November–December). It is divided into 6 phases, including Prelude, a mandatory pre-programme (August–October) introductory period. The next two phases—Pillars and Functional Management—are essentially the core. In phase 4 students can either undertake an in-company project and electives or opt for one of two "focuses" or specialisations, either business development and entrepreneurship or global financial management. Phase 5, general management, is common to all students and in phase 6 they may choose either an overseas exchange or further electives.

There are two separate language streams (Italian or English). Students in each are expected to study the other language. A guest-speaker series and careers management courses run throughout the programme.

Bocconi also offers a two-year part-time MBA (taught mainly in Italian) that includes distance-learning elements and some classroom work; a 15-month evening MBA taught entirely in Italian; and a Master in International Economics and Management (MIEM), a full-time, 13-month, interdisciplinary programme taught in English for young graduates and managers who want to work in the international economy.

	Full-time MBA
Student rating of programme	3.8 (90)
Number of overseas exchange programmes	30 (60)
Number of languages on offer	2 (78)

Students

	Full-time MBA
Annual intake	138
Applicants:places	5:1
Percentage of women students	22 (>100)
Percentage of foreign students	44 (62)
Average GMAT score	670 (36)
Average number of months' work experience	54 (82)
Age range of students	26-33
Average age	29
Student rating of culture and classmates	4.3 (39)

Student profile (full time)

- ■ EU
- ■ Non-EU Europe
- ▨ North America
- ■ Other Americas
- ■ Asia/Australasia
- ▨ Middle East

Which MBA? © The Economist Intelligence Unit Limited 2004

Recruiters/careers service

	Full-time MBA
Number of industry sectors that recruited graduates	7 (57)
Percentage of graduates in jobs 3 months after graduation	65 (100)
Percentage of graduates finding jobs through careers services	50 (46)
Student rating of careers service	2.9 (82)
Post-MBA salary, US$	80,682 (65)
Percentage increase in salary	58 (41)
Principal recruiters of graduates	Johnson & Johnson, Merloni Elettrodomestici, Boston Consulting Group

Cost

	Full-time MBA
Application fees	€100 (US$114)
Programme fees	€29,300 (US$33,295)
Comments	n/a
Accommodation costs (on campus, per year)	n/a
Accommodation costs (off campus, per year)	€10,000 (US$11,364)
Financial aid available	€1,170,000 (US$1,329,545)
Type of aid available	Scholarships and loans
Criteria on which aid is granted	Merit, financial need

Accreditation

AMBA, EQUIS

Application details

	Full-time MBA
Application deadline	May 15th
Programme dates	Oct start, 13 months
Admission requirements	First degree; work experience; TOEFL if first language not English; 2 references; interview; laptop

Executive education

Bocconi offers a large portfolio of open-enrolment short courses (taught in both Italian and English) and a wide range of customised courses in areas such as public administration and health, accounting and management control, banking and insurance, corporate finance, marketing, strategy and technology management.

Student/alumni quotes

"Value for money is unparalleled. I learned almost as much from fellow students as from the curriculum. The school handpicks an exceptional class."

"[Careers services]—very helpful for counselling and CV preparation but no widespread network and opportunities for foreign students."

"Too many Italian professors."

Bradford School of Management

Ranking	Rank (out of 100) Full-time
Overall rank	96
Regional rank	37

Criteria	Rank (out of 100) Full-time
Open new career opportunities	**80**
Diversity of recruiters	77
Number in jobs three months after graduation	>100
Jobs found through the careers service	40
Student assessment of careers service	38
Personal development and educational experience	**82**
Faculty quality	98
Student quality	76
Student diversity	66
Education experience	59
Increase in salary	**94**
Increase in salary	25
Post-MBA salary	>100
Potential to network	**>100**
Breadth of alumni network	63
Internationalism of alumni	62
Alumni effectiveness	99

Address
Emm Lane
Bradford
West Yorkshire
UK
BD9 4JL

Tel:
+44 1274 235 308

Fax:
+44 1274 546 866

E-mail:
mba@bradford.ac.uk

Website:
www.bradford.ac.uk/
management

Programme director:
Ms Jo Hardcastle

Figures in brackets
represent rank

Background

Bradford School of Management is one of Europe's largest full-range business schools. A full-time faculty of over 60 teaches undergraduate, postgraduate, doctoral and executive development programmes in the UK and overseas.

Bradford's MBA programmes are offered in various European locations through NIMBAS Graduate School of Management (see page 378) and in the Middle East, Singapore, Malaysia and India with local partners. Almost all students in the UK study a foreign language. UK students may be asked to take Bradford's own admissions test rather than the GMAT; others must take the GMAT.

Facilities

The school is self-contained, based in a number of different buildings on its own 14-acre site about two miles from the main university campus. There are lecture theatres, seminar and tutorial rooms, a management library, a bookshop, a language unit, computer facilities and careers services, as well as restaurant and bar facilities. The main university campus offers the full range of services and facilities for undergraduate and postgraduate study, including the J B Priestley Library, a larger bookshop, a computer centre and a language unit.

Some on-campus accommodation is available, but most students choose to live in the surrounding area, where housing is readily available at reasonable prices. Some students think that the school suffers because of its location in Bradford, but the surrounding countryside is very attractive.

	Full-time MBA
Student assessment of facilities	4.1 (69)

Which MBA? © The Economist Intelligence Unit Limited 2004

Faculty

Number of faculty: 53 full-time, 2 part-time, 40 visiting

	Full-time MBA	Distance Learning MBA	Executive Part Time MBA
Number of faculty per student	0.8 (29)	0.3	2.0
Percentage of faculty with PhD	70 (98)	70	70
Student rating of faculty	4.0 (94)	–	

Strengths and weaknesses

Strengths: strategy; human resource management; total quality management

Weaknesses: elective choice

Programme highlights

The Bradford MBA is a typical UK offering based around core courses, electives and an in-company or research-based project.

The full-time programme has three stages: six compulsory core subjects, a five-day introductory business environment course and a weekend course in interpersonal skills; six electives, two compulsory courses in strategic management and job-search skills, and a business game; the management project and dissertation. There is a good deal of group working. Case studies, although not the only teaching method, are used extensively. Although there are no overseas exchange programmes as such, there is a chance to study one of several foreign languages (French, German, Spanish and Japanese) throughout the programme.

The executive part-time MBA is identical to the full-time version and can be completed in two years or taken over a longer period up to a maximum of six years. Most students complete it in 3 years. First-year classes meet on campus on Wednesday evenings.

The Executive Modular MBA also has virtually the same curriculum. The first year is given over to four nine-day residential blocks (two weekends and a week), each covering two subjects. Each block is preceded by two weeks of preparatory work and followed by nine weeks of projects and assignments. The second year consists of six electives that can be taken over weekends or during the week as well as a project workshop. This followed by an applied management project.

Bradford's distance-learning MBA also has more or less the same curriculum. The programme starts in September and January each year and can be completed in a minimum of two or a maximum of six years. As well as written material for home study, the programme includes a three-day on-campus induction course, an optional two-day on-campus workshop on interpersonal skills and a five-day residential programme.

Other programmes include an MBA at NIMBAS in the Netherlands and Germany; an MBA in Dubai (full-time); an EMBA (modular) for organisations such as the BBC, CIBA and others; and an MBA in Engineering Management run in conjunction with the School of Engineering Management. The European Management Programme (EMP/MBA), offered jointly with the Universidad Comercial de Deusto-Bilbao and Groupe ESC Nantes Atlantique, is a trilingual programme taught and assessed in Spanish, French and English. Students spend a term at each institution.

	Full-time MBA	Distance Learning MBA	Executive Part Time MBA
Student rating of programme	3.9 (95)	–	–
Number of overseas exchange programmes	40 (16)	–	–
Number of languages on offer	4 (56)	–	–

The directory
Bradford School of Management

Students

	Full-time MBA	Distance Learning MBA	Executive Part Time MBA
Annual intake	80	240	48
Applicants:places	8:1	6:1	4:1
Percentage of women students	28 (47)	27	23
Percentage of foreign students	89 (11)	223	n/a
Average GMAT score	590 (97)	n/a	n/a
Average number of months' work experience	96 (12)	96	120
Age range of students	24–36	26–34	27–39
Average age	29	32	33
Student rating of culture and classmates	3.8 (>100)	–	–

Student profile (full time)

- ■ EU
- ■ Non-EU Europe
- ▨ North America
- ■ Other Americas
- ■ Asia/Australasia
- ▨ Middle East

Recruiters/careers service

	Full-time MBA	Distance Learning MBA	Executive Part Time MBA
Number of industry sectors that recruited graduates	7 (77)	–	–
Percentage of graduates in jobs 3 months after graduation	72 (103)	–	–
Percentage of graduates finding jobs through careers services	75 (40)	–	–
Student rating of careers service	3.7 (38)	–	–
Post-MBA salary, US$	57,377 (101)	–	–
Percentage increase in salary	107 (25)	–	–
Principal recruiters of graduates	Citibank, Habib Bank A G Zurich, Irwin Mitchell		

Cost

	Full-time MBA	Distance Learning MBA	Executive Part Time MBA
Application fees	None	None	None
Programme fees	£17,500 (US$28,689)	£9,500 (US$15,574)	£13,500 (US$22,131)
Comments	per year	–	–
Accommodation costs (on campus, per year)	£3,536 (US$5,797)	–	–
Accommodation costs (off campus, per year)	£3,640 (US$5,967)	–	–
Financial aid available	None	–	–
Type of aid available	n/a	–	–
Criteria on which aid is granted	n/a	–	–

Accreditation

AMBA, EQUIS

Application details

	Full-time MBA	Distance Learning MBA	Executive Part Time MBA
Application deadline	July 30th	–	July 30th
Programme dates	Sep start, 12 months	Jan start, 48 months	Jan start, 30 months
Admission requirements	First degree or equivalent; at least 3 years' work experience; GMAT; TOEFL or IELTS 6.5 if first language not English; 2 references; essay	First degree or equivalent; at least 3 years' work experience; TOEFL or IELTS if first language not English; 2 references	First degree or equivalent; at least 3 years' work experience; TOEFL or IELTS if first language not English; 2 references

Executive education

Bradford offers a range of customised in-company executive education programmes, many earning credits towards postgraduate qualifications.

Student/alumni quotes

"The things I remember best are the strength of our cohort and subsequent networking opportunities—students from a variety of industries and cultures, learning from each other and supporting each other throughout the year."

"Too many full-time MBA students for available facilities."

"A school with a good reputation, ranking and flexible programme with a wide choice of electives taught by experts (often with extensive industry experience)."

Brandeis International Business School

Ranking	Rank (out of 100) Full-time
Overall rank	n/a
Regional rank	55

Address
Mailstop 032
Waltham
Massachusetts
US
02454-9110

Tel:
+1 781 736 4829

Fax:
+1 781 736 2263

E-mail:
admission@lemberg.
brandeis.edu

Website:
www.brandeis.edu/
global

Programme director:
Ben Gomes-Casseres

Figures in brackets
represent rank

Background

Brandeis International Business School (IBS) is among the youngest business schools in the US. Its parent university, Brandeis (named after Louis Dembitz Brandeis, a Supreme Court judge), was formed only in 1948, although it did number Eleanor Roosevelt and Leonard Bernstein among its early faculty.

The school is determinedly international in approach and may be best compared with Thunderbird (page 477). It changed its name in 2003 from the Graduate School of International Economics and Finance, partly for marketing reasons but also to reflect a wider approach (although finance and economics still dominate). Brandeis University has 3,200 undergraduate and 1,100 graduate students.

Facilities

IBS is based on the 96-building, 235-acre university campus in Waltham, a 20-minute train ride from downtown Boston. Library, sports and other campus facilities are good. A small amount of on-campus housing is available for overseas students, but most students live off-campus.

	Full-time MBA
Student assessment of facilities	4.3 (n/a)

Faculty

Number of faculty: 20 full-time, 19 part-time, 0 visiting

	Full-time MBA
Number of faculty per student	1.2 (n/a)
Percentage of faculty with PhD	85 (n/a)
Student rating of faculty	4.4 (n/a)

Strengths and weaknesses

Strengths: international finance; international economics; international business and management

Weaknesses: small, relatively new, programme

Programme highlights

IBS's full-time two-year International MBA (MBAi) focuses exclusively on global management and international business. The first-year core curriculum reflects this, covering the major functional disciplines with a distinctive international twist. Students can take two electives in the first year if they have completed sufficient required courses. The second year involves three further required courses and six or seven electives. Electives can be grouped into a concentration of international finance or international economic policy, usually involving a minimum of four courses. Students who do not choose either option receive an MBA in international business, the "default" concentration.

Students must fulfil an international experience and foreign language requirement. This can be completed before (living outside the US for at least three years or working abroad in a professional post for at least three months) or during the programme. During the programme it involves an overseas internship or an exchange plus language training.

	Full-time MBA
Student rating of programme	4.2 (n/a)
Number of overseas exchange programmes	20 (n/a)
Number of languages on offer	>5 (n/a)

Which MBA? © The Economist Intelligence Unit Limited 2004

Students

Student profile (full time)

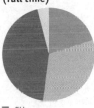

- ■ EU
- ■ Non-EU Europe
- ■ North America
- ■ Other Americas
- ■ Asia/Australasia
- ■ Middle East

	Full-time MBA
Annual intake	25
Applicants:places	3:1
Percentage of women students	50 (n/a)
Percentage of foreign students	64 (n/a)
Average GMAT score	600 (n/a)
Average number of months' work experience	40 (n/a)
Age range of students	24–31
Average age	27
Student rating of culture and classmates	4.1 (n/a)

Recruiters/careers service

	Full-time MBA
Number of industry sectors that recruited graduates	3 (n/a)
Percentage of graduates in jobs 3 months after graduation	74 (n/a)
Percentage of graduates finding jobs through careers services	21 (n/a)
Student rating of careers service	3.2 (n/a)
Post-MBA salary, US$	64,600 (n/a)
Percentage increase in salary	n/a
Principal recruiters of graduates	JP Morgan Chase, Standard & Poor's, Lewtan Technologies

Cost

	Full-time MBA
Application fees	US$50
Programme fees	US$30,450
Comments	–
Accommodation costs (on campus, per year)	US$12,000
Accommodation costs (off campus, per year)	US$12,000
Financial aid available	US$600,000
Type of aid available	Scholarships, loans
Criteria on which aid is granted	Merit, financial need

Accreditation

None

Application details

	Full-time MBA
Application deadline	April 15th
Programme dates	Sep start, 20 months
Admission requirements	Bachelor's degree or equivalent; at least 2 years' work experience; GMAT; TOEFL minimum if first language not English; 3 references; 2 essays; interview; laptop

Executive education

The only executive education programme offered by IBS is the two-week Executive Program on Macroeconomic Policy and Management, which was previously taught at the Harvard Institute for International Development (HIID) and the Kennedy School of Government at Harvard University.

Student/alumni quotes

"If you want international experience, it is the best school in the US that can offer it."

"The school's biggest weakness is its lack of focus other than being an international school. Its careers service is small but slowly developing."

"The school offers a truly international experience and a strong focus on finance and economics."

University of British Columbia—Sauder School of Business

Ranking	Rank (out of 100) Full-time
Overall rank	70
Regional rank	42

Criteria	Rank (out of 100) Full-time
Open new career opportunities	**57**
Diversity of recruiters	47
Number in jobs three months after graduation	43
Jobs found through the careers service	73
Student assessment of careers service	55
Personal development and educational experience	**26**
Faculty quality	59
Student quality	33
Student diversity	41
Education experience	26
Increase in salary	**95**
Increase in salary	33
Post-MBA salary	100
Potential to network	**73**
Breadth of alumni network	42
Internationalism of alumni	32
Alumni effectiveness	85

Address
2053 Main Mall
Vancouver, BC
Canada
V6T 1Z2

Tel:
+1 604 822 8345

Fax:
+1 604 822 1271

E-mail:
mba@sauder.ubc.ca

Website:
www.sauder.ubc.
ca/mba

Programme director:
Anne DeWolfe

Figures in brackets
represent rank

Background

Sauder is one of the less well known Canadian schools, although it is one of the largest, with more than 1,750 students on undergraduate, graduate and PhD programmes and 23,000 alumni in 60 countries.

In June 2003 the University of British Columbia (UBC) received the largest private donation made to a Canadian business school. William L Sauder, a local business leader and former UBC board chair and chancellor, endowed the university's Faculty of Commerce and Business Administration with a gift of C$20m. As a result, the university renamed it the Sauder School of Business.

The school has good partnerships with business and a strong reputation for research. It has also developed an interesting approach to MBA teaching and programme design.

Facilities

The school is based in its own complex on the university campus in three buildings that include faculty offices, administration, classrooms, business library and conference facilities. It also has offices and teaching space in downtown Vancouver

The attractive university campus, located on a forested peninsula overlooking the Pacific, is about 30 minutes' drive from Vancouver, one of North America's most attractive cities.

	Full-time MBA
Student assessment of facilities	4.2 (63)

Faculty

Number of faculty: 95 full-time, 42 part-time, 7 visiting

	Full-time MBA	UBC MBA Part time program
Number of faculty per student	1.1 (31)	3.2
Percentage of faculty with PhD	85 (67)	85
Student rating of faculty	4.3 (61)	–

Strengths and weaknesses

Strengths: finance and business economics; organisational behaviour and human resources; supply chain management and transportation

Weaknesses: job opportunities and internships in Vancouver; facilities

Programme highlights

Sauder's MBA is an unusually structured 15-month programme with core subjects offered as a single, team-taught 13-week foundation course covering basic management disciplines: finance, marketing, accounting, human resources, statistics, managerial economics and information systems. After the core, students can choose from seven areas of specialisation (entrepreneurship, finance, IT and management, marketing, organisational behaviour and human resources, strategic management and supply chain management), each consisting of both required and elective modules with sub-specialisations in e-business and international business.

The part-time 28-month MBA is similar to the full-time version. The first year is given over to the same integrated core. The second and third years vary, however, with electives offered across a wide range of areas rather than focused on specialisations. Students can have some input on the electives offered. The programme ends with a project, often within students' own organisations. Classes meet at weekends every three weeks beginning in January on Friday (5–9:30 pm), Saturday (8 am–5 pm) and Sunday (8 am–5 pm). Classes for the Professional Development Program, a series of seminars, guest speakers, discussion groups, career coaching and so on, may meet outside these times.

The International MBA is a variation on the full-time MBA with the core taught partly in Vancouver and partly at UBC's partner business school, the School of Management at Shanghai Jiao Tong University in China. Additional courses are taught in China.

	Full-time MBA	UBC MBA Part time program
Student rating of programme	4.2 (60)	–
Number of overseas exchange programmes	40 (22)	–
Number of languages on offer	>5 (1)	–

Students

Student profile (full time)

- ■ EU
- ■ Non-EU Europe
- ■ North America
- ■ Other Americas
- ■ Asia/Australasia
- ■ Middle East

	Full-time MBA	UBC MBA Part time program
Annual intake	106	45
Applicants:places	6:1	2:1
Percentage of women students	35 (24)	36
Percentage of foreign students	58 (49)	n/a
Average GMAT score	637 (62)	626
Average number of months' work experience	84 (17)	96
Age range of students	27–32	28–41
Average age	31	33
Student rating of culture and classmates	4.1 (62)	–

The directory
University of British Columbia—Sauder School of Business

Recruiters/careers service

	Full-time MBA	UBC MBA Part time program
Number of industry sectors that recruited graduates	7 (47)	–
Percentage of graduates in jobs 3 months after graduation	79 (43)	–
Percentage of graduates finding jobs through careers services	27 (73)	–
Student rating of careers service	3.5 (55)	–
Post-MBA salary, US$	53,250 (100)	–
Percentage increase in salary	64 (33)	–
Principal recruiters of graduates	Vancouver Coastal Health Authority, Best Buy, Business Objects (formerly Crystal Decisions)	

Cost

	Full-time MBA	UBC MBA Part time program
Application fees	C$125 (US$89)	C$125 (US$89)
Programme fees	C$36,000 (US$25,714)	C$36,000 (US$25,714)
Comments	Total programme	Total programme
Accommodation costs (on campus, per year)	C$7,200 (US$5,143)	–
Accommodation costs (off campus, per year)	C$8,400 (US$6,000)	–
Financial aid available	C$3,600,000 (US$2,571,429)	–
Type of aid available	Scholarships, loans	–
Criteria on which aid is granted	n/a	–

Accreditation

AACSB International, EQUIS

Application details

	Full-time MBA	UBC MBA Part time program
Application deadline	April 30th	September 30th
Programme dates	Aug start, 15 months	Jan start, 28 months
Admission requirements	First degree (generally a four year bachelor degree, with B+ average); at least 3 years' work experience; TOEFL (minimum of 600 paper or 250 computer) or IELTS and MELAB proficiency tests if first language not English; 3 references; 4 essays; interviews can be requested by Admissions Committee	First degree (generally a four year bachelor degree, with B+ average); at least 3 years' work experience; TOEFL (minimum of 600 paper or 250 computer) or IELTS and MELAB proficiency tests if first language not English; 3 references; 4 essays; interviews can be requested by Admissions Committee

Executive education

Sauder offers a large portfolio of short open-enrolment programmes (which it calls business seminars), in areas ranging from negotiation skills to managing professional service organisations, and a series of certificate programmes. It also offers customised in-company programmes.

Student/alumni quotes

"The school provided what I was looking for and all the new friends I made during the MBA programme will be one of the most important assets I will have for the rest of my life. If you ask me to do it all over again, I will choose the same school and same programme."

"The age of the building and facilities [means] there is not quite sufficient space for all students."

"Fantastic teachers, succinct and ideally paced programme, great career prospects within Canada afterwards."

Which MBA? © The Economist Intelligence Unit Limited 2004

Brunel Graduate Business School

Address
The Brunel MBA
Brunel University
Uxbridge, Middlesex
UK
UB8 3PH

Tel:
+44 1895 265 287

Fax:
+44 1895 203 075

E-mail:
BrunelMBA@brunel.
ac.uk

Website:
www.BrunelMBA.info

Programme director:
Dr Stephen Smith

Figures in brackets
represent rank

Ranking	Rank (out of 100) Full-time
Overall rank	n/a
Regional rank	n/a

Background

Brunel Graduate Business School is part of Brunel University's School of Business and Management, which although fairly new (it was set up in the early 1990s) is already among the largest schools within the university. It is a full-range school with about 1,000 undergraduates, 90 graduate students and 70 faculty, around 40 of whom teach on the MBA programme. The MBA is taught in the Graduate Business School.

Like the university (initially an engineering college named after the great Victorian engineer), the school emphasises what it calls "practical theory" and the role of people in business. It has good connections with business and, also like the university, strong overseas links. There is a high proportion of foreign students.

Facilities

The school is based in its own building on the university campus and there are dedicated facilities for the MBA programme, including lecture room, classrooms, break-out rooms, computer room, common room and faculty office. Some on-campus accommodation is available.

	Full-time MBA
Student assessment of facilities	n/a

Faculty

Number of faculty: 48 full-time, 20 part-time, 10 visiting	
	Full-time MBA
Number of faculty per student	1.8
Percentage of faculty with PhD	73
Student rating of faculty	n/a

Strengths and weaknesses

Strengths: management of innovation; business ethics; management and organisational learning

Weaknesses: careers services

Programme highlights

The Brunel MBA is offered in full-time and distance-learning versions. Both share more or less the same curriculum. The one-year full-time programme consists of two semesters (September–June) and a project. Students take all core subjects within the foundations of business management module and then choose two specialist modules from five options: information management; managing for the future; marketing; sports management; strategic accounting and finance. Students then take a final capstone core module, strategic integration and development, before starting their project.

The distance-learning programme has the same curriculum as the full-time version. The programme must be completed within five years but can be finished in two (based on an average of 15 hours per week, spread over 44 weeks each year). There are a number of three-day on-campus workshops during the programme, which has two start dates per year (February and September). The marketing and sports management specialisations are not available on the distance learning programme.

Language training is available in English, German, French, Spanish and Italian.

The directory
Brunel Graduate Business School

	Full-time MBA
Student rating of programme	n/a
Number of overseas exchange programmes	0
Number of languages on offer	5

Students

	Full-time MBA
Annual intake	40
Applicants:places	4:1
Percentage of women students	27
Percentage of foreign students	73
Average GMAT score	n/a
Average number of months' work experience	90
Age range of students	26-42
Average age	32
Student rating of culture and classmates	n/a

Recruiters/careers service

	Full-time MBA
Number of industry sectors that recruited graduates	n/a
Percentage of graduates in jobs 3 months after graduation	93
Percentage of graduates finding jobs through careers services	93
Student rating of careers service	n/a
Post-MBA salary, US$	n/a
Percentage increase in salary	n/a
Principal recruiters of graduates	n/a

Cost

	Full-time MBA
Application fees	None
Programme fees	£13,300 (US$21,803)
Comments	Total programme
Accommodation costs (on campus, per year)	£2,500 (US$4,098)
Accommodation costs (off campus, per year)	£3,000 (US$4,918)
Financial aid available	Not disclosed
Type of aid available	Scholarships
Criteria on which aid is granted	Merit, financial need

Accreditation

AMBA

Application details

	Full-time MBA
Application deadline	July 31st
Programme dates	Sep start, 12 months
Admission requirements	Good first degree; at least 3 years' work experience; GMAT; TOEFL or IELTS 7 if first language not English; 2 references; 4 essays; interview; laptop

**Student profile
(full time)**

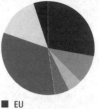

■ EU
■ Non-EU Europe
■ North America
■ Other Americas
■ Asia/Australasia
▨ Middle East
■ Other

Executive education

Brunel does not currently offer open-enrolment or customised in-company executive education programmes.

Student/alumni quotes

"I did enjoy my two years [part-time] at Brunel, but this was as much down to the people I met, and actually working with them, as it was the course content. This feedback is not meant to sound harsh— the finance, marketing and strategy courses have been invaluable. Overall the course was enjoyable, but it was very rough around the edges and would need improving if I were to recommend it."

"Good diversity and range [of recruiters] but most come because of engineering degrees/masters not MBA."

"Lots of extra curricular activities, as [Brunel is] a huge university. Particularly strong in sports."

University of Calgary—Haskayne School of Business

Ranking	Rank (out of 100) Full-time
Overall rank	n/a
Regional rank	54

Background

The business school at the University of Calgary was founded in 1967 so it is still quite young. In 2002 it was named after Richard F Haskayne, a Canadian businessman and benefactor. It is a full-range school, with over 1,800 full-time and part-time students on bachelor's, master's and PhD programmes, and more than 12,000 alumni in 50 countries. It has a strong commitment to developing leaders. In its recently developed strategic plan for future growth, one of the school's principal goals is to become a top 50 world business school by 2010.

Facilities

Haskayne is based in Scurfield Hall, which contains well-equipped classrooms, a management skills development laboratory, breakout and syndicate rooms, conference rooms and computer labs, and its own management library. Calgary is a lively, cosmopolitan oil town with a reputation for entrepreneurship, and a number of Canadian companies have their headquarters there. The winters can be very cold.

	Full-time MBA
Student assessment of facilities	4.3 (n/a)

Faculty

Number of faculty: 84 full-time, 0 part-time, 2 visiting

	Full-time MBA
Number of faculty per student	1.0 (n/a)
Percentage of faculty with PhD	82 (n/a)
Student rating of faculty	3.8 (n/a)

Strengths and weaknesses

Strengths: entrepreneurship and innovation; global energy management and sustainable development; finance

Weaknesses: elective choice; core structure

Programme highlights

Haskayne's MBA is a general management degree, but there is the opportunity to specialise. The programme consists of 20 courses (12 core and eight elective) over four terms. These can be taken consecutively including the summer to complete the programme in 16 months, or 20 months with a summer break. Most of the traditional core is completed in the first year. Students take electives and two required strategy courses in the second year. Electives can be grouped into concentrations (these are not available in the 16-month version). The MBA may also be studied in a "thesis-based" option, designed for students with a particular research interest.

The part-time MBA is taught in the evenings. The curriculum is exactly the same as the full-time version, but students can study at their own rate and have six years to complete the degree.

Haskayne's Executive MBA consists of 20 courses over 20 months. Classes meet every Friday and Saturday during term time and there is a one-week course at the beginning of each of the first three semesters. The programme begins in August and concludes with a ten-day international study tour in May. The EMBA is offered jointly by the University of Calgary and the University of Alberta, but almost all classes are held at Calgary's Scurfield Hall.

Address
Scurfield Hall
University of Calgary
2500 University Drive NW
Calgary, AB
Canada
T2N 1N4

Tel:
+1 403 220 8823

Fax:
+1 403 282 0095

E-mail:
penny.ohearn@
haskayne.ucalgary.ca

Website:
www.haskayne.
ucalgary.ca/mba

Programme director:
Wilfred Zerbe

Figures in brackets represent rank

	Full-time MBA
Student rating of programme	3.4 (n/a)
Number of overseas exchange programmes	10 (n/a)
Number of languages on offer	0 (n/a)

**Student profile
(full time)**

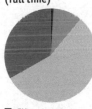

- ■ EU
- ■ Non-EU Europe
- ■ North America
- ■ Other Americas
- ■ Asia/Australasia
- ▨ Middle East

Students

	Full-time MBA
Annual intake	81
Applicants:places	2:1
Percentage of women students	36 (n/a)
Percentage of foreign students	44 (n/a)
Average GMAT score	632 (n/a)
Average number of months' work experience	72 (n/a)
Age range of students	23-46
Average age	30
Student rating of culture and classmates	3.3 (n/a)

Recruiters/careers service

	Full-time MBA
Number of industry sectors that recruited graduates	7 (n/a)
Percentage of graduates in jobs 3 months after graduation	88 (n/a)
Percentage of graduates finding jobs through careers services	n/a (n/a)
Student rating of careers service	3.1 (n/a)
Post-MBA salary, US$	52,889 (n/a)
Percentage increase in salary	38 (n/a)
Principal recruiters of graduates	City of Calgary, Nortel Networks, TD Canada Trust

Cost

	Full-time MBA
Application fees	C$60 (US$43)
Programme fees	C$$22,500 (US$16,071)
Comments	Per year. Fee for Canadian students is C$11,250
Accommodation costs (on campus, per year)	C$9,000 (US$6,429)
Accommodation costs (off campus, per year)	C$13,000 (US$9,286)
Financial aid available	C$339,000 (US$242,143)
Type of aid available	Scholarships, grants
Criteria on which aid is granted	GPA and GMAT

Accreditation

AACSB International

Application details

	Full-time MBA
Application deadline	November 1st
Programme dates	Sep start, 20 months
Admission requirements	Undergraduate 4-year degree; at least 3 years' work experience; GMAT; TOEFL minimum if first language not English; 3 references; essay

The directory
University of Calgary—Haskayne School of Business

Executive education

Haskayne offers open-enrolment executive programmes in areas such as leadership, finance, negotiation, strategy, organisational change, performance management, ethics and team performance. The school also offers customised programmes for both single companies and consortia of companies, in Canada and in other countries.

Student/alumni quotes

"As a full-time student, the course load is heavy but rewarding. Excellent value and career opportunities in Calgary, which is a dynamic and growing city."

"If you want to get into the oil and gas industry, this is a good programme."

"The Haskyane School of Business attempts to include members of the Calgary business community as much as possible in the education of its MBA students through mentorship programmes and work experience opportunities for the students. The tuition fees are reasonable and the class sizes are small."

University of California at Berkeley—Haas School of Business

Address
Haas School of
Business
University of
California, Berkeley
S430 Student Services
Bldg. #1902
Berkeley, CA
US
94720-1902

Tel:
+1 510 642 0342

Fax:
+1 510 642 4700

E-mail:
–

Website:
www.haas.berkeley.
edu

Programme director:
Dan Sullivan

Figures in brackets
represent rank

Ranking	Rank (out of 100) Full-time
Overall rank	19
Regional rank	16

Criteria	Rank (out of 100) Full-time
Open new career opportunities	**25**
Diversity of recruiters	n/a
Number in jobs three months after graduation	45
Jobs found through the careers service	38
Student assessment of careers service	24
Personal development and educational experience	**17**
Faculty quality	22
Student quality	20
Student diversity	43
Education experience	32
Increase in salary	**57**
Increase in salary	>100
Post-MBA salary	23
Potential to network	**35**
Breadth of alumni network	38
Internationalism of alumni	38
Alumni effectiveness	25

Background

Haas School of Business was established in 1898 and is the oldest business school at a public university in the US. It is named after the late Walter A Haas, who gained a bachelor's degree at the school in 1910. He was president of the San Francisco-based Levi Strauss & Company for nearly 30 years and a relative by marriage of the company's founder, Levi Strauss.

It is heavily influenced by the teaching and research ethos at Berkeley and by its strong connections with business in nearby Silicon Valley. On-campus visits by executives, including teaching stints, are regular events. The school has a strong research base but puts at least as much emphasis on the teaching abilities of faculty members. With an annual intake of under 250 students, the Haas MBA programme remains small and intimate compared with some other North American schools.

Facilities

The school is based in a mini-campus complex of three linked buildings that provide superb facilities for MBA students, undergraduates and participants on executive education programmes. The layout favours informal contacts between students and faculty. Faculty offices are designed to encourage "clusters" of teaching and research staff from different disciplines and so reinforce greater integration of core courses on the MBA programme. On-campus accommodation is available; private housing in the Berkeley area is expensive.

	Full-time MBA
Student assessment of facilities	4.2 (45)

The directory
University of California at Berkeley—Haas School of Business

Faculty

Number of faculty: 83 full-time, 87 part-time, 11 visiting

	Full-time MBA	Evening & Weekend MBA Program
Number of faculty per student	0.5 (76)	0.8
Percentage of faculty with PhD	98 (18)	98
Student rating of faculty	4.5 (21)	–

Strengths and weaknesses

Strengths: management of technology; entrepreneurship and innovation; finance

Weakness: elective choice

Programme highlights

Haas's full-time two-year MBA covers 11 core courses (including a required management communi-cations course) and two or three electives in the first year. There is a strong international content, and during each winter break students and faculty organise optional overseas study tours. The two first-year semesters are divided into seven-week mini-semesters, with most core courses meeting for four hours per week over seven weeks. There is a two-day career-planning seminar in the first-year fall semester. The second year is given over to electives, which make up around 60% of the pro-gramme. Courses are available both within Haas and in the wider university, although some students bemoan a lack of elective choice. There is no requirement to group electives into concentrations.

MBA students can opt to earn certificates in corporate environmental management, entrepreneur-ship, global management, health management, management of technology and real estate by com-pleting a designated number of courses and special projects. Special programmes in non-profit and public management and socially responsible business are also available.

The part-time programme has the same curriculum as the full-time version and is offered in two vari-ations: evening (two evenings a week, 6–9.30 pm, with a 45-minute break) and weekend (Saturdays, 9 am–6 pm, with two 15-minute class breaks and one 60-minute lunch break). Weekend classes alter-nate between the Haas campus and a facility in nearby Silicon Valley. Students take nine required core courses and eight electives. Between the third and fourth semesters, students must also take part in the mid-programme academic retreat. This is a major case study, conducted by faculty mem-bers off-site, that integrates the core curriculum material and prepares students for more in-depth studies in their advanced electives. Optional international study trips take place in the summer. Before beginning advanced course work, students must pass the writing requirement, demonstrating the ability to write effectively in a business context.

The 19-month Berkeley–Columbia Executive MBA is a joint venture between Haas and Columbia Busi-ness School in New York (see page 189).

	Full-time MBA	Evening & Weekend MBA Program
Student rating of programme	4.2 (45)	–
Number of overseas exchange programmes	22 (74)	–
Number of languages on offer	>5 (1)	–

Students

	Full-time MBA	Evening & Weekend MBA Program
Annual intake	241	234
Applicants:places	16:1	3:1
Percentage of women students	27 (57)	24
Percentage of foreign students	41 (69)	n/a
Average GMAT score	700 (10)	690
Average number of months' work experience	60 (63)	91.2
Age range of students	23-38	24-48
Average age	29	32
Student rating of culture and classmates	4.7 (12)	–

Student profile (full time)

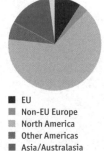

- ■ EU
- ■ Non-EU Europe
- ▨ North America
- ■ Other Americas
- ■ Asia/Australasia
- ▨ Middle East

Recruiters/careers service

	Full-time MBA	Evening & Weekend MBA Program
Number of industry sectors that recruited graduates	n/a (n/a)	–
Percentage of graduates in jobs 3 months after graduation	81 (45)	–
Percentage of graduates finding jobs through careers services	58 (38)	–
Student rating of careers service	3.7 (24)	–
Post-MBA salary, US$	84,345 (23)	–
Percentage increase in salary	7 (>100)	–
Principal recruiters of graduates	Wells Fargo Bank, McKinsey & Co, Deloitte	

Cost

	Full-time MBA	Evening & Weekend MBA Program
Application fees	US$150	US$150
Programme fees	US$33,020	US$1,800
Comments	Fee for California residents is US$20,774	Per unit; 42 units complete the degree
Accommodation costs (on campus, per year)	n/a	–
Accommodation costs (off campus, per year)	US$8,570	–
Financial aid available	US$9,767,668	
Type of aid available	Scholarships, loans, grants, teaching and research assistants	–
Criteria on which aid is granted	Merit, financial need	–

Accreditation

AACSB International

Application details

	Full-time MBA	Evening & Weekend MBA Program
Application deadline	April 3rd	January 3rd
Programme dates	Aug start, 19 months	Aug start, 33 months
Admission requirements	First degree; work experience; TOEFL if first language not English; references; essays; interview by invitation only	First degree; work experience; TOEFL if first language not English (minimum score of 230 required on computer-based test; minimum of 570 required on paper-based test); 2 references; essay; interview by invitation only

Executive education

Haas runs a suite of open-enrolment programmes that include the flagship four-week Berkeley Executive Program, one-day "Faculty Forums" on current trends and topics, and short certification courses. It also offers a range of customised in-company programmes.

Student/alumni quotes

"I learned more than I thought, yet did not have to work too hard and still was able to get to know almost every classmate—240 in total. MBAs are inherently competitive by nature, so Berkeley's highly co-operative atmosphere served as a check against back-stabbing and allowed close bonds to develop, whether looking for jobs, business research or the latest bar in San Francisco."

"The strategy course is taught at the end of the first year, too late to prepare students for consulting internship interviews."

"The unique questions Berkeley asks of prospective students result in a more interesting and higher-calibre student body. I received a merit scholarship covering my first year of tuition [but] I would have chosen Berkeley over competing schools even without the scholarship."

University of California at Davis—Graduate School of Management

Ranking	Rank (out of 100) Full-time
Overall rank	47
Regional rank	30

Criteria	Rank (out of 100) Full-time
Open new career opportunities	**32**
Diversity of recruiters	30
Number in jobs three months after graduation	39
Jobs found through the careers service	29
Student assessment of careers service	46
Personal development and educational experience	**49**
Faculty quality	25
Student quality	85
Student diversity	29
Education experience	53
Increase in salary	**87**
Increase in salary	>100
Post-MBA salary	76
Potential to network	**65**
Breadth of alumni network	74
Internationalism of alumni	98
Alumni effectiveness	44

Address
One Shields Avenue
Davis, CA
US
95616

Tel:
+1 530 754 5476

Fax:
+1 530 752 2924

E-mail:
admissions@gsm.
ucdavis.edu

Website:
www.gsm.ucdavis.edu

Programme director:
James R Stevens

Figures in brackets
represent rank

Background

The Graduate School of Management at the University of California at Davis is a young school. It was established in 1981 to provide management education in the northern California region. It says its aim is to be a leader in management research and education.

Facilities

The school is based on the main university campus and facilities are good. It has wireless and wired network access throughout its facilities. There are two student PC labs with access to school and university UNIX work stations, as well as access to over 1,000 scholarly and trade journals. The Graduate School of Management is due to begin work on a new management education centre in autumn 2004. Davis is a small college town with students making up more than half its population.

	Full-time MBA
Student assessment of facilities	4.2 (61)

Faculty

Number of faculty: 29 full-time, 18 part-time, 0 visiting

	Full-time MBA	UC Davis MBA for Working Professionals
Number of faculty per student	0.7 (58)	0.6
Percentage of faculty with PhD	100 (10)	100
Student rating of faculty	4.4 (37)	–

Strengths and weaknesses

Strengths: finance; marketing; general management

Weaknesses: small size and small alumni base

Programme highlights

Davis's full-time two-year MBA is an interesting variation on the traditional US model. Students take a total of 24 courses made up of six core courses, three breadth courses (chosen from a menu) and electives, which can be grouped into 11 offered concentrations or taken more broadly. Breadth courses are seen as a link between the required core and electives. The core is taken in the first year but breadth courses and electives are also studied early in the programme.

The part-time three-year MBA for Working Professionals has the same curriculum and structure as the full-time programme. Classes are held in downtown Sacramento on weekday evenings (6–9 pm) and Saturdays (9 am–12 pm or 1–4 pm).

	Full-time MBA	UC Davis MBA for Working Professionals
Student rating of programme	4.1 (65)	–
Number of overseas exchange programmes	4 (72)	–
Number of languages on offer	>5 (29)	–

Student profile (full time)

- ■ EU
- ■ Non-EU Europe
- ▨ North America
- ■ Other Americas
- ■ Asia/Australasia
- ▨ Middle East

Students

	Full-time MBA	UC Davis MBA for Working Professionals
Annual intake	57	83
Applicants:places	8:1	2:1
Percentage of women students	40 (11)	22
Percentage of foreign students	28 (100)	n/a
Average GMAT score	636 (65)	617
Average number of months' work experience	60 (62)	88
Age range of students	25-34	26-38
Average age	29	31
Student rating of culture and classmates	4.4 (28)	–

Recruiters/careers service

	Full-time MBA	UC Davis MBA for Working Professionals
Number of industry sectors that recruited graduates	8 (30)	–
Percentage of graduates in jobs 3 months after graduation	84 (39)	–
Percentage of graduates finding jobs through careers services	61 (29)	–
Student rating of careers service	3.5 (46)	–
Post-MBA salary, US$	71,000 (76)	–
Percentage increase in salary	19 (>100)	–
Principal recruiters of graduates	E&J Gallo Winery, Hewlett-Packard, Wells Fargo	

The directory
University of California at Davis—Graduate School of Management

Cost

	Full-time MBA	UC Davis MBA for Working Professionals
Application fees	US$95	US$95
Programme fees	US$16,667	US$39,840
Comments	–	Total programme
Accommodation costs (on campus, per year)	–	–
Accommodation costs (off campus, per year)	US$6,075 (US$6,075)	–
Financial aid available	Not disclosed	–
Type of aid available	Scholarships, loans, grants, private loans	–
Criteria on which aid is granted	Merit, financial need	–

Accreditation

AACSB International

Application details

	Full-time MBA	UC Davis MBA for Working Professionals
Application deadline	April 1st	July 1st
Programme dates	Sep start, 21 months	Sep start, 39 months
Admission requirements	First degree; TOEFL if first language not English; 3 references; 3 essays	First degree; work experience; 3 references; 3 essays; interview

Executive education

Davis does not offer open-enrolment or customised executive education programmes as such, but it does offer a life-long learning option to take MBA elective courses and a well-respected wine programme appropriate to its surroundings.

Student/alumni quotes

"UC Davis remains a rural academic environment in spite of its proximity to the greater Bay Area. Individuals interested in agricultural business issues have a wealth of resources at their fingertips. Urban individuals may have to adjust their expectations. The atmosphere was sometimes quite competitive although on the surface it appeared congenial and relaxed."

"Because the school is relatively small, it limits the number of recruiters who are willing to visit the school."

"Davis is the epicentre of an explosion in biotech entrepreneurship. UCD graduates more biotech PhDs than any other university in the world. The opportunity for life science pioneers is tremendous. I wouldn't be anywhere else right now."

University of Cambridge—Judge Institute of Management

Address
Judge Institute of
Management
Trumpington St
Cambridge
UK
CB2 1AG

Tel:
+44 1223 339 650

Fax:
+44 1223 339 581

E-mail:
mba-
enquiries@jims.cam.
ac.uk

Website:
www.jims.cam.ac.uk

Programme director:
Dr Richard Barker

Figures in brackets
represent rank

Ranking	Rank (out of 100) Full-time
Overall rank	62
Regional rank	23

Criteria	Rank (out of 100) Full-time
Open new career opportunities	**71**
Diversity of recruiters	46
Number in jobs three months after graduation	63
Jobs found through the careers service	78
Student assessment of careers service	60
Personal development and educational experience	**46**
Faculty quality	71
Student quality	23
Student diversity	7
Education experience	95
Increase in salary	**80**
Increase in salary	98
Post-MBA salary	68
Potential to network	**29**
Breadth of alumni network	>100
Internationalism of alumni	3
Alumni effectiveness	66

Background

Cambridge came fairly late to MBA education but the Judge Institute of Management, which teaches undergraduate, PhD and other masters programmes, has established itself as a leading European and world school. It has made full use of the close proximity of the high-tech entrepreneurial "Silicon Fen" around Cambridge and shrewd alliances such as the one with MIT in the US.

Facilities

The Judge Institute of Management is housed in a post-modern complex in central Cambridge, a university town that, like Oxford, will probably entrance most international students. The facilities are up to date and the atmosphere is invigorating. As members of the University of Cambridge, all students are also members of one of its colleges. About two-thirds of MBA students live in college accommodation, either in a college itself or in college-owned housing. The rest find accommodation (which can be expensive) in and around Cambridge.

	Full-time MBA
Student assessment of facilities	3.8 (91)

Faculty

Number of faculty: 78 full-time, 18 part-time, 8 visiting

	Full-time MBA
Number of faculty per student	0.9 (35)
Percentage of faculty with PhD	92 (45)
Student rating of faculty	3.8 (88)

The directory
University of Cambridge—Judge Institute of Management

Strengths and weaknesses
Strengths: international business; innovation; organisational behaviour

Weakness: elective choice

Programme highlights
The Cambridge MBA is divided into five phases. Phases 1–3 consist of mandatory core courses, assignments, projects and one elective. Phases 4 and 5 include a further four electives, an individual project and 12,000-word dissertation. Some electives can be taken in other parts of the university.

The MBA can also be taken as a two-year integrated, or sandwich, programme, with students studying for six months full-time at Cambridge, returning to their jobs for 12 months and then studying for a further six months. Students work alongside their full-time colleagues during their time at Cambridge and are expected to maintain e-mail contact with the school and student workgroups during their year back at work. They often base their projects on a work-related area.

	Full-time MBA
Student rating of programme	3.7 (91)
Number of overseas exchange programmes	0 (93)
Number of languages on offer	>5 (63)

Students

	Full-time MBA
Annual intake	104
Applicants:places	6:1
Percentage of women students	34 (32)
Percentage of foreign students	83 (15)
Average GMAT score	680 (33)
Average number of months' work experience	72 (31)
Age range of students	26-34
Average age	30
Student rating of culture and classmates	4.3 (31)

Student profile (full time)

- ■ EU
- ■ Non-EU Europe
- ■ North America
- ■ Other Americas
- ■ Asia/Australasia
- ■ Middle East

Recruiters/careers service

	Full-time MBA
Number of industry sectors that recruited graduates	8 (46)
Percentage of graduates in jobs 3 months after graduation	81 (63)
Percentage of graduates finding jobs through careers services	31 (78)
Student rating of careers service	3.0 (60)
Post-MBA salary, US$	85,246 (68)
Percentage increase in salary	33 (98)
Principal recruiters of graduates	Dell Computers, LEK Consulting, AT Kearney

Cost

	Full-time MBA
Application fees	None
Programme fees	£23,000 (US$37,705)
Comments	Total programme
Accommodation costs (on campus, per year)	£4,800 (US$7,869)
Accommodation costs (off campus, per year)	£4,800 (US$7,869)
Financial aid available	Potentially unlimited
Type of aid available	Scholarships, loans
Criteria on which aid is granted	Merit, financial need

Accreditation

AMBA, EQUIS

Application details

	Full-time MBA
Application deadline	May 31st
Programme dates	Sep start, 12 months
Admission requirements	First degree (although outstanding candidates are occasionally accepted without first degrees); at least 3 years' work experience; IELTS if first language not English (though TOEFL also accepted); 3 references; 3 essays; interview; laptop

Executive education

Judge's open-enrolment executive education programmes are run as part of the Cambridge-MIT Institute (CMI). Courses include creating strategic opportunities through ICT, strategic supply chain management, designing the customer experience for digital markets, building a software business and exploiting real options for profit; there are also a number of conferences. The school offers customised programmes but there is no fixed format or size.

Student/alumni quotes

"An extremely interesting university to be a part of; the college experience [makes it an] extremely agreeable place to live."

"The programme is only one year, which limits the number of courses and overall learning."

"Cambridge is more co-operative an environment than I ever imagined, beyond what any marketing brochure could ever communicate."

University of Cape Town—Graduate School of Business

Ranking	Rank (out of 100) Full-time
Overall rank	n/a
Regional rank	n/a

Address
Breakwater Campus
Portswood Rd
Greenpoint
Cape Town
South Africa
801

Tel:
+27 21 406 1466

Fax:
+27 21 406 1469

E-mail:
info@gsb.uct.ac.za

Website:
www.gsb.uct.ac.za

Programme director:
Elspeth Donovan

Figures in brackets
represent rank

Background

The University of Cape Town is a first-class university. The Graduate Business School has been teaching management for nearly 40 years and has a strong national, regional and international reputation. It says that it is well aware of the challenge it faces in developing distinctive approaches to management education that suit South Africa's position as the leading economy in sub-Saharan Africa and a culturally diverse society in the process of profound change. The school is closely linked to the university and is developing expertise in entrepreneurship, healthcare and education.

Facilities

The school is based near Cape Town's upmarket Waterfront development (it is housed in a converted prison) and facilities are very good. There are five lecture theatres, three function rooms and seminar rooms equipped with networked PCs. On-campus accommodation is available.

	Full-time MBA
Student assessment of facilities	n/a

Faculty

Number of faculty: 20 full-time; 6 part-time; 12 visiting

	Full-time MBA	Part Time MBA	MBA (Executive)
Number of faculty per student	0.3	0.76	1.0
Percentage of faculty with PhD	60	60	60
Student rating of faculty	n/a	–	–

Strengths and weaknesses

Strengths: entrepreneurship; leadership; emerging markets

Weaknesses: careers service

Programme highlights

Cape Town's 11-month full-time programme is based on 11 core courses and nine electives, which are grouped into four themed areas: knowledge management and information systems; entrepreneurship; adding shareholder value; and adding organisational and customer value. Students must also complete a report on a particular area of business research and a company analysis of an existing organisation

The 22-month part-time programme has exactly the same curriculum as the full-time version. Classes meet in the evenings and on Saturdays. There are two residential blocks at the beginning and in the middle of the first year.

Cape Town's Executive MBA has an unusual design. The two-year programme is divided into six two-week, full-time residential learning modules, each followed by a 14-week part-time block carried out in the student's workplace. The programme content is devised around three themes—human capital development, knowledge management, and leadership and change—which are said to represent the major challenges facing managers. The programme ends with a dissertation. For the EMBA the school uses its own system of teaching called SysTAL, which it claims is a combination of systems thinking and action learning.

	Full-time MBA	Part Time MBA	MBA (Executive)
Student rating of programme	n/a	–	–
Number of overseas exchange programmes	42	–	–
Number of languages on offer	0	–	–

Students

Student profile (full time)

- ■ EU
- ■ Non-EU Europe
- ■ North America
- ■ Other Americas
- ■ Asia/Australasia
- ▨ Middle East

	Full-time MBA	Part Time MBA	MBA (Executive)
Annual intake	79	34	25
Applicants:places	2:1	2:1	3:1
Percentage of women students	25	32	20
Percentage of foreign students	28	n/a	n/a
Average GMAT score	580	500	578
Average number of months' work experience	84	96	169
Age range of students	25-38	27-38	32-50
Average age	31	33	39
Student rating of culture and classmates	n/a	–	

Recruiters/careers service

	Full-time MBA	Part Time MBA	MBA (Executive)
Number of industry sectors that recruited graduates	3	–	–
Percentage of graduates in jobs 3 months after graduation	20	–	–
Percentage of graduates finding jobs through careers services	5	–	–
Student rating of careers service	n/a	–	–
Post-MBA salary, US$	n/a	–	–
Percentage increase in salary	n/a	–	–
Principal recruiters of graduates	Gemini Consulting, Nedcor, Shoprite/Checkers		

Cost

	Full-time MBA	Part Time MBA	MBA (Executive)
Application fees	R500 (US$66)	R500 (US$66)	R500 (US$66)
Programme fees	R80,000 (US$10,582)	R44,000 (US$5,820)	R66,000 (US$8,730)
Comments	Fee for non-African students is US$22,000	Per year; includes books and notes	Per year
Accommodation costs (on campus, per year)	R40,000 (US$5,291)	–	–
Accommodation costs (off campus, per year)	R50,000 (US$6,614)	–	–
Financial aid available	Varies	–	–
Type of aid available	Scholarships	–	–
Criteria on which aid is granted	Need, black South Africans	–	–

Accreditation

EQUIS

The directory
University of Cape Town—Graduate School of Business

Application details

	Full-time MBA	Part Time MBA	MBA (Executive)
Application deadline	November 30th	November 30th	January 1st
Programme dates	Jan start, 10 months	Jan start, 22 months	Feb start, 27 months
Admission requirements	First degree (though non-degree candidates are considered); at least 3 years' work experience; GMAT; TOEFL (or AARP—an internal test) if first language not English; 2 references; 9 essays; interview; laptop	First degree (though non-degree candidates are considered); at least 3 years' work experience; GMAT; TOEFL (or AARP—an internal test) if first language not English; 2 references; 9 essays; interview	At least 15 years' work experience; GMAT; 2 references; 9 essays; interview; Learning Diagnostic Test (English analytical and mathematical competency measurement)

Executive education

Cape Town's open programmes last 2–5 days, although general management programmes are full-time residential over 2–3 weeks. Some modular programmes run for periods of up to six months. Courses are offered in the following areas: executive and general management development; manufacturing and operations strategy; project management; financial decision-making; developing organisational strategy; leadership and personal mastery; marketing. The school also offers customised courses in areas such as post-merger integration, implementing corporate change, and creating a shared vision and unity of purpose.

Most of these programmes lead to qualifications such as a certificate in leadership and a postgraduate diploma in management practice. Graduates of certain programmes may proceed to a master's degree.

Student/alumni quotes

"The MBA at UCT is extremely challenging as it runs over a ten-month period. You are expected to work very long hours and breaks are taken up by studying."

"The school has one of the best locations in the world, with access to a modern life style on a third-world continent. This is unique, and the African flavour and the emerging market perspective are adding a dimension to the general management education."

"Although it is really important to ensure an international standard for the MBA, we also need to produce leaders and managers with relevant insight and skills to operate within an African context. In this respect the entrepreneurial electives were of most use to me personally. But I think that a core course (or a few lectures) on doing business in Africa would be most useful."

Carnegie Mellon University—Tepper School of Business

Address
5000 Forbes Avenue
Pittsburgh, PA
US
15213-3890

Tel:
+1 412 268 3486

Fax:
+1 412 268 7824

E-mail:
mba-admissions@andrew.cmu.edu

Website:
www.cmu.edu/mba

Programme director:
John Mather

Figures in brackets represent rank

Ranking	Rank (out of 100) Full-time
Overall rank	29
Regional rank	20

Criteria	Rank (out of 100) Full-time
Open new career opportunities	**36**
Diversity of recruiters	65
Number in jobs three months after graduation	60
Jobs found through the careers service	44
Student assessment of careers service	15
Personal development and educational experience	**25**
Faculty quality	17
Student quality	42
Student diversity	71
Education experience	20
Increase in salary	**40**
Increase in salary	71
Post-MBA salary	36
Potential to network	**56**
Breadth of alumni network	71
Internationalism of alumni	71
Alumni effectiveness	41

Background

In March 2004 Carnegie Mellon's Graduate School of Industrial Administration was renamed Tepper School of Business following a $55m gift (the largest in the university's history) from David A Tepper, an MBA alumnus from1982. The money will be used for faculty recruitment, research, enhancing academic programmes, improving facilities and other aspects of the student experience, and marketing.

The school (one of seven graduate schools of Carnegie Mellon University) was founded in 1949, and is best known for exploring the scientific principles of business management. It is famous for its quantitative skills and cutting-edge use of information technology; for example, it pioneered the use of computer simulation in the learning of business roles.

Having long been a leader in computer technology, the school has superb computer facilities. PCs and laptops are ubiquitous, and it was the first US school to set up a campus wireless network to allow students access to computer networks from anywhere in or around the building. It is not wholly quantitative and high-tech, however. Second-year project-based courses and the demanding management game teach leadership and interpersonal skills.

Facilities

Posner Hall provides excellent facilities, including classrooms, computer labs, a cafeteria, study lounges, conference rooms, and careers and faculty offices. The main campus library is next door. Carnegie Mellon University is small by US standards, with around 8,000 students, but its attractive campus is adjacent to the sprawling University of Pittsburgh. Most on-campus accommodation is for undergraduates; graduate students generally rent housing in surrounding neighbourhoods.

	Full-time MBA
Student assessment of facilities	4.4 (20)

The directory
Carnegie Mellon University—Tepper School of Business

Faculty

Number of faculty: 96 full-time, 37 part-time, 8 visiting

	Full-time MBA	Flex Mode MBA
Number of faculty per student	0.5 (78)	1.0
Percentage of faculty with PhD	97 (27)	97
Student rating of faculty	4.7 (8)	–

Strengths and weaknesses

Strengths: finance; production/operations; management strategy

Programme highlights

Tepper pioneered seven-and-a-half-week mini-semesters. Most courses last one mini-semester and generally students take four courses each mini-semester. Functional and broader core courses are taken during the first year. First-year students also take at least three and up to five electives.

Around 18 electives are taken in total, and one concentration (three electives) is required, although many students take more. Most courses have a high quantitative content. As well as concentrations, students must take one "breadth" option (one elective in two of six designated functional areas out-side their concentrations); one elective in the quantitative, organisational behaviour and strategy areas, if these are not part of their concentrations; and an "economics requirement", either busi-ness, government and strategy or macroeconomics. Soft skills courses and workshops are offered throughout the programme.

In autumn 2004 Tepper introduced eight "tracks" to increase the ability to customise the pro-gramme. These will be available in general management, asset management, integrated product development, biotechnology, entrepreneurship, computational marketing, operations management and e-business.

Students can fulfil the requirements for the degree in 16 months by taking courses during the sum-mer after the first year instead of undertaking an internship. Those studying throughout the summer can complete the course requirements by the end of December of the second year.

The part-time programme is called the Flex-time MBA and has the same curriculum as the full-time version. Students can transfer from one to the other. The three-year programme begins in August each year. Students take two courses per mini-semester and attend school throughout the year. All required courses meet for two hours twice a week. The school schedules two courses back-to-back on Tuesday and Thursday evenings, 6–10 pm. There are no classes on Friday evenings. Most elective courses meet once a week, 6–9 pm. Some parts of the programme may also be taken via a distance-learning option (FlexMode).

	Full-time MBA	Flex Mode MBA
Student rating of programme	4.5 (10)	–
Number of overseas exchange programmes	1 (91)	–
Number of languages on offer	5 (39)	–

Students

	Full-time MBA	Flex Mode MBA
Annual intake	236	45
Applicants:places	7:1	2:1
Percentage of women students	22 (93)	15
Percentage of foreign students	37 (71)	3
Average GMAT score	681 (24)	643
Average number of months' work experience	60 (63)	48
Age range of students	24–32	24–36
Average age	27	27
Student rating of culture and classmates	4.5 (25)	–

Student profile (full time)

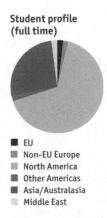

- ■ EU
- ■ Non-EU Europe
- ▨ North America
- ■ Other Americas
- ■ Asia/Australasia
- ▨ Middle East

Recruiters/careers service

	Full-time MBA	Flex Mode MBA
Number of industry sectors that recruited graduates	8 (65)	–
Percentage of graduates in jobs 3 months after graduation	77 (60)	
Percentage of graduates finding jobs through careers services	61 (44)	–
Student rating of careers service	3.9 (15)	–
Post-MBA salary, US$	80,000 (36)	–
Percentage increase in salary	45 (71)	
Principal recruiters of graduates	Deloitte Consulting, Honeywell, Citigroup	

Cost

	Full-time MBA	Flex Mode MBA
Application fees	US$100	US$100
Programme fees	US$37,000	US$407
Comments	–	Per unit
Accommodation costs (on campus, per year)	–	–
Accommodation costs (off campus, per year)	–	–
Financial aid available	US$2,400,000	–
Type of aid available	Scholarships	–
Criteria on which aid is granted	Merit	–

Accreditation

AACSB International

Application details

	Full-time MBA	Flex Mode MBA
Application deadline	March 22nd	April 30th
Programme dates	Aug start, 21 months	Aug start, 36 months
Admission requirements	First degree; TOEFL if first language not English; 2 references; 3 essays	First degree; TOEFL if first language not English; 2 references; 3 essays

Executive education

Tepper offers a small selection of open-enrolment programmes, including the flagship four-week Program for Executives, and shorter programmes in global treasury management, foundations for management excellence and management in technology organisations. It also offers customised programmes with various levels of tailoring from simple adaptation of existing open programmes to full-scale integration of educational content and business planning.

Case Western Reserve University—
Weatherhead School of Management

Ranking	Rank (out of 100) Full-time
Overall rank	71
Regional rank	43

Criteria	Rank (out of 100) Full-time
Open new career opportunities	**51**
Diversity of recruiters	61
Number in jobs three months after graduation	69
Jobs found through the careers service	33
Student assessment of careers service	63
Personal development and educational experience	**66**
Faculty quality	24
Student quality	94
Student diversity	81
Education experience	31
Increase in salary	**84**
Increase in salary	60
Post-MBA salary	82
Potential to network	**54**
Breadth of alumni network	24
Internationalism of alumni	97
Alumni effectiveness	60

Address
Weatherhead School of
Management
Case Western Reserve
University
10900 Euclid Avenue
Cleveland, OH
US
44106

Tel:
+1 216 368 3315

Fax:
+1 216 368 5548

E-mail:
MBA.Admission@
Weatherhead.case.edu

Website:
www.weatherhead.
case.edu

Programme director:
Robert Bricker

Figures in brackets
represent rank

Background

Cleveland College of Western Reserve University first offered MBA and BBA programmes in the 1920s, granting the region's first MBA degree in 1930. The college was named Weatherhead School of Management in 1980 in honour of one of Cleveland's outstanding entrepreneurial families. The student body is diverse and there is a strong emphasis on teamwork.

Facilities

In June 2002 the school moved to a new building, the Peter B Lewis Building designed by Frank Gehry, opposite the George S Dively Building (the executive education centre). Weatherhead says it now has some of the most advanced business school facilities in the world, and most students agree with this. The surrounding University Circle area is lively, with lots of museums, art galleries and concert halls. On-campus accommodation is available, but most students rent flats in the nearby Cleveland Heights area.

	Full-time MBA
Student assessment of facilities	4.4 (33)

Faculty

Number of faculty: 89 full-time, 9 part-time, 3 visiting

	Full-time MBA	The Evening MBA Program	Weatherhead Executive MBA Program
Number of faculty per student	0.8 (57)	1.0	4.8
Percentage of faculty with PhD	96 (29)	96	96
Student rating of faculty	4.4 (31)	–	–

Strengths and weaknesses

Strengths: organisational behaviour; entrepreneurship; non-profit management

Weaknesses: attracting recruiters to the area

Programme highlights

Weatherhead's two-year full-time MBA links a fairly traditional academic approach with a personalised scheme of education and development. The Leadership Assessment and Development (LEAD) course, for example, which runs over both years, allows students to assess their own strengths and weaknesses and develop a learning plan appropriate to their needs. Students take ten core courses plus workshops and ten electives, either in a concentration or more broadly based, beginning with two courses in the second semester of the first year.

Also of interest is the emphasis on action learning (very much a European concept), which culminates in a required project in the third semester of the programme. Students with an undergraduate business degree can opt for an accelerated track MBA. They start in June and graduate a year later.

The part-time evening programme is almost identical to the full-time version, but students take six electives rather than ten. Classes meet on campus once a week (twice a week in the short summer semester), either 6–8 pm or 8.15–10.15 pm. The programme is generally completed in three years, with a maximum of six. Students with an undergraduate business degree can follow a slightly accelerated programme that is completed in two years.

Weatherhead's Saturday MBA is a new 21-month part-time programme run bi-weekly on Saturdays during term. Alternating Saturdays are either on-campus class sessions or distance-learning interactive sessions. There are also two- or three-day residencies at the start of each term.

The Executive MBA is a traditional two-year programme. Classes are limited to 45 participants. They meet all day on alternate Fridays and Saturdays and the pace is intensive. Some 10–15 hours per week of additional study time is required, including a weekly study-group meeting. There are three short three- or four-day off-campus residential sessions during the programme and a ten-day overseas study tour in the second year. Classes are held at Weatherhead's executive education centre, the George S Dively Building. The school provides laptop computers for use on the programme.

	Full-time MBA	The Evening MBA Program	Weatherhead Executive MBA Program
Student rating of programme	4.3 (29)	–	–
Number of overseas exchange programmes	36 (53)	–	–
Number of languages on offer	>5 (51)	–	

Students

	Full-time MBA	The Evening MBA Program	Weatherhead Executive MBA Program
Annual intake	112	99	21
Applicants:places	4:1	1:1	1:1
Percentage of women students	28 (54)	28	19
Percentage of foreign students	42 (60)	n/a	n/a
Average GMAT score	615 (83)	570	n/a
Average number of months' work experience	54 (77)	n/a	176
Age range of students	23-33	23-35	33-48
Average age	27	28	39
Student rating of culture and classmates	4.0 (69)	–	–

Student profile (full time)

- ■ EU
- ■ Non-EU Europe
- ▨ North America
- ■ Other Americas
- ■ Asia/Australasia
- ▨ Middle East

The directory
Case Western Reserve University—Weatherhead School of Management

Recruiters/careers service

	Full-time MBA	The Evening MBA Program	Weatherhead Executive MBA Program
Number of industry sectors that recruited graduates	7 (61)	–	–
Percentage of graduates in jobs 3 months after graduation	78 (69)	–	–
Percentage of graduates finding jobs through careers services	46 (33)	–	–
Student rating of careers service	3.1 (63)	–	–
Post-MBA salary, US$	61,200 (82)	–	–
Percentage increase in salary	31 (60)	–	–
Principal recruiters of graduates	Johnson & Johnson, American Greetings Corporation, Samsung		

Cost

	Full-time MBA	The Evening MBA Program	Weatherhead Executive MBA Program
Application fees	US$50	US$50	US$50
Programme fees	US$30,000	US$3,698	US$80,000
Comments	Estimated, per academic year	Per course (total number of courses per program varies)	All inclusive
Accommodation costs (on campus, per year)	US$5,600	–	–
Accommodation costs (off campus, per year)	US$4,800	–	–
Financial aid available	US$8,500,000	–	–
Type of aid available	Scholarships, loans, assistantships	–	–
Criteria on which aid is granted	Merit , financial need	–	–

Accreditation

AACSB International

Application details

	Full-time MBA	The Evening MBA Program	Weatherhead Executive MBA Program
Application deadline	March 15th	July 1st for the fall entering class	July 17th
Programme dates	Aug start, 21 months	Aug start, 36 months	Aug start, 21 months
Admission requirements	First degree (must be 4-year degree or equivalent); at least 2 years' work experience; TOEFL if first language not English; 2 references; 4 essays; interview; laptop	First degree (must be four-year degree); at least 2 years' work experience; TOEFL if first language not English; 2 references; 4 essays; résumé	At least 10 years' work experience; 4 essays; interview; company endorsement

Executive education

Weatherhead offers a broad portfolio of open-enrolment short executive education programmes as well as customised in-company programmes.

Student/alumni quotes

"Weatherhead is on the verge of becoming a major player among b-schools because of the diverse student body and international programme offerings."

"The lead professors are fabulous. Some of the more junior-level professors are not as strong."

"The infrastructure (multimedia, computer technology, class equipment) is second to none. The action learning project is the highlight of the programme."

University of Chicago—Graduate School of Business

Ranking	Rank (out of 100) Full-time
Overall rank	6
Regional rank	5

Criteria	Rank (out of 100) Full-time
Open new career opportunities	**4**
Diversity of recruiters	37
Number in jobs three months after graduation	37
Jobs found through the careers service	9
Student assessment of careers service	1
Personal development and educational experience	**14**
Faculty quality	15
Student quality	35
Student diversity	68
Education experience	3
Increase in salary	**51**
Increase in salary	95
Post-MBA salary	31
Potential to network	**22**
Breadth of alumni network	16
Internationalism of alumni	53
Alumni effectiveness	15

Address
5807 South Woodlawn
Avenue
Chicago, IL
US
60637

Tel:
+1 773 702 4282

Fax:
+1 773 702 6420

E-mail:
admissions@gsb.
uchicago.edu

Website:
gsb.uchicago.edu

Programme director:
Stacey Kole

Figures in brackets
represent rank

Background

Chicago's Graduate School of Business (GSB) has been in existence since 1898 and has retained its reputation for research, scholarship and teaching ability in business education. The school has six Nobel laureates among its faculty and alumni, more than any other business school.

Finance is probably the most acclaimed subject at Chicago and students have a deserved reputation for number crunching. However, the GSB also offers a range of opportunities for study in other areas, such as strategy and entrepreneurship, with increased faculty and courses.

Facilities

The full-time MBA programme is currently housed in the Walker Museum, Rosenwald Hall, Stuart Hall and the Edelstone Building on the university's Hyde Park campus, about 20 minutes' drive from downtown Chicago. The part-time programmes are housed in the superbly equipped Gleacher Center in downtown Chicago. Students can take courses at the campus or at the downtown location. The Gleacher Center also houses the North American Executive MBA programme. The EMBA has buildings in Singapore for the Asian programme and in Barcelona for the European EMBA.

In late 2004 the full-time programme is scheduled to move from its various cramped locations to a new building going up in the middle of the university's historic campus, which will give it 60% more space.

	Full-time MBA
Student assessment of facilities	4.4 (21)

Faculty

Number of faculty: 121 full-time, 32 part-time, 13 visiting

	Full-time MBA	Evening MBA Program	Weekend MBA Program	Executive MBA Program North America	Executive MBA Program Europe	Executive MBA Program Asia
Number of faculty per student	0.3 (>100)	0.4	1.6	0.2	2.0	1.9
Percentage of faculty with PhD	97 (21)	97	97	97	97	97
Student rating of faculty	4.7 (4)	–	–	–	–	

Strengths and weaknesses

Strengths: finance; accounting; general management

Weaknesses: internationalism in teaching

Programme highlights

Chicago's full-time MBA is very flexible. The only required course is the LEAD (Leadership Effectiveness and Development) programme for first-year students, a series of workshops covering soft skills and teamwork during the first quarter. Students effectively design their own curriculum within broad guidelines: three courses or approved substitutes from the foundations core; four courses from the breadth requirements; one course from four of six areas (financial management, human resource management, macroeconomics, managerial accounting, marketing management, operations management); and two courses from managerial and organisational behaviour, organisations and markets, and strategic management.

All courses can be waived and replaced with electives or advanced versions. There is no requirement for a concentration (although it is an option) and students are encouraged to take electives (11 in all) from a wide range. Up to six electives can be taken in other university departments. Students must complete a minimum of 21 courses. There is a series of guest lectures by practising executives, and students can enrol in a series of laboratory courses that involve working with companies on real problems.

Students who are about to graduate from the College of the University of Chicago can apply immediately for admission to the GSB under the GSB Scholars Program. Successful applicants are admitted with an automatic deferral of two or three years during which they are expected to seek job experience.

The International MBA programme requires additional courses, including the IMBA Global Issues Seminar, international internship or study abroad and proficiency in a second language. Students must undertake five specifically international courses within the 21-course standard MBA, spend one university quarter studying abroad at one of the GSB's exchange partners and demonstrate mastery of a foreign language. The programme, which begins in the summer, generally takes 24 months to complete.

Concentrations (though not required) are offered in accounting; econometrics and statistics; economics; entrepreneurship; finance; analytic finance; general management; human resources management; international business; managerial and organisational behaviour; marketing management; operations management; strategic management.

Part-time programmes include the Evening MBA, which is identical to the full-time version and can be completed in 3–5 years, and the Weekend MBA, run all day on Saturdays. Classes for both are held at the GSB's Gleacher Center in downtown Chicago.

The GSB was the first school to launch an Executive MBA (in 1943) and now offers three distinct but linked programmes: the EMBA North America is run on alternate Fridays and Saturdays at the Gleacher Center; the EMBA Europe is based in Barcelona and involves 14 weeks of course work over 20 months in one- and two-week modules; and the EMBA Asia is based Singapore and involves 16 week-long course modules over 20 months. Each programme involves some shared classes with the others.

	Full-time MBA	Evening MBA Program	Weekend MBA Program	Executive MBA Program North America	Executive MBA Program Europe	Executive MBA Program Asia
Student rating of programme	4.7 (2)	–	–	–	–	–
Number of overseas exchange programmes	0 (41)	–	–	–	–	–
Number of languages on offer	>5 (1)	–	–	–	–	–

The directory
University of Chicago—Graduate School of Business

Students

	Full-time MBA	Evening MBA Program	Weekend MBA Program	Executive MBA Program North America	Executive MBA Program Europe	Executive MBA Program Asia
Annual intake	526	384	112	77	64	86
Applicants:places	n/a	n/a	n/a	n/a	n/a	n/a
Percentage of women students	29 (70)	25	19	21	10	26
Percentage of foreign students	27 (>100)	n/a	n/a	n/a	n/a	n/a
Average GMAT score	690 (15)	n/a	n/a	n/a	n/a	n/a
Average number of months' work experience	59 (86)	73	70	168	144	156
Age range of students	25-32	25-36	25-40	29-46	29-39	29-40
Average age	29	30	30	37	35	35
Student rating of culture and classmates	4.4 (23)	–	–	–	–	–

Student profile (full time)

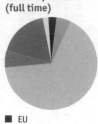

- ■ EU
- ■ Non-EU Europe
- ■ North America
- ■ Other Americas
- ■ Asia/Australasia
- ☐ Middle East
- ■ Other

Recruiters/careers service

	Full-time MBA	Evening MBA Program	Weekend MBA Program	Executive MBA Program North America	Executive MBA Program Europe	Executive MBA Program Asia
Number of industry sectors that recruited graduates	8 (37)	–	–	–	–	–
Percentage of graduates in jobs 3 months after graduation	85 (37)	–	–	–	–	–
Percentage of graduates finding jobs through careers services	74 (9)	–	–	–	–	–
Student rating of careers service	4.5 (1)	–	–	–	–	–
Post-MBA salary, US$	85,000 (31)	–	–	–	–	–
Percentage increase in salary	31 (95)	–	–	–	–	–
Principal recruiters of graduates	Citigroup, Booz-Allen & Hamilton Inc., Lehman Brothers, The Boston Consulting Group					

Cost

	Full-time MBA	Evening MBA Program	Weekend MBA Program	Executive MBA Program North America	Executive MBA Program Europe	Executive MBA Program Asia
Application fees	US$200	US$175	US$175	US$100	US$100	US$100
Programme fees	US$34,400	US$3,440	US$3,440	US$96,000	US$79,500	US$79,500
Comments	2003 entering class; 2004 or 2005 class fees not set	Per course	Per course	2003 tuition; includes tuition, books, residential hotels for one week in Singapore and one week in Barcelona. 2004 or 2005 class fees not set	2003 tuition; includes tuition, books, some meals and hotel for three residential weeks. 2004 or 2005 class fees not set	2003 tuition; 2004 or 2005 class fees not set
Accommodation costs (on campus, per year)	–	–	–	–	–	–
Accommodation costs (off campus, per year)	US$9,450	–	–	–	–	–
Financial aid available	Not disclosed	–	–	–	–	–
Type of aid available	Scholarships, loans	–	–	–	–	–
Criteria on which aid is granted	Merit, financial need	–	–	–	–	–

Accreditation

AACSB International

Application details

	Full-time MBA	Evening MBA Program	Weekend MBA Program	Executive MBA Program North America	Executive MBA Program Europe	Executive MBA Program Asia
Application deadline	2005 dates not set yet	2005 dates not set yet	2005 dates not set yet	2005 dates not set yet	2005 dates not set yet	2005 dates not set yet
Programme dates	Sep start, 21 months	Sep start, up to 60 months	Sep start, up to 60 months	Jul start, 20 months	Jul start, 20 months	Jul start, 20 months
Admission requirements	First degree; TOEFL if first language not English; 2 references; 3 essays; interview highly recommended; work experience not required but work history considered	First degree; TOEFL if first language not English; GMAT; 2 references; 3 essays; interview; employer's letter of support recommended	First degree; TOEFL if first language not English; 2 references; 3 essays; interview	First degree, work experience; TOEFL if first language not English; 3 references; interview; letter of support from employer	First degree; work experience; TOEFL if first language not English; 3 references; interview; letter of support from employer	First degree; work experience; TOEFL if first language not English; 3 references; interview; letter of support from employer

Executive education

The GSB offers a wide range of open-enrolment programmes in areas such as finance, general management, leadership and organisational behaviour, marketing and sales, and strategy. It also offers customised programmes covering similar areas.

Student/alumni quotes

"Chicago GSB still suffers from a very academic reputation. While the academic experience is certainly outstanding, the sense of community is also very strong and the student groups are great fun."

"People who are not sure of what they want to do can get into trouble with the extremely flexible curriculum."

"The classes are challenging and the flexible curriculum allows you to set your own course of study—ideal for motivated students. There is a co-operative atmosphere among students but you had better pull your weight. There is no room for slackers here!"

China Europe International Business School (CEIBS)

Ranking	Rank (out of 100) Full-time
Overall rank	95
Regional rank	8

Criteria	Rank (out of 100) Full-time
Open new career opportunities	**9**
Diversity of recruiters	40
Number in jobs three months after graduation	6
Jobs found through the careers service	14
Student assessment of careers service	29
Personal development and educational experience	**90**
Faculty quality	>100
Student quality	16
Student diversity	>100
Education experience	80
Increase in salary	**>100**
Increase in salary	n/a
Post-MBA salary	>100
Potential to network	**84**
Breadth of alumni network	95
Internationalism of alumni	>100
Alumni effectiveness	56

Address
699 Hongfeng Road
Pudong
Shanghai
China
201206

Tel:
+86 21 2890 5251

Fax:
+86 21 2890 5126

E-mail:
admissions@ceibs.edu

Website:
www.ceibs.edu/mba/

Programme director:
Gerald Fryxell

Figures in brackets
represent rank

Background

The Shanghai-based China Europe International Business School (CEIBS) is a non-profit joint venture by China's Ministry of Foreign Trade and Economic Co-operation, Shanghai municipal government and the EU. Shanghai Jiaotong University and the European Foundation for Management Development (EFMD) effectively run the school, which was set up in 1994.

Jiaotong University, which is over 100 years old, is one of China's leading universities. Its extensive and long-standing contacts with Chinese business have helped the CEIBS in its relationships with the Chinese corporate world and it has good backing from Chinese and international companies. Most of the faculty members are visiting professors from Western business schools.

Facilities

The CEIBS is based in a new campus in Pudong, Shanghai, with excellent facilities. The three-storey Academic Centre, built around a paved and landscaped courtyard, houses lecture rooms, discussion rooms, classrooms and administration areas. The Global Sources Information Centre is a business library. There are two on-campus dormitories that can accommodate a total of 260 students. The school also has offices in Beijing and Shenzhen.

	Full-time MBA
Student assessment of facilities	4.2 (62)

Faculty

Number of faculty: 18 full-time, 5 part-time, 27 visiting

	Full-time MBA	Executive MBA
Number of faculty per student	0.2 (99)	0.3
Percentage of faculty with PhD	67 (89)	67
Student rating of faculty	3.8 (100)	–

Strengths and weaknesses

Strengths: Chinese business and cross-cultural management; marketing; finance

Weaknesses: non-curricular activities; facilities

Programme highlights

The CEIBS has slightly revamped its full-time MBA programme in order, it says, to offer students more chance to customise it. The programme is divided into seven six-week teaching modules. There are compulsory core courses in the first four modules, eight electives in modules five and six (divided by an internship or overseas exchange), a group consulting project and a final module to integrate the whole programme.

Language training is available in Chinese (Mandarin) and Spanish.

The Executive MBA is divided into two specialisations: the general track and the finance track. The general track consists of 17 courses (15 compulsory core courses and two electives chosen from six offered). The finance track consists of 12 core courses and six finance courses. Students in both tracks also complete two projects. Both tracks use the same mix of visiting faculty as the full-time programme. Participants complete the degree within two years. The programme is delivered in four-day blocks covering one weekend each month (Friday–Monday).

The general track takes in two classes a year in Shanghai and Beijing. The finance track was launched in Shanghai in 2003. Although English is the teaching language, Chinese classes are equipped with sequential Chinese interpretation.

	Full-time MBA	Executive MBA
Student rating of programme	3.8 (99)	–
Number of overseas exchange programmes	58 (24)	–
Number of languages on offer	2 (74)	–

Students

Student profile (full time)

- ■ EU
- ■ Non-EU Europe
- ▨ North America
- ■ Other Americas
- ■ Asia/Australasia
- ▨ Middle East

	Full-time MBA	Executive MBA
Annual intake	112	182
Applicants:places	6:1	2:1
Percentage of women students	33 (36)	15
Percentage of foreign students	12 (>100)	n/a
Average GMAT score	669 (28)	n/a
Average number of months' work experience	71 (29)	168
Age range of students	26-33	31-41
Average age	30	36
Student rating of culture and classmates	4.0 (85)	–

The directory
China Europe International Business School (CEIBS)

Recruiters/careers service

	Full-time MBA	Executive MBA
Number of industry sectors that recruited graduates	8 (40)	–
Percentage of graduates in jobs 3 months after graduation	96 (6)	–
Percentage of graduates finding jobs through careers services	73 (14)	–
Student rating of careers service	3.8 (29)	–
Post-MBA salary, US$	9,029 (>100)	–
Percentage increase in salary	n/a	
Principal recruiters of graduates	Bearingpoint, Eli Lilly, Philips Consumer Electronic (China)	

Cost

	Full-time MBA	Executive MBA
Application fees	US$80	US$100
Programme fees	US$25,000	US$31,200
Comments	Total programme. For Mainland Chinese application fee and tuition fee are Rmb500 and Rmb138,000 respectively.	–
Accommodation costs (on campus, per year)	US$1,229	–
Accommodation costs (off campus, per year)	US$1,735	–
Financial aid available	US$444,434	–
Type of aid available	Scholarships, loans, grants plus loans provided by local banks for domestic students on request	–
Criteria on which aid is granted	Merit, financial need	–

Accreditation
EQUIS

Application details

	Full-time MBA	Executive MBA
Application deadline	February 28th	–
Programme dates	Jun start, 17 months	Nov start, 24 months
Admission requirements	Bachelor's degree or its equivalent from an accredited or state approved college or university; at least 2 years' work experience; TOEFL is recommended but not required if first language not English; 2 references; 6 essays; interview; laptop	Bachelor's degree; at least 8 years' work experience; 2 references; 3 essays; interview; written examination organised by the school

Executive education
The CEIBS's open-enrolment programmes focus on the main management disciplines, but the school says the teaching and learning processes take place with a general management perspective. Customised programmes are designed mainly to support organisational transformation and development.

Student/alumni quotes
"Consider this school if you want to develop your career in China. Strong network, good faculty and best value for money."

"The atmosphere is extremely co-operative. Because of the heaviness of the workload, there's a common sense that we all need to help each other as much as possible if we are to survive."

"The students have access to the frontline business leaders of present-day China."

The Chinese University of Hong Kong

Address
MBA Programmes
The Chinese University
of Hong Kong
Shatin, New Territories
Hong Kong

Tel:
+852 2609 7811

Fax:
+852 2603 6289

E-mail:
cumba@cuhk.edu.hk

Website:
www.cuhk.edu.hk/mba

Programme director:
Vincent S Lai

Figures in brackets
represent rank

Ranking	Rank (out of 100) Full time
Overall rank	n/a
Regional rank	11

Background

The MBA started by the graduate school of the Chinese University of Hong Kong (CUHK) in 1966 (the same year the school was established) is the oldest, and probably the most prestigious, full-time programme in Hong Kong. The university itself is predominantly for undergraduates and has over 8,000 students; there are only 30 full-time MBA students.

The school has a strong alumni base and good connections with the local business community. Guest lectures by local and international business leaders are a regular part of the MBA curriculum and most courses also involve project work. The programme particularly appeals to would-be entrepreneurs and is commonly used as a launching pad for new businesses. As the CUHK is a bilingual university, some knowledge of Chinese languages is useful. However, virtually all MBA classes are given in English. Only those directly related to markets in China or dealing in depth with Chinese issues are given in Chinese languages. Not all students have work experience. Placement advice is shared with undergraduates.

Facilities

CUHK is sited on a large split-level campus overlooking the scenic Tolo Harbour, near Shatin, some 40 minutes' drive from Hong Kong Island (there is a fast commuter rail link). Facilities are excellent. MBA administration and faculty offices are housed in the Leung Kau Kui Building on the central campus, where both the full-time and part-time (Weekend Mode) MBA classes are held. The modern classrooms provide good technology and computing support. There are also student common rooms and a behavioural science laboratory for scientific investigative research and skills development. On-campus accommodation is available but most MBA students live in rented apartments.

	Full-time MBA
Student assessment of facilities	4.2 (n/a)

Faculty

Number of faculty: 88 full-time, 22 part-time, 8 visiting

	Full-time MBA	MBA Programmes (Evening and Weekend Modes)	Executive MBA Programme
Number of faculty per student	1.8 (n/a)	0.9	2.7
Percentage of faculty with PhD	94 (n/a)	94	94
Student rating of faculty	3.9 (n/a)	–	–

Strengths and weaknesses

Strengths: finance; marketing; global business

Weaknesses: lack of elective choice

Programme highlights

The 18-month MBA has a single integrated core course, taught in modular format. After the core, students take advanced required, elective and capstone courses and a project, and have the option of an international exchange. Students also take required but non-credit courses that include talks from practising CEOs and executive development workshops. Pre-courses are required unless exemption is granted.

The school has an arrangement with HEC in Paris (see page 256) under which full-time MBA students complete required first-year MBA courses at CUHK and then study at HEC in their second year. They

The directory
The Chinese University of Hong Kong

are awarded MBA degrees from both CUHK and HEC.

The Evening programme is similar to the full-time version. Students take two courses in each trimester and one course in each session of the summer term and complete a Chinese business field study. Classes are held at CUHK's new downtown MBA centre once a week for each course. The Weekend programme is designed for non-business administration graduates. It is similar to the full-time version and the structure is the same as the Evening version. Students take two courses per semester. Classes are held on the main campus on Saturdays.

Both programmes are normally completed in two years. In special circumstances and with approval, students can extend their period of study for more than three years, but they must complete the programme within five consecutive years in order to qualify for the MBA degree.

CUHK's Executive MBA started in 1993 and was the first in Hong Kong. The first year is devoted to the major business functions and the second year to broader strategic and policy issues. The programme consists of eight ten-week quarters over two years. Chinese and English languages are used. There is a residence week in a local hotel at the beginning and end of the programme. Classes are held at CUHK's new downtown MBA centre on Friday evening and on Saturday afternoon.

CUHK also takes part in OneMBA, a joint global programme (see Rotterdam School of Management, page 441, for details) and offers specialised MBAs in finance and healthcare.

	Full-time MBA	MBA Programmes (Evening and Weekend Modes)	Executive MBA Programme
Student rating of programme	3.6 (n/a)	–	–
Number of overseas exchange programmes	31 (n/a)	–	–
Number of languages on offer	>5 (n/a)	–	–

Students

	Full-time MBA	MBA Programmes (Evening and Weekend Modes)	Executive MBA Programme
Annual intake	55	129	44
Applicants:places	4:1	5:1	1:1
Percentage of women students	35 (n/a)	38	36
Percentage of foreign students	62 (n/a)	n/a	n/a
Average GMAT score	618 (n/a)	600	n/a
Average number of months' work experience	62 (n/a)	78	168
Age range of students	23-32	26-36	33-43
Average age	27	30	37
Student rating of culture and classmates	3.8 (n/a)	–	–

Student profile (full time)

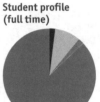

■ EU
■ Non-EU Europe
■ North America
■ Other Americas
■ Asia/Australasia
▨ Middle East

Recruiters/careers service

	Full-time MBA	MBA Programmes (Evening and Weekend Modes)	Executive MBA Programme
Number of industry sectors that recruited graduates	6 (n/a)	–	–
Percentage of graduates in jobs 3 months after graduation	70 (n/a)	–	–
Percentage of graduates finding jobs through careers services	25 (n/a)	–	–
Student rating of careers service	3.3 (n/a)	–	–
Post-MBA salary, US$	25,475 (n/a)	–	–
Percentage increase in salary	13 (n/a)	–	–
Principal recruiters of graduates	LVMH, JP Morgan Chase, Standard Chartered Bank		

Cost

	Full-time MBA	MBA Programmes (Evening and Weekend Modes)	Executive MBA Programme
Application fees	US$25	US$25	HK$180 (US$23)
Programme fees	US$17,890	US$25,730	HK$230,528 (US$29,593)
Comments	–	–	Total programme
Accommodation costs (on campus, per year)	US$4,000		–
Accommodation costs (off campus, per year)	US$9,000	–	–
Financial aid available	US$54,535	–	–
Type of aid available	Scholarships, exchange awards, loans	–	–
Criteria on which aid is granted	Scholarships are based on academic performance; loans on financial need	–	–

Accreditation

AACSB International

Application details

	Full-time MBA	MBA Programmes (Evening and Weekend Modes)	Executive MBA Programme
Application deadline	February 28th	February 28th	March 12th
Programme dates	Jul start, 18 months	Aug start, 24 months	Aug start, 24 months
Admission requirements	First degree (2nd lower honours/ grade B or above); TOEFL if first language not English; 2 references; essay; interview; laptop	First degree (2nd lower honours/ grade B or above); at least 3 years' work experience; TOEFL if first language not English; 2 references; essay; interview	First degree (bachelor's degree or equivalent professional qualification); at least 7 years' work experience; 2 references; interview

Executive education

CUHK runs executive education programmes through the Asia-Pacific Institute of Business (APIB), which was established in 1990. There is a series of courses offering diplomas (both open enrolment and customised), executive seminars and customised in-company programmes.

Student/alumni quotes

"It has a strong focus in Hong Kong and China, and has an aptitude for integrating its courses, network and guest lecturers into a broad business education of the region."

"There is still much room to better utilise the alumni network. I believe currently they are utilising just 20–30% of the potential benefits."

"Not enough electives."

City University—Cass Business School

Ranking	Rank (out of 100) Full-time
Overall rank	91
Regional rank	36

Criteria	Rank (out of 100) Full-time
Open new career opportunities	**98**
Diversity of recruiters	97
Number in jobs three months after graduation	68
Jobs found through the careers service	n/a
Student assessment of careers service	99
Personal development and educational experience	**89**
Faculty quality	94
Student quality	34
Student diversity	80
Education experience	>100
Increase in salary	**31**
Increase in salary	88
Post-MBA salary	17
Potential to network	**99**
Breadth of alumni network	20
Internationalism of alumni	65
Alumni effectiveness	>100

Address
106 Bunhill Row
London
UK
EC1Y 8TZ

Tel:
+44 20 7040 8662

Fax:
+44 20 7040 8898

E-mail:
cass-mba@city.ac.uk

Website:
www.cass.city.ac.uk/
mba

Programme director:
Vacant

Figures in brackets
represent rank

Background

Cass Business School makes the most of its location in the City of London, one of the world's leading financial centres. Its links with business are excellent and the list of visiting speakers is impressive. It also has good international links through its membership of the Alliance of Management Schools in European Capitals (AMSEC).

The full-range school is big by European standards, with 1,500 students, 100 full-time and more than 150 part-time staff, and nearly 10,000 alumni, including Stelios Haji-Iannou, founder of easyJet.

Facilities

Cass moved into a new eight-floor, 100,000 sq-ft building in the middle of the City of London in 2002. Facilities include classrooms, 22 lecture theatres and syndicate rooms. City University has some on-campus accommodation in halls of residence, but demand outstrips supply. Help is given to students seeking accommodation in London, but it is expensive and may be some way from the school.

	Full-time MBA
Student assessment of facilities	3.8 (>100)

Faculty

Number of faculty: 94 full-time, 4 part-time, 0 visiting	
	Full-time MBA
Number of faculty per student	1.5 (13)
Percentage of faculty with PhD	83 (95)
Student rating of faculty	3.8 (>100)

Strengths and weaknesses

Strengths: finance

Weaknesses: administration

Programme highlights

The City MBA begins with a traditional core followed by a choice of specialist subjects and additional electives. MBA students from overseas (of which the school has a large number) are offered a special introduction to MBA course work and English language skills during a four-week pre-programme course.

The core takes up the first term. In the second and third terms students take five courses in their field of specialisation (currently general and strategic management; strategic management of technology and electronic business; international business and management; and finance) and then select three elective courses from a range of approximately 30–40, which may or may not be in their specialisation. The programme is completed in the fourth term with an in-company business research project, which can be conducted individually or in small groups. Soft skills training is offered in lectures and workshops throughout the programme.

The Evening MBA is identical to the full-time version and is taken over two years. Classes meet two evenings a week (6–9 pm) in term time and the occasional weekend. Students take core courses in the first year and specialist and elective subjects plus a business project in the second year.

Cass has begun a part-time Executive MBA (with modules taught over weekends) in Shanghai, China, in co-operation with Bank of China and Shanghai University of Finance and Economics.

	Full-time MBA
Student rating of programme	3.9 (97)
Number of overseas exchange programmes	0 (41)
Number of languages on offer	0 (67)

Student profile (full time)

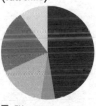

- ■ EU
- ■ Non-EU Europe
- ■ North America
- ■ Other Americas
- ■ Asia/Australasia
- ■ Middle East

Students

	Full-time MBA
Annual intake	63
Applicants:places	n/a
Percentage of women students	21 (66)
Percentage of foreign students	63 (41)
Average GMAT score	630 (69)
Average number of months' work experience	84 (13)
Age range of students	25-35
Average age	n/a
Student rating of culture and classmates	3.9 (100)

Recruiters/careers service

	Full-time MBA
Number of industry sectors that recruited graduates	6 (97)
Percentage of graduates in jobs 3 months after graduation	79 (68)
Percentage of graduates finding jobs through careers services	n/a (n/a)
Student rating of careers service	3.5 (99)
Post-MBA salary, US$	95,007 (17)
Percentage increase in salary	42 (88)
Principal recruiters of graduates	GE, Citigroup

The directory
City University—Cass Business School

Cost

	Full-time MBA
Application fees	£50 (US$82)
Programme fees	£22,000 (US$36,066)
Comments	–
Accommodation costs (on campus, per year)	–
Accommodation costs (off campus, per year)	–
Financial aid available	–
Type of aid available	–
Criteria on which aid is granted	–

Accreditation

AMBA, EQUIS

Application details

	Full-time MBA
Application deadline	–
Programme dates	Sep start, 12 months
Admission requirements	First degree (work experience may be taken instead of a degree for older applicants); at least 3 years' work experience; GMAT; 2 references; interview; laptop

Executive education

At the time of writing Cass was developing its portfolio of open-enrolment executive education courses and details were not available. It is an established and extensive provider of customised programmes.

Student/alumni quotes

"The course is good and there are great efforts being made to improve its weaker areas. Great facilities with strong academic credentials. International composition of students is impressive, as are standards."

"Some foreign students were admitted with poor English language skills, causing problems in team assignments."

"Cass continues to deliver outstanding teaching and is fast becoming a magnet for high-potential students."

Columbia Business School

Address
3022 Broadway
Uris Hall
New York, NY
USA
10027

Tel:
+1 212 854 2747

Fax:
+1 212 854 3050

E-mail:
apply@claven.gsb.
columbia.edu

Website:
www.gsb.columbia.edu

Programme director:
Safwan Masri

Figures in brackets
represent rank

Ranking	Rank (out of 100) Full-time
Overall rank	7
Regional rank	6

Criteria	Rank (out of 100) Full-time
Open new career opportunities	**5**
Diversity of recruiters	1
Number in jobs three months after graduation	35
Jobs found through the careers service	5
Student assessment of careers service	10
Personal development and educational experience	**32**
Faculty quality	67
Student quality	28
Student diversity	33
Education experience	46
Increase in salary	**17**
Increase in salary	59
Post-MBA salary	12
Potential to network	**28**
Breadth of alumni network	31
Internationalism of alumni	59
Alumni effectiveness	17

Background

Columbia Business School's location in New York City, which the school likes to call its own living laboratory, allows it to draw on high profile executives as guest speakers and adjunct faculty, and offer attractive internships and project opportunities. Many of the school's high-powered alumni live and work virtually on its doorstep. Finance, banking and Wall Street remain predominant, but the school also has good national and international links.

In July 2004 R Glenn Hubbard, a Columbia economics professor, took over as dean from the long-serving Meyer Feldberg. Hubbard joined Columbia in 1988.

Facilities

The business school is based in the recently refurbished Uris Hall, at the centre of the university campus, which provides classrooms, library, faculty and student lounges, offices and a delicatessen. Library, sports and leisure facilities are good. All students must have their own laptops and the school has over 300 network data jacks in study areas, conference rooms, classrooms, the library and even the delicatessen, providing access to the school's LAN, printing and university-based resources as well as external databases.

There are further facilities at Warren Hall, an eight-story building five minutes' walk from Uris and shared with the School of Law.

	Full-time MBA
Student assessment of facilities	3.9 (71)

The directory
Columbia Business School

Faculty

Number of faculty: 115 full-time, 89 part-time, 9 visiting

	Full-time MBA	Columbia Executive MBA Program	Berkeley-Columbia Executive MBA	EMBA-Global
Number of faculty per student	0.3 (93)	1.6	3.6	3.0
Percentage of faculty with PhD	98 (23)	98	98	98
Student rating of faculty	4.2 (60)	–	–	–

Strengths and weaknesses

Strengths: finance, entrepreneurship, general management

Weakness: facilities

Programme highlights

Columbia's two-year full-time MBA begins with a functional core of five full courses and eight half-term courses studied over the first two terms and then moves on to electives. Concentrations are not required, but students can group electives into offered areas of concentration or design their own. Some electives can be taken in other graduate schools of the university. Each entering class is divided into clusters of approximately 60 students who take all courses together for the first year.

The part-time Executive MBA has two start dates, January and September. Classes are on held Friday and Saturday of alternate weeks. The programme comprises five consecutive terms with four classes in each term. There is a five-day residential off-campus block at the start of the first and second terms. The EMBA, the EMBA–Global and Berkeley–Columbia Executive MBA are preceded by an online maths refresher course as well as an orientation.

The EMBA–Global is run in partnership with London Business School (LBS). The programme covers five terms over 20 months and mixes campus-based lectures, case studies, projects, teamwork, field trips and online learning. In the first year a once-a-month class schedule alternates between LBS and Columbia (a week at each). The second year (terms four and five) consists of a company project and electives at either or both schools; it also includes a one-week International Seminar in Asia, during which student groups conduct in-depth examinations of local firms. Participants earn an MBA degree from both institutions.

The Berkeley–Columbia Executive MBA is a 19-month programme taught jointly by faculty from Columbia and the University of California at Berkeley (Haas). Teaching is divided equally between Columbia and Berkeley faculty, but class sessions are held primarily in the San Francisco Bay area. During each of the five terms students attend four Thursday–Saturday blocks at Berkeley and one Wednesday–Saturday block at Columbia, staying in nearby accommodation. They study 11 typical core courses and eight advanced core courses. There are no electives. They also undertake a nine-day international study tour and a team project. Participants earn an MBA degree from both institutions.

	Full-time MBA	Columbia Executive MBA Program	Berkeley-Columbia Executive MBA	EMBA-Global
Student rating of programme	4.2 (46)	–	–	–
Number of overseas exchange programmes	50 (75)	–	–	–
Number of languages on offer	>5 (1)	–	–	–

Student profile
(full time)

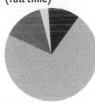

- ■ EU
- ■ Non-EU Europe
- ■ North America
- ■ Other Americas
- ■ Asia/Australasia
- ▨ Middle East
- ■ Other

Students

	Full-time MBA	Columbia Executive MBA Program	Berkeley-Columbia Executive MBA	EMBA-Global
Annual intake	517	133	60	70
Applicants:places	n/a	n/a	n/a	n/a
Percentage of women students	31 (34)	21	27	26
Percentage of foreign students	28 (88)	n/a	n/a	n/a
Average GMAT score	709 (4)	n/a	n/a	n/a
Average number of months' work experience	54 (98)	120	120	120
Age range of students	25-31	28-40	30-42	28-38
Average age	28	32	35	33
Student rating of culture and classmates	4.6 (15)	–	–	–

Recruiters/careers service

	Full-time MBA	Columbia Executive MBA Program	Berkeley-Columbia Executive MBA	EMBA-Global
Number of industry sectors that recruited graduates	8 (1)	–	–	–
Percentage of graduates in jobs 3 months after graduation	85 (35)	–	–	–
Percentage of graduates finding jobs through careers services	85 (5)	–	–	–
Student rating of careers service	4.1 (10)	–	–	–
Post-MBA salary, US$	89,091 (12)	–	–	–
Percentage increase in salary	61 (59)	–	–	–
Principal recruiters of graduates	–			

Cost

	Full-time MBA	Columbia Executive MBA Program	Berkeley-Columbia Executive MBA	EMBA-Global
Application fees	US$180	US$160	US$165	US$170
Programme fees	US$34,404	US$112,200	US$118,750	US$115,500
Comments	Per year	–	–	–
Accommodation costs (on campus, per year)	US$16,776	–	–	–
Accommodation costs (off campus, per year)	US$16,776	–	–	–
Financial aid available	Not disclosed	–	–	–
Type of aid available	Scholarships, fellowships, loans	–	–	–
Criteria on which aid is granted	Merit, financial need	–	–	–

Accreditation

AACSB International

The directory
Columbia Business School

Application details

	Full-time MBA	Columbia Executive MBA Program	Berkeley-Columbia Executive MBA	EMBA-Global
Application deadline	April 20th (domestic); March 1st (international)	June 1st (autumn); October 10th (spring)	March 1st	March 15th
Programme dates	Jan start, 20 months	Jan start, 20 months	Jun start, 19 months	May start, 20 months
Admission requirements	First degree; TOEFL if first language not English; 2 references; 4 essays	First degree; at least 5 years' work experience; TOEFL if first language not English; 2 references; essay; interview	First degree; TOEFL if first language not English; 2 references; 2 essays; interview	First degree; at least 10 years' work experience; TOEFL if first language not English; 2 references; 3 essays; interview

Executive education

Columbia offers open-enrolment courses in leadership and management, finance, and marketing as well as a wide range of customised in-company programmes.

Student/alumni quotes

"[Columbia's] biggest strength is access to and success in placing students with the premier firms in finance and consulting. Career-changers experience a great deal of success with these Wall Street and strategy firms."

"The facilities need to be updated, but as a New Yorker you are used to it."

"An especially lively and diverse group of students and faculty, A New York attitude means nothing is ever short of ambition and style."

Concordia University—John Molson School of Business

Address
GM 403-9
1455 de Maisonneuve
Blvd. W
Concordia University
Montreal, QC
Canada
H3G 1M8

Tel:
+1 514 848 2424
ext 2987

Fax:
+1 514 848 4502

E-mail:
mba@jmsb.concordia.
ca

Website:
www.johnmolson.
concordia.ca

Programme director:
Ronald Ferguson

Figures in brackets
represent rank

Ranking	Rank (out of 100) Full-time
Overall rank	n/a
Regional rank	56

Background

The business school at Concordia University is named after John Molson, an 18th-century Montreal brewer and banker. It is one of Canada's largest full-range business schools with around 5,000 undergraduate students, 1,000 postgraduates and over 30,000 alumni from the school as a whole (there are 3,350 registered MBA alumni). In French-speaking Montreal courses are taught in English, but undergraduate exams and papers can be written in French or English.

The school is determinedly multicultural, with 130 nationalities represented within the student body. The school has good links with local business and says its programmes focus on critical skills basic to effective communication, critical thinking, logical actions and lifelong learning.

Facilities

The school is currently based in downtown Montreal and MBA faculties, including "smart" class rooms, are good. Construction of a new C$60m building exclusively for the John Molson School of Business is scheduled to start in autumn 2004 with completion expected in winter 2007.

	Full-time MBA
Student assessment of facilities	4.4 (n/a)

Faculty

Number of faculty: 99 full-time, 40 part-time, 1 visiting

	Full-time MBA	Global Aviation MBA Program (GAMBA)	International Aviation MBA program
Number of faculty per student	1.8 (n/a)	4.2	9.3
Percentage of faculty with PhD	96 (n/a)	96	96
Student rating of faculty	4.0 (n/a)	–	–

Strengths and weaknesses

Strengths: finance; marketing; management

Weaknesses: low international content

Programme highlights

The Molson MBA is offered in identical full-time and part-time versions. All core courses are scheduled in both day and evening time slots, typically Monday–Thursday. In the summer, the courses are scheduled only in the evening and are offered twice a week over a six-week term.

The programme starts with an orientation and a quantitative skills course that must be taken, and passed, by students with a poor maths background (this programme can also be taken during the MBA programme proper). This is followed a traditional series of 12 core courses. The second part of the programme includes more specialised courses in finance, marketing, strategy, international business and e-business. The programme then splits into a number of options: seven elective courses; a research project plus four electives; or a consultancy-style project plus six electives.

Molson's Executive MBA meets one day a week, on alternate Fridays and Saturdays, for four semesters. Classes usually run from the last week of August to early May. During the summer between the first and second year, students participate in a ten-day international study trip. Although no classes are scheduled during the summer, students are expected to work on their research projects with faculty advisers once the trip is completed. One week before the start of classes, students attend a two-day orientation weekend. Free summer tutorials in accounting, mathematics and business English are available for new students.

The directory
Concordia University—John Molson School of Business

Montreal is an aviation centre and Molson offers an International Aviation MBA programme in two formats: one-year full-time or the Global Aviation MBA (GAMBA), a "virtual" programme lasting two years over four semesters.

	Full-time MBA	Global Aviation MBA Program (GAMBA)	International Aviation MBA program
Student rating of programme	3.8 (n/a)	–	–
Number of overseas exchange programmes	39 (n/a)	–	–
Number of languages on offer	3 (n/a)	–	–

Students

	Full-time MBA	Global Aviation MBA Program (GAMBA)	International Aviation MBA program
Annual intake	66	17	15
Applicants:places	6:1	10:1	10:1
Percentage of women students	32 (n/a)	22	27
Percentage of foreign students	91 (n/a)	12	n/a
Average GMAT score	666 (n/a)	550	550
Average number of months' work experience	70 (n/a)	108	72
Age range of students	25-33	23-48	25-41
Average age	30	35	31
Student rating of culture and classmates	3.8 (n/a)	–	–

Student profile (full-time)

n/a

Recruiters/careers service

	Full-time MBA	Global Aviation MBA Program (GAMBA)	International Aviation MBA program
Number of industry sectors that recruited graduates	6 (n/a)	–	–
Percentage of graduates in jobs 3 months after graduation	55 (n/a)	–	–
Percentage of graduates finding jobs through careers services	14 (n/a)	–	–
Student rating of careers service	3.0 (n/a)	–	–
Post-MBA salary, US$	40,621 (n/a)	–	–
Percentage increase in salary	26 (n/a)	–	–
Principal recruiters of graduates	Merck Frosst Canada, Janssen-Ortho, Novartis Pharmaceuticals Canada		

Which MBA? © The Economist Intelligence Unit Limited 2004

Cost

	Full-time MBA	Global Aviation MBA Program (GAMBA)	International Aviation MBA program
Application fees	C$50 (US$36)	–	
Programme fees	C$27,000 (US$19,285)	US$28,000	US$28,000
Comments	Total programme. Fee for Canadian residents is C$10,000. Fee for Quebec residents is C$5,500	–	–
Accommodation costs (on campus, per year)	C$3,996 (US$2,854)	–	–
Accommodation costs (off campus, per year)	C$6,000 (US$4,286)	–	–
Financial aid available	C$843,200 (US$602,286)	–	–
Type of aid available	Scholarships, tuition waiver, loans, bursaries	–	–
Criteria on which aid is granted	Merit, eligibility, financial need		–

Accreditation

AACSB International

Application details

	Full-time MBA	Global Aviation MBA Program (GAMBA)	International Aviation MBA program
Application deadline	June 1st	January 15th	June 15th
Programme dates	Sep start, 16 months	Apr start, 24 months	Sep start, 13 months
Admission requirements	First degree; at least 2 years' work experience; GMAT; TOEFL if first language not English (for international students); 3 references; essay; laptop; interview by invitation only	First degree; at least 3 years' work experience; GMAT; 2 references; 2 essays	First degree; at least 3 years' work experience; GMAT; 2 references; 2 essays

Executive education

Molson offers a range of open-enrolment seminars in both English and French and also customised in-company programmes (or open seminars delivered on company premises) in areas such as management and leadership, personal effectiveness, human resources, communications, marketing and sales, finance and accounting, supply chain management and operations management.

Student/alumni quotes

"JMSB is slowly learning its own strengths. The student body as well as the faculty are first rate—all that is missing is a catalyst to catapult JMSB to national prominence."

"Not enough real world, tying theory to practice."

"It is great value for money. The school is known locally as an excellent business school but is still building its reputation nationally and internationally. There is the opportunity to work with exciting and young up-and-coming faculty."

Cornell University—Johnson Graduate School of Management

Ranking	Rank (out of 100) Full-time
Overall rank	17
Regional rank	14

Criteria	Rank (out of 100) Full-time
Open new career opportunities	**22**
Diversity of recruiters	1
Number in jobs three months after graduation	58
Jobs found through the careers service	47
Student assessment of careers service	6
Personal development and educational experience	**18**
Faculty quality	26
Student quality	43
Student diversity	60
Education experience	5
Increase in salary	**38**
Increase in salary	87
Post-MBA salary	24
Potential to network	**38**
Breadth of alumni network	53
Internationalism of alumni	90
Alumni effectiveness	12

Address
Sage Hall
Cornell University
Ithaca, NY
US
14853

Tel:
+1 607 255 6379

Fax:
+1 607 255 1858

E-mail:
mba@cornell.edu

Website:
www.johnson.cornell.edu

Programme director:
Cathy S Dove

Figures in brackets represent rank

Background

Cornell University's Johnson Graduate School of Management is small and friendly with a co-operative, teamworking ethic and a commitment to business education that is readily applicable to the real world. Although it maintains a deliberately small MBA programme and is a bit out of the way (a five-hour drive from New York City), geographical isolation has not stopped it setting up international links, notably with Japan, and around one-third of students come from outside North America.

The school is closely linked to its parent, the prestigious Ivy League Cornell University, which has some 12,000–13,000 undergraduate and 6,000 postgraduate students. MBA students are encouraged to take advantage of the range of courses offered by the university as a whole.

Facilities

The school is based in Sage Hall, which is one of the original buildings at Cornell and a historic landmark (it was constructed to house Cornell's first women students). A US$35m renovation has effectively created an entirely new building within the old walls and provided outstanding facilities. The university is set in beautiful countryside in New York State's Finger Lakes region, and from November to March the weather is cold with a lot of snow. The centre of the scenic campus, built in the 1860s, is fairly quiet with pleasant lawns and some fine views.

Social life, which centres on the university, is good. Most MBA students live off campus, where accommodation is reasonably priced and fairly plentiful. Some foreign students live on campus. Ithaca is a small university town that makes the Johnson school an ideal location for students with families or international students nervous about American city life.

	Full-time MBA
Student assessment of facilities	4.8 (2)

Faculty

Number of faculty: 52 full-time, 15 part-time, 25 visiting

	Full-time MBA	Executive MBA Program
Number of faculty per student	0.2 (>100)	1.9
Percentage of faculty with PhD	94 (47)	94
Student rating of faculty	4.7 (6)	–

Strengths and weaknesses

Strengths: finance; marketing; entrepreneurship

Weaknesses: elective choice can be limited

Programme highlights

Cornell's full-time MBA programme follows the US tradition of a rigorous core (six required functional courses) in the first year and electives in the second, but it does have some interesting innovations. The most notable are the so-called immersion courses, taken during the spring semester of the first year, in which students work on real problems with real deadlines. Although these are optional, about 80% of students take them. Currently immersion courses are offered in strategic brand management, manufacturing, investment banking, managerial finance, entrepreneurship and private equity, and research, sales and trading. At least two electives can be taken in the first year. The programme also offers for-credit workshops in the softer areas of managerial skills.

There is also a one-year MBA (the Twelve Month Option), an accelerated programme designed specifically for fast-track business professionals with graduate degrees and proven quantitative skills.

The school is known for its small classes, easy access to faculty and a spirit of co-operation. The emphasis is probably more on education than at some other business schools, and extensive use is made of other university departments. Waivers by examination are encouraged to allow even more flexibility. There is an accelerated 12-month track for students with graduate degrees in scientific or technical fields. They join the second year directly after a ten-week summer term that covers the same areas as the first-year core.

The Executive MBA is held at IBM Palisades Executive Conference Center outside New York City. The programme includes a good deal of group project work, an international study trip and a management simulation. Classes are held every other weekend (all day Saturday and Sunday morning) and there is a one-week residential session on the Ithaca campus at the beginning of each of the four terms. The programme starts once a year in July.

	Full-time MBA	Executive MBA Program
Student rating of programme	4.5 (9)	–
Number of overseas exchange programmes	23 (73)	
Number of languages on offer	>5 (1)	–

Student profile (full time)

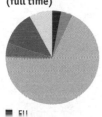

- ■ EU
- ■ Non-EU Europe
- ■ North America
- ■ Other Americas
- ■ Asia/Australasia
- Middle East

Students

	Full-time MBA	Executive MBA Program
Annual intake	273	49
Applicants:places	n/a	2:1
Percentage of women students	27 (67)	15
Percentage of foreign students	36 (84)	n/a
Average GMAT score	672 (25)	n/a
Average number of months' work experience	60 (63)	156
Age range of students	24–33	27–40
Average age	28	35
Student rating of culture and classmates	4.5 (18)	–

The directory
Cornell University—Johnson Graduate School of Management

Recruiters/careers service

	Full-time MBA	Executive MBA Program
Number of industry sectors that recruited graduates	8 (1)	–
Percentage of graduates in jobs 3 months after graduation	80 (58)	–
Percentage of graduates finding jobs through careers services	45 (47)	–
Student rating of careers service	4.3 (6)	–
Post-MBA salary, US$	83,300 (24)	–
Percentage increase in salary	28 (87)	
Principal recruiters of graduates	Johnson & Johnson, IBM, Avaya	

Cost

	Full-time MBA	Executive MBA Program
Application fees	US$180	US$200
Programme fees	US$34,400	US$107,600
Comments	Per year	Total programme
Accommodation costs (on campus, per year)	US$9,000	–
Accommodation costs (off campus, per year)	US$9,000	–
Financial aid available	US$3,547,600	–
Type of aid available	Merit scholarships, loans	–
Criteria on which aid is granted	Credit or financial need	–

Accreditation

AACSB International

Application details

	Full-time MBA	Executive MBA Program
Application deadline	March 15th	–
Programme dates	Aug start, 20 months	Jul start, 22 months
Admission requirements	First degree; work experience; TOEFL if first language not English; 2 references; 4 essays; laptop; interview by invitation only	First degree; at least 7 years' work experience; 2 references; essay; interview

Executive education

Cornell makes much both of its action-learning approach to executive education and the "retreat-like" setting of the beautiful surrounding countryside. It offers a range of open-enrolment courses in leadership, finance and human resources as well as customised in-company programmes.

Student/alumni quotes

"The Johnson School is the right school for you if you want to take advantage of Cornell University and its reputation as a premier Ivy League school. You have an opportunity to apply your business knowledge on research and technologies developed by different schools on campus."

"Location, at times, hurts for recruiting and guest speakers."

"It is an excellent school in a location that makes it easy to be effective. The faculty is very responsive and focused on our learning experience. The small number of people at the school makes it easy to get to know your classmates."

Cranfield School of Management

Address
Cranfield School of
Management
Cranfield
Bedford
UK
MK43 0AL

Tel:
+44 1234 754 386

Fax:
+44 1234 752 439

E-mail:
mbaadmissions@
cranfield.ac.uk

Website:
www.cranfield.ac.uk/
som/mba

Programme director:
Dr Pauline Weight

Figures in brackets
represent rank

Ranking	Rank (out of 100) Full-time
Overall rank	20
Regional rank	9

Criteria	Rank (out of 100) Full-time
Open new career opportunities	**72**
Diversity of recruiters	47
Number in jobs three months after graduation	86
Jobs found through the careers service	72
Student assessment of careers service	53
Personal development and educational experience	**16**
Faculty quality	86
Student quality	5
Student diversity	55
Education experience	4
Increase in salary	**16**
Increase in salary	43
Post-MBA salary	15
Potential to network	**14**
Breadth of alumni network	29
Internationalism of alumni	19
Alumni effectiveness	13

Background

Cranfield is one of the UK's longest-established business schools with a strong international orienta-tion. It has close links with companies, other schools and geographic regions. There is a strong emphasis on executive education and the school has research expertise in areas such as marketing strategy, change management and international human resources.

Facilities

The school occupies nine buildings with 29 teaching rooms. There are also 32 syndicate areas reserved for individual learning teams and a fully equipped TV recording studio that is used for the personal skills core courses and for project work. The main library is a three-minute walk away. The school's information centre is computer-based and there are good computer facilities for students. There is plenty of accommodation available on the sprawling campus, but many students live off cam-pus in the surrounding villages, where housing is easy to find and reasonably priced. Because the campus is isolated a car is almost essential.

	Full-time MBA
Student assessment of facilities	4.3 (29)

Faculty

Number of faculty: 81 full-time, 3 part-time, 117 visiting		
	Full-time MBA	Executive Part Time MBA Programme
Number of faculty per student	0.8 (27)	5.6
Percentage of faculty with PhD	58 (>100)	58
Student rating of faculty	4.3 (52)	–

The directory
Cranfield School of Management

Strengths and weaknesses
Strengths: entrepreneurship; finance; strategy

Weaknesses: remote location

Programme highlights
Cranfield's one-year full-time MBA consists of four taught terms rather than the more usual (in the UK) three. The first and second terms are devoted to core courses and the third and fourth terms to electives, projects (both in the UK and abroad) and capstone courses. The programme is intensive, especially in the first two terms. Some students may be required to attend pre-programme training in mathematics or English language and business culture.

The school's elective programme, with over 70 subjects, is one of the largest in Europe. Students choose around 12, either across a broad range or to form a specialisation. During the third and fourth terms students can exchange with European and other schools. They can also study a foreign language at various levels (training is offered in French, German, Spanish and Russian).

The part-time Executive MBA lasts two years, beginning in January and ending in November of the following year. The programme is virtually identical to the full-time version. Participants attend classes at Cranfield for 16 weekends (all day Friday and Saturday) and four one-week residential periods each year. Individual study is also required during the periods between residential weekends. An additional week is spent on an international study tour to China, Japan, Russia or the US. Participants are given a laptop computer for the duration of the programme and Lotus Notes software to allow communication with Cranfield and other students when working away from the school.

The two-year Executive Modular MBA programme combines on-campus sessions with off-campus distance learning. There are eight two-week blocks at Cranfield. Between modules students spend approximately two weeks in individual study, spread over the break, backed up by interactive learning sessions on the Internet and contact with Cranfield faculty. An in-company project runs throughout the programme and there is a week-long international study tour. The programme starts with an orientation weekend.

Cranfield also offers a double MBA programme with E.M. Lyon and a Public Sector MBA in association with the Civil Service College in full-time, part-time and modular versions.

	Full-time MBA	Executive Part Time MBA Programme
Student rating of programme	4.5 (12)	–
Number of overseas exchange programmes	136 (4)	–
Number of languages on offer	4 (50)	–

Students

	Full-time MBA	Executive Part Time MBA Programme
Annual intake	136	36
Applicants:places	3:1	2:1
Percentage of women students	16 (>100)	22
Percentage of foreign students	66 (46)	n/a
Average GMAT score	670 (41)	670
Average number of months' work experience	96 (7)	132
Age range of students	27-36	29-41
Average age	32	34
Student rating of culture and classmates	4.6 (14)	–

Student profile (full time)

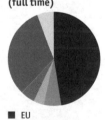

- ■ EU
- ■ Non-EU Europe
- ■ North America
- ■ Other Americas
- ■ Asia/Australasia
- ▨ Middle East

Recruiters/careers service

	Full-time MBA	Executive Part Time MBA Programme
Number of industry sectors that recruited graduates	7 (47)	–
Percentage of graduates in jobs 3 months after graduation	64 (86)	–
Percentage of graduates finding jobs through careers services	25 (72)	–
Student rating of careers service	3.1 (53)	–
Post-MBA salary, US$	91,803 (15)	–
Percentage increase in salary	44 (43)	–
Principal recruiters of graduates	Johnson & Johnson, Eli Lilly, GE Capital	

Cost

	Full-time MBA	Executive Part Time MBA Programme
Application fees	£75 (US$123)	£75 (US$123)
Programme fees	£25,000 (US$40,984)	£16,000 (US$26,230)
Comments	Total tuition	Per year
Accommodation costs (on campus, per year)	£4,000 (US$6,557)	–
Accommodation costs (off campus, per year)	£8,500 (US$13,934)	–
Financial aid available	£350,000 (US$573,770)	–
Type of aid available	Scholarships	–
Criteria on which aid is granted	Merit, financial need	–

Accreditation

AACSB International, AMBA, EQUIS

Application details

	Full-time MBA	Executive Part Time MBA Programme
Application deadline	September 1st	January 1st
Programme dates	Sep start, 12 months	Jan start, 24 months
Admission requirements	First degree (2.2 UK degree or overseas equivalent); at least 3 years' work experience; GMAT; TOEFL or IELTS if first language not English; 2 references; 4 essays; interview; laptop	First degree (2.2 UK degree or overseas equivalent); at least 3 years' work experience; GMAT; TOEFL or IELTS if first language not English; 2 references; 4 essays; interview

Executive education

Cranfield offers an extensive portfolio of executive education courses, including four flagship general management courses, and short courses in areas such as change management, corporate governance, supply chain management, customer service management, and soft skills and personal development. It also runs a centre for customised executive development that develops and runs customised in-company courses.

Student/alumni quotes

"Cranfield goes for slightly older students from the norm—the average age was 33 when I was there—and this gives you a very interesting mix of business and life experiences in the student body. In any MBA programme you learn as much from others as you do from the faculty, so this made it all the more rewarding. It's a great place for those with an entrepreneurial bent."

"Its location is very isolated."

"Excellent learning environment and process; varied knowledge of other students contributes greatly to classroom discussion."

Curtin University Graduate School of Business

Ranking	Rank (out of 100) Full-time
Overall rank	n/a
Regional rank	n/a

Background

Curtin University Graduate School of Business is one of seven schools that make up Curtin Business School. It has close links with business and industry, a good national brand name and a strong focus on Asian issues. As well as academic faculty, the school uses many senior executives as adjunct professors and teaching fellows.

Facilities

Curtin GSB is based in a refurbished 100-year-old building in the centre of Perth, formerly the government printing office. The facilities are especially designed for graduate students. Perth is hard to beat as a place in which to take an MBA. The climate is similar to that of southern California, the city is clean and the cost of living is low. Perth has superb food and wine and is near some of the loveliest beaches in the world. It also provides easier access to some of Asia's most thriving economies than many commercial centres on Australia's eastern seaboard.

	Full-time MBA
Student assessment of facilities	n/a

Faculty

28 full-time, 49 part-time, 8 visiting

	Full-time MBA	MBA (part time)	MBA (distance learning)	Executive MBA
Number of faculty per student	2.7	0.1	0.1	3.9
Percentage of faculty with PhD	80	80	80	80
Student rating of faculty	n/a	–	–	–

Strengths and weaknesses

Strengths: leadership; international business; scenario planning/decision science

Programme highlights

The Curtin MBA is offered in identical full-time and part-time options with the option to complete some courses via distance learning. The minimum time required to complete the basic MBA is 12 months full-time or two years part-time (including summer programmes), although taking a specialisation will add more time (an additional trimester full-time, or the equivalent part-time).

There are different tracks for students with an undergraduate business degree and those without. Before graduation students must also complete two non-core modules: critical and creative thinking, which includes an orientation retreat and a business speakers series, and business application, a series of in-company projects.

The Executive MBA is delivered via seven weekend modules and four one-week residential modules (including a South-east Asia study tour). All students must be sponsored by their employers.

Curtin also offers specialised MBAs in co-operation with CPA (certified practising accountant) Australia and Singapore Airlines.

	Full-time MBA	MBA (part time)	MBA (distance learning)	Executive MBA
Student rating of programme	n/a	–	–	–
Number of overseas exchange programmes	0	–	–	–
Number of languages on offer	1	–	–	–

Address
78 Murray Street
Perth, WA
Australia
6000

Tel:
+61 89 266 4184

Fax:
+61 89 266 3368

E-mail:
enquiries@gsb.curtin.edu.au

Website:
www.curtin.edu.au/gsb

Programme director:
Dr Robert Evans

Figures in brackets represent rank

Student profile (full time)

- ■ EU
- ■ Non-EU Europe
- ■ North America
- ■ Other Americas
- ■ Asia/Australasia
- ▦ Middle East

Students

	Full-time MBA	MBA (part time)	MBA (distance learning)	Executive MBA
Annual intake	20	370	450	14
Applicants:places	1:1	n/a	n/a	n/a
Percentage of women students	10	35	35	10
Percentage of foreign students	12	n/a	n/a	n/a
Average GMAT score	610	610	610	578
Average number of months' work experience	108	132	108	168
Age range of students	26-48	26-60	25-52	33-44
Average age	33	36	33	38
Student rating of culture and classmates	n/a	–	–	–

Recruiters/careers service

	Full-time MBA	MBA (part time)	MBA (distance learning)	Executive MBA
Number of industry sectors that recruited graduates	7	–	–	–
Percentage of graduates in jobs 3 months after graduation	86	–	–	–
Percentage of graduates finding jobs through careers services	25	–	–	–
Student rating of careers service	n/a	–	–	–
Post-MBA salary, US$	93,500	–	–	–
Percentage increase in salary	49	–	–	–
Principal recruiters of graduates	Rio Tinto, Australia Post, Telstra			

Cost

	Full-time MBA	MBA (part time)	MBA (distance learning)	Executive MBA
Application fees	A$50 (US$32) for non-Australians	None	None	None
Programme fees	A$32,000 (US$20,779)	A$32,000 (US$20,779)	$24,000 (US$15,584)	A$42,000 (US$27,273)
Comments	Fee for Australian residents is A$24,000	Fee for Australian residents is A$24,000		Includes all costs
Accommodation costs (on campus, per year)	A$5,250 (US$3,409)	–	–	–
Accommodation costs (off campus, per year)	A$10,000 (US$6,494)	–	–	–
Financial aid available	A$125,000 (US$81,169)	–	–	–
Type of aid available	Scholarships	–	–	–
Criteria on which aid is granted	Merit, international aid, Australian citizen	–	–	–

Accreditation

AMBA, EQUIS

The directory
Curtin University Graduate School of Business

Application details

	Full-time MBA	MBA (part time)	MBA (distance learning)	Executive MBA
Application deadline	December 17th	December 17th	December 17th	June 30th
Programme dates	Jan start, 12 months	Jan start, 12 months	Feb start, 12 months	Jul start, 15 months
Admission requirements	First degree; at least 3 years' work experience; GMAT; TOEFL, IELTS or CUTE if first language not English; 2 references; interview; laptop	First degree; at least 3 years' work experience; GMAT; TOEFL, IELTS or CUTE if first language not English; 2 references; interview; laptop	First degree; at least 3 years' work experience; GMAT; TOEFL, IELTS or CUTE if first language not English; 2 references; interview; laptop	At least 10 years' work experience; TOEFL if first language not English; reference; interview

Executive education

Curtin offers short open-entry (despite the name) graduate certificate courses, allowing participants to gain a qualification in a particular area. These are completed in one semester (or longer if needed) of evening classes.

Dartmouth College—Tuck School of Business

Address
100 Tuck Hall
Hanover, NH
US
03755

Tel:
+1 603 646 2733

Fax:
+1 603 646 1308

E-mail:
tuck.admissions@
dartmouth.edu

Website:
www.tuck.dartmouth.
edu

Programme director:
Paul Danos

Figures in brackets
represent rank

Ranking	Rank (out of 100) Full-time
Overall rank	3
Regional rank	3

Criteria	Rank (out of 100) Full-time
Open new career opportunities	**2**
Diversity of recruiters	1
Number in jobs three months after graduation	47
Jobs found through the careers service	4
Student assessment of careers service	9
Personal development and educational experience	**5**
Faculty quality	28
Student quality	22
Student diversity	34
Education experience	1
Increase in salary	**20**
Increase in salary	70
Post-MBA salary	13
Potential to network	**21**
Breadth of alumni network	68
Internationalism of alumni	66
Alumni effectiveness	1

Background

Tuck School of Business, part of the prestigious Dartmouth College, is the oldest graduate school of business in the world (founded in 1900). It offers only one degree programme, the full-time MBA, and claims this gives it added focus. The school is noted for general management, teamwork, close student–faculty relations and the Tuck "experience" of a small residential programme in a beautiful, semi-rural setting.

Almost all work is done in assigned teams and the ability to succeed in collaborative working is essential. Faculty members try hard to be accessible to students. This is backed up by students, who comment on Tuck's community spirit and, given the school's fairly remote location, the excellent job done by the careers service.

Facilities

The school consists of eight interconnected buildings combining traditional Georgian and modern architecture on a 13-acre site on the western edge of the Dartmouth campus. There are over 7,000 alumni, who are involved and helpful. Paul Danos, only the ninth dean in the school's long history, has invested heavily in faculty hiring, technology and building, and the facilities are excellent.

Most first-year students live on campus, further heightening the collegiate atmosphere. Whittemore Hall, a fairly new residence, includes lodgings for students and executives, study rooms, conference rooms, a gym and a distance-learning suite. There are approximately 75 public-access computers throughout the Tuck complex in the computer labs, study rooms and library.

Hanover is a tiny college town, about two hours' drive from Boston, in a beautiful country setting in New Hampshire. Despite its remoteness, Tuck has no difficulty in attracting recruiters and all the major organisations are represented on campus.

The directory
Dartmouth College—Tuck School of Business

	Full-time MBA
Student assessment of facilities	4.7 (4)

Faculty

Number of faculty: 47 full-time, 13 part-time, 7 visiting

	Full-time MBA
Number of faculty per student	0.2 (>100)
Percentage of faculty with PhD	96 (34)
Student rating of faculty	4.6 (12)

Strengths and weaknesses

Strengths: general management; accounting; finance

Weaknesses: range of electives

Programme highlights

The first year of Tuck's two-year full-time programme concentrates on the traditional basics of the MBA curriculum, but students also take two electives during the year. The Tuck Leadership Forum, which runs throughout the first year, focuses on developing general management knowledge and skills through projects, speakers and course work. Tuck alumni are often involved in teaching. The first year is divided into four mini-semesters and most of the work is carried out in four- or five-person study groups. Second-year students study 12 electives (four per term) and there is an optional international field project. There is no requirement to select a major but students are free to group electives if they wish.

Tuck also runs the Bridge Program, a summer school from June to August, which gives young liberal arts, sciences and engineering students an introduction to global business. Students spend four weeks studying business with Tuck MBA faculty.

	Full-time MBA
Student rating of programme	4.5 (14)
Number of overseas exchange programmes	241 (4)
Number of languages on offer	>5 (44)

Students

	Full-time MBA
Annual intake	241
Applicants:places	10:1
Percentage of women students	28 (65)
Percentage of foreign students	32 (73)
Average GMAT score	697 (13)
Average number of months' work experience	60 (63)
Age range of students	25-31
Average age	28
Student rating of culture and classmates	4.8 (5)

Recruiters/careers service

	Full-time MBA
Number of industry sectors that recruited graduates	8 (1)
Percentage of graduates in jobs 3 months after graduation	84 (47)
Percentage of graduates finding jobs through careers services	82 (4)
Student rating of careers service	4.2 (9)
Post-MBA salary, US$	86,736 (13)
Percentage increase in salary	41 (70)
Principal recruiters of graduates	Lehman Brothers, UBS, Bain & Co

Student profile (full time)

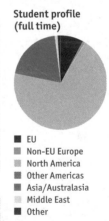

- ■ EU
- ▨ Non-EU Europe
- ▨ North America
- ■ Other Americas
- ■ Asia/Australasia
- ▨ Middle East
- ■ Other

Cost

	Full-time MBA
Application fees	US$190
Programme fees	US$36,390
Comments	Per year
Accommodation costs (on campus, per year)	US$7,500
Accommodation costs (off campus, per year)	US$9,000
Financial aid available	Varies
Type of aid available	Fellowships, loans, scholarships, work study
Criteria on which aid is granted	Merit, financial need

Accreditation

AACSB International

Application details

	Full-time MBA
Application deadline	April 19th
Programme dates	Aug start, 21 months
Admission requirements	Bachelor's degree or equivalent; TOEFL if first language not English; 2 references; 3 essays; interview; laptop

Executive education

Tuck offers a range of open-enrolment executive education programmes, including its three-week flagship Executive Program and specialised programmes in areas such as finance, and programmes for leaders of minority business. It also works with companies on customised programmes.

Student/alumni quotes

"Tuck will not admit you unless it is convinced you are a 'fit' with its programme. Regardless of your scores or background, if they think you aren't a fit you won't be admitted. Think about it: Tuck is buried in the New England forests and you will interact with other Tuckies 24/7. A bad fit is disastrous for both the school and the student."

"It's tough to specialise since it is a true generalist curriculum."

"It's the UN business school. You get the prestige, instruction, practice and access to world-class faculty, resources and alums without the snotty MBA attitude. The people here are accomplished yet grounded—that's true for both students and faculty."

University of Dublin—Trinity College— School of Business Studies

Ranking	Rank (out of 100) Full-time
Overall rank	n/a
Regional rank	44

Address
School of Business
Studies
Trinity College
College Green
Dublin 2
Ireland

Tel:
+353 1 608 2696

Fax:
+353 1 679 9503

E-mail:
trinitymba@tcd.ie

Website:
www.tcd.ie/Business–
Studies/MBA/

Programme director:
John Quilliam

Figures in brackets
represent rank

Background

The Trinity MBA is one of the oldest in Europe (it started in 1964) and Trinity College is one of Europe's oldest universities, founded by Elizabeth I. Illustrious alumni have included Jonathan Swift, Oliver Goldsmith, Oscar Wilde and Samuel Beckett.

The School of Business Studies, which teaches undergraduate and other masters programmes, is part of the Department of Business Studies of the Faculty of Business, Economic and Social Studies. The school has its own staff and also draws faculty from the other departments, from the university in general and from among practising managers. It has good international links, particularly within the EU, and good links with Irish and international business.

Facilities

The school is based on the Trinity campus, a collection of ancient and modern buildings and grassy or cobbled courtyards in the centre of Dublin. The MBA programme has its own 40-seat classroom, eight syndicate rooms, a common area, an adjacent kitchen and offices. The syndicate rooms are equipped with computer facilities providing Internet access. Students can use all the university facilities, including general and specialised databases. The college will advise on accommodation.

	Full-time MBA
Student assessment of facilities	3.8 (n/a)

Faculty

Number of faculty: 25 full-time, 2 part-time, 3 visiting

	Full-time MBA
Number of faculty per student	1.1 (n/a)
Percentage of faculty with PhD	96 (n/a)
Student rating of faculty	3.6 (n/a)

Strengths and weaknesses

Strengths: strategic management; international business; non-profit enterprises

Weaknesses: careers services; finance and accounting classes

Programme highlights

Trinity's one-year MBA programme has a tradition of personalised, tutorial-style learning and the class size (30–40 students) is deliberately kept small. In the second half of the programme students meet practising executives (and government ministers) in a series of seminars focusing on change management.

The programme is divided into five modules with typical core courses and more broadly based courses taught across most of them. Each module is deliberately linked to one of the stages of a team (5–6 students) in-company project that is the centrepiece of the programme and is worked on throughout most of the year. At each project stage the team must produce oral and written reports. Students also work on an individual research essay.

	Full-time MBA
Student rating of programme	3.5 (n/a)
Number of overseas exchange programmes	0 (n/a)
Number of languages on offer	0 (n/a)

Student profile (full time)

■ EU
■ Non-EU Europe
  North America
■ Other Americas
■ Asia/Australasia
  Middle East

Students

	Full-time MBA
Annual intake	26
Applicants:places	4:1
Percentage of women students	22 (n/a)
Percentage of foreign students	60 (n/a)
Average GMAT score	630 (n/a)
Average number of months' work experience	84 (n/a)
Age range of students	28-40
Average age	31
Student rating of culture and classmates	4.2 (n/a)

Recruiters/careers service

	Full-time MBA
Number of industry sectors that recruited graduates	4 (n/a)
Percentage of graduates in jobs 3 months after graduation	57 (n/a)
Percentage of graduates finding jobs through careers services	7 (n/a)
Student rating of careers service	2.4 (n/a)
Post-MBA salary, US$	90,909 (n/a)
Percentage increase in salary	33 (n/a)
Principal recruiters of graduates	n/a

Cost

	Full-time MBA
Application fees	€35 (US$40)
Programme fees	€20,500 (US$23,295)
Comments	–
Accommodation costs (on campus, per year)	€6,500 (US$7,386)
Accommodation costs (off campus, per year)	€9,000 (US$10,227)
Financial aid available	€30,000 (US$34,091)
Type of aid available	Scholarship
Criteria on which aid is granted	Exceptional and deserving Irish students

Accreditation

AMBA

Application details

	Full-time MBA
Application deadline	June 30th (late applications are considered)
Programme dates	Sep start, 11 months
Admission requirements	First degree (experienced non degree candidates can be considered); at least 3 years' work experience; GMAT; TOEFL if first language not English; 2 references; 2 essays

The directory
University of Dublin—Trinity College—School of Business Studies

Executive education

Trinity does not offer short executive courses. It does, however, run five master's (MSc) programmes for practising executives on a part-time basis (a two-day block release schedule over two years). The subjects offered are management practice, organisational behaviour, public-sector management, business administration and international business.

Student/alumni quotes

"The small class size and personal attention made this programme the best choice for me. This programme is especially good for the MBA student with a good deal of professional experience who's interested in personal growth and perhaps a bit averse to the perception of a 'typical MBA programme'."

"We should be put under more pressure to perform, some of the lecturers are too easy and 'academic' with us."

"The Trinity MBA is a boutique, intimate, one-year, intensive MBA course. The highlight of the programme is the company project, which is a wonderful consulting experience within an assigned company/industry."

Duke University—Fuqua School of Business

Address
1 Towerview Drive
Box 90120
Durham NC
US
27708

Tel:
+1 919 660 2923

Fax:
+1 919 660 2949

E-mail:
admissions-info@fuqua.duke.edu

Website:
www.fuqua.duke.edu

Programme director:
Liz Riley

Figures in brackets
represent rank

Ranking	Rank (out of 100) Full-time
Overall rank	13
Regional rank	11

Criteria	Rank (out of 100) Full-time
Open new career opportunities	**11**
Diversity of recruiters	1
Number in jobs three months after graduation	54
Jobs found through the careers service	26
Student assessment of careers service	12
Personal development and educational experience	**23**
Faculty quality	46
Student quality	8
Student diversity	32
Education experience	56
Increase in salary	**19**
Increase in salary	42
Post-MBA salary	19
Potential to network	**49**
Breadth of alumni network	96
Internationalism of alumni	81
Alumni effectiveness	22

Background

Fuqua School of Business, founded in 1970, began to emerge as a powerhouse in the 1980s after the first of a series of gifts from J B Fuqua, an Atlanta industrialist and philanthropist. (The name is pronounced few-qua, not foo-qua.) The school stresses collaboration and no single teaching method predominates, but there is an emphasis on functional skills and personal effectiveness through soft skills workshops and projects.

From an initial 12 students in 1970, Fuqua now has over 1,300 students on MBA programmes as well as a strong executive education arm. The school has embraced the use of technology in teaching and, like some other leading US schools, has set up satellite campuses abroad (for example, the Fuqua School of Business in Europe in Frankfurt, Germany). It has close links with business, benefiting from its base in the Raleigh–Durham–Chapel Hill triangle, which is a cluster of universities and high-tech businesses.

Facilities

Facilities are excellent. Nestling in a wooded area on the edge of Duke University's neo-Gothic campus, and linked to the executive education centre, the school's surroundings are idyllic. The Keller Center's 40,000 sq ft east wing houses the MBA programme with classrooms, seminar rooms and small rooms for group study. The building also contains the placement and faculty offices, a student lounge, two computer labs, a snack bar and the library. More faculty and other offices are located in the west wing.

	Full-time MBA
Student assessment of facilities	4.6 (7)

The directory
Duke University—Fuqua School of Business

Faculty

Number of faculty: 109 full-time, 0 part-time, 17 visiting

	Full-time MBA
Number of faculty per student	0.3 (104)
Percentage of faculty with PhD	91 (35)
Student rating of faculty	4.5 (26)

Strengths and weaknesses

Strengths: marketing; management; finance

Weakness: lack of quantitative input

Programme highlights

Duke's two-year full-time MBA combines a first year of largely required core courses followed by a second year of electives that can be either broadly based or concentrated into career paths. An individual effectiveness course covering communication, computing and career-planning runs throughout the first year. Formal concentrations are not required. The programme includes two integrative learning experiences (ILEs) designed to supplement traditional classroom learning. There is also an international business requirement, which can be met by a variety of elective courses. Courses are taught in long, two-and-a-quarter-hour classes that meet twice weekly during seven-week terms. First-year classes are divided into sections and further into small study groups.

The Duke MBA–Weekend is a cross between an executive MBA and a regular part-time programme. Students spend two weekends each month on campus and there is close liaison with their current jobs, a lot of projects being carried out in their own companies. There are also week-long residencies at Fuqua throughout the 20-month programme.

The Duke MBA–Global Executive is a 19-month programme with two- to three-week residencies in North America, Europe, Asia and South America. Between these sessions, students work via distance-learning technology that complements and extends the classroom experience. The programme is divided into five modules with three courses per module, involving 11 weeks of residential education on four continents and 50 weeks of distance learning.

The 20-month Duke MBA–Cross Continent is a variation on the Global Executive programme, using on-campus residencies and distance learning. Students complete 11 core courses, four elective courses and one integrative capstone course to earn their MBA degree. They attend nine weeks of residential sessions (eight one-week sessions and one week of orientation), six in North Carolina, one in Europe (residence three) and one in Asia (residence seven). During non-residential periods they spend 20 hours a week continuing their studies online using Internet-enabled learning.

	Full-time MBA
Student rating of programme	4.2 (40)
Number of overseas exchange programmes	112 (61)
Number of languages on offer	0 (94)

Students

	Full-time MBA
Annual intake	405
Applicants:places	8:1
Percentage of women students	31 (42)
Percentage of foreign students	36 (75)
Average GMAT score	705 (9)
Average number of months' work experience	68 (53)
Age range of students	27-33
Average age	28
Student rating of culture and classmates	4.6 (11)

**Student profile
(full time)**

- ■ EU
- ■ Non-EU Europe
- ▨ North America
- ■ Other Americas
- ■ Asia/Australasia
- ▨ Middle East

Recruiters/careers service

	Full-time MBA
Number of industry sectors that recruited graduates	8 (1)
Percentage of graduates in jobs 3 months after graduation	76 (54)
Percentage of graduates finding jobs through careers services	62 (25)
Student rating of careers service	3.7 (12)
Post-MBA salary, US$	85,000 (19)
Percentage increase in salary	44 (42)
Principal recruiters of graduates	Johnson & Johnson, IBM, Citigroup, Deloitte

Cost

	Full-time MBA
Application fees	US$175
Programme fees	US$33,500
Comments	Per year
Accommodation costs (on campus, per year)	–
Accommodation costs (off campus, per year)	US$4,700
Financial aid available	US$24,756,161
Type of aid available	Scholarships, loans
Criteria on which aid is granted	Merit, financial need

Accreditation

AACSB International

Application details

	Full-time MBA
Application deadline	March 15th
Programme dates	Aug start, 22 months
Admission requirements	Bachelor's degree or equivalent; at least 5 years' work experience; TOEFL if first language not English; 2 references; 3 essays; interview strongly recommended

Executive education

Fuqua runs a flagship Advanced Management Program and specialised programmes in business improvisation, financial reporting for non-financial managers, innovative leadership and managing customer value. Customised versions are available for individual companies.

Student/alumni quotes

"Fuqua's atmosphere is co-operative. I found that the workload was very heavy but appropriate to prepare me for my next career move. Fuqua's short terms can be intense but everyone survives and learns."

"A+ professors, but many of them are academic-oriented and relatively new in their field. Would like more instruction from the business community."

"Excellent two-year experience that I feel can't be matched by any other programme. Very responsive administration and superior classmates."

University of Durham—Durham Business School

Ranking	Rank (out of 100) Full-time
Overall rank	78
Regional rank	28

Criteria	Rank (out of 100) Full-time
Open new career opportunities	**95**
Diversity of recruiters	59
Number in jobs three months after graduation	23
Jobs found through the careers service	97
Student assessment of careers service	>100
Personal development and educational experience	**33**
Faculty quality	95
Student quality	3
Student diversity	27
Education experience	79
Increase in salary	**47**
Increase in salary	15
Post-MBA salary	70
Potential to network	**89**
Breadth of alumni network	55
Internationalism of alumni	43
Alumni effectiveness	93

Address
University of Durham
Mill Hill Lane
Durham City
UK
DH1 3LB

Tel:
+44 191 334 5265

Fax:
+44 191 334 5218

E-mail:
pg.bus@durham.ac.uk

Website:
www.dur.ac.uk/dbs

Programme director:
Dr Alan Jessop

Figures in brackets
represent rank

Background

Durham Business School, founded in 1965, has recently been restructured, absorbing Durham University's School of Economics and Finance and the Foundation for SME development, building on its strength in this area. Although still known as Durham Business School, it is now formally the School of Economics, Finance and Business and teaches business, economics and finance education at undergraduate, postgraduate and doctoral levels.

Facilities

Postgraduate business education including MBAs and specialist masters are offered at Mill Hill Lane campus, a dedicated site about a 20-minute walk from the centre of Durham. The town itself is over a thousand years old and has some of the most exceptional architectural and historical features in the UK.

The business school has its own library and there is 24-hour access to computer facilities. There are also 22 newly furnished syndicate rooms for study and discussion. Durham University (founded in 1832 and one of the oldest in the UK) operates a system of largely self-governing colleges to which all students, including graduates, must belong.

	Full-time MBA
Student assessment of facilities	4.0 (66)

Faculty

Number of faculty: 44 full-time, 2 part-time, 51 visiting

	Full-time MBA	Durham Distance Learning MBA	Durham Part-Time MBA
Number of faculty per student	0.9 (47)	0.1	2.2
Percentage of faculty with PhD	89 (75)	89	89
Student rating of faculty	3.7 (>100)	–	–

Strengths and weaknesses

Strengths: finance; entrepreneurship; strategy

Weaknesses: careers services

Programme highlights

The Durham full-time MBA programme groups core courses into five themed areas (managing people; managing information; managing in the competitive environment; managing finance; managing in the global context) and methods of inquiry (in preparation for the project and dissertation). Students choose six electives in the second term from about 20 offered, which can be grouped into a specialisation or taken across a broad area. The individual in company project, which requires a dissertation of 15,000 words, is undertaken in June–September. Managerial skills and personal development are strongly emphasised, both in the intensive pre-programme induction session and in an off-campus outdoor development course and various skills workshops. The guest-speaker series brings together students and leading authorities to discuss current business, political and economic issues.

The school has an exchange agreement with the China Europe Business School (CEIBS) in Shanghai (see page 180). It also offers language training in Arabic, French, German, Mandarin and Spanish.

In September 2004 Durham launched a specialised MBA in finance. Students follow the same core, but in the elective period they study three compulsory modules (corporate finance; financial planning and control; financial risk management) and three general electives from a selection. They also undertake a business finance project and dissertation.

Durham's two-year part-time MBA is virtually identical to the full-time programme. Students study the same foundation core subjects and electives, and undertake a project and dissertation. They can also voluntarily attend pre-programme workshops in quantitative and communications skills, the outdoor development course and other activities offered on the full-time programme. Classes meet all day Friday and Saturday every two or three weeks. The school advises that students will need to study for a further 12 hours a week.

The distance-learning MBA is similar in content to the full-time and part-time programmes and leads to same degree. Most of the course material is in written form, supplemented by CD-ROM and web-based material. Every student is allocated a tutor for each subject with whom communication can be by post, telephone, fax or e-mail. There are opportunities for contact among students in the same geographical area. Formal assessment is carried out at each stage and consists of written assignments and/or examinations, which can be taken at approved centres virtually anywhere in the world.

Durham also offers a part-time MBA in the Caribbean region in collaboration with Ernst & Young.

	Full-time MBA	Durham Distance Learning MBA	Durham Part-Time MBA
Student rating of programme	3.7 (94)	–	–
Number of overseas exchange programmes	4 (81)	–	–
Number of languages on offer	>5 (40)	–	–

The directory
University of Durham—Durham Business School

Students

	Full-time MBA	Durham Distance Learning MBA	Durham Part-Time MBA
Annual intake	67	190	45
Applicants:places	10:1	n/a	2:1
Percentage of women students	36 (23)	24	29
Percentage of foreign students	81 (27)	53	n/a
Average GMAT score	600 (91)	n/a	n/a
Average number of months' work experience	108 (4)	156	168
Age range of students	25-38	27-43	28-42
Average age	30	34	35
Student rating of culture and classmates	3.8 (87)	–	–

Student profile (full time)

- ■ EU
- ▨ Non-EU Europe
- ▨ North America
- ■ Other Americas
- ■ Asia/Australasia
- ▨ Middle East

Recruiters/careers service

	Full-time MBA	Durham Distance Learning MBA	Durham Part-Time MBA
Number of industry sectors that recruited graduates	8 (59)	–	–
Percentage of graduates in jobs 3 months after graduation	83 (23)	–	–
Percentage of graduates finding jobs through careers services	4 (97)	–	–
Student rating of careers service	2.6 (>100)	–	–
Post-MBA salary, US$	73,643 (70)	–	–
Percentage increase in salary	97 (15)	–	–
Principal recruiters of graduates	Shell, American Express, National Health Service		

Cost

	Full-time MBA	Durham Distance Learning MBA	Durham Part-Time MBA
Application fees	None	None	None
Programme fees	£16,000 (US$26,230)	£8,800 (US$14,426)	£11,950 (US$19,590)
Comments	Total programme. Fee for non-EU students is £18,000.	Fee for non-EU students is £9,200	Fee for non-EU students is £11,950
Accommodation costs (on campus, per year)	£4,000 (US$6,557)	–	–
Accommodation costs (off campus, per year)	£4,000 (US$6,557)	–	–
Financial aid available	£100,000 (US$163,934)	–	–
Type of aid available	Directors Scholarship, Shell Scholarship, Chevening Scholarship	–	–
Criteria on which aid is granted	Academic and/or professional achievement	–	–

Accreditation

AMBA

Application details

	Full-time MBA	Durham Distance Learning MBA	Durham Part-Time MBA
Application deadline	August 31st	October 30th	December 31st
Programme dates	Sep start, 12 months	Jan start, 24–96 months	Jan start, 24 months
Admission requirements	First degree; at least 3 years' work experience; GMAT; TOEFL or IELTS if first language not English; 2 references; laptop; interview may be replaced by an essay in certain circumstances	First degree; at least 3 years' work experience; TOEFL if first language not English; 2 references	First degree; at least 3 years' work experience; TOEFL if first language not English; 2 references; interview

Executive education

Durham has a small portfolio of specialised open-enrolment courses and offers a wider range of customised in-company courses.

Student/alumni quotes

"The administration listened to us and vastly improved things; alumni support is rapidly improving and has the commitment it needs from the director. What still needs to improve is careers support."

"The single challenge of covering many aspects of business in one year can lead to doing too much in too little time—this may be read as a criticism of one-year MBAs in general."

"Wonderful city, very international student and teaching body, good facilities."

EADA (Escuela de Alta Dirección y Administración)

Ranking	Rank (out of 100) Full-time
Overall rank	n/a
Regional rank	45

Address
Arago 204
Barcelona
Spain
8011

Tel:
+34 93 452 0844

Fax:
+34 93 323 7317

E-mail:
admisiones@eada.edu

Website:
www.eada.edu

Background

Escuela de Alta Dirección y Administración (EADA) is a commercial operation formed in 1957 in Barcelona. It was originally a consultancy in business management and administration and then expanded into customised in-company training. In 1960 it started its first open training courses, and in 1981 it gave up consulting to concentrate exclusively on training. The organisation has good contacts with business and has built up a large international branch network covering most of the world, with a special emphasis on Latin America.

Programme director:
David Dinwoodie

Facilities

EADA is based in an eight-storey building in the centre of Barcelona. Facilities include 24 classrooms, an auditorium, a library, computer labs and meeting rooms, a cafeteria and a restaurant. EADA also has a residential training centre in Collbató, about 40 km from Barcelona, which includes 18 classrooms, two auditoriums, meeting rooms, a library, a restaurant and a swimming pool.

Figures in brackets
represent rank

	Full-time MBA
Student assessment of facilities	3.9 (n/a)

Faculty

Number of faculty: 22 full-time, 10 part-time, 18 visiting

	Full-time MBA
Number of faculty per student	0.3 (n/a)
Percentage of faculty with PhD	36 (n/a)
Student rating of faculty	4.1 (n/a)

Strengths and weaknesses

Strengths: strategic management; leadership and managerial skills; international management

Weaknesses: low international profile

Programme highlights

EADA's full-time one-year MBA is offered in Spanish or English. The programme starts with a one-week orientation and foundation session. Students then study the extensive core (14 courses) between October and May, a set of integrative courses in May and June, and electives in July. Throughout the programme there are three team projects—a marketing plan, a business plan and new business venture—and students complete a corporate business project.

The part-time two-year Executive MBA programme consists of 17 courses, an international study week and a project. Classes meet two evenings a week (Monday 6–10 pm and Friday 5–9 pm). There are also nine residential modules (usually two days) at EADA's Collbató training centre.

	Full-time MBA
Student rating of programme	4.3 (n/a)
Number of overseas exchange programmes	29 (n/a)
Number of languages on offer	2 (n/a)

Student profile
(full time)

- ■ EU
- ■ Non-EU Europe
- North America
- ■ Other Americas
- ■ Asia/Australasia
- Middle East

Students

	Full-time MBA
Annual intake	95
Applicants:places	5:1
Percentage of women students	35 (n/a)
Percentage of foreign students	79 (n/a)
Average GMAT score	550 (n/a)
Average number of months' work experience	48 (n/a)
Age range of students	23-38
Average age	27
Student rating of culture and classmates	4.1 (n/a)

Recruiters/careers service

	Full-time MBA
Number of industry sectors that recruited graduates	6 (n/a)
Percentage of graduates in jobs 3 months after graduation	54 (n/a)
Percentage of graduates finding jobs through careers services	25 (n/a)
Student rating of careers service	3.5 (n/a)
Post-MBA salary, US$	55,909 (n/a)
Percentage increase in salary	76 (n/a)
Principal recruiters of graduates	Schneider Electric, Dupont, Hewlett-Packard

Cost

	Full-time MBA
Application fees	None
Programme fees	€20,500 (US$23,295)
Comments	–
Accommodation costs (on campus, per year)	–
Accommodation costs (off campus, per year)	€4,400 (US$5,000)
Financial aid available	€23,500 (US$26,705)
Type of aid available	Scholarship
Criteria on which aid is granted	Merit

Accreditation

AMBA, EQUIS

Application details

	Full-time MBA
Application deadline	May 31st
Programme dates	Sep start, 11 months
Admission requirements	First degree; at least 3 years' work experience; GMAT; TOEFL (minimum score 250 computer based/600 paper based) or interview with director of the English Department if first language not English; 2 references; 4 essays; interview; laptop

EADA (Escuela de Alta Dirección y Administración)

Executive education

EADA offers a range of open-enrolment and customised in-company executive education programmes.

Student/alumni quotes

"Very good investment compared to what you get out of it; emphasis on people and teamworking skills; extensive use of real-world examples that help to acquire new insights on a daily basis."

"For what the school offers and the accreditations it has, it has rather low recognition outside Spain and Latin America; alumni network could be better."

"Excellent, dynamic MBA programme with an unparalleled cultural diversity and a unique focus on leadership education."

The University of Edinburgh Management School

Address
University of
Edinburgh
Management School
7 Bristo Square
Edinburgh
UK
EH8 9AL

Tel:
+44 131 650 8067

Fax:
+44 131 650 6501

E-mail:
Management.School
@ed.ac.uk

Website:
www.ems.ed.ac.uk

Programme director:
Philip Bowers

Figures in brackets
represent rank

Ranking	Rank (out of 100) Full-time
Overall rank	32
Regional rank	12

Criteria	Rank (out of 100) Full-time
Open new career opportunities	**68**
Diversity of recruiters	1
Number in jobs three months after graduation	24
Jobs found through the careers service	94
Student assessment of careers service	72
Personal development and educational experience	**29**
Faculty quality	91
Student quality	9
Student diversity	30
Education experience	35
Increase in salary	**5**
Increase in salary	5
Post-MBA salary	8
Potential to network	**61**
Breadth of alumni network	78
Internationalism of alumni	30
Alumni effectiveness	62

Background

The Management School is closely integrated with Edinburgh University, one of the oldest and most highly respected universities in the UK. It draws its teaching staff primarily from the departments of Business Studies and Accounting and Business Methods. The university first offered a business degree in 1918 and the MBA was introduced in 1978.

The student body is international with nearly 70% coming from outside the UK. Although not strictly requiring the GMAT, the school says the test is preferred and will help applications.

Facilities

The school has its own building in the middle of the university campus, close to the city centre, which is used exclusively by postgraduate management students, researchers and executive course participants. There are four lecture theatres, two computer labs, six syndicate rooms, a research access centre and other specialised facilities for MBA students. The building has secure 24-hour access, giving increased flexibility for independent learning. Students use the main university library, which is close by. The university has excellent sporting and cultural amenities and on-campus accommodation is available. Edinburgh offers a wide variety of cultural and leisure activities.

	Full-time MBA
Student assessment of facilities	4.2 (60)

The directory
The University of Edinburgh Management School

Faculty

Number of faculty: 71 full-time, 0 part-time, 54 visiting

	Full-time MBA	UEMS Part-time programme
Number of faculty per student	0.8 (39)	2.5
Percentage of faculty with PhD	85 (78)	85
Student rating of faculty	3.9 (92)	–

Strengths and weaknesses

Strengths: finance and business economics; entrepreneurship; technology and innovation

Weaknesses: careers services; marketing the MBA programme

Programme highlights

The Edinburgh MBA programme covers eight functional core subjects in the first term. The second and third terms consist of a required strategic management course (in both terms), five electives and either a study tour or the Lothian Project, a group consultancy with a local company. In the fourth term students complete a project and dissertation.

Electives (which vary from year to year) can be taken across a wide range or grouped into specialisations. Depending on which electives are chosen, they can be taken as regular courses, in one-week intensive modules or in the evenings. Soft skills and careers workshops run throughout the first three terms. The strategic management course is based on small-group analysis and presentation of case studies and business games.

Edinburgh also offers an International MBA, a 15-month programme identical to the full-time programme but with an extra term that includes exchanges with and study visits to ENPC in Paris and a work placement in a country other than the student's country of origin. All teaching is in English.

From 2004 the part-time MBA will have one intake in October each year. The programme starts with an induction programme (two evenings a week for two weeks) followed by four core courses, an integrative module at the end of the second semester and a further core course.

	Full-time MBA	UEMS Part-time programme
Student rating of programme	4.1 (61)	–
Number of overseas exchange programmes	20 (28)	–
Number of languages on offer	5 (36)	–

Students

	Full-time MBA	UEMS Part-time programme
Annual intake	100	50
Applicants:places	5:1	3:1
Percentage of women students	27 (63)	32
Percentage of foreign students	73 (34)	n/a
Average GMAT score	n/a (n/a)	n/a
Average number of months' work experience	96 (11)	118
Age range of students	26-37	27-41
Average age	31	32
Student rating of culture and classmates	4.3 (40)	–

Recruiters/careers service

	Full-time MBA	UEMS Part-time programme
Number of industry sectors that recruited graduates	8 (1)	–
Percentage of graduates in jobs 3 months after graduation	78 (24)	–
Percentage of graduates finding jobs through careers services	7 (94)	–
Student rating of careers service	3.3 (72)	–
Post-MBA salary, US$	86,721 (8)	–
Percentage increase in salary	59 (5)	–
Principal recruiters of graduates	KPMG, HBOS, Securities Commission	

Student profile (full time)

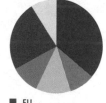

- ■ EU
- ■ Non-EU Europe
- North America
- ■ Other Americas
- ■ Asia/Australasia
- Middle East

Cost

	Full-time MBA	UEMS Part-time programme
Application fees	None	None
Programme fees	£21,400 (US$35,082)	£13,000 (US$21,311)
Comments	Total programme	Total programme
Accommodation costs (on campus, per year)	£3,614 (US$5,925)	–
Accommodation costs (off campus, per year)	£3,146 (US$5,157)	–
Financial aid available	None	–
Type of aid available	n/a	–
Criteria on which aid is granted	n/a	–

Accreditation

AMBA

Application details

	Full-time MBA	UEMS Part-time programme
Application deadline	July 31st	July 31st
Programme dates	Sep start, 12 months	Sep start, 30 months
Admission requirements	First degree; at least 4 years' work experience; TOEFL or IELTS if first language not English; 2 references; essay; applicants may be asked to attend an interview or a telephone interview may be conducted	First degree; at least 4 years' work experience; TOEFL or IELTS if first language not English; 2 references; essay; all applicants undertake an aptitude test, following this, they may be asked to attend an interview

Executive education

Edinburgh offers only customised in-company courses.

Student/alumni quotes

"Part-time students are well integrated with the full-time students, often sharing the same elective options. The class atmosphere is supportive rather than competitive. The dedicated building and library facilities for MBA students demonstrate the university's commitment to the programme."

"The school is one of the best management schools in Europe. However, it should devote more resources towards advertising the quality of its MBA programme in the international media."

Emory University—Goizueta Business School

Ranking	Rank (out of 100) Full-time
Overall rank	33
Regional rank	21

Criteria	Rank (out of 100) Full-time
Open new career opportunities	**31**
Diversity of recruiters	1
Number in jobs three months after graduation	46
Jobs found through the careers service	55
Student assessment of careers service	23
Personal development and educational experience	**44**
Faculty quality	58
Student quality	51
Student diversity	78
Education experience	10
Increase in salary	**74**
Increase in salary	75
Post-MBA salary	56
Potential to network	**46**
Breadth of alumni network	62
Internationalism of alumni	93
Alumni effectiveness	28

Address
1300 Clifton Road
Atlanta, GA
US
30322

Tel:
+1 404 727 8931

Fax:
+1 404 727 6313

E-mail:
Rosalyn–Robinson@
bus.emory.edu

Website:
www.goizueta.emory.
edu

Programme director:
Dr B Kembrel Jones

Figures in brackets
represent rank

Background

Goizueta Business School is a smallish school by US standards but it has big ambitions. These include continuing to hire faculty, establishing a PhD programme and planning a second building for faculty and classrooms. The school has close links with the local economy and the atmosphere is friendly, with an emphasis on local community service and volunteer action by students.

Facilities

The school is based on the main street of the Emory University campus and the facilities, which are shared with undergraduate business students, are excellent. They include an auditorium, an executive case classroom, eight case classrooms, four seminar rooms, three conference rooms and twelve breakout rooms. Most students live off campus, where rented apartments are easy to find and reasonably priced. Downtown Atlanta is only 15 minutes' drive away.

	Full-time MBA
Student assessment of facilities	4.8 (3)

Faculty

Number of faculty: 83 full-time, 13 part-time, 1 visiting

	Full-time MBA	Modular Executive MBA Program	Evening MBA Program	Weekend Executive MBA Program
Number of faculty per student	0.6 (77)	1.9	1.5	1.2
Percentage of faculty with PhD	93 (56)	93	93	93
Student rating of faculty	4.4 (34)	–	–	–

Strengths and weaknesses
Strengths: marketing; finance; organisation and management
Weaknesses: restricted elective choice

Programme highlights
Goizueta's two-year full-time MBA has a flexible curriculum, allowing students some choice in the sequence in which they take core courses during their first year (the so-called Flex/Core, which, says the school, allows students to begin looking at specific career tracks as early as their first semester). The programme begins with "lead weeks" at the start of each semester, which are followed by 12 weeks of traditional course work. In the two fall semesters the lead weeks involve students working in competitive teams. The two spring semesters are either overseas or domestic study tours or on-campus study.

Students take nine elective courses in the second year. These can be grouped into a specialisation or taken across a broad range, including some from other Emory schools; one elective must be in an international subject. The class size is small and the atmosphere is non-competitive.

An accelerated one-year track is available for students with a first degree in business or economics or a strong quantitative background, although some additional pre-programme courses may be required. Students in this option take summer courses and then join the regular second year of the programme.

The part-time evening MBA lasts three years, with three semesters each year. The programme is split in two: core courses are taken in the first 18 months and electives in the second 18 months. Classes meet two evenings a week. If their schedule permits, students may join daytime MBA courses.

Goizueta's Weekend Executive MBA lasts 16 months with classes held on alternate weekends (Fridays and Saturdays); a Thursday is sometimes added to this schedule. Participants will need to study for a further 25 hours a week. The programme ends with a ten-day international study tour.

The Modular Executive MBA has virtually the same curriculum as the Weekend programme. Students study over 20 months via a mix of distance learning and eight on-campus modules (one week per quarter, typically from Sunday lunchtime to Saturday afternoon) and a 10-day international module.

	Full-time MBA	Modular Executive MBA Program	Evening MBA Program	Weekend Executive MBA Program
Student rating of programme	4.3 (42)	–	–	–
Number of overseas exchange programmes	32 (58)	–	–	–
Number of languages on offer	>5 (1)	–	–	–

Student profile (full time)

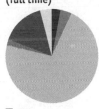

■ EU
■ Non-EU Europe
■ North America
■ Other Americas
■ Asia/Australasia
■ Middle East

Students

	Full-time MBA	Modular Executive MBA Program	Evening MBA Program	Weekend Executive MBA Program
Annual intake	157	35	66	80
Applicants:places	8:1	2:1	2:1	2:1
Percentage of women students	22 (99)	29	8	23
Percentage of foreign students	29 (93)	3	n/a	n/a
Average GMAT score	674 (27)	n/a	680	618
Average number of months' work experience	60 (63)	156	72	156
Age range of students	25-32	30-46	25-35	28-43
Average age	28	37	28	35
Student rating of culture and classmates	4.6 (20)	–	–	–

The directory
Emory University—Goizueta Business School

Recruiters/careers service

	Full-time MBA	Modular Executive MBA Program	Evening MBA Program	Weekend Executive MBA Program
Number of industry sectors that recruited graduates	8 (1)	–	–	–
Percentage of graduates in jobs 3 months after graduation	82 (46)	–	–	–
Percentage of graduates finding jobs through careers services	45 (55)	–	–	–
Student rating of careers service	4.0 (23)	–	–	–
Post-MBA salary, US$	75,068 (56)	–	–	–
Percentage increase in salary	34 (75)	–	–	–
Principal recruiters of graduates	Kimberly-Clark, Wachovia, IBM			

Cost

	Full-time MBA	Modular Executive MBA Program	Evening MBA Program	Weekend Executive MBA Program
Application fees	US$150	US$125	US$125	US$125
Programme fees	US$32,096	US$88,000	US$20,271	US$73,848
Comments	Per year; there is an additional US$422 per year payable for student activity, athletic and orientation	Total programme; includes all textbooks, materials, food, and lodging during residencies, and laptop computer	Per year	Includes all classes, fees, texts, materials, catered food during class sessions, and lodging on the international colloquium
Accommodation costs (on campus, per year)	US$9,750	–	–	–
Accommodation costs (off campus, per year)	US$15,000	–	–	–
Financial aid available	US$11,689,656	–	–	–
Type of aid available	Scholarships, loans	–	–	–
Criteria on which aid is granted	Merit, financial need	–	–	–

Accreditation

AACSB International

Application details

	Full-time MBA	Modular Executive MBA Program	Evening MBA Program	Weekend Executive MBA Program
Application deadline	March 15th	July 31st	March 15th	October 1st
Programme dates	Aug start, 21 months	Aug start, 20 months	Jul start, 36 months	Jan start, 16 months
Admission requirements	First degree (undergraduate transcripts required); at least 1 year's work experience; TOEFL if first language not English; 3 references; 3 essays; laptop; interviews are strongly recommended	First degree (exceptions will be made in the case of deserving candidates.); at least 7 years' work experience; TOEFL if first language not English (may be waived if functional in English); 2 references; 4 essays; interview (phone interviews on a case-by-case basis)	First degree; at least 6 years' work experience; TOEFL minimum if first language not English; 2 references; essays; interview	First degree (exceptions will be made in the case of deserving candidates); at least 7 years' work experience; TOEFL if first language not English (may be waived if functional in English); 2 references; 4 essays; interview (phone interviews on a case-by-case basis)

Executive education

Goizueta offers a three-week flag ship programme (the Goizueta Executive Program) as well as a range of open-enrolment programmes in management and leadership, finance and operations, and marketing. It also has a significant customised in-company training operation.

Student/alumni quotes

"The MBA at Goizueta is positively unique. The atmosphere is 'co-opetitive'. No words can explain the Goizueta School atmosphere. Like Roberto Goizueta, it has the Cuban party spirit with the Wall Street-like meanness."

"The biggest weakness in the curriculum is that several of the elective classes are not offered in each of the semesters, thus causing some scheduling difficulties."

"The school has excellent educators, a top-notch facility and programme directors who understand how to move the school up in the rankings."

ENPC School of International Management

Ranking	Rank (out of 100) Full-time
Overall rank	n/a
Regional rank	46

Background

ENPC School of International Management was founded in 1988 as part of the Ecole Nationale des Ponts et Chaussées (ENPC). This old and prestigious grande école was founded by a group of engineers in 1747 to train engineers to provide France with a reliable transport infrastructure. However, the school is less interested in bridges and roads than with training international business leaders for a global business environment.

The MBA programme is extremely flexible and very different from the traditional core-plus-electives model in that although there are constraints, students can choose the courses they wish to take (there is no core as such) from five "tracks". It is not suitable for those lacking maturity, so students need to be self-aware and confident about their aims. Work is done mainly in six-person teams designed to reflect a wide range of cultures, age and background.

The programme is strongly international, as are the student body and faculty. Most faculty are visiting (that is, part-time). They come from business schools in Europe, Asia and North America or are practising executives from the international corporate scene in France.

Facilities

The school is based in a 19th-century building in the Saint Germain des Prés district in the centre of Paris, an area of shops, cafés, restaurants and cultural monuments. MBA students have one main classroom with video/TV projectors, four study rooms, a bar/restaurant and an online library. They can also use other university facilities and classrooms and are full members of the école. There is no on-campus accommodation but the school helps students find housing.

	Full-time MBA
Student assessment of facilities	3.5 (n/a)

Faculty

Number of faculty: 7 full-time, 0 part-time, 31 visiting

	Full-time MBA	Part-Time MBA in International Business
Number of faculty per student	0.4 (n/a)	19.0
Percentage of faculty with PhD	71 (n/a)	71
Student rating of faculty	4.0 (n/a)	–

Strengths and weaknesses

Strengths: business development and new technologies; general management and entrepreneurship; individual and professional development

Weakness: low global profile

Programme highlights

The full-time programme takes 15 months to complete. Participants take courses from October to June and then undertake either a professional project (a four- to six-month internship in a company or research project) or specialised studies.

Students mainly work in assigned groups and take at least 18 full-credit courses chosen from about 45 full- and part-credit courses offered. These are grouped into five main study tracks: finance and accounting; economics and international business; marketing and strategy; management and leadership; and technology, innovation management and entrepreneurship (TIME). They must take a minimum of three full-credit courses in each track. The degree can be tailored as a specialisation in

Address
28 rue des Saints-Pères
Paris
France
75007

Tel:
+33 01 4458 2855

Fax:
+33 01 4015 9347

E-mail:
admissions@enpcmba
paris.com

Website:
www.enpcmbaparis.
com

Programme director:
Tawfik Jelassi

Figures in brackets
represent rank

TIME by taking extra courses in this track. Students also participate in some mandatory workshops and integration sessions designed to provide a common integrative experience for the entire class. There are also personal development workshops.

Because of the visiting faculty system, some courses may be taught as intensive modules, lasting one to two weeks. Others may be offered in the evening or on Saturdays to cater for part-time students. The taught courses last two semesters (September–July) and are followed by the project. The programme is taught entirely in English, but students are required to achieve a good knowledge of French before graduation.

Full-time and part-time MBA students work in tandem and share the same courses and schedule, which means that some courses are taught in the evening and also that part-time students can attend day-time classes if their schedule permits it. The part-time programme takes between 21 and 33 months to complete.

ENPC's 18-month Global Executive MBA is a rigorous general management programme with an emphasis on strategy and individual development. The entering class is limited to approximately 20 students. The programme starts in March and includes nine residential sessions (Monday–Saturday) in Paris and three international study trips. Each residential session covers two course topics. Between modules, participants keep in touch with faculty and other students via e-mail.

	Full-time MBA	Part-time MBA in International Business
Student rating of programme	4.1 (55)	–
Number of overseas exchange programmes	28 (19)	–
Number of languages on offer	1 (90)	–

Student profile (full time)

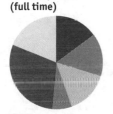

- ■ EU
- ■ Non-EU Europe
- ▨ North America
- ■ Other Americas
- ■ Asia/Australasia
- ▨ Middle East

Students

	Full-time MBA	Part-Time MBA in International Business
Annual intake	42	2
Applicants:places	4:1	1:1
Percentage of women students	38 (n/a)	50
Percentage of foreign students	64 (n/a)	n/a
Average GMAT score	600 (n/a)	600
Average number of months' work experience	72 (n/a)	72
Age range of students	22–43	29–32
Average age	30	30
Student rating of culture and classmates	3.7 (n/a)	–

Recruiters/careers service

	Full-time MBA	Part-Time MBA in International Business
Number of industry sectors that recruited graduates	7 (n/a)	–
Percentage of graduates in jobs 3 months after graduation	28 (n/a)	–
Percentage of graduates finding jobs through careers services	4 (n/a)	–
Student rating of careers service	2.9 (n/a)	–
Post-MBA salary, US$	54,811 (n/a)	–
Percentage increase in salary	28 (n/a)	
Principal recruiters of graduates	Bouygues Bâtiment International, GE Medical Systems, Agence Française du Developpement	

The directory
ENPC School of International Management

Cost

	Full-time MBA	Part-Time MBA in International Business
Application fees	€100 (US$114)	€100 (US$114)
Programme fees	€28,000 (US$31,818)	€34,000 (US$38,636)
Comments	Per year. Fee for company-sponsored students is €38 000	Fee for company-sponsored students is €42 000
Accommodation costs (on campus, per year)	–	–
Accommodation costs (off campus, per year)	€16,000 (US$18,182)	–
Financial aid available	Varies	–
Type of aid available	Partial tuition fee waivers	–
Criteria on which aid is granted	Merit, financial need	–

Accreditation

AMBA

Application details

	Full-time MBA	Part-Time MBA in International Business
Application deadline	August 15th	August 15th
Programme dates	Sep start, 15 months	Sep start, 27 months
Admission requirements	First degree; at least 3 years' work experience; GMAT; TOEFL, TOEIC, IELTS or Cambridge Certificate of Proficiency in English if first language not English; 3 references; 10 essays; interview; laptop; final project proposal	First degree; at least 3 years' work experience; GMAT; TOEFL, TOEIC, IELTS or Cambridge Certificate of Proficiency in English if first language not English; 3 references; 10 essays; interview; final project proposal

Executive Education

ENPC offers a customised MBA in co-operation with Edinburgh School of Management and KPMG.

Student/alumni quotes

"ENPC was one of the few schools that seemed actually to question the role of business in society; so many others appear to me to be management factories and little more than 'CV liner'. Above all, I was interested in the notion of visiting faculty and I liked the fact that the average age of the participants was 30 and not less. It meant that I would be exposed to many different ideas from my fellow participants."

"The school has such a good reputation in engineering that when recruiters come they search mainly for engineers."

"The faculty and the internationalism of the participants would be hard to beat."

ESADE Business School

Address
Av. Esplugues, 92-96
Barcelona
Spain
8034

Tel:
+34 93 280 6162

Fax:
+34 93 204 8105

E-mail:
mba@esade.edu

Website:
www.esade.edu/mba

Programme director:
Jaume Hugas

Figures in brackets
represent rank

Ranking	Rank (out of 100) Full-time
Overall rank	35
Regional rank	13

Criteria	Rank (out of 100) Full-time
Open new career opportunities	**21**
Diversity of recruiters	1
Number in jobs three months after graduation	40
Jobs found through the careers service	7
Student assessment of careers service	68
Personal development and educational experience	**69**
Faculty quality	>100
Student quality	77
Student diversity	35
Education experience	28
Increase in salary	**65**
Increase in salary	2
Post-MBA salary	90
Potential to network	**63**
Breadth of alumni network	43
Internationalism of alumni	40
Alumni effectiveness	70

Background

ESADE is a private academic institution set up in 1958 by the Catalan business community and the Jesuits to teach management and law and promote a scientific and humanistic approach to management research and education. The business school has a long tradition of internationalism and pluralism. It mixes a rigorous academic approach to business with a commitment to social responsibility and business ethics, a common characteristic of Spanish business schools.

Facilities

The ESADE campus in Barcelona (it also has facilities in Madrid) is split between three buildings (one is the language school) in the suburbs of the city. MBA students share some facilities with undergraduates. The school's multimedia technology includes a network of over 400 computers, online legal databases, satellite TV monitors and interactive videos, all available to students. There is no on-campus accommodation so most students share rented apartments.

	Full-time MBA
Student assessment of facilities	4.0 (79)

Faculty

Number of faculty: 82 full-time, 35 part-time, 28 visiting			
	Full-time MBA	Part-Time MBA	Executive MBA
Number of faculty per student	0.9 (38)	1.2	2.6
Percentage of faculty with PhD	71 (99)	71	71
Student rating of faculty	3.9 (97)	–	–

The directory
ESADE Business School

Strengths and weaknesses

Strengths: marketing; finance; business strategy

Weakness: low brand recognition

Programme highlights

ESADE's 18-month MBA starts with intensive Spanish-language training, an outdoor orientation and a one-month introduction to basic business principles. The programme is then divided into five stages. In the first year, the first three stages include general management and the business environment (a sort of expanded core); an integrative element concentrating largely on strategy; and global management. A summer section covers in-company experiences, language training and other elements. The six months of the second year include stages four and five, which cover electives and specialisations and an extensive exchange programme.

The programme is bilingual and students can choose between English and Spanish sections in their first academic year. By the beginning of stage five, all candidates are fluent enough in both languages to choose electives given in either.

ESADE also offers a part-time MBA, similar to the full-time version, and an Executive MBA in Barcelona and Madrid. Both programmes are taught in Spanish.

	Full-time MBA	Part Time MBA	Executive MBA
Student rating of programme	4.2 (58)	–	–
Number of overseas exchange programmes	120 (9)	–	–
Number of languages on offer	4 (48)	–	–

Students

	Full-time MBA	Part Time MBA	Executive MBA
Annual intake	115	120	55
Applicants:places	4:1	3:1	2:1
Percentage of women students	28 (91)	20	13
Percentage of foreign students	79 (31)	n/a	n/a
Average GMAT score	660 (53)	n/a	n/a
Average number of months' work experience	61 (78)	60	108
Age range of students	25-32	26-35	29-40
Average age	28	29	34
Student rating of culture and classmates	4.4 (34)	–	–

Student profile (full time)

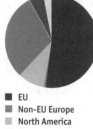

- ■ EU
- ■ Non-EU Europe
- ▨ North America
- ■ Other Americas
- ■ Asia/Australasia
- ▨ Middle East

Recruiters/careers service

	Full-time MBA	Part Time MBA	Executive MBA
Number of industry sectors that recruited graduates	8 (1)	–	–
Percentage of graduates in jobs 3 months after graduation	95 (40)	–	–
Percentage of graduates finding jobs through careers services	84 (7)	–	–
Student rating of careers service	3.5 (68)	–	–
Post-MBA salary, US$	79,407 (90)	–	–
Percentage increase in salary	132 (2)	–	–
Principal recruiters of graduates	Mckinsey & Co, Citibank, Danone		

Cost

	Full-time MBA	Part Time MBA	Executive MBA
Application fees	€100 (US$114)	€100 (US$114)	€100 (US$114)
Programme fees	€22,750 (US$25,852)	€38,000 (US$43,182)	€41,000 (US$46,591)
Comments	Per academic year	Total programme	Total programme
Accommodation costs (on campus, per year)	–	–	–
Accommodation costs (off campus, per year)	€5,700 (US$6,477)	–	–
Financial aid available	No limit, depends on demand	–	–
Type of aid available	Scholarships and loans	–	–
Criteria on which aid is granted	Qualifications, financial need	–	–

Accreditation

AACSB International, AMBA, EQUIS

Application details

	Full-time MBA	Part Time MBA	Executive MBA
Application deadline	June 30th	July 15th	November 22nd
Programme dates	Sep start, 18 months	Sep start, 21 months	Jan start, 18 months
Admission requirements	Bachelor's degree or equivalent; at least 2 years' work experience; TOEFL if first language not English (250 for English section/240 for Spanish section); 2 references; 4 essays; Interview; laptop	Bachelor's degree or equivalent; at least 3 years' work experience; TOEFL if first language not English (230); reference; 3 essays; interview	Bachelor's degree or equivalent; at least 5 years' work experience; TOEFL if first language not English (230); reference; 3 essays; interview; sponsoring letter from the candidate's company

Executive education

ESADE offers open executive programmes covering the main management disciplines at its Barcelona and Madrid campuses. Subjects covered include general management, strategy, leadership and management skills, entrepreneurship, and marketing management. It also offers custom-designed programmes.

Student/alumni quotes

"The atmosphere was very competitive and you could feel the tension in class at the beginning of the programme. This was a good experience but after some time we all became friends and towards the end of the programme the group had become one."

"The faculty is still predominantly Spanish and some are knowledgeable about their subject areas but have problems with English."

"A very open-minded school with a strong focus on emerging economies."

ESCP–EAP European School of Management

Ranking	Rank (out of 100) Full-time
Overall rank	82
Regional rank	32

Criteria	Rank (out of 100) Full-time
Open new career opportunities	**99**
Diversity of recruiters	94
Number in jobs three months after graduation	>100
Jobs found through the careers service	n/a
Student assessment of careers service	41
Personal development and educational experience	**34**
Faculty quality	1
Student quality	88
Student diversity	17
Education experience	86
Increase in salary	**61**
Increase in salary	37
Post-MBA salary	62
Potential to network	**79**
Breadth of alumni network	86
Internationalism of alumni	>100
Alumni effectiveness	53

Address
79 avenue de la
République
Paris
France
75011

Tel:
+33 1 4923 2791

Fax:
+33 1 4923 2290

E-mail:
mba@escp-eap.net

Website:
www.escp-eap.net

Programme director:
Frédéric Fréry

Figures in brackets
represent rank

Background

ESCP–EAP European School of Management is a highly international school with campuses in Paris, Oxford, Berlin and Madrid. With over 150 faculty members and nearly 200 support staff, it is the largest crossborder school of management in Europe. The school, which is part of the Paris Chamber of Commerce and Industry, has good links with European institutions and with industry.

Facilities

ESCP–EAP's main base is a modern building in the centre of Paris. Facilities are excellent and the small class size allows good relations among students and contact with faculty. In September 2004 the school moved its UK campus from Oxford to London (Parsifal College in Hampstead).

	Full-time MBA
Student assessment of facilities	3.8 (96)

Faculty

Number of faculty: 93 full-time, 27 part-time, 54 visiting

	Full-time MBA	Executive MBA in Paris
Number of faculty per student	3.9 (1)	3.9
Percentage of faculty with PhD	95 (79)	95
Student rating of faculty	4.2 (72)	–

Strengths and weaknesses

Strengths: internationalism

Weakness: lack of global profile

Programme highlights

The ESCP–EAP MBA is highly international, with over 20 nationalities in each intake (of around 30 students). It is an interesting programme for anyone contemplating an international career but wishing to avoid some of the more obvious international schools. The programme is based in Paris and is a fairly standard mix of core courses, electives and an international consultancy project carried out in small teams. Classes are taught in English, but students are expected to develop a good command of French.

ESCP–EAP runs a European Executive MBA linking its campuses. The programme lasts 18 months and includes six modules in Paris and four in Madrid, Berlin and (from 2004) London. There is a module every three weeks and each module lasts three days, from Thursday morning to Saturday lunchtime, with e-mail contact between modules. A Paris-based EMBA is delivered weekly (Thursday evenings, 5.30–8.30 pm) with workshops every three weeks (Friday afternoon and Saturday morning).

The school also offers a Global Executive MBA (International Masters in Management—IMM), a joint venture with Purdue University (Krannert Graduate School of Management) in the US, Tias Business School at Tilburg University in the Netherlands and IMC Graduate School of Management at Central European University in Budapest, Hungary. Graduates obtain a US MBA degree (Purdue) and a European MBA degree (Tilburg, Budapest or ESCP–EAP). There are six two-week residencies over two years rotating among the four campuses, with Internet support between sessions.

	Full-time MBA	Executive MBA in Paris
Student rating of programme	4.1 (75)	–
Number of overseas exchange programmes	0 (93)	–
Number of languages on offer	4 (55)	–

Students

Student profile (full time)

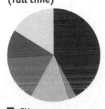

- ■ EU
- ■ Non-EU Europe
- ■ North America
- ■ Other Americas
- ■ Asia/Australasia
- ■ Middle East

	Full-time MBA	Executive MBA in Paris
Annual intake	31	45
Applicants:places	7:1	3:1
Percentage of women students	32 (25)	11
Percentage of foreign students	90 (12)	n/a
Average GMAT score	590 (96)	n/a
Average number of months' work experience	72 (27)	132
Age range of students	25-35	28-42
Average age	30	35
Student rating of culture and classmates	4.0 (80)	–

Recruiters/careers service

	Full-time MBA	Executive MBA in Paris
Number of industry sectors that recruited graduates	7 (94)	–
Percentage of graduates in jobs 3 months after graduation	50 (112)	–
Percentage of graduates finding jobs through careers services	n/a (n/a)	–
Student rating of careers service	3.9 (41)	–
Post-MBA salary, US$	76,617 (62)	–
Percentage increase in salary	44 (37)	
Principal recruiters of graduates	Vodafone, Publicis, Total	

The directory
ESCP–EAP European School of Management

Cost

	Full-time MBA	Executive MBA in Paris
Application fees	€120 (US$136)	€120 (US$136)
Programme fees	€30,000 (US$34,091)	€25,000 (US$28,409)
Comments	Tuition includes core course text books and expenses for international seminars	Plus €7,000 for international seminars
Accommodation costs (on campus, per year)	–	–
Accommodation costs (off campus, per year)	€8,500 (US$9,659)	–
Financial aid available	Not disclosed	–
Type of aid available	Scholarships	–
Criteria on which aid is granted	GMAT, merit, financial need	–

Accreditation

AACSB International, AMBA, EQUIS

Application details

	Full-time MBA	Executive MBA in Paris
Application deadline	October 11th	October 11th
Programme dates	Jan start, 12 months	Jan start, 18 months
Admission requirements	Bachelor's degree or equivalent; at least 3 years' work experience; TOEFL if first language not English (minimum TOEFL 600 paper-based, 250 computer-based); 2 references; 5 essays; interview; laptop	Bachelor's degree or equivalent; at least 5 years' work experience; TOEFL if first language not English (minimum TOEFL 600 paper-based, 250 computer-based); 2 references; 2 essays; interview

Executive education

ESCP–EAP offers four types of open programmes for executives in France: to introduce new management concepts and methods; to broaden and deepen knowledge and skills in an expert area; to specialise in a functional area; general management degree programmes. It also offers custom programmes are based on the following areas: leadership; general management; strategy; change management; human resources; finance, accounting, management control; marketing and sales; purchasing; research and development; and industrial management.

Student/alumni quotes

"Hard work but fun ... Ideally located in central Paris, it is nevertheless very open and international."

"The ESCP-EAP MBA programme is renowned for its international content and the study experience was competitive and rewarding. I would expect the school to further develop its job search activity."

"MBA far less known than the grande école *programmes; low awareness outside France."*

ESSEC Business School

Address
ESSEC Business
School
Avenue Bernard
Hirsch
BP 50105
Cergy-Pontoise
France
95021

Tel:
+33 1 3443 3125

Fax:
+33 1 3038 9898

E-mail:
dhalluin@essec.fr

Website:
www.essec.com

Programme director:
Nicolas Mottis

Figures in brackets
represent rank

Ranking	Rank (out of 100) Full-time
Overall rank	76
Regional rank	27

Criteria	Rank (out of 100) Full-time
Open new career opportunities	**15**
Diversity of recruiters	30
Number in jobs three months after graduation	42
Jobs found through the careers service	n/a
Student assessment of careers service	17
Personal development and educational experience	**>100**
Faculty quality	96
Student quality	>100
Student diversity	73
Education experience	70
Increase in salary	**>100**
Increase in salary	47
Post-MBA salary	>100
Potential to network	**68**
Breadth of alumni network	>100
Internationalism of alumni	46
Alumni effectiveness	30

Background

ESSEC, a grande école founded in Paris in 1907, has robustly embraced the American MBA model, though with a distinctively European twist. It is a full-range private institution offering business programmes from undergraduate to doctoral level as well as executive education programmes. In 1997 it became the first business school outside North America to be accredited by AACSB International.

The school is large, with about 3,500 students and 5,000 managers on various business programmes. It has excellent contacts with business and has increasingly internationalised itself via faculty recruitment, student intake and programme content.

Facilities

ESSEC's main campus is in Cergy, part of the new town of Cergy-Pontoise outside Paris. The facilities are good and there is plenty of on-campus accommodation. In 2002 the school launched a development campaign aiming raise €25m by 2006. The money will be used to fund chairs, institutes and scholarships, and will significantly increase the campus space available.

ESSEC also has an executive education centre in downtown Paris.

	Full-time MBA
Student assessment of facilities	3.6 (>100)

The directory
ESSEC Business School

Faculty

Number of faculty: 89 full-time, 17 part-time, 9 visiting

	Full-time MBA	ESSEC & Mannheim Executive MBA
Number of faculty per student	0.2 (>100)	1.6
Percentage of faculty with PhD	98 (26)	98
Student rating of faculty	3.9 (98)	–

Strengths and weaknesses

Strengths: finance; marketing; entrepreneurship

Weakness: part of a complex French educational system that is hard for outsiders to understand

Programme highlights

The ESSEC MBA is different from a traditional programme, offering a mix of academic and practical experiences, and students may be significantly younger than those on other MBA programmes. Some French students as young as 20 are accepted after taking a tough examination, and they then spend up to four years mixing the programme with work experience "apprenticeships".

The programme is flexible in length and format and offers a wide range of elective courses, professional experience and academic training, including a professional skills assessment. The length of the programme may vary from student to student but the minimum duration is two years, including course work and professional experience. The programme is bilingual in English and French with training available in both languages. Students can opt to specialise in certain areas (ESSEC calls them "specialised chair courses") in health economics, real estate, urban planning, luxury brand management, sales strategy, consumer goods and corporate governance. Students must also complete required periods in business and an international "experience" such as an exchange programme or an overseas internship.

The Executive MBA has an unashamed European focus. It has been jointly designed by ESSEC and the University of Mannheim in Germany, following the signing of a strategic alliance. The EMBA is offered in two formats. The 21-month Weekend EMBA is taught over 36 weekends and has five four-day residences. The 20-month Modular EMBA is taught over 14 intensive weeks, consisting of 10 five-day modules, three five-day residences and one ten-day residence.

ESSEC also offers an MBA in International Luxury Brand Management, an MBA in Agri-food and an MBA in International Hospitality Management (a joint programme with Cornell University's School of Hotel Administration). The school is working with the University of Mannheim School of Business Administration to develop a portfolio of joint executive MBA programmes.

	Full-time MBA	ESSEC & Mannheim Executive MBA
Student rating of programme	4.1 (74)	–
Number of overseas exchange programmes	222 (37)	–
Number of languages on offer	>5 (29)	–

Students

	Full-time MBA	ESSEC & Mannheim Executive MBA
Annual intake	615	71
Applicants:places	7:1	2:1
Percentage of women students	46 (5)	16
Percentage of foreign students	17 (>100)	n/a
Average GMAT score	668 (31)	610
Average number of months' work experience	12 (>100)	108
Age range of students	20-30	29-38
Average age	23	33
Student rating of culture and classmates	3.8 (98)	–

Student profile (full time)

- ■ EU
- ■ Non-EU Europe
- ■ North America
- ■ Other Americas
- ■ Asia/Australasia
- ■ Middle East

Recruiters/careers service

	Full-time MBA	ESSEC & Mannheim Executive MBA
Number of industry sectors that recruited graduates	8 (30)	–
Percentage of graduates in jobs 3 months after graduation	83 (42)	–
Percentage of graduates finding jobs through careers services	n/a (n/a)	–
Student rating of careers service	4.0 (17)	–
Post-MBA salary, US$	48,932 (104)	–
Percentage increase in salary	54 (47)	
Principal recruiters of graduates	L'Oréal, PricewaterhouseCoopers, Société Générale	

Cost

	Full-time MBA	ESSEC & Mannheim Executive MBA
Application fees	€160 (US$182)	€150 (US$170)
Programme fees	€7,800 (US$8,864)	€35,000 (US$39,773)
Comments	–	–
Accommodation costs (on campus, per year)	€2,800 (US$3,182)	–
Accommodation costs (off campus, per year)	€4,950 (US$5,625)	–
Financial aid available	€3,020,585 (US$3,432,483)	
Type of aid available	Grants, apprenticeships, assistantships	–
Criteria on which aid is granted	Financial need, merit	–

Accreditation

AACSB International, EQUIS

Application details

	Full-time MBA	ESSEC & Mannheim Executive MBA
Application deadline	February 1st	January 14th
Programme dates	Sep start, 30 months	Mar start, 20 months
Admission requirements	Bachelor's degree; at least 1 year's work experience; GMAT; TOEFL if first language not English (230 minimum); references; essays; interview; laptop	At least 5 years' work experience; GMAT; TOEFL if first language not English; 2 references; 4 essays; interview

Executive education

ESSEC offers a range of specialised open programmes, specialised masters programmes and customised in-company programmes.

Student/alumni quotes

"The ESSEC programme needs to strengthen its reputation in Europe to achieve its targets. I hope it will become a leading non-Anglo-Saxon MBA. Nevertheless, it is still a huge international opportunity at the career and training levels, especially for young French students."

"It may lack people old enough to have long, highly valuable work experience (a lot of students come from the French system of classes préparatoires, ie they have very good academic but little practical knowledge)."

"It is the best French business school after preparatory class and the only one providing a MBA."

University of Florida—Warrington College of Business

Ranking	Rank (out of 100) Full-time
Overall rank	89
Regional rank	50

Criteria	Rank (out of 100) Full-time
Open new career opportunities	**89**
Diversity of recruiters	99
Number in jobs three months after graduation	>100
Jobs found through the careers service	16
Student assessment of careers service	73
Personal development and educational experience	**53**
Faculty quality	4
Student quality	84
Student diversity	89
Education experience	44
Increase in salary	**92**
Increase in salary	61
Post-MBA salary	93
Potential to network	**77**
Breadth of alumni network	21
Internationalism of alumni	>100
Alumni effectiveness	90

Address
134 Bryan Hall
PO Box 117152
Gainesville, FL
US
32611-7152

Tel:
+1 352 392 7992

Fax:
+1 352 392 8791

E-mail:
floridamba@cba.ufl.
edu

Website:
www.floridamba.ufl.
edu

Programme director:
Alex Sevilla

Figures in brackets
represent rank

Background

The University of Florida was established in 1853, the College of Business Administration was founded in 1927 and the first MBA degree was awarded in 1946. In 1977 the Fisher School of Accounting was established, and in 1996, after receiving an endowment from alumnus Alfred C Warrington IV, it was renamed the Warrington College of Business.

Warrington can easily match many of the better known US schools in terms of the quality of its student body and faculty. It offers an impressive set of integrated programmes, with an emphasis on accelerated programmes and distance learning that puts it high on the list of innovative schools. Florida's balmy climate and subsidised tuition make the school a favourite for many out-of-state American and international students.

Facilities

The school is based on the 2,000-acre university campus in Gainesville, central Florida, between Orlando and Jacksonville. It consists of three buildings that house classrooms, faculty offices and student facilities, which are shared by students at the bachelor, master and PhD levels. MBA facilities include a study lounge, a graduate business computer lab and laptop hook-ups in many common areas. Some dedicated MBA classrooms are wired for multimedia presentations with laptop connections at every seat.

	Full-time MBA
Student assessment of facilities	4.5 (9)

Faculty

Number of faculty: 101 full-time, 0 part-time, 2 visiting

	Full-time MBA	Internet MBA (One year and Two year options)	Working Professional Programs	Executive MBA
Number of faculty per student	1.2 (20)	0.4	0.6	4.0
Percentage of faculty with PhD	95 (24)	95	95	95
Student rating of faculty	4.5 (25)	–	–	–

Strengths and weaknesses

Strengths: finance; technology; marketing

Weaknesses: careers services; alumni network

Programme highlights

In the Warrington full-time two-year MBA semesters are divided into two eight-week modules, including a week of exams. Students take 12 core courses in the first year, followed by one required strategy course and nine electives in the second year. Electives are generally grouped into concentrations and there is a wide choice of courses. To earn a concentration, students must complete a minimum of four courses within a field. Students are also free to choose electives from all concentrations. A global management concentration involves an overseas exchange and four electives at Warrington chosen from a specified list.

Students with any undergraduate degree (not just business) can opt to complete the programme in 12 months, effectively completing the core in the summer months (May–August) and then joining second-year students. Those with a business first degree may complete the programme in just nine months, joining second-year students to take elective courses and the required strategic management course.

Warrington's part-time MBA for Working Professionals programme is divided into seven 16-week terms, with students completing two courses per term. Students meet on the University of Florida campus one Saturday and Sunday per month for 27 months. The school says this programme is best suited to individuals at an earlier stage of their careers. A 16-month version for students with an undergraduate business degree is also available. From October 2004 the programme is offered in South Florida at the Wyndham Bonaventure Resort in Fort Lauderdale.

The Executive MBA is fairly traditional, although it relies on information technology for communications. The programme is divided into five four-month terms and classes meet on campus Friday–Sunday once a month. Students keep in touch with professors and fellow students via e-mail during off-campus periods.

Warrington's Internet (Flexible) MBA is one of the first online MBA degrees to be offered by a fully accredited business school. The degree earned on completion of the programme is equivalent to any other MBA offered by the University of Florida. The programme has a 27-month curriculum in which students meet for one weekend (Saturday and Sunday) at the end of each term (eight times). As well as time on campus, course work is offered electronically through Internet communications such as e-mail, web browsers, bulletin boards, synchronous group discussion software, asynchronous class presentation software, video and audio streaming, and interactive CD-ROM technology. The orientation exercises count for credit. A one-year Internet MBA for students with an undergraduate business degree is also available.

A specialised MBA Program for Engineers and Scientists is designed to provide a broad general management perspective while paying special attention to industries that require a high level of technological or scientific expertise. Students attend classes on Saturday and Sunday once a month for 20 months. Between campus visits, students keep in touch with professors, classmates and team members via Lotus Notes.

	Full-time MBA	Internet MBA (One year and Two year options)	Working Professional Programs	Executive MBA
Student rating of programme	4.3 (32)	–	–	–
Number of overseas exchange programmes	36 (23)	–	–	–
Number of languages on offer	0 (>100)	–	–	–

The directory
University of Florida—Warrington College of Business

Students

	Full-time MBA	Internet MBA (One year and Two year options)	Working Professional Programs	Executive MBA
Annual intake	84	96	171	26
Applicants:places	5:1	2:1	2:1	2:1
Percentage of women students	23 (95)	23	27	24
Percentage of foreign students	35 (80)	13	n/a	n/a
Average GMAT score	645 (52)	610	620	636
Average number of months' work experience	54 (97)	72	66	132
Age range of students	24-32	24-35	26-33	31-46
Average age	27	29	29	36
Student rating of culture and classmates	4.4 (35)	–	–	–

Student profile (full time)

- ■ EU
- ■ Non-EU Europe
- ▨ North America
- ■ Other Americas
- ■ Asia/Australasia
- ▨ Middle East

Recruiters/careers service

	Full-time MBA	Internet MBA (One year and Two year options)	Working Professional Programs	Executive MBA
Number of industry sectors that recruited graduates	6 (99)	–	–	–
Percentage of graduates in jobs 3 months after graduation	34 (>100)	–	–	–
Percentage of graduates finding jobs through careers services	88 (16)	–	–	–
Student rating of careers service	3.0 (73)	–	–	–
Post-MBA salary, US$	62,000 (93)	–	–	–
Percentage increase in salary	55 (61)	–	–	–
Principal recruiters of graduates	Citibank, Ernst & Young, DHL			

Cost

	Full-time MBA	Internet MBA (One year and Two year options)	Working Professional Programs	Executive MBA
Application fees	US$30	US$30	US$30	US$30
Programme fees	US$23,861	US$34,500	US$25,666	US$32,000
Comments	–	Total programme	Total programme	Total programme
Accommodation costs (on campus, per year)	US$5,000	–	–	–
Accommodation costs (off campus, per year)	US$5,500	–	–	–
Financial aid available	US$37,000	–	–	–
Type of aid available	Scholarships, loans, grants, waivers	–	–	–
Criteria on which aid is granted	Merit, financial need	–	–	–

Accreditation
AACSB International, EQUIS

Application details

	Full-time MBA	Internet MBA (One year and Two year options)	Working Professional Programs	Executive MBA
Application deadline	Details available from school	Details available from school	Details available from school	Details available from school
Programme dates	Aug start, 20 months	Jan start, 27 months	Aug start, 27 months	Sep start, 20 months
Admission requirements	US bachelor's degree or international equivalent; at least 4 years' work experience; TOEFL if first language not English; 2 references; 2 essays; interview; laptop	US bachelor's degree or international equivalent; at least 2 years' work experience; TOEFL if first language not English; 2 references; essay; interview	US bachelor's degree or international equivalent; at least 2 years' work experience; TOEFL if first language not English; 2 references; essay; interview	US bachelor's degree or international equivalent; at least 8 years' work experience; TOEFL minimum if first language not English; 2 references; essay; interview

Executive education

Warrington does not currently offer executive education programmes

Student/alumni quotes

"A Florida MBA is the best deal in the country. For very low tuition and cost of living, you can get a great MBA."

"Despite being the 'flagship MBA programme' in the state of Florida, facilities fall well short of expectations."

"My MBA experience in the two-year programme has been fantastic. The calibre of people and size of the programme make it a great place to make friends in the future business world. The class work, while challenging, is not overwhelming to the point where all aspects of a life outside school are lost."

Georgetown University—Robert Emmet McDonough School of Business

Ranking	Rank (out of 100) Full-time
Overall rank	41
Regional rank	27

Criteria	Rank (out of 100) Full-time
Open new career opportunities	**33**
Diversity of recruiters	28
Number in jobs three months after graduation	31
Jobs found through the careers service	41
Student assessment of careers service	50
Personal development and educational experience	**61**
Faculty quality	61
Student quality	57
Student diversity	59
Education experience	66
Increase in salary	**50**
Increase in salary	35
Post-MBA salary	54
Potential to network	**67**
Breadth of alumni network	>100
Internationalism of alumni	92
Alumni effectiveness	37

Address
3520 Prospect Street
Suite 215
Washington, DC
US
20057

Tel:
+1 202 687 4080

Fax:
+1 202 687 2017

E-mail:
mba@georgetown.edu

Website:
mba.georgetown.edu

Programme director:
Marilyn A Morgan

Figures in brackets
represent rank

Background

The MBA programme at Georgetown University's Robert Emmet McDonough School of Business is one of the more international MBA experiences on offer in the US. The small class size allows good inter-action between students and faculty as well as flexible teaching styles. The school's location above the Potomac River in Washington DC ensures an interesting list of guest speakers.

The university was established in 1789 as the first Jesuit institution of higher learning in the US, although freedom of religious belief among students has always been a principle. It is a bastion of the US's strong liberal arts tradition. In 1998 the business school was renamed in recognition of a US$30m endowment gift from an alumnus.

Facilities

The MBA programme is housed in the McDonough Graduate Center, which occupies over 32,000 sq ft in the historic Car Barn (built in the late 19th century to store streetcars). It includes classrooms, a student lounge, a computer lab, group meeting rooms, the careers management centre and adminis-trative offices. However, the school is planning and raising money to build a new home in the centre of the Georgetown campus. No on-campus accommodation is available for graduate students.

	Full-time MBA
Student assessment of facilities	3.9 (87)

Faculty

Number of faculty: 77 full-time, 76 part-time, 4 visiting

	Full-time MBA	International Executive MBA
Number of faculty per student	0.5 (82)	3.0
Percentage of faculty with PhD	95 (53)	95
Student rating of faculty	4.4 (36)	–

Strengths and weaknesses

Strengths: finance; international business; marketing

Weaknesses: facilities; careers services

Programme highlights

McDonough's full-time two-year MBA is generalised with a strong emphasis on the global nature of business and functional integration. The programme is divided into six-week modules and is strongly integrative, with four classes of 4–8 days covering three integrative areas: understanding international business and competing in international business in the first year; and global experience/residency, including a one-week international study tour, in the second year. Apart from this the core is generally traditional in design. Must of the second year is given over to electives, but there is no requirement to opt for a concentration or specialisation.

The curriculum focuses on global business, business-government relations, business ethics and management communications. The second year centres on a required international consulting project outside the US. A six-week summer school at Oxford University in the UK is available during the summer.

Students can also opt for an honours certificate in International Business Diplomacy (IBD) offered by McDonough and Georgetown's School of Foreign Service as part of their MBA curriculum.

The International Executive MBA consists of an 18-month sequence of courses and projects divided by four one-week periods of study, or residencies. Classes meet every other weekend, all day Friday and Saturday. The residencies include visits to Congress and to companies in Asia and Latin America. All involve a live case (a real-world strategic issue or problem affecting a company or industry), which teams of participants study in depth.

	Full-time MBA	International Executive MBA
Student rating of programme	4.4 (19)	–
Number of overseas exchange programmes	0 (41)	–
Number of languages on offer	2 (82)	–

Students

Student profile (full time)

- EU
- Non-EU Europe
- North America
- Other Americas
- Asia/Australasia
- Middle East

	Full-time MBA	International Executive MBA
Annual intake	252	52
Applicants:places	8:1	2:1
Percentage of women students	30 (45)	23
Percentage of foreign students	38 (79)	n/a
Average GMAT score	660 (38)	630
Average number of months' work experience	60 (72)	132
Age range of students	24–29	30–46
Average age	29	34
Student rating of culture and classmates	4.4 (33)	–

The directory
Georgetown University—Robert Emmet McDonough School of Business

Recruiters/careers service

	Full-time MBA	International Executive MBA
Number of industry sectors that recruited graduates	8 (28)	–
Percentage of graduates in jobs 3 months after graduation	90 (31)	–
Percentage of graduates finding jobs through careers services	52 (41)	–
Student rating of careers service	3.4 (50)	–
Post-MBA salary, US$	75,664 (54)	–
Percentage increase in salary	73 (35)	–
Principal recruiters of graduates	Citigroup, JP Morgan Chase, Lehman Brothers	

Cost

	Full-time MBA	International Executive MBA
Application fees	US$100	US$75
Programme fees	US$30,888	US$59,400
Comments	Per year. An additional US$4,000 per year is required for books and materials	An additional US$12,300 is required for meals, books and accommodation
Accommodation costs (on campus, per year)	–	–
Accommodation costs (off campus, per year)	US$16,000	–
Financial aid available	US$14,804,000	–
Type of aid available	Loans, work-study, grants, scholarships	–
Criteria on which aid is granted	Merit (grants/scholarships), financial need (loans/work-study)	–

Accreditation

AACSB International

Application details

	Full-time MBA	International Executive MBA
Application deadline	April 22nd	May 31st
Programme dates	Aug start, 24 months	Aug start, 18 months
Admission requirements	Bachelor's degree from accredited college or university; at least 2 years' work experience; TOEFL if first language not English (minimum score of 600, paper-based, or 250, computer-based required); 2 references; 3 essays; interview; laptop	Bachelor's degree from accredited college or university; at least 8 years' work experience; TOEFL if first language not English; 2 references; essay; interview; letter of support from current employer

Executive education

McDonough offers a range of customised in-company programmes as well as what it calls "public policy forums", drawing on its Washington location to host open programmes for business, government and academics.

Student/alumni quotes

"Every single course at the school is taught from an international perspective and Georgetown students really come into their own when faced with business challenges that require global thinking."

"The building is too small for the programme and there are not enough team rooms."

"It is a well-rounded school where you can learn from your profs as well as your peers. Teamwork is paramount in the programme, and it shows."

University of Georgia—Terry College of Business

Address
Brooks Hall
University of Georgia
Athens, GA
US
30602

Tel:
+1 706 542 5333

Fax:
+1 706 542 5351

E-mail:
terrymba@terry.uga.
edu

Website:
www.terry.uga.edu/
mba

Programme director:
Dr Melvin R Crask

Figures in brackets
represent rank

Ranking	Rank (out of 100) Full-time
Overall rank	97
Regional rank	52

Criteria	Rank (out of 100) Full-time
Open new career opportunities	**97**
Diversity of recruiters	>100
Number in jobs three months after graduation	55
Jobs found through the careers service	n/a
Student assessment of careers service	79
Personal development and educational experience	**80**
Faculty quality	10
Student quality	75
Student diversity	99
Education experience	89
Increase in salary	**83**
Increase in salary	51
Post-MBA salary	79
Potential to network	**55**
Breadth of alumni network	19
Internationalism of alumni	>100
Alumni effectiveness	64

Background

The University of Georgia's Terry College of Business began in 1912 as the School of Commerce and then became the College of Business Administration. In 1991 it was named after benefactors C Herman and Mary Virginia Terry. Although Terry has 5,500 undergraduate students, the MBA programme is relatively small, which encourages co-operation among students and allows fairly easy access to faculty. A third of students come from outside North America. As well as the low fees that are typical of some state universities, Terry offers significant merit-linked financial assistance (the school claims that a majority of students pay no more than $1,000 a year in tuition and fees).

Facilities

The university campus is pleasant and MBA students are close to all university amenities. Computer, library and sporting and leisure facilities are excellent. Faculty and staff offices, including the MBA admissions office, careers services office, interview rooms and an MBA lounge, are in the five-storey Brooks Hall. Most MBA classes are taught in Sanford Hall, a four-storey building next to Brooks Hall. Some classes are taught in nearby Caldwell Hall, which also houses the MBA computer lab. Most students live off campus where accommodation is plentiful and reasonably cheap. Athens is a medium-sized university town and the school is close to a lively café and restaurant area.

	Full-time MBA
Student assessment of facilities	4.3 (41)

The directory
University of Georgia—Terry College of Business

Faculty

Number of faculty: 150 full-time, 0 part-time, 0 visiting

	Full-time MBA
Number of faculty per student	3.1 (11)
Percentage of faculty with PhD	87 (62)
Student rating of faculty	4.2 (59)

Strengths and weaknesses

Strengths: management information systems, insurance and finance

Weaknesses: low profile; strides have been made with careers services, but there is still room for further improvement

Programme highlights

The Terry MBA is fairly traditional in structure with a strong emphasis on business leadership. During the pre-programme session students are assigned to four-member teams that work together throughout the first year. There is a team in-company project in the second year and an optional international study tour, which satisfies the requirement to take at least one elective in the international business area.

The second year is given over to electives. Limited waivers of core courses are allowed and these are replaced with electives or advanced courses. Students with approved undergraduate degrees in business can take an accelerated track, comprising a summer term and the second year. The programme is highly quantitative and students are advised to strengthen any weaknesses before arriving at Terry.

Terry's part-time MBA programme is offered at the Gwinnett University Center in Atlanta during the evening. It can be completed in eight semesters, although a maximum of 18 consecutive semesters is allowed. Classes meet 6–9 pm during the fall and spring semesters and 6–10 pm and one half day on Saturday during the 10-week summer semester. The programme has four parts: background courses; required courses in business skills and knowledge; globalisation and strategy; and electives. There is a required outdoor team-building exercise and an optional overseas study trip.

The 18-month Executive MBA emphasises both conceptual and practical development. Most classes are held at the UGA Alumni Club in Atlanta's Buckhead financial district. Two one-week sessions take place at Terry College of Business. At Buckhead the programme is divided into seven nine-week modules (three classroom sessions all day Friday and Saturday per module) with distance learning between classes. The last module is an international residency in which participants visit several countries to see how business processes are influenced by the prevailing economic, cultural and regulatory environment.

	Full-time MBA
Student rating of programme	4.0 (76)
Number of overseas exchange programmes	1 (90)
Number of languages on offer	0 (94)

Students

	Full-time MBA
Annual intake	49
Applicants:places	10:1
Percentage of women students	22 (84)
Percentage of foreign students	33 (98)
Average GMAT score	659 (40)
Average number of months' work experience	53 (95)
Age range of students	23-32
Average age	27
Student rating of culture and classmates	4.2 (51)

Student profile (full time)

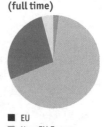

- EU
- Non-EU Europe
- North America
- Other Americas
- Asia/Australasia
- Middle East

Recruiters/careers service

	Full-time MBA
Number of industry sectors that recruited graduates	3 (>100)
Percentage of graduates in jobs 3 months after graduation	81 (55)
Percentage of graduates finding jobs through careers services	n/a (n/a)
Student rating of careers service	3.1 (79)
Post-MBA salary, US$	68,170 (79)
Percentage increase in salary	53 (51)
Principal recruiters of graduates	Cintas, C.B. Richard Ellis, Knowlagent

Cost

	Full-time MBA
Application fees	US$50
Programme fees	US$17,820
Comments	Per year; out-of-state
Accommodation costs (on campus, per year)	US$5,500
Accommodation costs (off campus, per year)	US$6,600
Financial aid available	US$2,263,143
Type of aid available	Assistantships, scholarships
Criteria on which aid is granted	Merit

Accreditation

AACSB International

Application details

	Full-time MBA
Application deadline	–
Programme dates	Aug start, 22 months
Admission requirements	Baccalaureate undergraduate degree from accredited university; at least 2 years' work experience; TOEFL if first language not English; 3 references, 3 essays; laptop; interview is encouraged

Executive education

Terry offers open-enrolment executive education programmes for directors and in finance and marketing as well as customised in-company programmes.

Student/alumni quotes

"Come to UGA, get an assistantship, pay next-to-nothing tuition, and enjoy living in the best college town in the US for two years."

"Too small for large recruiters to come to campus."

"Terry MBA gives the best value for money among the top 50 [US] programmes. With a graduate assistantship, it's practically free. The quality of teaching is very good and the administration is very active in improving the overall quality."

University of Glasgow—School of Business and Management

Ranking	Rank (out of 100) Full-time
Overall rank	79
Regional rank	29

Criteria	Rank (out of 100) Full-time
Open new career opportunities	**>100**
Diversity of recruiters	>100
Number in jobs three months after graduation	81
Jobs found through the careers service	80
Student assessment of careers service	67
Personal development and educational experience	**41**
Faculty quality	2
Student quality	>100
Student diversity	9
Education experience	43
Increase in salary	**15**
Increase in salary	16
Post-MBA salary	26
Potential to network	**72**
Breadth of alumni network	92
Internationalism of alumni	35
Alumni effectiveness	59

Address
University of Glasgow
School of Business
and Management
Gilbert Scott Building
Glasgow
UK
G12 8QQ

Tel:
+44 141 330 2550

Fax:
+44 141 330 4939

E-mail:
mbaadmissions@
gla.ac.uk

Website:
www.gla.ac.uk/
schools/business

Programme director:
Mrs Pamela Castledine

Figures in brackets
represent rank

Background

In early 2004 Glasgow's business school merged with the university's department of business and management to create the new School of Business and Management, headed by Robert Paton, previously head of the department of business and management. The school says its aim is to maintain and develop its international reach and that a number of initiatives and strategic alliances are under way that will sustain and provide the building blocks for future growth.

Glasgow University's business school was founded in 1952 linking four departments—urban studies and urban economy, management studies, finance and accountancy, and economics—from which it draws most of its teaching faculty. Glasgow was one of the first European business schools to introduce an international MBA, and it remains a highly international institution with excellent links to other schools and to business.

Facilities

The school is based in the Gilbert Scott Building on the main university campus, where it has its own dedicated facilities for teaching and administration, including an IT lab. As postgraduate students, MBA students have access to all university services, particularly the extensive library, IT facilities and accommodation.

	Full-time MBA
Student assessment of facilities	4.6 (11)

Faculty

Number of faculty: 93 full-time, 9 part-time, 22 visiting

	Full-time MBA	University of Glasgow Part Time MBA programme
Number of faculty per student	2.1 (7)	5.0
Percentage of faculty with PhD	87 (74)	87
Student rating of faculty	4.5 (19)	–

Strengths and weaknesses

Strengths: organisational transformation; international business; marketing

Weakness: low profile

Programme highlights

The Glasgow MBA consists of six core courses, six electives and an individual project and dissertation. Three electives are taken at a two-week winter school in Glasgow and three at a two-week spring school in Glasgow or at an international summer school elsewhere in Europe or Asia. Full-time and part-time students share elective courses.

The core is divided into three themes: foundation in management and research skills, strategic business analysis and review; and strategic business development. The project/dissertation is company-based and by agreement can be completed off-campus. Personal development and soft skills are covered in a core foundations in management course and throughout the programme. Electives can be grouped into specialisations in marketing, public sector and government, and international business.

The part-time MBA programme has the same curriculum as the full-time version, including winter and spring schools and the option of an international summer school. The project/dissertation is normally carried out within a student's own organisation. The programme lasts for two years and classes meet all day Friday or Saturday (sometimes these are consecutive). The programme begins with a two-day foundation session. Students without the required entry qualifications can join the part-time MBA via Glasgow's open-entry Certificate of Business Administration programme.

	Full-time MBA	University of Glasgow Part Time MBA programme
Student rating of programme	4.5 (17)	–
Number of overseas exchange programmes	0 (93)	–
Number of languages on offer	4 (73)	–

Students

	Full-time MBA	University of Glasgow Part Time MBA programme
Annual intake	50	25
Applicants:places	10:1	5:1
Percentage of women students	37 (30)	47
Percentage of foreign students	82 (18)	n/a
Average GMAT score	n/a (n/a)	n/a
Average number of months' work experience	48 (>100)	108
Age range of students	26-40	27-48
Average age	30	35
Student rating of culture and classmates	4.2 (43)	–

Student profile (full time)

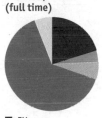

- ■ EU
- ■ Non-EU Europe
- ■ North America
- ■ Other Americas
- ■ Asia/Australasia
- ■ Middle East

The directory
University of Glasgow—School of Business and Management

Recruiters/careers service

	Full-time MBA	University of Glasgow Part Time MBA programme
Number of industry sectors that recruited graduates	5 (>100)	–
Percentage of graduates in jobs 3 months after graduation	80 (81)	–
Percentage of graduates finding jobs through careers services	25 (80)	–
Student rating of careers service	3.1 (67)	–
Post-MBA salary, US$	85,188 (26)	–
Percentage increase in salary	77 (16)	
Principal recruiters of graduates	n/a	

Cost

	Full-time MBA	University of Glasgow Part Time MBA programme
Application fees	None	None
Programme fees	£14,500 (US$23,770)	£5,000 (US$8,197)
Comments	Fee for EU students is £12, 500	Per year
Accommodation costs (on campus, per year)	£2,880 (US$4,721)	–
Accommodation costs (off campus, per year)	£3,000 (US$4,918)	–
Financial aid available	–	–
Type of aid available	–	–
Criteria on which aid is granted	–	–

Accreditation

AMBA

Application details

	Full-time MBA	University of Glasgow Part Time MBA programme
Application deadline	June 30th	September 31st
Programme dates	Sep start, 12 months	Sep start, 24 months
Admission requirements	Good UK honours degree or equivalent; at least 3 years' work experience; IELTS if first language not English (6.5 minimum); 2 references; interview; laptop	Good UK honours degree or equivalent; at least 3 years' work experience; IELTS if first language not English (6.5 minimum); 2 references; interview

Executive education

Glasgow offers a corporate Certificate of Business Administration programme lasting 12–15 months in either open-enrolment or customised in-company versions.

Student/alumni quotes

"Over the last few years the university has worked hard to establish the MBA programme. The facilities are superb, class sizes deliberately kept small so therefore more time with each professor/lecturer, the university is beautiful and the teaching staff of a very high quality. It is also very international."

"Overall recognition [is] less than it deserves."

"Glasgow is a great place to study and live. The university is stunning (founded 1451) and the business school is really moving the MBA programme along."

Harvard Business School

Address
Soldiers Field
Boston, MA
US
02163

Tel:
+1 617 495 6156

Fax:
+1 617 496 8180

E-mail:
admissions@hbs.edu

Website:
www.hbs.edu/mba

Programme director:
W Carl Kester

Figures in brackets
represent rank

Ranking	Rank (out of 100) Full-time
Overall rank	4
Regional rank	4

Criteria	Rank (out of 100) Full-time
Open new career opportunities	**7**
Diversity of recruiters	30
Number in jobs three months after graduation	9
Jobs found through the careers service	n/a
Student assessment of careers service	13
Personal development and educational experience	**10**
Faculty quality	6
Student quality	36
Student diversity	12
Education experience	40
Increase in salary	**12**
Increase in salary	58
Post-MBA salary	9
Potential to network	**23**
Breadth of alumni network	47
Internationalism of alumni	57
Alumni effectiveness	4

Background

Harvard Business School (HBS) is about halfway through the first fundraising effort in the school's 95-year history. "The Campaign for Harvard Business School" aims to raise $500m by the end of 2005 to support initiatives in student financial aid, global research (including setting up a range of overseas centres where faculty will be based to carry out research and case writing), faculty development and technology. The campaign will also fund a renewal of the HBS campus, including the first major renovation of the historic Baker Library and several student residences.

The school produces around 600 cases a year and they are used all over the world. It also supplies teaching material to many other schools around the world, including much of the intellectual capital developed in such subjects as general management, entrepreneurship, competition and strategy, and service management.

Facilities

Although steeped in tradition, HBS has enthusiastically embraced new technology, through both its own impressive on-campus IT systems and outside initiatives. The school is based on the Boston side of the Charles River, opposite Harvard University, which is in Cambridge, MA. The business school campus is large (32 buildings on a 35-acre campus) but compact, with a mix of traditional American academic architecture and more modern buildings. On-campus accommodation is available and about half of first-year students use it.

	Full-time MBA
Student assessment of facilities	4.8 (1)

The directory
Harvard Business School

Faculty

Number of faculty: 205 full-time, 0 part-time, 0 visiting	
	Full-time MBA
Number of faculty per student	0.1 (113)
Percentage of faculty with PhD	98 (28)
Student rating of faculty	4.9 (1)

Strengths and weaknesses

Strengths: field-based research in the practice of management

Programme highlights

The Harvard MBA starts with a pre-programme series of courses in accounting and finance, quantitative methods, business writing, class participation skills, computer and calculator skills, and general business knowledge designed to bring all students up to the same skills level. Some students may be required to take extra courses before arriving at HBS or the on-campus Analytics Program.

The programme proper starts with Foundations, a two-week course that launches the programme and leads into the beginning of the core curriculum. Subjects covered include applied leadership; a business simulation; economics; business history; ethics; and career development. The main programme comprises two terms of required courses followed by two terms of electives. Electives do not have to be grouped into concentrations and some can be taken in other areas of the university. During their second year, about half the class opt to undertake team projects. Entering classes are divided into sections of about 90 students who take all required courses together.

	Full-time MBA
Student rating of programme	4.6 (3)
Number of overseas exchange programmes	0 (86)
Number of languages on offer	0 (>100)

Students

	Full-time MBA
Annual intake	893
Applicants:places	9:1
Percentage of women students	35 (26)
Percentage of foreign students	37 (77)
Average GMAT score	707 (6)
Average number of months' work experience	48 (>100)
Age range of students	24-30
Average age	26
Student rating of culture and classmates	4.8 (2)

Student profile (full-time)

n/a

Recruiters/careers service

	Full-time MBA
Number of industry sectors that recruited graduates	8 (30)
Percentage of graduates in jobs 3 months after graduation	93 (9)
Percentage of graduates finding jobs through careers services	n/a (n/a)
Student rating of careers service	4.1 (13)
Post-MBA salary, US$	94,308 (9)
Percentage increase in salary	50 (58)
Principal recruiters of graduates	–

Cost

	Full-time MBA
Application fees	US$215
Programme fees	US$35,600
Comments	–
Accommodation costs (on campus, per year)	US$11,270
Accommodation costs (off campus, per year)	–
Financial aid available	US$10,200,000
Type of aid available	Need based fellowships, loans
Criteria on which aid is granted	HBS fellowship aid is based solely on financial need

Accreditation

AACSB International

Application details

	Full-time MBA
Application deadline	March 9th
Programme dates	Aug start, 18 months
Admission requirements	First degree; TOEFL if first language not English; 3 references; 6 essays; interview; laptop

Executive education

Harvard offers a large portfolio of open-enrolment programmes under the main headings of general management, owner-management, business strategy, financial management, personal development, social enterprise, technology and operations management, leadership and change, marketing, and negotiation and decision-making. It offers an equally wide range of customised in-company programmes.

HEC School of Management, Paris

Ranking	Rank (out of 100) Full-time
Overall rank	27
Regional rank	8

Criteria	Rank (out of 100) Full-time
Open new career opportunities	**47**
Diversity of recruiters	1
Number in jobs three months after graduation	>100
Jobs found through the careers service	36
Student assessment of careers service	25
Personal development and educational experience	**60**
Faculty quality	82
Student quality	50
Student diversity	76
Education experience	37
Increase in salary	**23**
Increase in salary	18
Post-MBA salary	43
Potential to network	**3**
Breadth of alumni network	4
Internationalism of alumni	16
Alumni effectiveness	10

Address
HEC Paris
MBA Program
1, rue de la Libération
Jouy-en-Josas cedex
France
78 351

Tel:
+33 1 39 67 74 84

Fax:
+33 1 39 67 94 46

E-mail:
admissionmba@
hec.fr

Website:
www.mba.hec.edu

Programme director:
Dr Valérie Gauthier

Figures in brackets
represent rank

Background

HEC School of Management, founded by the Paris Chamber of Commerce and Industry in 1881, is a leading French business school eager to be a real global player and expand its international contacts and reputation. French employers and students consider the school among the best in the country, and entry is tough. French is not a prerequisite for the programme, although a good knowledge of French is essential to get the best out of it. Students from outside France often choose HEC because they already have, or are looking for, personal or professional links with France. (As a grande école, HEC can provide an effective pathway into French business.)

Facilities

The large, modern, 25-acre campus is close to Versailles, about 20 km from central Paris. Facilities are excellent and include a fully equipped gym, sports fields and a nearby golf course. Most MBA students live in a new dedicated building, with 177 individual rooms and 24 apartments reserved for couples. Facilities include meeting rooms, lounge, gym and reserved parking. The surrounding Plateau de Saclay area is a centre for leading scientific research and teaching establishments.

	Full-time MBA
Student assessment of facilities	3.9 (86)

Faculty

Number of faculty: 101 full-time, 18 part-time, 40 visiting

	Full-time MBA	HEC Executive MBA
Number of faculty per student	0.6 (62)	0.5
Percentage of faculty with PhD	75 (93)	75
Student rating of faculty	4.3 (42)	–

Strengths and weaknesses

Strengths: finance; personal and professional development; strategy

Weakness: low profile outside France

Programme highlights

The core of HEC's 16-month full-time MBA is divided into parts, although both cover traditional core disciplines. During the core phase, one day a week is devoted to personal development issues. In the eight-month "personalised" phase, students choose electives (from around 70 offered) focusing on either management knowledge or managerial competencies and select one track from the following: international finance, marketing, entrepreneurship, strategies for growth, an individual professional or in company project, an international exchange. During the seven-week summer break all students undertake a further project.

Language training is available in English, French, Spanish, Italian and German.

HEC participates in the Trium Executive MBA, a programme run jointly with the London School of Economics and New York University (Stern, see page 371). It also offers a bilingual (French/English) Executive MBA.

	Full-time MBA	HEC Executive MBA
Student rating of programme	4.5 (20)	–
Number of overseas exchange programmes	88 (40)	–
Number of languages on offer	5 (42)	–

Student profile (full time)

- ■ EU
- ■ Non-EU Europe
- ▨ North America
- ■ Other Americas
- ■ Asia/Australasia
- ▨ Middle East

Students

	Full-time MBA	HEC Executive MBA
Annual intake	201	317
Applicants:places	5:1	8:1
Percentage of women students	17 (>100)	8
Percentage of foreign students	20 (57)	n/a
Average GMAT score	660 (49)	n/a
Average number of months' work experience	72 (41)	168
Age range of students	27-34	35-45
Average age	30	39
Student rating of culture and classmates	4.4 (30)	–

Recruiters/careers service

	Full-time MBA	HEC Executive MBA
Number of industry sectors that recruited graduates	8 (1)	–
Percentage of graduates in jobs 3 months after graduation	56 (>100)	–
Percentage of graduates finding jobs through careers services	60 (36)	
Student rating of careers service	3.8 (23)	–
Post-MBA salary, US$	93,436 (43)	–
Percentage increase in salary	76 (18)	
Principal recruiters of graduates	Michelin, Johnson & Johnson, Barclay's Capital	

The directory
HEC School of Management, Paris

Cost

	Full-time MBA	HEC Executive MBA
Application fees	€100 (US$114)	€300 (US$341)
Programme fees	€35,000 (US$39,773)	€30,500 (US$34,659)
Comments	Total programme	n/a
Accommodation costs (on campus, per year)	€7,400 (US$8,409)	–
Accommodation costs (off campus, per year)	€10,000 (US$11,364)	–
Financial aid available	€110,000 (US$125,000)	–
Type of aid available	Scholarships, loans	–
Criteria on which aid is granted	Merit and/or financial need	–

Accreditation

AACSB International, AMBA, EQUIS

Application details

	Full-time MBA	HEC Executive MBA
Application deadline	September 1st	–
Programme dates	Jan start, 16 months	Jan start, 15 months
Admission requirements	Bachelor's degree or higher; at least 2 years' work experience; GMAT; TOEFL or TOEIC if first language not English; 2 references; 5 essays; interview; laptop	Graduate degree; at least 8 years' work experience; reference; interview (2 steps: pre-interview and final admission jury)

Executive education

HEC runs a small number of open-enrolment programmes as well as customised in-company programmes. Often these are offered in conjunction with other business schools in Europe and the US.

Student/alumni quotes

"The atmosphere of the HEC MBA is definitely co-operative and non-competitive. Group workload is heavier than personal workload and participants spend a lot of time exchanging knowledge and working in formal or informal teams."

"Need to continue to build international reputation."

"The HEC MBA is a good path to penetrate the French business community, with its extensive alumni network."

Helsinki School of Economics

Address
Runeberginkatu 14-16
Helsinki
Finland
00100

Tel:
+358 9 4313 8208

Fax:
+358 9 4313 8841

E-mail:
mbafi@hkkk.fi

Website:
www.mbahelsinki.net

Programme director:
Dr Jyrki Wallenius

Figures in brackets
represent rank

Ranking	Rank (out of 100) Full-time
Overall rank	n/a
Regional rank	41

Background

Helsinki School of Economics was established by the local business community in 1904 and obtained university standing in 1911. It was privately run until 1974, when the Finnish state acquired financial responsibility for it. The International MBA is administered by the school's International Centre. The school is the largest institution of its kind in Finland with over 4,000 students and is full-range, offering degrees in economics and business administration at the bachelor, master, licentiate and doctoral levels.

Facilities

The MBA programme has its own recently renovated building with well-equipped classrooms, student lounge, cafeteria, and faculty and administration offices. The school has one of the largest scientific and business libraries in Scandinavia. MBA students have their own group workrooms and computers, as well as the use of other, generally available computing resources. They also have access to a well-equipped gymnasium in the main building. There is a small careers services centre for MBA students, which unfortunately does not get good reviews from students, who say most recruiting companies are Finnish. There is no on-campus accommodation, but students receive help in looking for housing.

	Full-time MBA
Student assessment of facilities	3.8 (n/a)

Faculty

Number of faculty: 5 full-time, 0 part-time, 36 visiting

	Full-time MBA	International Part-time MBA Program
Number of faculty per student	0.2 (n/a)	1.5
Percentage of faculty with PhD	80 (n/a)	80
Student rating of faculty	4.2 (n/a)	–

Strengths and weaknesses

Strengths: international business; international finance; high-technology management

Weakness: careers services

Programme highlights

The programme starts with an orientation session. Courses are offered as intensive sequential two- or three-week modules taught by visiting faculty. Full-time classes meet for four hours a day, five days a week. About half of the programme is devoted to 12 typical core courses. The rest is devoted to seven electives, which can be grouped into one of four concentrations: international finance, high technology, entrepreneurship and information technology management. A concentration is not required, but students who take a wide range of electives will be awarded a concentration in general management. Students also undertake an individual project, which may be completing a business project for a company or other organisation, writing a case or studying abroad.

The part-time MBA is identical to the full-time version. Classes meet on Monday, Wednesday and Friday evenings, and on Saturday. The programme can be completed in a minimum of two years and a maximum of four years.

The directory
Helsinki School of Economics

	Full-time MBA	International Part-time MBA Program
Student rating of programme	4.3 (n/a)	–
Number of overseas exchange programmes	40 (n/a)	–
Number of languages on offer	>5 (n/a)	–

Students

	Full-time MBA	International Part-time MBA Program
Annual intake	58	27
Applicants:places	2:1	2:1
Percentage of women students	28 (n/a)	15
Percentage of foreign students	60 (n/a)	n/a
Average GMAT score	555 (n/a)	580
Average number of months' work experience	60 (n/a)	120
Age range of students	26-41	28-46
Average age	31	35
Student rating of culture and classmates	4.1 (n/a)	–

Student profile (full time)

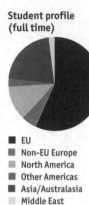

- ■ EU
- ■ Non-EU Europe
- ■ North America
- ■ Other Americas
- ■ Asia/Australasia
- ▨ Middle East

Recruiters/careers service

	Full-time MBA	International Part-time MBA Program
Number of industry sectors that recruited graduates	6 (n/a)	–
Percentage of graduates in jobs 3 months after graduation	75 (n/a)	–
Percentage of graduates finding jobs through careers services	n/a (n/a)	–
Student rating of careers service	3.1 (n/a)	–
Post-MBA salary, US$	65,227 (n/a)	–
Percentage increase in salary	13 (n/a)	–
Principal recruiters of graduates	Nokia, Accenture, IBM	

Cost

	Full-time MBA	International Part-time MBA Program
Application fees	None	None
Programme fees	€18,000 (US$20,455)	€23,000 (US$26,136)
Comments	Total programme	Includes books
Accommodation costs (on campus, per year)	–	–
Accommodation costs (off campus, per year)	€4,800 (US$5,455)	–
Financial aid available	€106 (US$120)	–
Type of aid available	Scholarships and grants for best students for study abroad	–
Criteria on which aid is granted	GMAT over 640 and excellent academic record	–

Accreditation

AMBA, EQUIS

Application details

	Full-time MBA	International Part-time MBA Program
Application deadline	Rolling admissions	September 30th
Programme dates	Mar start, 12 months	Jan start, 24 months
Admission requirements	Bachelor's degree; at least 2 years' work experience; GMAT; TOEFL if first language not English; 2 references; 4 essays; interview may be required	Bachelor's degree; at least 3 years' work experience; GMAT; TOEFL if first language not English; 2 references; 4 essays; interview may be required

Executive education

Helsinki operates The Small Business Centre (established in 1980), which has developed training and development services with the objectives of the long-term success of small and medium-sized enterprises and the maintenance of their competitiveness.

Student/alumni quotes

"Value for money is superb compared with the competition (eg UK schools); quality accreditations (EQUIS, AMBA); excellent infrastructure (libraries, buildings); very high educational level of Finns; exotic landscape!"

"They should sell their reputation outside Finland. They have a great advantage and they don't use it fully."

Henley Management College

Ranking	Rank (out of 100) Full-time
Overall rank	26
Regional rank	7

Criteria	Rank (out of 100) Full-time
Open new career opportunities	**>100**
Diversity of recruiters	96
Number in jobs three months after graduation	>100
Jobs found through the careers service	74
Student assessment of careers service	>100
Personal development and educational experience	**13**
Faculty quality	49
Student quality	2
Student diversity	>100
Education experience	92
Increase in salary	**2**
Increase in salary	>100
Post-MBA salary	2
Potential to network	**1**
Breadth of alumni network	1
Internationalism of alumni	1
Alumni effectiveness	72

Address
Greenlands
Henley-on-Thames
Oxfordshire
UK
RG9 3AU

Tel:
+44 1491 418 802

Fax:
+44 1491 418 899

E-mail:
kathy.jarvis@
henleymc.ac.uk

Website:
www.henleymc.ac.uk

Programme director:
Dr Susan Foreman

Figures in brackets
represent rank

Background

Henley Management College was established by business leaders in 1945, largely to deliver executive education. Its involvement in executive education continues and Henley is a major and innovative player in this market. However, it is also a considerable force in the MBA market through its large-scale international distance-learning programme, which was launched in 1984. The international reach of this programme is impressive. Henley has over 6,000 distance-learning students throughout the world. The programme can be studied in the UK or in any of the 21 countries where there is a Henley partner or office.

Facilities

The college is based in a mini-campus complex of three linked buildings that provide superb facilities for MBA students, undergraduates and participants in executive education programmes. The layout favours informal contacts between students and faculty. Faculty offices are designed to encourage "clusters" of teaching and research staff from different disciplines and so reinforce greater integration of core courses on the MBA programme.

	Full-time MBA
Student assessment of facilities	4.2 (65)

Faculty

Number of faculty: 51 full-time, 85 part-time, 15 visiting				
	Full-time MBA	Henley Distance Learning MBA	Flexible Evening MBA	Modular Two Year MBA Programme (Executive)
Number of faculty per student	2.9 (3)	<0.1	3.7	4.9
Percentage of faculty with PhD	61 (>100)	61	61	61
Student rating of faculty	3.9 (87)	–	–	–

Strengths and weaknesses

Strengths: strategy; leadership; knowledge management

Weakness: careers services

Programme highlights

Henley offers only one MBA, although there are numerous ways of studying for the degree all following the same curriculum and structure. There is scope for students to switch from one programme to another if their circumstances change. Henley also offers specialised MBAs in project management and telecommunications as well as company and consortium MBAs.

All programmes begin with the Foundations of Management course, which includes managing information and managing people. Part 2 covers the main functional core. Part 3 includes strategy issues, electives and the final dissertation.

Although designated a full-time programme, the one-year Executive MBA is designed to allow students to continue in employment if they so wish. The programme is divided into four four-week residential modules at Henley and other international business schools and includes international study trips to Spain, the US and Asia and Australasia, which account for four or five of the 16 weeks. Students have full use of Henley's web-based e-learning and e-library systems and there is a parallel skills development workshop including presentation and communication, negotiating and team-working. There is also a work placement scheme for students not in employment. The programme has a single annual intake in January.

The Modular two-year programme involves attendance at Henley through a series of four one-week residential periods and two study weeks, linked by a series of two- or three-day workshops and projects within students' own organisations. Students take part in a one-week European study trip in the first year (past destinations have included Barcelona, Turin, St Petersburg and Budapest) and a one-week international study trip in the second year (past destinations have included Cape Town, Boston and Hangzhou). They maintain contact outside residential modules via Henley's e-learning system.

The Flexible Evening MBA lasts two years and is studied at the British Bankers' Association facilities in the City of London and in Frankfurt. Both groups work together and with Henley's modular MBA students. Classes meet two evenings a week on Tuesday (for face-to-face teaching) and Thursday (for group-based activity).

The Distance Learning MBA typically takes about two and a half years to complete. Students attend a residential weekend at Henley at the start of the programme and a two-day residential module approximately every six months. Henley has more or less abandoned paper (except for textbooks), and the programme is delivered by a mixture of CDs and impressive online learning support. E-learning is supervised by two personal tutors per programme and online subject tutors. Administration and assignment submission is electronic.

	Full-time MBA	Henley Distance Learning MBA	Flexible Evening MBA	Modular Two Year MBA Programme (Executive)
Student rating of programme	4.0 (67)	–	–	–
Number of overseas exchange programmes	0 (93)	–	–	–
Number of languages on offer	0 (94)	–	–	–

The directory
Henley Management College

Students

	Full-time MBA	Henley Distance Learning MBA	Flexible Evening MBA	Modular Two Year MBA Programme (Executive)
Annual intake	33	240	41	31
Applicants:places	2:1	2:1	2:1	2:1
Percentage of women students	26 (81)	32	24	39
Percentage of foreign students	33 (95)	29	n/a	n/a
Average GMAT score	n/a (n/a)	n/a	n/a	n/a
Average number of months' work experience	120 (3)	120	108	132
Age range of students	31–47	26–44	27–42	27–46
Average age	34	34	33	35
Student rating of culture and classmates	4.0 (70)	–	–	–

Student profile (full time)

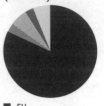

- ■ EU
- ■ Non-EU Europe
- ■ North America
- ■ Other Americas
- ■ Asia/Australasia
- ▨ Middle East

Recruiters/careers service

	Full-time MBA	Henley Distance Learning MBA	Flexible Evening MBA	Modular Two Year MBA Programme (Executive)
Number of industry sectors that recruited graduates	6 (96)	–	–	–
Percentage of graduates in jobs 3 months after graduation	18 (111)	–	–	–
Percentage of graduates finding jobs through careers services	29 (74)	–	–	–
Student rating of careers service	2.9 (103)	–	–	–
Post-MBA salary, US$	127,869 (2)	–	–	–
Percentage increase in salary	22 (101)	–	–	–
Principal recruiters of graduates	BT Retail, Co-op, Vodafone			

Cost

	Full-time MBA	Henley Distance Learning MBA	Flexible Evening MBA	Modular Two Year MBA Programme (Executive)
Application fees	None	None	None	None
Programme fees	£33,000 (US$54,098)	£13,700 (US$22,459)	£24,950 (US$40,902)	£24,950 (US$40,902)
Comments	Includes £2,000 for travel. A further £500 is required for text books	–	–	A further £700 is required for travel costs
Accommodation costs (on campus, per year)	£5,400 (US$8,852)	–	–	–
Accommodation costs (off campus, per year)	–	–	–	–
Financial aid available	£88,000 (US$144,262)	–	–	–
Type of aid available	Scholarships, bursaries	–	–	–
Criteria on which aid is granted	Normal admission criteria, plus essay- and diversity-based	–	–	–

Accreditation

AACSB International, AMBA, EQUIS

Application details

	Full-time MBA	Henley Distance Learning MBA	Flexible Evening MBA	Modular Two Year MBA Programme (Executive)
Application deadline	November 1st	Rolling admissions	July 15th	July 15th
Programme dates	Jan start, 12 months	Jan start, 36 months	Sep start, 24 months	Sep start, 24 months
Admission requirements	First degree; at least 5 years' work experience; TOEFL if first language not English; 2 references; essay; interview; laptop; group exercise at selection day	First degree; at least 3 years' work experience; TOEFL if first language not English; 2 references; candidates may be required to complete a questionnaire and attend an interview	First degree; at least 3 years' work experience; TOEFL if first language not English; 2 references; essay; interview; group exercise	First degree; at least 3 years' work experience; TOEFL if first language not English; 2 references; essay; interview, group exercise

Executive education

Henley has a strong executive education arm and offers open-enrolment programmes in general management, leadership, strategy, finance, marketing and personal skills as well as seminars and masterclasses in topical subjects. It also has extensive experience in running customised in-company programmes.

Student/alumni quotes

"The Henley MBA is without doubt an intensive experience but the friendly and high-contact faculty make it very relevant and personal—directly applicable to the working environment."

"Full-time MBA could be too intensive for some."

"Excellent student population, diverse programme with international components."

Heriot-Watt University—Edinburgh Business School

Address
Heriot-Watt
University
Riccarton Campus
Edinburgh
UK
EH14 4AS

Tel:
+44 131 451 3090

Fax:
+44 131 451 3002

E-mail:
oncampusmba@ebs.
hw.ac.uk

Website:
ebsmba.com

Programme director:
Keith G Lumsden

Figures in brackets
represent rank

Ranking	Rank (out of 100) Full-time
Overall rank	n/a
Regional rank	n/a

Background

Edinburgh Business School (EBS) is the Graduate School of Business of Heriot-Watt University. The school offers a portfolio of MBA programmes, each of which leads to the award of the Heriot-Watt University MBA. It also specialises in the design and delivery of tailored executive development programmes.

The school was created in 1995 as a centre for innovation in methods of delivering management education and is closely linked with Pearson Education, which administers the distance-learning programme (and which also publishes Which MBA?). Its offices around the world serve the needs of EBS distance-learning students (and prospective students), providing information, assistance, programme-planning hints and supplementary materials.

Facilities

EBS has its own building in the centre of the university campus, about 25 minutes' drive west of Edinburgh. Facilities are good. The school has two 60-seat teaching rooms, each with eight syndicate rooms attached, student dining facilities and faculty offices. On-campus accommodation is available for full-time students and also during part-time weekend teaching sessions, although this may be limited.

	Full-time MBA
Student assessment of facilities	n/a (n/a)

Faculty

12 full-time, 20 part-time, 6 visiting

	Full-time MBA	Distance learning MBA	Part Time MBA
Number of faculty per student	0.5 (n/a)	>0.1	0.7
Percentage of faculty with PhD	67	67	67
Student rating of faculty	n/a (n/a)	–	–

Strengths and weaknesses

Strengths: strategy; finance; project management

Weakness: involvement of alumni network

Programme highlights

The EBS MBA is modular and all variants of the degree (full-time, part-time and distance learning) are identical in content. Students can easily switch between the various delivery formats. All students complete the same seven core courses and choose at least two electives. Waivers may be available. Electives are chosen from a comparatively small, varying list.

The full-time programme is taught over one year of four terms. Normally, each course is taught for a full day once a week over a six-week term and is followed by examinations. Some courses are taught to full-time and part-time students together. Students use material from the distance-learning programme for self-study before each course. Generally, full-time students follow two courses per term. Students can specialise in a particular area (marketing, human resource management, finance and strategic planning) by completing the seven compulsory courses and four electives chosen from designated lists.

The part-time programme includes periods of self-study and two periods of on-campus classes (Friday, Saturday and Sunday) for each course. The programme can be completed in two years but this can be extended according to personal circumstances.

The distance-learning MBA is largely self-contained with both paper-based and online courses. There are also student self-help groups, a school helpline, local tuition, e-mail access and summer schools in Edinburgh. Distance learning students can also opt to take some modules on campus with full-time students. The maximum time allowed to take the degree is seven years.

EBS also runs a part-time consortium MBA for companies based in Scotland.

	Full-time MBA	Distance learning MBA	Part Time MBA
Student rating of programme	n/a (n/a)	–	–
Number of overseas exchange programmes	0 (n/a)	–	–
Number of languages on offer	0 (n/a)	–	–

Students

	Full-time MBA	Distance learning MBA	Part Time MBA
Annual intake	50	1,700	34
Applicants:places	7:1	–	3:1
Percentage of women students	24 (n/a)	32	24
Percentage of foreign students	88 (n/a)	–	–
Average GMAT score	n/a	n/a	n/a
Average number of months' work experience	72 (n/a)	144	144
Age range of students	24-37	26-45	24-46
Average age	28	35	34
Student rating of culture and classmates	n/a (n/a)	–	–

Recruiters/careers service

	Full-time MBA	Distance learning MBA	Part Time MBA
Number of industry sectors that recruited graduates	–	–	–
Percentage of graduates in jobs 3 months after graduation	–	–	–
Percentage of graduates finding jobs through careers services	–	–	–
Student rating of careers service	n/a	–	–
Post-MBA salary, US$	–	–	–
Percentage increase in salary	–	–	–
Principal recruiters of graduates	–		

Student profile (full time)

■ EU
■ Non-EU Europe
▨ North America
■ Other Americas
■ Asia/Australasia
▨ Middle East

The directory

Heriot-Watt University—Edinburgh Business School

Cost

	Full-time MBA	Distance learning MBA	Part Time MBA
Application fees	None	None	None
Programme fees	£13,185 (US$21,615)	£900 (US$1,475)	£13,185 (US$21,615)
Comments	Total programme	Per course. Completion of nine courses required for MBA	Total programme
Accommodation costs (on campus, per year)	£3,000 (US$4,918)	–	–
Accommodation costs (off campus, per year)	£2,800 (US$4,590)	–	–
Financial aid available	£25,000 (US$40,984)	–	–
Type of aid available	Scholarships	–	–
Criteria on which aid is granted	Merit, financial need	–	–

Accreditation

None

Application details

	Full-time MBA	Distance learning MBA	Part Time MBA
Application deadline	July 16th	n/a	July 31st
Programme dates	Oct start, 12 months	Start any time	Oct start, 24 months
Admission requirements	First degree; at least 3 years' work experience; TOEFL or IELTS if first language not English; 2 references	First degree; must have reasonable command of English if studying courses in English language	First degree; at least 3 years' work experience; TOEFL or IELTS if first language not English; 2 references

Executive education

EBS does not offer open-enrolment or customised in-company executive education programmes.

Student/alumni quotes

"To be honest, I was surprised at the high quality of the programme content and the expectations required to pass each exam. The EBS MBA is not for the faint at heart."

"Material dates very quickly, but they have introduced online materials now which should get round this."

"Flexibility of training and examinations, coupled with the wide availability of the programme in 150 countries, makes this the best option for the travelling or working professional."

University of Hong Kong—School of Business

Address
Faculty of Business &
Economics
The University of
Hong Kong
Room 733, Meng Wah
Complex
Pokfulam
Hong Kong

Tel:
+852 2241 5639

Fax:
+852 2549 3735

E-mail:
hkumba@fbe.hk.hk

Website:
www.fbe.hku.hk

Programme director:
K S Maurice Tse

Figures in brackets
represent rank

Ranking	Rank (out of 100) Full-time
Overall rank	68
Regional rank	3

Criteria	Rank (out of 100) Full-time
Open new career opportunities	**19**
Diversity of recruiters	45
Number in jobs three months after graduation	3
Jobs found through the careers service	11
Student assessment of careers service	71
Personal development and educational experience	**42**
Faculty quality	33
Student quality	62
Student diversity	36
Education experience	39
Increase in salary	**>100**
Increase in salary	3
Post-MBA salary	>100
Potential to network	**47**
Breadth of alumni network	>100
Internationalism of alumni	9
Alumni effectiveness	77

Background

The University of Hong Kong was founded in 1911 and is the oldest university in the territory. The School of Business was created in 1995 following the merger of the former department of management studies (which mainly taught undergraduate degrees) and the old business school (masters degrees and executive education) with the specific aim of developing Asian business education. Along with the School of Economics and Finance it is part of the university's Faculty of Business and Economics.

In a surprising move, in May 2004 Hong Kong University and Hong Kong University of Science and Technology (see page 272) announced that they were discussing the feasibility of collaborating to create a joint business school. At the time of going to press, no further details had emerged.

The school has strong research expertise in Asia and Australasia and, through the Poon Kam Kai Institute, its consulting arm, has good links with local and international industry. As well as its MBA and other master's programmes, the school teaches undergraduate and doctoral programmes.

Facilities

The school is located in the K K Leung building on the main university campus on Hong Kong Island, not far from the main business district. It also has a downtown campus at the Admiralty Centre, in the heart of the business community, where classes are taught for both the MBA and short executive education programmes.

	Full-time MBA	Part-time MBA
Student assessment of facilities	4.5 (17)	–

The directory
University of Hong Kong—School of Business

Faculty

Number of faculty: 72 full-time, 4 part-time, 30 visiting

	Full-time MBA	Part-time MBA
Number of faculty per student	2.0 (14)	1.6
Percentage of faculty with PhD	92 (71)	92
Student rating of faculty	4.2 (63)	–

Strengths and weaknesses

Strengths: business strategy; finance and accounting control; China business and China marketing

Weakness: elective range and choice

Programme highlights

The MBA is offered in full-time and part-time versions. The full-time programme must be completed within a minimum of one academic year and a maximum of two. The part-time programme lasts a minimum of two academic years and a maximum of four. The programme features five themes: doing business in China and the region; accounting, financial control and corporate governance; information technology; e-business; and managing people and change. Students take five typical core courses, one course from each theme area, six electives and a capstone strategy course plus executive workshops.

Courses are taught in modules of 5–7 weeks followed by examinations. Classes meet two or three times a week (weekday evenings, 6.30–9.30 pm, at HKU Town Centre and Saturday afternoons, 1.00–7.00 pm on the main campus).

The MBA is also offered in conjunction with the School of Management of Fudan University in Shanghai. Some transfer between programmes is available.

	Full-time MBA	Part-time MBA
Student rating of programme	3.8 (>100)	–
Number of overseas exchange programmes	30 (20)	–
Number of languages on offer	>5 (25)	–

Students

	Full-time MBA	Part-time MBA
Annual intake	40	65
Applicants:places	4:1	8:1
Percentage of women students	45 (17)	38
Percentage of foreign students	90 (8)	n/a
Average GMAT score	610 (81)	600
Average number of months' work experience	84 (23)	100
Age range of students	25-36	25-42
Average age	28	31
Student rating of culture and classmates	3.4 (112)	–

Recruiters/careers service

	Full-time MBA	Part-time MBA
Number of industry sectors that recruited graduates	8 (45)	–
Percentage of graduates in jobs 3 months after graduation	100 (3)	–
Percentage of graduates finding jobs through careers services	60 (11)	–
Student rating of careers service	3.5 (71)	–
Post-MBA salary, US$	15,942 (>100)	–
Percentage increase in salary	91 (3)	–
Principal recruiters of graduates	–	

Student profile (full time)

- ■ EU
- ▨ Non-EU Europe
- ▨ North America
- ■ Other Americas
- ■ Asia/Australasia
- ▨ Middle East

Cost

	Full-time MBA	Part-time MBA
Application fees	US$19	US$19
Programme fees	US$21,350	US$24,230
Comments	Total programme. Payable in three instalments	–
Accommodation costs (on campus, per year)	US$3,800	–
Accommodation costs (off campus, per year)	US$3,000	–
Financial aid available	US$64,000	
Type of aid available	Scholarships	–
Criteria on which aid is granted	Undergraduate academic performance, GMAT, work experience, interview performance	–

Accreditation

None

Application details

	Full-time MBA	Part-time MBA
Application deadline	February 28th	February 28th
Programme dates	Sep start, 12 months	Sep start, 24 months
Admission requirements	First degree; at least 3 years' work experience; GMAT; TOEFL if degree is not from an English-speaking country; 2 references; essay; interview; laptop	First degree; at least 3 years' work experience; GMAT; TOEFL if degree is not from an English-speaking country; 2 references; essay; interview

Executive education

The school's executive education is organised through the Poon Kam Kai Institute of Management, a non-profit management consultancy established in 1990 and owned by the University of Hong Kong. The institute offers a wide range of open-enrolment courses, customised in-company courses and consultancy.

Student/alumni quotes

"I think the programme is good. I like the arrangement of the courses. The cases used in the courses are very effective in our study and the lecturers are very professional. But it [would be] better to provide more career service and internships for the students."

"Limited variety of electives."

"Overall, the MBA programme has been an enjoyable one, with co-operative staff and fellow students. Group projects and class interaction are definitely reasons for choosing either a part-time or full-time (only if not currently employed) MBA over distance-learning."

Hong Kong University of Science and Technology—School of Business and Management

Ranking	Rank (out of 100) Full-time
Overall rank	n/a
Regional rank	9

Address
MBA Program, HKUST
Room 5601, Annex
Clearwater Bay
Kowloon
Hong Kong

Tel:
+852 2358 7535

Fax:
+852 2705 9596

E-mail:
mba@ust.hk

Website:
www.bm.ust.hk/mba

Programme director:
Steven DeKrey

Figures in brackets
represent rank

Background

The School of Business and Management at Hong Kong University of Science and Technology (HKUST) was founded in 1991 with help from the Anderson School at UCLA in the US. Although the school stresses its regional expertise, it has always aimed to be seen as a mainstream international business school, an ambition that it is achieving.

HKUST is highly specialised. It has only four schools: Business and Management (which enrols almost 40% of the university's undergraduate students and approximately 30% of its postgraduate students); Science; Engineering; and Humanities and Social Sciences (which supports the others by offering, for example, language courses).

Facilities

HKUST's campus is spectacularly sited above Clearwater Bay, about 30 minutes' drive from downtown Hong Kong. Library and computer facilities are excellent and the whole university is wired with fibre optics, allowing access to the computer network, including the library, from virtually anywhere. The technological bias of the university means that students have access to an impressive range of laboratories and design equipment, including an operations management simulation laboratory and a behavioural laboratory. On-campus accommodation is available.

	Full-time MBA
Student assessment of facilities	4.1 (n/a)

Faculty

Number of faculty: 101 full-time, 1 part-time, 29 visiting

	Full-time MBA	HKUST MBA Program (part-time)	Kellogg-HKUST Executive MBA Program
Number of faculty per student	2.2 (n/a)	1.1	2.7
Percentage of faculty with PhD	100 (n/a)	100	100
Student rating of faculty	4.0 (n/a)	–	–

Strengths and weaknesses

Strengths: China business; finance; information technology management

Weakness: marketing courses; elective choice

Programme highlights

The 18-month full-time programme starts with a required five-day orientation course in managerial problem solving that stresses interpersonal skills, teamwork, the case study approach and group working. This is followed by core courses and electives, which take up about one-third of the programme. Most electives are offered on Saturdays to allow full-time and part-time students to mix. Concentrations are not required but are available in China business, information technology management and financial services. To complete the concentration, students take ten credits of elective courses in the relevant area.

As well as traditional courses, the school organises a series of enrichment programmes. These are workshops, seminars and presentations designed to develop creativity, self-awareness, leadership and other soft skills.

Core courses for the part-time programme (which can be completed in a minimum of two years) are identical to the full-time version, but fewer electives are required. Classes are held on campus on Saturdays.

HKUST also runs a part-time MBA programme in Shenzhen. This two-year programme is jointly administered with Peking University. The curriculum is similar to the Hong Kong part-time MBA and is taught in English by HKUST faculty. Classes meet on Saturdays in Shenzhen.

HKUST's Executive MBA is offered jointly with Kellogg School of Management (see page 386) and Kellogg faculty teach half of the courses. The degree is awarded jointly by both universities. The programme lasts 16 months and participants meet twice a month (Friday midday–Sunday evening), staying on the HKUST campus. There are two six-day live-in, or residential, sessions. The first is at HKUST in Hong Kong at the start of the programme in January, and the second is at Kellogg in the US (near Chicago) in September and includes a marketing simulation game. Participants take 28 courses with no electives.

	Full-time MBA	HKUST MBA Program (part-time)	Kellogg-HKUST Executive MBA Program
Student rating of programme	3.6 (n/a)	–	–
Number of overseas exchange programmes	90 (n/a)	–	–
Number of languages on offer	0 (n/a)	–	–

Student profile (full time)

- ■ EU
- ■ Non-EU Europe
- ▨ North America
- ■ Other Americas
- ■ Asia/Australasia
- ▨ Middle East

Students

	Full-time MBA	HKUST MBA Program (part-time)	Kellogg-HKUST Executive MBA Program
Annual intake	50	122	48
Applicants:places	5:1	3:1	–
Percentage of women students	48 (n/a)	44	29
Percentage of foreign students	82 (n/a)	n/a	n/a
Average GMAT score	633 (n/a)	593	n/a
Average number of months' work experience	60 (n/a)	84	168
Age range of students	24-33	26-35	32-43
Average age	28	30	37
Student rating of culture and classmates	3.4 (n/a)	–	–

Recruiters/careers service

	Full-time MBA	HKUST MBA Program (part-time)	Kellogg-HKUST Executive MBA Program
Number of industry sectors that recruited graduates	5 (n/a)	–	–
Percentage of graduates in jobs 3 months after graduation	86 (n/a)	–	–
Percentage of graduates finding jobs through careers services	25 (n/a)	–	–
Student rating of careers service	2.8 (n/a)	–	–
Post-MBA salary, US$	45,154 (n/a)	–	–
Percentage increase in salary	45 (45)	–	–
Principal recruiters of graduates	American Appraisal, Emerson Electric, HSBC		

The directory
Hong Kong University of Science and Technology—School of Business and Management

Cost

	Full-time MBA	HKUST MBA Program (part-time)	Kellogg-HKUST Executive MBA Program
Application fees	US$64	US$64	US$200
Programme fees	US$25,900	US$25,900	US$70,500
Comments	Total programme	Total programme	Total programme
Accommodation costs (on campus, per year)	US$2,800	–	–
Accommodation costs (off campus, per year)	US$6,200	–	–
Financial aid available	Varies	–	–
Type of aid available	Scholarships	–	–
Criteria on which aid is granted	Merit, financial need	–	–

Accreditation
AACSB International, EQUIS

Application details

	Full-time MBA	HKUST MBA Program (part-time)	Kellogg-HKUST Executive MBA Program
Application deadline	March 30th	March 30th	September 30th
Programme dates	Aug start, 18 months	Aug start, 24 months	Jan start, 15 months
Admission requirements	First degree; at least 1 year's work experience; TOEFL if degree is not from an English-speaking country; 2 references; essay; interview; laptop	First degree; at least 3 years' work experience; 2 references; essay; interview	Bachelor degree from a recognised university or an approved institution; at least 10 years' work experience; GMAT if degree is not from an English-speaking country; 2 references; essay; interview; company sponsorship and support

Executive education
HKUST runs executive open programmes, including diplomas in management and e-commerce, and shorter programmes in finance, marketing, management and technology. It also offers customised in-company programmes in areas such as leadership, finance and accounting, technology, marketing, strategy and China business.

Student/alumni quotes

"For a westerner wanting to figure out what is going on in China, HKUST is a great choice. It is still 'western' in teaching style but has many mainland China students and faculty and has strong links with mainland China."

"Reputation is growing, faculty quality is good, international content is good—tuition cost is comparatively cheap to get all these."

"[There is an] absence of electives outside finance, accounting and China business."

Hult International Business School

Address
1 Education Street
Cambridge, MA
USA
02141

Tel:
+1 617 619 1040

Fax:
+1 617 746 1991

E-mail;
susan.adler@
hult.edu

Website:
www.hult.edu

Programme director:
Lynne Rosansky

Figures in brackets
represent rank

Ranking	Rank (out of 100) Full-time
Overall rank	59
Regional rank	37

Criteria	Rank (out of 100) Full-time
Open new career opportunities	**63**
Diversity of recruiters	1
Number in jobs three months after graduation	90
Jobs found through the careers service	71
Student assessment of careers service	37
Personal development and educational experience	**86**
Faculty quality	97
Student quality	79
Student diversity	39
Education experience	87
Increase in salary	**35**
Increase in salary	11
Post-MBA salary	72
Potential to network	**13**
Breadth of alumni network	6
Internationalism of alumni	10
Alumni effectiveness	82

Background

The former Arthur D Little School of Management, operating since 1964, has been taken over by EF Education, the world's largest privately held education organisation. EF has over 20,000 teachers and staff and offices in 50 different countries. The school has been renamed after Bertil Hult, EF's founder, who started the business in 1965 teaching Swedish children to speak English.

As yet the school has made few changes to the MBA programme, but it does stress the high proportion of foreign students (98%), which was an Arthur D Little trademark. It is therefore not surprising that English-language training is high on its agenda.

Facilities

Hult has new, modern facilities on two campuses in Boston: a downtown site on the Charles River and the Brighton campus in the suburbs about 20 minutes from downtown. On-campus accommodation is available and the school will help students find other housing.

	Full-time MBA
Student assessment of facilities	3.9 (68)

Faculty

Number of faculty: 3 full-time, 22 part-time, 20 visiting

	Full-time MBA
Number of faculty per student	0.5 (41)
Percentage of faculty with PhD	67 (>100)
Student rating of faculty	4.2 (69)

The directory
Hult International Business School

Strengths and weaknesses

Strengths: international business; global consulting; strategy

Weakness: low profile

Programme highlights

Hult's one-year MBA has a modular format based on three central themes: managing a high-perform-ance organisation; sustaining competitive advantage; and creating the future. Teaching methods include case studies, lectures, exercises, simulations and a project. There is a strong emphasis on action-learning techniques.

The core is covered in the first two modules, with the third given over to six electives chosen from a small offering including an individual project. The programme starts with a four-week foundation session covering basic business skills. There are optional study tours to New York, Europe or Asia.

	Full-time MBA
Student rating of programme	4.1 (70)
Number of overseas exchange programmes	0 (93)
Number of languages on offer	1 (83)

Students

	Full-time MBA
Annual intake	42
Applicants:places	3:1
Percentage of women students	22 (>100)
Percentage of foreign students	98 (2)
Average GMAT score	580 (>100)
Average number of months' work experience	96 (8)
Age range of students	25–40
Average age	32
Student rating of culture and classmates	4.2 (61)

Student profile (full time)

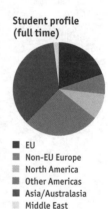

- ■ EU
- ■ Non-EU Europe
- ■ North America
- ■ Other Americas
- ■ Asia/Australasia
- ■ Middle East

Recruiters/careers service

	Full-time MBA
Number of industry sectors that recruited graduates	8 (1)
Percentage of graduates in jobs 3 months after graduation	60 (90)
Percentage of graduates finding jobs through careers services	25 (71)
Student rating of careers service	3.8 (37)
Post-MBA salary, US$	72,000 (72)
Percentage increase in salary	125 (11)
Principal recruiters of graduates	Johnson & Johnson, Siemens, IBM

Cost

	Full-time MBA
Application fees	US$75
Programme fees	US$36,000
Comments	–
Accommodation costs (on campus, per year)	–
Accommodation costs (off campus, per year)	US$8,000
Financial aid available	US$350,000
Type of aid available	Scholarships, fellowships, loans
Criteria on which aid is granted	Academic and professional merit, financial need

Accreditation

None

Application details

	Full-time MBA
Application deadline	June 15th
Programme dates	Sep start, 11 months
Admission requirements	First degree; work experience; TOEFL if first language not English (minimum 240, computer-based); 2 references; essays; interview; laptop

Executive education

Hult does not currently offer executive education programmes.

Student/alumni quotes

"Hult suited what I was looking for as I would obtain a good general MBA with no particular speciality, meet students from other countries and complete the programme in a year."

"[There is a] lack of time—11 months is a short period."

"Diverse experience and the accelerated programme save time and money—[it is] cost effective."

IE—Instituto de Empresa

Ranking	Rank (out of 100) Full-time
Overall rank	21
Regional rank	5

Criteria	Rank (out of 100) Full-time
Open new career opportunities	**10**
Diversity of recruiters	1
Number in jobs three months after graduation	64
Jobs found through the careers service	12
Student assessment of careers service	5
Personal development and educational experience	**21**
Faculty quality	47
Student quality	37
Student diversity	5
Education experience	63
Increase in salary	**100**
Increase in salary	24
Post-MBA salary	>100
Potential to network	**10**
Breadth of alumni network	14
Internationalism of alumni	18
Alumni effectiveness	16

Address
María de Molina
11-13-15
Madrid
Spain
28006

Tel:
+34 91 745 2124

Fax:
+34 91 745 2147

E-mail:
admissions@ie.edu

Website:
www.ie.edu

Programme director:
Camino de Paz

Figures in brackets
represent rank

Background

Instituto de Empresa (IE) is a private academic institution set up in 1973 by business leaders and academics. It has strong links with Latin America and the Philippines and as well as its European and North American counterparts. It also has good links with industry through a division devoted to consultancy and in-company training. Like many other schools in Spain, IE is a strong advocate of the case method and group work.

In summer 2004, the dean, Angel Cabrera, who has done much to put IE on the global business school map, left to take over as head of Thunderbird (see page 477). He was replaced by Santiago Iñiguez, professor of strategic management and director of external relations at IE, who has played a major role in expanding the institution in Latin America.

Facilities

The school is based in the centre of Madrid's financial district, and its greatly enlarged and improved premises include 39 classrooms with laptop access and 65 team rooms. The main library facilities are in a recently opened building that operates as the nerve centre of IE's information system. The virtual library is also managed from this building. There is no on-campus accommodation.

	Full-time MBA
Student assessment of facilities	4.0 (56)

Faculty

Number of faculty: 95 full-time, 200 part-time, 29 visiting			
	Full-time MBA	International Executive MBA	Executive MBA
Number of faculty per student	1.0 (25)	10.8	1.0
Percentage of faculty with PhD	82 (87)	82	82
Student rating of faculty	4.3 (27)	–	–

Strengths and weaknesses

Strengths: entrepreneurship; strategy; general management

Weakness: on-campus facilities could be improved further

Programme highlights

IE's full-time MBA lasts 13 months. The first part of the programme is taught wholly in English, but non-Spanish speakers must undergo intensive language training. In later periods courses may be taught in Spanish. The programme proper begins in November, but students can take online pre-programme analytical and quantitative courses (and Spanish language training) during September and October before going to Madrid.

The first period of the programme aims to bring students from different academic backgrounds up to speed and also introduce them to entrepreneurial studies, an important element of IE's approach. The second period is essentially the core. The third period focuses on global strategies; bilingual classes start in this period. The final period consists of electives and/or an exchange programme. A guest-speaker and conference series runs throughout the first three periods and there are a number of self-development workshops. The World Reality Seminar in September analyses the major regional markets.

IE's International Executive MBA also lasts 13 months. There are three intensive two-week residential periods (two in Madrid and one in Miami) and two six-month online periods. Additional study requirements are 12 hours per day in residential periods and some 15 hours per week in online periods. The course is divided into two modules: basics and integration. Both combine residential and online sessions to present most of the subject matter. The residential sessions are rounded off with seminars designed to develop essential management skills while providing an up to the minute vision of business realities. The online sessions take place between the three planned residential periods. Before the programme starts, students take an introductory online course in the basics of financial accounting.

The school also offers a Spanish-language MBA (full-time and part-time) and two Executive MBAs in Spanish.

	Full-time MBA	International Executive MBA	Executive MBA
Student rating of programme	4.3 (21)	–	–
Number of overseas exchange programmes	21 (70)	–	–
Number of languages on offer	1 (83)	–	–

Students

Student profile (full time)

- ■ EU
- ▨ Non-EU Europe
- ▨ North America
- ■ Other Americas
- ■ Asia/Australasia
- ▨ Middle East

	Full-time MBA	International Executive MBA	Executive MBA
Annual intake	208	30	311
Applicants:places	4:1	3:1	2:1
Percentage of women students	38 (14)	35	35
Percentage of foreign students	83 (19)	25	n/a
Average GMAT score	670 (29)	670	670
Average number of months' work experience	66 (49)	85	84
Age range of students	27–34	32–38	32–38
Average age	30	35	36
Student rating of culture and classmates	3.9 (44)	–	–

The directory
IE—Instituto de Empresa

Recruiters/careers service

	Full-time MBA	International Executive MBA	Executive MBA
Number of industry sectors that recruited graduates	8 (1)	–	–
Percentage of graduates in jobs 3 months after graduation	71 (64)	–	–
Percentage of graduates finding jobs through careers services	75 (12)	–	–
Student rating of careers service	4.1 (5)	–	–
Post-MBA salary, US$	56,818 (>100)	–	–
Percentage increase in salary	67 (24)	–	–
Principal recruiters of graduates	Telefónica, Accenture, Endesa		

Cost

	Full-time MBA	International Executive MBA	Executive MBA
Application fees	€120 (US$136)	€120 (US$136)	€120 (US$136)
Programme fees	€36,900 (US$41,932)	€36,000 (US$40,909)	€28,000 (US$31,818)
Comments	–	–	–
Accommodation costs (on campus, per year)	–	–	–
Accommodation costs (off campus, per year)	€20,000 (US$22,727)	–	–
Financial aid available	€275 (US$313)	–	–
Type of aid available	Scholarships, loans	–	–
Criteria on which aid is granted	Merit	–	–

Accreditation

AACSB International, AMBA, EQUIS

Application details

	Full-time MBA	International Executive MBA	Executive MBA
Application deadline	Rolling admissions	Rolling admissions	Rolling admissions
Programme dates	Nov start, 13 months	Nov start, 13 months	Oct start, 10 months
Admission requirements	Bachelor's degree; at least 5 years' work experience; GMAT; TOEFL if first language not English; 3 references; essay; interview; laptop	Bachelor's degree; at least 6 years' work experience; GMAT; TOEFL if first language not English; 3 references; essay; interview	First degree; at least 6 years' work experience; GMAT; TOEFL if first language not English; 3 references; essay; interview

Executive education

IE's open-enrolment executive education programmes include general management programmes such as the flagship English-language Advanced Management Program for senior executives of international companies, the China International Executive Program for senior executives seeking an integral view of global business and understanding of the Chinese business environment, and the Program for Management Development for managers of international companies at an early stage in their career. It also offers shorter specialised programmes that provide an in-depth analysis of a specific business area and customised in-company programmes. Many programmes are offered in Spanish.

Student/alumni quotes

"Great opportunity to learn from other students and great faculty. Programme format (EMBA) is good for working professionals."

"Professors were excellent, very involved."

"Excellent programme, with full personal and professional satisfaction. Too early yet to tell any results from having attended it."

IESE Business School—University of Navarra

Address
Avda. Pearson, 21
Barcelona
Spain
08034

Tel:
+ 34 617 301 914

Fax:
+ 34 91 357 2913

E-mail:
MBAAdmissions@
iese.edu

Website:
www.iese.edu/en/
Programs/MBA/
Admission/
Admissions.asp

Programme director:
Francisco Iniesta

Figures in brackets
represent rank

Ranking	Rank (out of 100) Full-time
Overall rank	9
Regional rank	2

Criteria	Rank (out of 100) Full-time
Open new career opportunities	**8**
Diversity of recruiters	1
Number in jobs three months after graduation	7
Jobs found through the careers service	2
Student assessment of careers service	43
Personal development and educational experience	**47**
Faculty quality	55
Student quality	46
Student diversity	26
Education experience	75
Increase in salary	**11**
Increase in salary	13
Post-MBA salary	28
Potential to network	**41**
Breadth of alumni network	67
Internationalism of alumni	33
Alumni effectiveness	33

Background

Part of the University of Navarra, IESE Business School offers an MBA, a Global Executive MBA, an Executive MBA (in Spanish) and a doctoral programme as well as a wide range of open-enrolment and customised programmes for corporate clients and continuing education programmes for alumni. IESE is a leading European school and Jordi Canals, the dean, has a persuasive view of its future. This involves building alliances in key areas such as Latin America, China and eastern Europe in the belief that IESE must combine a global campus with global reach and at the same time recruit and develop faculty and expand its facilities.

IESE, like its parent university, is an institution of Opus Dei, a personal prelature of the Catholic Church founded in 1928. Opus Dei promotes the pursuit of "personal holiness through work, family and social life". But there is no proselytising and the atmosphere is the same as in any modern business school.

Facilities

IESE has campuses in both Madrid and Barcelona. The MBA is taught at the small, attractive Barcelona campus in the leafy, largely residential, western suburbs of the city. Both campuses are being developed: in Madrid a €13m project will effectively double the size of the campus and in Barcelona a new €24m executive education centre is being developed near the main campus. Library and other facilities are excellent. There are no on-campus accommodation or sports facilities, but these are readily available in the city, one of the most attractive of the Mediterranean.

	Full-time MBA
Student assessment of facilities	3.8 (92)

The directory
IESE Business School—University of Navarra

Faculty

Number of faculty: 85 full-time, 47 part-time, 24 visiting

	Full-time MBA	IESE Executive MBA	IESE Global Executive MBA
Number of faculty per student	0.6 (70)	2.2	5.2
Percentage of faculty with PhD	99 (30)	99	99
Student rating of faculty	4.3 (54)	–	–

Strengths and weaknesses

Strengths: general management and strategy; entrepreneurship; leadership and organisational behaviour

Weakness: small campus

Programme highlights

During the first year of IESE's 19-month full-time MBA students are divided into all-English or English/Spanish streams for the core programme. Language training in either Spanish or English (both before and during the programme) is mandatory for those who are not bilingual. Second-year electives may be taught in either language; students are expected to take elective classes in both languages. The summer is spent in a company internship.

The programme is a traditional and rigorous general management education based entirely on the case method. Group working is widespread, with groups deliberately set up to be as diverse as possible. Each group has an academic adviser and meets daily to analyse cases that will be discussed in full-class sessions. Pre-programme courses in Spanish, accounting and quantitative methods are available. Students take 21 core courses in the first year (no waivers are allowed) and 12 electives (from around 70 on offer) in the second year.

The 15-month Global Executive MBA centres on seven two-week residential learning modules: five at IESE in Barcelona, one at the China Europe International Business School (CEIBS) in Shanghai and one in Silicon Valley. Each module is separated by an eight-week period during which participants continue to learn and maintain contact with each other via IESE's "Global Campus", an interactive Internet system developed by IESE in collaboration with Duke Corporate Education. The online element of the programme (accessed via laptops supplied by IESE) includes work groups, bulletin boards, live chats and multimedia lectures.

IESE also offers a bilingual two-year Executive MBA at its Madrid campus.

	Full-time MBA	IESE Executive MBA	IESE Global Executive MBA
Student rating of programme	4.4 (28)	–	–
Number of overseas exchange programmes	86 (36)	–	–
Number of languages on offer	1 (83)	–	–

Students

	Full-time MBA	IESE Executive MBA	IESE Global Executive MBA
Annual intake	202	72	30
Applicants:places	8:1	4:1	3:1
Percentage of women students	28 (72)	13	15
Percentage of foreign students	75 (35)	n/a	n/a
Average GMAT score	685 (19)	n/a	670
Average number of months' work experience	56 (85)	82.8	120
Age range of students	26-30	30-35	29-41
Average age	28	33	34
Student rating of culture and classmates	4.5 (24)	–	–

Student profile (full time)

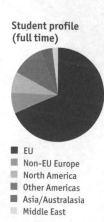

- ■ EU
- ■ Non-EU Europe
- ▨ North America
- ■ Other Americas
- ■ Asia/Australasia
- ▨ Middle East

Recruiters/careers service

	Full-time MBA	IESE Executive MBA	IESE Global Executive MBA
Number of industry sectors that recruited graduates	8 (1)	–	–
Percentage of graduates in jobs 3 months after graduation	96 (7)	–	–
Percentage of graduates finding jobs through careers services	97 (2)	–	–
Student rating of careers service	3.5 (43)	–	–
Post-MBA salary, US$	97,492 (28)	–	–
Percentage increase in salary	126 (13)	–	–
Principal recruiters of graduates	Morgan Stanley, McKinsey, Johnson & Johnson		

Cost

	Full-time MBA	IESE Executive MBA	IESE Global Executive MBA
Application fees	€100 (US$114)	€100 (US$114)	€100 (US$114)
Programme fees	€56,700 (US$64,432)	€23,500 (US$26,705)	€79,500 (US$90,341)
Comments		Per year. Fee covers academic tuition, teaching material and food and accommodation during week of residence at Michigan Business School	Fee includes tuition, laptop computer, course materials, lunch and dinner during residential modules (except Sundays), access to IESE Business Center
Accommodation costs (on campus, per year)	–	–	–
Accommodation costs (off campus, per year)	€7,200 (US$8,182)	–	–
Financial aid available	€260,000 (US$295,455)	–	–
Type of aid available	Loans, scholarships	–	–
Criteria on which aid is granted	Merit, financial need	–	–

Accreditation

AMBA, EQUIS

Application details

	Full-time MBA	IESE Executive MBA	IESE Global Executive MBA
Application deadline	April 28th	May 1st	May 10th
Programme dates	Sep start, 19 months	Sep start, 20 months	Jun start, 16 months
Admission requirements	First degree; at least 4 years' work experience, TOEFL if first language not English; 2 references; 7 essays; interview; laptop	First degree; at least 5 years' work experience; reference; interview	First degree; at least 7 years' work experience; GMAT; 2 references; 4 essays; interview; letter of support from employer; digital photo or four passport-size pictures

Executive education

Executive education has played a large part in the development of IESE. Its open-enrolment programmes include general management programmes (in both English and Spanish), shorter functional programmes and industry seminars devoted to specific topics for companies in Europe and around the world. IESE also offers customised in-company programmes to a wide range of multinational companies.

Student/alumni quotes

"The two years of the MBA programme at IESE have been the toughest of my entire life, but at the same time the most rewarding. The learning experience was exceptional; now I see the world with new eyes. And I met a bunch of incredible people. Even considering the heavy workload, I would do it all over again."

"No extra-curricular facilities; no sports ground; no student dorms; practically no campus. Could also do better on supporting social clubs."

"The opportunity to learn a global curriculum in an international non-English-speaking environment surrounded by the most diverse, interesting and international fellow students is a once-in-a-lifetime experience."

University of Illinois at Urbana-Champaign—College of Commerce and Business Administration

Address
407 David Kinley Hall
1407 West Gregory
Drive
Urbana, IL
US
61801

Tel:
+1 312 575 7896

Fax:
+1 312 575 7909

E-mail:
mba@uiuc.edu

Website:
www.mba.uiuc.edu

Programme director:
Lawrence DeBrock

Figures in brackets
represent rank

Ranking	Rank (out of 100) Full-time
Overall rank	36
Regional rank	23

Criteria	Rank (out of 100) Full-time
Open new career opportunities	**27**
Diversity of recruiters	35
Number in jobs three months after graduation	14
Jobs found through the careers service	27
Student assessment of careers service	48
Personal development and educational experience	**54**
Faculty quality	20
Student quality	92
Student diversity	77
Education experience	22
Increase in salary	**45**
Increase in salary	10
Post-MBA salary	75
Potential to network	**86**
Breadth of alumni network	66
Internationalism of alumni	70
Alumni effectiveness	76

Background

The College of Business at the University of Illinois is a leader in information technology (an area in which the university has always been strong). With more than 3,200 undergraduates and 1,000 MBA students, other master's students and doctoral candidates, the college is large.

Facilities

The school is based in two buildings, Commerce West and David Kinley Hall, and facilities are good. It has a high reputation for computer education and research, and the Office for Information Management provides exceptional computer facilities. The university offers good sports and recreational amenities and on-campus accommodation is available.

	Full-time MBA
Student assessment of facilities	4.1 (54)

Faculty

Number of faculty: 95 full-time, 21 part-time, 17 visiting

	Full-time MBA
Number of faculty per student	0.6 (73)
Percentage of faculty with PhD	100 (5)
Student rating of faculty	4.4 (22)

Strengths and weaknesses

Strengths: finance; marketing; general management

Weakness: elective choice

The directory

University of Illinois at Urbana-Champaign—College of Commerce and Business Administration

Programme highlights

In the first year of Illinois's two-year full-time MBA students follow required core courses grouped into foundations of business, principles and processes of management, and topics in management. Classes are taught in seven-week blocks. For one week of each semester in the first year students take the applied business perspectives seminar, a competitive team simulation. There is an executive-speaker series running throughout the first semester.

The second year is more traditional, with students gearing course selection to their career objectives. They can design their own suite of courses or opt for standardised concentrations: finance, marketing, information technology management, operations management and general management. In addition, students take free electives or a second concentration. They can also opt for an exchange visit in either semester in the second year.

The 15-month Executive MBA is traditional in structure. Classes meet on alternate weekends (Fridays and Saturdays (8 am–4.30 pm). There are three one-week residential on-campus sessions (all other classes are held in downtown Chicago) and a required international study trip. Students are assigned to study groups that meet once a week in the evening. Summer review courses in accounting and quantitative skills are available. Classes are televised live and recorded so that students who miss them can catch up.

	Full-time MBA
Student rating of programme	4.2 (44)
Number of overseas exchange programmes	173 (4)
Number of languages on offer	>5 (63)

Students

	Full-time MBA
Annual intake	173
Applicants:places	5:1
Percentage of women students	29 (51)
Percentage of foreign students	56 (53)
Average GMAT score	648 (63)
Average number of months' work experience	52 (>100)
Age range of students	24-33
Average age	27
Student rating of culture and classmates	3.8 (88)

Recruiters/careers service

	Full-time MBA
Number of industry sectors that recruited graduates	8 (35)
Percentage of graduates in jobs 3 months after graduation	90 (14)
Percentage of graduates finding jobs through careers services	63 (27)
Student rating of careers service	3.3 (48)
Post-MBA salary, US$	73,859 (75)
Percentage increase in salary	83 (10)
Principal recruiters of graduates	Whirlpool Corporation, Johnson & Johnson, Samsung

Cost

	Full-time MBA
Application fees	US$50
Programme fees	US$23,100
Comments	For out-of-state students
Accommodation costs (on campus, per year)	US$4,700
Accommodation costs (off campus, per year)	US$6,200
Financial aid available	US$4,500,000
Type of aid available	Scholarships, loans, internships, work/study programmes
Criteria on which aid is granted	Merit, financial need

Student profile (full time)

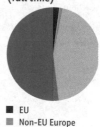

- ■ EU
- ■ Non-EU Europe
- ■ North America
- ■ Other Americas
- ■ Asia/Australasia
- ░ Middle East

University of Illinois at Urbana-Champaign—College of Commerce and Business Administration

Accreditation
AACSB International

Application details

	Full-time MBA
Application deadline	March 15th
Programme dates	Aug start, 21 months
Admission requirements	First degree; work experience; TOEFL if first language not English; 3 references; 3 essays; interviews encouraged, but not required

Executive education
Illinois does not currently offer executive education programmes.

Student/alumni quotes
"The faculty really cared whether or not we learned. I've often met with faculty members to get career advice as well."

"I don't consider a student body consisting of mostly international Asians and domestic Caucasians to be diverse. The programme, while challenging, could have done without so much focus on earning on points and more on learning concepts thoroughly. The competitiveness went way over the top. While some professors taught concepts well, others made no attempt to explain terms clearly or try to help students who were having trouble."

"The Illinois MBA programme does an excellent job of preparing its students to be top performers in the working world. By incorporating an integrated curriculum the student can get a more holistic view of how the major disciplines work together in a successful business. Furthermore, the team-oriented culture helps develop the student into a professional who will be highly successful in the business world."

IMD—International Institute for Management Development

Ranking	Rank (out of 100) Full-time
Overall rank	5
Regional rank	1

Criteria	Rank (out of 100) Full-time
Open new career opportunities	**26**
Diversity of recruiters	37
Number in jobs three months after graduation	11
Jobs found through the careers service	61
Student assessment of careers service	22
Personal development and educational experience	**15**
Faculty quality	53
Student quality	7
Student diversity	8
Education experience	69
Increase in salary	**4**
Increase in salary	49
Post-MBA salary	3
Potential to network	**6**
Breadth of alumni network	57
Internationalism of alumni	7
Alumni effectiveness	19

Address
Ch. de Bellerive 23
PO Box 915
1001 Lausanne
Switzerland

Tel:
+41 21 618 0594

Fax:
+41 21 618 0615

E-mail:
mbainfo@imd.ch

Website:
www.imd.ch/mba

Programme director:
Sean Meehan

Figures in brackets
represent rank

Background

IMD is well known and admired, and also relatively small compared with other leading schools. It believes in an integrated faculty (that is, without departments) and feels this can only be achieved with modest faculty numbers. The MBA programme is also small (IMD puts a lot of effort into executive education). Its contacts with global business are superb and its numerous corporate partners are keen supporters of the school, sending their managers there on short courses and recruiting MBA graduates.

Facilities

The facilities are excellent. A large new building for executive education classrooms was completed in 2002. A school sports centre next to IMD is available in the evenings. The MBA is based in its own building across the road from the main campus. There is a part-time on-campus kindergarten that provides a bilingual (French/English) environment for children aged 2–5. An MBA Partner Programme helps participants' partners to get to know each other, organise activities during their stay in Switzerland and become more fully integrated within the IMD community.

Lausanne, on the shores of Lake Geneva, is an attractive but somewhat quiet town.

	Full-time MBA
Student assessment of facilities	4.5 (25)

Faculty

Number of faculty: 42 full-time, 8 part-time, 0 visiting

	Full-time MBA	Executive MBA Program
Number of faculty per student	0.5 (65)	0.8
Percentage of faculty with PhD	95 (44)	95
Student rating of faculty	4.3 (45)	–

Strengths and weaknesses

Strengths: general management; leadership; entrepreneurship

Weakness: limited elective choice

Programme highlights

The 10-month full-time MBA is deliberately focused on producing future corporate leaders because IMD believes that what recruiters really want is not administrators or managers but leaders. The programme is complex and challenging. Core courses, which IMD calls "building blocks", are covered during the first half of the programme, mainly through case studies.

Leadership experiences—on- and off-campus activities, including team building, personal coaching and leading in a variety of situations—are also covered in the first half. One experience is a required off campus "discovery expedition" for the entire class to work with the government of Bosnia and Herzegovina, a European country disrupted by conflict and trying to get its economy back on track, which IMD organises with the IEDC Bled School of Management in Slovenia. The principal objectives are to allow participants to develop a "real-world" understanding of the challenges facing the country and to give them a realistic perspective of political and economic risk.

Teams also work outside the classroom with start-up ventures, helping them develop a business plan and sell an existing entrepreneurial idea to venture capitalists. This is followed by eight-week international consulting projects, where different teams work with senior managers of global companies on strategic issues. Students take four or five electives (from 10–15 offered each year). These classes are shared with participants on the Executive MBA programme.

IMD's Executive MBA combines a modular structure with elements of distance learning, study trips and close links between the school and sponsoring companies. The first two modules comprise the highly successful 10-week Programme for Executive Development (PED). EMBA and PED participants share the same classrooms and lessons. EMBA participants join full-time MBA students for the electives module. There are also overseas study trips, typically at a location in Europe, or overseas in Silicon Valley or in Shanghai.

The 18 weeks of classroom teaching and study trips can be completed in as little as 16 months or spread over a period of up to three years. All participants also undertake a major project in their own company. Between modules participants stay in touch with IMD faculty and fellow students via e-mail.

	Full-time MBA	Executive MBA Program
Student rating of programme	4.4 (24)	–
Number of overseas exchange programmes	0 (93)	–
Number of languages on offer	0 (94)	–

Student profile
(full time)

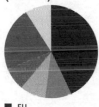

- ■ EU
- ■ Non EU Europe
- ■ North America
- ■ Other Americas
- ■ Asia/Australasia
- ■ Middle East

Students

	Full-time MBA	Executive MBA Program
Annual intake	89	65
Applicants:places	7:1	n/a
Percentage of women students	20 (>100)	8
Percentage of foreign students	98 (5)	n/a
Average GMAT score	680 (26)	580
Average number of months' work experience	84 (17)	156
Age range of students	28-33	32-44
Average age	30	38
Student rating of culture and classmates	4.8 (6)	–

The directory
IMD—International Institute for Management Development

Recruiters/careers service

	Full-time MBA	Executive MBA Program
Number of industry sectors that recruited graduates	8 (37)	–
Percentage of graduates in jobs 3 months after graduation	95 (11)	–
Percentage of graduates finding jobs through careers services	46 (61)	–
Student rating of careers service	4.0 (22)	–
Post-MBA salary, US$	123,000 (3)	–
Percentage increase in salary	64 (49)	
Principal recruiters of graduates	McKinsey, Merloni, Samsung	

Cost

	Full-time MBA	Executive MBA Program
Application fees	Swfr300 (US$222)	Swfr200 (US$148)
Programme fees	Swfr75,000 (US$55,556)	Swfr115,000 (US$85,185)
Comments	Includes all programme and project related fees	–
Accommodation costs (on campus, per year)	–	–
Accommodation costs (off campus, per year)	Swfr13,000 (US$9,630)	–
Financial aid available	Swfr1,519,000 (US$1,125,185)	–
Type of aid available	Scholarships, loans	–
Criteria on which aid is granted	Merit, financial need	–

Accreditation
AMBA, EQUIS

Application details

	Full-time MBA	Executive MBA Program
Application deadline	September 1st	Rolling admissions
Programme dates	Jan start, 10 months	Jan start, 16 months minimum
Admission requirements	Bachelor's degree or equivalent from an accredited institution; at least 3 years' work experience; 3 references; 10 essays; interview; laptop; strong command of written and spoken English	First degree (waived in exceptional circumstances); at least 10 years' work experience; 3 references; 4 essays; applicants are encouraged to visit IMD and sit in on a class before applying

Executive education
IMD has a large and comprehensive portfolio of open-enrolment executive education, ranging from short "Top Management Forums" for senior executives through general management courses to leadership and practical "execution capability" courses. The school's involvement in customised in-company programmes (it calls them "partnership programmes") is equally extensive, and in a typical year it will work with some 60 companies.

Student/alumni quotes
"Everything does work like a Swiss watch from admission process to schedule of classes."

"The programme is too short; it should be a full year with more time for other activities."

"The sharing of experience with other students in their 30s with eight years' decent work experience is the main asset. [There's] no school that comes close."

Imperial College London—Tanaka Business School

Address
Tanaka Business
School
Imperial College
London
South Kensington
campus
London
UK
SW7 2AZ

Tel:
+44 20 7594 9207

Fax:
+44 20 7594 9184

E-mail:
fthiba@imperial.
ac.uk

Website:
www.imperial.ac.uk/
tanaka

Programme director:
Stefan Szymanski

Figures in brackets
represent rank

Ranking	Rank (out of 100) Full-time
Overall rank	42
Regional rank	15

Criteria	Rank (out of 100) Full-time
Open new career opportunities	**50**
Diversity of recruiters	1
Number in jobs three months after graduation	95
Jobs found through the careers service	n/a
Student assessment of careers service	26
Personal development and educational experience	**56**
Faculty quality	84
Student quality	65
Student diversity	20
Education experience	68
Increase in salary	**14**
Increase in salary	44
Post-MBA salary	11
Potential to network	**58**
Breadth of alumni network	65
Internationalism of alumni	34
Alumni effectiveness	58

Background

With a new name, a new building and a new principal (dean), David Begg, an economist and former faculty member, 2004 has been an important year for the former Imperial College Business School. In 2000 it received a £27m gift from Gary Tanaka, an American technology investment manager and alumnus. The donation, one of the largest made to a European university, financed a new building and accounts for the school's new name, Tanaka Business School.

Imperial College, situated next to London's Science Museum, is famous for science and engineering. Its technological heritage is to an extent reflected in the school's concentration, in both teaching and research, on the interaction of management, technology and innovation. The school has close links with industry, and an especially strong position in entrepreneurship.

Facilities

In 2004 the school moved into a new £25m building within the main college campus. It contains net worked lecture theatres, breakout rooms, a central forum with café and bar, and study areas in the converted 19th century vaults. Faculty offices and careers services are in a neighbouring wing.

Imperial College offers all the usual academic and sporting facilities. There are excellent libraries within the college and university, and the school has good computer facilities. On-campus accommodation is available. Many of London's cultural highlights, such as the Victoria and Albert Museum, the Natural History Museum, the Albert Hall and Hyde Park are within walking distance of the school.

	Full-time MBA
Student assessment of facilities	4.1 (82)

The directory
Imperial College London—Tanaka Business School

Faculty

Number of faculty: 34 full-time, 8 part-time, 30 visiting

	Full-time MBA	Executive MBA programme
Number of faculty per student	0.5 (71)	1.2
Percentage of faculty with PhD	91 (73)	91
Student rating of faculty	4.2 (67)	–

Strengths and weaknesses

Strengths: innovation and entrepreneurship; technology; finance

Weakness: marketing classes

Programme highlights

The Tanaka full-time one-year MBA mixes traditional core subjects, electives (students take six out of 24 offered and can group them in a concentration or take a wide range) and an in-company project. The programme runs over three academic terms and the summer. Core courses are covered in the first and second terms and electives in the third term. The project must be completed by September. Each element is examined and assessed separately and each must be passed.

Tanaka's two-year part-time Executive EMBA is virtually identical to the full-time programme. It is run on a day-release basis with classes normally meeting on alternate Fridays (for a lengthy ten hours from 9 am to 7 pm). Every six weeks there is a mandatory three-day block (Wednesday, Thursday and Friday). The project takes two or three months and is usually carried out in the student's sponsoring organisation. It ends with a 20,000-word report.

The distance-learning MBA, which is similar in content to the full-time and part-time programmes, is offered under the auspices of the University of London External System and leads to the award of the degree of MBA of the University of London. The programme can be completed in three years.

There is also a 27-month part-time MBA programme in Singapore. The degree is identical to that awarded in London and the syllabus is almost the same as the London version. London-based Tanaka faculty do most of the teaching. Students spend two weeks each year at Tanaka.

	Full-time MBA	Executive MBA programme
Student rating of programme	4.0 (82)	–
Number of overseas exchange programmes	0 (93)	–
Number of languages on offer	>5 (1)	–

Students

	Full-time MBA	Executive MBA programme
Annual intake	100	62
Applicants:places	5:1	2:1
Percentage of women students	34 (31)	37
Percentage of foreign students	68 (42)	n/a
Average GMAT score	620 (82)	n/a
Average number of months' work experience	76 (26)	72
Age range of students	25-36	28-41
Average age	30	32
Student rating of culture and classmates	4.4 (36)	–

Student profile (full time)

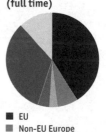

■ EU
■ Non-EU Europe
■ North America
■ Other Americas
■ Asia/Australasia
■ Middle East

Recruiters/careers service

	Full-time MBA	Executive MBA programme
Number of industry sectors that recruited graduates	8 (1)	–
Percentage of graduates in jobs 3 months after graduation	47 (95)	–
Percentage of graduates finding jobs through careers services	n/a (n/a)	–
Student rating of careers service	4.0 (26)	–
Post-MBA salary, US$	90,164 (11)	–
Percentage increase in salary	15 (44)	–
Principal recruiter of graduates	Shell	

Cost

	Full-time MBA	Executive MBA programme
Application fees	£50 (US$82)	None
Programme fees	£22,000 (US$36,066)	£30,000 (US$49,180)
Comments	–	–
Accommodation costs (on campus, per year)	£5,500 (US$9,016)	–
Accommodation costs (off campus, per year)	£6,250 (US$10,246)	–
Financial aid available	£11,000 (US$18,033)	–
Type of aid available	Bursary	–
Criteria on which aid is granted	Outstanding application	–

Accreditation

AMBA

Application details

	Full-time MBA	Executive MBA programme
Application deadline	July 31st	November 30th
Programme dates	Oct start, 12 months	Dec start, 24 months
Admission requirements	First degree; at least 3 years' work experience; GMAT; TOEFL or IELTS if first language not English; 2 references; interview; laptop	First degree (minimum 2:2 honours degree); at least 3 years' work experience; TOEFL or IELTS if first language not English; 2 references; interview

Executive education

Tanaka runs a small series of specialist open-enrolment programmes (such as intellectual property and pensions) as well as customised in-company programmes.

Student/alumni quotes

"The programme is currently in a time of massive change and development. Once the administration has completed the restructuring I have no doubt the programme will follow in the Imperial tradition of world-class education. The fundamentals and commitment are already present. The international student body, the alumni network and the careers services department have been truly exceptional."

"A few of the classes were too academic and not as practical as they could have been and there was not enough feedback given on assignments."

"Excellent student and camaraderie, great faculty, world-class facilities, both at the business school and Imperial itself, and, of course, its location."

Indian Institute of Management— Ahmedabad

Ranking	Rank (out of 100) Full-time
Overall rank	64
Regional rank	2

Criteria	Rank (out of 100) Full-time
Open new career opportunities	**1**
Diversity of recruiters	40
Number in jobs three months after graduation	2
Jobs found through the careers service	1
Student assessment of careers service	2
Personal development and educational experience	**>100**
Faculty quality	50
Student quality	>100
Student diversity	>100
Education experience	29
Increase in salary	**>100**
Increase in salary	n/a
Post-MBA salary	108
Potential to network	**44**
Breadth of alumni network	77
Internationalism of alumni	86
Alumni effectiveness	21

Address
Indian Institute of
Management
Ahmedabad
Vastrapur
Ahmedabad
India
380015

Tel:
+91 79 2632 4917

Fax:
+91 79 2630 6896

E-mail:
admission@iimahd.
ernet.in

Website:
www.iimahd.ernet.in

Programme director:
Samir Barua

Figures in brackets
represent rank

Background

The Indian Institute of Management at Ahmedabad (IIM-A; there are several other IIMs at various locations around India) is reckoned by most national surveys to be the leading business school in the subcontinent. It has close links with industry and with state and national authorities. The Indian national government, the government of the state of Gujarat and Indian industry and business were key players in its formation. The IIM-A has a good research base and an active involvement in management development in a number of important fields.

Like many other business schools around the world, the IIM-A was set up (in 1961) with help and collaboration from Harvard Business School and is a great promoter of the case method of teaching. However, it promotes itself as a school of management, aiming to promote effective management in both the public and private sectors and to concentrate on areas especially applicable to the Indian economy, notably agriculture.

Facilities

Facilities are good. The school is based on a 60-acre campus designed by Louis Kahn, an American architect. It includes six classrooms, five seminar rooms, offices for faculty and research staff and accommodation for students (only in special circumstances are they allowed to live off campus) in 18 multi-storey dormitories.

	Full-time MBA
Student assessment of facilities	4.4 (39)

Faculty

Number of faculty: 73 full-time, 0 part-time, 31 visiting

	Full-time MBA
Number of faculty per student	0.3 (89)
Percentage of faculty with PhD	96 (36)
Student rating of faculty	4.5 (32)

Strengths and weaknesses

Strengths: production and operations management; marketing; organisational behaviour

Weaknesses: lack of internationalism; lack of diversity among student body

Programme highlights

IIM-A's two-year full-time Postgraduate Diploma in Management is generally accepted as equivalent to an MBA. As well as imparting functional knowledge, the programme aims to provide conceptual and interpersonal skills, encourage entrepreneurial capabilities and equip students to set standards of excellence in managerial life. Most teaching is done by the case method, although other methods are used. There is a strong project element in most courses.

The two-year programme is similar in structure to the American model, with required core courses in the first year and two more in the second year, followed by electives, which can be grouped into concentrations. These include business policy, computers and information systems, economics, finance and accounting, international management, marketing, organisational behaviour, personnel and industrial relations, production and quantitative methods and public systems. There are non-credit classes in communications and writing throughout the first year.

Few students have much work experience. As a result the summer assignment (internship) is seen as a key part of the programme and is required for all students. Around 50 students spend one term in the second year on exchange.

	Full-time MBA
Student rating of programme	4.5 (18)
Number of overseas exchange programmes	45 (56)
Number of languages on offer	4 (63)

Students

	Full-time MBA
Annual intake	258
Applicants:places	373:1
Percentage of women students	13 (>100)
Percentage of foreign students	0 (>100)
Average GMAT score	n/a (n/a)
Average number of months' work experience	12 (>100)
Age range of students	21-25
Average age	23
Student rating of culture and classmates	4.4 (37)

Recruiters/careers service

	Full-time MBA
Number of industry sectors that recruited graduates	8 (40)
Percentage of graduates in jobs 3 months after graduation	100 (2)
Percentage of graduates finding jobs through careers services	100 (1)
Student rating of careers service	4.4 (2)
Post-MBA salary, US$	33,439 (>100)
Percentage increase in salary	n/a
Principal recruiters of graduates	PricewaterhouseCoopers, Lehman Brothers, Procter & Gamble

The directory
Indian Institute of Management—Ahmedabad

Cost

	Full-time MBA
Application fees	Rs1,100 (US$24)
Programme fees	Rs100,000 (US$2,147)
Comments	Per year
Accommodation costs (on campus, per year)	Rs32,500 (US$698)
Accommodation costs (off campus, per year)	–
Financial aid available	Rs4,420,000 (US$94,891)
Type of aid available	Scholarships
Criteria on which aid is granted	Merit, financial need

Accreditation

None

Application details

	Full-time MBA
Application deadline	September 20th
Programme dates	Jun start, 22 months
Admission requirements	First degree; interview; laptop; Common Admission Test (specialised admission test for management studies, designed and administered by IIM faculty); group discussions

Executive education

IIM-A offers open-enrolment programmes, seminars and workshops in general management and functional areas including communications, computers and information systems, finance and accounting, marketing, strategic management, and so on, as well as sectoral programmes in agriculture and public systems.

Student/alumni quotes

"IIM-A's full time MBA programme is undoubtedly the best in India. The admission process is probably the toughest in the world where only the best of the best can survive."

"Needs more international interface."

"This is among the toughest b-schools to get into in the world, with only the cream of Indian students studying here ... The faculty are among the best in the academic world and the infrastructure in place is the best in India."

Indiana University—Kelley School of Business

Address
1275 E Tenth Street
Suite 2010
Indiana University
Bloomington
IN
US
47405

Tel:
+1 812 855 8006

Fax:
+1 812 855 9039

E-mail:
mbaoffice@indiana.
edu

Website:
www.kelley.indiana.
edu/mba

Programme director:
Idie Kesner

Figures in brackets
represent rank

Ranking	Rank (out of 100) Full-time
Overall rank	54
Regional rank	34

Criteria	Rank (out of 100) Full-time
Open new career opportunities	**59**
Diversity of recruiters	89
Number in jobs three months after graduation	75
Jobs found through the careers service	60
Student assessment of careers service	18
Personal development and educational experience	**50**
Faculty quality	54
Student quality	74
Student diversity	83
Education experience	8
Increase in salary	**70**
Increase in salary	65
Post-MBA salary	60
Potential to network	**45**
Breadth of alumni network	35
Internationalism of alumni	75
Alumni effectiveness	42

Background

Kelley School of Business offers basic advantages such as value for money, a readily accessible faculty and a good careers office. It also has an innovative approach to management education that emphasises integration, teamwork and co-operation while maintaining a strong belief in individual effort and, especially, leadership. The school teaches undergraduate and graduate programmes to nearly 5,000 full-time students on its Bloomington campus and approximately 1,200 students on its Indianapolis campus. The school is named after E W "Ed" Kelley, who received his undergraduate degree from Indiana University in 1939.

Facilities

The MBA programme is housed in a new US$33m, 200,000 sq ft Graduate and Executive Education Center, which includes all resources for graduate education on three floors, with executive education on the fourth. There are classrooms, student lounges, team breakout rooms, conference rooms and careers services. The building has wireless and wired infrastructure, two full computer labs and 2,600 data ports for laptops.

Indiana University's sports, recreational and on-campus accommodation facilities are all excellent. However, most students live off campus where housing is easy to find and reasonably priced. Bloomington is a small town in the Midwest, an hour's drive from Indianapolis. It has plenty of amenities and many students like the quiet atmosphere. A strong interest in basketball is almost essential, but there are other cultural attractions.

	Full-time MBA
Student assessment of facilities	4.5 (13)

The directory
Indiana University—Kelley School of Business

Faculty

Number of faculty: 189 full-time, 23 part-time, 12 visiting

	Full-time MBA	Evening MBA Program
Number of faculty per student	0.8 (56)	1.9
Percentage of faculty with PhD	76 (91)	76
Student rating of faculty	4.7 (7)	–

Strengths and weaknesses

Strengths: marketing; finance; strategic management and international business

Programme highlights

Kelley's MBA curriculum is one of the most innovative and integrated in the US. The programme starts with a two-week orientation with a strong emphasis on leadership. The core itself is taught as an integrated unit over 15 weeks. The first year also features extensive career sessions that are aimed at helping students to choose the right combination of academic courses. The second year consists of electives. Interestingly, Kelley offers second-year students the option to continue via the online programme if, for example, they are offered a full-time position after their internship or a sponsored student is required to return to his or her organisation.

The part-time MBA is taught by the school's faculty at its urban campus in Indianapolis. It is usually completed in three years or less and must be finished within five. Students are required to take pre-programme courses in either financial accounting or statistics by studying either web-based courses or on-campus courses. The programme is run in modules over 15-week semesters with classes held two nights a week. There are also three one-day seminars. Students can major in either general administration or finance.

Kelley's Direct Online MBA is a two-year programme centred on web-based courses and a one-week residential session at the beginning of each year. This programme is also offered in a customised version for a number of US companies. The school also offers a specialised MBA in accounting.

	Full-time MBA	Evening MBA Program
Student rating of programme	4.4 (15)	–
Number of overseas exchange programmes	40 (62)	–
Number of languages on offer	>5 (1)	–

Students

	Full-time MBA	Evening MBA Program
Annual intake	250	120
Applicants:places	7:1	2:1
Percentage of women students	26 (89)	25
Percentage of foreign students	30 (96)	n/a
Average GMAT score	651.5 (46)	630
Average number of months' work experience	55 (81)	60
Age range of students	27-35	24-35
Average age	30	29
Student rating of culture and classmates	4.4 (27)	–

Student profile (full time)

- ■ EU
- ■ Non-EU Europe
- ■ North America
- ■ Other Americas
- ■ Asia/Australasia
- ■ Middle East

Recruiters/careers service

	Full-time MBA	Evening MBA Program
Number of industry sectors that recruited graduates	6 (89)	–
Percentage of graduates in jobs 3 months after graduation	77 (75)	–
Percentage of graduates finding jobs through careers services	41 (60)	–
Student rating of careers service	4.0 (18)	–
Post-MBA salary, US$	74,050 (60)	–
Percentage increase in salary	41 (65)	–
Principal recruiters of graduates	Eli Lilly, Johnson & Johnson, Guidant Corp	

Cost

	Full-time MBA	Evening MBA Program
Application fees	US$75	US$45
Programme fees	US$24,200	US$18,870
Comments	Per year	Total programme, in-state students
Accommodation costs (on campus, per year)	US$5,400	–
Accommodation costs (off campus, per year)	US$6,750	–
Financial aid available	Not disclosed	–
Type of aid available	Scholarships, fellowships, assistantships	–
Criteria on which aid is granted	Merit	–

Accreditation

AACSB International

Application details

	Full-time MBA	Evening MBA Program
Application deadline	March 1st	November 1st
Programme dates	Aug start, 21 months	Jan start, 32 months
Admission requirements	US bachelor's degree or equivalent; TOEFL if first language not English (237 minimum, computer-based); 2 references; 3 essays	4-year bachelor's degree from an accredited institution; at least 2 years' work experience; GMAT; 3 essays; 2 recommendations; TOEFL if first language not English (other ESL may substitute)

Executive education

Kelley offers open-enrolment executive programmes in finance and accounting, management and leadership, project management, supply chain management, and sales and marketing. Customised in-company programmes are offered in similar areas. Kelley also organises consortium programmes for groups of companies.

INSEAD

Ranking	Rank (out of 100) Full-time
Overall rank	20
Regional rank	4

Criteria	Rank (out of 100) Full-time
Open new career opportunities	**43**
Diversity of recruiters	1
Number in jobs three months after graduation	79
Jobs found through the careers service	48
Student assessment of careers service	45
Personal development and educational experience	**6**
Faculty quality	65
Student quality	6
Student diversity	13
Education experience	7
Increase in salary	**25**
Increase in salary	62
Post-MBA salary	20
Potential to network	**37**
Breadth of alumni network	88
Internationalism of alumni	44
Alumni effectiveness	11

Address
INSEAD
Boulevard de
Constance
Fontainebleau
France
77305

Tel:
+33 1 6072 4402

Fax:
+33 1 6074 5530

E-mail:
mba.info@insead.edu

Website:
www.insead.edu/mba

Programme director:
Doris Sohmen-Pao

Figures in brackets
represent rank

Background

INSEAD offers a strong international experience that promotes a lasting attachment to the school. It has some 14,000 MBA alumni and on-campus class reunions are exceptionally well attended. The networking opportunities offered by INSEAD are a major attraction for some students.

The school was among the first to open a parallel campus and students can opt to study in Fontainebleau or Singapore. Since 1996 the intake has been steadily increasing, and faculty members on both campuses now teach over 800 MBA students and nearly 7,000 executives from over 75 countries.

Facilities

Facilities on the large modern campuses in Fontainebleau (about 65 km from Paris) and Singapore are excellent. Campus life is lively and informal with lots of social activities. The two campuses operate on the same internal IT network and are linked by videoconference facilities for lectures, classes and other events; many students take both core courses and electives on both campuses.

On-campus accommodation at Fontainebleau is available but rarely used. Nearby rented housing, including attractive farmhouse-style accommodation, is popular but can be expensive, as is the area generally.

	Full-time MBA
Student assessment of facilities	3.8 (90)

Faculty

Number of faculty: 147 full-time, 0 part-time, 55 visiting	
	Full-time MBA
Number of faculty per student	0.2 (107)
Percentage of faculty with PhD	98 (14)
Student rating of faculty	4.2 (57)

Strengths and weaknesses

Strengths: international business; strategy; entrepreneurship

Weakness: school administration

Programme highlights

The INSEAD full-time MBA is divided into five periods taught over five eight-week terms or "periods", each followed by examinations and a short break. The first three periods cover core courses grouped under themes: business fundamentals, core functional skills, and global and IT challenges in management. Part of period three and periods four and five are given over to electives. Students take 13 core courses and a minimum of 10 electives (chosen from around 80 offered), and attend topic days on specific subjects, such as ethics or entrepreneurship. They can also take half-credit mini-electives. A faculty-approved project and report may be substituted for one elective. Although almost all classes are taught in English, languages are important. INSEAD requires fluent English and a working knowledge of a second language for admission and students must learn a third language before graduation.

There are two MBA intakes, in January and late August, on both the Fontainebleau and Singapore campuses. The January entry has a seven-week summer break. The programmes in Fontainebleau and Singapore are identical and require students to work in groups of five or six, chosen to maximise diversity and the potential for conflict. Groups work together to produce analyses, reports and presentations. Students can switch between the Fontainebleau and Singapore campuses during elective periods and are guaranteed the opportunity of spending at least one eight-week period on the other campus. Students can also apply to take one elective period at Wharton (Pennsylvania) in the US.

INSEAD's 14-month Executive MBA programme, which began in 2003, runs simultaneously on the Fontainebleau and Singapore campuses. The two groups of participants meet three times during the programme. The format is modular with nine on-campus modules totalling 12 weeks. The first, middle and last modules consist of joint sessions of two weeks. Between modules students keep in contact electronically.

	Full-time MBA
Student rating of programme	4.4 (20)
Number of overseas exchange programmes	909 (2)
Number of languages on offer	>5 (1)

Students

Student profile (full time)

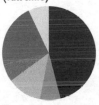

- ■ EU
- ■ Non-EU Europe
- ▨ North America
- ■ Other Americas
- ■ Asia/Australasia
- ▨ Middle East

	Full-time MBA
Annual intake	839
Applicants:places	4:1
Percentage of women students	19 (>100)
Percentage of foreign students	89 (9)
Average GMAT score	707 (7)
Average number of months' work experience	72 (41)
Age range of students	23-35
Average age	29
Student rating of culture and classmates	4.6 (13)

The directory
INSEAD

Recruiters/careers service

	Full-time MBA
Number of industry sectors that recruited graduates	8 (1)
Percentage of graduates in jobs 3 months after graduation	77 (79)
Percentage of graduates finding jobs through careers services	65 (48)
Student rating of careers service	3.3 (45)
Post-MBA salary, US$	88,068 (20)
Percentage increase in salary	35 (62)
Principal recruiters of graduates	McKinsey & Co, Bain & Co, Booz Allen & Hamilton

Cost

	Full-time MBA
Application fees	€200 (US$227)
Programme fees	€43,500 (US$49,432)
Comments	–
Accommodation costs (on campus, per year)	–
Accommodation costs (off campus, per year)	€8,000 (US$9,091)
Financial aid available	Not disclosed
Type of aid available	Full and partial scholarships, loans
Criteria on which aid is granted	Financial need, merit, and occasionally for specific backgrounds

Accreditation

AMBA

Application details

	Full-time MBA
Application deadline	July 7th
Programme dates	Jan start, 12 months
Admission requirements	First degree; work experience; TOEFL, IELTS, TOEIC or CPE if first language not English; 2 references; 6 essays; interview; laptop; 2 languages required for admission, one of which must be English

Executive education

INSEAD has a strong executive education arm, offering open-enrolment programmes in top management, leadership, general management, finance, marketing, strategy, operations management and so on. It also offers an extensive portfolio of customised, in-company programmes.

Student/alumni quotes

"If you want to build an international network of intelligent, ambitious and worldly persons look no further than INSEAD. It is hands down the best school in the world for this.".

"Some inexperienced professors teaching core courses."

"INSEAD is without doubt the most international MBA and is without doubt the best school for people with a passion for an international career, not only because of the programme but as well because of the alumni network. Further, the ten-month programme is all you need."

Institut d'Etudes Politiques de Paris— MBA Sciences Po

Address
174 Boulevard Saint-Germain
Paris
France
75006

Tel:
+33 1 4544 8743

Fax:
+33 1 4544 8892

Email:
mba@sciences-po.fr

Website:
mba.sciences-po.fr

Programme director:
Jean-Jacques Rosa

Figures in brackets
represent rank

Ranking	Rank (out of 100) Full-time
Overall rank	100
Regional rank	40

Criteria	Rank (out of 100) Full-time
Open new career opportunities	>100
Diversity of recruiters	>100
Number in jobs three months after graduation	>100
Jobs found through the careers service	n/a
Student assessment of careers service	51
Personal development and educational experience	88
Faculty quality	89
Student quality	80
Student diversity	>100
Education experience	54
Increase in salary	68
Increase in salary	>100
Post-MBA salary	39
Potential to network	40
Breadth of alumni network	>100
Internationalism of alumni	11
Alumni effectiveness	49

Background

Institut d'Etudes Politiques de Paris (known as Sciences Po), founded in 1872, is one of Europe's most distinguished universities as well as being a grande école. It started offering an MBA in the early 1990s. One of Sciences Po's distinctive characteristics is its teaching faculty. Approximately 1,200 individuals teach at the university each year and the majority are also involved in outside career activities. The MBA programme also includes quite a few visiting faculty from outside France.

Facilities

The school is based in Paris's Latin Quarter (Saint Germain des Prés) with MBA classes held in boulevard Saint Germain, rue Saint Guillaume and the prestigious ENA (Ecole Nationale d'Administration). The school leases a large building on campus for postgraduate students, which has a specialised management library and a computer room. MBA students have their own classroom, Internet access and rooms where they can work together, separate from the rest of the institution. They can use all Sciences Po's services, including a library (housing more than 700,000 volumes and receiving 6,000 French and foreign periodicals) and a number of computer rooms connected to the Internet. No on-campus accommodation is available but the school offers advice on finding housing.

	Full-time MBA
Student assessment of facilities	3.8 (97)

Faculty

Number of faculty: 5 full-time, 0 part-time, 31 visiting	
	Full-time MBA
Number of faculty per student	0.4 (54)
Percentage of faculty with PhD	40 (100)
Student rating of faculty	4.3 (56)

Strengths and weaknesses

Strengths: finance; international environment of firms

Weakness: careers services

Programme highlights

The MBA Sciences Po is a bilingual programme. Students are expected to be reasonably fluent in both English and French before admission, but most class material is in English. The class size is limited to 40 students.

The intensive and international programme lasts just nine months. It is built around three main areas: economics, finance, accounting and valuation; management, strategy and marketing; and organisations, institutions and human resources. These are taught via ten modules that include core functional disciplines such as accounting and marketing and also strategy, geopolitics and business law, key Sciences Po strengths.

Students work in small groups and are formed into different groups for an in-company project, which is worked on throughout the programme. Workshops in public speaking, writing skills and project work are held for small groups throughout the course, and there is a series of guest lectures. A careers forum and organised meetings with companies take place in the second trimester.

A language laboratory is available for MBA students offering the possibility of learning or improving any language.

	Full-time MBA
Student rating of programme	4.1 (68)
Number of overseas exchange programmes	0 (41)
Number of languages on offer	>5 (1)

Students

	Full-time MBA
Annual intake	34
Applicants:places	3:1
Percentage of women students	26 (77)
Percentage of foreign students	35 (86)
Average GMAT score	616 (84)
Average number of months' work experience	72 (41)
Age range of students	27-33
Average age	31
Student rating of culture and classmates	4.0 (84)

Recruiters/careers service

	Full-time MBA
Number of industry sectors that recruited graduates	5 (>100)
Percentage of graduates in jobs 3 months after graduation	30 (>100)
Percentage of graduates finding jobs through careers services	n/a (n/a)
Student rating of careers service	3.6 (51)
Post-MBA salary, US$	87,007 (39)
Percentage increase in salary	25 (>100)
Principal recruiters of graduates	–

Student profile (full time)

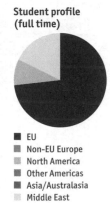

- ■ EU
- ■ Non-EU Europe
- ■ North America
- ■ Other Americas
- ■ Asia/Australasia
- ■ Middle East

Cost

	Full-time MBA
Application fees	€70 (US$80)
Programme fees	€22,000 (US$25,000)
Comments	–
Accommodation costs (on campus, per year)	–
Accommodation costs (off campus, per year)	€9,000 (US$10,227)
Financial aid available	n/a
Type of aid available	n/a
Criteria on which aid is granted	n/a

Accreditation

AMBA

Application details

	Full-time MBA
Application deadline	October 15th
Programme dates	Jan start, 9 months
Admission requirements	First degree; at least 3 years' work experience; GMAT; TOEFL if first language not English; 3 references; 1 essay; interview; laptop; fluency in French

Executive education

Sciences Po offers open-enrolment executive education programmes that include diplomas (2–3 days a month over 20 months) in areas such as corporate finance and capital markets, healthcare management, non-profit management and public-sector management, and non-diploma seminars (2–5 days) in economics and finance, communications management, new technologies and public-sector management. It also offers customised in-company programmes. As well as its Paris base, Sciences Po operates such programmes from satellite campuses in Dijon, Nancy and Poitiers.

Student/alumni quotes

"For me, the MBA Sciences Po is a programme with an incredible return on investment: I made a +55% increase in salary with a nine-month programme costing just €20,000. Moreover, the MBA experience was fantastic. I met co-operative talented professionals that, I hope, will remain lifelong friends."

"Students have to live in downtown Paris (nice but expensive)."

"This programme is a good balance of French, European and US business approaches."

University of Iowa—Henry B Tippie School of Management

Ranking	Rank (out of 100) Full-time
Overall rank	38
Regional rank	25

Criteria	Rank (out of 100) Full-time
Open new career opportunities	**34**
Diversity of recruiters	72
Number in jobs three months after graduation	22
Jobs found through the careers service	21
Student assessment of careers service	32
Personal development and educational experience	**65**
Faculty quality	9
Student quality	100
Student diversity	94
Education experience	21
Increase in salary	**49**
Increase in salary	6
Post-MBA salary	77
Potential to network	**50**
Breadth of alumni network	28
Internationalism of alumni	>100
Alumni effectiveness	51

Address
Henry B Tippie College
of Business
The University of Iowa
C108 PBB
Iowa City IA
US
52242-1000

Tel:
+1 319 335 0867

Fax:
+1 319 335 0860

Email:
tippiemba@uiowa.
edu

Website:
www.biz.uiowa.edu/
fulltimemba

Programme director:
Gary Gaeth

Figures in brackets
represent rank

Background

Iowa has offered an MBA for over 30 years and the business school has a highly rated faculty. The school is named after Henry B Tippie, an alumnus, who made a $30m donation in 1999. The small scale of the school allows good contact between students and faculty. As at many schools based in state universities the fees are quite low, but the quality is high.

Facilities

The school is based in the John Pappajohn Business Administration Building in the middle of the university campus. Facilities, including a business library and computer lab, are good. Each classroom is equipped with a computer, projector and video recorder. There are study areas throughout the building, and in the second-floor lounges students can access their e-mail at standing PC stations. A new building, the Pomerantz Center, is scheduled for completion in spring 2005. It will house offices, the Executive MBA programme and careers services, and it will contain a 400-seat auditorium and six classrooms.

Iowa City is small but with plenty of cultural and social attractions.

	Full-time MBA
Student assessment of facilities	4.6 (6)

Faculty

Number of faculty: 95 full-time, 41 part-time, 5 visiting

	Full-time MBA	MBA for Professionals and Managers (MBA-PM)	International Executive MBA	Executive MBA Program
Number of faculty per student	1.3 (23)	0.6	3.8	3.7
Percentage of faculty with PhD	94 (43)	94	94	94
Student rating of faculty	4.4 (30)	–	–	–

Strengths and weaknesses

Strengths: finance; marketing; non-profit

Weakness: few on-campus recruiters

Programme highlights

The Tippie two-year full-time MBA is fairly traditional with an interdisciplinary core followed by a concentration. Students can take a concentration in a specific area or devise their own, drawing on other graduate schools of the university. Concentrations are offered in accounting, entrepreneurship, finance, strategic management and consulting, management information systems, marketing and operations management. There is a capstone strategy course in the first semester of the second year that focuses on competitive strategy from a manager's perspective.

The part-time MBA for Professionals and Managers is a strong, traditional American programme. Classes generally meet one evening a week (usually 6–10 pm) during term time (13-week semesters plus a summer term). The programme is offered in three separate locations in Iowa (Cedar Rapids/Iowa City, Des Moines/Newton and Quad Cities) and includes ten core courses and five electives. Most students take two courses in the fall and spring semesters and one in the summer, which allows the programme to be completed in three years. Students can select from an array of elective courses that develop depth in a broad choice of business disciplines. Electives can be taken in one or several different business areas. There is a capstone strategy course in the third year as well as a series of guest-speaker presentations.

The 21-month EMBA is fairly traditional in style and is taught in Des Moines and Iowa City. All participants are sponsored by their companies (or at least have their permission and support). There is a five-day residency week at the beginning of each year. Classes meet on alternate Fridays and Saturdays during term time, and there is a three-month summer break between the two years. The second year includes an intensive business simulation, electives, an international seminar (7–10 days) and a capstone course in strategic management. The EMBA is also offered in an international version in Hong Kong.

	Full-time MBA	MBA for Professionals and Managers (MBA-PM)	International Executive MBA	Executive MBA Program
Student rating of programme	4.2 (49)	–	–	–
Number of overseas exchange programmes	6 (76)	–	–	–
Number of languages on offer	>5 (1)	–	–	–

Students

	Full-time MBA	MBA for Professionals and Managers (MBA-PM)	International Executive MBA	Executive MBA Program
Annual intake	87	220	37	38
Applicants:places	3:1	–	1:1	1:1
Percentage of women students	21 (100)	31	47	27
Percentage of foreign students	39 (65)	n/a	n/a	n/a
Average GMAT score	638 (59)	565	n/a	550
Average number of months' work experience	40 (>100)	77	84	168
Age range of students	24-33	25-35	27-38	31-45
Average age	28	28	31	37
Student rating of culture and classmates	4.3 (45)	–	–	–

Student profile (full time)

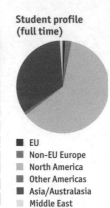

- ■ EU
- ■ Non-EU Europe
- ▨ North America
- ■ Other Americas
- ■ Asia/Australasia
- ▨ Middle East

Recruiters/careers service

	Full-time MBA	MBA for Professionals and Managers (MBA-PM)	International Executive MBA	Executive MBA Program
Number of industry sectors that recruited graduates	8 (72)	–	–	–
Percentage of graduates in jobs 3 months after graduation	82 (22)	–	–	–
Percentage of graduates finding jobs through careers services	63 (21)	–	–	–
Student rating of careers service	3.5 (32)	–	–	–
Post-MBA salary, US$	65,000 (77)	–	–	–
Percentage increase in salary	82 (6)	–	–	–
Principal recruiters of graduates	AEGON USA, John Deere Credit Company, Kimberly-Clark			

Cost

	Full-time MBA	MBA for Professionals and Managers (MBA-PM)	International Executive MBA	Executive MBA Program
Application fees	US$50	US$50	HK$500 (US$64)	None
Programme fees	US$10,500	US$425	HK$219,000 (US$28,113)	US$43,000 (US$43,000)
Comments	Application/programme fees apply to US residents only; application fee is US$75 and programme fees $19,362 for international students	Per semester hour of credit. US$1,275 per 3 semester-hour course. Application fee is for US students; fee for international students is $75		
Accommodation costs (on campus, per year)	US$5,600	–	–	–
Accommodation costs (off campus, per year)	US$7,200	–	–	–
Financial aid available	US$481,000	–	–	–
Type of aid available	Scholarships, graduate assistantships	–	–	–
Criteria on which aid is granted	Merit, admission criteria	–	–	–

Accreditation

AACSB International

Application details

	Full-time MBA	MBA for Professionals and Managers (MBA-PM)	International Executive MBA	Executive MBA Program
Application deadline	July 15th (US applicants); April 15th (international applicants)	Rolling admissions	Not yet determined	April 15th
Programme dates	Aug start, 21 months	Jan/Aug start, 36 months	Sep start, 18 months	Aug start, 21 months
Admission requirements	First degree; at least 2 years' work experience; TOEFL if first language not English; GMAT (no minimum score); 3 references; 2 essays; interview; laptop	First degree; at least 3 years' work experience; TOEFL if first language not English; 3 references; 2 essays	First degree; at least 5 years' work experience; TOEFL if first language not English; 2 references; essay; interview	First degree (one exceptional candidate without a degree, but with unique work experience, is considered for admission per class); at least 10 years' work experience; GMAT (no minimum score); 2 references; essays; interview

Executive education

Tippie does not currently offer open-enrolment or customised in-company executive education programmes.

Student/alumni quotes

"The atmosphere at the University of Iowa is great. The smaller class sizes give the programme a very friendly and co-operative spirit. The ability to get financing and the admission process were much easier than anticipated. Getting my MBA at Iowa was the best choice I could have made."

"A stereotypical reputation based on location. If you moved the Tippie MBA programme to the east or west coast in a major city it would be ranked as one of the top MBA programmes in the US."

"The University of Iowa is a great school especially when considering the economic costs of obtaining an MBA. The school provides great opportunities to obtain financial aid through assistantships. Students who want to work in the Midwest should strongly consider Iowa. People throughout the programme are committed to helping students succeed."

International University of Japan—Graduate School of International Management

Address
777 Anaji Shinden
Yamato-machi
Minami Uonuma-gun
Niigata
Japan
9497277

Tel:
+81 25 779 1500

Fax:
+81 25 779 1187

Email:
admgsim@iuj.ac.jp

Website:
www.ibs.iuj.ac.jp/

Programme director:
Dr Jay R Rajasekera

Figures in brackets
represent rank

Ranking	Rank (out of 100) Full-time
Overall rank	84
Regional rank	5

Criteria	Rank (out of 100) Full-time
Open new career opportunities	**30**
Diversity of recruiters	92
Number in jobs three months after graduation	3
Jobs found through the careers service	32
Student assessment of careers service	74
Personal development and educational experience	**>100**
Faculty quality	>100
Student quality	97
Student diversity	91
Education experience	91
Increase in salary	**>100**
Increase in salary	100
Post-MBA salary	97
Potential to network	**64**
Breadth of alumni network	>100
Internationalism of alumni	41
Alumni effectiveness	97

Background

The Graduate School of International Management (GSIM) is one of two graduate schools at the International University of Japan (IUJ); the other is the Graduate School of International Relations (GSIR). The GSIM offers two master's programmes: a two-year MBA and a one-year master of e-business management. Both schools teach entirely in English.

The GSIM was originally developed in 1988 in collaboration with Dartmouth College (Tuck School of Business, see page 205) although it now has its own curriculum. The IUJ was created by business leaders, and the school's connections with Japanese and international business are excellent. There is a good range of guest speakers.

Facilities

The school is about 230 km north-west of Tokyo in quiet rural surroundings with hot summers and snowy winters. Facilities on campus are good and most students stay in on-campus housing. First-year MBA students have their own exclusive classroom.

	Full-time MBA
Student assessment of facilities	4.2 (75)

Faculty

Number of faculty: 17 full-time, 0 part-time, 18 visiting

	Full-time MBA
Number of faculty per student	0.4 (83)
Percentage of faculty with PhD	53 (>100)
Student rating of faculty	3.9 (>100)

Strengths and weaknesses

Strengths: financial strategy; IT management; consumer marketing

Weaknesses: elective choice, remote location

Programme highlights

The GSIM's two-year full-time MBA is based firmly on the traditional US model (although it is taken over six terms rather than four semesters). The first year consists of core courses, which follow the traditional model, and electives, which start in the spring term. There is also a year-long group in-company project. In the second year students take ten or more electives that can be grouped (specialisations are offered in finance, IT, strategic management and marketing) or taken from a variety of areas to form a general degree. The second year also contains a required project and report. Elective courses can be chosen from the E-Business programme and from some courses offered by the GSIR. Soft skills courses and language training in English and Japanese are offered.

The E-Business Management Programme is a one-year master's programme, incorporating some elements of the MBA, designed for young managers wanting to enter the e-commerce area.

	Full-time MBA
Student rating of programme	3.9 (>100)
Number of overseas exchange programmes	39 (14)
Number of languages on offer	2 (79)

Students

	Full-time MBA
Annual intake	54
Applicants:places	55:1
Percentage of women students	16 (>100)
Percentage of foreign students	80 (28)
Average GMAT score	592 (94)
Average number of months' work experience	60 (72)
Age range of students	24-34
Average age	28
Student rating of culture and classmates	3.9 (97)

Student profile (full time)

- ■ EU
- ■ Non-EU Europe
- ▨ North America
- ■ Other Americas
- ■ Asia/Australasia
- ▨ Middle East

Recruiters/careers service

	Full-time MBA
Number of industry sectors that recruited graduates	6 (92)
Percentage of graduates in jobs 3 months after graduation	100 (3)
Percentage of graduates finding jobs through careers services	56 (32)
Student rating of careers service	3.9 (74)
Post-MBA salary, US$	60,366 (97)
Percentage increase in salary	25 (100)
Principal recruiters of graduates	Eiken Chemical, Lehman Brothers (Japan), DaimlerChrysler (Japan)

Cost

	Full-time MBA
Application fees	¥5,000 (US$43)
Programme fees	¥1,900,000 (US$16,385)
Comments	–
Accommodation costs (on campus, per year)	¥384,000 (US$3,311)
Accommodation costs (off campus, per year)	¥720,000 (US$6,209)
Financial aid available	¥61,556,000 (US$530,838)
Type of aid available	Scholarships
Criteria on which aid is granted	Academic standing, financial status

Accreditation

None

Application details

	Full-time MBA
Application deadline	End March
Programme dates	Sep start, 21 months
Admission requirements	Bachelor's degree or equivalent (minimum of 16 years of formal schooling); TOEFL or IELTS if first language not English; 2 references; 2 essays; Japanese applicants are required to atend an interview

Executive education

The school offers customised in-company short executive programmes, often based on investing and managing in Asian markets.

Student/alumni quotes

"If you want to study an MBA programme with a real international environment and many cross-cultural experiences, International University of Japan is the right place. You will learn much more than you expected."

"[Too] far from Tokyo, Japan's biggest MBA job market."

"It's an excellent programme, well balanced, and provides terrific career-growth opportunities. The scholarships are a welcome bonus."

Lancaster University Management School

Ranking	Rank (out of 100) Full-time
Overall rank	52
Regional rank	18

Criteria	Rank (out of 100) Full-time
Open new career opportunities	**82**
Diversity of recruiters	62
Number in jobs three months after graduation	53
Jobs found through the careers service	96
Student assessment of careers service	57
Personal development and educational experience	**11**
Faculty quality	5
Student quality	54
Student diversity	14
Education experience	23
Increase in salary	**22**
Increase in salary	12
Post-MBA salary	50
Potential to network	**>100**
Breadth of alumni network	83
Internationalism of alumni	>100
Alumni effectiveness	94

Address
Lancaster University
Management School
Lancaster University
Bailrigg
Lancaster
UK
LA1 4YX

Tel:
+44 1524 593 708

Fax:
+44 1524 592 417

Email:
mba@lancaster.ac.uk

Website:
www.lums.lancs.ac.uk

Programme director:
Steve Kempster

Figures in brackets
represent rank

Background

Lancaster University Management School is a full-range school covering undergraduate programmes, the MBA, specialist master's programmes, doctoral programmes and short executive courses. The school is large, with around 100 faculty, 2,000 undergraduate students and over 1,000 postgraduates. The school has been established for over 30 years and has a strong reputation for research. It also has good international and regional industry links and was a pioneer of company-specific and consortium MBA programmes in the UK.

Facilities

The facilities are excellent and the school is currently building an extension, which should open in early 2005. At present the school occupies modern buildings in the south-west corner of the sprawling, low-rise university campus. The MBA and other taught master's programmes are housed in the Management School. Dedicated MBA facilities include a lecture theatre, seminar rooms, computer room, and careers and library resources. Students have 24-hour access to a number of university computer laboratories and there is a well-equipped sports centre next to the school.

Lancaster is a small city with good transport links. It is close to the sea and the picturesque Lake District. Social life is limited, especially during the hectic first term.

	Full-time MBA
Student assessment of facilities	4.5 (30)

Faculty

Number of faculty: 114 full-time, 6 part-time, 73 visiting

	Full-time MBA	Lancaster Executive MBA
Number of faculty per student	3.4 (4)	12.1
Percentage of faculty with PhD	72 (>100)	72
Student rating of faculty	4.5 (35)	–

Strengths and weaknesses

Strengths: finance; leadership; entrepreneurship

Weakness: effectiveness of alumni network

Programme highlights

Lancaster's full-time MBA is one of a wide range of general and specialist master's programmes offered by the school. The programme lasts 12 months, including a summer project, and is divided into four modules (including the project). Students undertake six foundation courses in the first module, three strategy courses (business economics, human resource management and strategic management) and an in-company consultancy project in the second module, and four electives in the third (they can take an additional four non-assessed courses). The fourth module is the project. A "managing in action" course (action learning is an important element at Lancaster) and a career management course run throughout the programme.

The two-year Executive MBA has a similar curriculum to the full-time version. Students attend eight five-day (Monday–Friday) intensive residential modules based at an off-campus hotel and training centre in Lancaster or at an executive training facility in the south of England. Work-based assignments follow each module, enabling participants to apply the theory to their own organisations. There are also small-group tutorials, approximately every month, which bring together cross-organisational and cross-functional groups of managers and their tutor.

	Full-time MBA	Lancaster Executive MBA
Student rating of programme	4.3 (43)	–
Number of overseas exchange programmes	18 (39)	–
Number of languages on offer	5 (43)	–

Students

	Full-time MBA	Lancaster Executive MBA
Annual intake	40	16
Applicants:places	8:1	25:1
Percentage of women students	52 (12)	20
Percentage of foreign students	73 (23)	n/a
Average GMAT score	620 (74)	n/a
Average number of months' work experience	84 (22)	144
Age range of students	24-34	27-39
Average age	29	34
Student rating of culture and classmates	4.1 (82)	–

Student profile (full time)

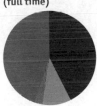

- ■ EU
- ■ Non-EU Europe
- ■ North America
- ■ Other Americas
- ■ Asia/Australasia
- ■ Middle East

Recruiters/careers service

	Full-time MBA	Lancaster Executive MBA
Number of industry sectors that recruited graduates	7 (62)	–
Percentage of graduates in jobs 3 months after graduation	88 (53)	–
Percentage of graduates finding jobs through careers services	12 (96)	–
Student rating of careers service	3.7 (57)	–
Post-MBA salary, US$	78,689 (50)	–
Percentage increase in salary	78 (12)	–
Principal recruiters of graduates	Ernst & Young, Deutsche Bank, Citibank	

Cost

	Full-time MBA	Lancaster Executive MBA
Application fees	None	None
Programme fees	£16,500 (US$27,049)	£16,500 (US$27,049)
Comments	–	–
Accommodation costs (on campus, per year)	£3,640 (US$5,967)	–
Accommodation costs (off campus, per year)	£2,700 (US$4,426)	–
Financial aid available	£80,000 (US$131,148)	–
Type of aid available	Scholarship, bursary	–
Criteria on which aid is granted	Merit, financial need	–

Accreditation

AMBA, EQUIS

Application details

	Full-time MBA	Lancaster Executive MBA
Application deadline	June 30th	August 30th
Programme dates	Sep start, 12 months	Oct start, 22 months
Admission requirements	Good first degree or equivalent professional qualification; at least 3 years' work experience; GMAT; TOEFL if first language not English (minimum 600 paper-based; 250 computer-based); 2 references; interview; laptop	Good first degree or equivalent professional qualification; at least 5 years' work experience; TOEFL if first language not English; 2 references; interview

Executive education

Lancaster is a specialist in customised in-company programmes, mainly carried out through its Management Development and Entrepreneurship and Enterprise divisions. The school has developed customised programmes for a number of organisations, including British Airways, Royal & SunAlliance, the National Health Service, Total and Zetex.

Student/alumni quotes

"Lancaster stood apart from other schools because of the responsiveness and positive attitude of the staff."

"I suppose the school's location is not the best and this may sway people to make the wrong decision about Lancaster."

"It is great value for money and treats every student as an individual."

Leeds University Business School

Address
Maurice Keyworth
Building
University of Leeds
Leeds
UK
LS2 9JT

Tel:
+44 113 343 4884

Fax:
+44 113 343 4885

Email:
mba@lubs.leeds.ac.uk

Website:
www.leeds.ac.uk/lubs

Programme director:
John March

Figures in brackets
represent rank

Ranking	Rank (out of 100) Full-time
Overall rank	81
Regional rank	31

Criteria	Rank (out of 100) Full-time
Open new career opportunities	**87**
Diversity of recruiters	73
Number in jobs three months after graduation	50
Jobs found through the careers service	90
Student assessment of careers service	>100
Personal development and educational experience	**77**
Faculty quality	88
Student quality	48
Student diversity	24
Education experience	96
Increase in salary	**36**
Increase in salary	17
Post-MBA salary	59
Potential to network	**>100**
Breadth of alumni network	>100
Internationalism of alumni	73
Alumni effectiveness	>100

Background

Leeds University Business School has grown in size and reputation during the last decade and is now among the leading UK university business schools. It is closely linked to the university, but with over 80 faculty it has its own high reputation for research. It is a full-range school with 1,300 undergraduate and 500 postgraduate students.

Facilities

The school is based in a newly refurbished building close to the university campus that once housed Leeds grammar school. Facilities, including lecture theatre, seminar and syndicate rooms, café and common rooms, are excellent. MBA students have access to all university libraries and sporting facilities. Leeds is a lively, cosmopolitan city in the UK's northern hilly region.

	Full-time MBA
Student assessment of facilities	4.2 (78)

Faculty

Number of faculty: 78 full-time, 5 part-time, 23 visiting

	Full-time MBA	Executive MBA
Number of faculty per student	0.9 (40)	5.4
Percentage of faculty with PhD	81 (84)	81
Student rating of faculty	4.0 (96)	–

Strengths and weaknesses

Strengths: international business; finance; organisational development and strategy

Weakness: industry links

Programme highlights

The Leeds MBA is in the mainstream UK and European tradition of a one-year programme consisting of taught core courses and electives followed by an individual project. It starts with a ten-subject core including soft skills training. Students then choose three option modules (effectively electives) from 15 offered (management of projects, international finance, management decision-making, international management, marketing communications, e-business, managing and exploiting intellectual capital, financial analysis, financial derivatives, multinational business strategy, marketing strategy, business excellence, international marketing, knowledge management, European business). After this they complete their project.

The 30-month Executive MBA is made up of 11 core modules and three optional modules (from management decision-making, knowledge management, e-business, business excellence) followed by a project and dissertation usually in a student's own organisation. Each module involves open learning preceding a three- or four-day workshop followed by further study or a work-based assignment. One core module—executive skills: thinking and acting for effective practice—involves shorter workshops scheduled before or after other module workshops.

	Full-time MBA	Executive MBA
Student rating of programme	4.0 (96)	–
Number of overseas exchange programmes	0 (93)	–
Number of languages on offer	>5 (25)	–

Students

	Full-time MBA	Executive MBA
Annual intake	95	20
Applicants:places	10:1	1:1
Percentage of women students	30 (20)	25
Percentage of foreign students	88 (10)	n/a
Average GMAT score	n/a (n/a)	n/a
Average number of months' work experience	72 (35)	144
Age range of students	25-37	30-43
Average age	30	38
Student rating of culture and classmates	3.8 (>100)	–

Student profile (full time)

- ■ EU
- ■ Non-EU Europe
- ▨ North America
- ■ Other Americas
- ■ Asia/Australasia
- ▨ Middle East

Recruiters/careers service

	Full-time MBA	Executive MBA
Number of industry sectors that recruited graduates	6 (73)	–
Percentage of graduates in jobs 3 months after graduation	92 (50)	–
Percentage of graduates finding jobs through careers services	28 (90)	–
Student rating of careers service	3.1 (110)	–
Post-MBA salary, US$	73,770 (59)	–
Percentage increase in salary	114 (17)	–
Principal recruiters of graduates	De Puy, Johnson & Johnson, HBOS, Tetrapak	

Cost

	Full-time MBA	Executive MBA
Application fees	None	None
Programme fees	£17,500 (US$28,689)	£15,500 (US$25,410)
Comments	Total programme in 2004. Fee for EU citizens is £15,500	Total programme
Accommodation costs (on campus, per year)	£4,160 (US$6,820)	–
Accommodation costs (off campus, per year)	£5,200 (US$8,525)	–
Financial aid available	£65,200 (US$106,885)	–
Type of aid available	Scholarships	–
Criteria on which aid is granted	Merit	–

Accreditation

AMBA, EQUIS

Application details

	Full-time MBA	Executive MBA
Application deadline	June 30th	July 31th
Programme dates	Sep start, 12 months	Oct start, 30 months
Admission requirements	First degree, at least 3 years' work experience; TOEFL or IELTS if first language not English; 2 references; laptop; interview for UK applicants (and for others when feasible); GMAT minimum 600 (when required)	First degree (non-graduates considered on basis of career and potential); at least 5 years' work experience; TOEFL or IELTS if first language not English; 2 references; interview

Executive education

Leeds offers a series of short customised in-company programmes delivered either on campus or on the company's premises.

Student/alumni quotes

"I have no regrets about leaving a well-paid job to take part in the Leeds MBA. I feel I have grown as an individual, and will be better placed to serve the needs of my next employer."

"[The school] hasn't built enough contact with many companies."

"Excellent teaching, great facilities and a growing reputation."

London Business School

Ranking	Rank (out of 100) Full-time
Overall rank	31
Regional rank	11

Criteria	Rank (out of 100) Full-time
Open new career opportunities	**67**
Diversity of recruiters	51
Number in jobs three months after graduation	84
Jobs found through the careers service	50
Student assessment of careers service	70
Personal development and educational experience	**7**
Faculty quality	38
Student quality	14
Student diversity	15
Education experience	18
Increase in salary	**13**
Increase in salary	57
Post-MBA salary	10
Potential to network	**60**
Breadth of alumni network	99
Internationalism of alumni	31
Alumni effectiveness	46

Address
London Business School
Sussex Place
Regent's Park
London
UK
NW1 4SA

Tel:
+44 20 7706 6861

Fax:
+44 20 7724 7875

Email:
mbainfo@london.edu

Website:
www.london.edu

Programme directors:
Julia Tyler/
Craig Smith

Figures in brackets
represent rank

Background

London Business School (LBS) is one of the world's leading schools. As one of only a handful of European schools that follow the North American two-year MBA model, LBS combines many of the best aspects of the North American and European traditions. In common with the leading US schools, for example, it has a strong summer internship programme; and like other leading European schools it prides itself on attracting a diverse mix of nationalities.

Facilities

LBS benefits greatly from its location in the centre of London (although it is actually closer to the West End, London's entertainment centre, than to the City, the financial centre) and takes full advantage of this by inviting business leaders as guest speakers and lecturers. Facilities are universally good although the main building is less "high-tech" in appearance (both inside and outside) than some of its US competitors. A separate building across the road provides excellent IT and sports facilities.

	Full-time MBA
Student assessment of facilities	4.2 (57)

Faculty

Number of faculty: 93 full-time, 16 part-time, 17 visiting			
	Full-time MBA	**EMBA-Global**	**Executive MBA**
Number of faculty per student	0.3 (91)	1.8	0.9
Percentage of faculty with PhD	99 (12)	99	99
Student rating of faculty	4.4 (29)	–	–

Strengths and weaknesses

Strengths: entrepreneurship; finance; strategic and international management

Weaknesses: operations management classes; lack of space

Programme highlights

The LBS MBA is a strongly academic and intensive general management programme with a good deal of practical emphasis. It is international in philosophy and scope (although American in design), and every student must master a second language other than English in order to graduate. Some students may have to take pre-programme courses in quantitative areas such as accounting, economics and statistics.

In the first year, students take 16 required courses, a number of soft skills and language workshops and a one-week shadowing project in which they work with a practising manager and produce a report that is graded by faculty. In the second year, they take 12 electives from around 70 on offer, which can be grouped into a career track or "stream of learning" (becoming an independent thinker, making things happen, becoming a leader and becoming an international citizen) and a concentration (change management, entrepreneurial management, finance, marketing, strategy, technology management and international business) are offered. A concentration consists of five electives. Elective courses are studied alongside students from other LBS programmes and those on international exchanges.

Students also complete an in-company consultancy project (usually in a two-person team) on which they must write a management report. Free or subsidised language training is available in Arabic, French, Catalan, German, Greek, Italian, Japanese, Mandarin Chinese, Polish, Portuguese, Russian and Spanish.

The Executive MBA leads to the same degree as the full-time version and the programme details are similar. There are two start dates, January and September. Students take 15 core courses during the first year and choose 6–8 electives from the same large portfolio as full-time students in the second year. There are five block weeks to allow in-depth study of a particular topic. The first of these at the start of the programme is residential and two are field trips, one in Europe and one outside Europe, and include a mini-consultancy project. Classes meet all day on Fridays and Saturdays every two weeks with breaks at Christmas and Easter and in the summer.

The EMBA–Global is run in partnership with Columbia Business School in New York (see page 189 for details).

	Full-time MBA	EMBA-Global	Executive MBA
Student rating of programme	4.5 (16)		–
Number of overseas exchange programmes	140 (30)	–	–
Number of languages on offer	>5 (35)	–	–

Student profile (full time)

■ EU
■ Non-EU Europe
■ North America
■ Other Americas
■ Asia/Australasia
▨ Middle East

Students

	Full-time MBA	EMBA-Global	Executive MBA
Annual intake	303	69	148
Applicants:places	6:1	2:1	2:1
Percentage of women students	24 (85)	25	20
Percentage of foreign students	87 (14)	n/a	n/a
Average GMAT score	684 (17)	n/a	660
Average number of months' work experience	72 (41)	120	108
Age range of students	26-31	28-38	28-39
Average age	28	33	33
Student rating of culture and classmates	4.6 (19)	–	–

Recruiters/careers service

	Full-time MBA	EMBA-Global	Executive MBA
Number of industry sectors that recruited graduates	8 (51)	–	–
Percentage of graduates in jobs 3 months after graduation	65 (84)	–	–
Percentage of graduates finding jobs through careers services	36 (50)	–	–
Student rating of careers service	3.2 (70)	–	–
Post-MBA salary, US$	92,566 (10)	–	–
Percentage increase in salary	53 (57)	–	–
Principal recruiters of graduates	McKinsey & Co, Barclays Capital, Johnson & Johnson, American Express		

Cost

	Full-time MBA	EMBA-Global	Executive MBA
Application fees	£120 (US$197)	US$170	£75 (US$123)
Programme fees	£41,970 (US$68,803)	US$115,000	£42,500 (US$69,672)
Comments	Total programme	Payable by US$3,000 commitment fee and two instalments of US$66,000 and $46,000	Total programme
Accommodation costs (on campus, per year)	–	–	–
Accommodation costs (off campus, per year)	£12,636 (US$20,715)	–	–
Financial aid available	£400,000 (US$655,738)	–	–
Type of aid available	Scholarships	–	–
Criteria on which aid is granted	Formal scholarship application process, predominantly merit-based	–	–

Accreditation

AACSB International, AMBA, EQUIS

Application details

	Full-time MBA	EMBA-Global	Executive MBA
Application deadline	April 20th	To be confirmed	Rolling admissions
Programme dates	Sep start, 21 months	May start, 20 months	Jan start, 24 months
Admission requirements	Good undergraduate degree or equivalent qualification; work experience; TOEFL or IELTS if first language not English; 2 references; 6 essays; laptop; interview by invitation	First degree; at least 5 years' work experience; 2 references; 3 essays; interview; résumé	First degree (or significant work experience and professional qualifications); at least 4 years' work experience; GMAT; 2 references; 5 essays; interview

Executive education

LBS has a strong tradition of excellence in executive education. Its open-enrolment programmes are grouped in the areas of general management, strategy, and leadership and finance. Customised in-company programmes are equally well developed and the school has over 60 client companies around the world.

Student/alumni quotes

"LBS is a very international, open, intellectually challenging and welcoming community. You can feel it once you start the application process. I was really happy to have spent two years there and made lots of friends."

"Capacity constraints in facilities."

"International student body and strong faculty."

University of London—Royal Holloway School of Management

Ranking	Rank (out of 100) Full-time
Overall rank	n/a
Regional rank	n/a

Address
School of
Management
Royal Holloway
University of London
Egham
Surrey
UK
TW20 0EX

Background

Royal Holloway College was opened by Queen Victoria in 1886 and became part of the University of London at the end of the 19th century. The School of Management was established in 1990 and is one of the largest academic departments at Royal Holloway. It has dedicated facilities for teaching undergraduate and graduate degree programmes.

Facilities

The college has over 5,000 undergraduate and postgraduate students on its striking neo-gothic campus outside London, not far from Heathrow Airport. Facilities are generally good and on-campus accommodation is available.

	Full-time MBA
Student assessment of facilities	n/a (n/a)

Faculty

Number of faculty: 36 full-time, 0 part-time, 3 visiting

	Full-time MBA
Number of faculty per student	0.9 (n/a)
Percentage of faculty with PhD	– (n/a)
Student rating of faculty	n/a (n/a)

Strengths and weaknesses

Strengths: management information systems; human resources management; international management

Weakness: effectiveness of alumni

Programme highlights

The Royal Holloway MBA in International Management has a fairly standard European format. Students take six core courses (each assessed separately by a 3,000-word assignment and an exam), two electives (assessed in the same way) concentrating on either business in a particular geographic region or a particular area of business such as global financial markets, and finish with a 12,000–15,000-word dissertation. They must also undertake two group projects and two case studies. The programme is very international in character and has some interesting additional elements, including masterclasses given by practising executives and soft skills workshops and seminars.

The distance-learning programme is essentially the same as the full-time version, with the same core courses and electives and a final project. Participants can take a maximum of six courses and a minimum of two in any one study year (September–April). They can start the programme at any time, but as examinations are held every May and October the school advises starting in March for October exams and in October for May exams. The programme can be completed in a minimum of 28 months and a maximum of five years.

	Full-time MBA
Student rating of programme	n/a (n/a)
Number of overseas exchange programmes	0 (n/a)
Number of languages on offer	0 (n/a)

Tel:
+44 1784 414 350

Fax:
+44 1784 439 854

Email:
laura.henocq@
rhul.ac.uk

Website:
www.rhul.ac.uk/
management

Programme director:
Brendan McSweeney

Figures in brackets
represent rank

Student profile (full time)

- ■ EU
- ■ Non-EU Europe
- ■ North America
- ■ Other Americas
- ■ Asia/Australasia
- ░ Middle East

Students

	Full-time MBA
Annual intake	42
Applicants:places	9:1
Percentage of women students	50 (n/a)
Percentage of foreign students	40 (n/a)
Average GMAT score	n/a (n/a)
Average number of months' work experience	84
Age range of students	25-41
Average age	30
Student rating of culture and classmates	n/a (n/a)

Recruiters/careers service

	Full-time MBA
Number of industry sectors that recruited graduates	– (n/a)
Percentage of graduates in jobs 3 months after graduation	– (n/a)
Percentage of graduates finding jobs through careers services	– (n/a)
Student rating of careers service	– (n/a)
Post-MBA salary, US$	– (n/a)
Percentage increase in salary	– (n/a)
Principal recruiters of graduates	–

Cost

	Full-time MBA
Application fees	None
Programme fees	£11,450 (US$18,770)
Comments	Fee for EU citizens. Fee for non-EU students is £12,600
Accommodation costs (on campus, per year)	–
Accommodation costs (off campus, per year)	–
Financial aid available	£11,450 (US$18,770)
Type of aid available	Scholarship
Criteria on which aid is granted	Strength of application

Accreditation

None

Application details

	Full-time MBA
Application deadline	August 1st
Programme dates	Sep start, 12 months
Admission requirements	First degree (in exceptional circumstances, applicants without a first degree will be considered); at least 3 years' work experience; TOEFL or IELTS if first language not English; 2 references

Executive education

Royal Holloway offers a number of customised company degree programmes.

E.M. Lyon

Ranking	Rank (out of 100) Full-time
Overall rank	53
Regional rank	19

Criteria	Rank (out of 100) Full-time
Open new career opportunities	**86**
Diversity of recruiters	79
Number in jobs three months after graduation	85
Jobs found through the careers service	83
Student assessment of careers service	58
Personal development and educational experience	**79**
Faculty quality	79
Student quality	87
Student diversity	74
Education experience	41
Increase in salary	**60**
Increase in salary	31
Post-MBA salary	69
Potential to network	**2**
Breadth of alumni network	2
Internationalism of alumni	5
Alumni effectiveness	48

Address
23, ave. Guy de
Collongue
BP 174
Lyon Ecully
France
69134

Tel:
+33 04 7833 7740

Fax:
+33 04 7833 7755

E-mail:
mba@em-lyon.com

Website:
www.em-lyon.com

Programme director:
Christian Gérard

Figures in brackets
represent rank

Background

E.M. Lyon, founded in 1872 by the local Lyon business community (the Lyon Chamber of Commerce is a main stakeholder), is a French school with global ambitions. It is boosting the number of non-French students and the faculty is increasingly Anglophone, with staff offered in-hours language training (this has always been open to students). There is a keen desire to form overseas alliances. It has, for example, formed a strategic alliance with leading business schools in Brazil, Canada, the UK and the US. It is also concentrating on three strategic areas: internationalism, entrepreneurship and technology.

Facilities

The modern campus is located just outside Lyon and has excellent facilities, including a major library, a computer centre, restaurants and cafeterias, and an audio-visual and language laboratory. There are two residential complexes housing 350 students and good sports facilities. MBA students share most resources with other students, but they have a separate area with two lecture rooms and nine classrooms. Lyon says there is campus-wide handicap access, parking and classroom.

Despite its reputation as an industrial powerhouse, the centre of Lyon is attractive and full of character, as well as being a centre of French gastronomy. It is an important transport hub with good rail and air links and easy access to the Alps, the Mediterranean and other European countries.

	Full-time MBA
Student assessment of facilities	4.0 (77)

Faculty

Number of faculty: 67 full-time, 21 part-time, 24 visiting

	Full-time MBA	EM Lyon Executive MBA
Number of faculty per student	1.2 (18)	2.9
Percentage of faculty with PhD	81 (92)	81
Student rating of faculty	4.0 (78)	–

Strengths and weaknesses

Strengths: entrepreneurship; corporate finance; personal and managerial development

Weakness: lack of international profile (especially outside Europe)

Programme highlights

E.M. Lyon's International MBA programme starts with an optional Basics course, involving statistics and language courses. This is followed by 12 Foundation courses (essentially the core) interspersed with a series of seminars focusing on major issues in entrepreneurship and intrapreneurship, and then Gateways (three set specialised tracks: business-to-business marketing, international business, or corporate restructuring), although students can opt to take a range of general electives. Students take the first part of the programme in either French or English and courses in the other language (or a third if they are already fluent in both). They then continue with a project, an exchange visit or an in-company placement.

The school offers a two-year part-time MBA mainly in French but with some courses in English. The content is identical to the International MBA and students from both programmes take some courses together.

There is also a joint MBA programme with Cranfield School of Management, UK.

	Full-time MBA	EM Lyon Executive MBA
Student rating of programme	4.2 (56)	–
Number of overseas exchange programmes	43 (21)	–
Number of languages on offer	>5 (37)	–

Students

Student profile (full time)

- ■ EU
- ■ Non-EU Europe
- ▨ North America
- ■ Other Americas
- ■ Asia/Australasia
- ▨ Middle East

	Full-time MBA	EM Lyon Executive MBA
Annual intake	72	39
Applicants:places	3:1	3:1
Percentage of women students	39 (50)	15
Percentage of foreign students	50 (58)	n/a
Average GMAT score	610 (87)	605
Average number of months' work experience	60 (38)	84
Age range of students	27-36	31-40
Average age	31	35
Student rating of culture and classmates	4.0 (65)	–

Recruiters/careers service

	Full-time MBA	EM Lyon Executive MBA
Number of industry sectors that recruited graduates	7 (79)	–
Percentage of graduates in jobs 3 months after graduation	60 (85)	–
Percentage of graduates finding jobs through careers services	38 (83)	–
Student rating of careers service	3.5 (58)	–
Post-MBA salary, US$	61,364 (69)	–
Percentage increase in salary	57 (31)	–
Principal recruiters of graduates	General Electric, Sara Lee, Renault VI	

Cost

	Full-time MBA	EM Lyon Executive MBA
Application fees	€110 (US$125)	€110 (US$125)
Programme fees	€28,000 (US$31,818)	€28,000 (US$31,818)
Comments	Total programme	Total programme
Accommodation costs (on campus, per year)	€2,830 (US$3,216)	–
Accommodation costs (off campus, per year)	€3,390 (US$3,852)	–
Financial aid available	€63,000 (US$71,591)	–
Type of aid available	International student scholarships	–
Criteria on which aid is granted	Merit, financial need	–

Accreditation

AMBA, EQUIS

Application details

	Full-time MBA	EM Lyon Executive MBA
Application deadline	May 1st	Rolling admissions
Programme dates	Sep start, 12 months	Jan start, 24 months
Admission requirements	First degree; at least 3 years' work experience; GMAT; TOEFL if first language not English; references; essays; interview; laptop	First degree; at least 5 years' work experience; GMAT; TOEFL if first language not English; references; essays; interview

Executive education

E.M. Lyon offers open-enrolment programmes at diploma (1–2 years), certificate (6–22 days) and seminar (1–5 days) levels that correspond to the target audiences of young managers, senior managers and top executives. It also offers an extensive range of language courses as well as customised in-company programmes.

Student/alumni quotes

"E.M. Lyon is an excellent school in a very special place in France. It is often overlooked and swamped by the other grande écoles ... It is a travesty that this school is not considered in the same category ... and amounts to some degree of snobbery within the French education system and nothing else. E.M. Lyon is a great place to take a full-time MBA."

"Some organisational problems—materials not always on time, scheduling of the electives not very well thought out."

"Very good atmosphere and quality of students, good academic quality, international focus."

Maastricht School of Management

Address
Endepolsdomein 150
P.O. Box 1203
BE Maastricht
The Netherlands
6201

Tel:
+31 43 387 0875

Fax:
+31 43 387 0800

Email:
admissions@msm.nl

Website:
www.msm.nl

Programme director:
Dr E L Maes

Figures in brackets
represent rank

Ranking	Rank (out of 100) Full-time
Overall rank	n/a
Regional rank	n/a

Background

Maastricht School of Management (MSM) was established in 1952 as the Researchinstituut Voor Bedrijfswetenschappen (RVB) at the Technical University of Delft (the Netherlands' premier engineering school). It moved its campus to Maastricht in 1989 and began a full-time MBA in 1990. The school is quite small, with 30 full-time MBA students and 12 EMBA students on its Maastricht campus in 2003, but around 1,600 students participate in its postgraduate business degree programmes worldwide through an extensive network of affiliated institutions.

MSM was originally set up to provide management education for sponsored students from emerging economies, which partly explains the high proportion of foreign students. The school has a strong MBA Outreach programme that allows it, in conjunction with local partners, to deliver full-time and part-time MBAs around the world. Students on the full-time programme at Maastricht can apply to study part of the time on an overseas Outreach programme.

Facilities

Based in a business park on the outskirts of Maastricht, the school has excellent facilities. Computer facilities are superb, and the school provides laptop computers. On-campus accommodation, for single people, couples and families, is linked to the school and is widely used. Rented housing in Maastricht is scarce and expensive.

	Full-time MBA
Student assessment of facilities	n/a (n/a)

Faculty

Number of faculty: 9 full-time, 11 part-time, 1 visiting

	Full-time MBA	Executive MBA
Number of faculty per student	0.5 (n/a)	1.2
Percentage of faculty with PhD	79 (n/a)	78
Student rating of faculty	n/a (n/a)	–

Strengths and weaknesses

Strengths: globally networked knowledge community; international management; cross cultural

Programme highlights

MSM's full-time one-year MBA programme begins with a short preparation or induction period including a week of training in interpersonal skills and then moves into the Foundation Segment, a set of largely function-based core courses, followed by the Integration Segment, which stresses strategy, and then the Focus Segment or chosen specialisation. Students must complete four courses in one of the specialisations offered (these include accounting and finance, globalisation, e-business and information technology, corporate strategy and economic policy, and management of government). The programme is completed with an individual project/research paper (the Performance Segment).

There is a six-month full-time pre-MBA programme for students who need to improve their English language skills or who seek additional skills and management training to reach the MBA admission level required at MSM or other business schools.

The part-time two-year Executive MBA, which leads to the same degree as the full-time version, specialises in general and strategic management. It focuses on strategy design and strategic behaviour with an emphasis on international trade and competition. The programme consists of seven nine-day residential modules with a break of about three months between each module. The aim is to help prepare middle managers for general management posts and to give them the tools to cope with the increasing rate of change within business and the world at large. The programme structure is similar to the full-time version, but the specialisations offered are general and strategic management, e-business and information technology, technology facility management (Dutch programme) and aviation management.

MSM offers its MBA via Outreach programmes in around 20 countries. The degree is the same as that offered in Maastricht, but it generally takes longer to complete (18–24 months) and classes are usually held in the evenings or at weekends. The pre-MBA is also offered on this basis.

	Full-time MBA	Executive MBA
Student rating of programme	n/a (n/a)	–
Number of overseas exchange programmes	6 (n/a)	–
Number of languages on offer	0 (n/a)	–

Students

	Full-time MBA	Executive MBA
Annual intake	30	12
Applicants:places	6:1	3:1
Percentage of women students	47 (n/a)	15
Percentage of foreign students	100 (n/a)	n/a
Average GMAT score	n/a	n/a
Average number of months' work experience	60 (n/a)	120
Age range of students	24-45	32-54
Average age	30	37
Student rating of culture and classmates	n/a (n/a)	–

Student profile (full time)

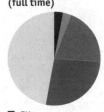

- ■ EU
- ▨ Non-EU Europe
- ▨ North America
- ■ Other Americas
- ■ Asia/Australasia
- ▨ Middle East

Recruiters/careers service

	Full-time MBA	Executive MBA
Number of industry sectors that recruited graduates	– (n/a)	–
Percentage of graduates in jobs 3 months after graduation	100 (n/a)	–
Percentage of graduates finding jobs through careers services	– (n/a)	–
Student rating of careers service	n/a (n/a)	–
Post-MBA salary, US$	– (n/a)	–
Percentage increase in salary	– (n/a)	–
Principal recruiters of graduates	–	

Cost

	Full-time MBA	Executive MBA
Application fees	€75 (US$85)	€75 (US$85)
Programme fees	€10,500 (US$12,273)	€19,500 (US$22,159)
Comments	–	–
Accommodation costs (on campus, per year)	€5,000 (US$5,682)	–
Accommodation costs (off campus, per year)	–	–
Financial aid available	–	–
Type of aid available	Scholarships, student loans	–
Criteria on which aid is granted	GMAT	–

Accreditation

None

Application details

	Full-time MBA	Executive MBA
Application deadline	June 1st	Rolling admissions
Programme dates	Sep start, 12 months	Feb start, 24 months
Admission requirements	Bachelor's degree or academic equivalent from a recognised university, with a foundation in economics and management; at least 3 years' work experience; GMAT; TOEFL or IELTS if first language not English; 3 references	Bachelor's degree or academic equivalent from a recognised university; at least 3 years' work experience; GMAT; TOEFL or IELTS if first language not English; 3 references

Executive education

MSM offers open-enrolment executive education programmes lasting 3–12 weeks and covering most management areas, as well as customised in-company programmes. Executive education is also offered via Maastricht's Outreach partners.

Macquarie Graduate School of Management

Ranking	Rank (out of 100) Full-time
Overall rank	50
Regional rank	1

Criteria	Rank (out of 100) Full-time
Open new career opportunities	**81**
Diversity of recruiters	1
Number in jobs three months after graduation	18
Jobs found through the careers service	76
Student assessment of careers service	>100
Personal development and educational experience	**3**
Faculty quality	>100
Student quality	1
Student diversity	64
Education experience	>100
Increase in salary	**58**
Increase in salary	>100
Post-MBA salary	25
Potential to network	**>100**
Breadth of alumni network	69
Internationalism of alumni	77
Alumni effectiveness	96

Address
Macquarie University
NSW
Australia
2109

Tel:
+61 2 9850 9052

Fax:
+61 2 9850 9022

Email:
mgsminfo@mgsm.
edu.au

Website:
www.mgsm.edu.au

Programme director:
Guy Ford

Figures in brackets
represent rank

Background

Established as part of Macquarie University in 1969, Macquarie Graduate School of Management (MGSM) is the oldest continuously operating graduate school of business in New South Wales. An innovative school, it has a strong social science and psychology orientation. MGSM has satellite campuses in the Sydney business area, Hong Kong and Singapore. Around 2,500 students are currently enrolled in postgraduate programmes supported by over 100 permanent and adjunct faculty. Like many Australian schools, MGSM prides itself on the flexibility of its delivery of programmes.

Facilities

The modern, well-equipped school is sited in a group of seven low-rise buildings separated by English-style gardens on the edge of the university's park-like campus in Ryde, about 30 minutes' drive north of downtown Sydney. Students use the main university library, where they have their own librarian. There are good computer facilities and students have access to the university sports and recreational amenities.

	Full-time MBA
Student assessment of facilities	3.6 (>100)

Faculty

Number of faculty: 39 full-time, 60 part-time, 14 visiting		
	Full-time MBA	**Part-time MBA**
Number of faculty per student	0.6 (59)	0.4
Percentage of faculty with PhD	87 (86)	87
Student rating of faculty	3.6 (>100)	–

Strengths and weaknesses

Strengths: finance; marketing; strategy

Weakness: some weak teaching

Programme highlights

The Macquarie MBA is offered in one-, two- or three-year variations. The difference between the various options is the number of courses taken in each term. In the one-year version, which is similar to a regular full-time programme, students take four courses per term. Elective courses are usually offered in block format (over one week, for example) and may be scheduled in the evenings. In the two-year version students take two or three courses per term, and in the three-year version they take one or two courses per term.

It is a generalised programme with a good range of electives. There are ten fairly traditional core courses and six electives, which include in-company consulting and research projects. Students can follow a particular stream, or concentration, or take electives across a wide range of subjects. Concentrations are offered in general management; financial management; human resource management; information technology management; international management; logistics, operations and technology management; marketing management; strategic management; research. Core courses can be waived and replaced with electives.

The MBA is offered in downtown Sydney as well as Singapore and Hong Kong, where it is taught by Sydney faculty. Classes are given in eight-day blocks.

	Full-time MBA	Part-time MBA
Student rating of programme	3.9 (93)	–
Number of overseas exchange programmes	0 (41)	–
Number of languages on offer	1 (83)	–

Students

Student profile (full time)

- ■ EU
- ■ Non-EU Europe
- ■ North America
- ■ Other Americas
- ■ Asia/Australasia
- ■ Middle East

	Full-time MBA	Part-time MBA
Annual intake	113	306
Applicants:places	2:1	2:1
Percentage of women students	38 (16)	38
Percentage of foreign students	46 (63)	n/a
Average GMAT score	n/a (n/a)	n/a
Average number of months' work experience	144 (1)	144
Age range of students	28-40	28-40
Average age	34	34
Student rating of culture and classmates	3.9 (91)	–

Recruiters/careers service

	Full-time MBA	Part-time MBA
Number of industry sectors that recruited graduates	8 (1)	–
Percentage of graduates in jobs 3 months after graduation	87 (18)	–
Percentage of graduates finding jobs through careers services	25 (76)	
Student rating of careers service	2.3 (>100)	–
Post-MBA salary, US$	85,416 (25)	–
Percentage increase in salary	24 (>100)	
Principal recruiters of graduates	Singtel Optus, PricewaterhouseCoopers, Dell Computer	

Cost

	Full-time MBA	Part-time MBA
Application fees	A$110 (US$71)	–
Programme fees	A$44,800 (US$29,090)	A$42,400 (US$27,532)
Comments	Fee for Australian citizens is A$42,400	Different rates apply for students studying in Hong Kong and Singapore
Accommodation costs (on campus, per year)	A$9,240 (US$6,000)	–
Accommodation costs (off campus, per year)	A$7,800 (US$5,064)	–
Financial aid available	Not disclosed	–
Type of aid available	Scholarships, company sponsorships	–
Criteria on which aid is granted	Varies	–

Accreditation

None

Application details

	Full-time MBA	Part-time MBA
Application deadline	October 22nd and May 6th	October 22nd and May 6th
Programme dates	Jan start, 12 months	Jan start, 24 months
Admission requirements	First degree; at least 5 years' work experience; TOEFL or IELTS if first language not English; 3 references; essay; laptop; interview may be required	First degree; at least 5 years' work experience; TOEFL or IELTS if first language not English; 3 references; essay; interview may be required

Executive education

MGSM's open-enrolment executive education programmes are grouped into six main management areas: general management and strategy; leadership and change; individual development; finance and marketing; operations; conferences and special events. In-company programmes can be either fully customised or adapted from existing open programmes, and some offer participants credits leading to postgraduate degrees. The main areas covered include: general management, leadership and change; individual development; performance management; financial management; corporate governance; strategic marketing; competition and strategy in Asia; operations and logistics management; coaching.

Student/alumni quotes

"A demanding, rigorous programme that is cost-effective; very strong, capable and supportive student body (not as competitive as I had anticipated)."

"Reliance on American (especially Harvard) ideas and case studies. There needs to be a broader exposure of ideas and more Australian case studies."

"I believe they deliver the best course within Australia (including Asia) and with some curriculum tweaks and faculty tweaks could challenge for a top-ten place globally."

Manchester Business School

Address
Manchester Business
School
Booth Street West
Manchester
UK
M15 6PB

Tel:
+44 161 275 6498

Fax:
+44 161 275 6556

Email:
manchester_mba@
mbs.ac.uk

Website:
www.mbs.ac.uk

Programme director:
Jikyeong Kang

Figures in brackets
represent rank

Ranking	Rank (out of 100) Full-time
Overall rank	58
Regional rank	21

Criteria	Rank (out of 100) Full-time
Open new career opportunities	**49**
Diversity of recruiters	1
Number in jobs three months after graduation	32
Jobs found through the careers service	59
Student assessment of careers service	83
Personal development and educational experience	**87**
Faculty quality	>100
Student quality	56
Student diversity	84
Education experience	57
Increase in salary	**21**
Increase in salary	29
Post-MBA salary	38
Potential to network	**76**
Breadth of alumni network	50
Internationalism of alumni	42
Alumni effectiveness	80

Background

The creation of a new university in Manchester, scheduled for October 2004, formed by the merger of the University of Manchester and the University of Manchester Institute of Science and Technology (UMIST) will have major implications for Manchester Business School (MBS). It will effectively merge with UMIST's (mainly undergraduate) School of Management and some other departments to form the biggest full-range business school in the UK, with 2,000 students and nearly 200 faculty, allowing greater choice and variety on the MBA, more specialised master's programme, and expanded research and executive education activity. At the time of writing the school was searching for a new dean.

Facilities

MBA programmes will continue to be taught in the old business school, which is housed in a self-contained modern building near the city-centre university campus. Facilities are good. MBA students have their own lecture rooms, group rooms, bar and restaurants, library and IT facilities. A sponsorship deal with Sony has provided videoconferencing for meeting rooms and lecture theatres. MBS's 35,000-volume management library is considered to be one of the best in Europe. There are plenty of PCs and the school has its own language centre. All full-time MBA students receive a laptop computer, loaned by the school, for the duration of their studies.

Sports and cultural facilities on the university campus are good. MBS is friendly and relaxed and recognises that Manchester, one of the most vibrant and lively cities in the UK, is a great bonus. There is no on-campus accommodation (except for some incoming exchange students), but reasonably priced accommodation within commuting distance is available.

	Full-time MBA
Student assessment of facilities	4.2 (76)

Faculty

Number of faculty: 44 full-time, 0 part-time, 42 visiting

	Full-time MBA	Distance Learning MBA Programme	Executive (part-time) MBA
Number of faculty per student	0.4 (80)	0.0	1.4
Percentage of faculty with PhD	80 (82)	80	80
Student rating of faculty	3.7 (>100)	–	–

Strengths and weaknesses

Strengths: international business; entrepreneurship and innovation; finance

Weaknesses: facilities; some teaching

Programme highlights

The 18-month full-time MBA programme at MBS is based on a diploma/MBA system and is preceded by a mandatory (unassessed) four-week introductory module. The first two terms, effectively the core, make up the diploma stage; three further terms, including the summer, make up the MBA stage. The diploma stage consists of 13 courses and two projects, as well as a range of personal and career development workshops. The MBA stage offers a varied menu of assessed internship, study tours to Europe and Asia, electives and an international project. In the MBA stage, only the ten-week international business project is mandatory. Students choose from the other options to make up the required credits. The programme reflects MBS's heavy emphasis on project work—the so-called "Manchester method".

The part-time Executive MBA draws heavily on the traditional MBS approach of project-based learning. It is divided into core subjects, project work and some electives. Students take ten core credit courses, at least two from each subject area, and a project-based course in the diploma stage, and eight credits (from a menu including a three-month overseas exchange) in the MBA stage. Classes are held on Tuesday and Thursday evenings (5.30–8 pm), Friday morning (9 am–12.30 pm) and Friday afternoon (2–5.30 pm). Most students choose either two evenings or all day Friday, but any combination is possible, starting in September, January or March. Most students are sponsored by their companies, but careers management services and all other school and university amenities are available.

The Distance Learning MBA is delivered via Manchester Business School Worldwide, which as well as its UK base has support offices in Singapore and Hong Kong and affiliations in Jamaica and India. Distance learning is combined with residential workshops each semester in the UK and at overseas facilities. Teaching includes regular face-to-face contact with students and senior faculty.

MBS also offers a range of corporate MBAs.

	Full-time MBA	Distance Learning MBA Programme	Executive (part-time) MBA
Student rating of programme	3.9 (85)	–	–
Number of overseas exchange programmes	0 (64)	–	–
Number of languages on offer	>5 (1)	–	–

Students

	Full-time MBA	Distance Learning MBA Programme	Executive (part-time) MBA
Annual intake	127	344	61
Applicants:places	4:1	–	2:1
Percentage of women students	29 (82)	33	20
Percentage of foreign students	27 (52)	n/a	n/a
Average GMAT score	615 (80)	n/a	625
Average number of months' work experience	84 (17)	120	120
Age range of students	25–35	25–45	27–43
Average age	29	36	33
Student rating of culture and classmates	4.0 (68)	–	–

Student profile (full time)

- ■ EU
- ▨ Non-EU Europe
- ▨ North America
- ■ Other Americas
- ■ Asia/Australasia
- ▨ Middle East

Recruiters/careers service

	Full-time MBA	Distance Learning MDA Programme	Executive (part-time) MBA
Number of industry sectors that recruited graduates	8 (1)	–	–
Percentage of graduates in jobs 3 months after graduation	80 (32)	–	–
Percentage of graduates finding jobs through careers services	53 (59)	–	–
Student rating of careers service	3.0 (83)	–	–
Post-MBA salary, US$	83,607 (38)	–	–
Percentage increase in salary	79 (29)	–	–
Principal recruiters of graduates	Barclays Capital, DHL, AT Kearney		

Cost

	Full-time MBA	Distance Learning MBA Programme	Executive (part-time) MBA
Application fees	£50 (US$82)	None	£50 (US$82)
Programme fees	£25,500 (US$41,803)	£12,600 (US$20,656)	£20,600 (US$33,770)
Comments	Fee is for EU citizens. Fee for non-EU citizens is £29,500	Total fees covering course work and project stages	Payable in three annual instalments
Accommodation costs (on campus, per year)	£4,600 (US$7,541)	–	–
Accommodation costs (off campus, per year)	£4,600 (US$7,541)	–	–
Financial aid available	£50,000 (US$81,967)	–	–
Type of aid available	Scholarships	–	–
Criteria on which aid is granted	Merit	–	–

Accreditation

AACSB International, AMBA, EQUIS

Application details

	Full-time MBA	Distance Learning MBA Programme	Executive (part-time) MBA
Application deadline	June 30th	December 1st	September 2nd
Programme dates	Sep start, 18 months	Jan start, 36 months	Sep start, 30 months
Admission requirements	First degree (candidates aged 27 and over without an undergraduate degree are considered depending on professional qualifications and work experience); at least 3 years' work experience; TOEFL or IELTS if first language not English; 2 references; interview; laptop	First degree (candidates aged 27 and over without an undergraduate degree are considered depending on professional qualifications and work experience); at least 3 years' work experience; reference	First degree (candidates aged 27 and over without an undergraduate degree are considered depending on professional qualifications and work experience); at least 3 years' work experience; TOEFL or IELTS if first language not English; 2 references; interview

Executive education

MBS's open-enrolment programmes are headed by the Programme for High Value Managers, a sort of mini-MBA. This comes in various options: a core programme (two five-day modules); an extended programme (the core programme followed by five three-day modules chosen from a range); or selected three-day modules (any number chosen on a stand-alone basis). Another is The plc Board—Meeting the Challenges, a three-day programme for directors of publicly quoted UK companies run in co-operation with Ashridge and Henley Management College. Specialist three-day modules are offered in areas such as strategy, finance, marketing, operations and human resources. MBS also runs an extensive portfolio of customised in-company programmes.

Student/alumni quotes

"Manchester offers the best combination of opportunities of any of the major business schools, particularly in the UK. You can do an internship and an exchange visit, and the course is only 18 months long."

"A handful of lecturers were very poor, although this was often offset by strong performers within the same subject area."

"It is very practical, giving everyone an opportunity to learn in the classroom then apply in real-life situations."

University of Maryland—Robert H Smith School of Business

Address
2308 Van Munching Hall
University of Maryland
College Park, MD
US
20742

Tel:
+1 301 405 9469

Fax:
+1 301 314 6685

Email:
mba_info@rhsmith
umd.edu

Website:
www.rhsmith.umd.edu

Programme director:
Cherie Scricca

Figures in brackets
represent rank

Ranking	Rank (out of 100) Full-time
Overall rank	48
Regional rank	31

Criteria	Rank (out of 100) Full-time
Open new career opportunities	**52**
Diversity of recruiters	51
Number in jobs three months after graduation	66
Jobs found through the careers service	63
Student assessment of careers service	42
Personal development and educational experience	**37**
Faculty quality	13
Student quality	58
Student diversity	46
Education experience	47
Increase in salary	**72**
Increase in salary	64
Post-MBA salary	63
Potential to network	**70**
Breadth of alumni network	56
Internationalism of alumni	>100
Alumni effectiveness	57

Background

The University of Maryland's Robert H Smith School of Business focuses on management information systems as a key area of strength. As well as teaching undergraduate and graduate business programmes, the school is closely involved with the Maryland–Washington DC–Northern Virginia corporate and government nexus through consulting, research and executive education. The Smith School is one of 13 colleges and schools of the University of Maryland. It is named after Robert H Smith, an alumnus and co-chairman and co-CEO of the Charles E Smith Companies, following a US$15m endowment.

Facilities

The school is based in Van Munching Hall on the university's large suburban campus. An extension to the building in 2002 doubled the size of the business school and brought most of the undergraduate and graduate classes under one roof. It contains classrooms, a café, a computer lab and interview rooms for recruiters. Some on-campus accommodation is available.

	Full-time MBA
Student assessment of facilities	4.3 (35)

Faculty

Number of faculty: 125 full-time, 30 part-time, 6 visiting			
	Full-time MBA	Part-time MBA	Executive MBA
Number of faculty per student	0.9 (55)	0.4	6.0
Percentage of faculty with PhD	95 (22)	95	95
Student rating of faculty	4.5 (17)	–	–

Strengths and weaknesses
Strengths: entrepreneurship; finance; information systems management
Weakness: careers services

Programme highlights
Smith's full-time MBA is a fairly traditional two-year programme with the first year largely taken up with 11 required courses and the second year devoted to electives. The first year also includes soft skills such as leadership, teamwork, communication and analysis, and there is a strong emphasis on group in-company projects. Each semester is divided into two terms of seven and a half weeks with integrative exercises concentrated into week-long "experiential learning modules" (ELM). Electives can be grouped into offered concentrations or taken across a wider area. Second-year students also take part in the MBA consulting project, a team-based in-company consultancy exercise.

Smith's Evening MBA and Weekend MBA share the same curriculum as the full-time programme. The Evening MBA is offered at three locations in the Greater Baltimore/Washington DC Area: Washington DC, Shady Grove Campus (Rockville, Maryland) and Baltimore, Maryland. Classes meet on Mondays and Wednesdays or Tuesdays and Thursdays, 6.25–10 pm. Elective classes usually meet once a week, 7–9.40 pm. The Weekend programme is offered at the Ronald Reagan Building and International Trade Center in Washington DC. Core classes meet on alternate Saturdays, 9 am–6 pm. Students can take electives on alternate Saturdays or join Evening MBA elective classes. Both programmes take 28–36 months to complete.

Smith launched an Executive MBA in January 2003. The 18-month programme is limited to 35 participants and includes three modules: foundation, project and mastery. Core courses are followed by four "mastery skills" courses (technology, communications, ethics and corporate citizenship, and leadership and creativity) and the programme concludes with an action-learning project in participants' own companies. Classes are held from Friday (8 am) to Saturday (7 pm) every other weekend. Students stay on campus.

	Full-time MBA	Part-time MBA	Executive MBA
Student rating of programme	4.4 (22)	–	–
Number of overseas exchange programmes	10 (77)	–	–
Number of languages on offer	>5 (63)	–	–

Students

	Full-time MBA	Part-time MBA	Executive MBA
Annual intake	160	370	27
Applicants:places	8:1	2:1	3:1
Percentage of women students	35 (35)	29	15
Percentage of foreign students	34 (85)	n/a	n/a
Average GMAT score	656 (42)	616	n/a
Average number of months' work experience	62 (60)	68	180
Age range of students	25-33	25-35	31-47
Average age	28	29	37
Student rating of culture and classmates	4.4 (26)	–	–

Student profile (full time)

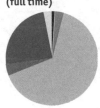

- ■ EU
- ■ Non-EU Europe
- North America
- ■ Other Americas
- ■ Asia/Australasia
- Middle East

Recruiters/careers service

	Full-time MBA	Part-time MBA	Executive MBA
Number of industry sectors that recruited graduates	8 (51)	–	–
Percentage of graduates in jobs 3 months after graduation	55 (66)	–	–
Percentage of graduates finding jobs through careers services	40 (63)	–	–
Student rating of careers service	3.5 (42)	–	–
Post-MBA salary, US$	75,790 (63)	–	–
Percentage increase in salary	50 (64)	–	–
Principal recruiters of graduates	CapitalOne, PricewaterhouseCoopers, Citigroup		

Cost

	Full-time MBA	Part-time MBA	Executive MBA
Application fees	US$50	US$50	US$50
Programme fees	US$17,223	US$803	US$77,500
Comments	Yearly resident tuition and fees	Tuition per credit; fees differ by location (details from website)	Total programme including residency costs. Does not include travel and living costs for optional China visit
Accommodation costs (on campus, per year)	–	–	–
Accommodation costs (off campus, per year)	–	–	–
Financial aid available	US$1,376,000	–	–
Type of aid available	Scholarships, assistantships	–	–
Criteria on which aid is granted	Merit		–

Accreditation

AASCB International

Application details

	Full-time MBA	Part-time MBA	Executive MBA
Application deadline	January 5th	June 15th	February 1st
Programme dates	Aug start, 22 months	Aug start, 36 months	Mar start, 18 months
Admission requirements	First degree; TOEFL if first language not English; 2 references; 3 essays	First degree; TOEFL if first language not English; references; essays	First degree (applicants without a Bachelor's degree can apply for a waiver if they have sufficient non-degree academic experience); at least 8 years' work experience; TOEFL, IELTS or Maryland English Institute test if first language not English; 2 references; 5 essays; interview

Executive education

Smith offers a range of open-enrolment executive education and customised in-company programmes.

Student/alumni quotes

"I would highly recommend this school to anyone wanting to go part-time. The part-time students receive the same quality education as full-time students and have the flexibility of attending classes at one of four campuses in the region."

"The careers centre could still be better but is rapidly improving."

"It's a better school than you might think, especially in terms of the quality of the professors and the students around you. That said, R H Smith is not a "top five" school and you won't get any credit from potential hiring companies for going there. I feel I have a better job and a better toolkit (in terms of knowledge and skill) now than I would have had if I did not get my MBA. Overall, I was pleasantly surprised by the value I got from this school."

Massachusetts Institute of Technology— MIT Sloan School of Management

Address
50 Memorial Drive
Cambridge, MA
US
02142

Tel:
+1 617 253 7750

Fax:
+1 617 258 6796

Email:
mbaadmissions@
sloan.mit.edu

Website:
www.mitsloan.mit.
edu/mba/admissions/
apply.php

Programme director:
David Capodilupo

Figures in brackets
represent rank

Ranking	Rank (out of 100) Full-time
Overall rank	16
Regional rank	13

Criteria	Rank (out of 100) Full-time
Open new career opportunities	**16**
Diversity of recruiters	51
Number in jobs three months after graduation	34
Jobs found through the careers service	10
Student assessment of careers service	20
Personal development and educational experience	**31**
Faculty quality	21
Student quality	21
Student diversity	48
Education experience	67
Increase in salary	**27**
Increase in salary	90
Post-MBA salary	14
Potential to network	**43**
Breadth of alumni network	64
Internationalism of alumni	79
Alumni effectiveness	26

Background

Massachusetts Institute of Technology (MIT) started to offer business training for engineers in 1914, establishing the Department of Business and Engineering Administration, which began a Masters in Management programme in 1925. In 1931, with the support of Alfred P Sloan Jr, chairman of General Motors and an alumnus, MIT created the Sloan Fellows Program, becoming the world's first provider of university-based executive education. In 1952, through his foundation, Sloan established the MIT School of Industrial Management, and in 1964 the school was renamed in his honour. It is a fairly small school, with around 1,000 students, including doctoral students and undergraduates.

Although the institute's technological, manufacturing and engineering background is reflected in the Sloan School's programmes, they are not just for technical engineering undergraduates. There is an emphasis on soft skills, with required courses in communications and leadership, and Sloan has always had a strong organisational and human resources department. It aims to use the innovative techniques and creative thinking that come naturally to scientists and engineers to give managers a competitive edge. Sloan regards itself as a global school with a good international intake and wide-ranging contacts, notably in China.

Facilities

MIT sits on the Cambridge side of the Charles River, just north of the historic city of Boston and within easy walking distance of downtown. The Sloan School is sited on the eastern edge of the campus, flanking the river, in a network of eight buildings. It is in the process of expanding. Some on-campus accommodation is available.

	Full-time MBA
Student assessment of facilities	4.2 (52)

Faculty

Number of faculty: 96 full-time, 1 part-time, 7 visiting	
	Full-time MBA
Number of faculty per student	0.2 (>100)
Percentage of faculty with PhD	100 (1)
Student rating of faculty	4.5 (14)

Strengths and weaknesses

Strengths: finance; entrepreneurship; operations

Programme highlights

Sloan's full-time two-year MBA packs a seven-course core into the first semester, based on two six-week sessions of classes with a one-week "Sloan Innovation Period" (basically soft skills and leadership training) in between. The "First Year Challenge", a team-based project, starts in the fall semester of the first year and is completed early in the spring semester. The rest of the programme is given over to electives, which students can structure as they wish.

Sloan continues to offer the alternative of an MBA to its long-standing Master of Science in Management. The normal programme leads to an MBA; add a thesis and the degree becomes an MSM or, if preferred, remains an MBA.

The Sloan Fellows Program is a one-year full-time programme for experienced executives leading to a Master of Science or MBA. The school has also integrated the Fellows Program with its Management of Technology Program to create the Sloan Fellows in Innovation and Global Leadership, a flexible (one year full-time or two years part-time) global programme.

The Leaders for Manufacturing (LFM) Program is a 24-month joint degree programme that offers an MBA or a Master of Science (SM) from Sloan and an SM degree in engineering from MIT's School of Engineering. It includes a six-and-a-half month internship at an LFM partner company.

	Full-time MBA
Student rating of programme	4.5 (8)
Number of overseas exchange programmes	2 (92)
Number of languages on offer	0 (94)

Students

	Full-time MBA
Annual intake	408
Applicants:places	8:1
Percentage of women students	26 (76)
Percentage of foreign students	41 (72)
Average GMAT score	710 (3)
Average number of months' work experience	54 (92)
Age range of students	25-32
Average age	28
Student rating of culture and classmates	4.7 (8)

Recruiters/careers service

	Full-time MBA
Number of industry sectors that recruited graduates	8 (51)
Percentage of graduates in jobs 3 months after graduation	88 (34)
Percentage of graduates finding jobs through careers services	77 (10)
Student rating of careers service	3.9 (20)
Post-MBA salary, US$	88,217 (14)
Percentage increase in salary	30 (90)
Principal recruiters of graduates	McKinsey & Co, Bain & Co, Boston Consulting Group

Student profile (full time)

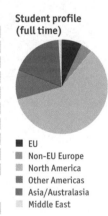

- ■ EU
- ■ Non-EU Europe
- ▨ North America
- ■ Other Americas
- ■ Asia/Australasia
- ▨ Middle East

Cost

	Full-time MBA
Application fees	US$210
Programme fees	US$37,050
Comments	–
Accommodation costs (on campus, per year)	–
Accommodation costs (off campus, per year)	–
Financial aid available	Not disclosed
Type of aid available	Tuition assistance, stipend, loans, outside scholarships
Criteria on which aid is granted	Merit, financial need

Accreditation

AACSB International

Application details

	Full-time MBA
Application deadline	–
Programme dates	Jan start, 24 months
Admission requirements	First degree; 2 references; 5 essays; interview by invitation; laptop

Executive education

Sloan offers a series of open-enrolment programmes under the main headings of strategic thinking, leading across the value chain, building enabling capability and entrepreneurship/intrapreneurship. It also offers a portfolio of customised in-company programmes.

McGill University—Faculty of Management

Ranking	Rank (out of 100) Full-time
Overall rank	n/a
Regional rank	53

Background

The Faculty of Management, which is integrated with the university, has good links with business. The campus is in the middle of the Montreal business sector and many senior executives visit the faculty. Like most Canadian schools, McGill offers extremely good value for money for in-state and other Canadian residents, although for others tuition fees are generally in line with those at most North American schools.

Facilities

The Samuel Bronfman building, which houses the Faculty of Management, borders McGill's sprawling campus. It is shared with undergraduate students so space is limited, but MBA students have their own lounge and computer lab. The faculty has its own computer centre and management library, but some subjects, such as economics and social science, may be found in one of the other 17 libraries on campus. Students have access to the excellent university sporting and cultural amenities. There is no on-campus accommodation for graduates. MBA students rent local housing, which is plentiful and reasonably priced. Montreal is a pleasant city with a European atmosphere and local transport is good.

	Full-time MBA
Student assessment of facilities	3.6 (n/a)

Faculty

Number of faculty: 49 full-time, 25 part-time, 1 visiting

	Full-time MBA	McGill Part-time MBA
Number of faculty per student	0.5 (n/a)	1.2
Percentage of faculty with PhD	93 (n/a)	93
Student rating of faculty	3.8 (n/a)	–

Strengths and weaknesses

Strengths: finance; international business; strategy

Weakness: facilities

Programme highlights

McGill's two-year full-time MBA mixes a highly integrative core in the first year with intensive specialisation in the second. Core courses are taught in three nine-week modules, linked by an integrative core course, a team project that runs throughout the year. In the second year, students can focus on one of eight tailored concentrations (entrepreneurship, finance, information systems, international business, management for developing economies, marketing, operations management, strategic management) or create their own wider general management option. A concentration consists of five courses within a chosen subject area. Students also select five free electives from within other faculty concentrations, support/elective courses (from other management fields) or other graduate programmes at McGill. Course lectures and assignments are supplemented by seminars and guest speakers.

Students with an undergraduate business degree (from a recognised North American university) can take an accelerated 15-month track, and other full-time students can work throughout the summer semester and complete their programme the following December.

The part-time MBA is identical to the full-time version. Students can complete the core year requirements in about two years. After that they can either join the full-time programme to complete their

Address
1001 Sherbrooke
Street West
Montreal, QC
Canada
H3A 1G5

Tel:
+1 514 398 4030

Fax:
+1 514 398 5116

Email:
mba.mgmt@mcgill.ca

Website:
www.management.
mcgill.ca

Programme director:
Alfred Jaeger

Figures in brackets
represent rank

Which MBA? © The Economist Intelligence Unit Limited 2004

degree at an accelerated pace or continue part-time, with up to five years to complete the programme. Students with an undergraduate business degree (from a recognised North American university) can take an accelerated 36-month track. All core courses and most electives are available in the evening, and part-time students can choose to take classes during the day or in the evening. Evening classes meet once a week (6–9 pm) and the programme starts in September or January.

McGill's Executive MBA is the somewhat oddly named MBA3 (MBA Cubed). It is based on learning weeks, executive MBA-style weekends and part-time MBA evening courses. The first year of the two-year programme is the core, taught over five modules. The first module is a three-week "jump start" session (full-time Monday to Friday) held in July/August. Classes are then held one evening a week (6–9 pm) between September and May. The year concludes with a module held over six weekends in May/June (full-time Fridays and Saturdays). In the second year students can choose from the same concentrations as the full-time and part-time programmes. There are four modules beginning with a full-time three-week session in July/August. During the next two semesters, participants select five electives from regular MBA courses. The programme ends with a six-week summer module, with classes held two days a week.

	Full-time MBA	McGill Part-time MBA
Student rating of programme	3.8 (n/a)	–
Number of overseas exchange programmes	40 (n/a)	–
Number of languages on offer	0 (n/a)	–

Student profile (full time)

- EU
- Non-EU Europe
- North America
- Other Americas
- Asia/Australasia
- Middle East

Students

	Full-time MBA	McGill Part-time MBA
Annual intake	136	64
Applicants:places	6:1	3:1
Percentage of women students	31 (n/a)	23
Percentage of foreign students	63 (n/a)	n/a
Average GMAT score	640 (n/a)	635
Average number of months' work experience	53 (n/a)	72
Age range of students	25-34	25-36
Average age	28	30
Student rating of culture and classmates	3.7 (n/a)	–

Recruiters/careers service

	Full-time MBA	McGill Part-time MBA
Number of industry sectors that recruited graduates	7 (n/a)	–
Percentage of graduates in jobs 3 months after graduation	66 (n/a)	–
Percentage of graduates finding jobs through careers services	53 (n/a)	–
Student rating of careers service	3.3 (n/a)	–
Post-MBA salary, US$	52,857 (n/a)	–
Percentage increase in salary	40 (n/a)	–
Principal recruiters of graduates	CIBC, Bombardier, Deloitte & Touche	

Cost

	Full-time MBA	McGill Part-time MBA
Application fees	C$100 (US$71)	C$100 (US$71)
Programme fees	C$20,000 (US$14,286)	C$139 (US$99)
Comments	Per year. Fee for Canadian residents is C$4,173; fee for Quebec residents is C$1,668	Per credit, Canadian residents; fee for Quebec residents is C$56
Accommodation costs (on campus, per year)	–	
Accommodation costs (off campus, per year)	C$650 (US$464)	–
Financial aid available	C$197,168 (US$140,834)	–
Type of aid available	Scholarships, awards	–
Criteria on which aid is granted	Academic credentials	–

Accreditation

None

Application details

	Full-time MBA	McGill Part-time MBA
Application deadline	February 15th	Rolling admissions
Programme dates	Sep start, 16 months	Sep start, 52 months
Admission requirements	First degree (minimum GPA of 3.0/4.0); at least 2 years' work experience; GMAT; TOEFL if first language not English (minimum 250 computer-based, 600 paper-based); 2 references; 2 essays; computer strongly recommended	First degree (minimum GPA of 3.0/4.0); at least 2 years' work experience; GMAT; TOEFL if first language not English (minimum 250 computer-based, 600 paper-based); 2 references; 2 essays; computer highly recommended

Executive education

McGill's flagship open-enrolment executive course is the Executive Training Program, which is unusual in that it is delivered on a part-time evening basis. The programme is a typical "mini-MBA", covering much the same areas as the full MBA. It is divided into two levels: the Executive Development Course, which covers core-like functional subjects; and the Advanced Management Course, which is more integrative. Each level consists of ten evening sessions (on a Monday) and two weekend sessions. McGill also offers short seminars in areas such as general management, leadership, marketing and organisational effectiveness as well as customised in-company programmes.

Which MBA? © The Economist Intelligence Unit Limited 2004

University of Melbourne—Melbourne Business School

Address
200 Leicester Street
Carlton VIC
Australia
3053

Tel:
+61 3 9349 8143

Fax:
+61 3 9349 8271

Email:
enquiries@mbs.edu

Website:
www.mbs.edu

Programme director:
Ian Harper

Figures in brackets
represent rank

Ranking	Rank (out of 100) Full-time
Overall rank	92
Regional rank	6

Criteria	Rank (out of 100) Full-time
Open new career opportunities	**93**
Diversity of recruiters	47
Number in jobs three months after graduation	99
Jobs found through the careers service	77
Student assessment of careers service	80
Personal development and educational experience	**63**
Faculty quality	78
Student quality	66
Student diversity	57
Education experience	48
Increase in salary	**90**
Increase in salary	>100
Post-MBA salary	81
Potential to network	**80**
Breadth of alumni network	73
Internationalism of alumni	50
Alumni effectiveness	69

Background

Melbourne Business School celebrated its 40th birthday in 2004. It marked the occasion by quietly merging with Mt Eliza Business School, another Australian school, and creating the biggest school in Australia. The school is a private limited company (owned 45% by the University of Melbourne and 55% by Australian businesses) and has excellent links with business (many executives sit on its board of directors), which has largely financed its growth in recent years. The school controls all academic issues.

Facilities

The school's building in Melbourne is spacious and impressive with excellent facilities. It is a ten-minute walk from the downtown business area and borders the southern edge of the university's extensive campus. The surrounding district of Carlton has plenty of cafés and shops and a strong Italian influence. Accommodation in Carlton is plentiful and reasonably cheap.

	Full-time MBA
Student assessment of facilities	4.1 (80)

Faculty

Number of faculty: 29 full-time, 0 part-time, 27 visiting			
	Full-time MBA	**Part-time MBA**	**Executive MBA**
Number of faculty per student	0.3 (97)	0.6	1.6
Percentage of faculty with PhD	97 (20)	97	97
Student rating of faculty	4.1 (76)	–	

Strengths and weaknesses

Strengths: economics; marketing; finance

Weakness: elective choice

Programme highlights

Melbourne's full-time 16-month MBA operates a continuous 13-week, three-term year, with all students starting the programme in January and finishing the following year in May. About one-third of students can go on exchange visits, which take place in the September term. Electives can be taken across a broad range or grouped into specialisations (entrepreneurship and innovation, finance and economics, general management, human resource management, international business, marketing, public-sector management, strategic management, technology and operations management). Leadership qualities and the ability to act through other people are covered during the first two terms.

The programme has a high Australian content as well as good international, especially regional, coverage. Case studies are used extensively and the school has written many cases on the international operations of Australian companies. There is a good deal of group work, and the list of industry guest speakers is impressive.

The part-time MBA is similar to the full-time version with 11 core subjects and nine electives. Students generally complete the programme in three years, studying two courses per term. Part-time students can apply to convert to full-time study in the third term if they have completed the core courses. They then have two consecutive terms to complete the MBA. Students who transfer to the full-time programme are eligible to go on an international exchange (this option is not available to students who study only part-time).

Melbourne's Executive MBA is run in collaboration with WHU Otto Beisheim Graduate School of Management, Koblenz, Germany. The 14-month programme consists of four one-month fully residential taught modules, the second of which is held in Koblenz.

	Full-time MBA	Part-time MBA	Executive MBA
Student rating of programme	4.0 (79)	–	–
Number of overseas exchange programmes	75 (27)	–	–
Number of languages on offer	6 (1)	–	–

Students

	Full-time MBA	Part-time MBA	Executive MBA
Annual intake	126	100	35
Applicants:places	4:1	1:1	1:1
Percentage of women students	25 (87)	31	18
Percentage of foreign students	80 (25)	n/a	n/a
Average GMAT score	627 (70)	616	n/a
Average number of months' work experience	70 (34)	84	180
Age range of students	25-34	25-36	31-50
Average age	29	30	40
Student rating of culture and classmates	4.1 (71)	–	–

Student profile (full time)

- EU
- Non-EU Europe
- North America
- Other Americas
- Asia/Australasia
- Middle East

Recruiters/careers service

	Full-time MBA	Part-time MBA	Executive MBA
Number of industry sectors that recruited graduates	7 (47)	–	–
Percentage of graduates in jobs 3 months after graduation	66 (99)	–	–
Percentage of graduates finding jobs through careers services	29 (77)	–	–
Student rating of careers service	3.2 (80)	–	–
Post-MBA salary, US$	66,883 (81)	–	–
Percentage increase in salary	7 (>100)	–	–
Principal recruiters of graduates	AT Kearney, Boston Consulting Group, Booz Allen Hamilton		

Cost

	Full-time MBA	Part-time MBA	Executive MBA
Application fees	None	None	None
Programme fees	A$48,000 (US$31,169)	A$48,000 (US$31,169)	A$88,000 (US$57,143)
Comments	Total programme	Total programme	Total programme (includes materials, all meals and accommodation during residential programme)
Accommodation costs (on campus, per year)	–	–	–
Accommodation costs (off campus, per year)	A$9,620 (US$6,247)	–	–
Financial aid available	A$370,000 (US$240,260)	–	–
Type of aid available	Scholarships	–	–
Criteria on which aid is granted	Excellent applicant		–

Accreditation

None

Application details

	Full-time MBA	Part-time MBA	Executive MBA
Application deadline	September 30th	November 30th	June 16th
Programme dates	Jan start, 16 months	Jan start, 36 months	Oct start, 14 months
Admission requirements	First degree; at least 2 years' work experience; GMAT; TOEFL if first language not English (minimum 610 paper-based, 253 computer-based); 2 references; 4 essays; interview recommended	First degree; at least 2 years' work experience; GMAT; TOEFL if first language not English (minimum 610 paper-based, 253 computer-based); 2 references; 4 essays; interview recommended	First degree; at least 10 years' work experience; GMAT; TOEFL or IELTS if first language not English; 4 essays; interview

Executive education

Melbourne's merger with Mt Eliza means that most executive education programmes are now run at the Mt Eliza Centre for Executive Education in Victoria (Mt Eliza has dropped its MBA programmes), although some are run in downtown Melbourne. Open-enrolment courses cover areas such as general management, leadership, strategy and functional programmes and customised in-company programmes.

Student/alumni quotes

"I commenced studies at the Melbourne Business School in January 2002; at this time it was considered the number two business school in Australia and had moderate international acclaim. I believe the school is now clearly first in Australia and has significantly improved its international standing."

"Limited electives available to part-time students."

"Excellent quality of academic programme. Strong brand. Good calibre of candidates."

University of Michigan Business School

Ranking	Rank (out of 100) Full-time
Overall rank	11
Regional rank	9

Criteria	Rank (out of 100) Full-time
Open new career opportunities	**13**
Diversity of recruiters	1
Number in jobs three months after graduation	71
Jobs found through the careers service	26
Student assessment of careers service	3
Personal development and educational experience	**22**
Faculty quality	18
Student quality	30
Student diversity	63
Education experience	34
Increase in salary	**32**
Increase in salary	83
Post-MBA salary	21
Potential to network	**25**
Breadth of alumni network	33
Internationalism of alumni	60
Alumni effectiveness	8

Address
701 Tappan Street
D0253
Ann Arbor, MI
US
48109

Tel:
+1 734 936 2150

Fax:
+1 734 647 2401

Email:
umbsmba@umich.edu

Website:
www.bus.umich.edu

Programme director:
Eugene Anderson

Figures in brackets
represent rank

Background

The University of Michigan Business School was founded in 1924 and is a world leader in business education at all levels: undergraduate, graduate and executive (a particularly strong area). Through its executive education arm, the school has unusually good links with industry, especially the automobile industry. This is not surprising given its location near Detroit. It does not, however, specialise in the motor industry.

Facilities

The business school campus comprises seven interconnected buildings surrounding the Alessi Courtyard and the Executive Residence Patio. The entire complex occupies a city block on the southern tip of the university campus. The school is well equipped with large classrooms, study rooms, computer labs and a 211,000-volume library (one of the biggest business libraries in the country). Some on-campus accommodation is available, but most students prefer to live in the university town of Ann Arbor, even though housing there can be expensive.

	Full-time MBA
Student assessment of facilities	4.4 (19)

Faculty

Number of faculty: 128 full-time, 69 part-time, 0 visiting

	Full-time MBA	Evening MBA Program	Executive MBA Program
Number of faculty per student	0.4 (86)	0.9	3.3
Percentage of faculty with PhD	100 (9)	100	100
Student rating of faculty	4.6 (10)	–	–

Strengths and weaknesses

Strengths: general management; finance; marketing

Weakness: some facilities are out-dated

Programme highlights

Michigan's two-year full-time MBA consists of ten core courses and one elective in the first year and elective courses in the second. Students also participate in a seven-week Multidisciplinary Action Program (MAP), a real-life case study within a company that rounds off the first year and aims to integrate previous learning. Teams of 6–7 students work together in a company (in the US or overseas) on a real project. Multidisciplinary faculty teams act as consultants and mentors to the student teams. Executive skills workshops, based on action-learning techniques and similar in approach to executive education, run throughout the year (often taught by outside non-academics). Their aim is to develop effective executive skills such as multicultural awareness and conflict resolution. They are based on students' performance during the five-day Leadership Development Program, a wide-ranging series of events that is Michigan's version of an orientation week.

All students take a managerial writing assessment on entry, which may result in them having to take a managerial writing course. Passing either the assessment or course is a requirement of graduation. Core courses can be waived and replaced by electives. Incoming students take voluntary quantitative skills workshops to refresh basic quantitative skills. A focus of the workshops, offered during the week before the Leadership Development Program, is to apply these skills to business situations. Students are mailed an assessment test to help them decide whether their skill level is up to that required for the MBA programme. They can then choose to attend one of two workshops offered.

Electives can be drawn from a variety of areas or grouped into concentrations, although there is no requirement to do so. Some may be taken in other graduate schools of the university and at least one elective must be in the area of ethics or business law.

The structure of the part-time Evening MBA programme varies slightly from the full-time version, although the degree awarded is exactly the same. The main difference is that the MAP project is not available. However, part-time students take the executive skills courses and must complete the managerial writing assessment and take remedial courses if appropriate. They also have full use of all amenities, including careers services.

Classes are held in two locations: at the main campus in Ann Arbor; and at the Commerce Park satellite in Dearborn (which has five classrooms, a study area and a small computer lab linked to the main campus that is used exclusively by Evening MBA students). Classes are held all year round (fall/winter full terms and spring/summer half terms), and core classes are offered each fall and winter at both locations, allowing students to take all their required classes at the most convenient location. Most classes are offered once a week, Monday–Thursday, 6–9 pm or 7–10 pm. Several courses each term are taught either in a series of intensive weekend classes or in classes that meet one weekday and one weekend day. Students can opt for an overseas exchange once they have completed core courses.

Michigan's 20-month Executive MBA programme starts with a ten-day residency in Ann Arbor at the beginning of each year. Students then take courses on campus for two-day weekends (8 am Friday–5.30 pm Saturday) approximately every four weeks. Between residencies there is Internet-based learning and team collaboration. A typical workload requires participants to study for 10–12 hours per week. The first year ends with team consulting projects.

Michigan also offers a corporate Global MBA, similar to its regular MBA but not for open enrolment.

	Full-time MBA	Evening MBA Program	Executive MBA Program
Student rating of programme	4.6 (5)	–	–
Number of overseas exchange programmes	8 (83)	–	–
Number of languages on offer	2 (71)	–	–

University of Michigan Business School

Students

	Full-time MBA	Evening MBA Program	Executive MBA Program
Annual intake	419	231	59
Applicants:places	8:1	2:1	–
Percentage of women students	26 (80)	23	29
Percentage of foreign students	27 (97)	n/a	n/a
Average GMAT score	692 (14)	653	n/a
Average number of months' work experience	60 (63)	72	168
Age range of students	25-32	25-35	32-49
Average age	28	30	38
Student rating of culture and classmates	4.7 (7)	–	–

Student profile (full time)

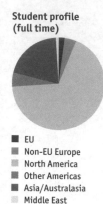

- ■ EU
- ■ Non-EU Europe
- ▨ North America
- ■ Other Americas
- ■ Asia/Australasia
- ▨ Middle East

Recruiters/careers service

	Full-time MBA	Evening MBA Program	Executive MBA Program
Number of industry sectors that recruited graduates	8 (1)	–	–
Percentage of graduates in jobs 3 months after graduation	75 (71)	–	–
Percentage of graduates finding jobs through careers services	62 (26)	–	–
Student rating of careers service	4.4 (3)	–	–
Post-MBA salary, US$	85,000 (21)	–	–
Percentage increase in salary	37 (83)	–	–
Principal recruiters of graduates	McKinsey & Company, Johnson & Johnson, Ford Motor Company, Medtronic		

Cost

	Full-time MBA	Evening MBA Program	Executive MBA Program
Application fees	US$180	US$180	US$125
Programme fees	US$36,688	US$965	US$100,000
Comments	Per year	Per credit. First credit is US$1,150	Total programme. Fee for out-of-state students is US$105,000
Accommodation costs (on campus, per year)	US$7,200	–	–
Accommodation costs (off campus, per year)	US$7,200	–	–
Financial aid available	US$47,933	–	–
Type of aid available	Scholarships, loans	–	–
Criteria on which aid is granted	Merit, financial need	–	–

Accreditation

AACSB International

Application details

	Full-time MBA	Evening MBA Program	Executive MBA Program
Application deadline	March 1st	October 1st	May 1st
Programme dates	Sep start, 20 months	Jan start, 42 months	Aug start, 20 months
Admission requirements	First degree (must be equivalent to US Bachelor's degree); at least 2 years' work experience; TOEFL if first language not English; 2 references; 3 essays; interview; laptop; college level calculus course; interview is required for admission but not application	First degree; at least 2 years' work experience; TOEFL if first language not English, 2 references; 3 essays; interview	First degree; at least 10 years' work experience; TOEFL if first language not English (waived if work conducted in English); 3 references; 4 essays; interview

Executive education

Michigan's executive education arm is claimed to be one of the largest affiliated with a university anywhere in the world. It runs open-enrolment executive education programmes ranging from the four-week flagship Executive Program to short programmes both on campus and around the world. It also offers customised in-company programmes.

Student/alumni quotes

"Michigan is a great place for hands-on experience. I went to India to study corporate citizenship for GE and P&G and will be presenting our findings to the CEOs of both companies; not many programmes pro vide such an opportunity. You can get classroom learning everywhere—all the top-ten schools teach the same material."

"The physical campus needs to be improved."

"Scholarship opportunities are more abundant at Michigan than I would have guessed. Even though I submitted an application in the third round, I still received a scholarship from the University of Michigan. Also, there is much more opportunity to explore non-profit issues through course work and interna tional consulting projects included in the curriculum than at any other top-ten school."

University of Minnesota—Carlson School of Management

Ranking	Rank (out of 100) Full-time
Overall rank	46
Regional rank	29

Criteria	Rank (out of 100) Full-time
Open new career opportunities	**29**
Diversity of recruiters	n/a
Number in jobs three months after graduation	13
Jobs found through the careers service	39
Student assessment of careers service	30
Personal development and educational experience	**84**
Faculty quality	43
Student quality	82
Student diversity	107
Education experience	>100
Increase in salary	**46**
Increase in salary	28
Post-MBA salary	61
Potential to network	**81**
Breadth of alumni network	49
Internationalism of alumni	95
Alumni effectiveness	73

Address
Carlson Full-Time MBA
Program
2-210 Carlson School
of Management
321 19th Avenue South
Minneapolis, MN
US
55455

Tel:
+1 612 625 9562

Fax:
+1 612 626 7785

Email:
full-timembainfo@
csom.umn.edu

Website:
www.carlsonmba.umn.
edu

Programme director:
Carleen Kerttula

Figures in brackets
represent rank

Background

Founded in 1919, Carlson School of Management is a big, traditional US school with more than 3,500 students and 40,000 alumni. It has strong links with the vibrant local business community, which is a keen recruiter. The alumni base in the local area is said to be some 20,000. Each year, more than 80% of Carlson undergraduates and 95% of full-time MBA students take part in internships, mentorships and other activities with local businesses. Even so, the school has ambitions to strengthen its global coverage and is building international links.

Facilities

The school is housed in a 243,000 sq ft building that includes 33 classrooms, 35 meeting rooms, a graduate and undergraduate career centre, five computer labs, Internet access from MBA classrooms, two large lecture halls, an atrium that acts as a "town square" and a dining room with courtyard on the lower level. The Wilson Library is adjacent to the business school, giving access to 500,000 publications as well as online databases and publications. On-campus accommodation is available.

	Full-time MBA
Student assessment of facilities	4.1 (58)

Faculty

Number of faculty: 133 full-time, 30 part-time, 0 visiting

	Full-time MBA	Part-Time MBA Program	Carlson Executive MBA Program
Number of faculty per student	0.7 (49)	0.3	3.6
Percentage of faculty with PhD	95 (37)	95	95
Student rating of faculty	4.3 (49)	–	–

Strengths and weaknesses

Strengths: finance; marketing; information technology

Weakness: elective choice

Programme highlights

Carlson's two-year full-time MBA is flexible. Students take the integrated core and attend personal development and career management workshops in the first semester and start on electives, either grouped into pre-selected concentrations or self-designed, in the second semester. The second year consists of electives and a capstone strategy course. Carlson is closely involved with the local business community and students meet executives throughout the programme via an executive mentoring programme, the Top Management Perspective guest speaker course and in-company projects.

The part-time MBA programme has a similar core to the full time version, but concentrations will end in 2005. Instead students are offered electives grouped into "professional portfolios" linked to career objectives. Portfolios include consulting, finance, marketing, information systems and technology, supply chain and operations. Students can choose electives from any portfolio and are not restricted to one area.

Carlson's Executive MBA programme lasts 18 months and is a traditional in structure. Classes meet on campus on Friday and Saturday every two weeks during term time. There are residential sessions at the beginning of each year and an overseas study trip at the end of the programme.

	Full-time MBA	Part-Time MBA Program	Carlson Executive MBA Program
Student rating of programme	3.9 (86)	–	–
Number of overseas exchange programmes	40 (57)	–	–
Number of languages on offer	0 (67)	–	–

Student profile (full time)

- ■ EU
- ■ Non-EU Europe
- ▨ North America
- ■ Other Americas
- ■ Asia/Australasia
- ▨ Middle East

Students

	Full-time MBA	Part-Time MBA Program	Carlson Executive MBA Program
Annual intake	213	471	45
Applicants:places	6:1	1:1	2:1
Percentage of women students	24 (71)	33	23
Percentage of foreign students	15 (109)	n/a	n/a
Average GMAT score	656 (47)	600	600
Average number of months' work experience	49 (91)	72	168
Age range of students	25-32	24-36	31-42
Average age	28	28	38
Student rating of culture and classmates	3.9 (78)	–	–

Recruiters/careers service

	Full-time MBA	Part-Time MBA Program	Carlson Executive MBA Program
Number of industry sectors that recruited graduates	n/a (n/a)	–	–
Percentage of graduates in jobs 3 months after graduation	93 (13)	–	–
Percentage of graduates finding jobs through careers services	58 (39)	–	–
Student rating of careers service	3.6 (30)	–	–
Post-MBA salary, US$	76,306 (61)	–	–
Percentage increase in salary	60 (28)	–	–
Principal recruiters of graduates	Honeywell, 3M, Medtronic		

Cost

	Full-time MBA	Part-Time MBA Program	Carlson Executive MBA Program
Application fees	US$90	US$60	US$60
Programme fees	US$28,685	US$750	US$72,500
Comments	Per year, non resident	Per credit	Total programme
Accommodation costs (on campus, per year)	US$7,200	–	–
Accommodation costs (off campus, per year)	US$13,400	–	–
Financial aid available	US$1,600,000	–	–
Type of aid available	Scholarships, fellowships	–	–
Criteria on which aid is granted	Merit	–	–

Accreditation

AACSB International

Application details

	Full-time MBA	Part-Time MBA Program	Carlson Executive MBA Program
Application deadline	March 1st for international candidates	May 1st	April 1st
Programme dates	Aug start, 22 months	Sep start, up to 7 years	Aug start, 18 months
Admission requirements	First degree (comparable to a US bachelor's degree); work experience; TOEFL if first language not English; 2 references; 3 essays; laptop	First degree; at least 2 years' work experience; TOEFL if first language not English (waived if last two years of baccalaureate degree or one year of graduate school taken in the US, Australia or Canada); 2 references; 5 essays	First degree; at least 8 years' work experience; TOEFL if first language not English; 3 references; 5 essays; interview

Executive education

The Carlson Executive Development Center offers various open-enrolment programmes including the flagship four-week Minnesota Executive Program, the three-week Minnesota Management Institute (a mini-MBA), the one-week Minnesota Management Academy and various short programmes in areas such as strategy, leadership, finance, sales and marketing. The school also offers a range of customised programmes.

Student/alumni quotes

"Carlson [MBA] is an amazing feeder programme to companies located in Minnesota. However, many options exist outside of the Minneapolis/St Paul area if so desired."

"Recruiting outside the Midwest is very minimal."

"The school overall is very good and the faculty are very nurturing with students and most have outstanding credentials. The diversity of the student body does need improvement and the lack of students from the east and west coasts limits networking opportunities."

International University of Monaco

Address
2 Avenue Prince
Héréditaire Albert
MC
Monaco
98000

Tel:
+377 9798 6986

Fax:
+377 9205 2830

Email:
jmrouhier@monaco.edu

Website:
www.monaco.edu

Programme director:
William S Lightfoot

Figures in brackets
represent rank

Ranking	Rank (out of 100) Full-time
Overall rank	99
Regional rank	39

Criteria	Rank (out of 100) Full-time
Open new career opportunities	**100**
Diversity of recruiters	>100
Number in jobs three months after graduation	38
Jobs found through the careers service	65
Student assessment of careers service	96
Personal development and educational experience	**64**
Faculty quality	93
Student quality	>100
Student diversity	1
Education experience	61
Increase in salary	**79**
Increase in salary	93
Post-MBA salary	64
Potential to network	**>100**
Breadth of alumni network	>100
Internationalism of alumni	80
Alumni effectiveness	91

Background

Formerly known as the University of Southern Europe—Monaco Business School, the International University of Monaco has undergone many changes in recent years. In its former incarnation it seemed to be losing its way, but a new management and faculty team under Maxime Crener, president and dean, is restoring its potential. The team has revamped the infrastructure and added new young faculty and new programmes. It retains, however, a strong commitment to practical business: many classes are taught by practising executives and many of the small in-house faculty have extensive business experience. Although Monaco is a full-range (undergraduate and postgraduate) business university, there are no plans to increase the number of students beyond 500.

The university's location in the tiny principality of Monaco is seen as a niche strength, and there are plans to exploit this through specialisations in areas such as luxury goods and hedge funds. Despite its exotic image, the surrounding area of the Côte d'Azur has become a leading centre of international business.

Facilities

The university occupies three floors of the office complex of the Louis II sports stadium in central Monaco, which is not as odd as it sounds. Facilities are very good and include a real-time stock trading room. A new complex for MBA students across the road includes an auditorium, breakout rooms and a lounge area. There are plans to move to a new building in the near future. There is no on-campus accommodation but help is available for students seeking housing. Monaco and the surrounding area are not as expensive as many people think.

	Full-time MBA
Student assessment of facilities	4.3 (42)

Faculty

Number of faculty: 24 full-time, 14 part-time, 14 visiting		
	Full-time MBA	Executive MBA
Number of faculty per student	1.0 (26)	2.1
Percentage of faculty with PhD	50 (>100)	50
Student rating of faculty	4.2 (40)	–

Strengths and weaknesses

Strengths: finance; luxury goods management; entrepreneurship

Weakness: low profile

Programme highlights

Monaco's revamped MBA is firmly in the European tradition, being a short (ten months) intensive programme with a limited range of specialisations. It starts with a short orientation (which has included a tough hike in the hills around Monaco) and pre-programme training in financial accounting, economics and mathematics. This is followed by foundation and core courses; integrative courses in areas such as government, entrepreneurship and negotiations; "environmental factors" modules covering a broad range of issues; and applied research modules in students' fields of interest or a specialisation, providing them with in-depth knowledge and practical hands-on experience. The specialisations offered (which involve a minimum of four elective courses) include corporate finance, hedge funds, luxury goods, international marketing, international organisation and information technology. Students can also create their own track by choosing electives from all those offered. A series of workshops and forums runs throughout the programme.

Monaco's Executive MBA began in September 2003. The 18-month programme consists of six two-week residential sessions in Monaco. Between these sessions students stay in touch with the school and each other via the Internet. The programme starts in June, September, December and March each year and ends with a project in students' own organisations.

	Full-time MBA	Executive MBA
Student rating of programme	4.1 (62)	–
Number of overseas exchange programmes	0 (67)	–
Number of languages on offer	3 (61)	–

Students

	Full-time MBA	Executive MBA
Annual intake	36	25
Applicants:places	4:1	40:1
Percentage of women students	55 (1)	40
Percentage of foreign students	100 (1)	n/a
Average GMAT score	570 (>100)	570
Average number of months' work experience	60 (47)	168
Age range of students	24-35	30-45
Average age	28	37
Student rating of culture and classmates	4.0 (75)	–

Student profile (full time)

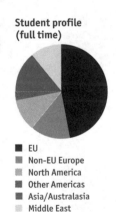

- ■ EU
- ■ Non-EU Europe
- ■ North America
- ■ Other Americas
- ■ Asia/Australasia
- ■ Middle East

Recruiters/careers service

	Full-time MBA	Monaco MBA 22 Month Option	Executive MBA
Number of industry sectors that recruited graduates	6 (>100)	–	–
Percentage of graduates in jobs 3 months after graduation	73 (38)	–	–
Percentage of graduates finding jobs through careers services	33 (65)	–	–
Student rating of careers service	2.9 (96)	–	–
Post-MBA salary, US$	79,545 (64)	–	–
Percentage increase in salary	27 (93)		–
Principal recruiters of graduates	EFG, SAP, Alpstar Group		

Cost

	Full-time MBA	Monaco MBA – 22 Month Option	Executive MBA
Application fees	€50 (US$57)	€50 (US$57)	€50 (US$57)
Programme fees	€21,300 (US$24,205)	_1,150 (US$1,307)	€24,485 (US$27,824)
Comments	–	Per course. A minimum of 20 courses required	–
Accommodation costs (on campus, per year)	–	–	–
Accommodation costs (off campus, per year)	€8,000 (US$9,091)	–	–
Financial aid available	€100,000 (US$113,636)	–	–
Type of aid available	Merit scholarships	–	–
Criteria on which aid is granted	Background, test scores	–	–

Accreditation

None

Application details

	Full-time MBA	Monaco MBA – 22 Month Option	Executive MBA
Application deadline	June 30th	Rolling admissions	Rolling admissions
Programme dates	Sep start, 10 months	Jan start, 22 months	Jan start, 18 months
Admission requirements	Undergraduate degree; at least 2 years' work experience; TOEFL, Cambridge, TOEIC or 3 years of study in English degree programme required if first language not English; 2 references; 10 essays; interview; laptop	Undergraduate degree; at least 2 years' work experience; TOEFL, Cambridge, TOEIC or 3 years of study in English degree programme required if first language not English; 2 references; essays; interview	First degree; at least 7 years' work experience; TOEFL, Cambridge or TOEIC if first language not English; 2 references; 10 essays; interview (by telephone or in person)

Executive education

Monaco does not currently offer open-enrolment or customised in-company executive education programmes.

Student/alumni quotes

"This is a young school which is striving for excellence and taking advantage of its key strength: its people."

"The smallness of the school is a two-edged sword that can be or a pro or a con depending on the particular needs and wants of a student. For me it was the key to all the networking I did during the year."

Monash University—Faculty of Business and Economics

Ranking	Rank (out of 100) Full-time
Overall rank	n/a
Regional rank	n/a

Address
MBA Programs
Monash University
27 Sir John Monash Drive
Caulfield East, VIC
Australia
3145

Tel:
+61 3 9903 1897

Fax:
+61 3 9903 1800

Email:
MBA@buseco.monash.edu.au

Website:
www.mba.monash.edu.au

Programme director:
Robert Willis

Figures in brackets represent rank

Background

Monash University is one of Australia's leading academic institutions with six campuses in Australia, one in Malaysia and one in South Africa, as well as outposts in London and Italy. It has over 40,000 students in ten faculties. Being part of a large business and economics faculty means that the MBA can draw on research strengths in the core areas of business, such as accounting and finance, economics, econometrics, marketing management, and business law and taxation. The departments of accounting and finance, marketing and management, and information technology are the major contributors to the MBA programme. It also draws on other parts of the university to offer a diverse range of professional tracks as a part of the MBA elective programme.

Facilities

Caulfield campus, near Melbourne, has a good reputation as a centre for training and developing senior business people. It hosts a range of visual arts, educational and sporting events and has well-established links with industry, government and the local community. The MBA building on the Caulfield campus has lecture theatres for the exclusive use of MBA students, student lounges and seminar rooms and computer labs.

	Full-time MBA
Student assessment of facilities	n/a (n/a)

Faculty

Number of faculty: 50 full-time, 2 part-time, 10 visiting

	Full-time MBA	Part-time MBA
Number of faculty per student	0.4 (n/a)	0.4
Percentage of faculty with PhD	94	94
Student rating of faculty	n/a (n/a)	–

Strengths and weaknesses

Strengths: marketing; Asian business; finance

Weakness: lack of internationalism

Programme highlights

The Monash MBA consists of 16 semester-length subjects based on five themes: technology, strategy, internationalisation, personal development and innovation. There are ten foundation core subjects and six elective subjects. Electives can be taken across a range of subjects or grouped into professional tracks, making use of other areas of expertise within the university. Tracks are available in the following areas: business law and taxation; management; accounting and finance; cross functional; health; marketing; and IT.

Full-time students can complete the programme in two years. Part-time students take two subjects per semester and can take up to nine years to complete their studies. Both versions of the programme can be accelerated by taking courses in summer and/or winter schools.

	Full-time MBA	Part-time MBA
Student rating of programme	n/a (n/a)	–
Number of overseas exchange programmes	12 (n/a)	–
Number of languages on offer	6 (n/a)	–

Which MBA? © The Economist Intelligence Unit Limited 2004

Student profile (full time)

- ■ EU
- ■ Non-EU Europe
- ▨ North America
- ■ Other Americas
- ■ Asia/Australasia
- ▨ Middle East

Students

	Full-time MBA	Part-time MBA
Annual intake	152	152
Applicants:places	7:1	7:1
Percentage of women students	42 (n/a)	42
Percentage of foreign students	n/a (n/a)	n/a
Average GMAT score	640 (n/a)	640
Average number of months' work experience	108 (n/a)	108
Age range of students	27-36	27-36
Average age	32	32
Student rating of culture and classmates	n/a (n/a)	–

Recruiters/careers service

	Full-time MBA	Part-time MBA
Number of industry sectors that recruited graduates	8 (n/a)	–
Percentage of graduates in jobs 3 months after graduation	89 (n/a)	–
Percentage of graduates finding jobs through careers services	65 (n/a)	–
Student rating of careers service	n/a (n/a)	–
Post-MBA salary, US$	90,909	–
Percentage increase in salary	87	
Principal recruiters of graduates	Telstra, IBM, General Motors	

Cost

	Full-time MBA	Part-time MBA
Application fees	A$50 (US$32)	None
Programme fees	A$44,000 (US$28,571)	A$36,800 (US$23,896)
Comments	Total programme. Fee for Australian students is A$36,800	Total programme
Accommodation costs (on campus, per year)	–	
Accommodation costs (off campus, per year)	A$8,500 (US$5,519)	–
Financial aid available	A$160,000 (US$103,896)	–
Type of aid available	Scholarships and Australian government loans for local post graduate students	–
Criteria on which aid is granted	Scholarships based on academic performance in the MBA programme	–

Accreditation

None

Application details

	Full-time MBA	Part-time MBA
Application deadline	November 30th	November 30th
Programme dates	Feb start, 24 months	Feb start, 48 months
Admission requirements	First degree (credit average minimum from a recognised university); at least 4 years' work experience, TOEFL or IELTS if first language not English; 2 references; GMAT is not mandatory but is recommended; interview when appropriate	First degree (credit average minimum from a recognised university); at least 4 years' work experience; TOEFL or IELTS if first language not English; 2 references; GMAT is not mandatory but is recommended; interview when appropriate

Executive education

Monash does not currently offer open-enrolment or customised in-company executive education programmes.

Student/alumni quotes

"If you know what you want and need, the flexibility of the Monash MBA programme allows that."

"There is a gap between the local and the international students."

"Regular careers seminars; excellent careers advice."

Nanyang Technological University— Nanyang Business School

Address
The Nanyang MBA
Nanyang Business
School
Nanyang
Technological
University
Nanyang Avenue
Singapore
639798

Tel:
+65 6790 4899

Fax:
+65 6791 3561

Email:
nbsmba@ntu.edu.sg

Website:
www.nanyangmba.
ntu.edu.sg

Programme director:
Choo Teck Min

Figures in brackets
represent rank

Ranking	Rank (out of 100) Full-time
Overall rank	93
Regional rank	7

Criteria	Rank (out of 100) Full-time
Open new career opportunities	**60**
Diversity of recruiters	28
Number in jobs three months after graduation	62
Jobs found through the careers service	70
Student assessment of careers service	>100
Personal development and educational experience	**51**
Faculty quality	73
Student quality	60
Student diversity	22
Education experience	60
Increase in salary	**>100**
Increase in salary	>100
Post-MBA salary	>100
Potential to network	**>100**
Breadth of alumni network	89
Internationalism of alumni	76
Alumni effectiveness	>100

Background

Nanyang Technological University (NTU) was formed in 1955 when Singapore was still a British colony. The university is big, with around 25,000 undergraduate and graduate students. The business school (more properly the School of Accountancy and Business) was created in 1990. The school is well connected with industry and business, both locally and internationally. There are plenty of opportunities to meet business leaders, professionals and entrepreneurs, and there is a good guest-speaker series.

Facilities

The school is based on the landscaped campus of NTU in Jurong, about 25 km from the city centre. The 200-hectare site contains more than 50 buildings, including 15 halls of residence with accommodation for more than 8,500 students. The school also has a downtown executive centre where some MBA teaching takes place. Facilities for MBA students are excellent and include a financial trading room and an e-commerce laboratory for teaching and researching e-commerce. The university campus is well equipped with wireless technology, an impressive library and goods sports facilities.

	Full-time MBA
Student assessment of facilities	4.6 (40)

Faculty

Number of faculty: 79 full-time, 5 part-time, 3 visiting		
	Full-time MBA	**The Nanyang MBA**
Number of faculty per student	1.1 (34)	1.8
Percentage of faculty with PhD	92 (64)	92
Student rating of faculty	4.1 (93)	–

Strengths and weaknesses
Strengths: accounting; finance; strategic management

Weakness: networking potential

Programme highlights
Nanyang's MBA is flexible and can be taken full-time or part-time. The full-time version is normally completed in four trimesters (trimesters last around 13 weeks) and the part-time version in eight trimesters. Full-time students usually take four courses per trimester and part-time students take two courses per trimester. Students can switch between full-time and part-time or vice versa at any point in the programme. Leave of absence (up to a maximum of two years) is also available.

The programme is divided into nine core courses and seven electives. Electives can be grouped into specialisations (accountancy, banking and finance, IT, human capital management, international business, marketing, strategic management, technology and operations management) or taken across a wide field as a General MBA. (Specialisations involve taking five functional subjects within that specialisation and up to two subjects from any area.) Students must also complete an individual or group dissertation or complete an overseas business study mission (a short group overseas study tour).

Nanyang offers a joint programme with the University of St Gallen in Switzerland or ESSEC Business School in France. Students spend one year studying at Nanyang and another year studying at St Gallen or ESSEC. The programme is taught in English.

The Nanyang Executive MBA is a bilingual English/Chinese programme for experienced managers taught part-time over 18 months.

	Full-time MBA	Part-time MBA
Student rating of programme	4.3 (83)	–
Number of overseas exchange programmes	72 (13)	–
Number of languages on offer	5 (58)	–

Students

	Full-time MBA	Part-time MBA
Annual intake	73	49
Applicants:places	5:1	3:1
Percentage of women students	34 (18)	36
Percentage of foreign students	84 (21)	n/a
Average GMAT score	651 (48)	625
Average number of months' work experience	60 (54)	96
Age range of students	24-35	28-40
Average age	28	34
Student rating of culture and classmates	3.9 (>100)	–

Student profile (full time)

- ■ EU
- ■ Non-EU Europe
- ▨ North America
- ■ Other Americas
- ■ Asia/Australasia
- ▨ Middle East

Recruiters/careers service

	Full-time MBA	Part-time MBA
Number of industry sectors that recruited graduates	8 (28)	–
Percentage of graduates in jobs 3 months after graduation	81 (62)	–
Percentage of graduates finding jobs through careers services	47 (70)	–
Student rating of careers service	3.1 (>100)	–
Post-MBA salary, US$	37,632 (>100)	–
Percentage increase in salary	28 (>100)	–
Principal recruiters of graduates	Bayer AG, Dell Computer, Mercer HR Consulting	

Cost

	Full-time MBA	Part-time MBA
Application fees	S$50 (US$29)	S$50 (US$29)
Programme fees	S$24,000 (US$13,793)	S$28,000 (US$16,092)
Comments	Total programme	Total programme
Accommodation costs (on campus, per year)	S$4,200 (US$2,414)	–
Accommodation costs (off campus, per year)	S$4,800 (US$2,759)	–
Financial aid available	S$255,100 (US$146,609)	–
Type of aid available	Scholarships	–
Criteria on which aid is granted	Strong academic record, high GMAT and TOEFL scores, relevant work experience	–

Accreditation

EQUIS

Application details

	Full-time MBA	The Nanyang MBA
Application deadline	March 31st	March 31st
Programme dates	Jul start, 16 months	Jul start, 32 months
Admission requirements	First degree; at least 2 years' work experience; GMAT; TOEFL if first language not English; 2 references; 4 essays; interview; laptop	First degree; at least 2 years' work experience, GMAT; TOEFL if first language not English; 2 references; 4 essays; interview

Executive education

Nanyang offers an extensive portfolio of open-enrolment programmes covering such areas as finance, China business, performance measurement, supply chain management, negotiation and many others. It also offers a range of customised in-company programmes.

Student/alumni quotes

"Great place to gain knowledge. The school is great and the staff are dedicated. However, [it] needs to spend more time and resources on its marketing and publicity effort."

"It's one of the best schools in Asia and its tuition is very reasonable when compared to other MBA programmes in the world."

"Companies do not yet consider Asian business schools as 'good enough'. They would rather hire a mediocre person with no Asian experience who is from a somewhat higher-rated business school (and I do not even mean Ivy League schools)."

National University of Singapore—The NUS Business School

Ranking	Rank (out of 100) Full-time
Overall rank	n/a
Regional rank	10

Address
BIZ 2 Building
1 Business Link
Singapore
117592

Tel:
+65 6874 4821

Fax:
+65 6872 1438

Email:
nusmba@nus.edu.sg

Website:
www.mba.nus.edu.sg

Programme directors:
Sum Chee Chuong
Ho Yew Kee

Background

Business teaching started at the National University of Singapore in 1961 and the NUS Business School (part of the Faculty of Business Administration) has ambitions to be the best in Asia. It has a large faculty and also draws teachers from the university. Senior executives from the public and private sectors are used to add variety to teaching and to deliver guest lectures. It is a full-range school, teaching an undergraduate BBA, MBA and doctoral programmes, and executive development courses. There are good exchange agreements with leading schools in the US, Canada and Europe.

Facilities

The school is based within the Faculty of Business Administration and uses most of its facilities (largely shared with business undergraduates). There is an excellent computerised 60,000-volume business library next door (which also serves undergraduates), as well as four PC labs and a mainframe terminal room. The university itself has the largest and most up-to-date computer network in the region. Staff and student computers are networked together. There are six conference rooms and 15 seminar rooms, all equipped with audio and visual facilities. Students have access to all the main university facilities, including libraries and sports and recreational amenities. On-campus accommodation is available.

	Full-time MBA
Student assessment of facilities	3.9 (n/a)

Figures in brackets represent rank

Faculty

Number of faculty: 105 full-time, 9 part-time, 6 visiting

	Full-time MBA	Part-time MBA	Asia-Pacific Executive MBA
Number of faculty per student	1.3 (n/a)	2.9	2.2
Percentage of faculty with PhD	96 (n/a)	96	96
Student rating of faculty	3.8 (n/a)	–	–

Strengths and weaknesses

Strengths: finance; marketing; decision science

Weakness: careers services

Programme highlights

The NUS full-time MBA is a fairly standard US-style programme. It normally takes two years (four semesters and an optional summer term) to complete, although in special circumstances students can graduate in 16 months. There are 12 core courses covering the main management disciplines (waivers are occasionally given) and five electives, chosen from around 50 offered. Elective courses are grouped under such headings as finance and banking, accounting and control, management and organisation, marketing, international business, management information systems, operations management/operations research and strategic management. Classes are based on case studies and group discussion.

The part-time programme has exactly the same curriculum as the full-time version. Students can complete the programme in as little as 28 months or a maximum of six years. Classes meet on campus during the evenings (6–9 pm).

The International Master of Business Administration (IMBA) is a joint programme between NUS and Beijing University and is one of the first to offer modules in both English and Chinese. The aim is to develop future global business leaders and professionals in the context of Singapore and the Asia-Pacific region. Students complete 11 modules at Beijing and Singapore. The programme is completed in 2–4 years.

The UCLA–NUS EMBA is a 15-month course leading to two MBA degrees, one awarded by UCLA and one by NUS. Students attend six two-week segments conducted in residence at NUS, UCLA and Shanghai. The Asia-Pacific Executive (APEX) MBA is available in Chinese and English.

	Full-time MBA	Part-time MBA	Asia-Pacific Executive MBA
Student rating of programme	3.6 (n/a)	–	–
Number of overseas exchange programmes	65 (n/a)	–	–
Number of languages on offer	>5 (n/a)	–	–

Students

	Full-time MBA	Part-time MBA	Asia-Pacific Executive MBA
Annual intake	84	42	55
Applicants:places	11:1	6:1	3:1
Percentage of women students	24 (n/a)	22	6
Percentage of foreign students	80 (n/a)	n/a	n/a
Average GMAT score	662 (n/a)	633	n/a
Average number of months' work experience	60 (n/a)	84	180
Age range of students	24-36	26-51	32-45
Average age	30	32	40
Student rating of culture and classmates	3.5 (n/a)	–	–

Recruiters/careers service

	Full-time MBA	Part-time MBA	Asia-Pacific Executive MBA
Number of industry sectors that recruited graduates	8 (n/a)	–	–
Percentage of graduates in jobs 3 months after graduation	81 (n/a)	–	–
Percentage of graduates finding jobs through careers services	4 (n/a)	–	–
Student rating of careers service	2.6 (n/a)	–	–
Post-MBA salary, US$	39,714 (n/a)	–	–
Percentage increase in salary	16 (n/a)	–	–
Principal recruiters of graduates	OCBC Bank, Inland Revenue Authority of Singapore, Citigroup		

Student profile (full time)

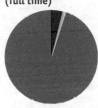

- ■ EU
- ▦ Non-EU Europe
- ▨ North America
- ■ Other Americas
- ■ Asia/Australasia
- ▢ Middle East

Cost

	Full-time MBA	Part-time MBA	Asia-Pacific Executive MBA
Application fees	S$50 (US$29)	S$50 (US$29)	S$50 (US$29)
Programme fees	S$24,000 (US$13,793)	S$28,000 (US$16,092)	S$48,000 (US$27,586)
Comments	–	–	Accommodation, out of pocket and travelling expenses can amount to about S$10,000 to S$25,000
Accommodation costs (on campus, per year)	S$7,680 (US$4,414)	–	–
Accommodation costs (off campus, per year)	S$3,600 (US$2,069)	–	–
Financial aid available	S$1,540,000 (US$885,057)	–	–
Type of aid available	Loans	–	–
Criteria on which aid is granted	Admission to programme	–	–

Accreditation

AACSB International

Application details

	Full-time MBA	Part-time MBA	Asia-Pacific Executive MBA
Application deadline	February 28th	February 28th	March 31st
Programme dates	Aug start, 16-48 months	Aug start, 28-72 months	Jul start, 18 months
Admission requirements	First degree; at least 2 years' work experience; GMAT; TOEFL minimum if first language not English; 2 references; 5 essays; interview; laptop	First degree; at least 2 years' work experience; GMAT; TOEFL if first language not English; 2 references; 5 essays; interview	First degree; at least 10 years' work experience; 3 references; 2 essays; interview

Executive education

The NUS offers open-enrolment executive education programmes in English and Chinese. Topics covered in English include general management, finance, human resources, decision sciences and marketing, as well as programmes for senior managers. It also offers a portfolio of customised in-company programmes in English and Chinese.

Student/alumni quotes

"The school offers value for money. Everybody gets a loan. Some of the exchange programmes are with renowned business schools. Atmosphere is the right mix of competitive and co-operative."

"The attitude of NUS Business School towards MBA students needs to change. They need to start to accept the fact that students look for an MBA mostly to advance their career and enter into a big company riding on their school's shoulder. Massive investment in careers services is required."

"The course work involves many practical projects, with much opportunity for determining individual abilities and group efforts. Classroom discussions are usually dynamic and the lecturers are inspiring."

New York University—Leonard N Stern School of Business

Address
Henry Kaufman
Management Center
44 West Fourth Street
New York, NY
US
10012

Tel:
+1 212 998 0995

Fax:
+1 212 995 4950

Email:
sternmba@stern.nyu.edu

Website:
www.stern.nyu.edu

Programme director:
Russell Winer

Figures in brackets
represent rank

Ranking	Rank (out of 100) Full-time
Overall rank	10
Regional rank	8

Criteria	Rank (out of 100) Full-time
Open new career opportunities	**14**
Diversity of recruiters	1
Number in jobs three months after graduation	44
Jobs found through the careers service	n/a
Student assessment of careers service	11
Personal development and educational experience	**9**
Faculty quality	14
Student quality	27
Student diversity	31
Education experience	17
Increase in salary	**48**
Increase in salary	91
Post-MBA salary	33
Potential to network	**16**
Breadth of alumni network	7
Internationalism of alumni	63
Alumni effectiveness	29

Background

The Stern school's location in a large building in New York City's Greenwich Village area highlights its close bonds with New York's financial community. There is a good mix of nationalities in both the faculty and the student body. It makes full use of its New York location and its guest-speaker series includes some of the world's leading executives. Finance is one of the main reasons people are attracted to Stern. The finance department is exceptional and is frequently at the forefront of knowledge of the latest techniques and concepts. But the school has strengths in other areas, most notably international business and information systems.

Facilities

Facilities are excellent. The school occupies two buildings, the Henry Kaufman Management Center and Tisch Hall. It shares Tisch Hall with the undergraduate business programme. There are plans to expand into Shimkin Hall, which is adjacent to Kaufman. Some on-campus accommodation is available, and Stern owns a number of apartments in the surrounding area for students to rent.

	Full-time MBA
Student assessment of facilities	4.3 (31)

Faculty

Number of faculty: 167 full-time, 174 part-time, 18 visiting			
	Full-time MBA	Part-Time MBA for Working Professionals	Executive MBA
Number of faculty per student	0.7 (67)	0.9	3.9
Percentage of faculty with PhD	99 (19)	99	99
Student rating of faculty	4.6 (13)	–	–

Strengths and weaknesses

Strengths: finance; marketing; entertainment, media and technology

Weaknesses: urban campus lacks camaraderie; dominance of finance

Programme highlights

Stern's two-year full-time MBA starts with a first year of mainly core courses (with one elective in the second semester) including three "breadth" courses: marketing concepts, foundations of finance and operations. In the second year students can (but need not) follow up to three specialisations and complete the capstone core course, professional responsibility. The programme is quantitative and rigorous and a good prior knowledge of most of the quantitative disciplines is assumed.

An important element of the programme is an intensive two-week required pre-programme session, covering areas such as ethics, computing, mathematics and data analysis, as well as team building and social events. During this session the annual intake is divided into blocks (or classes) of around 65 students who spend the first year together. Students further organise themselves into study groups of about five people. Some students may be required to take a business writing course depending on their performance in the written section of the GMAT.

The part-time Langone Program is identical to the full-time MBA. Most students complete it in three years, although the maximum allowed is six years. Students have access to all the school's facilities, including careers services. Various options are available: classes that meet once a week; intensive courses and mini-courses that supplement more traditional class offerings and accelerate the programme (one-week intensive courses can be completed over the winter holiday or spring break; mini-courses meet several times per semester, relying on the Internet and assignments and projects to extend learning between classes); Saturday and Sunday classes that allow the entire programme to be completed on weekends. All courses take advantage of the flexibility of the Internet.

Stern's two-year Executive MBA has two modes: an August start with classes meeting on alternating Fridays and Saturdays, 8.30 am–4.30 pm; and a January start with classes on Friday and Saturday, two weekends a month. Both programmes include four one-week residencies: two in New York at the start of each year and two international. Students take two courses at a time in two classes a day. The programme can be studied as a general management option or as a specialisation in finance (available in the August start programme) or with a healthcare track (January start). All students complete the core curriculum and then take advanced core courses (specific to the concentration chosen) and electives based on their field of study.

The TRIUM Executive MBA is a joint programme with the London School of Economics (LSE) and HEC Paris (see page 256) and two other international business schools. The programme includes ten residential weeks divided into six one- or two-week modules held over a 16-month period. Modules are hosted at Stern (two modules), LSE and HEC Paris, as well as two other international business schools (chosen annually).

Stern also offers company MBA programmes.

	Full-time MBA	Part-Time MBA for Working Professionals	Executive MBA
Student rating of programme	4.5 (11)	–	–
Number of overseas exchange programmes	101 (51)	–	–
Number of languages on offer	>5 (44)	–	–

Student profile (full time)

- ■ EU
- ■ Non-EU Europe
- ■ North America
- ■ Other Americas
- ■ Asia/Australasia
- ▪ Middle East

Students

	Full-time MBA	Part-Time MBA for Working Professionals	Executive MBA
Annual intake	393	384	91
Applicants:places	11:1	3:1	5:1
Percentage of women students	37 (21)	33	28
Percentage of foreign students	32 (90)	n/a	n/a
Average GMAT score	700 (12)	673	621
Average number of months' work experience	54 (82)	60	104
Age range of students	25-30	24-32	27-40
Average age	27	28	32
Student rating of culture and classmates	4.6 (21)	–	–

Recruiters/careers service

	Full-time MBA	Part-Time MBA for Working Professionals	Executive MBA
Number of industry sectors that recruited graduates	8 (1)	–	
Percentage of graduates in jobs 3 months after graduation	80 (44)	–	–
Percentage of graduates finding jobs through careers services	n/a (n/a)	–	–
Student rating of careers service	4.1 (11)	–	–
Post-MBA salary, US$	83,439 (33)	–	–
Percentage increase in salary	30 (91)	–	–
Principal recruiters of graduates	Citigroup, Lehman Brothers, American Express		

Cost

	Full-time MBA	Part-Time MBA for Working Professionals	Executive MBA
Application fees	US$175	US$175	US$150
Programme fees	US$32,400	US$1,190	US$111,300
Comments	Per year	Per credit; credit load is flexible	–
Accommodation costs (on campus, per year)	–	–	–
Accommodation costs (off campus, per year)	US$11,700	–	–
Financial aid available	US$5,000,000	–	–
Type of aid available	Scholarships, fellowships	–	–
Criteria on which aid is granted	Scholarships are merit-based	–	–

Accreditation

AACSB International

Application details

	Full-time MBA	Part-Time MBA for Working Professionals	Executive MBA
Application deadline	March 15th	Rolling admissions	May 27th
Programme dates	Sep start, 21 months	Sep start, 36-72 months	Aug start, 22 months
Admission requirements	First degree; work experience; TOEFL if first language not English (not required if student has degree from university that teaches in English); 2 references; 3 essays; interview by invitation of the admissions committee	First degree; work experience; TOEFL if first language not English (not required if student has degree from university that teaches in English); 2 references; 3 essays; interview by invitation of the admissions committee	First degree (may be waived in certain circumstances); work experience; 2 references; 2 essays; interview

Executive education

Stern offers open-enrolment executive education programmes in finance and accounting and customised in-company programmes.

Student/alumni quotes

"Being in NYC is a critical resource for students to meet with potential recruiters."

"Most of the electives were offered during the evening in my second year. They need more day classes for full-time students."

"NYU is a great school for self-motivated individuals who do not need someone to hold their hand through the process. I felt that the more mature students did quite well throughout with some of the less experienced or younger students feeling frustrated. It takes a strong individual to pick up and move to New York."

University of Newcastle upon Tyne Business School

Address
University of
Newcastle upon Tyne
Business School
Ridley Building
Newcastle upon Tyne
UK
NE1 7RU

Tel:
+44 191 222 5678

Fax:
+44 191 222 6838

Email:
yang.lu@ncl.ac.uk

Website:
www.ncl.ac.uk/nubs/

Programme director:
Dr Andrew Simpson

Figures in brackets
represent rank

Ranking	Rank (out of 100) Full-time
Overall rank	60
Regional rank	22

Criteria	Rank (out of 100) Full-time
Open new career opportunities	**83**
Diversity of recruiters	>100
Number in jobs three months after graduation	8
Jobs found through the careers service	98
Student assessment of careers service	56
Personal development and educational experience	**19**
Faculty quality	66
Student quality	22
Student diversity	2
Education experience	81
Increase in salary	**34**
Increase in salary	23
Post-MBA salary	52
Potential to network	**96**
Breadth of alumni network	>100
Internationalism of alumni	>100
Alumni effectiveness	65

Background

University of Newcastle upon Tyne Business School was formed in 2002 following a university restructuring. It has some 50 faculty, over 1,000 undergraduates and over 150 postgraduate students studying ten taught master's and research programmes. The university has been teaching management subjects since the 1920s and the MBA started in the 1980s. Newcastle has ambitions to become one of the top ten business schools in the UK.

Facilities

The school is housed in the 19th-century Armstrong Building. However, the majority of the teaching is conducted in newly refurbished teaching suites. The university has a large, well-equipped library. Accommodation, in both the private rental sector and the university, is reasonably priced. Newcastle is a lively city with plenty of nightlife.

	Full-time MBA
Student assessment of facilities	4.5 (24)

Faculty

Number of faculty: 60 full-time, 0 part-time, 7 visiting

	Full-time MBA	Executive MBA
Number of faculty per student	2.3 (10)	6.7
Percentage of faculty with PhD	83 (69)	83
Student rating of faculty	3.9 (>100)	–

Strengths and weaknesses

Strengths: technology and innovation management; human resource management; e-business

Weaknesses: careers service; low profile

Programme highlights

The Newcastle MBA is a typical one-year European programme with a strong core, a range of electives and a final dissertation. The programme structure is modular, with eight core modules and five elective modules chosen from a varying list (which generally mirror the main themes covered in the core). It starts with a mandatory induction week. The core is based on themes rather than functional disciplines. The themes are the global business environment; organisations in transition; managing financial performance; managing innovation, technology and operations; and strategy, marketing and business relationships. Case studies and group work are used extensively and there is a good list of visiting speakers.

The Executive MBA is taught in 12 three-day blocks spread over two years. There is an international study trip at the end of each year. The programme ends with a dissertation. Managers are encouraged to bring work-based projects to the classes to assist the transfer of learning from classroom to workplace. The programme is aimed at fully sponsored students.

	Full-time MBA	Executive MBA
Student rating of programme	4.1 (92)	–
Number of overseas exchange programmes	0 (93)	–
Number of languages on offer	4 (56)	–

Students

	Full-time MBA	Executive MBA
Annual intake	27	10
Applicants:places	15:1	2:1
Percentage of women students	48 (4)	40
Percentage of foreign students	96 (6)	n/a
Average GMAT score	n/a (n/a)	n/a
Average number of months' work experience	72 (30)	180
Age range of students	24-53	31-47
Average age	30	35
Student rating of culture and classmates	4.1 (76)	–

**Student profile
(full time)**

- ■ EU
- ■ Non-EU Europe
- ▨ North America
- ■ Other Americas
- ■ Asia/Australasia
- ▨ Middle East

Recruiters/careers service

	Full-time MBA	Executive MBA
Number of industry sectors that recruited graduates	5 (>100)	–
Percentage of graduates in jobs 3 months after graduation	90 (8)	–
Percentage of graduates finding jobs through careers services	0 (98)	–
Student rating of careers service	3.4 (56)	–
Post-MBA salary, US$	77,571 (52)	–
Percentage increase in salary	82 (23)	–
Principal recruiters of graduates	–	

Cost

	Full-time MBA	Executive MBA
Application fees	None	None
Programme fees	£14,175 (US$23,238)	£14,200 (US$23,279)
Comments	Fees include standard text books for core modules	–
Accommodation costs (on campus, per year)	£2,600 (US$4,262)	–
Accommodation costs (off campus, per year)	£2,600 (US$4,262)	–
Financial aid available	Not disclosed	–
Type of aid available	Scholarships	–
Criteria on which aid is granted	Academic merit	–

Accreditation

AMBA

Application details

	Full-time MBA	Executive MBA
Application deadline	August 31st	August 31st
Programme dates	Sep start, 12 months	Sep start, 24 months
Admission requirements	Good first degree from recognised university; at least 3 years' work experience; GMAT; TOEFL or IELTS if first language not English; 2 references; personal statement outlining the purpose of study and career plan	Good first degree; at least 3 years' work experience; TOEFL or IELTS if first language not English; 2 references; interview; personal statement outlining the purpose of study and career plan

Executive education

Newcastle offers a good portfolio of both open-enrolment and customised in-company programmes based on themes such as e-business, negotiations, finance and accounting, and economics.

Student/alumni quotes

"A fantastic year that has taught me a lot of additional aspects of business that I only had a basic understanding of. However, the main benefit was the international focus of the course and the personal development associated with working with many other cultures. This course has given me a higher level of confidence and built international relations."

"The school has amazing facilities and very good teaching quality. Unfortunately, they are not good in marketing approach. They do not sell the MBA course in an effective way."

"Prospective students should give Newcastle serious consideration. The academic team are world class, the business school is focused on becoming one of the best in the world and the connections with London Business School and international assignments make it a high-value academy. The 'Toon', as we locals call Newcastle, is already on the map, of course, for academic antidotes."

NIMBAS Graduate School of Management

Ranking	Rank (out of 100) Full-time
Overall rank	56
Regional rank	20

Criteria	Rank (out of 100) Full-time
Open new career opportunities	**70**
Diversity of recruiters	51
Number in jobs three months after graduation	10
Jobs found through the careers service	75
Student assessment of careers service	86
Personal development and educational experience	**39**
Faculty quality	81
Student quality	15
Student diversity	6
Education experience	84
Increase in salary	**52**
Increase in salary	39
Post-MBA salary	53
Potential to network	**85**
Breadth of alumni network	51
Internationalism of alumni	48
Alumni effectiveness	88

Address
Kromme
Nieuwegracht 39
Utrecht
The Netherlands
3512 HD

Tel:
+31 30 230 3058

Fax:
+31 30 236 7320

Email:
admissions@nimbas.
com

Website:
www.nimbas.com

Programme director:
Gretchen van der Spek

Figures in brackets
represent rank

Background

NIMBAS Graduate School of Management was set up in 1988 and is based in Utrecht in the Netherlands. It is essentially an associate institute of the University of Bradford in the UK and awards the Bradford School of Management MBA (see page 142) in various formats in the Netherlands and Germany. The school is strongly international and has good links with industry.

NIMBAS draws faculty from leading business schools in Europe and a large number come from Bradford. Students and alumni are very enthusiastic about the school.

Facilities

Facilities at NIMBAS in Utrecht are good. Students have access to the University of Utrecht library. For full-time students, the school has a limited number of furnished bedrooms available in IJsselstein, a pleasant residential suburb a short distance from Utrecht. Foreign students have priority in the allocation of rooms. The school can also help students to find accommodation. Utrecht is a pleasant city with excellent transport and communication links.

	Full-time MBA
Student assessment of facilities	3.8 (98)

Faculty

Number of faculty: 2 full-time, 57 part-time, 5 visiting

	Full-time MBA	Two-year Part-time and Modular MBA	Executive MBA
Number of faculty per student	0.8 (36)	0.7	2.7
Percentage of faculty with PhD	100 (68)	100	100
Student rating of faculty	4.1 (84)	–	–

Strengths and weaknesses

Strengths: financial management; international marketing management; environmental management

Weakness: low profile

Programme highlights

The full-time one-year NIMBAS MBA is divided into three stages plus a project. Following an introductory session students follow six typical core courses in the first stage (up to Christmas) and five "advanced" courses and three electives (which can be taken as part of an exchange) in stage 2. Stage 3 (June to September) is given over to the project. Specialisations are offered in environmental management, financial management, international marketing management and legal practice (with advanced diploma in international legal studies). Students choosing to specialise are required to complete two modules or electives and the project in their area of specialisation. About 25% of the students opt to specialise.

The various MBA programmes offered by NIMBAS are validated by Bradford School of Management and students are awarded the Bradford MBA (including specialisations). The programme places considerable emphasis on pre-course reading, tutorials and small study groups. As well as the required courses, electives and projects there are a number of workshops linked to project research and presentation, communication skills and careers development.

NIMBAS has exchange agreements with Bradford, Schulich School of Business at York University in Canada and Brisbane Graduate School of Business at Queensland University of Technology in Australia.

The part-time MBA programme has the same content and essentially the same structure as the full-time version and lasts two years. It concludes with a project, normally carried out in the student's own organisation. The programme is taught at NIMBAS's headquarters in Utrecht and starts in September with an introductory full-time one-week session, which includes the first of the six core subjects. The rest of the first year is given over to the remaining five core courses and one elective, or advanced, course. The second year starts with a residential week followed by six electives. The project is completed during the summer of the second year. Classes are generally held on Tuesday evenings (4.30–10.30 pm) and occasionally on Friday and/or Saturday.

The part-time modular MBA is offered in Bonn, Berlin and Mainz and is identical in structure and content to the full-time and part-time programmes. The programme begins in September with a full-time one-week session. After that, students attend eight Friday–Sunday sessions annually. Lectures begin at 9.30 am on Friday and run through to 4.30 pm on Sunday, including the evenings. Students may study electives as part of an exchange. The programme concludes with the project.

The curriculum of the NIMBAS Executive MBA is again similar to its other MBA programmes. The difference comes in the delivery methods. Students study seven nine-day modules (a working week with two weekends at either end) over two years. The modules rotate among four European countries: the Netherlands, Germany, Spain and the UK.

	Full-time MBA	Two-year Part-time and Modular MBA	Executive MBA
Student rating of programme	4.1 (63)	–	–
Number of overseas exchange programmes	32 (17)	–	–
Number of languages on offer	0 (94)	–	–

Students

	Full-time MBA	Two-year Part-time and Modular MBA	Executive MBA
Annual intake	42	96	24
Applicants:places	3:1	3:1	3:1
Percentage of women students	39 (13)	22	4
Percentage of foreign students	64 (26)	n/a	n/a
Average GMAT score	640 (45)	640	670
Average number of months' work experience	84 (16)	96	156
Age range of students	26-39	27-46	32-52
Average age	32	34	38
Student rating of culture and classmates	4.3 (47)	–	–

Student profile (full time)

- ■ EU
- ■ Non-EU Europe
- ■ North America
- ■ Other Americas
- ■ Asia/Australasia
- ■ Middle East

Recruiters/careers service

	Full-time MBA	Two-year Part-time and Modular MBA	Executive MBA
Number of industry sectors that recruited graduates	8 (51)	–	–
Percentage of graduates in jobs 3 months after graduation	91 (10)	–	–
Percentage of graduates finding jobs through careers services	28 (75)	–	–
Student rating of careers service	2.9 (86)	–	–
Post-MBA salary, US$	92,500 (53)	–	–
Percentage increase in salary	73 (39)	–	–
Principal recruiters of graduates	KPMG, Mitsubishi Fuso Truck & Bus Corporation, Arcelor		

Cost

	Full-time MBA	Two-year Part-time and Modular MBA	Executive MBA
Application fees	€150 (US$170)	€150 (US$170)	€150 (US$170)
Programme fees	€26,000 (US$29,545)	€15,750 (US$17,898)	€18,250 (US$20,739)
Comments	Enrolment fee is €3,000	Enrolment fee is €3,000	Enrolment fee is €3,000
Accommodation costs (on campus, per year)	–	–	–
Accommodation costs (off campus, per year)	€5,500 (US$6,250)	–	–
Financial aid available	€65,000 (US$73,864)	–	–
Type of aid available	Scholarships	–	–
Criteria on which aid is granted	Ability and background	–	–

Accreditation

AMBA

Application details

	Full-time MBA	Two-year Part-time and Modular MBA	Executive MBA
Application deadline	June 15th (EU and North America), May 15th (other countries)	June 15th	June 15th
Programme dates	Sep start, 13 months	Sep start, 24 months	Sep start, 24 months
Admission requirements	First degree; at least 3 years' work experience; GMAT; NIMBAS test if first language not English (the school reserves the right to also ask for either IELTS or TOEFL test); 2 references; 5 essays; interview; laptop; NIMBAS personality test and review	First degree; at least 3 years' work experience; GMAT; NIMBAS test if first language not English (the school reserves the right to also ask for either IELTS or TOEFL test); 2 references; 5 essays; interview; NIMBAS personality test and review	First degree; at least 5 years' work experience; GMAT; NIMBAS test if first language not English (the school reserves the right to also ask for either IELTS or TOEFL test); 2 references; 5 essays; interview; NIMBAS personality test and review

Executive education

NIMBAS does not currently offer non-degree executive education programmes.

Student/alumni quotes

"It's small, flexible, attracts great international students, good value for money and is located in a beautiful town with lots of other students."

"NIMBAS is a personal MBA school with an international student body with wide experiences ... from non-business sectors such as NGOs. Compared with other MBA programmes there is a high emphasis on educating students rather than just producing alumni."

"The atmosphere is competitive but I wonder whether this is just a consequence of doing an MBA? MBA students are generally pushy, forward looking and strong-minded people. NIMBAS, I think, can handle this quite well by means of a sociable staff and supportive social activities and workshops."

University of North Carolina at Chapel Hill—Kenan-Flagler Business School

Ranking	Rank (out of 100) Full-time
Overall rank	37
Regional rank	24

Criteria	Rank (out of 100) Full-time
Open new career opportunities	**39**
Diversity of recruiters	89
Number in jobs three months after graduation	80
Jobs found through the careers service	13
Student assessment of careers service	14
Personal development and educational experience	**27**
Faculty quality	35
Student quality	41
Student diversity	72
Education experience	13
Increase in salary	**63**
Increase in salary	72
Post-MBA salary	46
Potential to network	**48**
Breadth of alumni network	82
Internationalism of alumni	94
Alumni effectiveness	24

Address
CB 3490, McColl
Building
Chapel Hill, NC
US
27599-3490

Tel:
+4 919 962 7235

Fax:
+1 919 962 7732

Email:
mba_info@unc.edu

Website:
www.kenan-flagler.
unc.edu/Programs/
MBA/index.cfm

Programme director:
Dr Valarie Zeithaml

Figures in brackets
represent rank

Background

The University of North Carolina at Chapel Hill's Kenan-Flagler Business School began in 1919 as the Department of Commerce of the College of Arts (it is one of the oldest accredited business schools in the US). It was renamed in 1991 following a gift from Frank Hawkins Kenan in honour of Mary Lily Kenan-Flagler, a philanthropist, and her husband, Henry Morrison Flagler. It is particularly known for its focus on team-based learning.

Facilities

Facilities at the McColl Building, where the school is based, are very good. They include classrooms, a careers services library, a technology centre, a 500-seat auditorium, a trading room and a 40-work-station multimedia classroom. All undergraduate and masters programmes as well as students, faculty and staff are housed in the building, which is on the edge of the university campus. On-campus accommodation is available but most students live off campus in Chapel Hill. The university is in the middle of the Raleigh–Durham–Chapel Hill Triangle area, a booming part of North Carolina that has attracted many leading US companies.

	Full-time MBA
Student assessment of facilities	4.4 (23)

Faculty

Number of faculty: 93 full-time, 20 part-time, 1 visiting

	Full-time MBA	Executive MBA Weekend Program	Executive MBA Evening Program
Number of faculty per student	0.4 (87)	2.0	1.7
Percentage of faculty with PhD	94 (31)	94	94
Student rating of faculty	4.5 (20)	–	–

Strengths and weaknesses

Strengths: management; marketing; finance

Weakness: somewhat isolated location

Programme highlights

The first-year core of the Kenan-Flagler two-year full time MBA is based on a series of themes: analysing capabilities and resources; monitoring the marketplace and external environment; formulating strategy; implementing strategy and assessing firm performance. First-year courses (including two electives) are covered in four modules arranged around these themes. Each module contains a theme-based integrative exercise. Each student is assigned to a study group of five to six people who stay together all year. The leading and managing and communication skills courses address leadership, sensitivity to cultural differences, and written, verbal and non-verbal communication.

In the second year students can if they wish follow career concentrations (customer and product management, corporate finance, global supply chain management, investment management, management consulting, real estate, and entrepreneurship and venture development) and/or enrichment concentrations (sustainable enterprise, international business, and electronic business and digital commerce). The latter cut across different career paths. The second year also includes a faculty-led team project.

Kenan-Flagler's Executive MBA is similar to the full-time MBA and is offered in two versions, evening and weekend. They both have the same curriculum, but Weekend MBA classes are more concentrated with longer preparation periods in between. Classes meet twice a month, all day Friday and Saturday. The 20-month programme begins in January with a six-day mandatory immersion week from Sunday evening to Saturday afternoon with overnight stays required.

For an EMBA the programme has a good range of electives. Participants take 8–10 electives from approximately 30 offered. There is also the option of global immersion courses, offered in March and May, which highlight many of the most dynamic economies in Asia, Europe, Latin America and South Africa. Before the trips (which last 10–14 days) students attend classroom lectures and complete readings focusing on the business, political and cultural issues affecting the region. There is an additional charge for these courses. A communications skills course runs throughout the programme.

Evening MBA classes start in August and meet on campus on Monday and Thursday evenings (6–9.15 pm) over 24 months with breaks for holidays. The programme begins with a two-day mandatory immersion weekend that lays the foundation for future classes. Occasional Saturday sessions are held for course reviews, exams or workshops.

The school also offers OneMBA, a joint global programme designed for executives with at least seven years' experience (see Rotterdam School of Management, page 441).

	Full-time MBA	Executive MBA Weekend Program	Executive MBA Evening Program
Student rating of programme	4.4 (25)	–	–
Number of overseas exchange programmes	60 (25)	–	–
Number of languages on offer	35 (37)	–	–

University of North Carolina at Chapel Hill—Kenan-Flagler Business School

Students

	Full-time MBA	Executive MBA Weekend Program	Executive MBA Evening Program
Annual intake	264	56	68
Applicants:places	8:1	3:1	2:1
Percentage of women students	27 (60)	21	15
Percentage of foreign students	28 (102)	n/a	n/a
Average GMAT score	671 (23)	600	610
Average number of months' work experience	60 (63)	132	132
Age range of students	25-33	27-42	27-55
Average age	28	33	34
Student rating of culture and classmates	4.4 (29)	–	–

Student profile (full time)

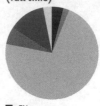

- ■ EU
- ■ Non-EU Europe
- ■ North America
- ■ Other Americas
- ■ Asia/Australasia
- ■ Middle East

Recruiters/careers service

	Full-time MBA	Executive MBA Weekend Program	Executive MBA Evening Program
Number of industry sectors that recruited graduates	6 (89)	–	–
Percentage of graduates in jobs 3 months after graduation	71 (80)	–	–
Percentage of graduates finding jobs through careers services	69 (13)	–	–
Student rating of careers service	3.9 (14)	–	–
Post-MBA salary, US$	77,788 (46)	–	–
Percentage increase in salary	38 (72)	–	–
Principal recruiters of graduates	Johnson & Johnson, IBM, Lehman Brothers		

Cost

	Full-time MBA	Executive MBA Weekend Program	Executive MBA Evening Program
Application fees	US$100	US$110	US$110
Programme fees	US$31,980	US$61,500	US$48,000
Comments	Per year	Total programme	Includes tuition, texts, socials and immersion weekend accommodations for the entire programme
Accommodation costs (on campus, per year)	US$10,588	–	–
Accommodation costs (off campus, per year)	US$10,392	–	–
Financial aid available	Not disclosed	–	–
Type of aid available	Fellowships, loans	–	–
Criteria on which aid is granted	Merit, financial need	–	–

Accreditation

AACSB International

Application details

	Full-time MBA	Executive MBA Weekend Program	Executive MBA Evening Program
Application deadline	May 1st	September 22nd	May 3rd
Programme dates	Aug start, 21 months	Jan start, 20 months	Aug start, 24 months
Admission requirements	First degree; at least 2 years' work experience; TOEFL if first language not English; references; essays; interview; laptop	First degree; at least 5 years' work experience; TOEFL if first language not English; 3 references; 5 essays; interview	First degree; at least 5 years' work experience; TOEFL if first language not English; 3 references; 6 essays; interview

Executive education

Kenan-Flagler's open-enrolment executive education programmes are headed by the four-week Senior Executive Institution, a leadership programme, the Executive Development Institute, a development programme for high-potential managers, and the four-day Business of Human Development programme for HR executives. Shorter (two- or three-day) specialist seminars cover areas such as managing scientifically oriented organisations, marketing, finance, negotiation, leadership, and strategic leadership for senior executives. The school offers a portfolio of customised in-company programmes.

Student/alumni quotes

"General business education is strong. Marketing and sustainability programmes are top notch."

"Branding was a problem because Kenan-Flagler was not immediately associated with UNC Chapel Hill. This has now been corrected with the rebranding initiative (now UNC's Kenan-Flagler Business School)."

"The atmosphere of teamwork, leadership quality of the students, and high quality of the student body from a knowledge standpoint are second to none. The faculty is spectacular and only getting better. The administration is very student-focused and is attempting to increase student awareness of its initiatives. The location and weather don't hurt, either."

Northwestern University—Kellogg School of Management

Ranking	Rank (out of 100) Full-time
Overall rank	1
Regional rank	1

Criteria	Rank (out of 100) Full-time
Open new career opportunities	**3**
Diversity of recruiters	1
Number in jobs three months after graduation	21
Jobs found through the careers service	6
Student assessment of careers service	4
Personal development and educational experience	**4**
Faculty quality	19
Student quality	12
Student diversity	38
Education experience	2
Increase in salary	**7**
Increase in salary	56
Post-MBA salary	4
Potential to network	**17**
Breadth of alumni network	11
Internationalism of alumni	49
Alumni effectiveness	14

Address
Donald P. Jacobs Center
2001 Sheridan Road
Evanston, IL
US
60208-2001

Tel:
+1 847 491 2112

Fax:
+1 847 467 3140

Email:
MBAadmissions@ kellogg.northwestern. edu

Website:
www.kellogg. northwestern.edu

Programme director:
Dipak C Jain

Figures in brackets represent rank

Background

Kellogg is one of the most engaging top-ranked schools in the world. A commitment to student needs in every programme from the full-time MBA to executive courses, coupled with top-notch faculty and high-powered staff, creates a culture of loyalty. MBA students and alumni are involved in interviewing every applicant just to make sure it stays that way.

The school accepts its deserved reputation as a marketing powerhouse, but points out that finance and general management are more popular majors (and have been for some time). The school is not (as some think) named after a breakfast cereal but after John L and Helen Kellogg, who made a gift of US$10m in 1979.

Facilities

Kellogg's facilities are superb. The three-building Donald P Jacobs Center could hardly offer students more, and executives live and learn in some style at the James L Allen Center. Some MBA student residences are available in the nearby McManus Living-Learning Center, but most students find apartments easily enough in pleasant (in parts, posh) Evanston, bordering Lake Michigan and about 30 minutes north of downtown Chicago.

	Full-time MBA
Student assessment of facilities	4.6 (10)

Faculty

Number of faculty: 145 full-time, 81 part-time, 7 visiting

	Full-time MBA	The Managers' Program (TMP)	Executive Master's Program
Number of faculty per student	0.4 (90)	0.6	1.3
Percentage of faculty with PhD	99 (13)	99	99
Student rating of faculty	4.6 (11)	–	–

Strengths and weaknesses

Strengths: management and strategy; finance; marketing

Weakness: international focus

Programme highlights

Kellogg's full-time two-year (known as "the 2Y") MBA curriculum is a strong and flexible model in the US mainstream. The programme is taught over six quarters with students attending classes during the fall, winter and spring quarters for two academic years and completing an internship during the summer. The first two quarters are largely taken up by traditional core courses, which make up nine of the required 24 courses. Courses can be waived and replaced by electives. Electives can be taken from the second quarter of the first year. Group work pervades every aspect of the curriculum, and most students will spend all their time in small groups.

The post-core programme is broad and flexible. Students must major in at least one discipline but are encouraged to take several (95% major in at least two). As well as the major business disciplines, Kellogg offers nine professional fields of study (biotechnology; health industry management; public/non-profit management; transport and logistics management; entrepreneurship and innovation; real estate management; international business and markets; technology industry management; and media management). Many courses involve in-company project work in the Chicago area.

Students generally take four courses a quarter but can study more at no extra cost. Core courses in the winter and spring quarters can be interchanged to allow time for electives. Students with undergraduate business degrees can complete the programme in one year (four quarters). During the summer quarter, they take catch-up courses and then join the second year.

The part-time Managers' Program is identical in content and teaching to the full-time MBA. Students are encouraged to waive core courses and must have their own approved laptop computers. Classes are held at Northwestern's Chicago campus in the evenings, 6–9 pm. Students take a maximum of two courses a quarter. The programme, which can start in any quarter, can be completed in two-and-a half to five years. Some electives can be taken in the evening on the Evanston campus with full-time students.

Kellogg's Executive Master's Programme (EMP) is based on six-week modules typically covering two courses each. Students take 12 modules during the two-year programme. In modules 9 and 10 participants choose four electives from around 12 on offer. Classes are held on alternate Fridays and Saturdays. Two sections start in September and one in January. The programme is also offered in a variation called the North American Program (NAP), which is designed for long-distance students. Classes for the NAP are held on alternate weekends (Friday afternoon, all day Saturday and Sunday morning). All sections begin each year with a six-day live-in residential block. Classes are held at Kellogg's executive education facility, the James L Allen Center, where NAP students are accommodated. Students are assigned to study groups, which meet once a week outside of class.

Kellogg also offers joint degree programmes with Tel Aviv University in Israel, an EMBA in conjunction with WHU Koblenz in Germany, and a joint EMBA with Hong Kong University of Science and Technology and York University's Schulich School of Business in Canada.

	Full-time MBA	The Managers' Program (TMP)	Executive Master's Program
Student rating of programme	4.7 (4)	–	–
Number of overseas exchange programmes	519 (4)	–	–
Number of languages on offer	>5 (63)	–	–

Students

	Full-time MBA	The Managers' Program (TMP)	Executive Master's Program
Annual intake	519	385	182
Applicants:places	10:1	3:1	n/a
Percentage of women students	28 (52)	32	20
Percentage of foreign students	28 (94)	n/a	n/a
Average GMAT score	703 (8)	690	n/a
Average number of months' work experience	62 (60)	84	168
Age range of students	–	–	33–43
Average age	28	29	37
Student rating of culture and classmates	4.8 (4)	–	–

Student profile (full time)

- ■ EU
- ■ Non-EU Europe
- ▨ North America
- ■ Other Americas
- ■ Asia/Australasia
- ▨ Middle East
- ■ Other

Recruiters/careers service

	Full-time MBA	The Managers' Program (TMP)	Executive Master's Program
Number of industry sectors that recruited graduates	8 (1)	–	–
Percentage of graduates in jobs 3 months after graduation	86 (21)	–	–
Percentage of graduates finding jobs through careers services	68 (6)	–	–
Student rating of careers service	4.4 (4)	–	–
Post-MBA salary, US$	88,000 (4)	–	–
Percentage increase in salary	41 (56)	–	–
Principal recruiters of graduates	McKinsey & Company, Bain & Company, Boston Consulting Group		

Cost

	Full-time MBA	The Managers' Program (TMP)	Executive Master's Program
Application fees	US$200	US$200	US$150
Programme fees	US$34,314	US$3,204	See comments
Comments	Per year	Per credit	Total tuition by programme: US$102,000 Regional Program; US$114,000 September North American Program; $112,000 January North American
Accommodation costs (on campus, per year)	–	–	–
Accommodation costs (off campus, per year)	–	–	–
Financial aid available	Not disclosed	–	–
Type of aid available	Scholarships, loans	–	–
Criteria on which aid is granted	Merit, financial need	–	–

Accreditation

AACSB International

Application details

	Full-time MBA	The Managers' Program (TMP)	Executive Master's Program
Application deadline	March 12th	July 16th	Rolling Admissions
Programme dates	Sep start, 21 months	Sep start, 36 months	Sep start, 21 months
Admission requirements	First degree; work experience; TOEFL if first language not English; references; essays; interview; laptop	First degree; work experience; TOEFL if first language not English; references; essays; interview	First degree; at least 10 years' work experience; TOEFL if first language not English (based on evaluation during the interview); 2 references; 4 essays; interview; letter of organisation support

Executive education

Kellogg offers a wide variety of open-enrolment executive education courses in areas such as general management, finance and accounting, leadership and strategy, marketing and sales, technology management and manufacturing management. General management programmes generally last 3–4 weeks and functional programmes 3–5 days. Kellogg also has a strong portfolio of customised in-company programmes, which make up around 40% of its executive education output.

Student/alumni quotes

"The atmosphere is co-operative, but group expectations are high. Plan on putting in double the effort if that's what it takes to contribute your fair share of the work."

"Cases could be more internationally oriented."

"Kellogg provides a terrific education and experience—the chance to learn in an open, collegial atmosphere with an astonishing collection of bright, interesting and motivated people."

Norwegian School of Management BI

Ranking	Rank (out of 100) Full-time
Overall rank	n/a
Regional rank	43

Address
BI Norwegian School
of Managment
Executive School
Box 9386, Gronland
0135 Olso
Norway
0135

Tel:
+47 2257 6212

Fax:
+47 2257 6282

Email:
mba@bi.no

Website:
www.mba.no/mba

Programme director:
Pal Korsvold

Figures in brackets
represent rank

Background

The Norwegian School of Management BI (NSM), set up in 1943, is one of Europe's largest private business schools, with 10,500 full-time students, 11,500 part-timers and 365 faculty. The MBA, programme, though, is very small. Students like the small class size and the emphasis on strategy and leadership, but say the MBA programme is not well marketed to employers and that the careers service needs improvement.

Besides the Sandvika campus, the school operates 15 business colleges across Norway as well as the Norwegian School of Marketing, the Norwegian School of Trade and Retail Management, the Executive School, the Distance Learning Centre and the Financial Services Studies. NSM is also the major shareholder in Lithuania's first business school and has been granted permission to offer higher university degree courses in China. The school says it is determined to become a major player in the knowledge economy.

Facilities

The MBA and EMBA programmes are housed on the Executive School (which is exclusively postgraduate) campus, a refurbished educational conference centre in Oslo overlooking the Oslo Fjord. Teaching takes place in the MBA auditorium. Group rooms, each with two PCs, and the MBA lounge are solely for the use of MBA participants. They have access to a common PC room as well as free photocopying and printing facilities. Library facilities at the Executive School are good, and more library resources are available on the Sandvika campus to the west of Oslo.

NSM is currently building a new campus in central Oslo and this should open in mid-2005.

	Full-time MBA
Student assessment of facilities	3.7 (n/a)

Faculty

Number of faculty: 32 full-time, 5 part-time, 7 visiting

	Full-time MBA	Executive MBA
Number of faculty per student	1.3 (n/a)	2.0
Percentage of faculty with PhD	40 (n/a)	40
Student rating of faculty	4.2 (n/a)	–

Strengths and weaknesses

Strengths: finance; strategy; marketing

Weakness: careers service

Programme highlights

NSM offers an intensive 11-month (August–June) MBA programme, which includes a comprehensive 15-course core, four electives, a five-month project culminating in a presentation to the client organisation and a one-week overseas study tour combining lectures with excursions, case studies and meetings with local business leaders and government officials.

The programme consists of four ten-week terms. There is a strong emphasis on leadership, strategy and group orientation, with two sets of core courses each in leadership and strategy. The strategy project is an in-company team consulting experience concentrating on industry analysis, company analysis and issue analysis.

The programme is geared to teaching general management, but there is some opportunity to specialise via a small range of electives. It is highly regarded for its international focus and emphasis on multicultural learning. Soft management issues, such as cross-cultural management and change management, are handled well. The programme starts with an "introduction week", comprising cultural, social and academic events and culminating in an activity-based learning weekend including outdoor exercises.

In January 2005 NSM is launching an Executive MBA in co-operation with ESCP–EAP. The programme will consist of 18 short modules (Thursday morning to Saturday lunchtime) over 18 months, with distance-learning elements between modules and five week-long international seminars. Classes will meet in Norway and at ESCP–EAP campuses in Paris, London, Berlin and Madrid.

The school is also involved in a part-time MBA programme in China in co-operation with Fudan University.

	Full-time MBA	Executive MBA
Student rating of programme	4.0 (n/a)	–
Number of overseas exchange programmes	0 (n/a)	–
Number of languages on offer	1 (n/a)	–

Student profile (full time)

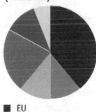

- ■ EU
- ■ Non-EU Europe
- ■ North America
- ■ Other Americas
- ■ Asia/Australasia
- ▨ Middle East

Students

	Full-time MBA	Executive MBA
Annual intake	28	22
Applicants:places	5:1	3:1
Percentage of women students	11 (n/a)	27
Percentage of foreign students	64 (n/a)	n/a
Average GMAT score	600 (n/a)	550
Average number of months' work experience	72 (n/a)	162
Age range of students	26-37	29-43
Average age	30	36
Student rating of culture and classmates	4.1 (n/a)	–

Recruiters/careers service

	Full-time MBA	Executive MBA
Number of industry sectors that recruited graduates	5 (n/a)	–
Percentage of graduates in jobs 3 months after graduation	60 (n/a)	–
Percentage of graduates finding jobs through careers services	n/a (n/a)	–
Student rating of careers service	2.5 (n/a)	–
Post-MBA salary, US$	85,206 (n/a)	–
Percentage increase in salary	21 (n/a)	–
Principal recruiters of graduates	Norsk Hydro, DnB	

Cost

	Full-time MBA	Executive MBA
Application fees	None	None
Programme fees	Nkr199,400 (US$28,164)	Nkr210,000 (US$29,661)
Comments	–	–
Accommodation costs (on campus, per year)	–	–
Accommodation costs (off campus, per year)	Nkr44,000 (US$6,215)	–
Financial aid available	Nkr250,000 (US$35,311)	–
Type of aid available	Scholarship	–
Criteria on which aid is granted	Strong academic record, financial need	

Accreditation

AACSB International, EQUIS

Application details

	Full-time MBA	Executive MBA
Application deadline	October 17th	September 15th
Programme dates	Aug start, 11 months	Jan start, 18 months
Admission requirements	First degree; at least 3 years' work experience; GMAT; 3 references; essay; interview; laptop	First degree; at least 3 years' work experience; GMAT; 2 references; essay; interview

Executive education

NSM does not currently offer non-degree executive education programmes.

Student/alumni quotes

"I would advise prospective students to attend this programme, but be pushy about careers services questions so as to stimulate changes in this area."

"It is fun but demanding, and you should definitely have some and various work experience before attending. The atmosphere has been co-operative and that has increased the learning very much. Because it is a 'safe' work space we have tested out much more than we would have done if it had been more competitive."

"Good professors, focus on group processes and strategy focus."

University of Notre Dame—Mendoza College of Business

Address
204 Mendoza College
of Business
University of Notre
Dame
Notre Dame, IN
US
46556

Tel:
+1 574 631 9295

Fax:
+1 574 631 4825

Email:
mba.1@nd.edu

Website:
www.nd.edu/~mba

Programme director:
Edward J Conlon

Figures in brackets
represent rank

Ranking	Rank (out of 100) Full-time
Overall rank	39
Regional rank	26

Criteria	Rank (out of 100) Full-time
Open new career opportunities	**40**
Diversity of recruiters	37
Number in jobs three months after graduation	56
Jobs found through the careers service	43
Student assessment of careers service	54
Personal development and educational experience	**73**
Faculty quality	41
Student quality	68
Student diversity	>100
Education experience	55
Increase in salary	**42**
Increase in salary	9
Post-MBA salary	74
Potential to network	**12**
Breadth of alumni network	60
Internationalism of alumni	17
Alumni effectiveness	5

Background

Established in 1921, with antecedents going back to 1913, Mendoza College of Business is a full-range school with over 2,000 students. It offers undergraduate degrees in accountancy, finance, management, management information systems and marketing, graduate degrees in business administration (MBA), accountancy and administration, and executive education programmes.

Like its parent, the University of Notre Dame, Mendoza is a Catholic institution (although there are no restrictions on entry) with a strong ethical foundation. In this way it is similar to Spanish schools such as IESE and offers an added dimension for many students. The Notre Dame Center for Ethics, established in 1975, runs some MBA elective courses as well as bringing distinguished executives on campus to discuss business issues with students and faculty.

Facilities

The school occupies a modern, four-building complex that includes a multimedia amphitheatre, a computer lab, a two-storey MBA lounge and team rooms equipped with networked computers. On-campus accommodation is available.

	Full-time MBA
Student assessment of facilities	4.2 (55)

Faculty

Number of faculty: 122 full-time, 40 part-time, 0 visiting

	Full-time MBA	Notre Dame – South Bend EMBA	Notre Dame – Chicago EMBA
Number of faculty per student	1.1 (43)	2.7	2.7
Percentage of faculty with PhD	90 (39)	90	90
Student rating of faculty	4.3 (48)	–	–

Strengths and weaknesses

Strengths: ethical leadership; corporate finance and investments; marketing and public policy

Weakness: careers services needs to show some improvement

Programme highlights

Mendoza's two-year full-time MBA is a fairly traditional mix of core and electives. The first year is mainly traditional core subjects with two required electives in management communications chosen from nine offered. The second year is mainly given over to electives and concentrations (corporate finance, investments, entrepreneurship, information technology, management development, manufacturing management, business-to-business marketing, consumer marketing and consulting), as well as required courses in ethics and international business (again chosen from an offered list).

A one-year MBA programme allows students who hold undergraduate degrees from accredited business programmes to earn the MBA degree in 11 months. They take an intensive ten-week summer semester in core disciplines and then move directly into the second year of the two-year programme.

Mendoza's main 21-month Executive MBA is delivered both on and off campus via an online video link. Classes are held once a month, Wednesday–Saturday, on the main Mendoza campus and via video links to classrooms in Ohio (Toledo and Cincinnati) for four semesters. Each semester begins with a week-long residency either on campus or at a sponsoring partner. There are also in-company residencies and a one-week international study tour.

The EMBA is also offered in downtown Chicago as a classroom-based 18-month programme. Classes are held all day on Fridays and Saturdays on alternating weekends. The programme lasts from January to May of the following year and includes four one-week residencies: three at Notre Dame's campus in South Bend, Indiana, and one at IBM's Advanced Business Institute in Palisades, New York. Study teams are a central element of the programme.

	Full-time MBA	Notre Dame – South Bend EMBA	Notre Dame – Chicago EMBA
Student rating of programme	4.1 (71)	–	–
Number of overseas exchange programmes	58 (32)	–	–
Number of languages on offer	>5 (59)	–	–

Students

	Full-time MBA	Notre Dame – South Bend EMBA	Notre Dame – Chicago EMBA
Annual intake	129	60	59
Applicants:places	6:1	2:1	2:1
Percentage of women students	19 (98)	22	31
Percentage of foreign students	36 (89)	n/a	n/a
Average GMAT score	664 (32)	n/a	n/a
Average number of months' work experience	54 (92)	165	172
Age range of students	24-32	29-46	31-44
Average age	27	36	36
Student rating of culture and classmates	4.2 (50)	–	–

Student profile (full time)

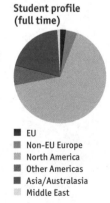

- ■ EU
- ■ Non-EU Europe
- ▨ North America
- ■ Other Americas
- ■ Asia/Australasia
- ▨ Middle East

Recruiters/careers service

	Full-time MBA	Notre Dame South Bend EMBA	Notre Dame – Chicago EMBA
Number of industry sectors that recruited graduates	8 (37)	–	–
Percentage of graduates in jobs 3 months after graduation	78 (56)	–	–
Percentage of graduates finding jobs through careers services	48 (43)	–	–
Student rating of careers service	3.4 (54)	–	–
Post-MBA salary, US$	70,245 (74)	–	–
Percentage increase in salary	88 (9)	–	–
Principal recruiters of graduates	Honeywell, General Electric, IBM		

Cost

	Full-time MBA	Notre Dame – South Bend EMBA	Notre Dame – Chicago EMBA
Application fees	US$100	US$50	US$50
Programme fees	US$30,215	US$67,500	US$66,000
Comments	Per year	Total programme	Total programme
Accommodation costs (on campus, per year)	US$425	–	–
Accommodation costs (off campus, per year)	US$500	–	–
Financial aid available	US$9,810,000	–	–
Type of aid available	Fellowships, private loans, federal loans	–	–
Criteria on which aid is granted	Merit	–	–

Accreditation

AACSB International

Application details

	Full-time MBA	Notre Dame – South Bend EMBA	Notre Dame – Chicago EMBA
Application deadline	March 17th	June 1st	November 15th
Programme dates	Aug start, 21 months	Aug start, 21 months	Jan start, 18 months
Admission requirements	First degree; work experience; GMAT; TOEFL if first language not English; 2 references; 3 essays; interview; laptop	First degree (5% accepted without degree – GMAT required); at least 5 years' work experience; TOEFL may be required by admissions committee; interview	First degree (5% accepted without degree – GMAT required); at least 5 years' work experience; TOEFL may be required by admissions committee; interview

Executive education

Mendoza's flagship open-enrolment executive programme is the Executive Integral Leadership Program, a session conducted on campus. Other non-degree programmes include Supervisory Development and the Certificate in Executive Management. Mendoza has also offered a portfolio of customised in-company programmes since 1982.

Student/alumni quotes

"The school work can be quite challenging and time-consuming but the incredibly co-operative atmosphere within the student body makes it enjoyable."

"I feel they could be doing more to leverage the ND name. Companies come to recruit undergrads but not MBAs."

"Notre Dame's Graduate School of Business is a well-funded and supported business school, leveraging all of the strengths of the university, from dedicated alumni to football to public service. I had looked at one-year programmes abroad but decided on Notre Dame because of the ND programme and the opportunities to intern and study abroad. The experience thus far has been overwhelmingly positive."

University of Nottingham Business School

Address
Jubilee Campus
Wollaton Road
Nottingham
UK
NG8 1BB

Tel:
+44 115 846 6974

Fax:
+44 115 846 6667

Email:
mba@nottingham.ac.
uk

Website:
www.nottingham.ac.
uk/business

Programme director:
Scott Goddard

Figures in brackets
represent rank

Ranking	Rank (out of 100) Full-time
Overall rank	80
Regional rank	30

Criteria	Rank (out of 100) Full-time
Open new career opportunities	**84**
Diversity of recruiters	66
Number in jobs three months after graduation	78
Jobs found through the careers service	67
Student assessment of careers service	89
Personal development and educational experience	**75**
Faculty quality	90
Student quality	72
Student diversity	25
Education experience	82
Increase in salary	**24**
Increase in salary	40
Post-MBA salary	30
Potential to network	**>100**
Breadth of alumni network	94
Internationalism of alumni	85
Alumni effectiveness	95

Background

Nottingham Business School was created in 1998 from the old School of Management and Finance. In 1999 it moved to new purpose-built premises on the university's Jubilee Campus, bringing together teaching staff, researchers and students who were previously scattered over three sites. As well as its own faculty, it draws academics and expertise from the rest of the university, offering students a good choice. The school has strong links with industry through research, consulting work and sponsored chairs.

Facilities

As current students overwhelmingly agree, facilities are excellent, with resource rooms, seminar rooms, a boardroom, computer suites, two large atria, and administrative and staff offices. The adjacent teaching block and resource centre have lecture theatres seating up to 300, videoconferencing facilities, a library and 24-hour computer access. There is a postgraduate residence 50 metres away with 150 en-suite rooms (generally reserved for overseas students). The careers service gets mixed reviews from students. The university has comprehensive sports facilities and Nottingham is an old city with plenty of amenities.

	Full-time MBA
Student assessment of facilities	4.1 (73)

Faculty

Number of faculty: 90 full-time, 7 part-time, 22 visiting

	Full-time MBA	Part-time MBA Programme	Executive MBA Programme
Number of faculty per student	1.2 (28)	7.9	5.2
Percentage of faculty with PhD	76 (96)	76	76
Student rating of faculty	4.1 (79)	–	–

Strengths and weaknesses

Strengths: corporate social responsibility and business ethics; finance; entrepreneurship

Weakness: can be over-academic, rather than practical

Programme highlights

The Nottingham MBA is a strong, UK-style programme. The school has gone further than most in the provision of specialised MBAs, offering a suite of different programmes through a variety of delivery routes (full-time, part-time and modular): general MBA; MBA in financial studies; executive MBA; specialised MBAs in corporate social responsibility, and risk and insurance management (full-time and part-time); international MBA (full-time); executive MBA and financial MBA in Singapore; MBA in Malaysia. Most of the UK-based programmes share a number of common courses, with core courses in specialised programmes often doubling up as electives in others, although the elective choice is generally wide.

The full-time general MBA programme lasts 12 months and is divided into three terms. Students take eight core courses and six electives, some of which can be taken in other schools of the university. They then complete group or individual in-company projects, culminating in written reports and oral presentations to the companies, or an individual dissertation. Each student is assigned to a faculty member who acts as a personal tutor throughout the programme.

Nottingham's part-time programmes are identical to the full-time versions and to an extent are taught alongside them. Students can take 2–4 years to complete their degree. They must attend the school when core and elective courses are being held. Core subjects are normally offered twice during an academic year, once during the day and once in the evening. Most elective subjects are taught in the evening at least every two years. Students must complete group or individual projects or an individual dissertation.

	Full-time MBA	Part-time MBA Programme	Executive MBA Programme
Student rating of programme	4.0 (89)	–	–
Number of overseas exchange programmes	4 (78)	–	–
Number of languages on offer	4 (53)	–	–

Students

	Full-time MBA	Part-time MBA Programme	Executive MBA Programme
Annual intake	84	15	23
Applicants:places	n/a	n/a	2:1
Percentage of women students	32 (19)	40	17
Percentage of foreign students	82 (16)	n/a	n/a
Average GMAT score	600 (86)	600	600
Average number of months' work experience	84 (21)	108	120
Age range of students	27–39	29–37	28–42
Average age	31	28	34
Student rating of culture and classmates	3.9 (94)	–	–

Student profile (full time)

- ■ EU
- ■ Non-EU Europe
- ■ North America
- ■ Other Americas
- ■ Asia/Australasia
- ▢ Middle East
- ■ Other

Recruiters/careers service

	Full-time MBA	Part-time MBA Programme	Executive MBA Programme
Number of industry sectors that recruited graduates	7 (66)	–	–
Percentage of graduates in jobs 3 months after graduation	90 (78)	–	–
Percentage of graduates finding jobs through careers services	40 (67)	–	–
Student rating of careers service	3.2 (89)	–	–
Post-MBA salary, US$	77,049 (30)	–	–
Percentage increase in salary	34 (40)		
Principal recruiters of graduates	The Boots Company, BT plc, National Health Service		

Cost

	Full-time MBA	Part-time MBA Programme	Executive MBA Programme
Application fees	None	None	None
Programme fees	£16,500 (US$27,049)	£16,500 (US$27,049)	£16,500 (US$27,049)
Comments	Total programme, non-EU students; fee for EU citizens is £15,500	Total programme, non-EU students; fee for EU citizens is £15,500	Total programme, non-EU students; fee for EU citizens is £15,500
Accommodation costs (on campus, per year)	£7,500 (US$12,295)	–	–
Accommodation costs (off campus, per year)	£7,500 (US$12,295)	–	–
Financial aid available	£246,000 (US$403,279)	–	–
Type of aid available	10 half-fee scholarships on full time MBA for UK/EU applicants		
Criteria on which aid is granted	Merit	–	–

Accreditation

AMBA

Application details

	Full-time MBA	Part-time MBA Programme	Executive MBA Programme
Application deadline	September 25th	September 25th	–
Programme dates	Sep start, 12 months	Sep start, 24 months	Jan start, 24 months
Admission requirements	First degree (or relevant professional qualification deemed equivalent to a degree); at least 4 years' work experience; GMAT; TOEFL or IELTS if first language not English; 2 references; interviews are offered to applicants resident in the UK (other applicants will be considered for admission on their written application)	First degree (or relevant professional qualification deemed to be equivalent to a degree); at least 4 years' work experience; GMAT; TOEFL or IELTS if first language not English; 2 references; interviews are offered to applicants resident in the UK (other applicants will be considered for admission on their written application)	First degree (or relevant professional qualification deemed to be equivalent to a degree); at least 5 years' work experience; GMAT; TOEFL or IELTS if first language not English; 2 references; interviews are offered to applicants resident in the UK (other applicants will be considered for admission on their written application)

Executive education

Nottingham does not currently offer non-degree executive education programmes.

Student/alumni quotes

"Although [there is] a good international mix of students, a good proportion of the students during my years are not ready to engage [in] the MBA because of lack of experience and language command. I would encourage the school to control the quality of the student intake because this is vital to the reputation and interest of participants."

"It is not full of alpha males. Good male/female balance and this reflects on co-operative nature."

"Unique programme and value for money, very enthusiastic and friendly staff."

Universiteit Nyenrode—The Netherlands Business School

Address
Universiteit Nyenrode
Straatweg 25
Breukelen
The Netherlands
3621 BG

Tel:
+31 346 291 681

Fax:
+31 346 291 450

Email:
imba@nyenrode.nl

Website:
www.nyenrode.nl

Programme director:
Dr Jack van der Veen

Figures in brackets
represent rank

Ranking	Rank (out of 100) Full-time
Overall rank	98
Regional rank	38

Criteria	Rank (out of 100) Full-time
Open new career opportunities	**96**
Diversity of recruiters	100
Number in jobs three months after graduation	83
Jobs found through the careers service	85
Student assessment of careers service	76
Personal development and educational experience	**99**
Faculty quality	45
Student quality	>100
Student diversity	42
Education experience	>100
Increase in salary	**82**
Increase in salary	32
Post-MBA salary	85
Potential to network	**19**
Breadth of alumni network	81
Internationalism of alumni	8
Alumni effectiveness	27

Background

Nyenrode is the only private university in the Netherlands and was one of the first to be financed by the business community (it was founded by Shell, Unilever and Philips among others). The school retains excellent links with industry and prides itself on close student–faculty relations. In April 2004 Nyenrode and the University of Rochester (Simon) in the US ended their long-standing joint Executive MBA programme.

Facilities

The large wooded campus on the Nyenrode estate is in Breukelen on the River Vecht. It consists of several modern buildings and a 13th-century moated castle, which is mainly used for administrative offices (student access is limited to a cellar bar). Facilities are good. There are extensive amenities for MBA students, with refurbished lecture rooms, good group workrooms and first-class computer facilities. Students are encouraged to live on campus to strengthen the community atmosphere. On-campus sports and restaurant facilities are good and there is a small, well-equipped library.

	Full-time MBA
Student assessment of facilities	3.9 (95)

Faculty

Number of faculty: 41 full-time, 34 part-time, 12 visiting

	Full-time MBA
Number of faculty per student	1.6 (8)
Percentage of faculty with PhD	78 (83)
Student rating of faculty	4.0 (85)

Strengths and weaknesses

Strengths: entrepreneurship; finance; strategy

Weaknesses: administration; some weak teaching

Programme highlights

Nyenrode's 13-month International MBA programme is divided into six blocks, with the first five covering a wide-ranging and slightly idiosyncratic core (including, for example, international monetary environment and organisational dynamics). Blocks three, four and five each contain an elective choice. Personal development issues are included as core subjects. The project takes place in block six. Small-group work is mandatory. In 2004 Nyenrode introduced a two-week module, shared with part-time students, at Northwestern University's Kellogg School of Management in the US.

The two-year part-time programme is aimed at sponsored students and has a lot in common with what many schools would call an executive MBA (although Nyenrode's target student body is somewhat younger). The curriculum is broadly similar to the full-time MBA with assignments and projects carried out in students' own workplaces. The programme is divided into six two-week full-time modules. Four of these take place on the Nyenrode campus, one at Kellogg and one at the University of Stellenbosch in South Africa. Online learning and contact with classmates and faculty back up the taught modules. Soft skills training and a guest-speaker series are also covered.

Nyenrode also offers a number of specialised company MBA programmes in English and Dutch.

	Full-time MBA
Student rating of programme	4.0 (81)
Number of overseas exchange programmes	0 (93)
Number of languages on offer	0 (94)

Students

	Full-time MBA
Annual intake	39
Applicants:places	3:1
Percentage of women students	33 (41)
Percentage of foreign students	77 (32)
Average GMAT score	570 (>100)
Average number of months' work experience	60 (55)
Age range of students	25-32
Average age	29
Student rating of culture and classmates	3.9 (81)

Student profile (full time)

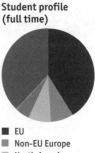

- ■ EU
- ■ Non-EU Europe
- ■ North America
- ■ Other Americas
- ■ Asia/Australasia
- ■ Middle East

Recruiters/careers service

	Full-time MBA
Number of industry sectors that recruited graduates	5 (100)
Percentage of graduates in jobs 3 months after graduation	54 (83)
Percentage of graduates finding jobs through careers services	10 (85)
Student rating of careers service	3.2 (76)
Post-MBA salary, US$	61,868 (85)
Percentage increase in salary	34 (32)
Principal recruiters of graduates	ABN AMRO, Deutsche Post, Shell

Cost

	Full-time MBA
Application fees	€80 (US$91)
Programme fees	€28,500 (US$32,386)
Comments	€
Accommodation costs (on campus, per year)	€5,500 (US$6,250)
Accommodation costs (off campus, per year)	€
Financial aid available	€
Type of aid available	Tuition waivers, scholarships
Criteria on which aid is granted	Merit, candidate profile

Accreditation

AMBA, EQUIS

Application details

	Full-time MBA
Application deadline	July 15th
Programme dates	Oct start, 13 months
Admission requirements	Bachelor's degree or equivalent; at least 2 years' work experience; GMAT; TOEFL or IELTS if first language not English; 2 references; 5 essays; interview; laptop

Executive education

Nyenrode offers open-enrolment executive education programmes but many of these are in Dutch. It also offers Dutch and English customised in-company programmes for individual managers (largely competency-based) and for whole organisations.

Student/alumni quotes

"The atmosphere is very vibrant and dynamic ... Discussions with fellow students are open and interesting and there is a feeling of entrepreneurship that permeates everything."

"Too Dutch oriented for an international MBA. There are minor opportunities for good networking of international students. The school needs to get away from its traditional Dutch programmes and invite international companies [for recruiting] ... the only major multinationals I recall visiting us were the Dutch ones. It's a great opportunity to improve the name of the school among the plethora of multinationals with European HQs in the Netherlands."

"The size of the programme and its intensity brings out the best and the worst in everyone, and the predominance of on-campus living makes it hard to get away from. This means that interpersonal skills are honed in the most difficult and stressful of times. If you can survive this MBA you are intimidated by nothing any more."

The Ohio State University—Fisher College of Business

Ranking	Rank (out of 100) Full-time
Overall rank	24
Regional rank	19

Criteria	Rank (out of 100) Full-time
Open new career opportunities	**12**
Diversity of recruiters	1
Number in jobs three months after graduation	26
Jobs found through the careers service	15
Student assessment of careers service	27
Personal development and educational experience	**57**
Faculty quality	36
Student quality	67
Student diversity	96
Education experience	36
Increase in salary	**56**
Increase in salary	55
Post-MBA salary	49
Potential to network	**74**
Breadth of alumni network	34
Internationalism of alumni	96
Alumni effectiveness	71

Address
2100 Neil Avenue
Columbus, OH
US
43210-1144

Tel:
+1 614 292 8022

Fax:
–

Email:
fishergrad@cob.osu.
edu

Website:
www.fisher.osu.edu

Programme director:
Karen Hopper Wruck

Figures in brackets
represent rank

Background

Fisher College of Business was founded in the 1920s and expanded dramatically during the 1990s under Joseph Alutto, the current dean, following a major financial gift from industrialist Max M Fisher in 1993 (when the school also adopted its present name). The college has narrowed the focus of its programmes to promote higher academic quality and added over 60 new faculty. The school is recognised in the US as being excellent value for money. It is fairly small by US standards, with an intake of 125 full-time students.

Fisher has good links with industry and plenty of executives visit the campus. In a regular series, small groups of students have lunch with visiting executives. The school is two miles from the downtown area of Columbus, which is home to many regional and national corporate headquarters and notable for some of the high-tech companies based there. There is an innovative first-year executive mentoring scheme for women, minority and foreign students.

Facilities

The Fisher campus is made up of five academic buildings and an executive residence. Fisher Hall contains offices for faculty, graduate associates, administration and academic departments, as well as the college's research groups. MBA students attend classes in Gerlach Hall, which includes classrooms, computer labs, seminar and breakout rooms, an investment management laboratory, a student lounge and the careers services centre. On-campus accommodation is available but most students live in Columbus, where housing is plentiful and reasonably priced.

	Full-time MBA
Student assessment of facilities	4.5 (14)

Faculty

Number of faculty: 102 full-time, 20 part-time, 4 visiting

	Full-time MBA	Part-time MBA Program	Executive MBA
Number of faculty per student	0.9 (52)	0.9	3.5
Percentage of faculty with PhD	90 (58)	90	90
Student rating of faculty	4.6 (24)	–	–

Strengths and weaknesses

Strengths: finance; marketing; operations and strategy

Weakness: elective choice

Programme highlights

The Fisher MBA starts with the "Super September Start-Up", a mandatory orientation programme that includes team-building exercises, case analyses, plant visits, simulations and social events, as well as a community service project. The main programme consists of core courses in the first year and electives (four per quarter) in the second. These are grouped into a major area of concentration and an optional minor or a series of free electives. Group work is heavily emphasised and team skills workshops run throughout the first year. During the fall and winter quarters, small student teams carry out in-company consulting projects. The majors offered are corporate financial management, investment management, marketing management, operations and logistics, consulting, and interdisciplinary studies. An interesting feature is that students can complete the first year at Fisher, join the US Peace Corps for two years, and then return to a guaranteed place at the school to finish their MBA.

The part-time MBA is similar but not identical to the full-time version. (There are no majors, for example.) The programme is taught over eight quarters, with two core courses covered in each of the first five quarters and electives in the remaining three. Students can attend core courses two evenings a week (6–10 pm), but this can be varied to extend the time taken to complete the degree. The core includes a two-course sequence in strategy formulation and implementation to analyse the role of top management. Elective courses (five are required but students can take more) are taught at varying times, including during the day. Electives are offered in accounting, information systems management, finance, management sciences, marketing, logistics and human resources management. Student teams also work on in-company consultancy-like projects and there are regular guest-speaker seminars.

Fisher's Executive MBA can be completed in 18 months with three days of classes each month (Thursday, Friday and Saturday, 8 am–5 pm). The programme starts in January. Between classes participants have access to lecture notes, course content exercises and tests, and can contact colleagues and professors through web-based online news and chat rooms. The programme is modular: modules 1–3 cover foundation courses, and modules 4–6 integrate these to provide an overall business perspective.

	Full-time MBA	Part-time MBA Program	Executive MBA
Student rating of programme	4.4 (37)	–	–
Number of overseas exchange programmes	38 (54)	–	–
Number of languages on offer	3 (60)	–	–

Student profile (full time)

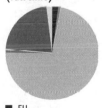

- ■ EU
- ■ Non-EU Europe
- ▨ North America
- ■ Other Americas
- ■ Asia/Australasia
- ▨ Middle East

Students

	Full-time MBA	Part-time MBA Program	Executive MBA
Annual intake	125	135	36
Applicants:places	6:1	2:1	2:1
Percentage of women students	25 (56)	21	25
Percentage of foreign students	26 (>100)	n/a	n/a
Average GMAT score	670 (37)	629	n/a
Average number of months' work experience	51 (88)	67.2	156
Age range of students	23-32	29-34	29-48
Average age	27	29	36
Student rating of culture and classmates	4.2 (57)	–	–

Recruiters/careers service

	Full-time MBA	Part-time MBA Program	Executive MBA
Number of industry sectors that recruited graduates	8 (1)	–	–
Percentage of graduates in jobs 3 months after graduation	88 (26)	–	–
Percentage of graduates finding jobs through careers services	72 (15)	–	–
Student rating of careers service	3.8 (27)	–	–
Post-MBA salary, US$	75,985 (49)	–	–
Percentage increase in salary	43 (55)	–	–
Principal recruiters of graduates	Nationwide, Abbott, Ford Motor Company		

Cost

	Full-time MBA	Part-time MBA Program	Executive MBA
Application fees	US$40	US$40	US$200
Programme fees	US$24,846	US$14,544	US$58,000
Comments	Fee for Ohio students is US$13,365	–	–
Accommodation costs (on campus, per year)	US$5,736	–	–
Accommodation costs (off campus, per year)	US$7,200	–	–
Financial aid available	US$1,118,205	–	–
Type of aid available	Scholarships, assistantships, fellowships	–	–
Criteria on which aid is granted	Merit	–	–

Accreditation

AACSB International

Application details

	Full-time MBA	Part-time MBA Program	Executive MBA
Application deadline	April 30th	April 1st	September 17th
Programme dates	Sep start, 21 months	Jun start, 48 months	Jan start, 18 months
Admission requirements	Baccalaureate or professional degree; TOEFL if first language not English; 3 references; 2 essays; interview; laptop	Baccalaureate or professional degree; TOEFL if first language not English; 3 references; 3 essays; interview	First degree; at least 7 years' work experience; TOEFL if first language not English; references; essay; interview

Executive education

Fisher offers open-enrolment executive programmes in accounting and finance, general management, logistics and distribution, marketing and sales, management information systems, and operations and supply chain management. It also offers customised programmes in wide range of functional and soft skills areas.

Student/alumni quotes

"If there is an uncut gem among the top MBA programmes in the US, it is Fisher. The faculty was top-notch and the material covered relevant to everyday business. The Graduate Programs Office is very responsive to student needs."

"By forcing students to select and complete a 'Major' students are limited regarding the time available for free electives beyond their area of study. Our school offers many neat electives and sometimes it's just not possible to fit everything in."

"Small, intimate programme; guaranteed faculty and administrative attention; chance to shine."

The Open University Business School

Address
Michael Young
Building
Walton Hall
Milton Keynes
UK
MK43 0XA

Tel:
+44 8700 100 311

Email:
oubs-
ilgen@open.ac.uk

Website:
oubs.open.ac.uk

Programme director:
Keith Dixon

Figures in brackets
represent rank

Ranking	Rank (out of 100) Full-time
Overall rank	n/a
Regional rank	n/a

Background

The Open University Business School (OUBS), founded in 1983, now has over 13,000 MBA graduates. With over 30,000 managers a year signing up for its courses, it is Europe's largest business school. The OUBS is a faculty of the Open University (OU), a far-sighted UK government initiative of the late 1960s to allow anyone, irrespective of qualifications or lack of them, to study for a degree through a mixture of distance learning, summer-school residential modules, BBC radio and TV programmes, and now, increasingly, the Internet.

The OUBS offers a similar mix of modular, multimedia distance learning, local tutorials, short residential blocks, local student self-help groups and electronic conferencing. It also has a large base of corporate clients that have sponsored students on courses or use OUBS material in their own in-house training. Like other university-linked business schools, the OUBS operates with a strong research base and a small number of doctoral students on the large (though student-less) OU campus in Milton Keynes. It has a strong student base in Europe, Africa and Asia. Overall, the OUBS has students in 44 countries outside the UK.

Facilities

The school has no student facilities of its own but uses public and private management schools, as well as hotels and conference centres, to provide meeting places for tutorials and residential schools. Students need regular and ready access to a PC, modem and CD player.

Faculty

Number of faculty: 60 full-time, 350 part-time, 3 visiting

	Distance learning MBA
Number of faculty per student	0.03
Percentage of faculty with PhD	40
Student rating of faculty	–

Strengths and weaknesses

Strengths: creativity; human resource management; financial strategy

Programme highlights

The OUBS is a long-standing and experienced player in the distance-learning market. The MBA is available via open access, which allows students to enter the course without any previous qualifications. Graduates follow an accelerated track.

Open-access students must first attain the OUBS Professional Certificate and Professional Diploma in Management, which count as Stage I of the open-access MBA. Graduates join with a single course, fundamentals of senior management, which covers the main functional areas of business; those with a business first degree take managing performance and change, a course from the Professional Diploma in Management. Stage II of the MBA focuses on strategy, involving a required strategy course and two electives. (A second required course is to be added in 2005.) Students usually study two courses a year. Most courses involve project work in students' own organisations.

The certificate–diploma–MBA route (the open-access route) may take five years to complete. Graduate entry allows the MBA to be completed in three years. Students who have studied the foundation courses of an MBA elsewhere or who have other relevant qualifications may be allowed to go straight into Stage II. Some credit transfers may be available, but this must be discussed with OUBS regional offices.

The OUBS limits the number of courses students can take in any year, but study time is likely to be 8–16 hours a week with additional time for tutor and self-help groups, day schools and residential weekends.

	Distance learning MBA
Student rating of programme	–
Number of overseas exchange programmes	–
Number of languages on offer	–

Students

	Distance learning MBA
Annual intake	7,800
Applicants:places	1:1
Percentage of women students	40
Percentage of foreign students	21
Average GMAT score	n/a
Average number of months' work experience	144
Age range of students	26-55
Average age	36
Student rating of culture and classmates	–

Student profile (full time)

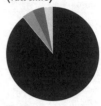

- ■ EU
- ■ Non-EU Europe
- ■ North America
- ■ Other Americas
- ■ Asia/Australasia
- ■ Middle East

Recruiters/careers service

	Distance learning MBA
Number of industry sectors that recruited graduates	–
Percentage of graduates in jobs 3 months after graduation	–
Percentage of graduates finding jobs through careers services	–
Student rating of careers service	–
Post-MBA salary, US$	–
Percentage increase in salary	–
Principal recruiters of graduates	–

Cost

	Distance learning MBA
Application fees	None
Programme fees	£2,500 (US$4,098)
Comments	Average per year assuming a 2-year completion schedule
Accommodation costs (on campus, per year)	–
Accommodation costs (off campus, per year)	–
Financial aid available	–
Type of aid available	–
Criteria on which aid is granted	–

Accreditation

AMBA, EQUIS

Application details

	Distance learning MBA
Application deadline	Rolling admissions
Programme dates	May start, 30 months
Admission requirements	At least 3 years' work experience

Executive education

The OUBS does not offer executive education courses as such but elements of the MBA programme can be studied as standalone courses.

University of Otago—School of Business

Address
School of Business
University of Otago
PO Box 56
Dunedin
New Zealand
9001

Tel:
+64 3 479 8640

Fax:
+ 64 3 479 8045

Email:
mbainfo@business.
otago.ac.nz

Website:
www.otagomba.co.nz

Programme director:
Garry Heaton

Figures in brackets
represent rank

Ranking	Rank (out of 100) Full-Time
Overall rank	n/a
Regional rank	n/a

Background

Otago University dates back to 1869 and business education started 1912. Originally restricted to accounting, the School of Business now teaches business law, economics, finance, information science, management, marketing management, quantitative methods and tourism. It is a full-range school, teaching undergraduate, postgraduate and executive education programmes. There is a strong emphasis on experiential learning and group work.

Facilities

Although the main campus is Victorian, the business school is housed in a separate, modern building. Facilities are good and the full-time MBA programme has its own dedicated space including two purpose-built, fully equipped and networked lecture theatres, several small group teaching rooms and student group-study rooms, and computer labs. The campus is close to the business district of Dunedin, a small university town set up by Scottish settlers in the middle of the 19th century, in attractive countryside close to the Southern Alps and lakes.

On-campus accommodation is not recommended for graduate students as it is geared to undergraduates, but rented housing close to the campus in Dunedin is easy to find and reasonably priced.

	Full-time MBA
Student assessment of facilities	n/a (n/a)

Faculty

Number of faculty: 140 full-time, 21 part-time, 18 visiting

	Full-time MBA
Number of faculty per student	9 (n/a)
Percentage of faculty with PhD	51 (n/a)
Student rating of faculty	n/a (n/a)

Strengths and weaknesses

Strengths: economics; tourism; marketing

Weaknesses: lack of integration with university; remote location

Programme highlights

The Otago full-time MBA programme lasts 16 months: 12 months of taught courses followed by a three-month consulting project and research essay. It is divided into five modules (including the project) and emphasises the process and experience of learning, using small groups. There are no electives as such but plenty of integrative courses. The programme stresses critical analysis and effective argument. There is a lot of case work, but teaching is not done exclusively by this method. Business leaders are involved throughout the programme as both teachers and mentors.

Students are expected to be competent in basic accounting, basic maths and personal computing before commencing the programme. Those who are not may be required to attend pre-programme preparatory courses. Most students have considerable work experience and see the MBA as a way of broadening from functional to general management. The small intake is divided into assigned study groups or syndicates, designed to reflect diversity, which are rotated each term.

The two-year Executive MBA run at Otago's Auckland campus is currently suspended.

University of Otago—School of Business

	Full-time MBA
Student rating of programme	n/a (n/a)
Number of overseas exchange programmes	5 (n/a)
Number of languages on offer	0 (n/a)

Students

	Full-time MBA
Annual intake	17
Applicants:places	2:1
Percentage of women students	29 (n/a)
Percentage of foreign students	76 (n/a)
Average GMAT score	580 (n/a)
Average number of months' work experience	72 (n/a)
Age range of students	25-36
Average age	28
Student rating of culture and classmates	n/a (n/a)

Student profile (full time)

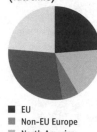

- ■ EU
- ■ Non-EU Europe
- ■ North America
- ■ Other Americas
- ■ Asia/Australasia
- ■ Middle East

Recruiters/careers service

	Full-time MBA
Number of industry sectors that recruited graduates	6 (n/a)
Percentage of graduates in jobs 3 months after graduation	76 (n/a)
Percentage of graduates finding jobs through careers services	32 (n/a)
Student rating of careers service	n/a (n/a)
Post-MBA salary, US$	n/a (n/a)
Percentage increase in salary	n/a (n/a)
Principal recruiters of graduates	Fonterra

Cost

	Full-time MBA
Application fees	US$100
Programme fees	US$25,500
Comments	Total programme, international students. Covers tuition, texts and teaching materials plus some additional resource materials. Fee for domestic students is NZ$22,500
Accommodation costs (on campus, per year)	NZ$9,000 (US$5,233)
Accommodation costs (off campus, per year)	NZ$7,800 (US$4,535)
Financial aid available	None
Type of aid available	n/a
Criteria on which aid is granted	n/a

Accreditation

None

Application details

	Full-time MBA
Application deadline	July 1st (international students); August 1st (domestic students)
Programme dates	Sep start, 16 months
Admission requirements	First degree or equivalent professional qualification; at least 3 years' work experience; GMAT; TOEFL or IELTS if first language not English; 2 references; 5 essays; interview; laptop; leadership potential

Executive education

Otago offers open-enrolment executive education courses in the following areas: corporate governance; general management; human capital; competitive strategy; leadership; corporate entrepreneurship; marketing management; financial decision-making; and professional practice
development. The general management programme is the foundation for the Certificate of Business
Administration (CBA). The school does not currently offer customised in-company programmes.

Student/alumni quotes

*"The atmosphere here is fantastic—welcoming, generous, caring, fair and challenging—all at the same
time. Having the flexibility to consider student needs through a smaller programme has clearly enabled
this university to offer something truly unique."*

*"Great for personal development. However, don't expect it to deliver much in terms of career move,
especially in New Zealand."*

*"What I liked about it so much is that there is a real emphasis on personal growth and reflecting on
one's own strengths and weaknesses; this is crucial in terms of leadership. I would strongly recommend
the course to anyone. It is also in one of the most beautiful places in the world, if you have time to look
around, that is; it is a very demanding course and you can't get away with things because of the small
class size."*

University of Oxford—Saïd Business School

Ranking	Rank (out of 100) Full-time
Overall rank	40
Regional rank	14

Criteria	Rank (out of 100) Full-time
Open new career opportunities	**66**
Diversity of recruiters	1
Number in jobs three months after graduation	82
Jobs found through the careers service	82
Student assessment of careers service	52
Personal development and educational experience	**40**
Faculty quality	74
Student quality	11
Student diversity	23
Education experience	74
Increase in salary	**10**
Increase in salary	82
Post-MBA salary	6
Potential to network	**59**
Breadth of alumni network	>100
Internationalism of alumni	25
Alumni effectiveness	45

Address
Park End Street
Oxford
Oxfordshire
UK
OX1 1HP

Tel:
+44 1865 288 852

Fax:
+44 1865 288 850

Email:
enquiries@sbs.ox.ac.uk

Website:
www.sbs.ox.ac.uk

Programme director:
Roy Westbrook

Figures in brackets represent rank

Background

Saïd Business School (named after Wafic Saïd, who donated £20m to the school) is growing rapidly, now taking in over 150 students from all over the world for its MBA and also hosting an active undergraduate and doctoral series of courses. The Oxford "brand" is a huge attraction, particularly in North America. The school is closely integrated with the university and draws on its resources, although it also has its own faculty. The programme is highly international, in terms of both the students and the programme content. MBA students become members of one of Oxford's many colleges, which provide accommodation, meals, sports and social facilities. The school has a dedicated MBA careers service, which is also a subsidiary of the university careers service.

Facilities

Facilities at the school's £25m home near Oxford railway station are lavish, with four "case" lecture theatres, a 300-seat lecture theatre, a 300-seat open-air amphitheatre, seminar and project rooms, a two-floor library, careers management centre, common room, bar, restaurant, and faculty and administration offices. In the Oxford tradition, there are lots of open spaces, cloistered walkways and a large internal courtyard, all designed to foster informal interaction.

	Full-time MBA
Student assessment of facilities	4.5 (18)

Faculty

Number of faculty: 40 full-time, 0 part-time, 0 visiting

	Full-time MBA	Executive MBA
Number of faculty per student	0.2 (94)	1.3
Percentage of faculty with PhD	90 (57)	90
Student rating of faculty	4.2 (55)	–

Strengths and weaknesses

Strengths: finance; entrepreneurship

Weakness: elective choice

Programme highlights

The MBA at Saïd is in the one-year European tradition, mixing core courses, electives and projects with a strong international emphasis. The fairly typical core is covered in the first two ten-week terms. Two electives are taken in the second term and six in the third. Personal and group development, careers and computer workshops and a guest-speaker series run throughout the first two terms. There are two projects: an entrepreneurial new business development project (either working on students' own ideas or with outside entrepreneurs) in the spring; and a major two-month consultancy project in the summer (often carried out outside the UK). After this students return for a final two-week session back at Oxford for project presentations and exams. The school follows the Oxford tradition of small group tutorials, and there is also a good deal of other group working.

Saïd launched its Executive MBA in January 2004. The programme consists of 14 one-week residential modules over 21 months and closely mirrors the full-time programme, with 11 core courses, six electives, an entrepreneurial project and a consultancy-style project.

	Full-time MBA	Executive MBA
Student rating of programme	4.3 (36)	–
Number of overseas exchange programmes	0 (93)	–
Number of languages on offer	0 (94)	–

**Student profile
(full time)**

■ EU
■ Non-EU Europe
■ North America
■ Other Americas
■ Asia/Australasia
■ Middle East

Students

	Full-time MBA	Executive MBA
Annual intake	167	31
Applicants:places	4:1	1:1
Percentage of women students	21 (>100)	10
Percentage of foreign students	87 (13)	n/a
Average GMAT score	692 (16)	620
Average number of months' work experience	72 (41)	168
Age range of students	25-34	24-58
Average age	29	37
Student rating of culture and classmates	4.6 (22)	–

Recruiters/careers service

	Full-time MBA	Executive MBA
Number of industry sectors that recruited graduates	8 (1)	–
Percentage of graduates in jobs 3 months after graduation	76 (82)	–
Percentage of graduates finding jobs through careers services	27 (82)	–
Student rating of careers service	3.4 (52)	–
Post-MBA salary, US$	103,279 (6)	–
Percentage increase in salary	43 (82)	–
Principal recruiters of graduates	McKinnsey & Co, Johnson & Johnson, Microsoft	

Cost

	Full-time MBA	Executive MBA
Application fees	£120 (US$197)	£120 (US$197)
Programme fees	£23,000 (US$37,705)	£37,000 (US$60,656)
Comments	Plus an additional college fee of approximately £2,500	Total programme; can be paid in two instalments
Accommodation costs (on campus, per year)	£3,000 (US$4,918)	–
Accommodation costs (off campus, per year)	£5,000 (US$8,197)	–
Financial aid available	£46,000 (US$75,410)	–
Type of aid available	SBS Scholarships	–
Criteria on which aid is granted	Prior academic performance, breadth and depth of work experience, interpersonal skills	–

Accreditation

AMBA

Application details

	Full-time MBA	Executive MBA
Application deadline	May 27th	November 16th
Programme dates	Oct start, 12 months	Jan start, 21 months
Admission requirements	First degree; at least 2 years' work experience; TOEFL if first language not English; 2 references; 2 essays; interview; laptop	First degree; at least 5 years' work experience; TOEFL if first language not English; 2 references; 5 essays; interview

Executive education

Executive education is run through Oxford Executive Education (OEE)—an independent company set up by the university that pools resources from Saïd and Templeton College—which was previously the centre for executive education. Open-enrolment programmes include the four-week flagship Oxford Advanced Management Programme and others of varying length covering leadership, finance, consulting and coaching, negotiation, scenarios, competing through people and, somewhat oddly, global pension reform. OEE also offers customised in-company programmes.

Student/alumni quotes

"The Oxford brand name carries as much or more weight in the US as any other international business school. Although the school is young (1996 start), the quality of students is excellent. The international range of students and professors is unparalleled. I would strongly recommend the programme to an American looking for a solid international experience. The class is a good mix of Asian, European and North American, with 44 countries represented this year. This exposure in the Oxford environment is worth as much as any course work."

"It pays a price for newness. It needs to be more independent from the university, which on the other hand is another great strength. The balance needs to be tuned."

"I have been amazed at the quality of people who have come in to speak to us. CEOs of so many companies in so many industries, leading economists, politicians and industry observers."

Pennsylvania State University—Smeal College of Business

Address
The Pennsylvania
State University
The Mary Jean and
Frank P. Smeal
College of Business
Administration
MBA Program, 106
Business
Administration
Building
University Park, PA
US
16802-3000

Tel:
+1 814 863 0448

Fax:
+1 814 865 7064

Email:
smealmba@psu.edu

Website:
www.smeal.psu.edu/
mba

Programme director:
F. Robert Wheeler III

Figures in brackets
represent rank

Ranking	Rank (out of 100) Full-time
Overall rank	40
Regional rank	32

Criteria	Rank (out of 100) Full-time
Open new career opportunities	**46**
Diversity of recruiters	n/a
Number in jobs three months after graduation	59
Jobs found through the careers service	29
Student assessment of careers service	100
Personal development and educational experience	**95**
Faculty quality	37
Student quality	70
Student diversity	>100
Education experience	>100
Increase in salary	**30**
Increase in salary	30
Post-MBA salary	44
Potential to network	**33**
Breadth of alumni network	46
Internationalism of alumni	82
Alumni effectiveness	61

Background

Smeal College of Business may not be well known outside the US, but it is a strong, well-respected institution. It offers undergraduate, masters and doctoral programmes and has a good research base, excellent links with business and good faculty, all promoted by Judy Olian, its energetic dean. The MBA programme is small by US standards and is also reckoned to be very good value for money. It claims one of the lowest student:faculty ratios in the US. Even so, Smeal's alumni network is large at over 52,000. Students are enthusiastic about the commitment of alumni and about the school in general.

Facilities

A new building is being constructed for the business school. Scheduled to open in summer 2005, this will be the largest academic facility at Penn State, bringing together students, faculty departments, research centres and staff under one roof for the first time.

	Full-time MBA
Student assessment of facilities	4.3 (70)

Faculty

Number of faculty: 89 full-time, 0 part-time, 0 visiting

	Full-time MBA	Executive MBA Program
Number of faculty per student	0.9 (48)	4.7
Percentage of faculty with PhD	100 (4)	100
Student rating of faculty	4.2 (81)	–

Strengths and weaknesses

Strengths: finance; supply chain management; marketing

Weaknesses: careers services; location

Programme highlights

Smeal's full-time two-year MBA begins with a traditional core curriculum. Students then have the option of six areas of expertise, or "portfolios" (as the school calls them): corporate financial analysis and planning, entrepreneurship, investment management and portfolio analysis, product and market development, strategic management and consulting, and supply chain management. The scheduling is somewhat unusual, based on a "7–1–7" modular format. Each semester is divided into three periods consisting of seven weeks, one week and seven weeks, with different courses being offered in each module. The first set of courses is taught in the first seven-week session; this is followed by a one-week immersion course (usually set in a real business environment); then there is a second a set of courses for another seven weeks. This approach is used in all semesters of both years. Each seven-week session is referred to as modules I–VII. Students study core subjects in modules I–III and part of module IV, which is also used as a lead-in to specialisations. Exchange places are available only during the summer.

Smeal's Executive MBA is based on the full-time version. The programme is divided into four 15-week segments over 22 months. Each of the first three segments contains a five-day residence at Penn State's University Park Campus. The final segment includes an international study trip. Classes meet on alternating weekends (Friday overnight to Saturday) at the Gregg Conference Center in Bryn Mawr, Pennsylvania. The programme is based on four themes: communications, community, customisation and convergence.

	Full-time MBA	Executive MBA Program
Student rating of programme	3.9 (>100)	–
Number of overseas exchange programmes	3 (89)	–
Number of languages on offer	0 (93)	–

Students

	Full-time MBA	Executive MBA Program
Annual intake	103	19
Applicants:places	6:1	25:1
Percentage of women students	29 (61)	6
Percentage of foreign students	34 (83)	n/a
Average GMAT score	653 (50)	571
Average number of months' work experience	60 (72)	115
Age range of students	24-33	28-37
Average age	28	33
Student rating of culture and classmates	3.9 (>100)	–

Student profile (full time)

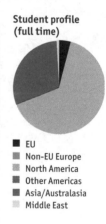

- ■ EU
- ■ Non-EU Europe
- ▨ North America
- ■ Other Americas
- ■ Asia/Australasia
- ▥ Middle East

Recruiters/careers service

	Full-time MBA	Executive MBA Program
Number of industry sectors that recruited graduates	n/a (n/a)	–
Percentage of graduates in jobs 3 months after graduation	74 (59)	–
Percentage of graduates finding jobs through careers services	61 (29)	–
Student rating of careers service	3.3 (100)	–
Post-MBA salary, US$	84,857 (44)	–
Percentage increase in salary	74 (30)	
Principal recruiters of graduates	PricewaterhouseCoopers, General Electric, IBM	

Cost

	Full-time MBA	Executive MBA Program
Application fees	–	US$60
Programme fees	US$24,796	US$82,000
Comments	Per year. Fee for Pennsylvania students is US$14,500	–
Accommodation costs (on campus, per year)	US$7,650	–
Accommodation costs (off campus, per year)		–
Financial aid available	Not disclosed	–
Type of aid available	Graduate assistantships, loans, scholarships	–
Criteria on which aid is granted	Academic and professional qualifications	–

Accreditation

AACSB International

Application details

	Full-time MBA	Executive MBA Program
Application deadline	April 15th	June 15th
Programme dates	Jan start, 21 months	Aug start, 22 months
Admission requirements	First degree (US baccalaureate or 4-year equivalent); at least 2 years' work experience; TOEFL if first language not English (minimum requirement 250, computer-based; 600 paper-based); 2 references; 3 essays; interview; laptop	First degree (US baccalaureate or 4-year equivalent); at least 4 years' work experience; TOEFL if first language not English (minimum requirement 250, computer-based; 600 paper-based); 2 references; 4 essays; interview

Executive education

Smeal offers open-enrolment executive education programmes in areas such as finance and accounting, general management, specific industries, marketing, supply chain and operational efficiency, as well as "hot topic" workshops. It also offers customised in-company programmes.

Student/alumni quotes

"Anyone looking for a full time MBA programme on the east coast would make a mistake if they did not take a look at PSU, especially if they are looking for marketing, finance or supply chain expertise."

"The geographic location is a slight disadvantage related to corporate recruitment."

"There are a lot of engineers here and you have to be comfortable with quantitative analysis; but [the school is] also building more activities and programmes to learn more of the soft skills of business. Penn State faculty and administration are very open-minded, transparent and responsive."

University of Pennsylvania—Wharton School

Ranking	Rank (out of 100) Full-time
Overall rank	8
Regional rank	7

Criteria	Rank (out of 100) Full-time
Open new career opportunities	**18**
Diversity of recruiters	30
Number in jobs three months after graduation	33
Jobs found through the careers service	34
Student assessment of careers service	21
Personal development and educational experience	**1**
Faculty quality	11
Student quality	4
Student diversity	19
Education experience	12
Increase in salary	**44**
Increase in salary	85
Post-MBA salary	34
Potential to network	**18**
Breadth of alumni network	8
Internationalism of alumni	64
Alumni effectiveness	23

Address
420 Jon M. Huntsman Hall
3730 Walnut Street
Philadelphia, PA
US
19104-6430

Tel:
+1 215 898 7640

Fax:
+1 215 898 1883

Email:
mba.admissions@
wharton.upenn.edu

Website:
www.wharton.upenn.
edu/mba

Programme director:
Rosemaria Martinelli

Figures in brackets
represent rank

Background

Founded in 1881 as one of the graduate schools of the University of Pennsylvania, Wharton was the first collegiate school of business in the world. Although it has a deserved reputation as a financial powerhouse, the school offers a huge range of subject areas (there are over 200 MBA elective courses) and has a highly international approach. There is a good mix of nationalities and most students travel widely during their MBA programme. Wharton is a big school, with around 200 full-time faculty in 11 academic departments teaching business to over 1,500 undergraduates and MBA students and approximately 7,500 executives. The large intake means that the school has some 77,000 alumni in 139 countries.

Facilities

Facilities are generally good and the university campus is pleasant. MBA students have access to the university computer network and several well-equipped computer labs. The university libraries contain 3.6m volumes, 200,000 of them specific to business. The MBA programme is housed in a complex of five buildings. Some facilities are shared with undergraduate and PhD programmes, as well as executive education and the Executive MBA programme. Huntsman Hall, a new US$120m, 320,000 sq ft building, opened in summer 2002. It provides classroom and academic support services for undergraduates and MBA students and contains 48 classrooms, 57 group-study rooms, four teaching labs, two study lounges and two social lounges. On-campus housing is available and there are good sports and recreational amenities.

	Full-time MBA
Student assessment of facilities	4.4 (27)

Faculty

Number of faculty: 212 full-time, 95 part-time, 8 visiting

	Full-time MBA	Wharton MBA Program for Executives
Number of faculty per student	0.3 (>100)	1.5
Percentage of faculty with PhD	100 (10)	100
Student rating of faculty	4.7 (2)	–

Strengths and weaknesses

Strengths: finance and accounting; strategic management and marketing; entrepreneurship

Programme highlights

The Wharton two-year full-time MBA begins with an intensive four-week pre-programme session designed to bring students to an equal level in areas such as accounting, microeconomics and statistics. It includes courses in the humanities and business history and seminars in areas such as communications and career management. The main programme is divided into a first year of fairly straightforward core courses (including courses in ethics, leadership and communications skills that cannot be waived) and a second year of electives. Within the core, students work individually and in small teams in the Foundations of Leadership course to examine areas such as personal development, communications and ethics, and on 12-week project. The Global Immersion Program is an optional four-week overseas study tour.

In the second year students choose at least one major from those on offer. They can take dual majors or design their own. They also undertake a project related to their field of interest. Students are allocated to cohorts of around 60, who take classes together, and into smaller teams for group work.

The Wharton Executive MBA (WEMBA) has more or less the same curriculum, the same faculty and confers the same degree as the full-time programme. Classes meet on campus on alternate Fridays and Saturdays for the two years of the programme; in the second year there are some three-day sessions and a one-week international study tour. Each year is divided into three terms of approximately 16 weeks, or eight WEMBA weekends. The first year is essentially the core and most of the second year is devoted to electives. Leadership and personal skills development are covered through a course that emphasises effective teamwork and self-learning. This programme is also offered at Wharton's San Francisco campus.

	Full-time MBA	Wharton MBA Program for Executives
Student rating of programme	4.7 (1)	–
Number of overseas exchange programmes	12 (82)	–
Number of languages on offer	>5 (29)	–

Student profile (full time)

- ■ EU
- ■ Non-EU Europe
- ■ North America
- ■ Other Americas
- ■ Asia/Australasia
- ■ Middle East
- ■ Other

Students

	Full-time MBA	Wharton MBA Program for Executives
Annual intake	892	204
Applicants:places	9:1	5:1
Percentage of women students	33 (33)	16
Percentage of foreign students	36 (78)	n/a
Average GMAT score	713 (2)	700
Average number of months' work experience	73 (32)	120
Age range of students	26-32	27-40
Average age	28	33
Student rating of culture and classmates	4.8 (3)	–

Recruiters/careers service

	Full-time MBA	Wharton MBA Program for Executives
Number of industry sectors that recruited graduates	8 (30)	–
Percentage of graduates in jobs 3 months after graduation	85 (33)	–
Percentage of graduates finding jobs through careers services	58.8 (34)	–
Student rating of careers service	3.9 (21)	–
Post-MBA salary, US$	85,000 (34)	–
Percentage increase in salary	34 (85)	–
Principal recruiters of graduates	McKinsey & Company, Bain & Company, Boston Consulting Group	

Cost

	Full-time MBA	Wharton MBA Program for Executives
Application fees	US$200	US$150
Programme fees	US$35,203	US$122,000
Comments	–	Total programme; cost includes tuition, books, materials, fees, room and board
Accommodation costs (on campus, per year)	US$14,200	–
Accommodation costs (off campus, per year)	US$14,200	–
Financial aid available	US$64,338	–
Type of aid available	Fellowships, grants, loans	–
Criteria on which aid is granted	Merit & need-based	–

Accreditation

AACSB International

Application details

	Full-time MBA	Wharton MBA Program for Executives
Application deadline	March 25th	February 1st
Programme dates	Aug start, 18 months	May start, 24 months
Admission requirements	First degree; TOEFL if first language not English; 2 references; 5 essays; interview; laptop; interview by invitation only	At least 5 years' work experience (if applicant does not have minimum work/management experience, they should be sponsored fully by employer); 2 references; 3 essays; letter of sponsorship from employer

Executive education

Wharton offers a range of open-enrolment executive education programmes in areas such as corporate governance, general management, leadership, strategy, finance and marketing. It also offers industry-specific and customised in-company programmes.

University of Pittsburgh—Joseph M Katz Graduate School of Business

Address
Joseph M. Katz
Graduate School of
Business
University of
Pittsburgh
372 Mervis Hall
Pittsburgh, PA
US
15260

Tel:
+1 412 648 1566

Fax:
+1 412 648 1552

Email:
krwilson@katz.pitt.
edu

Website:
www.katz.pitt.edu

Programme director:
Cathy Vargo

Figures in brackets
represent rank

Ranking	Rank (out of 100) Full-time
Overall rank	73
Regional rank	44

Criteria	Rank (out of 100) Full-time
Open new career opportunities	**53**
Diversity of recruiters	82
Number in jobs three months after graduation	52
Jobs found through the careers service	17
Student assessment of careers service	75
Personal development and educational experience	**93**
Faculty quality	42
Student quality	>100
Student diversity	95
Education experience	77
Increase in salary	**81**
Increase in salary	36
Post-MBA salary	83
Potential to network	**20**
Breadth of alumni network	3
Internationalism of alumni	55
Alumni effectiveness	83

Background

Katz Graduate School of Management offers a unique 11-month MBA programme that, unlike other short US programmes, requires no undergraduate business degree. Nevertheless, it ranks highly against the competition. The school is increasingly stressing the need for a solid business background and substantial work experience to applicants and has now introduced a more traditional two-year programme.

Katz has close contact with local business as Pittsburgh is a popular location for corporate headquarters, and it organises an extensive series of events for students to meet executives. Business leaders from all over the US come to the school for lectures, lunches and off-the-record chats. The school has good international connections (some elective courses involve overseas trips) and good links with industry. Scholarships are available for MBA students.

Facilities

Mervis Hall, the school's home, is a sleek glass building that has undergone a major refurbishment. There is a streamlined business library with expanded access to online databases, and Katz has a partnership with the University of Pittsburgh Library System and the Carnegie Library. There are three other business school buildings on the University of Pittsburgh campus: Alumni Hall, which houses executive education offices; Posvar Hall, which houses the school's Institute for Entrepreneurial Excellence and alumni and development offices; and Sennott Square, completed in May 2002, home of Katz's undergraduate arm, the College of Business Administration. There is no on-campus accommodation but plenty of student housing is available close by. Pittsburgh is a lively city and social life both on and off campus is good.

	Full-time MBA
Student assessment of facilities	4.3 (59)

Faculty

Number of faculty: 71 full-time, 21 part-time, 4 visiting

	Full-time MBA	Part-time MBA	Executive MBA
Number of faculty per student	0.5 (63)	0.6	2.5
Percentage of faculty with PhD	93 (33)	93	93
Student rating of faculty	4.5 (39)	–	–

Strengths and weaknesses

Strengths: finance; management information systems; marketing

Weakness: integration of alumni network

Programme highlights

The Katz one-year MBA programme lasts from August to July with just two short breaks. Students can declare a traditional MBA concentration or "major" or choose elective courses to fit a self-designed goal. About half of the total programme is made up of electives. There is also a series of professional workshops based on a student's self-evaluation in areas such as time management or communication. The school says that this programme is primarily aimed at students with a strong economics or business background and plenty of work experience. It has recently added a more traditional two-year full-time programme. This has more or less the same academic core as the one-year programme but offers more electives, a traditional summer internship and the Executive Coaching Plan, an individualised programme of professional development.

The part-time MBA is virtually identical to the full-time version and has long been an important recruiting source for the corporate offices of Pittsburgh. There are three start dates in January, April and September. Generally, students take two courses per module to complete the programme within three years. The programme runs throughout the year with fall, spring and summer trimesters of 14 weeks each. Classes are held on weekday evenings, and some may be available on Saturday.

The Executive MBA lasts 21 months. Classes meet one day a week on alternating Fridays and Saturdays (8.15 am–5.30 pm). In the second year there is a ten-day international research project. As well as required and elective courses, during their second year students take part in a series of "total immersion" activities, multiple-day courses that provide an in-depth focus. These include electives, interactive capstone courses and the annual "Global Executive Forum", in which EMBA students are integrated with their European and South American counterparts from Katz's International Executive MBA Programmes.

Katz runs an International Executive MBA in Prague, Czech Republic, and in São Paulo, Brazil. The programme consists of eight residence periods of 5–7 days every two months and one three-week session in Pittsburgh.

	Full-time MBA	Part-time MBA	Executive MBA
Student rating of programme	4.2 (50)	–	–
Number of overseas exchange programmes	0 (41)	–	–
Number of languages on offer	1 (92)	–	–

Students

	Full-time MBA	Part-time MBA	Executive MBA
Annual intake	164	164	39
Applicants:places	4:1	2:1	1:1
Percentage of women students	25 (74)	27	20
Percentage of foreign students	38 (64)	n/a	n/a
Average GMAT score	635 (68)	570	537
Average number of months' work experience	36 (>100)	66	144
Age range of students	23-49	23-49	32-36
Average age	30	30	35
Student rating of culture and classmates	4.1 (77)	–	–

Student profile (full time)

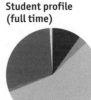

- ■ EU
- ■ Non-EU Europe
- ■ North America
- ■ Other Americas
- ■ Asia/Australasia
- ■ Middle East

Recruiters/careers service

	Full-time MBA	Part-time MBA	Executive MBA
Number of industry sectors that recruited graduates	7 (82)	–	–
Percentage of graduates in jobs 3 months after graduation	84 (52)	–	–
Percentage of graduates finding jobs through careers services	66 (17)	–	–
Student rating of careers service	3.2 (75)	–	–
Post-MBA salary, US$	64,000 (83)	–	–
Percentage increase in salary	73 (36)	–	–
Principal recruiters of graduates	Ford Motor Company, Bayer, PNC Bank		

Cost

	Full-time MBA	Part-time MBA	Executive MBA
Application fees	US$50	US$50	None
Programme fees	US$39,693	US$63,000	US$50,000
Comments	Per year. Fee for Pennsylvania students is US$24,595	Total programme. Fee for Pennsylvania students is US$24,595	Fee for US students. The programme occurs simultaneously on 3 continents and fees may vary slightly in Europe and South America.
Accommodation costs (on campus, per year)	–	–	–
Accommodation costs (off campus, per year)	US$6,000	–	–
Financial aid available	Not disclosed	–	–
Type of aid available	Scholarship, loan	–	–
Criteria on which aid is granted	Merit (for scholarship)	–	–

Accreditation
AACSB International

Application details

	Full-time MBA	Part-time MBA	Executive MBA
Application deadline	April 15th	March 1st	August
Programme dates	Aug start, 11 months	Aug start, 36 months	Mar start, 15 months
Admission requirements	US Bachelor's degree or equivalent; TOEFL if first language not English; 2 references; 2 essays; interview; laptop	US Bachelor's degree or equivalent; TOEFL if first language not English; 2 references; 2 essays	US Bachelor's degree or equivalent; at least 5 years' work experience; must be able to speak English at a high level, TOEFL may be required; 2 references; essay

Executive education

Katz runs two interesting open-enrolment executive programmes: MBA Essentials, a sort of mini-MBA lasting 11 weeks with classes meeting two evenings a week or two weeks full-time; and the International Executive Fellows Program, which allows overseas executives to spend one seven-week term, full-time, on Katz's regular MBA programme. It also offers shorter courses in areas such as creativity and innovation, decision technologies, finance, leadership, marketing, strategy and project management as well as a large portfolio of customised in-company programmes.

Student/alumni quotes

"I liked the small size of the programme and the environment is totally co-operative. The fall semester is brutal but I got the hang of it very quickly and now spring semester feels like a walk in the park, even though the effort I need to put in is essentially the same."

"Many students without any prior work experience."

"Because of the smaller class size and short academic year, electives were typically only offered once; so if you couldn't fit it in, you missed out."

Purdue University—Krannert Graduate School of Management

Address
100 S. Grant Street
Rawls Hall, Suite 2020
West Lafayette, IN
US
47907-2076

Tel:
+1 765 496 3668

Fax:
+1 765 494 9841

Email:
masters@krannert.
purdue.edu

Website:
www.krannert.purdue.
edu/programs/masters

Programme director:
Chuck Johnson

Figures in brackets
represent rank

Ranking	Rank (out of 100) Full-time
Overall rank	51
Regional rank	33

Criteria	Rank (out of 100) Full-time
Open new career opportunities	**45**
Diversity of recruiters	89
Number in jobs three months after graduation	61
Jobs found through the careers service	18
Student assessment of careers service	36
Personal development and educational experience	**78**
Faculty quality	44
Student quality	83
Student diversity	>100
Education experience	33
Increase in salary	**26**
Increase in salary	14
Post-MBA salary	51
Potential to network	**91**
Breadth of alumni network	54
Internationalism of alumni	>100
Alumni effectiveness	78

Background

Krannert Graduate School of Management was founded in 1958 and teaches undergraduate, masters and doctoral programmes. It is relatively small by North American standards and the small classes foster a good team spirit and a close relationship between students and faculty. The school's size, supportive atmosphere and low fees make it good value for money and the international content is well up to the North American average.

Facilities

The school is based in Rawls Hall, which opened in 2003. It houses classrooms, a careers centre, a multimedia-based auditorium, a reception area, student club offices and breakout rooms, distance-learning facilities and computer labs. The university has indoor and outdoor swimming pools, tennis courts and a range of sports facilities, including an 18-hole golf course. Accommodation is available both on and off campus. Off-campus rents are reasonable in the local area of Lafayette/West Lafayette, between Chicago and Indianapolis.

	Full-time MBA
Student assessment of facilities	4.5 (22)

Faculty

Number of faculty: 101 full-time, 6 part-time, 23 visiting

	Full-time MBA	Executive MBA
Number of faculty per student	0.7 (64)	2.9
Percentage of faculty with PhD	97 (16)	97
Student rating of faculty	4.3 (47)	–

Strengths and weaknesses

Strengths: operations management; corporate finance; technology

Weakness: location

Programme highlights

Krannert's two-year MBA has a largely functional core covered in the first year in four half-semester modules (although two electives are offered in the fourth module). The second year consists of three required courses and electives. A management development series, a set of Friday courses aimed at introducing students to leading-edge practices and emerging topics, runs throughout the first year. Specialisations are offered in accounting, finance, marketing, strategic management, operations management, information systems, e-business and human resource management. There are also three interdisciplinary options: general management, international management and manufacturing management.

The school also offers a one-year Master of Science in Industrial Administration (MSIA). This shares the same required core as the MBA but has fewer electives. The MSIA is completed in just 11 months (two semesters and a summer session) and includes the option of an eight-week exchange allowing study in Hannover, Germany.

The Executive Masters in Business (EMB) is effectively an executive MBA (it leads to the Master of Business Administration degree). The programme comprises six two-week residencies over 22 months coupled with Internet-supported off-campus assignments between residencies (allowing a wide geographical range of participants). The programme begins each July with an orientation session. Students enter as a cohort, taking the same set of courses together and graduating together. The final residency session is an international trip with class sessions, plant visits and guest speakers. Asia and Europe have been the sites of recent trips.

Other degree programmes include: International Master's in Management (IMM), modelled on the EMB, based on an alliance between Krannert and the Ecole Supérieure de Commerce de Rouen (ESC Rouen); Weekend EMBA, which follows the same curriculum as the EMB but takes three years to complete; Executive Master's in Business in Germany (EMBG), a collaboration between Krannert and the German International Graduate School of Management and Administration in Hannover (the students come from Europe, primarily from Germany; Executive MBA in Agribusiness (AgEMBA), designed for professionals from the food industry and agribusiness sector.

	Full-time MBA	Executive MBA
Student rating of programme	4.1 (53)	–
Number of overseas exchange programmes	60 (33)	–
Number of languages on offer	5 (49)	–

Students

	Full-time MBA	Executive MBA
Annual intake	160	45
Applicants:places	7:1	2:1
Percentage of women students	21 (>100)	14
Percentage of foreign students	38 (74)	n/a
Average GMAT score	659 (44)	600
Average number of months' work experience	49 (99)	144
Age range of students	24-34	30-40
Average age	28	35
Student rating of culture and classmates	4.0 (79)	–

Student profile (full time)

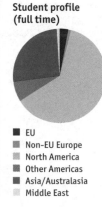

- ■ EU
- ■ Non-EU Europe
- ▨ North America
- ■ Other Americas
- ■ Asia/Australasia
- ▨ Middle East

Recruiters/careers service

	Full-time MBA	Executive MBA
Number of industry sectors that recruited graduates	6 (89)	–
Percentage of graduates in jobs 3 months after graduation	75 (61)	–
Percentage of graduates finding jobs through careers services	67 (18)	–
Student rating of careers service	3.4 (36)	–
Post-MBA salary, US$	78,120 (51)	–
Percentage increase in salary	95 (14)	–
Principal recruiters of graduates	Ford, Procter & Gamble, Guidant	

Cost

	Full-time MBA	Executive MBA
Application fees	US$55	None
Programme fees	US$24,988	US$54,000
Comments	Per year, out-of-state students	Includes books, course materials, lodging and most meals
Accommodation costs (on campus, per year)	US$3,200	–
Accommodation costs (off campus, per year)	US$5,000	–
Financial aid available	US$3,789,305	–
Type of aid available	Scholarships, assistantships, fellowships, loans	–
Criteria on which aid is granted	Merit, financial need	–

Accreditation

AACSB International

Application details

	Full-time MBA	Executive MBA
Application deadline	February 1st (international students); May 1st (US students)	June 1st
Programme dates	Aug start, 21 months	Jul start, 22 months
Admission requirements	US Bachelor's degree or equivalent; work experience; TOEFL if first language not English; 2 references; 3 essays; interview recommended and may be requested	First degree; at least 5 years' work experience; GMAT; TOEFL if first language not English; 3 references; 6 essays

Executive education

Krannert's open-enrolment executive education programmes include a series of short "mini-MBA" programmes, courses covering manufacturing and life sciences (information technology, medical device development, and clinical pharmaceutical trials) and specialised sponsored programmes. The school also offers customised in-company programmes.

Student/alumni quotes

"Krannert is a very analytical business school that demands hard work but rewards the student with a true academic experience that is immediately applicable."

"While I loved the small-town atmosphere around campus, someone who wanted a big-city atmosphere could view West Lafayette as a weakness."

"The faculty are extraordinary, the programme is great value at the current tuition rates, and there is a very strong push for diversity."

Queen's University—Queen's School of Business

Ranking	Rank (out of 100) Full-time
Overall rank	69
Regional rank	41

Criteria	Rank (out of 100) Full-time
Open new career opportunities	**76**
Diversity of recruiters	83
Number in jobs three months after graduation	89
Jobs found through the careers service	54
Student assessment of careers service	44
Personal development and educational experience	**48**
Faculty quality	40
Student quality	18
Student diversity	82
Education experience	62
Increase in salary	**97**
Increase in salary	97
Post-MBA salary	91
Potential to network	**4**
Breadth of alumni network	22
Internationalism of alumni	4
Alumni effectiveness	20

Address
143 Union St
Goodes Hall
Queen's University
Kingston, ON
Canada
K7L 3N6

Tel:
+1 613 533 2319

Fax:
+1 613 533 6978

Email:
admin@mbast.
queensu.ca

Website:
www.business.
queensu.ca/mbast

Programme director:
Dr Jeff McGill

Figures in brackets
represent rank

Background

Queen's University was founded in Kingston, Ontario, in 1842 (with a royal charter from Queen Victoria) and in 1919 launched the first commerce degree in Canada. Queen's School of Business effectively dates from 1963, when it was formed as a faculty within the university. It is a full-range school, with a strong undergraduate component and a successful doctoral programme. Teamworking is a central part of its programmes.

Facilities

The school is based in Goodes Hall, a C$25.5m, 110,000 sq ft building opened in 2002, near the heart of the university campus. MBA students have their own dedicated facilities in the building, including a student lounge.

	Full-time MBA
Student assessment of facilities	4.7 (5)

Faculty

Number of faculty: 48 full-time, 0 part-time, 0 visiting

	Full-time MBA
Number of faculty per student	0.6 (53)
Percentage of faculty with PhD	90 (60)
Student rating of faculty	4.5 (23)

Strengths and weaknesses

Strengths: new venture management; leadership; management of technology

Weakness: lack of student diversity

Programme highlights

Queen's one-year MBA aims to combine a grounding in the fundamentals of management with an emphasis on the special challenges of managing technology-driven organisations. There is a strong emphasis on careers services and teamwork. Applicants need an undergraduate degree in science or engineering.

The programme is intensive and intelligently put together, dividing into business fundamentals and functions, strategy and a final concentration. Despite the emphasis on science, concentrations are not all in science-based areas. The programme is divided into four 11-week stages, each of which begins with a one-week careers programme, separated by one-week breaks. Stages one and two essentially cover core subjects. Stage three concentrates on strategy formulation and implementation. In stage four students opt for one of four concentrations offered (strategy and management consulting, finance and investment banking, marketing management, management of operations and information technology) and either a new venture project or management consulting project.

Queen's Executive MBA is a traditional 15-month programme taught on alternate weekends (all day Friday and Saturday morning). It is offered in two versions: the "national" programme, delivered by videoconferencing to major cities across Canada; and the "Ottowa" programme, a traditional classroom programme held at Queen's facilities in downtown Ottowa. The programme is divided into what is effectively a core, covering business fundamentals, and advanced topics dealing with issues such as strategy, globalisation and leadership. There are projects in both years (one is global) and assignments that are normally carried out in participants' own organisations.

Queen's new one-year Accelerated MBA is aimed specifically at students with an undergraduate degree in business and at least two years' work experience. It combines three one-week on-campus sessions and classes (all day Sunday and Monday morning of every other week) delivered using the same online interactive video technology used in the school's national EMBA.

	Full-time MBA
Student rating of programme	4.3 (38)
Number of overseas exchange programmes	0 (93)
Number of languages on offer	0 (94)

Student profile (full time)

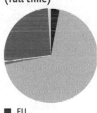

- ■ EU
- ■ Non-EU Europe
- North America
- ■ Other Americas
- ■ Asia/Australasia
- Middle East

Students

	Full-time MBA
Annual intake	74
Applicants:places	4:1
Percentage of women students	20 (>100)
Percentage of foreign students	31 (99)
Average GMAT score	684 (20)
Average number of months' work experience	72 (41)
Age range of students	24-43
Average age	31
Student rating of culture and classmates	4.6 (17)

Recruiters/careers service

	Full-time MBA
Number of industry sectors that recruited graduates	6 (83)
Percentage of graduates in jobs 3 months after graduation	69 (89)
Percentage of graduates finding jobs through careers services	55 (54)
Student rating of careers service	3.5 (44)
Post-MBA salary, US$	57,143 (91)
Percentage increase in salary	19 (97)
Principal recruiters of graduates	Bell Canada, RBC Financial Group, Eli Lilly Pharmaceuticals

Cost

	Full-time MBA
Application fees	C$100 (US$71)
Programme fees	C$51,000 (US$36,429)
Comments	Total programme
Accommodation costs (on campus, per year)	C$7,014 (US$5,010)
Accommodation costs (off campus, per year)	C$11,280 (US$8,057)
Financial aid available	Not disclosed
Type of aid available	Loan programme with Royal Bank of Canada
Criteria on which aid is granted	–

Accreditation

AACSB International, AMBA, EQUIS

Application details

	Full-time MBA
Application deadline	January 15th
Programme dates	May start, 12 months
Admission requirements	Undergraduate degree in science or engineering; at least 2 years' work experience; GMAT; TOEFL if first language not English; 3 references; essays; interview; laptop

Executive education

Queen's Executive Development Centre is one of North America's largest providers of non-degree executive education. Open-enrolment courses include the three-week Executive Program, the two-week Public Executive Program and shorter programmes in areas such as leadership, finance, strategy, IT, marketing, operations leadership, sales management and human resources. It also offers a range of customised in-company programmes.

Student/alumni quotes

"Without question [its strength is] the camaraderie developed by a team-based learning model and fostered by the small class size. The spirit and extra-curricular participation was phenomenal, especially given the magnitude of the workload imposed by classes."

"Small class size resulted in limited exposure to organised company recruiting efforts."

"The workload is absolutely tremendous, and anyone will curse it while going through it. My health and lifestyle seriously suffered, relationships were harmed. But it never stopped being worth it ... and I'm a much better, more self-reflective person for it."

University of Queensland Business School

Address
UQ Business School
Colin Clark Building
The University of
Queensland
St. Lucia Q
Australia
4072

Tel:
+61 7 3365 6179

Fax:
+61 7 3365 7582

Email:
postgrad_enquiries@
business.uq.edu.au

Website:
www.business.uq.edu.
au

Programme director:
Dr Peter Lynch

Figures in brackets
represent rank

Ranking	Rank (out of 100) Full-time
Overall rank	n/a
Regional rank	n/a

Background

The University of Queensland (UQ) Business School is part of the faculty of business, economics and law. It is a large full-range school with more than 5,000 students enrolled on undergraduate and postgraduate programmes. The school's ambition is to be a centre of excellence in business, providing quality education and leadership in research. Teaching and research are clustered into a number of functional areas (accounting and accountability, business information systems, enterprise and international business, finance, marketing, and organisation and communication), each led by a professor.

Facilities

UQ's main campus is located in the suburb of St Lucia, about 7 km from downtown Brisbane, on a picturesque 285-acre site. Facilities at the school and the university are excellent. In early 2004 the school expanded into additional premises in the Brisbane central business district, responding, it says, to demand. The MBA will now be taught at this location.

	Full-time MBA
Student assessment of facilities	n/a (n/a)

Faculty

Number of faculty: 87 full-time, 16 part-time, 11 visiting

	Full-time MBA	Part-time MBA
Number of faculty per student	1.3 (n/a)	2.2
Percentage of faculty with PhD	91 (n/a)	91
Student rating of faculty	n/a (n/a)	–

Strengths and weaknesses

Strengths: finance and accounting; marketing and international business; organisational behaviour

Weakness: some students lack work experience

Programme highlights

Not unusually for an Australian school, Queensland offers the same MBA in full time and part-time formats. The full-time programme lasts 4–5 semesters and the part-time programme 8–10 semesters. The variation in time is because two types of programme are offered: MBA and MBA (Advanced). Both programmes start with a management development workshop and conclude with a leadership workshop, and both share the same straightforward 11-course core. MBA students then choose four electives. The MBA (Advanced) programme includes either a research project and seven electives or a research thesis and five electives. Electives can be grouped into specialisations in marketing, international business, business economics, accounting and finance.

	Full-time MBA	Part-time MBA
Student rating of programme	n/a (n/a)	–
Number of overseas exchange programmes	74 (n/a)	–
Number of languages on offer	0 (n/a)	–

University of Queensland Business School

Students

	Full-time MBA	Part-time MBA
Annual intake	78 (n/a)	45
Applicants:places	4:1	4:1
Percentage of women students	33 (n/a)	33
Percentage of foreign students	62 (n/a)	n/a
Average GMAT score	n/a (n/a)	n/a
Average number of months' work experience	96 (n/a)	96
Age range of students	25-45	25-44
Average age	32	34
Student rating of culture and classmates	n/a (n/a)	–

Student profile (full time)

- ■ EU
- ■ Non-EU Europe
- ▨ North America
- ■ Other Americas
- ■ Asia/Australasia
- ▨ Middle East

Recruiters/careers service

	Full-time MBA	Part-time MBA
Number of industry sectors that recruited graduates	6 (n/a)	–
Percentage of graduates in jobs 3 months after graduation	90 (n/a)	–
Percentage of graduates finding jobs through careers services	42 (n/a)	–
Student rating of careers service	n/a (n/a)	–
Post-MBA salary, US$	54,256	–
Percentage increase in salary	43	
Principal recruiters of graduates	Telstra, KPMG, Commonwealth Bank	

Cost

	Full-time MBA	Part-time MBA
Application fees	A$50 (US$32)	A$50 (US$32)
Programme fees	A$34,400 (US$22,338)	A$34,400 (US$22,338)
Comments	Total programme	Total programme
Accommodation costs (on campus, per year)	A$10,536 (US$6,842)	–
Accommodation costs (off campus, per year)	A$6,842 (US$4,443)	–
Financial aid available	A$160,000 (US$103,896)	–
Type of aid available	Scholarships	–
Criteria on which aid is granted	Academic merit, financial need, at least 16 units completed	–

Accreditation

AACSB International

Application details

	Full-time MBA	Part-time MBA
Application deadline	January 31st	January 31st
Programme dates	Feb start, 21 months	Feb start, 34 months
Admission requirements	Approved Bachelor's degree; at least 2 years' work experience; TOEFL or IELTS if first language not English; 2 references	Approved Bachelor's degree; at least 2 years' work experience; TOEFL or IELTS if first language not English; 2 references

Executive education

Queensland offers open-enrolment seminars, short courses and executive education programmes in areas such as leadership, marketing, strategy and change, cost benefit analysis, communication, accounting and corporate governance.

Student/alumni quotes

"The part-time course fits around my work schedule and the university has recently opened a teaching centre in the middle of the city, making it more accessible. The university campus is fantastic and the facilities are excellent."

"An indicator of how the local business community values the MBA is that the classes comprise mostly international students. This is OK but it reveals that Queensland business doesn't value the MBA. Another problem is that too many of these international students have little or no business or work experience and therefore don't add a lot to the value of the classes."

"I am really enjoying the subject content. I manage a business unit in the public sector and everything we study has some relevance to my workplace."

Rice University—Jesse H Jones Graduate School of Administration

Ranking	Rank (out of 100) Full-time
Overall rank	57
Regional rank	36

Criteria	Rank (out of 100) Full-time
Open new career opportunities	**38**
Diversity of recruiters	86
Number in jobs three months after graduation	16
Jobs found through the careers service	20
Student assessment of careers service	39
Personal development and educational experience	**85**
Faculty quality	52
Student quality	96
Student diversity	70
Education experience	83
Increase in salary	**55**
Increase in salary	38
Post-MBA salary	57
Potential to network	**82**
Breadth of alumni network	>100
Internationalism of alumni	>100
Alumni effectiveness	47

Address
PO Box 2932
Houston, TX
US
77252-2932

Tel:
+1 713 348 6343

Fax:
+1 713 348 6228

Email:
ricemba@rice.edu

Website:
www.jonesgsm.rice.edu

Programme director:
George Kanatas

Figures in brackets represent rank

Background

The Jones Graduate School of Management, founded in 1974, is young by US standards. It is also quite small, enrolling about 165 students a year, so there is a good student:faculty ratio. The school is named after the late Jesse Holman Jones, a Houston business and civic leader, and is one of seven academic units of Rice University, which has around 4,000 students. It is one of the few US schools to be a devotee of action learning and experiential learning techniques. The school has close links with local Houston and Texan industry and uses a number of practising managers and executives to teach on the programme. It says it is dedicated to improving its global reputation.

Facilities

Jones is based in a US$60m building, opened in September 2002, which includes innovative class-rooms, a high-tech trading room, breakout rooms, a "cyber-commons" (where students and faculty can meet with refreshments and ports for computer and network connectivity), a careers centre and a business information centre. Students also have access to the resources and facilities of Rice University. On-campus accommodation is available but nearby housing is fairly plentiful and reasonably priced.

	Full-time MBA
Student assessment of facilities	4.3 (38)

Faculty

Number of faculty: 49 full-time, 41 part-time, 4 visiting

	Full-time MBA	Rice MBA for Executives
Number of faculty per student	0.4 (85)	1.1
Percentage of faculty with PhD	98 (49)	98
Student rating of faculty	4.4 (28)	–

Strengths and weaknesses

Strengths: finance; entrepreneurship; marketing

Weakness: lack of international students and recruiters can lead to the perception that Rice is a regional school

Programme highlights

The Jones full-time MBA mixes core courses and an action-learning project in the first year and five required courses and electives (as well as a required entrepreneurship elective course) in the second year. There is an emphasis on communications and career management throughout the programme. The school has an interesting series of courses on the impact of government and the legal framework on business (power, influence and politics) as well as a required communications course. Overall, the programme is rigorous and fairly quantitative. A lot of work is done in small groups, based on projects, case studies and developing oral presentations and written reports. In the first year's action-learning project, teams of 4–6 students undertake a ten-week in-company consulting project, including five weeks on site. Students provide written recommendations in a presentation to senior managers.

The Executive MBA is divided into 11 mini-semesters over 21 months with breaks at Christmas and in the summer. Classes are held every other Friday and Saturday. Students can also participate in an optional elective international trip in January of the second year or a four-day seminar on business and politics in Washington, DC. Throughout the year students participate in "extended learning labs", which apply learning areas to real-world issues and encourage cross-functional thinking.

	Full-time MBA	Rice MBA for Executives
Student rating of programme	4.2 (41)	–
Number of overseas exchange programmes	0 (93)	–
Number of languages on offer	0 (94)	–

Students

	Full-time MBA	Rice MBA for Executives
Annual intake	166	84
Applicants:places	4:1	–
Percentage of women students	31 (38)	–
Percentage of foreign students	23 (>100)	–
Average GMAT score	625 (67)	–
Average number of months' work experience	48 (100)	–
Age range of students	25–31	–
Average age	28	–
Student rating of culture and classmates	4.2 (46)	–

Student profile (full time)

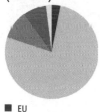

- ■ EU
- ■ Non-EU Europe
- ▨ North America
- ■ Other Americas
- ■ Asia/Australasia
- ▨ Middle East

Recruiters/careers service

	Full-time MBA	Rice MBA for Executives
Number of industry sectors that recruited graduates	7 (86)	–
Percentage of graduates in jobs 3 months after graduation	85 (16)	–
Percentage of graduates finding jobs through careers services	45 (20)	–
Student rating of careers service	3.5 (39)	–
Post-MBA salary, US$	76,745 (57)	–
Percentage increase in salary	52 (38)	–
Principal recruiters of graduates	Deloitte & Touche, Sabre, British Petroleum	

Cost

	Full-time MBA	Rice MBA for Executives
Application fees	US$100	US$100
Programme fees	US$31,746	US$77,000
Comments		Total programme. Includes laptop computer, all course materials, meals and parking while on campus. Does not include fees for the international business briefing elective or for an optional seminar on public policy
Accommodation costs (on campus, per year)	US$5,640	–
Accommodation costs (off campus, per year)	US$9,200	–
Financial aid available	US$1,000,000	–
Type of aid available	Scholarships, loans	–
Criteria on which aid is granted	Merit, financial need	–

Accreditation

AACSB International

Application details

	Full-time MBA	Rice MBA for Executives
Application deadline	March 15th	June 15th
Programme dates	Aug start, 21 months	Jul start, 22 months
Admission requirements	First degree; TOEFL if first language not English; 2 references; 3 essays; interview; laptop	First degree; at least 10 years' work experience; TOEFL if first language not English; 2 references; 4 essays; interview; statement of organisational support

Executive education

Jones runs a wide range of open-enrolment programmes in areas such as finance and marketing, and, not surprisingly given its location, the energy industry. Executives who follow a predetermined set of courses can gain certificates in areas such as finance and accounting, energy management and leadership. The school also offers customised in-company programmes.

Student/alumni quotes

"Rice is a fantastic school which is quickly becoming a national leader. However, it is still a work in progress and is a little rough around the edges."

"Module system limits the depth of knowledge in some subjects."

"Because of small school size, cost of living and programme, [it's] great for people who would like to stay in the Texas region."

University of Rochester—William E Simon Graduate School of Business

Address
Schlegel Hall
Rochester, NY
US
14627

Tel:
+1 585 275 3735

Fax:
+1 585 275 9331

Email:
mbaadm@simon.rochester.edu

Website:
www.simon.rochester.edu

Programme director:
Stacey R Kole

Figures in brackets represent rank

Ranking	Rank (out of 100) Full-time
Overall rank	61
Regional rank	38

Criteria	Rank (out of 100) Full-time
Open new career opportunities	**54**
Diversity of recruiters	51
Number in jobs three months after graduation	57
Jobs found through the careers service	56
Student assessment of careers service	61
Personal development and educational experience	**68**
Faculty quality	56
Student quality	52
Student diversity	98
Education experience	58
Increase in salary	**69**
Increase in salary	50
Post-MBA salary	67
Potential to network	**57**
Breadth of alumni network	37
Internationalism of alumni	78
Alumni effectiveness	55

Background

The Simon Graduate School of Business was founded in 1958 as the School of Business Administration at the University of Rochester. It awarded its first MBA in 1962. In 1986 it was renamed after the late William E Simon, a financial entrepreneur and former US Treasury secretary. The school takes the view that students need to learn a coherent, scientific way to analyse management problems and that economics is the key discipline governing business and human behaviour. This makes the school somewhat intensive, quantitative and academic. But it is also international, with a high percentage of foreign students. It is also relatively small by US standards, with around 160 students entering in September and a further 40 in January.

Facilities

Facilities are first-class, with Schlegel Hall providing nine case classrooms, 21 group-study rooms and a large computer lab. Carol G Simon Hall houses the school's administration, faculty and PhD students. James S Gleason Hall, an extension to Carol G Simon Hall, includes five classrooms, 16 study rooms and a careers services suite, including eight interview rooms. Management library facilities occupy one floor in a nearby university library. Students have access to all university sporting and cultural amenities and on-campus accommodation is available.

	Full-time MBA
Student assessment of facilities	4.3 (43)

Faculty

Number of faculty: 56 full-time, 11 part-time, 0 visiting

	Full-time MBA	Part-time MBA Program	Rochester Executive MBA Program
Number of faculty per student	0.3 (100)	2.2	2.8
Percentage of faculty with PhD	89 (61)	89	89
Student rating of faculty	4.5 (15)	–	–

Strengths and weaknesses

Strengths: finance; economics; accounting

Weaknesses: careers services; location

Programme highlights

The Simon MBA, especially the demanding core, is highly quantitative, given the school's belief that management is essentially economics-based. During the two-week orientation session, students participate in a statistics review workshop, self-assessment exercises, personal selling and communications skills instruction, corporate leadership training and one-to-one careers counselling. They also take several VISION modules, designed to enhance leadership skills in the areas of team-building, training in diversity issues, ethical decision-making and social responsibility. The programme consists of nine core courses, two electives and a required sequence of communication courses in the first year and nine electives in the second year. There is no requirement to specialise in a concentration (14 are offered) although most students do so. They can take electives or an internship during the summer. Entry in January allows students to take an accelerated 18-month track (there is usually no summer internship).

Under an agreement with the university, students can study for three years at undergraduate level and then immediately join other full-time MBA participants. Students from any academic major can apply for this "3-2 programme", but course work in economics and statistics is desirable and summer internships and/or part-time business work experience are expected.

The part-time programme is virtually identical to the full-time version. There are nine core and 11 elective courses. Classes are held one evening a week. Some electives are shared with full-time students. Students generally take one or two courses per quarter and can start in any quarter. Up to four courses can be taken before joining the programme and these count towards graduation requirements. The programme can be completed in 30 months but most students take just over three years. The maximum time allowed is seven years.

In the two-year Executive MBA, classes are held all day Friday from September to July in the first year and from September to June in the second year. In addition to academic study, there is a parallel series of seminars conducted by academics and government and industry leaders as well as European study trips (held in conjunction with Simon's International EMBA, run in partnership with the University of Bern in Switzerland).

	Full-time MBA	Part-time MBA Program	Rochester Executive MBA Program
Student rating of programme	4.3 (27)	–	–
Number of overseas exchange programmes	20 (34)	–	–
Number of languages on offer	0 (94)	–	–

Students

	Full-time MBA	Part-time MBA Program	Rochester Executive MBA Program
Annual intake	203	30	24
Applicants:places	–	–	–
Percentage of women students	22 (94)	28	38
Percentage of foreign students	41 (59)	n/a	n/a
Average GMAT score	647 (57)	590	0
Average number of months' work experience	72 (36)	60	132
Age range of students	25-35	26-38	30-43
Average age	29	31	35
Student rating of culture and classmates	3.9 (64)	–	–

Student profile (full time)

- ■ EU
- ■ Non-EU Europe
- ■ North America
- ■ Other Americas
- ■ Asia/Australasia
- ■ Middle East

Recruiters/careers service

	Full-time MBA	Part-time MBA Program	Rochester Executive MBA Program
Number of industry sectors that recruited graduates	8 (51)	–	–
Percentage of graduates in jobs 3 months after graduation	83 (57)	–	–
Percentage of graduates finding jobs through careers services	46 (56)	–	–
Student rating of careers service	3.1 (61)	–	–
Post-MBA salary, US$	70,824 (67)	–	–
Percentage increase in salary	50 (50)	–	–
Principal recruiters of graduates	Johnson & Johnson, Bausch & Lomb Inc, Deloitte & Touche I I P		

Cost

	Full-time MBA	Part-time MBA Program	Rochester Executive MBA Program
Application fees	US$125	US$125	None
Programme fees	US$33,720	US$1,124	US$78,500
Comments	Per year	Per credit hour	Includes class day meals, events, textbooks, software and computer
Accommodation costs (on campus, per year)	US$5,250	–	–
Accommodation costs (off campus, per year)	US$5,250	–	–
Financial aid available	No specific amount	–	–
Type of aid available	Scholarships	–	–
Criteria on which aid is granted	Merit	–	–

Accreditation

AACSB International

Application details

	Full-time MBA	Part-time MBA Program	Rochester Executive MBA Program
Application deadline	June 1st	Rolling admissions	January 7th
Programme dates	Sep start, 22 months	Up to seven years	Sep start, 22 months
Admission requirements	First degree; TOEFL if first language not English; 2 references; 3 essays; interview; laptop	First degree; TOEFL if first language not English; 2 references; 3 essays; interview	First degree; at least 6 years' work experience; 2 references; 3 essays; interview; sponsorship-work release

Executive education

Simon offers non-degree programmes (which it calls graduate-level certificate programmes) in financial analysis, e-commerce strategies, health sciences management, design of effective organisations and service management, as well as a specialised healthcare leadership programme.

Student/alumni quotes

"Simon Graduate School of Business is a great place to do the MBA; the faculty is excellent, as well as students and alumni. The school is really strong in finance, and the small class size gives you a perfect place to learn and contribute to the school, making a positive impact."

"[The school] is aggressively approaching the main problems and I anticipate the programme will improve greatly in the next two to three years. The instruction is excellent; it is the other stuff that is lacking, but easily corrected."

"It's very selective, has a small group of students, and you get a lot of hands-on attention from top-notch faculty. Faculty is very willing to help and work with you."

Rotterdam School of Management— Erasmus Graduate School of Business

Address
J Building
Burg. Oudlaan 50
Rotterdam
The Netherlands
3062 PA

Tel:
+31 10 408 2222

Fax:
+31 10 452 9509

Email:
info@rsm.nl

Website:
www.rsm.nl

Programme director:
Dianne Cleton

Figures in brackets
represent rank

Ranking	Rank (out of 100) Full-time
Overall rank	AA
Regional rank	34

Criteria	Rank (out of 100) Full-time
Open new career opportunities	**88**
Diversity of recruiters	71
Number in jobs three months after graduation	48
Jobs found through the careers service	89
Student assessment of careers service	93
Personal development and educational experience	**>100**
Faculty quality	92
Student quality	78
Student diversity	50
Education experience	>100
Increase in salary	**37**
Increase in salary	19
Post-MBA salary	58
Potential to network	**71**
Breadth of alumni network	80
Internationalism of alumni	22
Alumni effectiveness	74

Background

Rotterdam School of Management (RSM) was established in 1970 and soon after began offering an MBA. In 1985, when RSM moved to the Erasmus campus, the programme was transformed into the present English-language International MBA.

The school is resolutely international, with a good international mix of students, yet it retains a Dutch atmosphere. It has a friendly and youthful faculty and staff.

Facilities

RSM is based in a new, somewhat slab-sided building (opened in March 2000) that fits in well with Erasmus's functional campus, but inside it is spacious and well appointed. It includes eight large theatre-style classrooms, breakout rooms, student lounges, a business library, a cafeteria and staff offices, as well as three computer labs with 70 desktop PCs and connections for 55 laptop computers. All students are given an account to access the Internet from home.

The Business Information Centre (BIC) holds books, annual reports, directories and periodicals to support the MBA and MBA/MBI curriculum and offers free access to all relevant online publications and CD-ROM databases. Students can also use the library and information services available at Erasmus University.

There is no on-campus accommodation, but rented housing is available, subsidised by the government for students. Most students live in special housing complexes. Rotterdam is a lively, sophisticated city with lots of attractions.

	Full-time MBA
Student assessment of facilities	2.9 (>100)

Rotterdam School of Management—Erasmus Graduate School of Business

Faculty

Number of faculty: 165 full-time, 63 part-time, 70 visiting

	Full-time MBA	Part-time Weekend Executive MBA (EMBA)	The Global Executive OneMBA
Number of faculty per student	1.4 (19)	3.7	3.8
Percentage of faculty with PhD	74 (72)	74	74
Student rating of faculty	3.5 (>100)	–	–

Strengths and weaknesses

Strengths: finance; information technology; strategy

Weaknesses: administration; careers services

Programme highlights

RSM offers a 15-month MBA or a joint MBA/MBI (Master of Business Informatics) that focuses on the strategic use of IT. The two programmes follow slightly different tracks, but both are intensive and diverse and offer good exchange opportunities. Personal development and career workshops run throughout the first and second semesters.

The programme starts with a series of short, pre-programme refresher courses in quantitative areas. The first year consists of mandatory core courses covering management basics and functional areas. After the second semester, students on the MBA/MBI take four additional MBI courses focusing on strategic issues of information technology. During the summer, all students undertake an internship culminating in an assessed company analysis. The fourth semester consists of electives (many taken alongside part-time students) or an international exchange programme, though competition for places is strong (40 places were available in the last academic year).

The part-time Executive MBA, which lasts two years, consists of four terms and a one-month in-company project. Classes are held on Friday evening and all day Saturday, generally every two weeks. There is a one-week residential block in January and a one-week overseas trip in June each year. Electives can be studied concurrently with full-time students. Soft skills and careers workshops run throughout the programme. A high proportion of students on the part-time programme come from outside the Netherlands, mainly because of the large number of international workers in Rotterdam and the Netherlands generally.

OneMBA is a joint global programme designed for executives with at least seven years' experience. The 21-month programme involves a partnership of five business schools on four continents. Participants meet for 11 residential blocks, the first and last of two or three days and the other nine of one week, of which four are held in Asia, Europe, and North and South America. Co-ordinated courses comprise the core and occur concurrently on all OneMBA campuses. These courses include assignments that give participants experience working in separate global virtual teams made up of OneMBA executives spread across the world. The partner schools are: The Chinese University of Hong Kong; Fundação Getulio Vargas, Escola de Administração de Empresas de São Paulo (FGV-EAESP), Brazil; Monterrey Tech Graduate School of Business Administration and Leadership (EGADE-ITESM), Mexico; Rotterdam School of Management, Netherlands; and University of North Carolina, Kenan-Flagler Business School, US.

	Full-time MBA	Part-time Weekend Executive MBA (EMBA)	The Global Executive OneMBA
Student rating of programme	3.9 (88)	–	–
Number of overseas exchange programmes	40 (55)	–	–
Number of languages on offer	0 (94)	–	–

Student profile (full time)

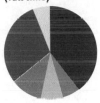

- ■ EU
- ■ Non-EU Europe
- ▨ North America
- ■ Other Americas
- ■ Asia/Australasia
- ▨ Middle East

Students

	Full-time MBA	Part-time Weekend Executive MBA (EMBA)	The Global Executive OneMBA
Annual intake	158	80	78
Applicants:places	4:1	1:1	–
Percentage of women students	17 (>100)	17	14
Percentage of foreign students	97 (3)	n/a	n/a
Average GMAT score	630 (66)	590	n/a
Average number of months' work experience	68 (50)	108	132
Age range of students	25-34	30-40	29-44
Average age	29	34	36
Student rating of culture and classmates	4.0 (73)	–	–

Recruiters/careers service

	Full-time MBA	Part-time Weekend Executive MBA (EMBA)	The Global Executive OneMBA
Number of industry sectors that recruited graduates	6 (71)	–	–
Percentage of graduates in jobs 3 months after graduation	80 (48)	–	–
Percentage of graduates finding jobs through careers services	20 (89)	–	–
Student rating of careers service	2.8 (93)	–	–
Post-MBA salary, US$	79,545 (58)	–	–
Percentage increase in salary	75 (19)	–	–
Principal recruiters of graduates	Johnson & Johnson, General Electric, Cargill		

Cost

	Full-time MBA	Part-time Weekend Executive MBA (EMBA)	The Global Executive OneMBA
Application fees	€75 (US$85)	€75 (US$85)	€75 (US$85)
Programme fees	€34,000 (US$38,636)	€38,500 (US$43,750)	€48,000 (US$54,545)
Comments	–	–	–
Accommodation costs (on campus, per year)	–	–	–
Accommodation costs (off campus, per year)	€6,000 (US$6,818)	–	–
Financial aid available	€500,000 (US$568,182)	–	–
Type of aid available	Scholarships	–	–
Criteria on which aid is granted	Merit	–	–

Accreditation

AACSB International, AMBA, EQUIS

Application details

	Full-time MBA	Part-time Weekend Executive MBA (EMBA)	The Global Executive OneMBA
Application deadline	June 15th	December 6th	August 20th
Programme dates	Oct start, 15 months	Jan start, 24 months	Sep start, 21 months
Admission requirements	First degree; work experience; TOEFL if first language not English; 2 references; 4 essays; interview; laptop	First degree; work experience; 2 references; 4 essays; interview	First degree; work experience; 2 references; essays; interview

Executive education

Rotterdam's open-enrolment courses include interim management (Dutch language), business valuation, international account management and the TEG series, which is based on the core courses of its existing MBA programme (see above) and leads to a management diploma.

Customised in-company training courses include competence building, talent development, executive development and senior executives programmes.

Student/alumni quotes

"The school is a diamond in the rough: it needs a little polish before it truly shines but it will. The classmates you have are the biggest asset you could ever ask for. Where else can you have classmates from 50 countries and also know them all by name?"

"I would recommend the OneMBA programme as one of the most up-to-date programmes in terms of access to understanding the essence of global business environment."

"School administration (with the notable positive exception of the admissions office) was too rigid, treating students as solicitants, with inconvenient office hours and low responsiveness."

Sheffield University Management School

Address
9 Mappin Street
Sheffield
S Yorks
UK
S1 4DT

Tel:
+44 114 222 3368

Fax:
+44 114 222 3348

Email:
c.ford@sheffield.ac.
uk

Website:
www.shef.ac.uk/rao/
admissions/pgadmit/
index.html

Programme director:
David Shearn

Figures in brackets
represent rank

Ranking	Rank (out of 100) Full-time
Overall rank	66
Regional rank	24

Criteria	Rank (out of 100) Full-time
Open new career opportunities	**48**
Diversity of recruiters	66
Number in jobs three months after graduation	5
Jobs found through the careers service	66
Student assessment of careers service	81
Personal development and educational experience	**94**
Faculty quality	>100
Student quality	>100
Student diversity	16
Education experience	85
Increase in salary	**18**
Increase in salary	21
Post-MBA salary	32
Potential to network	**>100**
Breadth of alumni network	70
Internationalism of alumni	56
Alumni effectiveness	>100

Background

Sheffield University Management School was set up in 1970 and teaches management and business at undergraduate, postgraduate and doctoral levels. It has a good research base and attracts large numbers of international students. Students like the value-for-money offered by the programme but claim that careers services could be improved, especially for international students.

Facilities

The school has its own purpose-built building on the university campus, close to the city centre. Dedicated facilities for MBA students include lecture and seminar rooms, an IT laboratory, and a social and reading room. A comprehensive range of computing services is available, including library catalogues and CD-ROM databases. There is a specialised management library opposite the school.

The university provides accommodation, careers services and sports and social facilities. There is plenty of reasonably priced accommodation both on-campus and off-campus. Sheffield is a pleasant city set in attractive countryside. The Peak District National Park is easily accessible and cultural and social amenities are good.

	Full-time MBA
Student assessment of facilities	3.9 (83)

Faculty

Number of faculty: 48 full-time, 12 part-time, 1 visiting	
	Full-time MBA
Number of faculty per student	0.7 (51)
Percentage of faculty with PhD	75 (94)
Student rating of faculty	3.7 (>100)

Strengths and weaknesses

Strengths: human resources management; technology; ecological business

Weakness: extracurricular activities

Programme highlights

Sheffield offers a general management and four specialist MBAs: e-business; accounting and financial management; marketing; and technology management. All programmes share a common set of ten core courses taught over the first and second seminars. In the second seminar, students take two courses from the options offered in each module. (General management students can take any two courses.) Some options can also be selected to suit individual needs with the co-operation of other university departments (for example, the School of East Asian Studies offers business and social options). The final project and dissertation must be submitted by December following the second semester. Research methodology is included in a series of skills workshops beginning in the pre-programme introduction week and continuing throughout the programme. There is also a series of guest speakers.

The school has introduced an MBA in EcoBusiness, consisting of two taught semesters followed by a dissertation. Although it is called an MBA, the programme does not have a recognisable MBA core and most courses relate to "sustainable development"—for example, green knowledge and green marketing.

Students can take the programme at diploma level by completing only its taught elements.

	Full-time MBA
Student rating of programme	3.5 (>100)
Number of overseas exchange programmes	0 (93)
Number of languages on offer	>5 (28)

Students

	Full-time MBA
Annual intake	73
Applicants:places	8:1
Percentage of women students	42 (10)
Percentage of foreign students	93 (7)
Average GMAT score	600 (89)
Average number of months' work experience	60 (63)
Age range of students	24-37
Average age	28
Student rating of culture and classmates	3.6 (>100)

Student profile (full time)

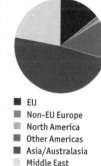

- ■ EU
- ■ Non-EU Europe
- ▨ North America
- ■ Other Americas
- ■ Asia/Australasia
- ▨ Middle East

Recruiters/careers service

	Full-time MBA
Number of industry sectors that recruited graduates	7 (66)
Percentage of graduates in jobs 3 months after graduation	99 (5)
Percentage of graduates finding jobs through careers services	30 (66)
Student rating of careers service	2.9 (81)
Post-MBA salary, US$	85,188 (32)
Percentage increase in salary	77 (21)
Principal recruiters of graduates	Rolls Royce, M&S, Avesta

Cost

	Full-time MBA
Application fees	None
Programme fees	£12,000 (US$19,672)
Comments	Fee for EU citizens is £8,500
Accommodation costs (on campus, per year)	£2,700 (US$4,426)
Accommodation costs (off campus, per year)	£2,005 (US$3,287)
Financial aid available	£2,000 (US$3,279)
Type of aid available	Scholarship
Criteria on which aid is granted	–

Accreditation

None

Application details

	Full-time MBA
Application deadline	August 31st
Programme dates	Sep start, 12 months
Admission requirements	Good first degree; at least 3 years' work experience; GMAT; TOEFL or IELTS if first language not English; 2 references

Executive education

Sheffield does not currently offer open-enrolment or customised in-company executive education programmes.

Student/alumni quotes

"I was expecting to be loaded with much more work and assignments. The university was offered by the British Council, which provides me with a scholarship. The selection process was smooth and with little bureaucracy. Overall, I believe I am having a very interesting and useful experience of studying in MBA. The atmosphere is friendly enough and co-operative."

"There is an overemphasis on overseas students (only one local British student in 2001), and I hope this is not because of the higher fees that overseas students have to pay."

"Well, it's cheaper than others, the city is safe, they have a good quality in teaching and make interesting case studies."

Solvay Business School—Université Libre de Bruxelles

Ranking	Rank (out of 100) Full-time
Overall rank	90
Regional rank	35

Criteria	Rank (out of 100) Full-time
Open new career opportunities	**79**
Diversity of recruiters	40
Number in jobs three months after graduation	29
Jobs found through the careers service	95
Student assessment of careers service	78
Personal development and educational experience	**>100**
Faculty quality	85
Student quality	>100
Student diversity	28
Education experience	100
Increase in salary	**73**
Increase in salary	22
Post-MBA salary	78
Potential to network	**100**
Breadth of alumni network	>100
Internationalism of alumni	24
Alumni effectiveness	>100

Address
Avenue F.D. Roosevelt
21
Brussels
Belgium
1050

Tel:
+32 2 650 4183

Fax:
+32 2 650 4199

Email:
leclercq@ulb.ac.be

Website:
www.solvay.edu/mba

Programme director:
Bruno van Pottelsberghe

Figures in brackets
represent rank

Background

Solvay Business School, founded in 1903 by Ernest Solvay of the eponymous chemicals company, is one of the oldest business schools in Europe and offers a wide range of undergraduate and graduate programmes (mostly taught in French). Part of Brussels University (Université Libre de Bruxelles or ULB), it makes the most of its location in what many call "the capital of Europe". Its English-language MBA programme (introduced in the late 1980s) has a strong underlying emphasis on the economies and business of the EU.

The school is closely integrated with its 14,000-strong parent university and MBA students use most of its facilities. Faculty members are drawn from the university and from other business schools in Europe and the US.

Facilities

The MBA is taught in one of the older buildings on the large campus, which is a short drive from the centre of Brussels. Students are expected to have their own computers. For students who do not live in Brussels or the surrounding area, the university's accommodation office offers rooms on its three campuses (Solbosch, Plaine and Erasme). Private accommodation is also available in houses on the Plaine and Erasme campuses.

	Full-time MBA
Student assessment of facilities	3.0 (>100)

Faculty

Number of faculty: 33 full-time, 16 part-time, 0 visiting

	Full-time MBA	Part-time MBA
Number of faculty per student	0.7 (45)	0.3
Percentage of faculty with PhD	91 (65)	91
Student rating of faculty	4.0 (86)	–

Strengths and weaknesses

Strengths: finance, control and accounting; European management; business intelligence

Weakness: administration

Programme highlights

The Solvay MBA is a 10-month programme split into ten core courses and a number of electives (usually about eight, depending on the concentration chosen). Teaching takes place over five six-week periods with a week of exams and a week off at the end of each period. Students can take optional pre-programme courses in quantitative analysis and presentation writing. Specialisations are offered in finance, control and accounting, European management, strategy and marketing, technology and entrepreneurship, and business intelligence.

Students can opt to undertake an in-company team project equivalent to two elective courses.

The part-time MBA is fairly new and is virtually identical to the full-time version, with ten six-week periods of courses and seminars over two years. Each period ends with an exam week and a one-week break. Students take ten core and around eight elective courses. Specialisations are the same as for the full-time programme. Classes meet on weekday evenings and Saturday morning (9 am–12 pm).

	Full-time MBA	Part-time MBA
Student rating of programme	4.3 (48)	–
Number of overseas exchange programmes	0 (93)	–
Number of languages on offer	>5 (44)	–

Students

Student profile (full time)

- ■ EU
- ■ Non-EU Europe
- ■ North America
- ■ Other Americas
- ■ Asia/Australasia
- ■ Middle East

	Full-time MBA	Part-time MBA
Annual intake	55	150
Applicants:places	4:1	–
Percentage of women students	44 (9)	19
Percentage of foreign students	78 (22)	n/a
Average GMAT score	580 (>100)	610
Average number of months' work experience	60 (96)	96
Age range of students	23-48	24-56
Average age	28	33
Student rating of culture and classmates	3.5 (>100)	–

Recruiters/careers service

	Full-time MBA	Part-time MBA
Number of industry sectors that recruited graduates	8 (40)	–
Percentage of graduates in jobs 3 months after graduation	90 (29)	–
Percentage of graduates finding jobs through careers services	5 (95)	–
Student rating of careers service	3.1 (78)	–
Post-MBA salary, US$	67,001 (78)	–
Percentage increase in salary	76 (22)	–
Principal recruiters of graduates	General Electric, Procter & Gamble, Accenture	

Cost

	Full-time MBA	Part-time MBA
Application fees	None	None
Programme fees	€16,000 (US$18,182)	€20,000 (US$22,727)
Comments	–	–
Accommodation costs (on campus, per year)	€5,000 (US$5,682)	–
Accommodation costs (off campus, per year)	€6,500 (US$7,386)	–
Financial aid available	€5,000 (US$5,682)	–
Type of aid available	Scholarships, loans	–
Criteria on which aid is granted	Merit, financial need. Justification letter required	–

Accreditation

None

Application details

	Full-time MBA	Part-time MBA
Application deadline	August 1st	August 1st
Programme dates	Jan start, 10 months	Jan start, 20 months
Admission requirements	First degree (diploma and grade transcripts required); at least 2 years' work experience; GMAT; TOEFL if first language not English; 2 references; essays; interview; laptop	First degree (diploma and grade transcripts required); at least 3 years' work experience; GMAT; TOEFL if first language not English; 2 references; essays; interview

Executive education

Solvay offers a large portfolio of open-enrolment executive education programmes in areas such as general management, finance, marketing, strategy, leadership, entrepreneurship, technology and IT management, and public management. It also offers customised in-company programmes and online and e-learning courses.

Student/alumni quotes

"Solvay has the best professors coming from all over the world and a very international student body. And all this for a reasonable price."

"I believe the Solvay Business School MBA to be one of the most up-and-coming MBAs in the world. They are going to great lengths to improve their programme and strengthen their output of students. It's an impressive uphill battle that they are winning."

"The school's range of courses is excellent, the lecturers are generally very good to excellent. Administration needs improving."

University of South Carolina—Moore School of Business

Address
1705 College Street
Columbia, SC
US
29208

Tel:
+1 803 777 5035

Fax:
+1 803 777 9123

Email:
imba@mmore.sc.edu

Website:
mmoreschool.sc.edu

Programme director:
Dr Robert Rolfe

Figures in brackets
represent rank

Ranking	Rank (out of 100) Full-time
Overall rank	94
Regional rank	51

Criteria	Rank (out of 100) Full-time
Open new career opportunities	**92**
Diversity of recruiters	62
Number in jobs three months after graduation	>100
Jobs found through the careers service	58
Student assessment of careers service	88
Personal development and educational experience	**96**
Faculty quality	63
Student quality	>100
Student diversity	>100
Education experience	76
Increase in salary	**91**
Increase in salary	54
Post-MBA salary	95
Potential to network	**9**
Breadth of alumni network	75
Internationalism of alumni	2
Alumni effectiveness	84

Background

The University of South Carolina's Moore School of Business was founded in 1919 as the School of Commerce, and in 1998 became the first major business school to be named after a woman (in recognition of a US$25m gift from Darla Moore, a business woman and alumna). In April 2004 the school announced that Ms Moore was donating a further US$45m. The total of US$70m is the largest private gift ever given to a US business school. Ms Moore wants the university to match her donation. The funds will go toward a major renovation of the school's facilities and support scholarships and endowed professorships.

The Moore school is large, with around 3,000 undergraduate, graduate and doctoral students; it offers one undergraduate, five master's and two PhD programmes. It has more than 30,000 alumni around the world, although the majority live in the south-east of the US. The student body is diverse and fully supportive of the school's emphasis on internationalism.

Facilities

The school is based in a nine-storey, 330,000 sq ft building with its own library, placement centre and executive education centre. Graduate students have their own designated facilities. Students have access to the university's 2,500-seat main library as well as all other university facilities. The state of South Carolina is a southern US growth spot with beautiful scenery, an interesting history and good recreational and cultural amenities.

	Full-time MBA
Student assessment of facilities	3.4 (>100)

Faculty

Number of faculty: 123 full-time, 38 part-time, 2 visiting

	Full-time MBA	Professional MBA
Number of faculty per student	1.1 (44)	1.5
Percentage of faculty with PhD	85 (76)	85
Student rating of faculty	4.3 (44)	–

Strengths and weaknesses

Strengths: operations management; marketing; international business

Weaknesses: administration; low profile

Programme highlights

Moore's International MBA (IMBA) has a standard core of ten courses, four communications workshops and then an option of three specialised and highly international tracks: the Language Track, the Global Track and the Vienna Program. All tracks include a five-month international internship.

The Language Track combines business education with intensive language training in one of seven languages: Chinese, French, German, Italian, Japanese, Portuguese or Spanish. Students also have an internship in a country that speaks the language they have studied. All language tracks take two years, with the exception of Chinese and Japanese, which require three years of study.

The Global Track involves additional course work that focuses on the political, economic and business factors affecting the investment climate of various regions throughout the world such as Europe, Latin America, South-east Asia and Africa, rather than languages. Students take a special three-week course at an overseas university and have an internship in a country where English is the native language. International students on the Global Track typically have their internship in the US.

After their internships are completed, students on both these tracks return to the Moore school and in the second year acquire depth in their areas of interest. As well as a required management class, students take elective classes. All students can undertake a concentration in a designated area such as finance, marketing, supply chain management and e-commerce.

The Vienna Program, a partnership between the Moore school and Wirtschaftsuniversität Wien (Vienna University of Business and Economics), is a 15-month, two-campus, English-language variation on the programme designed for experienced managers. Students study core subjects in Vienna for six months then return to Moore for two semesters, joining language and global track students returning from their internships.

The part-time Professional MBA programme lasts 28 months. Students take ten core courses and six electives, at least one of which must be in international business or international economics. Classes are held on campus in the evenings from Monday to Thursday, and there are some Saturday sessions. Classes are also broadcast live via closed-circuit television to 22 receiving stations around the state and (by arrangement) to company premises. Students at receiving stations can talk to lecturers during the broadcasts via classroom audio equipment.

	Full-time MBA	Professional MBA
Student rating of programme	4.2 (54)	–
Number of overseas exchange programmes	14 (71)	–
Number of languages on offer	>5 (1)	–

Students

	Full-time MBA	Professional MBA
Annual intake	128	112
Applicants:places	3:1	2:1
Percentage of women students	27 (55)	30
Percentage of foreign students	28 (92)	n/a
Average GMAT score	630 (71)	589
Average number of months' work experience	48 (>100)	67
Age range of students	24-31	23-38
Average age	28	29
Student rating of culture and classmates	4.0 (83)	–

Student profile (full time)

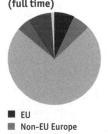

- ■ EU
- ■ Non-EU Europe
- ▨ North America
- ■ Other Americas
- ■ Asia/Australasia
- ▨ Middle East

Recruiters/careers service

	Full-time MBA	Professional MBA
Number of industry sectors that recruited graduates	7 (62)	
Percentage of graduates in jobs 3 months after graduation	65 (>100)	–
Percentage of graduates finding jobs through careers services	25 (58)	–
Student rating of careers service	3.2 (88)	–
Post-MBA salary, US$	61,500 (95)	–
Percentage increase in salary	54 (54)	
Principal recruiters of graduates	Citigroup, Ingersoll Rand, B B & T	

Cost

	Full-time MBA	Professional MBA
Application fees	US$40	US$40
Programme fees	US$47,000	US$410
Comments	Total programme	Per credit hour for South Carolina residents, US$450 for out-of-state students
Accommodation costs (on campus, per year)	US$9,000	–
Accommodation costs (off campus, per year)	US$11,000	–
Financial aid available	US$1,600,000	–
Type of aid available	Fellowships, fee reductions, work grants	–
Criteria on which aid is granted	Merit	–

Accreditation

AACSB International

Application details

	Full-time MBA	Professional MBA
Application deadline	April 1st	July 15th
Programme dates	May start, 27 months	Sep start, 28 months
Admission requirements	4-year Bachelor's degree from an accredited university; at least 2 years' work experience; GMAT; TOEFL if first language not English; 2 references; essay; interview; laptop	First degree; at least 2 years' work experience; GMAT; TOEFL if first language not English; 2 references; essay

Executive education

Executive education is organised through the Daniel Management Center. There are short open-enrolment programmes in leadership, business skills and communication skill, longer programmes in front-line management and mid-management, and specialised seminars in finance and international business.

Student/alumni quotes

"I chose the Moore School of Business because it has the most innovative and unique approach to international business. It is the only global business programme in the US that focuses on hands-on international experience and training. If this school were in a major metropolitan area and surrounded by a thriving business community, it would be a premier business school."

"Lack of co-ordination among administrative sectors."

"The internship abroad is a unique, invaluable experience—not only culturally, but educationally and professionally. This, coupled with the excellent faculty, is the strength of the programme that should be fully promoted."

University of Southampton—School of Management

Address
School of
Management
University of
Southampton
Highfield
Southampton
UK
SO17 1BJ

Tel:
+44 23 8059 6872

Fax:
+44 23 8059 3844

Email:
mbamail5@soton.ac.
uk

Website:
www.management.
soton.ac.uk

Programme director:
Dr Charlie Wilkinson

Figures in brackets
represent rank

Ranking	Rank (out of 100) Full-time
Overall rank	n/a
Regional rank	n/a

Background

Southampton's School of Management is a typical UK university-based business school with good teaching, research and consulting links with industry and government. As well as the MBA, it offers undergraduate degrees in accounting, finance and management science, postgraduate degrees in accounting, banking, finance, information systems, risk management and management science, and doctoral programmes. The school has grown rapidly in recent years and now has over 700 students. Its ambition is to be seen as one of Europe's leading business schools by 2010.

Facilities

The school occupies a refurbished building on the university campus. Facilities include dedicated postgraduate study and computer rooms, a lecture room, a meeting room and a suite of rooms for small-group work and seminars. On-campus accommodation is available. Southampton is a pleasant and lively city, reasonably close to London and (by ferry) the Continent, in an attractive rural area.

	Full-time MBA
Student assessment of facilities	n/a (n/a)

Faculty

Number of faculty: 40 full-time, 10 part-time, 10 visiting	
	Full-time MBA
Number of faculty per student	0.6 (n/a)
Percentage of faculty with PhD	80 (n/a)
Student rating of faculty	n/a (n/a)

Strengths and weaknesses

Strengths: entrepreneurship; risk; accounting, accountability and governance

Programme highlights

Southampton's MBA programme is unusual and interesting and is offered in three separate streams: a traditional full-time stream for students with at least two years' work experience; an executive stream (full-time and part-time) for students with at least five years' managerial experience; and a full-time MBA for recent graduates aimed at students without previous work experience.

The traditional full-time MBA is a typical European one-year programme of core, electives and a dissertation. It begins in late September with an induction programme and the integrated "The Effective Manager" core unit. Three further core units and one or two electives are taught during the rest of the first semester. The second semester begins in February and includes the last two core units and the remainder of six electives. The programme ends with a dissertation based on an individual piece of research, chosen by the student, submitted in mid-September.

The Executive MBA admits students in late September or early February (for part-time students only) and lasts between two and three years. Students must complete the six core units and any six electives within a three-year period. A further six months is allowed for the dissertation. The school says that it is unlikely that anyone much under the age of 30 would be deemed to have sufficient managerial experience to obtain maximum benefit from this stream. During each academic year, half of the core units will be scheduled during the day (9 am–5 pm), normally on Fridays, and the remainder on weekday evenings (6–9 pm), Monday–Thursday. Core units delivered during the day one year will normally be delivered in the evening in the following year, and vice versa. Over three years, the average attendance time is one core unit and one option unit per semester, which is equivalent to eight days (or 16 evenings) spread across approximately 12 teaching weeks.

The MDA for recent graduates is a set of taught courses assessed by a mixture of course work and formal examinations. Following successful completion of the taught element, students gain a diploma. They then move on to a group project and dissertation, which leads to the MBA.

	Full-time MBA
Student rating of programme	n/a (n/a)
Number of overseas exchange programmes	0 (n/a)
Number of languages on offer	6 (n/a)

Students

Student profile (full time)

- ■ EU
- ■ Non-EU Europe
- ■ North America
- ■ Other Americas
- ■ Asia/Australasia
- ▨ Middle East

	Full-time MBA
Annual intake	62
Applicants:places	14:1
Percentage of women students	35 (n/a)
Percentage of foreign students	85 (n/a)
Average GMAT score	–
Average number of months' work experience	120 (n/a)
Age range of students	28-45
Average age	33
Student rating of culture and classmates	n/a (n/a)

Recruiters/careers service

	Full-time MBA
Number of industry sectors that recruited graduates	8 (n/a)
Percentage of graduates in jobs 3 months after graduation	85 (n/a)
Percentage of graduates finding jobs through careers services	– (n/a)
Student rating of careers service	n/a (n/a)
Post-MBA salary, US$	– (n/a)
Percentage increase in salary	– (n/a)
Principal recruiters of graduates	– (n/a)

Cost

	Full-time MBA
Application fees	None
Programme fees	£12,875 (US$21,107)
Comments	2004 fee as 2005 fee not yet available
Accommodation costs (on campus, per year)	£3,000 (US$4,918)
Accommodation costs (off campus, per year)	£3,200 (US$5,246)
Financial aid available	–
Type of aid available	–
Criteria on which aid is granted	–

Accreditation

None

Application details

	Full-time MBA
Application deadline	July 31st
Programme dates	Oct start, 12 months
Admission requirements	First degree (normally a first or second class honours degree from a UK university, or an equivalent professional or overseas qualification); at least 2 years' work experience; TOEFL, IELTS or Cambridge Certificate if first language not English; 2 references

Executive education

Southampton does not currently offer open-enrolment or customised in-company executive education programmes.

Student/alumni quotes

"The standard and experience of the other students was exceptionally high. The atmosphere was supportive and used much of the experience available in the class."

"My experience is that you need to work very, very hard to complete the MBA—much more work than my previous degrees. Having said that it is well worth the effort (very rewarding), especially when there is a good and competitive class spirit that leads to continuous and lively debate."

University of Southern California—
Marshall School of Business

Address
University of Southern California
Marshall School of Business
701 Exposition Boulevard
Los Angeles, CA
US
90089-1425

Tel:
+1 213 740 7146

Fax:
+1 213 740 9876

Email:
marshallmba@marshall.usc.edu

Website:
www.marshall.usc.edu

Programme director:
Dr Carl Voigt

Figures in brackets represent rank

Ranking	Rank (out of 100) Full-time
Overall rank	23
Regional rank	18

Criteria	Rank (out of 100) Full-time
Open new career opportunities	**28**
Diversity of recruiters	40
Number in jobs three months after graduation	36
Jobs found through the careers service	31
Student assessment of careers service	28
Personal development and educational experience	**52**
Faculty quality	83
Student quality	38
Student diversity	56
Education experience	50
Increase in salary	**67**
Increase in salary	46
Post-MBA salary	66
Potential to network	**11**
Breadth of alumni network	17
Internationalism of alumni	67
Alumni effectiveness	3

Background

Marshall School of Business began as the College of Commerce and Business Administration in 1920. The Graduate School of Business Administration was established in 1960. In 1997 the school was renamed following a US$35m donation from Gordon S Marshall, an alumnus. The school has particular faculty strength in Pacific Rim economies and, given its location a few miles south of Los Angeles, the entertainment industry. It has a strong international approach that permeates most of its programmes but is especially prominent in the IBEAR MBA. The class size is small and there is a good student:faculty ratio.

Facilities

The school occupies four well-equipped multistorey buildings—Hoffman Hall, Bridge Hall, the School of Accounting building and Popovich Hall (the MBA building)—on the University of Southern California (USC) campus. Popovich Hall contains state-of-the-art technology and eight case-study rooms with audio-video teleconferencing facilities. Students have access to all university facilities. Most students live off-campus and a car is a necessity.

	Full-time MBA
Student assessment of facilities	4.2 (49)

Faculty

Number of faculty: 186 full-time, 29 part-time, 5 visiting

	Full-time MBA	Marshall MBA for Professionals & Managers	Marshall Executive MBA Program
Number of faculty per student	0.8 (61)	0.8	3.0
Percentage of faculty with PhD	79 (88)	79	79
Student rating of faculty	4.2 (58)	–	–

Strengths and weaknesses

Strengths: finance; marketing; entrepreneurship

Programme highlights

Marshall's two-year full-time MBA comprises a straightforward intensive core delivered in the four-term first year followed by a wide range of electives and concentrations in the second year. The emphasis is on entrepreneurship, a global perspective and technology. The core concludes with PRIME, a required research trip to Pacific Rim countries to visit selected companies, both domestic and multinational, and governmental institutions. The aim is to train students as global managers by allowing them to compare and contrast the US business experience with that of Pacific Rim countries and industries. The second year is devoted to electives and concentrations and is shared with part-time and IBEAR students. Students can choose from over 20 offered concentrations or design their own. The school recommends that students choose a primary concentration in a functional area such as marketing or finance and a secondary one in a career area, such as the entertainment industry.

The 33-month part-time MBA for Professionals and Managers (MBA.PM) programme consists of 12 months of core classes followed by electives. The core can be taken at either the USC University Park campus in Los Angeles or the USC Orange County Center in Irvine. All elective courses are taught at the main University Park campus. Regardless of location, students attend classes two evenings a week on either Monday and Wednesday (University Park) or Tuesday and Thursday (Orange County). After the core all students take PM Globe, a semester-long macroeconomics course that includes a one-week overseas trip to a Pacific Rim country. Elective classes offer the same options as the full-time programme and may be scheduled at various times and with students from other Marshall MBA programmes. Students usually take two electives at a time for four semesters plus one summer.

Marshall's Executive MBA is a 21-month programme. Classes meet one day a week on alternating Fridays and Saturdays. Class meetings include three off-campus residential sessions, two domestic and one international. The curriculum focuses on ten integrated themes rather than functional disciplines. The domestic sessions, lasting six and two days respectively, are taken at the start of the first year and the end of the second year. The international off-site session is a seven-day overseas study in the fall of the second year. During the summer break between the first and second years students must write a publishable paper for a trade journal of their choice on a topic of personal and professional interest. In May 2004 Marshall launched its Executive MBA in Shanghai in collaboration with Jiao Tong University.

The IBEAR (International Business Education and Research) MBA is a 12-month full-time programme in international management aimed at mid-career managers. Participants come from many different countries and have an average of ten years' work experience. They can opt to take electives outside of the programme during the spring and summer with students on other Marshall MBA programmes. During the final two terms they undertake an overseas group consulting project. IBEAR courses emphasise business in and between Asia, North America and South America but, says the school, this does not exclude other regions. Classes meet 9.30–11.45 am and 1.45–4 pm, Monday–Thursday, in Popovich Hall in IBEAR's own multimedia case room. Each course meets twice a week. The programme starts with orientation and transition sessions to develop teamwork and refresh statistical and computer skills.

	Full-time MBA	Marshall MBA for Professionals & Managers	Marshall Executive MBA Program
Student rating of programme	4.1 (52)	–	–
Number of overseas exchange programmes	12 (79)	–	–
Number of languages on offer	>5 (41)	–	–

Students

	Full-time MBA	Marshall MBA for Professionals & Managers	Marshall Executive MBA Program
Annual intake	262	287	74
Applicants:places	8:1	2:1	3:1
Percentage of women students	31 (42)	30	22
Percentage of foreign students	50 (76)	n/a	n/a
Average GMAT score	689 (18)	622	602
Average number of months' work experience	60 (79)	63	168
Age range of students	26-32	25-33	32-43
Average age	28	28	37
Student rating of culture and classmates	4.4 (32)	–	–

Student profile (full-time)

n/a

Recruiters/careers service

	Full-time MBA	Marshall MBA for Professionals & Managers	Marshall Executive MBA Program
Number of industry sectors that recruited graduates	8 (40)	–	–
Percentage of graduates in jobs 3 months after graduation	84 (36)	–	–
Percentage of graduates finding jobs through careers services	63 (31)	–	–
Student rating of careers service	3.6 (28)	–	–
Post-MBA salary, US$	70,979 (66)		–
Percentage increase in salary	71 (46)	–	–
Principal recruiters of graduates	Mattel, Deloitte, Wells Fargo		

Cost

	Full-time MBA	Marshall MBA for Professionals & Managers	Marshall Executive MBA Program
Application fees	US$125	US$125	US$125
Programme fees	US$32,175	US$32,175	US$29,250
Comments	Per year	Per year	Per year
Accommodation costs (on campus, per year)	US$7,200	–	–
Accommodation costs (off campus, per year)	US$9,600	–	–
Financial aid available	Not discolsed	–	–
Type of aid available	Scholarships, loans	–	–
Criteria on which aid is granted	Merit	–	–

Accreditation

AACSB International

Application details

	Full-time MBA	Marshall MBA for Professionals & Managers	Marshall Executive MBA Program
Application deadline	January 4th	April 29th	April 29th
Programme dates	Aug start, 18 months	Aug start, 33 months	Aug start, 21 months
Admission requirements	First degree; TOEFL if first language not English; 2 references; 3 essays	First degree; at least 2 years' work experience; TOEFL if first language not English; 2 references; essay	First degree; at least 8 years' work experience; TOEFL if first language not English or if first degree not received from an institution where the primary instruction was in English; 2 references; essay; interview

Executive education

Marshall offers a range of specialised open-enrolment and customised in-company programmes. Many of these can be delivered via distance learning.

Southern Methodist University—Cox School of Business

Address
P.O. Box 750333
Dallas, TX
US
75275-0333

Tel:
+1 214 768 3562

Fax:
+1 214 768 3331

Email:
mbainfo@mail.cox.
smu.edu

Website:
www.coxmba.com

Programme director:
Dr Marci Armstrong

Figures in brackets
represent rank

Ranking	Rank (out of 100) Full-time
Overall rank	74
Regional rank	45

Criteria	Rank (out of 100) Full-time
Open new career opportunities	**61**
Diversity of recruiters	97
Number in jobs three months after graduation	70
Jobs found through the careers service	42
Student assessment of careers service	31
Personal development and educational experience	**92**
Faculty quality	70
Student quality	55
Student diversity	>100
Education experience	93
Increase in salary	**77**
Increase in salary	63
Post-MBA salary	73
Potential to network	**15**
Breadth of alumni network	9
Internationalism of alumni	26
Alumni effectiveness	34

Background

The Cox School of Business began as the Department of Commerce of Southern Methodist University (SMU) in 1920. It was established as a school of business in 1941 and the graduate programme began in 1949. The emphasis is on soft management skills, such as teamwork and communications, career development and contact with business, and the school has a solid base in academic research.

Practising executives are closely involved in the tuition and support of MBA students (the school was renamed in 1978 in honour of Edwin L. Cox, a Dallas businessman). The Business Leadership Center, for example, was established after market research suggested employers wanted MBA graduates with more leadership skills. Corporate executives and outside consultants are used to teach non-credit courses in communications and teamwork that complement the more theoretical concepts taught by the academic faculty. This interaction can also increase opportunities for career contacts in the future. Executives are involved in an innovative mentoring programme that gives students regular access to business leaders in some 200 leading corporations.

Facilities

The school is housed in a three-building complex and the facilities are excellent, with up-to-date equipment and dedicated classrooms. The class size is small by North American standards and there is a lot of interaction among students and between students and faculty.

	Full-time MBA
Student assessment of facilities	4.0 (67)

Faculty

Number of faculty: 74 full-time, 7 part-time, 1 visiting

	Full-time MBA	Professional MBA Program	Executive MBA
Number of faculty per student	1.0 (50)	0.4	1.0
Percentage of faculty with PhD	91 (55)	91	91
Student rating of faculty	4.1 (68)	–	–

Strengths and weaknesses

Strengths: finance; marketing; entrepreneurship

Weakness: elective choice

Programme highlights

Cox's full-time MBA is a two-year programme with each semester divided into two eight-week "modules". The first year consists of a mix of compulsory core courses, workshops, four electives and the Global Leadership Program (sponsored by American Airlines), a two-week overseas study tour preceded by six months of intensive preparation. Core courses can be waived by exam and replaced with electives. The second year is completely devoted to electives. Students may declare up to two concentrations from: accounting; finance; information technologies and operations management; management and organisations; marketing; strategy and entrepreneurship or opt for the general management concentrations, which allows a wide variety of study options. The Business Leadership Center offers a wide range of courses as well as a series of career enhancement workshops.

The part-time MBA (the Professional MBA or PMBA) is unusual in that it is taught over two-and-a-half years of seven consecutive semesters (spring, summer, fall). Each semester is divided into two eight-week modules, A and B. Again unusually, 17 electives are available in the second half of the programme. Electives can be grouped into a concentration or taken more widely. Some of the principal elements of the full-time programme, such as the Business Leadership Center, the Associate Board Mentoring Program and an exchange programme, are also available on the PMBA. Classes are held on weekday evenings and, on the Dallas campus only, Saturday mornings. The SMU campus in Legacy (Plano) offers core classes on Monday and Wednesday evenings.

The 21-month Executive MBA programme begins in August each year. Classes are held every other Friday and Saturday. Participants meet in small assigned study groups outside the classroom. A ten-day international trip to Europe or Asia, meeting top executives and companies, is an important part of the final semester. As well as an opening orientation session, there are a number of pre-programme workshops in business fundamentals.

	Full-time MBA	Professional MBA Program	Executive MBA
Student rating of programme	3.9 (80)	–	–
Number of overseas exchange programmes	15 (65)	–	–
Number of languages on offer	0 (94)	–	–

Students

	Full-time MBA	Professional MBA Program	Executive MBA
Annual intake	79	213	85
Applicants:places	4:1	–	2:1
Percentage of women students	24 (75)	26	18
Percentage of foreign students	15 (>100)	n/a	n/a
Average GMAT score	665 (34)	600	n/a
Average number of months' work experience	60 (63)	60	156
Age range of students	25-32	25-34	33-41
Average age	28	28	37
Student rating of culture and classmates	3.9 (63)	–	–

Student profile (full time)

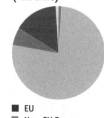

- ■ EU
- ■ Non-EU Europe
- North America
- ■ Other Americas
- ■ Asia/Australasia
- Middle East

Recruiters/careers service

	Full-time MBA	Professional MBA Program	Executive MBA
Number of industry sectors that recruited graduates	6 (97)	–	–
Percentage of graduates in jobs 3 months after graduation	78 (70)	–	–
Percentage of graduates finding jobs through careers services	44 (42)	–	–
Student rating of careers service	3.6 (31)	–	–
Post MBA salary, US$	69,407 (73)	–	–
Percentage increase in salary	22 (63)	–	–
Principal recruiters of graduates	Vartec Telecom, Inc. , Deloitte Consulting, On-Target Supplies & Logistics		

Cost

	Full-time MBA	Professional MBA Program	Executive MBA
Application fees	US$75	US$75	US$75
Programme fees	US$31,204	US$25,644	US$67,685
Comments	–	Per year	Total programme, except airfare and meals for two international trips
Accommodation costs (on campus, per year)	–	–	–
Accommodation costs (off campus, per year)	–	–	–
Financial aid available	Not disclosed	–	–
Type of aid available	Scholarships, graduate assistantships, loans	–	–
Criteria on which aid is granted	Merit, financial need	–	–

Accreditation

AACSB International

Application details

	Full-time MBA	Professional MBA Program	Executive MBA
Application deadline	April 30th	Rolling admission	July 1st
Programme dates	Aug start, 22 months	Aug start, 28 months	Aug start, 21 months
Admission requirements	First degree (US 4-year or equivalent); at least 2 years' work experience; TOEFL if first language not English; 2 references; 2 essays; laptop; interview by invitation only	First degree; at least 2 years' work experience; TOEFL if first language not English (minimum 600); 2 references; 2 essays; interview at discretion of admissions committee	At least 8 years' work experience; 2 references; 2 essays; interview

Executive education

Cox offers short (two-day to two-week) open-enrolment courses in sales and marketing, accounting and finance, management and leadership, and oil and gas/energy. It also offers longer (several months) certificate programmes in marketing and finance. Executive education at Cox will soon have a new home, the James M Collins Executive Education Center, currently under construction.

Student/alumni quotes

"The programme is especially strong in the applicable areas of finance and economics, and has a very good reputation for placement in the south-west, and Texas in particular."

"I found the entire faculty to be very knowledgeable and well respected in their field; however, a few of the faculty were not strong teachers."

"The number-one reason I chose to attend Cox was the non-curriculum programmes that enhanced my education. The Global Leadership Program is by far one of the best experiences in learning."

Stanford Graduate School of Business

Address
518 Memorial Way
Stanford, CA
US
94305

Tel:
+1 650 723 1771

Fax:
+1 650 725 6750

Email:
mba@gsb.stanford.
edu

Website:
www.gsb.stanford.
edu/mba/

Programme director:
Sharon Hoffman

Figures in brackets
represent rank

Ranking	Rank (out of 100) Full-time
Overall rank	2
Regional rank	2

Criteria	Rank (out of 100) Full-time
Open new career opportunities	**6**
Diversity of recruiters	1
Number in jobs three months after graduation	27
Jobs found through the careers service	3
Student assessment of careers service	8
Personal development and educational experience	**2**
Faculty quality	8
Student quality	10
Student diversity	11
Education experience	14
Increase in salary	**9**
Increase in salary	81
Post-MBA salary	5
Potential to network	**24**
Breadth of alumni network	52
Internationalism of alumni	58
Alumni effectiveness	2

Background

Stanford Business School was founded in 1925 by a group of Californian business leaders organised by Herbert Hoover, an alumnus of Stanford University and 31st president of the US. Hoover wanted to stem the tide of students going east to get a business education, and Stanford was the first graduate school of business west of the Mississippi.

Stanford's reputation for research, its location on the Pacific coast near Silicon Valley, close contacts with industries large and small, high academic standards and an enviable careers services record make it one of the most sought-after business schools in the world. The school makes great efforts to ensure a diverse student body, which gives it a cosmopolitan and international flavour. Students are almost unhealthily enthusiastic about the school and themselves. In response to a question in the 2004 Economist Intelligence Unit survey for Which MBA? designed to elicit what was a problem with a school or programme, one Stanford student replied: "I'd be nit-picking."

The school's long-standing expertise in public-sector management attracts students from diverse backgrounds such as government, health management, arts administration, museums, charities and other non-profit areas. Contacts with industry, notably in Silicon Valley but also internationally, are excellent and executives regularly visit the campus. Indeed, some help to teach elective courses. This ensures that Stanford has a strong entrepreneurial focus.

Facilities

The campus is built in a low-rise Spanish style, making Stanford one of the most striking business schools in North America (although one or two students suggest that the buildings are starting to show their age). The J Hugh Jackson library has more than 400,000 business volumes and there is a high-tech Reference Center offering electronic access to business and financial databases. San Francisco and the Bay Area offer many opportunities for sports, arts and leisure, but the campus is some distance from the city. Nevertheless, on-campus sports facilities are superb. There is also an impressive on-campus block of student apartments, the Schwab Residential Center.

	Full-time MBA
Student assessment of facilities	4.5 (16)

Faculty

Number of faculty: 100 full-time, 40 part-time, 8 visiting	
	Full-time MBA
Number of faculty per student	0.3 (95)
Percentage of faculty with PhD	99 (6)
Student rating of faculty	4.8 (3)

Strengths and weaknesses

Strengths: general management and strategy; finance and economics; organisational behaviour

Weakness: marketing classes have room for improvement

Programme highlights

The Stanford MBA is offered only as a full-time programme. Students study over six academic quarters beginning in the fall. The first year is mainly core courses (for three-quarters of the first year the focus is on foundations, functions and capstone), but some electives may be taken. The second year is all elective courses. Generally, students take around 14 electives chosen from around 100 within the school; four can be taken in other schools of the university. The emphasis is on general management and there is no requirement to specialise. The programme starts with a two-week pre-term academic programme designed to introduce students to the academic environment and covering such areas as career management, ethics and group working.

The Stanford Sloan Program is a full-time, ten-month academic programme leading to a Master of Science in Management degree. It is designed for mid-career executives, who are generally sponsored by their companies.

	Full-time MBA
Student rating of programme	4.6 (7)
Number of overseas exchange programmes	0 (93)
Number of languages on offer	>5 (1)

Students

	Full-time MBA
Annual intake	374
Applicants:places	14:1
Percentage of women students	35 (22)
Percentage of foreign students	35 (87)
Average GMAT score	716 (1)
Average number of months' work experience	50 (89)
Age range of students	–
Average age	–
Student rating of culture and classmates	4.9 (1)

Student profile (full time)

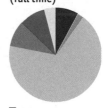

- ■ EU
- ■ Non-EU Europe
- ▨ North America
- ■ Other Americas
- ■ Asia/Australasia
- ▨ Middle East

Recruiters/careers service

	Full-time MBA
Number of industry sectors that recruited graduates	8 (1)
Percentage of graduates in jobs 3 months after graduation	86 (27)
Percentage of graduates finding jobs through careers services	86 (3)
Student rating of careers service	4.2 (8)
Post-MBA salary, US$	96,000 (5)
Percentage increase in salary	30 (81)
Principal recruiters of graduates	McKinsey & Co, The Boston Consulting Group, Booz Allen & Hamilton

Cost

	Full-time MBA
Application fees	US$225
Programme fees	US$37,998
Comments	Per year
Accommodation costs (on campus, per year)	US$17,751
Accommodation costs (off campus, per year)	US$19,071
Financial aid available	US$46,500,000
Type of aid available	Fellowships, loans
Criteria on which aid is granted	–

Accreditation

AACSB International

Application details

	Full-time MBA
Application deadline	March 17th
Programme dates	Sep start, 22 months
Admission requirements	TOEFL if first degree obtained from an institution where the primary language is not English; 3 references; 2 essays; laptop; interview by invitation only; transcripts; employment history (if previously employed)

Executive education

Stanford's flagship general management open-enrolment executive education programmes include the Stanford Executive Program, the Executive Program for Growing Companies and the Executive Management Program. There are also shorter programmes in financial management, leadership and strategy, marketing, negotiation, non profit and philanthropy, technology and operations. The school offers a range of customised in-company programmes.

Student/alumni quotes

"Stanford is one of the most selective MBA programmes in the country. Each person is hand-picked and given the support that is needed to develop on an individual basis."

"The school has a phenomenal network, a quality that I didn't even consider before attending. An amazing group of people—current students, alums, professors and administrators."

"The business school attracts some of the most charismatic, fascinating, diverse (for a b school!) people I have ever encountered. Everyone is very motivated (no slacking), happy (due to the weather) and collaborative (not competitive at all). All of these things make the GSB a wonderful place to spend two years."

University of Strathclyde Graduate School of Business

Ranking	Rank (out of 100) Full-time
Overall rank	67
Regional rank	25

Criteria	Rank (out of 100) Full-time
Open new career opportunities	**77**
Diversity of recruiters	51
Number in jobs three months after graduation	20
Jobs found through the careers service	62
Student assessment of careers service	>100
Personal development and educational experience	**58**
Faculty quality	32
Student quality	69
Student diversity	58
Education experience	72
Increase in salary	**29**
Increase in salary	67
Post-MBA salary	22
Potential to network	**88**
Breadth of alumni network	18
Internationalism of alumni	36
Alumni effectiveness	>100

Address
199 Cathedral Street
Glasgow
UK
G4 0QU

Tel:
+44 141 553 6104

Fax:
+44 141 553 6162

Email:
admissions@gsb.
strath.ac.uk

Website:
www.gsb.strath.ac.uk

Programme director:
Dr Robert McIntosh

Figures in brackets
represent rank

Background

The University of Strathclyde Graduate School of Business (GSB) is part of Strathclyde Business School, one of the largest in Europe, and itself a faculty of the University of Strathclyde. It has good links with industry and good international connections.

Facilities

Although the GSB is an integral part of the university, it is financially separate. It has funded its own development, notably the excellent facilities at its purpose-built city-centre site, which includes teaching and administration blocks, two computer laboratories, and business information and audio-visual centres. The building is not open to undergraduates. MBA students have access to the main university library (with 350,000 volumes and 1,250 seats) and to good on-campus sports facilities. The GSB also has a fully equipped two-star Campus Conference and Hotel Centre with 108 bedrooms. There is plenty of on-campus accommodation.

	Full-time MBA
Student assessment of facilities	4.2 (46)

Faculty

Number of faculty: 186 full-time, 4 part-time, 52 visiting

	Full-time MBA
Number of faculty per student	3.1 (2)
Percentage of faculty with PhD	53 (>100)
Student rating of faculty	4.1 (71)

Strengths and weaknesses

Strengths: strategy and strategic management; collaboration; leadership

Weakness: careers services

Programme highlights

The Strathclyde MBA can be earned full-time and part-time and through open-learning, in-company and consortium programmes. There is considerable flexibility in moving between the various delivery options. A mix of teaching and learning methods is employed. The main MBA versions have the same structure whatever their delivery system and all have an emphasis on strategic management. There is a good deal of group work and all delivery methods lead to the same MBA degree.

The full-time programme lasts one year and consists of three academic terms and an in-company project (July–September). It is divided into five modules, progressing from a compulsory grounding in basic business to specialised or generalist elective courses and then the final project. Students take three electives in module 4, either across a wide field or as a concentration. If they follow a specialisation their project is expected to be in that area. A project methodology course in module 5 is compulsory.

The evening part-time programme lasts for three years with classes meeting on two evenings a week (6.30–9.30 pm). Study groups may hold another weekly meeting. The programme can be fast-tracked to take two to two-and-a-half years via summer project work and full-time summer schools.

The flexible-learning (distance-learning) programme can be completed in 2–5 years (three years is the norm). Course materials consist of study guides, audiocassettes, videotapes and computer disks. Each student has a tutor, who provides guidance and support by phone, for each unit studied. Students must attend at least four weekend schools, covering business simulations and management skills.

The MBA is also offered part-time at one of nine international centres: Bahrain, Dubai, Greece, Hong Kong, Malaysia, Oman, Shanghai, Singapore, Switzerland. Teaching is by Strathclyde's full-time MBA faculty with support from open learning materials and approved local counsellors. The programme is completed in 2–3 years and requires on average 15–20 hours' study per week. Electives can be taken in the UK, together with students on the full-time and part-time programmes, and at other international centres.

Strathclyde also offers an MBA in leadership, in conjunction with the Leadership Trust Foundation, which is normally taken part-time on a modular basis over three years.

	Full-time MBA
Student rating of programme	4.0 (72)
Number of overseas exchange programmes	0 (68)
Number of languages on offer	5 (72)

Student profile (full time)

- ■ EU
- ■ Non-EU Europe
- ■ North America
- ■ Other Americas
- ■ Asia/Australasia
- ■ Middle East

Students

	Full-time MBA
Annual intake	64
Applicants:places	4.5:1
Percentage of women students	27 (69)
Percentage of foreign students	69 (30)
Average GMAT score	590 (95)
Average number of months' work experience	92 (10)
Age range of students	26–40
Average age	31
Student rating of culture and classmates	3.9 (86)

Recruiters/careers service

	Full-time MBA
Number of industry sectors that recruited graduates	8 (51)
Percentage of graduates in jobs 3 months after graduation	98 (20)
Percentage of graduates finding jobs through careers services	45 (62)
Student rating of careers service	2.3 (>100)
Post-MBA salary, US$	98,361 (22)
Percentage increase in salary	67 (67)
Principal recruiters of graduates	Royal Bank of Scotland, PriceWaterhouseCooper, Honeywell

Cost

	Full-time MBA
Application fees	None
Programme fees	£17,300 (US$28,361)
Comments	Total programme, including commitment fee
Accommodation costs (on campus, per year)	£2,500 (US$4,098)
Accommodation costs (off campus, per year)	£3,800 (US$6,230)
Financial aid available	£130,000 (US$213,115)
Type of aid available	Scholarships, partial awards
Criteria on which aid is granted	Merit

Accreditation

AACSB International, AMBA, EQUIS

Application details

	Full-time MBA
Application deadline	June 30th
Programme dates	Oct start, 12 months
Admission requirements	First degree; at least 3 years' work experience; GMAT; TOEFL or IELTS if first language not English; 2 references; 3 essays; interview; laptop

Executive education

Strathclyde does not currently offer open-enrolment or in-company executive education programmes.

Student/alumni quotes

"I am really happy with Strathclyde. One of the main reasons for choosing the university was the fact that it had amazing faculty ... though I feel the school needs to stress the GMAT. For prospective students, well it's a brilliant education, world-class faculty, the teaching techniques are excellent, brilliant business library ... the quality of students well experienced. But the flipside is that the careers services have more to do."

"It's a great school but it needs to be promoted better and the students must be required to take a GMAT."

"The high quality and extent of work experience of the class is the most valuable asset of this programme. The average age of the class is 31 and lots of my classmates have several years' managerial experience. It provides a good arena for critical review and to integrate theory and practice based on work experience from different cultures and nationalities."

Which MBA? © The Economist Intelligence Unit Limited 2004

University of Texas at Austin—McCombs School of Business

Address
One University Station
Stop B6000
Austin, TX
US
78712

Tel:
+1 512 475 6423

Fax:
+1 512 232 9167

Email:
McCombsMBA@
mccombs.utexas.edu

Website:
mba.mccombs.utexas.
edu/
admissions/

Programme director:
Steve Salbu

Figures in brackets
represent rank

Ranking	Rank (out of 100) Full-time
Overall rank	45
Regional rank	28

Criteria	Rank (out of 100) Full-time
Open new career opportunities	37
Diversity of recruiters	73
Number in jobs three months after graduation	n/a
Jobs found through the careers service	8
Student assessment of careers service	97
Personal development and educational experience	81
Faculty quality	75
Student quality	47
Student diversity	69
Education experience	99
Increase in salary	53
Increase in salary	53
Post-MBA salary	45
Potential to network	62
Breadth of alumni network	58
Internationalism of alumni	83
Alumni effectiveness	>100

Background

McCombs School of Business at the University of Texas at Austin is one of the best-regarded business schools in the burgeoning US south-west with ambitions to become a national player. In 2000 Red McCombs, a Texan entrepreneur, invested US$50m in the school, allowing it to launch an aggressive expansion plan that will include adding 30 new tenure-track faculty over the next five academic years, starting in 2003–04, and significantly improving its undergraduate programmes.

Mcombs is already a big, full-range school with over 6,000 students and 2,000 executive education participants each year and more than 75,000 alumni. Links with local business are strong and are fully utilised. MBA students have, for example, launched "Austin Power", a scheme that helps local companies recruit students who want to stay in Austin.

Facilities

The school is housed in three interconnected buildings at the heart of the university campus with 26 classrooms, 500 offices, 19 research centres, five computer laboratories with 300 computers and over 1,000 network ports as well as wireless network access. The new MBA Carpenter Center Lounge offers private study space for students as well as work rooms and conference rooms for student organisations and ten private meeting rooms. The Ford Career Interview Center has 43 private interviewing suites with nearby changing rooms and suit lockers. The EDS Trading and Technology Center is a state-of-the art trading, research and teaching facility equipped with the same technology that serves Wall Street

	Full-time MBA
Student assessment of facilities	4.2 (84)

Faculty

Number of faculty: 143 full-time, 43 part-time, 6 visiting

	Full-time MBA	Texas Evening MBA Program	Texas Executive MBA Program at DFW	Option II Executive MBA Program
Number of faculty per student	0.4 (84)	2.4	6.4	2.6
Percentage of faculty with PhD	90 (59)	90	90	90
Student rating of faculty	4.3 (77)	–	–	–

Strengths and weaknesses

Strengths: finance, marketing, technology

Weaknesses: marketing classes; perception that it is a regional school

Programme highlights

In the McCombs two-year full-time MBA, core courses and electives overlap. The nine-course core is taken during the first year and the first semester of the second, and electives start in the second semester of the first year. There is also a good programme of soft skills training such as written and oral communications. Core courses are fairly traditional, although there is some choice. For example, there is an option of art and science of negotiation, creating and managing human capital, or managing people and organisations: consultant's perspective. The Plus Program is a series of team-oriented, non-graded seminars covering such things as sales and negotiation and the complexities of business ethics and global trade.

There is no requirement to group electives into a concentration although several are offered (accounting, finance, management, information technology and marketing). Students can also choose a specialisation, a specifically designed set of courses geared to particular employment markets (accounting; finance; management; management science and information systems; marketing; marketing/management science and information systems; social enterprise).

The three-year part-time Texas Evening MBA (TEMBA) has the same curriculum as the full-time version. Students attend classes in the fall, spring and summer semesters. Classes meet on Monday and Tuesday evenings, with three one-week residential "business immersion courses".

The Executive MBA is a traditional two-year programme for mid-career professionals with classes scheduled on campus on alternate weekends (Friday and Saturday). The programme is also held in the downtown Dallas/Fort Worth area at the American Airlines Training and Conference Center @ DFW over five sequential semesters for 21 months, and in Mexico City, offering an MBA from McCombs and a Master's of Administration from Tecnológico de Monterrey-Campus Ciudad de México.

	Full-time MBA	Texas Evening MBA Program	Texas Executive MBA Program at DFW	Option II Executive MBA Program
Student rating of programme	4.2 (77)	–	–	–
Number of overseas exchange programmes	70 (63)	–	–	–
Number of languages on offer	3 (76)	–	–	–

Student profile (full time)

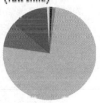

- ■ EU
- ■ Non-EU Europe
- ■ North America
- ■ Other Americas
- ■ Asia/Australasia
- ▒ Middle East

Students

	Full time MBA	Texas Evening MBA Program	Texas Executive MBA Program at DFW	Option II Executive MBA Program
Annual intake	387	79	30	73
Applicants:places	5:1	2:1	–	2:1
Percentage of women students	24 (90)	17	14	11
Percentage of foreign students	50 (70)	n/a	n/a	na
Average GMAT score	677 (22)	664	620	667
Average number of months' work experience	60 (72)	72	108	132
Age range of students	25-32	26-36	26-38	29-42
Average age	28	26	30	35
Student rating of culture and classmates	4.4 (55)	–	–	–

Recruiters/careers service

	Full-time MBA	Texas Evening MBA Program	Texas Executive MBA Program at DFW	Option II Executive MBA Program
Number of industry sectors that recruited graduates	6 (73)	–	–	–
Percentage of graduates in jobs 3 months after graduation	n/a (n/a)	–	–	–
Percentage of graduates finding jobs through careers services	80 (8)	–	–	–
Student rating of careers service	3.4 (97)	–	–	–
Post-MBA salary, US$	79,787 (45)	–	–	–
Percentage increase in salary	57 (53)	–	–	–
Principal recruiters of graduates	Dell, IBM, Citigroup			

Cost

	Full-time MBA	Texas Evening MBA Program	Texas Executive MBA Program at DFW	Option II Executive MBA Program
Application fees	US$125	US$125	US$125	US$125
Programme fees	US$27,599	US$6,900	US$13,000	US$51,000
Comments	Per year. Fee for Texas residents is US$13,063. Fee for other US residents is US$26,953	Per semester	Per semester	Fee for Texas residents. Fee for non-Texas residents is US$72,000
Accommodation costs (on campus, per year)		–	–	–
Accommodation costs (off campus, per year)	US$12,212	–	–	–
Financial aid available	US$19,700 (maximum per student)	–	–	–
Type of aid available	Scholarships, grants, loans	–	–	–
Criteria on which aid is granted	Need analysis, merit, non-need aid/ loan awarded	–	–	–

Accreditation

AACSB International

Application details

	Full-time MBA	Texas Evening MBA Program	Texas Executive MBA Program at DFW	Option II Executive MBA Program
Application deadline	April 15th	June 15th	June 15th	June 15th
Programme dates	Aug start, 22 months	Aug start, 33 months	Aug start, 22 months	Aug start, 22 months
Admission requirements	Bachelor's degree or equivalent; at least 2 years' work experience; TOEFL if first language not English (minimum 260,computer-based; 620 paper-based); 2 references; 3 essays; interview; laptop	First degree; at least 2 years' work experience; TOEFL if first language not English; 3 references; essay; interview	First degree; at least 5 years' work experience; TOEFL if first language not English; 2 references; essay; interview	First degree (equivalent to a four-year undergraduate degree from a college/university in the US); at least 5 years' work experience; GMAT; letter of commitment from employer; references; essay; interviews are conducted at the discretion of the director

Executive education

McCombs offers short open-enrolment executive education courses in areas such as organisation, people, marketing management, accounting and finance, and operational excellence. It also runs programmes leading to a General Management Certificate involving two required courses (leveraging culture and organisational change, and accounting and finance for non-financial managers) and seven days of elective courses taken in one or two-and-a-half-day courses. The school offers a range of customised in-company programmes.

Student/alumni quotes

"An excellent programme in an exquisite city. Austin is very nice, specially for married students. The cost of living is not high and the quality of the academic experience is outstanding. When choosing among different schools take a closer look at McCombs Plus Program; it makes a difference."

"The graduate business school is co-mingled with the undergraduates."

"My classmates are bright, ambitious and fun to be around. The administration is extraordinarily receptive to new ideas but has occasionally been asleep at the wheel by allowing a less than stellar professor to teach a core class. Regardless, I've been extremely happy with the programme and wouldn't have chosen differently with the benefit of hindsight. McCombs will be the best public business school in the US within the next five years."

Theseus International Management Institute

Address
903 rue Albert
Einstein
BP 169
Sophia Antipolis
France
06903

Tel:
+33 4 9294 5107

Fax:
+33 4 9365 3837

Email:
travia@theseus.fr

Website:
www.theseus.edu

Programme director:
Francis Bidault

Figures in brackets
represent rank

Ranking	Rank (out of 100) Full-time
Overall rank	n/a
Regional rank	42

Background

Theseus was set up in 1989 as a joint venture by the French government and leading European (largely French) companies, including Aerospatiale, France Telecom and Hewlett-Packard. The aim was to redefine management for the information age. Although IT is a strong element of its MBA, the school stresses that it is concerned with the management of information, not just the technology.

Theseus has a small core faculty, but affiliated and visiting faculty, consisting of a mixture of academics and practising managers, teach many courses. The annual intake is also small.

Facilities

The school is based in a modern building in Sophia Antipolis, a science park between Nice and Cannes on the French Côte d'Azur—an attractive location for a business school. There is no on-campus accommodation but the school helps students find housing.

	Full-time MBA
Student assessment of facilities	3.5 (n/a)

Faculty

Number of faculty: 7 full-time, 0 part-time, 20 visiting

	Full-time MBA
Number of faculty per student	0.4 (n/a)
Percentage of faculty with PhD	14 (n/a)
Student rating of faculty	4.1 (n/a)

Strengths and weaknesses

Strengths: innovation; technology management; strategy

Weakness: careers service

Programme highlights

Theseus's ten-month programme starts with an orientation week, followed by six three-week modules during autumn and winter. These cover what the school calls the fundamentals of management and technology and are equivalent to a core programme, with a strong emphasis on technology. The spring schedule is built around four consecutive three-week "clusters" relating to issues and external developments that have an impact on business life. The first three clusters are mandatory and cover entrepreneurial leadership, knowledge and people management, and customer-centric management. Students then have a choice of either innovation management or managing alliances and partnerships. The programme finishes with a group consultancy project lasting eight weeks. There is a wide range of personal and group development and careers workshops throughout the taught programme.

There is no part-time MBA but working managers can attend MBA courses on a for-credit basis to gain the MBA over a maximum of three consecutive academic years.

	Full-time MBA
Student rating of programme	4.1 (n/a)
Number of overseas exchange programmes	0 (n/a)
Number of languages on offer	1 (n/a)

Students

	Full-time MBA
Annual intake	33
Applicants:places	4:1
Percentage of women students	25 (n/a)
Percentage of foreign students	61 (n/a)
Average GMAT score	620 (n/a)
Average number of months' work experience	96 (n/a)
Age range of students	28-36
Average age	33
Student rating of culture and classmates	4.2 (n/a)

Student profile (full time)

- ■ EU
- ■ Non-EU Europe
- ▨ North America
- ■ Other Americas
- ■ Asia/Australasia
- ▨ Middle East

Recruiters/careers service

	Full-time MBA
Number of industry sectors that recruited graduates	3 (n/a)
Percentage of graduates in jobs 3 months after graduation	50 (n/a)
Percentage of graduates finding jobs through careers services	20 (n/a)
Student rating of careers service	2.8 (n/a)
Post-MBA salary, US$	90,909 (n/a)
Percentage increase in salary	38 (n/a)
Principal recruiters of graduates	–

Cost

	Full-time MBA
Application fees	€65 (US$74)
Programme fees	€23,500 (US$26,705)
Comments	Total programme
Accommodation costs (on campus, per year)	–
Accommodation costs (off campus, per year)	€4,500 (US$5,114)
Financial aid available	€62,400 (US$70,909)
Type of aid available	Scholarships
Criteria on which aid is granted	Essays, merit

Accreditation

AMBA

Application details

	Full-time MBA
Application deadline	May 31st
Programme dates	Sep start, 10 months
Admission requirements	First degree; at least 3 years' work experience; GMAT; interview in English; 2 references; 8 essays; laptop

Executive education

Theseus offers a range of open-enrolment and customised in-company programmes largely based on action-learning concepts.

Student/alumni quotes

"Theseus is different from the other MBA schools I researched because it has a totally different business model. By using visiting professors to get amazing faculty talent, sourced on a course-by-course basis from around the world for their expertise, the school is viable with a small class size that means everyone gets individual attention and the whole school feels like a start-up."

"Occasionally the 'French' delivery style/approach overpowers the group learning dynamics."

"The recruitment climate during and after my MBA has been very tough. This was made more difficult by the fact that Theseus is a small school in a somewhat out-of-the-way location."

Thunderbird—The Garvin School of International Management

Address
15249 N. 59th Avenue
Glendale, AZ
US
85306

Tel:
+1 602 978 7114

Fax:
+1 602 978 7626

Email:
admissions@thunderbird.edu

Website:
www.thunderbird.edu

Programme director:
Dr Olufemi Babarinde

Figures in brackets
represent rank

Ranking	Rank (out of 100) Full-time
Overall rank	83
Regional rank	47

Criteria	Rank (out of 100) Full-time
Open new career opportunities	**85**
Diversity of recruiters	47
Number in jobs three months after graduation	>100
Jobs found through the careers service	64
Student assessment of careers service	35
Personal development and educational experience	**72**
Faculty quality	72
Student quality	99
Student diversity	54
Education experience	30
Increase in salary	**93**
Increase in salary	77
Post-MBA salary	92
Potential to network	**7**
Breadth of alumni network	10
Internationalism of alumni	27
Alumni effectiveness	9

Background

Thunderbird virtually invented the teaching of international business education in the US (it was formed in 1946 on a second world war pilot training base outside Phoenix, hence the rather odd name). Although it no longer has the field to itself, it has proved nimble in reacting to increased pressure from other schools moving into its "global" focus and in responding to the growth of global-isation. It has modernised its programmes and invested heavily in a new campus in France and facilities in Japan, China and Russia. It also teaches students through partnership programmes in Brazil, Mexico, Peru and Taiwan.

In April 2004 Thunderbird received a gift of $60m (the biggest of its kind to a business school) from alumnus Samuel S. Garvin and his wife Rita, which will be used to increase scholarships and attract faculty. Also in 2004, the school said goodbye to Roy Herberger, its long-serving (since 1989) president (dean). He was replaced by Angel Cabrera, formerly dean of IE in Madrid.

Thunderbird's international reputation, strong corporate links, opportunities to study abroad and large alumni network (33,000 managers in 135 countries) make it highly attractive for students and recruiters. However, students say that careers services can be weak.

Facilities

A US$15m building programme has provided excellent facilities. The school is mainly residential. It has plenty of student clubs and good staff–student interaction, so social activity is strongly focused on the school. Sports facilities are superb. The lifestyle is relaxed and Phoenix offers good cultural, sporting and leisure amenities. Arizona is extremely hot in summer and comfortably balmy in winter.

	Full-time MBA
Student assessment of facilities	4.4 (44)

Faculty

Number of faculty: 70 full-time, 14 part-time, 5 visiting

	Full-time MBA	Global MBA for Latin American Managers	Executive MBA in International Management
Number of faculty per student	0.2 (>100)	0.3	0.5
Percentage of faculty with PhD	93 (52)	93	93
Student rating of faculty	4.3 (46)	–	–

Strengths and weaknesses

Strengths: marketing; finance; international development

Weakness: located some distance from commercial/industrial hubs

Programme highlights

Thunderbird's MBA is divided into two tracks. Track 1 is a four-trimester programme that includes for-eign language study. Track 2 is a shorter three-trimester programme for students who already speak a foreign language and have some international business experience, designed to be completed in one calendar year. Students must take a "Winterim" programme, preferably outside the US, in place of language studies. Both tracks share the same core subjects and focuses.

After the core, students choose a functional focus in global marketing, global finance or internation-al development, or a customised focus. Each focus consists of a mix of required and elective courses. All students must have completed pre-programme courses in macroeconomics and microeconomics. The programme begins with the one-week required Foundations, which provides personal and pro-fessional tools and insights necessary for success and career effectiveness in the global economy.

Thunderbird's 21-month Executive MBA has almost exactly the same curriculum as the full-time ver-sion. Classes meet all day Friday and Saturday on alternate weekends. The programme begins with a one-week residential session and there are three further one-week residencies: language camp; study tour to Mexico; study tour to Europe or Asia.

The school also runs an EMBA in central and eastern Europe and in Latin America; a Global MBA for Latin American Managers with the Instituto Tecnológico y de Estudios Superiores de Monterrey (ITESM); and a Post MBA Program for students who already hold an MBA to further internationalise their knowledge of business practices and business environments. This programme leads to a Masters of International Management.

	Full-time MBA	Global MBA for Latin American Managers	Executive MBA in International Management
Student rating of programme	4.3 (30)	–	–
Number of overseas exchange programmes	10 (84)	–	–
Number of languages on offer	>5 (1)	–	–

Students

	Full-time MBA	Global MBA for Latin American Managers	Executive MBA in International Management
Annual intake	320	–	177
Applicants:places	2:1	1:1	–
Percentage of women students	27 (62)	18	20
Percentage of foreign students	58 (47)	–	n/a
Average GMAT score	600 (90)	600	n/a
Average number of months' work experience	66 (58)	24	96
Age range of students	25-35	24-35	30-45
Average age	30	29	37
Student rating of culture and classmates	4.2 (49)	–	–

Student profile (full time)

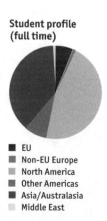

- ■ EU
- ■ Non-EU Europe
- North America
- ■ Other Americas
- ■ Asia/Australasia
- Middle East

Recruiters/careers service

	Full-time MBA	Global MBA for Latin American Managers	Executive MBA in International Management
Number of industry sectors that recruited graduates	7 (47)	–	–
Percentage of graduates in jobs 3 months after graduation	37 (>100)	–	–
Percentage of graduates finding jobs through careers services	30 (64)	–	–
Student rating of careers service	3.7 (35)	–	–
Post-MBA salary, US$	60,111 (92)	–	–
Percentage increase in salary	30 (77)		–
Principal recruiters of graduates	Johnson & Johnson, Citigroup, LG Electronics		

Cost

	Full-time MBA	Global MBA for Latin American Managers	Executive MBA in International Management
Application fees	US$125	US$250	US$100
Programme fees	US$14,648	US$33,500	US$58,000
Comments	Per trimester	–	Total programme. The fee for the 16 month class in Prague, Czech Republic is US$34,000
Accommodation costs (on campus, per year)	US$4,500	–	–
Accommodation costs (off campus, per year)	US$6,900	–	–
Financial aid available	US$4,200,000	–	–
Type of aid available	Scholarships, grants, loans, student employment	–	–
Criteria on which aid is granted	Financial need, academic merit, letters of recommendation, work history, essays	–	–

Accreditation

AACSB International, EQUIS

Application details

	Full-time MBA	Global MBA for Latin American Managers	Executive MBA in International Management
Application deadline	Rolling admissions	April 30th	Rolling admissions, but May 14th is the preferred deadline
Programme dates	Sep start, 16 months	Aug start, 24 months	Aug start, 21 months
Admission requirements	4-year first degree or equivalent; at least 2 years' work experience; TOEFL if first language not English; pre-requisite courses (macroeconomics and microeconomics at an accredited university or college); 2 references; 2 essays	First degree (minimum grade point average of 3.0); at least 2 years' work experience; TOEFL if first language not English; references; interview may be required, based on the application	First degree; at least 8 years' work experience; 3 references; essay; interview; the school reserves the right to ask for TOEFL or GMAT scores

Executive education

Thunderbird offers a wide portfolio of open-enrolment programmes including language and culture training and leadership, strategy, project management and finance. It also offers customised in-company programmes.

Student/alumni quotes

"Thunderbird has an excellent programme with global appeal, but it doesn't have high US brand awareness."

"If you want to go into global business management, this is the place to go. Aside from course content, a 30,000+ global alumni network is invaluable."

"The trimester system creates too rigorous a workload, which leaves limited time to take advantage of the cultural experience with peers, participate in campus groups, and attend all the events and speakers."

UCLA—Anderson School

Address
110 Westwood Plaza
Box 951481
Los Angeles, CA
US
90095-1481

Tel:
+1 310 825 9883

Fax:
+1 310 825 7977

Email:
mba.admissions@and
erson.ucla.edu

Website:
www.mba.anderson.
ucla.edu

Programme director:
David Lewin

Figures in brackets
represent rank

Ranking	Rank (out of 100) Full-time
Overall rank	18
Regional rank	15

Criteria	Rank (out of 100) Full-time
Open new career opportunities	**23**
Diversity of recruiters	1
Number in jobs three months after graduation	73
Jobs found through the careers service	n/a
Student assessment of careers service	16
Personal development and educational experience	**20**
Faculty quality	48
Student quality	19
Student diversity	61
Education experience	15
Increase in salary	**43**
Increase in salary	78
Post-MBA salary	35
Potential to network	**31**
Breadth of alumni network	36
Internationalism of alumni	68
Alumni effectiveness	18

Background

The Anderson School at UCLA began in 1935 as the College of Commerce with just seven faculty to teach business fundamentals and basic skills such as typing, shorthand and penmanship to high-school graduates. Now it concentrates on business leadership in the context of globalisation, entre-preneurship and technology. The school teaches some 1,300 students on various degree and non-degree programmes annually. It is an international powerhouse with good links with local and international business (practising executives frequently visit the campus) and numerous research centres, such as The Center for Management in the Information Economy, that promote and share applied research.

Facilities

The school is based in a purpose-built, seven-building academic village on the UCLA campus, close to Santa Monica, Malibu, Bel Air and Beverly Hills. The complex provides superb teaching, library and technology facilities. Information technology is pervasive and students must have a laptop comput-er. Students have access to all university facilities, which include a full range of sports and leisure amenities. Limited on-campus accommodation is available in the graduate residence hall and in married-student apartments.

	Full-time MBA
Student assessment of facilities	4.4 (26)

Faculty

Number of faculty: 83 full-time, 36 part-time, 4 visiting

	Full-time MBA	Fully Employed MBA Program	Executive MBA Program
Number of faculty per student	0.3 (96)	0.6	1.7
Percentage of faculty with PhD	100 (7)	100	100
Student rating of faculty	4.4 (38)	–	–

Strengths and weaknesses

Strengths: finance; marketing; entrepreneurship

Programme highlights

The Anderson MBA starts with the five-day, two-course Management Foundations, which acts as an orientation week and prepares students for the MBA programme. This is followed by the ten-course core, which is studied over three quarters. Students then take 12 electives, divided into nine "advanced electives", which allow students to concentrate on one or more areas of study, and three "free electives", which can be taken as advanced management courses or in other departments at UCLA. In the core, students study in assigned sections of 65. The programme concludes with the Management Field Study, a six-month team consultancy-like project designed to allow students to apply their knowledge and skills in a professional setting outside the classroom. Soft skills workshops run alongside the regular curriculum.

The part-time MBA (known as the Fully Employed MBA) offers a curriculum very similar to the full-time version. Three class sections of 60 students each are admitted in September. Classes are held on campus, and core courses are offered either twice weekly or all day Saturday. Section 1 meets on Thursdays (1.30–5 pm) and Saturdays (8.30 am–12 pm); Section 2 meets on Saturdays (8.30 am–5 pm); and Section 3 meets on Monday evenings (6–9.30 pm) and Saturday mornings (8.30 am–12 pm). Elective courses are generally held on weekday afternoons.

The two-year Executive MBA is fairly traditional in structure but does include an overseas study session in Europe in the second year. Classes meet on alternate weekends, 9.30 am–5 pm on Friday and 8.30 am–4 pm on Saturday, with three-week breaks after each 16-week trimester. The programme proper begins with managerial problem solving, a five-day, off-campus orientation session that introduces the case method.

	Full-time MBA	Fully Employed MBA Program	Executive MBA Program
Student rating of programme	4.3 (34)	–	–
Number of overseas exchange programmes	340 (3)	–	–
Number of languages on offer	2 (75)	–	–

Students

	Full-time MBA	Fully Employed MBA Program	Executive MBA Program
Annual intake	333	197	72
Applicants:places	11:1	2:1	2:1
Percentage of women students	30 (49)	23	23
Percentage of foreign students	26 (>100)	n/a	n/a
Average GMAT score	705 (5)	664	659
Average number of months' work experience	54 (82)	72	168
Age range of students	23-37	24-46	32-45
Average age	27	30	37
Student rating of culture and classmates	4.6 (16)	–	–

Student profile (full time)

- ■ EU
- ▨ Non-EU Europe
- ▨ North America
- ■ Other Americas
- ■ Asia/Australasia
- ▨ Middle East

Recruiters/careers service

	Full-time MBA	Fully Employed MBA Program	Executive MBA Program
Number of industry sectors that recruited graduates	8 (1)	–	–
Percentage of graduates in jobs 3 months after graduation	74 (73)	–	–
Percentage of graduates finding jobs through careers services	n/a (n/a)	–	–
Student rating of careers service	3.9 (16)	–	–
Post-MBA salary, US$	85,000 (35)	–	–
Percentage increase in salary	55 (78)		–
Principal recruiters of graduates	–		

Cost

	Full-time MBA	Fully Employed MBA Program	Executive MBA Program
Application fees	US$150	US$150	US$150
Programme fees	$29,218	US$24,000	US$38,610
Comments	Per year. Fee for California residents is US$16,973	Per year	Per year
Accommodation costs (on campus, per year)	US$11,670	–	–
Accommodation costs (off campus, per year)	US$11,670	–	–
Financial aid available	US$7,406,496	–	–
Type of aid available	Scholarships, fellowships, loans, assistantships	–	–
Criteria on which aid is granted	Merit, financial need	–	–

Accreditation

AACSB International

Application details

	Full-time MBA	Fully Employed MBA Program	Executive MBA Program
Application deadline	April 14th	–	–
Programme dates	Sep start, 21 months	Sep start, 33 months	Aug start, 21 months
Admission requirements	4-year Bachelor's degree or equivalent; work experience; TOEFL if first language not English (no minimum score, but few applicants are admitted with scores lower than 600 paper-based, 260 computer-based); 2 references; 4 essays	4-year Bachelor's degree; work experience; TOEFL if first language not English (no minimum score, but few applicants are admitted with scores lower than 600 paper-based, 275 computer-based); 2 references; 3 essays	First degree; work experience; TOEFL if first language not English (no minimum score, but few applicants are admitted with scores lower than 600 paper-based, 275 computer-based); 3 references; 3 essays

Executive education

Anderson runs around 40 executive education courses each year for some 2,000 participants. Its open-enrolment programmes are most notable for their emphasis on leadership, particularly for African-American executives, women, gay, lesbian and bisexual executives and so on. Customised programmes cover areas such as general management, global management, financial management, marketing management, leadership and diversity, operations and technology management, and human resource management and leadership.

Student/alumni quotes

"Anderson is very much underrated. The curriculum and atmosphere is very competitive. And the tuition was such a good deal."

"Excellent reputation on the west coast but not as respected on the east coast."

"Just as academically challenging as any other school, with the friendliest student body of any school I have visited and the largest variety of activities to participate in outside of school."

Vanderbilt University—Owen Graduate School of Management

Address
401 21st Avenue
South
Nashville, TN
US
37067

Tel:
+1 615 322 2316

Fax:
+1 615 343 7110

Email:
admissions@owen.
vanderbill.edu

Website:
mba.vanderbilt.edu

Programme director:
William G Christie

Figures in brackets
represent rank

Ranking	Rank (out of 100) Full-time
Overall rank	55
Regional rank	36

Criteria	Rank (out of 100) Full-time
Open new career opportunities	**41**
Diversity of recruiters	57
Number in jobs three months after graduation	49
Jobs found through the careers service	49
Student assessment of careers service	33
Personal development and educational experience	**67**
Faculty quality	62
Student quality	90
Student diversity	97
Education experience	16
Increase in salary	76
Increase in salary	69
Post-MBA salary	71
Potential to network	**53**
Breadth of alumni network	79
Internationalism of alumni	87
Alumni effectiveness	31

Background

Vanderbilt University's Graduate School of Business, founded in 1969 by local Tennessee businesses to be a regional centre of excellence, began with just ten students and ten faculty. It has remained determinedly small. The school has a strong emphasis on entrepreneurship and leadership and there is a lot of teamwork. In 1977 the business school was named after Ralph (a former chairman of American Express) and Lulu Owen in recognition of their contributions to its development.

Facilities

The school is based in Management Hall, an attractive modern block that also incorporates the Victorian exterior of one of the university's oldest buildings, Mechanical Engineering Hall, built in 1888. Library and computer facilities are excellent and students have access to all the university's sports and recreational amenities. On-campus housing is available but most MBA students stay off campus, where housing is plentiful and reasonably priced.

	Full-time MBA
Student assessment of facilities	4.5 (15)

Faculty

Number of faculty: 44 full-time, 30 part-time, 2 visiting

	Full-time MBA	Vanderbilt Executive MBA Program
Number of faculty per student	0.3 (>100)	1.5
Percentage of faculty with PhD	91 (42)	91
Student rating of faculty	4.3 (41)	–

Strengths and weaknesses

Strengths: finance; human resources and organisational behaviour; operations management

Weakness: marketing courses

Programme highlights

The Owen MBA is based on a solid core and concentrations. Concentrations are typically six courses in a particular field and students can choose to follow more than one. Work on concentrations (accounting, finance, electronic commerce, human and organisational performance, information technology, marketing, operations and strategy) starts in the second semester of the first year, with core courses largely completed in the first semester. Each semester is divided into two seven-week modules. Students can work with faculty to develop a customised "general management" concentration. Concentrations can be complemented with "emphases"—additional approved course work—in brand management, entrepreneurship, environmental management, healthcare or international studies. Students can also take "free" electives, not linked to concentrations or emphases, often in other schools of the university. One elective must be taken in the international business field.

The programme is rigorous and quantitative. First-year students must demonstrate their competence in calculus, linear algebra, statistics and basic computing. The school offers pre-programme "camps" in calculus and statistics. There is a significant amount of project and group work.

The Executive MBA is traditional in style and content. Participants meet on campus on alternate weekends (Friday and Saturday) over 21 months. The programme begins in August with a full week of instruction at an off-campus site. This is an intensive introduction and allows students and faculty to get to know each other. There is a group strategy project and an international study trip in the second year as part of the global management course. There are three electives in the second year.

	Full-time MBA	Vanderbilt Executive MBA Program
Student rating of programme	4.3 (39)	–
Number of overseas exchange programmes	72 (49)	–
Number of languages on offer	>5 (1)	–

Students

	Full-time MBA	Vanderbilt Executive MBA Program
Annual intake	209	52
Applicants:places	5:1	3:1
Percentage of women students	25 (86)	25
Percentage of foreign students	27 (>100)	n/a
Average GMAT score	644 (56)	590
Average number of months' work experience	54 (n/a)	144
Age range of students	25-33	26-57
Average age	28	34
Student rating of culture and classmates	4.4 (38)	–

Student profile (full time)

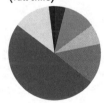

- ■ EU
- ■ Non-EU Europe
- ▨ North America
- ■ Other Americas
- ■ Asia/Australasia
- ▨ Middle East
- ■ Other

Recruiters/careers service

	Full-time MBA	Vanderbilt Executive MBA Program
Number of industry sectors that recruited graduates	7 (57)	–
Percentage of graduates in jobs 3 months after graduation	87 (49)	–
Percentage of graduates finding jobs through careers services	53 (49)	–
Student rating of careers service	3.8 (33)	–
Post-MBA salary, US$	70,097 (71)	–
Percentage increase in salary	35 (69)	–
Principal recruiters of graduates	AIM Healthcare, Citigroup, American Express	–

Cost

	Full-time MBA	Vanderbilt Executive MBA Program
Application fees	US$100	US$100
Programme fees	US$30,345	US$38,210
Comments	–	–
Accommodation costs (on campus, per year)	US$5,830	–
Accommodation costs (off campus, per year)	US$7,340	–
Financial aid available	US$8,890,000	–
Type of aid available	Scholarships, assistantships, loans	–
Criteria on which aid is granted	Merit, financial need	–

Accreditation

AACSB International

Application details

	Full-time MBA	Vanderbilt Executive MBA Program
Application deadline	May 1st	June 18th
Programme dates	Aug start, 21 months	Aug start, 21 months
Admission requirements	4-year US Bachelor's degree or equivalent; TOEFL or IELTS if first language not English; 2 references; 3 essays; interview; laptop; official transcripts in English	First degree; at least 5 years' work experience; GMAT; TOEFL if first language not English; 3 references; essays; interview

Executive education

Owen's portfolio of open-enrolment executive education programmes includes finance and accounting for non-financial managers, leadership, strategic innovation, marketing, and growing and managing the biotech enterprise. The Vanderbilt Executive Development Institute offers short courses based on the MBA programme. Executives who take four courses are awarded the Vanderbilt Executive Development Institute Certificate. Customised in-company programmes follow similar lines in areas such as strategy and leadership.

Student/alumni quotes

"The location is both a strength and weakness. I grew up in NJ and had some reservations about Nashville. I can assure you that Nashville is a terrific place to spend a few years and, while a small town, has all of the amenities of a larger city without the hassles."

"A great learning experience, both inside and outside the classroom. Faculty and staff are extremely helpful and competent. Fellow students are very amicable and the school provides a family-like atmosphere."

"Relatively small size and location makes it more difficult to attract recruiters."

University of Virginia—Darden Graduate School of Business Administration

Ranking	Rank (out of 100) Full-time
Overall rank	12
Regional rank	10

Criteria	Rank (out of 100) Full-time
Open new career opportunities	35
Diversity of recruiters	60
Number in jobs three months after graduation	1
Jobs found through the careers service	51
Student assessment of careers service	64
Personal development and educational experience	8
Faculty quality	7
Student quality	29
Student diversity	44
Education experience	11
Increase in salary	66
Increase in salary	79
Post-MBA salary	47
Potential to network	5
Breadth of alumni network	5
Internationalism of alumni	6
Alumni effectiveness	68

Address
Darden Graduate
School of Business
Administration
P.O. Box 6550
100 Darden Boulevard
Charlottesville, VA
US
22906

Tel:
+1 434 924 4791

Fax:
+1 434 924 4724

Email:
darden@virginia.edu

Website:
www.darden.edu

Programme director:
Elliott Weiss

Figures in brackets
represent rank

Background

Darden Graduate School of Business Administration has a strong general management approach and an unyielding commitment to the case method as its principal teaching philosophy. It is well known for its close community spirit, supportive faculty and close links with local and international business. Founded in 1954, the school is named after Colgate Whitehead Darden, Jr., former governor, congressman, and president of the University of Virginia.

Facilities

Facilities at Darden have been continuously upgraded for the past decade, and the school has stunning buildings packed with high-tech features. Although self-contained, it is closely integrated with the University of Virginia, founded by Thomas Jefferson in 1819. The university dominates the historic university town of Charlottesville and there is no campus as such. But Jefferson's original and beautiful "academical village", known as The Lawn and one of the most important architectural sites in the US, still exists and is used as a residence for favoured faculty and students. Housing is available both on and off campus but can be expensive. The state of Virginia, which is close to the power centres of Washington and New York, offers plenty of leisure activities.

	Full-time MBA
Student assessment of facilities	4.5 (8)

Faculty

Number of faculty: 61 full-time, 13 part-time, 18 visiting

	Full-time MBA
Number of faculty per student	0.2 (>100)
Percentage of faculty with PhD	97 (32)
Student rating of faculty	4.6 (9)

Strengths and weaknesses

Strengths: general management; entrepreneurship; ethics

Weaknesses: can be a lack of international content; somewhat isolated location

Programme highlights

The integrated first-year curriculum of Darden's 21-month full-time MBA consists of ten functional core courses (including business communication) and is particularly intensive. Virtually all teaching is done by the case method and students prepare up to 14 cases a week. All students are expected to prepare for every class and are cold-called (chosen randomly) to start case discussions. First-year students are divided into sections of around 60 (rotated after the first semester) which meet daily to discuss cases. Students are also assigned to five- or six-person learning teams in which they analyse cases before and after class. The second year consists of electives, one of which must be in the leadership area. No majors are required, although students can group electives into areas of interest. Students can also opt for an in-company or entrepreneurial project.

	Full-time MBA
Student rating of programme	4.6 (6)
Number of overseas exchange programmes	0 (85)
Number of languages on offer	0 (94)

Students

Student profile (full time)

- ■ EU
- ■ Non-EU Europe
- ▨ North America
- ■ Other Americas
- ■ Asia/Australasia
- ▨ Middle East

	Full-time MBA
Annual intake	316
Applicants:places	11:1
Percentage of women students	27 (64)
Percentage of foreign students	25 (>100)
Average GMAT score	678 (21)
Average number of months' work experience	72 (51)
Age range of students	25-32
Average age	28
Student rating of culture and classmates	4.7 (10)

Recruiters/careers service

	Full-time MBA
Number of industry sectors that recruited graduates	8 (1)
Percentage of graduates in jobs 3 months after graduation	65 (77)
Percentage of graduates finding jobs through careers services	61 (22)
Student rating of careers service	4.2 (7)
Post-MBA salary, US$	90,180 (16)
Percentage increase in salary	41 (84)
Principal recruiters of graduates	Citigroup Global, Lehman Brothers, McKinsey

Cost

	Full-time MBA
Application fees	US$140
Programme fees	US$35,000
Comments	Per year
Accommodation costs (on campus, per year)	–
Accommodation costs (off campus, per year)	US$4,545
Financial aid available	US$32,256,000
Type of aid available	Scholarships, grants, loans
Criteria on which aid is granted	Merit for scholarship, financial need for grants, all students eligible for loans

Accreditation

AACSB International

Application details

	Full-time MBA
Application deadline	April 1st
Programme dates	Aug start, 21 months
Admission requirements	At least 2 years' work experience; TOEFL if first language not English; references; 4 essays; interview; laptop

Executive education

Darden offers open-enrolment courses in the following areas: general management; leadership and change; marketing and sales; financial excellence; innovations and operations excellence; and capability development: individual and organisational. It also offers customised courses in such areas as developing general managers, developing high-potential managers, leading the total enterprise, strategic leadership and transformational change.

Student/alumni quotes

"The case method of teaching compounds the learning experience more than I ever expected. It is hard to teach that way, therefore the professors are here because they love teaching. They are energetic, enthusiastic, and go above and beyond to help students. Additionally, because of the case method structure, your learning is compounded by other students' perspectives and experiences."

"The remote location is both a weakness and strength. Because we were far from major cities, fewer recruiters were willing to visit. The school needs to put some energy towards non-traditional recruiting to make students accessible in other ways."

"Darden isn't for everyone, but for those who are ready and willing, it's everything."

Vlerick Leuven Gent Management School

Address
Vlamingenstraat 83
Leuven
Belgium
3020

Tel:
+32 479 950 754

Fax:
+32 16 323 581

Email:
mba@vlerick.be

Website:
www.Vlerick.com

Programme director:
Dr Dirk Buyens

Figures in brackets
represent rank

Ranking	Rank (out of 100) Full-time
Overall rank	15
Regional rank	3

Criteria	Rank (out of 100) Full-time
Open new career opportunities	**35**
Diversity of recruiters	60
Number in jobs three months after graduation	1
Jobs found through the careers service	51
Student assessment of careers service	64
Personal development and educational experience	**8**
Faculty quality	7
Student quality	29
Student diversity	44
Education experience	11
Increase in salary	**66**
Increase in salary	79
Post-MBA salary	47
Potential to network	**5**
Breadth of alumni network	5
Internationalism of alumni	6
Alumni effectiveness	68

Background

Vlerick Leuven Gent Management School was created by the 1999 merger of Vlerick School of Management (at Gent University) and the management education elements of Katholieke Universiteit Leuven. With autonomous university status, the school is the biggest in Belgium with strong links to industry. Not surprisingly, given its location, the school focuses on all things European.

The constituent parts of the school have a long history of MBA education. Vlerick, for example, was founded in 1953 and when it was converted into a business school in 1988 it became Belgium's leading school. Katholieke Universiteit Leuven started its MBA in 1968.

Facilities

The school has two campuses: Leuven and Gent. The full-time MBA is taught at Leuven, an ancient university town. The university was founded in 1425 and counts Erasmus and Mercator among its alumni. The management school is based in a refurbished building in the centre of Leuven. It is self-contained and dedicated to postgraduate management students, with three lecture theatres and private workrooms, all equipped with projection and computer technology. There is no on-campus accommodation.

	Full-time MBA
Student assessment of facilities	4.4 (36)

Faculty

Number of faculty: 47 full-time, 11 part-time, 14 visiting

	Full-time MBA	Executive International MBA
Number of faculty per student	1.7 (15)	0.7
Percentage of faculty with PhD	98 (15)	98
Student rating of faculty	4.2 (62)	–

Strengths and weaknesses

Strengths: doing business in Europe; entrepreneurship; corporate social responsibility

Weakness: very Euro-centric

Programme highlights

Vlerick Leuven Gent's full-time one-year International MBA is strongly European in content but somewhat unusual in its structure. This programme is only offered at the Leuven campus. The core (divided into introductory, basic and advanced courses) is large with 20 courses, and there are just two elective course options: management of technology, innovation and entrepreneurship; and doing business in Europe (although additional electives are offered at partner institutions in Europe and North America). The programme ends with a business game and an in-company project. A number of soft skills, project preparation and European business seminars run throughout the programme.

The two-year part-time MBA is offered at the Gent and Leuven campuses in English (a Dutch-language version is also offered in Gent). The programme is essentially a series of core courses (the Main Module) followed by a project carried out in the student's own company. A six-week pre-programme introductory module covers basic concepts and skills; experienced students can waive this. Classes take place twice a week. At Gent they are on Monday evenings (7–10.30 pm) and Tuesday afternoons and evenings (2.30–6 pm and 7–10.30 pm). There is a group dinner on Tuesday evenings. At Leuven they are on Thursday evenings (7–10.30 pm) and Friday afternoons and evenings (2.30–6 pm and 7–10.30 pm). There is a group dinner on Friday evenings.

	Full-time MBA	Executive International MBA
Student rating of programme	4.0 (87)	–
Number of overseas exchange programmes	33 (4)	–
Number of languages on offer	>5 (25)	–

Students

	Full-time MBA	Executive International MBA
Annual intake	33	100
Applicants:places	6:1	4:1
Percentage of women students	21 (78)	13
Percentage of foreign students	67 (33)	n/a
Average GMAT score	634 (61)	640
Average number of months' work experience	96 (9)	96
Age range of students	26-38	28-44
Average age	32	33
Student rating of culture and classmates	4.2 (48)	–

Student profile (full time)

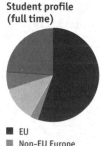

- ■ EU
- ■ Non-EU Europe
- ▨ North America
- ■ Other Americas
- ■ Asia/Australasia
- ▧ Middle East

Recruiters/careers service

	Full-time MBA	Executive International MBA
Number of industry sectors that recruited graduates	8 (60)	–
Percentage of graduates in jobs 3 months after graduation	100 (1)	–
Percentage of graduates finding jobs through careers services	60 (51)	–
Student rating of careers service	3.3 (64)	–
Post-MBA salary, US$	80,682 (47)	–
Percentage increase in salary	42 (79)	–
Principal recruiters of graduates	DHL, Picanol, GE Finance	

Cost

	Full-time MBA	Executive International MBA
Application fees	€50 (US$57)	€50 (US$57)
Programme fees	€11,500 (US$13,068)	€6,500 (US$7,386)
Comments	Total programme. Includes books, seminar costs and access to library and social services	Per year. Includes books and seminars
Accommodation costs (on campus, per year)	€2,200 (US$2,500)	–
Accommodation costs (off campus, per year)	€2,200 (US$2,500)	–
Financial aid available	€60 (US$68)	–
Type of aid available	Scholarships, bursaries	–
Criteria on which aid is granted	Merit, financial need.	–

Accreditation

AMBA, EQUIS

Application details

	Full-time MBA	Executive International MBA
Application deadline	June 30th	June 30th
Programme dates	Aug start, 11 months	Sep start, 22 months
Admission requirements	First degree; at least 3 years' work experience; GMAT; TOEFL if first language not English (in-house and by-arrangement language testing services available); 2 references; 11 essays; interview; laptop	First degree; at least 3 years' work experience; GMAT; TOEFL if first language not English (in-house and by-arrangement language testing services available); 2 references; 11 essays; interview

Executive education

Vlerick offers open-enrolment executive seminars in accounting and finance, entrepreneurship, general management, information management, human resources management, marketing management, operations management and services management. The school also runs customised in-company seminars.

Student/alumni quotes

"An excellent school, value for money, dedicated, experienced and knowledgeable faculty. A very healthy and conducive atmosphere for learning."

"School could do more outside the Flemish community."

"Value for your money; a top MBA in one year in the coolest student town in the world. The lowest risk for your investment."

Wake Forest University—Babcock Graduate School of Management

Ranking	Rank (out of 100) Full-time
Overall rank	63
Regional rank	39

Criteria	Rank (out of 100) Full-time
Open new career opportunities	**41**
Diversity of recruiters	n/a
Number in jobs three months after graduation	12
Jobs found through the careers service	19
Student assessment of careers service	94
Personal development and educational experience	**93**
Faculty quality	72
Student quality	98
Student diversity	>100
Education experience	44
Increase in salary	**68**
Increase in salary	20
Post-MBA salary	76
Potential to network	**42**
Breadth of alumni network	30
Internationalism of alumni	97
Alumni effectiveness	38

Address
P. O. Box 7659
Winston-Salem, NC
US
27109-7659

Tel:
+1 336 758 5421

Fax:
+1 336 758 5830

Email:
admissions@mba.wfu.edu

Website:
www.mba.wfu.edu

Programme director:
Stacy Owen

Figures in brackets represent rank

Background

Wake Forest University's Babcock Graduate School of Management, founded in 1969, is relatively new and small by US standards, with around 550 enrolled students. Its location in Winston-Salem puts it close to the University of North Carolina (Kenan-Flagler) and Duke University (Fuqua) in a vibrant area of the country. The school is named after Charles Babcock, a local businessman and philanthropist. who made an initial donation to found the school. It has a strong international emphasis and a good guest-speaker series.

Facilities

The school is based in the Worrell Professional Center for Law and Management on Wake Forest University's Winston-Salem campus. The building opened in 1993 and facilities are good. They include 30 private study rooms open 24 hours a day, library, computer lab, student lounge, cafés and a bookstore. Saturday MBA and executive education programmes and some Evening MBA classes are based at the school's One Morrocroft Center in the South Park area of Charlotte. The centre, which is networked to the Worrell Center, has classrooms, seminar and study rooms and is accessible to students 24 hours a day.

	Full-time MBA
Student assessment of facilities	4.6 (8)

Faculty

Number of faculty: 42 full-time, 9 part-time, 1 visiting

	Full-time MBA	Evening MBA – Winston-Salem	Evening MBA Program – Charlotte	Saturday MBA Program – Charlotte	Fast-Track Executive MBA
Number of faculty per student	0.4 (82)	0.9	1.0	1.1	0.9
Percentage of faculty with PhD	93 (52)	93	93	93	93
Student rating of faculty	4.2 (61)	–	–	–	–

Strengths and weaknesses

Strengths: finance; operations; entrepreneurship

Weakness: careers service

Programme highlights

Babcock's full-time two-year MBA is traditional in design with a first year of mainly core courses (which include a required communications course) and two electives. No waivers of the core are allowed. The second year is largely devoted to electives, although there are required courses in international competitive policy (continuing a first-year course) and law and ethics, as well as an in-company consulting project. Electives can be grouped into "career" concentrations in finance, consulting, marketing, operations management, information technology management or entrepreneurship. Classes are small, with three sections of around 38 students, and teamworking (first-year students are assigned to teams of four or five) is widespread. A lot of teaching is done via the case method.

The MBA is also taught part-time over six semesters (24 months) as an evening programme on campus and at the One Morrocroft Center in Charlotte. Students take 14 core courses and three elective courses. There is a two-day residential session in the fourth and final semesters as well as an optional international study tour. Charlotte also hosts the Saturday MBA, a similar programme with classes meeting for 42 Saturdays a year over two years.

The Babcock Executive MBA is a 17-month programme with classes meeting every other weekend (Friday and Saturday). There is an international study trip included in the tuition fees.

	Full-time MBA	Evening MBA – Winston-Salem	Evening MBA Program – Charlotte	Saturday MBA Program – Charlotte	Fast-Track Executive MBA
Student rating of programme	4.0 (90)	–	–	–	–
Number of overseas exchange programmes	10 (70)	–	–	–	–
Number of languages on offer	>5 (29)	–	–	–	–

Students

Student profile (full time)

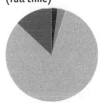

- ■ EU
- ■ Non-EU Europe
- ■ North America
- ■ Other Americas
- ■ Asia/Australasia
- ■ Middle East

	Full-time MBA	Evening MBA – Winston-Salem	Evening MBA Program – Charlotte	Saturday MBA Program – Charlotte	Fast-Track Executive MBA
Annual intake	105	60	50	46	55
Applicants:places	5:1	1:1	1:1	1:1	2:1
Percentage of women students	27 (68)	23	21	30	23
Percentage of foreign students	20 (>100)	n/a	n/a	n/a	n/a
Average GMAT score	642 (58)	n/a	n/a	n/a	n/a
Average number of months' work experience	43 (>100)	74	90	70	150
Age range of students	23-30	25-35	26-36	25-33	29-47
Average age	26	29	30	28	36
Student rating of culture and classmates	4.0 (82)	–	–	–	–

Wake Forest University—Babcock Graduate School of Management

Recruiters/careers service

	Full-time MBA	Evening MBA – Winston-Salem	Evening MBA Program – Charlotte	Saturday MBA Program – Charlotte	Fast-Track Executive MBA
Number of industry sectors that recruited graduates	n/a (n/a)	–	–	–	–
Percentage of graduates in jobs 3 months after graduation	91 (12)	–	–	–	–
Percentage of graduates finding jobs through careers services	65 (19)	–	–	–	–
Student rating of careers service	2.9 (94)	–	–	–	–
Post-MBA salary, US$	71,000 (76)	–	–	–	–
Percentage increase in salary	76 (20)	–	–	–	–
Principal recruiters of graduates	Lowes Home Improvement, Wachovia, BB&T				

Cost

	Full-time MBA	Evening MBA – Winston-Salem	Evening MBA Program – Charlotte	Saturday MBA Program – Charlotte	Fast-Track Executive MBA
Application fees	US$75	US$75	US$75	US$75	US$75
Programme fees	US$28,000	US$27,000	US$27,000	US$27,000	US$59,500
Comments	Per year	Per year	Per year	Per year	Total programme
Accommodation costs (on campus, per year)	–	–	–	–	–
Accommodation costs (off campus, per year)	US$3,600	–	–	–	–
Financial aid available	US$1,940,000	–	–	–	–
Type of aid available	Scholarships, stipends	–	–	–	–
Criteria on which aid is granted	Merit	–	–	–	–

Accreditation

AACSB International, EQUIS

Application details

	Full-time MBA	Evening MBA – Winston-Salem	Evening MBA Program – Charlotte	Saturday MBA Program – Charlotte	Fast-Track Executive MBA
Application deadline	April 1st (priority date, not a strict deadline)	–	–	–	–
Programme dates	Aug start, 21 months	Aug start, 24 months	Aug start, 24 months	Jan start, 24 months	Aug start, 17 months
Admission requirements	First degree; TOEFL if first language not English; 2 references; 2 essays; laptop; an interview is required for domestic applicants, interviews are by invitation only for international applicants	First degree; at least 3 years' work experience; 3 references; 2 essays; interview	First degree; at least 5 years' work experience; 3 references; 2 essays; interview	First degree; at least 3 years' work experience; 3 references; 2 essays; interview	First degree; work experience; 3 references; 2 essays; interview; letter of support from employer

Executive education

Babcock provides customised in-company executive education programmes through its Institute for Executive Education at the One Morrocroft Center in Charlotte.

Student/alumni quotes

"Very impressive faculty with unsurpassed teaching methods. The integrative and facilitative environment within the classroom helps all students learn from each other as well."

"The program is small which is beneficial but with limited alumni and less students, often people have not heard of the programme."

"The quality of the people and the academic preparation is as good or better than schools ranked much higher, and at a lower cost also (both tuition and cost of living)."

Warwick Business School

Ranking	Rank (out of 100) Full-time
Overall rank	30
Regional rank	10

Criteria	Rank (out of 100) Full-time
Open new career opportunities	**75**
Diversity of recruiters	35
Number in jobs three months after graduation	28
Jobs found through the careers service	87
Student assessment of careers service	92
Personal development and educational experience	**36**
Faculty quality	57
Student quality	45
Student diversity	49
Education experience	27
Increase in salary	**6**
Increase in salary	8
Post-MBA salary	7
Potential to network	**27**
Breadth of alumni network	15
Internationalism of alumni	14
Alumni effectiveness	63

Address
Warwick Business School
University of Warwick
Coventry
UK
CV4 7AL

Tel:
+44 24 7652 8225

Fax:
+44 24 7652 4969

Email:
warwickmba@wbs.ac.uk

Website:
www.wbs.ac.uk

Programme director:
John McGee

Figures in brackets represent rank

Background

Warwick Business School is a full-range school, teaching undergraduates, postgraduates and doctoral students, and has close links to its parent university. It has a strong reputation in the UK for research and has excellent links with industry.

The school has a large full-time teaching staff and offers a variety of MBA delivery modes, including full-time, part-time, distance-learning and modular, all with considerable flexibility and the opportunity to switch between them. Careers advice is given by a careers manager on the full-time programme as well as the main university careers office.

Facilities

Located just outside Coventry, the school occupies a large modern building on the University of Warwick campus. Teaching and computer facilities are good. MBA students have access to the university library business section. The university has excellent sports and cultural facilities. On-campus accommodation is available in special postgraduate residences and flats.

	Full-time MBA
Student assessment of facilities	4.3 (48)

Faculty

Number of faculty: 102 full-time, 1 part-time, 15 visiting

	Full-time MBA	MBA by Distance Learning	MBA by Evening Study	MBA by Modular Study
Number of faculty per student	1.1 (33)	0.1	3.9	1.3
Percentage of faculty with PhD	84 (71)	84	84	84
Student rating of faculty	4.3 (53)	–	–	–

Strengths and weaknesses

Strengths: strategic management; marketing; operations management

Weakness: careers services

Programme highlights

Warwick's full-time one-year MBA consists of three university terms (nine months) of class teaching and an individual in-company project during the summer term (three months), which can be undertaken outside the UK. Students take six core courses in the first term, one required course and four electives in the second term, and one required course and four electives in the third term. The programme includes the MBA Forum guest-speakers' session. Careers and personal development are covered in series of workshops.

The school offers a variation on the full-time programme called the European MBA, which involves six months at Warwick followed by three months at the University of Mannheim in Germany and three months consulting in a European company.

The Executive Evening and Modular MBAs have a similar curriculum to the full-time version, consisting of eight core modules, five elective modules, and a project and dissertation. The evening programme can be completed in a minimum of 27 months and a maximum of eight years; the average is three years. Classes meet on campus two evenings a week (6.30–9.30 pm) during term time (30 weeks per year). The programme starts with a required one-week residential session and there is a further residential week towards the end of the programme. Students can switch easily between the part-time programme and the modular or distance-learning programmes if their circumstances change.

The modular programme is based on intensive one-week (Monday–Friday) residential modules that cover one subject area. Students are usually given an assignment to complete following the modules and this plays a part in their assessment. There are 13 modules and two weekend workshops. Students take eight core modules and five elective modules and attend a required two-day workshop on research methods before starting an in-company project. There is also a required induction weekend at the start of the programme. The modular programme is designed to be completed in three years, but it can be accelerated (by joining the end of the full-time programme) or extended to a maximum of eight years (by joining the evening or distance-learning programmes).

Warwick's distance-learning MBA has the same flexibility as the other delivery methods and is broadly similar in approach and curriculum. The programme is divided into three parts, designed to be followed consecutively over three to three and a half years, although it can be extended to eight years. It is easily interchangeable with other Warwick delivery methods. Students take eight core courses and five electives and complete a project and dissertation.

	Full-time MBA	MBA by Distance Learning	MBA by Evening Study	MBA by Modular Study
Student rating of programme	4.1 (66)	–	–	–
Number of overseas exchange programmes	44 (38)	–	–	–
Number of languages on offer	>5 (1)	–	–	–

Students

	Full-time MBA	MBA by Distance Learning	MBA by Evening Study	MBA by Modular Study
Annual intake	98	300	30	90
Applicants:places	4:1	2:1	2:1	2:1
Percentage of women students	22 (73)	25	27	24
Percentage of foreign students	76 (37)	n/a	n/a	n/a
Average GMAT score	620 (75)	n/a	n/a	n/a
Average number of months' work experience	78 (15)	72	102	96
Age range of students	26-36	28-41	29-42	28-39
Average age	30	33	33	33
Student rating of culture and classmates	4.1 (53)	–	–	–

Student profile (full time)

- ■ EU
- ■ Non-EU Europe
- ■ North America
- ■ Other Americas
- ■ Asia/Australasia
- ■ Middle East
- ■ Other

Recruiters/careers service

	Full-time MBA	MBA by Distance Learning	MBA by Evening Study	MBA by Modular Study
Number of industry sectors that recruited graduates	8 (35)	–	–	–
Percentage of graduates in jobs 3 months after graduation	87 (28)	–	–	–
Percentage of graduates finding jobs through careers services	21 (87)	–	–	–
Student rating of careers service	3.0 (92)	–	–	–
Post-MBA salary, US$	109,977 (7)	–	–	–
Percentage increase in salary	126 (8)	–	–	–
Principal recruiters of graduates	Prudential, Liberata, Johnson & Johnson			

Cost

	Full-time MBA	MBA by Distance Learning	MBA by Evening Study	MBA by Modular Study
Application fees	£80 (US$131)	None	None	None
Programme fees	£23,700 (US$38,852)	£4,100 (US$6,721)	£5,850 (US$9,590)	£6,500 (US$10,656)
Comments	–	–	–	–
Accommodation costs (on campus, per year)	£4,900 (US$8,033)	–	–	–
Accommodation costs (off campus, per year)	£5,200 (US$8,525)	–	–	–
Financial aid available	£25,000 (US$40,984)	–	–	–
Type of aid available	Dean's Bursaries	–	–	–
Criteria on which aid is granted	Merit	–	–	–

Accreditation

AACSB International, AMBA, EQUIS

Application details

	Full-time MBA	MBA by Distance Learning	MBA by Evening Study	MBA by Modular Study
Application deadline	June 30th	May 31st	March 31st	Rolling admissions
Programme dates	Sep start, 12 months	Jan start, 36 months	Apr start, 36 months	Oct start, 36 months
Admission requirements	Good university degree, or equivalent professional qualification; at least 3 years' work experience; TOEFL (minimum 620 paper-based, 260 computer-based) or IELTS (minimum 7.0) if first language not English; 2 references; 2 essays; interview; laptop	First degree or equivalent professional qualification; at least 4 years' work experience; TOEFL (minimum 620 paper-based, 260 computer-based) or IELTS (minimum 7.0) if first language not English; 2 references; 2 essays	First degree or equivalent professional qualification; at least 4 years' work experience; TOEFL (minimum 620 paper-based, 260 computer-based) or IELTS (minimum 7.0) if first language not English; 2 references; 2 essays; interview	First degree or equivalent professional qualification; at least 4 years' work experience; TOEFL (minimum 620 paper-based, 260 computer-based) or IELTS (minimum 7.0) if first language not English; 2 references; 2 essays; interview

Executive education

Warwick runs a number of open-enrolment short executive education programmes, covering areas such as finance and marketing, including three-day "MBA Refresher" courses for MBA graduates. It also offers customised in-company programmes.

Student/alumni quotes

"Initially I started on the Executive (Modular) part-time course, suspecting that I might transfer full-time. After completing one year I did. The curriculum was complementary and I slotted in as though I had been there since the beginning of the full-time course. The ease of transfer between the MBA courses was excellent."

"Week-long electives make it difficult to take in all the content over such a short period of time. "

"For me the highest value gained from my year at Warwick was the multinational element of the student base and the friendliness of everyone—it made the whole year a unique and supportive experience."

Washington University in St Louis—Olin School of Business

Ranking	Rank (out of 100) Full-time
Overall rank	34
Regional rank	22

Criteria	Rank (out of 100) Full-time
Open new career opportunities	**45**
Diversity of recruiters	1
Number in jobs three months after graduation	87
Jobs found through the careers service	57
Student assessment of careers service	34
Personal development and educational experience	**43**
Faculty quality	31
Student quality	64
Student diversity	90
Education experience	6
Increase in salary	**41**
Increase in salary	27
Post-MBA salary	55
Potential to network	**30**
Breadth of alumni network	31
Internationalism of alumni	20
Alumni effectiveness	35

Address
Olin School of
Business
Campus Box 1133
1 Brookings Drive
Saint Louis, MO
US
63130

Tel:
+1 314 935 4214

Fax:
+1 314 935 8891

Email:
mba@olin.wustl.edu

Website:
www.olin.wustl.edu

Programme director:
Joe Fox

Figures in brackets
represent rank

Background

Washington University in St Louis dates back to 1853 and the business school was founded in 1917, mainly as an undergraduate school. It added an MBA in 1950. The John M Olin School of Business, named in 1988 in honour of the chairman of the Olin Corporation, a major benefactor of Washington University, has a strong research base and good contacts with industry. St Louis is a centre for large US corporations, and the school has a good range of visiting speakers.

Olin is a full-range school, teaching business subjects from undergraduate to doctorate level.

Facilities

The school is based in the John E Simon Hall, an 80,000 sq ft building opened in 1986. It contains student lounges, classrooms, seminar rooms, faculty offices, a library, a 70-unit computer lab, rooms for small-group study, offices for student organisations and clubs, and a deli. It also makes extensive use of the Charles F Knight Executive Education Center, a five-storey, 135,000 sq ft building with conference rooms, classrooms and breakout rooms

	Full-time MBA
Student assessment of facilities	4.6 (13)

Faculty

Number of faculty: 68.5 full-time, 13.5 part-time, 1 visiting

	Full time MBA	PMBA	Residential EMBA	Weekend EMBA
Number of faculty per student	0.6 (68)	0.6	2.6	1.9
Percentage of faculty with PhD	91 (55)	91	91	91
Student rating of faculty	4.6 (16)	–	–	–

Strengths and weaknesses

Strengths: finance; strategy/consulting; marketing

Weakness: relatively small programme can lead to a dearth of on-campus recruiters

Programme highlights

Olin's full-time programme is in the mainstream American tradition but offers considerable flexibility. The four semesters are each divided into two mini-terms. The first semester concentrates on business fundamentals, and electives begin in the second semester. There is a required career management course in the fall term of the first semester. There is no requirement to nominate a major but concentration tracks (finance, marketing, organisational behaviour, operations and manufacturing management, management strategy, accounting analysis, entrepreneurship and international business) are offered. Some electives can be taken in other schools of the university. Extracurricular workshops, self-development courses, guest-speaker series and other activities run throughout the programme.

The Professional MBA (PMBA) is a three-year part-time programme taught over nine semesters (autumn, spring and summer each year). Each semester is divided into two mini-terms covering two subjects. Most of the core courses are taught in the first year. Over half of the programme consists of elective courses. Classes meet two evenings a week (6.15–9.15 pm). As with the full-time programme, there is no requirement to declare a major area of study or concentration. Some electives can be taken in other schools of the university.

Olin's 18-month Executive MBA programme is taught at the school's Charles F Knight executive education centre and can be studied in the evening or at weekends. The evening programme begins in August with classes meeting once a month on Thursday, Friday and Saturday (8.30 am–5.30 pm). The weekend programme begins in January with classes meeting on alternate weekends (Friday and Saturday). Both programmes include two one-week on-campus residencies, a required two-week residency in China and an optional London, UK, summer programme.

The 18-month Shanghai Executive MBA is a partnership between Washington University and Fudan University in Shanghai. Students attend classes four consecutive days per month, Friday–Monday, in Shanghai. The programme ends with a two-week study session at Olin.

	Full-time MBA	PMBA	Residential EMBA	Weekend EMBA
Student rating of programme	4.5 (23)	–	–	
Number of overseas exchange programmes	12 (35)	–	–	
Number of languages on offer	6 (1)	–	–	–

Students

Student profile (full time)

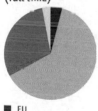

- ■ EU
- ■ Non-EU Europe
- ■ North America
- ■ Other Americas
- ■ Asia/Australasia
- ▢ Middle East

	Full-time MBA	PMBA	Residential EMBA	Weekend EMBA
Annual intake	134	132	32	43
Applicants:places	7:1	2:1	–	–
Percentage of women students	24 (83)	28	22	12
Percentage of foreign students	37 (81)	n/a	n/a	n/a
Average GMAT score	650 (51)	601	n/a	n/a
Average number of months' work experience	60 (55)	60	168	132
Age range of students	24-34	25-34	28-45	27-42
Average age	28	28	37	34
Student rating of culture and classmates	4.3 (41)	–	–	–

Recruiters/careers service

	Full-time MBA	PMBA	Residential EMBA	Weekend EMBA
Number of industry sectors that recruited graduates	8 (1)	–	–	–
Percentage of graduates in jobs 3 months after graduation	71 (87)	–	–	–
Percentage of graduates finding jobs through careers services	53 (57)	–	–	–
Student rating of careers service	3.7 (34)	–	–	–
Post-MBA salary, US$	75,000 (55)	–	–	–
Percentage increase in salary	76 (27)	–	–	–
Principal recruiters of graduates	Guidant Corporation, Citigroup, IBM			

Cost

	Full-time MBA	PMBA	Residential EMBA	Weekend EMBA
Application fees	US$100	US$100	US$100	US$100
Programme fees	US$33,000	US$975	US$88,600	US$79,200
Comments	–	Per credit hour	Per year	Per year
Accommodation costs (on campus, per year)	–	–	–	–
Accommodation costs (off campus, per year)	US$9,600	–	–	–
Financial aid available	Not disclosed	–	–	–
Type of aid available	Scholarships, loans	–	–	–
Criteria on which aid is granted	Merit, financial need	–	–	–

Accreditation

AACSB

Application details

	Full-time MBA	PMBA	Residential EMBA	Weekend EMBA
Application deadline	April 22nd	Rolling admissions	Rolling admissions	Rolling admissions
Programme dates	Aug start, 21 months	Jan start, 36 months	Aug start, 18 months	Jan start, 18 months
Admission requirements	First degree; at least 5 years' work experience; TOEFL if first language not English; 2 references; 4 essays; interview required for most students	First degree; at least 2 years' work experience; TOEFL if first language not English; 2 references; 4 essays; interview is usual	First degree; at least 7 years' work experience; 2 references; 4 essays; interview	First degree; at least 5 years' work experience; 2 references; 4 essays; interview

Executive education

Olin's open-enrolment executive education programmes, which it calls "ExecEdge", are deliberately specialised, currently concentrating on corporate governance. Customised in-company and consortium programmes are similarly highly focused and generally concentrate on leadership.

Student/alumni quotes

"The Olin name doesn't open doors like Harvard or Stanford but the co-operative environment, excellent faculty, and flexibility of the programme more than offset any shortcomings. I received four consulting and strategic planning offers in a down economy and credit much of my success to the support of the faculty and administration."

"As a small school with such a responsive administration, it's easier to do whatever you need, and there's less stress. Also, the quality of the teaching staff and the rigour of the academic programme are surprisingly top-notch."

"Small size of the class leads to low campus recruiting activities from big firms."

University of Western Ontario—Richard Ivey School of Business

Ranking	Rank (out of 100) Full-time
Overall rank	75
Regional rank	46

Criteria	Rank (out of 100) Full-time
Open new career opportunities	**63**
Diversity of recruiters	1
Number in jobs three months after graduation	96
Jobs found through the careers service	n/a
Student assessment of careers service	59
Personal development and educational experience	**74**
Faculty quality	68
Student quality	53
Student diversity	91
Education experience	65
Increase in salary	**87**
Increase in salary	53
Post-MBA salary	88
Potential to network	**32**
Breadth of alumni network	26
Internationalism of alumni	37
Alumni effectiveness	32

Address
Richard Ivey School of Business
University of Western Ontario
1151 Richmond Street North
London, ON
Canada
N6A 3K7

Tel:
+1 519 661 4222

Fax:
+1 519 850 2321

Email:
swalker@ivey.ca

Website:
www.ivey.ca/mba

Programme director:
Murray Bryant

Figures in brackets represent rank

Background

The Richard Ivey School of Business is predominantly a case-method school and about 80% of the programme is taught in this way. It is a leading world producer of business case studies, and students are exposed to over 600 cases during their programme. The school was named after a local entrepreneur who donated C$11m in 1995, and it launched a fund-raising campaign in the same year that had raised C$78m by the time it closed in 2001. This allowed Ivey to increase faculty numbers and student scholarships and create the Cheng Yu Tung Management Institute in Hong Kong.

Facilities

The school is housed in two buildings on the main university campus, 15 minutes' drive from the centre of London, a town of parkland and tree-lined avenues with a population of around 300,000. MBA students have access to all university facilities. Ivey has its own library and two computer labs. The IT network is wireless-based, allowing students to access it from any location. On-campus accommodation is available, although rented housing in London is plentiful and reasonably priced.

	Full-time MBA
Student assessment of facilities	4.1 (75)

Faculty

Number of faculty: 81 full-time, 10 part-time, 3 visiting

	Full-time MBA	Ivey Executive MBA Program
Number of faculty per student	0.4 (93)	1.0
Percentage of faculty with PhD	90 (48)	90
Student rating of faculty	4.3 (51)	–

Strengths and weaknesses

Strengths: general management; global strategy; entrepreneurship

Weakness: somewhat homogenous student body

Programme highlights

Ivey has redesigned its full-time MBA programme—the changes became effective for the incoming fall 2004 class—but it maintains its dedication to the case method. It starts with a short pre-programme session on basic quantitative and business issues. The main programme is divided into eight seven-week terms, which are grouped into themes (people and quantitative skills; formulating strategy and understanding basic business processes; international issues and strategy), and electives, which can be grouped into concentrations or taken across a wide range. Terms 1–3 focus on core courses, terms 4–6 mix core and elective courses, and terms 6–8 are devoted to electives. Students also undertake an individual research project designed with faculty input and there is a lengthy eight-month in-company group project as part of the required core.

Former graduates of Ivey's Honours Business Administration (HBA) programme at the University of Western Ontario can apply for MBA 2 Direct, a one-year accelerated MBA. Admission is not automatic and applicants must have at least two years' full-time work experience.

The Executive MBA is fairly traditional in structure and content. The programme includes three projects (normally in the participant's own organisation) in the functional, general management and best practice areas. There are also two optional international study tours. Classes are held at Ivey's executive development centre in Mississauga, either every other weekend on Friday and Saturday during term time or every two weeks on Sunday and Monday. The programme is also offered at a downtown facility in Toronto, where classes meet every two weeks on Friday and Saturday, and in Hong Kong at Ivey's Cheng Yu Tung Management Institute. The programme is a combination of short residential and weekend sessions. There is a one-week residential session at the beginning of each term. E-mail is used to maintain contact between students and faculty and among students. There are two start times during the year: September (a 22-month programme) and January (a 17-month programme).

	Full-time MBA	Ivey Executive MBA Program
Student rating of programme	4.3 (33)	–
Number of overseas exchange programmes	87 (52)	
Number of languages on offer	1 (81)	–

Students

Student profile (full time)
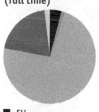

- ■ EU
- ■ Non-EU Europe
- ■ North America
- ■ Other Americas
- ■ Asia/Australasia
- ■ Middle East

	Full-time MBA	Ivey Executive MBA Program
Annual intake	231	92
Applicants:places	4:1	–
Percentage of women students	21 (96)	22
Percentage of foreign students	35 (66)	n/a
Average GMAT score	662 (35)	n/a
Average number of months' work experience	60 (59)	156
Age range of students	24–46	32–41
Average age	29	36
Student rating of culture and classmates	4.2 (42)	–

Recruiters/careers service

	Full-time MBA	Ivey Executive MBA Program
Number of industry sectors that recruited graduates	8 (1)	–
Percentage of graduates in jobs 3 months after graduation	70 (96)	–
Percentage of graduates finding jobs through careers services	n/a (n/a)	–
Student rating of careers service	3.4 (59)	–
Post-MBA salary, US$	55,511 (88)	–
Percentage increase in salary	40 (53)	–
Principal recruiters of graduates	McKinsey, CIBC, Johnson & Johnson	

Cost

	Full-time MBA	Ivey Executive MBA Program
Application fees	C$150 (US$107)	US$150 (US$150)
Programme fees	C$56,000 (US$40,000)	US$56,250 (US$56,250)
Comments	–	–
Accommodation costs (on campus, per year)	–	–
Accommodation costs (off campus, per year)	C$5,600 (US$4,000)	–
Financial aid available	C$607,000 (US$433,571)	–
Type of aid available	Scholarships, private and government loans	–
Criteria on which aid is granted	Financial need, merit, career aspirations	–

Accreditation

EQUIS

Application details

	Full-time MBA	Ivey Executive MBA Program
Application deadline	May 1st	Rolling admissions
Programme dates	Sep start, 20 months	Sep start, 16 months
Admission requirements	4-year undergraduate degree; at least 2 years' work experience; GMAT; TOEFL or IELTS if first language not English; 3 references; 5 essays; interview; laptop	First degree preferred; at least 8 years' work experience; GMAT (sometimes waived); TOEFL if first language not English; references; 3 essays

Executive education

Ivey's open-enrolment executive programmes include the flagship three-week Executive Program and shorter programmes in areas such as strategy, negotiation, finance and marketing. It also offers a range of customised in-company programmes. As with the MBA, executive education makes a lot of use of the case method and small-group working.

The College of William & Mary—School of Business

Address
P.O. Box 8795
Williamsburg, VA
US
23187-8795

Tel:
+1 757 221 2963

Fax:
+1 757 221 2958

Email:
admissions@business.
wm.edu

Website:
business.wm.edu/mha

Programme director:
John J Dittrick, Jr.

Figures in brackets
represent rank

Ranking	Rank (out of 100) Full-time
Overall rank	85
Regional rank	48

Criteria	Rank (out of 100) Full-time
Open new career opportunities	**76**
Diversity of recruiters	30
Number in jobs three months after graduation	>100
Jobs found through the careers service	37
Student assessment of careers service	91
Personal development and educational experience	**76**
Faculty quality	49
Student quality	73
Student diversity	86
Education experience	66
Increase in salary	**97**
Increase in salary	97
Post-MBA salary	90
Potential to network	**67**
Breadth of alumni network	62
Internationalism of alumni	86
Alumni effectiveness	52

Background

The College of William & Mary, a state-assisted public college, was founded in 1693 and is the second oldest college in the US. Thomas Jefferson, James Monroe and many others were alumni. Business studies started in 1919 and a graduate degree programme in 1967. The School of Business Administration teaches undergraduate, graduate and executive education programmes.

Facilities

The school is based on the college's 1,200-acre rural campus in Williamsburg, Virginia, 150 miles south of Washington, DC. Currently, MBA programs are conducted in Blow Memorial Hall on the main campus at the College of William and Mary. Covering nearly 16,000 sq ft, there are four tiered classrooms, two seminar rooms, a student lounge, eight group study rooms, a computer lab, and administrative offices. Every seat is wired for Internet access and all areas have wireless access.

The School of Business is in the development phase of a 175,000 sq ft new facility that will provide state-of-the-art technology, classrooms, office and public/private meeting space for students and faculty.

	Full-time MBA
Student assessment of facilities	3.8 (>100)

Faculty

Number of faculty: 36 full-time, 11 part-time, 1 visiting

	Full-time MBA	Evening MBA Program	The Executive MBA Program
Number of faculty per student	0.5 (75)	0.8	0.9
Percentage of faculty with PhD	n/a (n/a)	n/a	n/a
Student rating of faculty	4.5 (18)	–	–

Strengths and weaknesses

Strengths: finance; marketing; operations

Weaknesses: elective choice; careers service

Programme highlights

The full-time two-year MBA at William and Mary starts with a two-week foundations session. The first year consists of a ten-course core (which includes courses such as management communications and business, government and the global economy) and two electives. The second year includes the required global strategic management course, an in-company team project and electives. These can be grouped into a focus or concentration (entrepreneurship, finance, general management, human resources, information technology, international business, marketing or operations).

The three-year part-time Evening MBA has a similar curriculum to the full-time programme. Students take 13 core courses in the first two years and five electives and the required global strategic management course in the third year. Classes are held at the William and Mary Peninsula Center in the Oyster Point section of Newport News throughout the year and students complete the degree over nine semesters. Classes meet one evening a week (7–10 pm) during the fall and spring semesters and two evenings a week during the summer.

The 20-month part-time Executive MBA is fairly traditional. The programme is divided into five semesters of 10–15 weeks and includes three residency sessions and an international study tour. Classes meet on campus on alternating Fridays and Saturdays. The EMBA is also offered at Reston, near Washington, DC, and classes meet on alternating Saturdays and Sundays.

	Full-time MBA	Evening MBA Program	The Executive MBA Program
Student rating of programme	4.1 (64)	–	–
Number of overseas exchange programmes	15 (59)	–	–
Number of languages on offer	6 (29)	–	–

Students

	Full-time MBA	Evening MBA Program	The Executive MBA Program
Annual intake	81	61	51
Applicants:places	–	–	–
Percentage of women students	28 (59)	28	29
Percentage of foreign students	42 (61)	n/a	n/a
Average GMAT score	623 (77)	613	555
Average number of months' work experience	72 (33)	84	132
Age range of students	24-32	24-39	29-44
Average age	28	29	35
Student rating of culture and classmates	4.1 (72)	–	–

Student profile (full time)

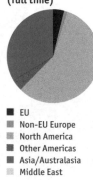

- ■ EU
- ■ Non-EU Europe
- ▨ North America
- ■ Other Americas
- ■ Asia/Australasia
- ▨ Middle East

Recruiters/careers service

	Full-time MBA	Evening MBA Program	The Executive MBA Program
Number of industry sectors that recruited graduates	8 ('10)	–	–
Percentage of graduates in jobs 3 months after graduation	59 (>100)	–	–
Percentage of graduates finding jobs through careers services	58 (37)	–	–
Student rating of careers service	2.9 (91)	–	–
Post-MBA salary, US$	64,000 (90)	–	–
Percentage increase in salary	29 (97)	–	–
Principal recruiters of graduates	Capital One, IBM, Wachovia		

Cost

	Full-time MBA	Evening MBA Program	The Executive MBA Program
Application fees	US$80	US$80	US$50
Programme fees	US$23,362	US$4,020	US$49,500
Comments	Fee for Virginia residents is US$11,860	Fee for Virginia residents is US$2,100 Fees are based upon a 6-credit-hour semester	–
Accommodation costs (on campus, per year)	US$8,330	–	–
Accommodation costs (off campus, per year)	US$8,330	–	–
Financial aid available	US$1,275,863	–	–
Type of aid available	Scholarships, graduate assistantships	–	–
Criteria on which aid is granted	Merit	–	–

Accreditation

AACSB International

Application details

	Full-time MBA	Evening MBA Program	The Executive MBA Program
Application deadline	March 15th for non-US candidates; May 15th for US candidates	November 15th	Rolling admissions
Programme dates	Aug start, 21 months	Jan start, 36 months	Jan start, 20 months
Admission requirements	First degree; at least 2 years' work experience; TOEFL if first language not English (minimum 250 computer-based); 2 references; 3 essays; interview; laptop; résumé	First degree; at least 2 years' work experience; TOEFL if first language not English (minimum 250computer-based); 2 references; 3 essays; interview; résumé	First degree; at least 10 years' work experience; 3 references; interview

Executive education

William and Mary's Center for Corporate Education offers one annual open-enrolment executive education programme, strategic planning and management in retailing (six days), and a range of customised in-company seminars and programmes in areas such as strategic planning, negotiation skills, financial and productivity analysis, organisational leadership and change management.

Student/alumni quotes

"I like this school because of the small size and attention students get from the teachers. I went to a large undergraduate programme and felt really lost; I was looking for a small programme where I could get more attention. I am naturally shy and this environment has forced me to speak up. You simply can't hide at William and Mary."

"[The careers services were] definitely the weakest part of the programme—but the college has hired a new director to adress shortcomings."

"My family responsibilities drove me to seek a part-time MBA and I was very concerned about earning a 'second rate' [degree]. The College of William & Mary was the only school I considered where the administration viewed the W&M MBA as one degree offering ... not as one real MBA (full-time) and a second-class substitute (part-time)."

University of Wisconsin-Madison— Graduate School of Business

Address
Grainger Hall
975 University Ave.
Madison, WI
US
53706-1323

Tel:
+1 608 262 9213

Fax:
+1 608 265 4194

Email:
uwmadmba@bus.wisc.
edu

Website:
www.wisc.edu

Programme director:
Dr Donald Hausch

Figures in brackets
represent rank

Ranking	Rank (out of 100) Full time
Overall rank	65
Regional rank	40

Criteria	Rank (out of 100) Full-time
Open new career opportunities	**65**
Diversity of recruiters	79
Number in jobs three months after graduation	74
Jobs found through the careers service	53
Student assessment of careers service	49
Personal development and educational experience	**59**
Faculty quality	27
Student quality	86
Student diversity	88
Education experience	25
Increase in salary	**76**
Increase in salary	28
Post-MBA salary	81
Potential to network	**39**
Breadth of alumni network	12
Internationalism of alumni	100
Alumni effectiveness	40

Background

The Graduate School of Business at the University of Wisconsin-Madison is one of the oldest business schools in the US, offering its first business programme in 1900. It is a full-range school teaching from undergraduate to doctoral level and the MBA is just one of a raft of graduate degrees that offer a comprehensive coverage of the business scene. Teaching faculty at Wisconsin-Madison have a good reputation for research and scholarly publishing, but the school also puts a strong emphasis on teaching skills, with student evaluations, teaching skills classes and promotion based partly on classroom performance.

Facilities

The school's home, Grainger Hall—a 260,000 sq ft, five-storey building with 30 well-equipped class-rooms, several large theatre-style lecture halls and many student-friendly features—provides excellent computer, teaching, study and administrative facilities. A new $40m extension to Grainger Hall is expected to open in 2007. Students are well catered for, and there are separate communal areas for graduates and undergraduates. The university campus comprises 1,000 acres of rolling hills, picturesque buildings and lakefront scenery. Madison, often rated among the country's most agreeable cities, offers a wide variety of sports, cultural and recreational amenities. On-campus accommodation is available.

	Full-time MBA
Student assessment of facilities	4.5 (33)

Faculty

Number of faculty: 99 full-time, 1 part-time, 4 visiting

	Full-time MBA	Evening MBA Program	Executive MBA Program
Number of faculty per student	0.9 (60)	2.4	3.5
Percentage of faculty with PhD	100 (2)	100	100
Student rating of faculty	4.4 (43)	–	–

Strengths and weaknesses

Strengths: marketing research; applied security analysis; real estate

Weakness: careers services

Programme highlights

The Wisconsin-Madison MBA was revised in 2004 to provide a high level of career specialisation for students. Electives are grouped into 14 career-linked specialisations rather than majors and start as early as the first semester. (The specialisations are accounting, applied corporate finance, applied security analysis, arts administration, entrepreneurial management, information systems, marketing research, operations and technology management, product management, real estate and urban land economics, risk management and insurance, strategic human resource management, management in the life and engineering science, and supply chain management.) There are two required courses, strategy and ethics, in the second year.

Wisconsin's three-year part-time Evening MBA is a general management programme. Classes meet every Monday and Thursday (6.15–9 pm), including summer semesters. Students take two courses at a time. Some courses last 15 weeks (semester long) and some last eight weeks (modules). A semester may consist of two semester-long courses or one semester-long course and two modular courses.

The Executive MBA is fairly typical in content and structure. Classes meet on campus on Friday and Saturday on alternate weeks during the academic year, and there is a one-week residence at the beginning of the programme. The two-year programme consists of 16 five-week terms (modules) and during each term students take two courses. Group working is widespread. Study teams, which generally stay together throughout the programme, usually meet one night a week.

	Full-time MBA	Evening MBA Program	Executive MBA Program
Student rating of programme	4.2 (59)	–	–
Number of overseas exchange programmes	85 (12)	–	–
Number of languages on offer	2 (62)	–	–

Students

	Full-time MBA	Evening MBA Program	Executive MBA Program
Annual intake	118	43	30
Applicants:places	4:1	2:1	–
Percentage of women students	33 (40)	32	32
Percentage of foreign students	28 (91)	n/a	n/a
Average GMAT score	662 (54)	600	n/a
Average number of months' work experience	51 (>100)	63	163
Age range of students	23-32	26-48	31-45
Average age	28	29	37
Student rating of culture and classmates	4.1 (66)	–	–

Student profile (full time)

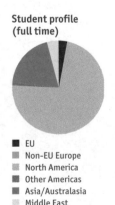

- ■ EU
- ▨ Non-EU Europe
- ▨ North America
- ■ Other Americas
- ■ Asia/Australasia
- ▨ Middle East

Recruiters/careers service

	Full-time MBA	Evening MBA Program	Executive MBA Program
Number of industry sectors that recruited graduates	7 (79)	–	–
Percentage of graduates in jobs 3 months after graduation	75 (74)	–	–
Percentage of graduates finding jobs through careers services	46 (53)	–	–
Student rating of careers service	3.7 (49)	–	–
Post-MBA salary, US$	68,852 (81)	–	–
Percentage increase in salary	70 (28)	–	–
Principal recruiters of graduates	Kraft Foods, General Mills, Schreiber Foods		

Cost

	Full-time MBA	Evening MBA Program	Executive MBA Program
Application fees	US$45	US$45	US$50
Programme fees	US$49,004	US$41,000	US$50,000
Comments	Fee for Wisconsin residents is US$18,128	Total programme	Total programme
Accommodation costs (on campus, per year)	US$7,800	–	–
Accommodation costs (off campus, per year)	US$7,800	–	–
Financial aid available	US$953,722	–	–
Type of aid available	Fellowships, research assistantships, scholarships, project assistantships, teaching assistantships	–	–
Criteria on which aid is granted	Merit	–	–

Accreditation

AACSB International

Application details

	Full-time MBA	Evening MBA Program	Executive MBA Program
Application deadline	April 4th	January 4th	June 1st
Programme dates	Aug start, 21 months	Sep start, 34 months	Aug start, 18 months
Admission requirements	First degree; at least 2 years' work experience; TOEFL if first language not English; 3 references; 3 essays; interview is recommended	First degree; at least 2 years' work experience; TOEFL if first language not English; 3 references; 2 essays; interview	At least 8 years' work experience; 3 references; essay; interview

Executive education

Wisconsin-Madison offers a range of open-enrolment executive education programmes in areas such as general management, strategy, finance and marketing as well as customised in-company programmes.

Student/alumni quotes

"My MBA experience at UW-Madison has been wonderful. The focused curriculum will give me real-world experience while being in school, which is an added edge against other schools. Also, with a little work, it was possible to find more than affordable financing resources to limit the amount of student loans that I had to take out."

"The location can be a deterrent to some larger, coastal companies."

"There is a new University of Wisconsin on the horizon thanks to the vision of a new dean. With specialised centres of excellence, Wisconsin is perfect for students who know exactly what they want to do upon graduation. For example, I want to be a brand manager for a world-class consumer packaged goods company and there was no better place in the world than Wisconsin and the Center for Product Management. We all rave about our school; we just wish more people knew about the new Wisconsin!"

University of Witwatersrand—Wits Business School

Address
2 St Davids Place
Parktown
Johannesburg
South Africa
2000

Tel:
+27 11 717 3657

Email:
facreg@mgmt.wits.ac.
za

Website:
www.wits.ac.za

Programme director:
John Luiz

Figures in brackets
represent rank

Ranking	Rank (out of 100) Full-time
Overall rank	n/a
Regional rank	n/a

Background

Wits Business School, as it is universally known, was founded in 1968 so it is still quite young. However, it is now well established with over 700 students registered on academic programmes and more than 1,000 executives on various short courses. The business school and the School of Public and Development Management make up the Faculty of Management. Within the business school there are a number of Associate centres, including the Management Development Unit and the South African Management Project.

The school has excellent links with national and international business and is also closely integrated with its parent university.

Facilities

Wits is based in Outeniqua, an impressive house built in the early 1900s, in the leafy Johannesburg suburb of Parktown, within easy reach of much of the South African business community. Facilities include a 230-seat auditorium, a 140-seat auditorium, three 75-seat lecture rooms and 30 syndicate rooms.

	Full-time MBA
Student assessment of facilities	n/a (n/a)

Faculty

Number of faculty: 25 full-time, 15 part-time, 3 visiting

	Full-time MBA	MBA (Part-time)
Number of faculty per student	0.6 (n/a)	0.8
Percentage of faculty with PhD	16 (n/a)	16
Student rating of faculty	n/a (n/a)	–

Strengths and weaknesses

Strengths: finance; research; marketing

Weakness: quality of teaching can be variable

Programme highlights

The Wits MBA is taught full-time, part-time or as a combination of the two. The full-time programme last 14 months (April through to May the following year), although the school says this is equivalent to a two-year programme (classes meet six days a week and some evenings and there is no long summer vacation). The first half of the programme is taken up with the fundamental and core courses (both are essentially traditional core courses) and the second half with a research report and five electives. Electives can be grouped into specialist streams such as finance, information management and human resources. The programme starts with a one-week induction, which is also mandatory for part-time students.

The part-time programme (which is identical to the full-time version) lasts three years with classes normally meeting two evenings a week, Monday and Thursday, from 5.30 pm to 9 pm. Occasional Saturday morning classes may be scheduled. The fundamental and core courses are completed in the first two years, and five electives and the research report in the third year. There are two entry dates in January and April.

The programme is also taught as a combined full-time and part-time programme over 20 months with students attending full-time for the first eight months and then switching to the part-time programme for a further year.

Wits offers a modular version of its MBA programme in association with De Chazal Du Mee Business School in Mauritius.

	Full-time MBA	MBA (Part-time)
Student rating of programme	n/a (n/a)	–
Number of overseas exchange programmes	6 (n/a)	–
Number of languages on offer	1 (n/a)	–

Students

	Full-time MBA	MBA (Part-time)
Annual intake	60	40
Applicants:places	3:1	–
Percentage of women students	33 (n/a)	20
Percentage of foreign students	10 (n/a)	n/a
Average GMAT score	n/a (n/a)	n/a
Average number of months' work experience	84 (n/a)	96
Age range of students	24-40	24-54
Average age	31	31
Student rating of culture and classmates	n/a (n/a)	–

Student profile (full-time)

n/a

Recruiters/careers service

	Full-time MBA	MBA (Part-time)
Number of industry sectors that recruited graduates	4 (n/a)	–
Percentage of graduates in jobs 3 months after graduation	– (n/a)	–
Percentage of graduates finding jobs through careers services	– (n/a)	–
Student rating of careers service	– (n/a)	–
Post-MBA salary, US$	– (n/a)	–
Percentage increase in salary	– (n/a)	–
Principal recruiters of graduates	–	

Cost

	Full-time MBA	MBA (Part-time)
Application fees	None	None
Programme fees	R60,000 (US$7,937)	R90,000 (US$11,905)
Comments	–	Total programme
Accommodation costs (on campus, per year)	R24,000 (US$3,175)	–
Accommodation costs (off campus, per year)	R36,000 (US$4,762)	–
Financial aid available	R500,000 (US$66,138)	–
Type of aid available	Scholarship	–
Criteria on which aid is granted	65% aggregate mark on first degree	–

Accreditation

None

Application details

	Full-time MBA	MBA (Part-time)
Application deadline	December 24th	August 27th
Programme dates	Apr start, 14 months	Jan start, 36 months
Admission requirements	First degree; at least 3 years' work experience; GMAT; TOEFL if first language not English; 2 references; 2 essays	First degree; at least 3 years' work experience; GMAT; TOEFL if first language not English; 2 references; 2 essays

Executive education

Wits offers a range of open-enrolment executive education programmes in areas such as finance, marketing and human resources. It also runs a four-week Executive Development Programme and customised in-company programmes.

Student/alumni quotes

"I really enjoyed my courses at Wits and the people I studied with. I think I laughed more times in the year than in all my previous university studies. In terms of value for money, Wits has no equal. Compared with the money US students pay, I feel I came out way ahead."

"Not international enough. Too much focus on South Africa/Africa."

"It is the top school in South Africa with an excellent calibre of staff and students."

Yale School of Management

Ranking	Rank (out of 100) Full-time
Overall rank	14
Regional rank	12

Criteria	Rank (out of 100) Full-time
Open new career opportunities	**24**
Diversity of recruiters	1
Number in jobs three months after graduation	67
Jobs found through the careers service	35
Student assessment of careers service	19
Personal development and educational experience	**12**
Faculty quality	16
Student quality	24
Student diversity	37
Education experience	19
Increase in salary	**33**
Increase in salary	69
Post-MBA salary	29
Potential to network	**26**
Breadth of alumni network	94
Internationalism of alumni	23
Alumni effectiveness	7

Address
135 Prospect Street
Box 208200
New Haven, CT
US
06520-8200

Tel:
+1 203 432 5949

Fax:
+1 203 432 9992

Email:
mba.admissions@yale.edu

Website:
mba.yale.edu

Programme director:
Stanley Garstka

Figures in brackets represent rank

Background

Yale School of Management has traditionally taught the benefits of best-practice management in the public and non-profit sectors as well as the commercial world (its MBA used to be an MPPM—Masters in Public and Private Management). Although this emphasis has eased a little in recent years, it remains a central tenet of the school and the MBA curriculum reflects this. As a result, Yale continues to provide a noticeably broader educational experience than some other US schools.

As befits its venerable age (Yale University was founded by a group of Connecticut clergy in 1701), its name has an unusual provenance. In 1717 Elihu Yale, an English merchant, donated nine bales of "goods" valued at £562 12s (shillings), including books and a portrait of King George. Although he apparently never saw the university, this makes it possibly the first instance of an American academic institution naming itself after a benefactor.

Facilities

The school is closely integrated with the university and students have access to all libraries and sporting and recreational facilities. It is located in the northern, less urban area of Yale's sprawling campus in four historic mansions at the top of Hillhouse Avenue, a street Yale claims was referred to by Charles Dickens as the most beautiful in the US. Three of those mansions hold classrooms, faculty offices and study halls. The International Center for Finance includes faculty offices, conference areas, a finance library and state-of-the-art computer facilities with extensive financial databases for research.

Some on-campus accommodation is available but most students rent apartments.

	Full-time MBA
Student assessment of facilities	4.5 (28)

Faculty

Number of faculty: 53 full-time, 33 part-time, 3 visiting

	Full-time MBA
Number of faculty per student	0.3 (99)
Percentage of faculty with PhD	98 (17)
Student rating of faculty	4.7 (5)

Strengths and weaknesses

Strengths: finance; strategy and economics; non-profit management

Weakness: facilities

Programme highlights

Yale's two-year full-time MBA programme consists of 12 core courses in the first year and six electives in the second. In the second year students undertake a three-course concentration in finance, strategy, marketing, leadership, operations management, public management or non-profit management. Courses are available in other schools of Yale University. Core courses can be waived by examination and replaced by electives. Yale's non-competitive grading system of distinction, proficient, pass or fail supposedly encourages students to take risks and collaborate more effectively.

	Full-time MBA
Student rating of programme	4.5 (13)
Number of overseas exchange programmes	0 (93)
Number of languages on offer	>5 (1)

Students

	Full-time MBA
Annual intake	239
Applicants:places	9:1
Percentage of women students	31 (48)
Percentage of foreign students	31 (82)
Average GMAT score	703 (11)
Average number of months' work experience	60 (79)
Age range of students	–
Average age	–
Student rating of culture and classmates	4.7 (9)

Student profile (full time)

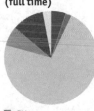

- ■ EU
- ■ Non-EU Europe
- North America
- Other Americas
- ■ Asia/Australasia
- Middle East

Recruiters/careers service

	Full-time MBA
Number of industry sectors that recruited graduates	8 (1)
Percentage of graduates in jobs 3 months after graduation	73 (67)
Percentage of graduates finding jobs through careers services	51 (35)
Student rating of careers service	3.9 (19)
Post-MBA salary, US$	82,500 (29)
Percentage increase in salary	42 (69)
Principal recruiters of graduates	IBM/IBM Strategy and Change, Standard & Poor's, McKinsey, Lohman, Bank of America

Cost

	Full-time MBA
Application fees	US$180
Programme fees	US$35,000
Comments	Per year
Accommodation costs (on campus, per year)	–
Accommodation costs (off campus, per year)	US$10,580
Financial aid available	Not disclosed
Type of aid available	Grants, scholarships, loans
Criteria on which aid is granted	Merit, financial need

Accreditation

AACSB International

Application details

	Full-time MBA
Application deadline	–
Programme dates	Aug start, 21 months
Admission requirements	First degree; work experience; TOEFL if first language not English (Indian citizens are exempt); 2 references; 2 essays

Executive education

Yale offers only customised in-company programmes, which either concentrate on a single functional area or are more broadly cross-discipline. Input from other schools of Yale University is sometimes used.

Student/alumni quotes

"The biggest asset at Yale SOM is the size of the school and wealth of faculty. If students go to SOM just for getting an MBA degree they are wasting their money. The real value at SOM is bringing what is taught in the classroom to life by engaging the faculty on personal business projects and developing ideas."

"The facility has not grown at the same rate as the size of the student body."

"Yale SOM is a small and supportive community. People live up to their values and highly honour business ethics. Besides taking business classes, you have access to the best law school in the world."

York University—Schulich School of Business

Address
Schulich School of Business
4700 Keele Street
Toronto, ON
Canada
M3J 1P3

Tel:
+1 416 736 5546

Fax:
+1 416 736 5763

Email:
intladmissions@
schulich.yorku.ca

Website:
www.schulich.yorku.ca

Programme director:
David Dimick

Figures in brackets
represent rank

Ranking	Rank (out of 100) Full-time
Overall rank	22
Regional rank	17

Criteria	Rank (out of 100) Full-time
Open new career opportunities	**20**
Diversity of recruiters	1
Number in jobs three months after graduation	17
Jobs found through the careers service	23
Student assessment of careers service	47
Personal development and educational experience	**35**
Faculty quality	69
Student quality	25
Student diversity	51
Education experience	38
Increase in salary	**72**
Increase in salary	7
Post-MBA salary	85
Potential to network	**52**
Breadth of alumni network	48
Internationalism of alumni	51
Alumni effectiveness	50

Background

York University's Schulich School of Business was formerly the Faculty of Administrative Studies (founded in 1966). In 1995 Seymour Schulich donated C$15m to the university for the business school, which was named in his honour. It is highly international, with strategic alliances in more than 45 countries that include academic exchange agreements with leading management schools in the Americas, Asia and Europe.

Facilities

In August 2003 the school moved into an impressive new C$102m building on the main campus of York University in Toronto. The new building houses 1,500 graduate and 1,250 undergraduate business students as well as executive education programmes. As might be expected, facilities are pretty good. Schulich also has a downtown campus, the Miles S Nadal Management Center, in the city's financial district.

	Full-time MBA
Student assessment of facilities	3.7 (94)

Faculty

Number of faculty: 94 full-time, 41 part-time, 10 visiting

	Full-time MBA
Number of faculty per student	0.4 (89)
Percentage of faculty with PhD	99 (8)
Student rating of faculty	4.1 (71)

Strengths and weaknesses

Strengths: international management; finance and financial services; marketing and strategy

Weakness: some teaching

Programme highlights

Schulich's MBA programme consists of a first year of core courses and a second year that includes a strategy capstone course, electives and a project (the Strategy Field Study). An international variation of the project (the Global Leadership Program) can be studied with students from overseas business schools. The programme starts with a required one-week skills development session. Students can join the programme in September or January, although January admission usually means attending a summer term. The programme can be completed in a minimum of 16 months over four consecutive terms; the average is 20 months with a summer break. The maximum time allowed is 24 months over six terms. Students with a four-year honours undergraduate business degree such as a BComm or BBA and two years' full-time work experience can reduce the programme length by about a half.

Students are not required to group electives into a major. Instead, they are encouraged to select electives that best suit their backgrounds and career interests. However, 19 areas lead to specialisations, and students can also develop a formal concentration in a functional programme area, completing a graduate diploma programme concurrently with a degree programme, or taking a specialised degree programme such as Master of Public Administration.

Schulich's part-time MBA has the same curriculum as the full-time version and it is possible to switch between the two. Students with a business degree can take an accelerated track and there are also opportunities for exchanges during MBA 2 (the equivalent of the second year of the full-time programme). The part-time programme typically takes a minimum of 40 months over 10 consecutive terms or a maximum of 72 months over 18 terms. It can be studied at the main campus or at the school's downtown campus in central Toronto (but only core courses are taught there). In September 2004 Schulich launched a weekend version of the part-time programme. Students attend classes on alternate weekends (Saturdays and Sundays 9.30 am–12.30 pm and 2–5 pm) at the new Seymour campus building.

The International MBA (IMBA) builds on the general MBA but includes specialist areas such as regional studies, languages and an overseas internship.

Schulich also runs a joint Executive MBA, the Kellogg–Schulich Executive MBA. This is a two-year part-time sponsored programme with classes on alternate weekends. Graduates receive a Kellogg–Schulich EMBA degree and become alumni of both Northwestern and York universities.

	Full-time MBA
Student rating of programme	4.3 (31)
Number of overseas exchange programmes	148 (31)
Number of languages on offer	>5 (1)

Students

	Full-time MBA
Annual intake	314
Applicants:places	5:1
Percentage of women students	34 (28)
Percentage of foreign students	70 (38)
Average GMAT score	660 (43)
Average number of months' work experience	84 (24)
Age range of students	26-35
Average age	30
Student rating of culture and classmates	3.7 (96)

Student profile (full time)

- ■ EU
- ■ Non-EU Europe
- ■ North America
- ■ Other Americas
- ■ Asia/Australasia
- ■ Middle East
- ■ Other

Recruiters/careers service

	Full-time MBA
Number of industry sectors that recruited graduates	8 (1)
Percentage of graduates in jobs 3 months after graduation	87 (17)
Percentage of graduates finding jobs through careers services	87 (23)
Student rating of careers service	3.6 (47)
Post-MBA salary, US$	67,000 (85)
Percentage increase in salary	103 (7)
Principal recruiters of graduates	CIBC & CIBC , TD Bank Financial Group, IBM

Cost

	Full-time MBA
Application fees	C$125 (US$89)
Programme fees	C$50,000 (US$35,714)
Comments	International student fees
Accommodation costs (on campus, per year)	C$10,000 (US$7,143)
Accommodation costs (off campus, per year)	C$12,500 (US$8,929)
Financial aid available	C$4,800,000 (US$3,428,571)
Type of aid available	Grants, scholarships, awards, bursaries, interest-free loans, graduate assistanceships
Criteria on which aid is granted	Academic merit, demonstrated financial need

Accreditation

None

Application details

	Full-time MBA
Application deadline	March 1st
Programme dates	Jan start, 16 months
Admission requirements	First degree; at least 2 years' work experience; GMAT; TOEFL or IELTS if first language not English; 2 references; 5 essays; laptop; one-third of applicants are interviewed; random application audits are carried out

Executive education

Schulich offers a huge range of open-enrolment and e-learning executive education programmes as well as customised in-company programmes.

Student/alumni quotes

"The environment (building) and faculty are world class but the main reason for attending Schulich is the quality of the student body."

"Schulich has a vast number of scholarships, awards and financial programmes to help students finance their MBA. I found I was easily able to support myself and then double my salary when I graduated. It was money well spent."

"The grading system placed everyone around the same B- to B+ range. Exceptional efforts would earn you a B+ and minimal effort would earn you a B-. It is not an environment that rewards effort and creativity."

Appendix
Comparative tables

Comparative data, full-time programmes

School	Key data				Admissions requirements	
	Average number of months' work experience of students	Average GMAT score	Post-MBA salary	Percentage of faculty with a PhD	Number of years' work experience required	Minimum GMAT score required
American (Kogod)	60	590	62,403	95	2	n/a
Arizona (Eller)	42	639	65,171	95	2	n/a
Ashridge	120	580	177,049	35	3	550
Aston	90	620	90,164	79	3	550
Australian GSM	60	654	78,064	98	2	550
Bath	96	580	88,505	79	3	n/a
Birmingham	84	n/a	85,188	60	5	n/a
Bocconi	54	670	80,682	80	n/a	n/a
Bradford	96	590	57,377	70	3	580
Brandeis	48	600	64,600	85	2	500
British Columbia (Sauder)	84	637	53,250	85	3	n/a
Brunel	90	n/a	n/a	73	3	560
Calgary (Haskayne)	72	632	52,889	82	3	550
California at Berkeley (Haas)	60	700	84,345	98	n/a	n/a
California at Davis	60	636	71,000	100	n/a	n/a
Cambridge (Judge)	72	680	85,246	92	3	n/a
Cape Town	84	580	n/a	60	3	550
Carnegie Mellon	60	681	80,000	97	n/a	n/a
Case Western Reserve (Weatherhead)	54	615	61,200	96	2	n/a
Chicago	59	690	85,000	97	n/a	n/a
China Europe International Business School	71	669	9,029	67	2	n/a
Chinese University of Hong Kong	62	618	25,475	94	n/a	n/a
City (Cass)	84	630	95,007	83	3	600
Columbia	54	709	89,091	98	n/a	n/a
Concordia (Molson)	70	666	40,621	96	2	600
Cornell (Johnson)	60	672	83,300	94	n/a	n/a
Cranfield	96	670	91,803	58	3	600
Curtin	n/a	n/a	n/a	n/a	3	550
Dartmouth (Tuck)	60	697	86,736	96	n/a	n/a
Dublin (Trinity)	84	630	90,909	96	3	520
Duke (Fuqua)	68	705	85,000	91	5	n/a
Durham	108	600	73,643	89	3	600
EADA	48	550	55,909	36	3	550
Edinburgh	96	n/a	86,721	85	4	n/a
Emory (Goizueta)	60	674	75,068	93	1	n/a
ENPC	72	600	54,811	71	3	600
ESADE	61	660	79,407	71	2	n/a
ESCP-EAP	72	590	76,617	95	3	n/a

	Class characteristics				Programme fees	
Ratio of applicants to places	Student intake	Average age	Age range	Percentage women students	Programme fees	Comments
6:1	78	27	24-30	40	US$25,766	Per year
5:1	64	27	24-30	19	US$22,828	Per year. Fee for Arizona students is US$13,848
3:1	17	32	29-41	12	£29,500 (US$48,361)	
9:1	30	30	27-36	38	£18,380 (US$30,131)	Total programme
2:1	89	30	26-35	25	A$56,280 (US$36,545)	Total programme. Fee for Australian students is A$49,140.
5:1	51	30	25-36	48	£20,000 (US$32,787)	
8:1	134	30	26-38	43	£12,500 (US$20,492)	£13,800 for non-EU students
5:1	138	29	26-33	22	€29,300 (US$33,295)	
8:1	80	29	24-36	28	£17,500 (US$28,689)	Per year
3:1	25	27	24-31	50	US$30,450	
6:1	106	31	27-32	35	C$36,000 (US$25,714)	Total programme
4:1	40	32	26-42	n/a	£13,300 (US$21,803)	Total programme
2:1	81	30	23-46	36	C$22,500 (US$16,072)	Per year. Fee for Canadian students is C$11,250
16:1	241	29	23-38	27	US$33,020	Fee for California students is US$20,774
8:1	57	29	25-34	40	US$16,667	Per year
6:1	104	30	26-34	34	£23,000 (US$37,705)	Total programme
2:1	79	31	25-38	n/a	R80,000 (US$10,582)	Fee for non-African students is $US22,000
7:1	236	27	24-32	22	US$37,000	
4:1	112	27	23-33	28	US$30,000	Per year
n/a	526	29	25-32	29	US$34,400	
6:1	112	30	26-33	33	US$25,000	Total programme. Fee for Mainland Chinese students is Rmb138,000
4:1	55	27	23-32	35	US$17,890	
n/a	63	n/a	25-35	21	£22,000 (US$36,066)	
n/a	517	28	25-31	31	US$34,404	Per year
6:1	66	30	25-33	32	C$27,000 (US$19,285)	Total programme. Fee for Canadian students is C$10,000. Fee for Quebec residents is C$5,500
n/a	273	28	24-33	27	US$34,400	Per year
3:1	136	32	27-36	16	£25,000 (US$40,984)	Total programme
1:1	20	33	26-48	n/a	A$32,000 (US$20,779)	Fee for Australian students is A$24,000
10:1	241	28	25-31	28	US$36,390	Per year
4:1	25	31	28-40	22	€20,500 (US$23,295)	
8:1	405	28	27-33	31	US$33,500	
10:1	67	30	25-38	36	£16,000 (US$26,230)	Total programme. Fee for non-EU students is £18,000.
5:1	95	27	23-38	35	€20,500 (US$23,295)	
5:1	100	31	26-37	27	£21,400 (US$35,082)	Total programme
8:1	157	28	25-32	22	US$32,096	Per year
4:1	42	30	22-43	38	€28,000 (US$31,818)	Per year. Fee for company-sponsored students is €38,000
4:1	115	28	25-32	28	€22,750 (US$25,852)	Per year
7:1	31	30	25-35	32	€30 (US$34)	

Comparative data, full-time programmes continues

School	Key data				Admissions requirements	
	Average number of months' work experience of students	Average GMAT score	Post-MBA salary	Percentage of faculty with a PhD	Number of years' work experience required	Minimum GMAT score required
ESSEC	12	668	48,932	98	1	600
Florida (Warrington)	54	645	62,000	95	5	n/a
Georgetown (McDonough)	60	660	75,664	95	2	n/a
Georgia (Terry)	53	659	68,170	87	2	n/a
Glasgow	48	n/a	85,188	87	3	n/a
Harvard	48	707	94,308	98	n/a	n/a
HEC, Paris	72	660	93,436	75	2	600
Helsinki	60	555	65,227	80	2	500
Henley	120	n/a	127,869	61	5	n/a
Heriot Watt	72	n/a	n/a	67	3	n/a
Hong Kong UST	60	633	45,154	100	1	n/a
Hong Kong BS	84	610	15,942	92	3	550
Hult	96	580	72,000	67	0	n/a
IE	66	670	56,818	82	5	n/a
IESE	56	685	97,492	99	5	n/a
Illinois at Urbana-Champaign	52	648	73,859	100	n/a	n/a
IMD	84	680	123,000	95	3	n/a
Imperial (Tanaka)	76	620	90,164	91	3	600
Indian Institute (Ahmedabad)	12	n/a	33,439	96	n/a	720
Indiana (Kelley)	55	651.5	74,050	76	n/a	n/a
INSEAD	72	707	88,068	98	n/a	n/a
Institut d'Etudes Politiques	72	616	87,007	40	3	550
International University of Japan	60	592	60,366	53	n/a	n/a
Iowa (Tippie)	40	638	65,000	94	2	n/a
Lancaster	84	620	78,689	72	3	600
Leeds	72	n/a	73,770	81	3	n/a
London	72	684	92,566	99	n/a	n/a
London, Royal Holloway	84	n/a	n/a	n/a	3	n/a
E.M. Lyon	60	610	61,364	81	3	550
Maastricht	n/a	n/a	n/a	n/a	3	500
Macquarie	144	n/a	85,416	87	5	n/a
Manchester	84	615	83,607	80	3	n/a
Maryland (Smith)	62	656	75,799	95	n/a	n/a
MIT (Sloan)	54	710	88,217	100	n/a	n/a
McGill	53	640	52,857	93	2	570
Melbourne	70	627	66,883	97	2	550
Michigan	60	692	85,000	100	2	n/a
Minnesota	49	656	76,306	95	n/a	n/a
Monaco	60	570	79,545	50	2	n/a

	Class characteristics				Programme fees	
Ratio of applicants to places	Student intake	Average age	Age range	Percentage women students	Programme fees	Comments
7:1	615	23	20-30	46	€7,800 (US$8,864)	
5:1	84	27	24-32	23	US$23,861	
8:1	252	29	24-29	30	US$30,888	Per year
10:1	49	26.9	23-32	22	US$17,820	
10:1	50	30	26-40	37	£14,500 (US$23,770)	Fee for EU students is £12,500
9:1	893	26	24-30	35	US$35,600	
5:1	201	30	27-34	17	€35,000 (US$39,773)	Total programme
2:1	58	31	26-41	28	€18,000 (US$20,455)	Total programme
2:1	33	34	31-47	26	£33,000 (US$54,098)	
7:1	50	28	24-37	n/a	£13,185 (US$21,615)	Total programme
5:1	50	27.5	24-33	48	US$25,900	Total programme
4:1	40	28	25-36	45	US$21,350	Total programme
3:1	42	32	25-40	22	US$50,000	
4:1	208	30	27-34	38	€36,900 (US$41,932)	
8:1	202	28	26-30	28	€56,700 (US$64,432)	
5:1	173	27	24-33	29	US$23,100	
7:1	89	30	28-33	20	Swfr75,000 (US$55,556)	
5:1	100	30	25-36	34	£22,000 (US$36,066)	
373:1	258	23	21-25	13	Rs100,000 (US$2,147)	Per year
7:1	250	30	27-35	26	US$24,200	Per year
4:1	839	29	23-35	19	€43,500 (US$49,432)	
3:1	34	31	27-33	26	€22,000 (US$25,000)	
55:1	54	28	24-34	16	¥1,900,000 (US$16,385)	
3:1	87	28	24-33	21	US$10,500	Fee for non-US students is US$19,362
8:1	40	29	24-34	52	£16,500 (US$27,049)	
10:1	95	30	25-37	30	£17,500 (US$28,689)	Total programme. Fee for EU students is £15,500
6:1	303	28	26-31	24	£41,970 (US$68,803)	Total programme
9:1	42	30	25-41	n/a	£11,450 (US$18,770)	Fee for non-EU students is £12,600
3:1	72	31	27-36	39	€28,000 (US$31,818)	Total programme
6:1	30	30	24-45	n/a	€10,800 (US$12,273)	
2:1	113	34	28-40	38	A$44,800 (US$29,090)	Fee for Australian students is A$42,400
4:1	127	29	25-35	29	£25,500 (US$41,803)	Fee for non-EU students is £29,500
8:1	160	28	25-33	35	US$17,223	Per year
8:1	408	28	25-32	26	US$37,050	
6:1	136	28	25-34	31	C$20,000 (US$14,286)	Per year. Fee for Canadian students is C$4,173; fee for Quebec students is C$1,668
4:1	126	29	25-34	25	A$48,000 (US$31,169)	
8:1	419	28	25-32	26	US$36,688	Per year
6:1	213	28	25-32	24	US$28,685	Per year
4:1	36	28	24-35	55	€21,300 (US$24,205)	

Comparative data, full-time programmes continues

| School | Key data | | | | Admissions requirements | |
	Average number of months' work experience of students	Average GMAT score	Post-MBA salary	Percentage of faculty with a PhD	Number of years' work experience required	Minimum GMAT score required
Monash	108	640	90,909	94	4	n/a
Nanyang	60	651	37,632	92	2	600
Singapore	60	662	39,714	96	2	600
New York (Stern)	54	700	83,439	99	n/a	n/a
Newcastle	72	n/a	77,571	83	3	550
NIMBAS	84	640	92,500	100	3	600
North Carolina (Kenan-Flagler)	60	671	77,788	94	2	n/a
Northwestern (Kellogg)	62	703	88,000	99	n/a	n/a
Norwegian School of Management BI	72	600	85,206	40	3	600
Notre Dame (Mendoza)	54	664	70,245	90	n/a	500
Nottingham	84	600	77,049	76	4	600
Nyenrode	60	570	61,868	78	2	500
Ohio (Fisher)	51	670	75,985	90	n/a	n/a
Otago	n/a	n/a	n/a	n/a	3	550
Oxford, (Saïd)	72	692	103,279	90	2	n/a
Penn State (Smeal)	60	653	84,857	100	2	n/a
Pennsylvania (Wharton)	73	713	85,000	100	n/a	n/a
Pittsburgh (Kat)	36	635	64,000	93	2	n/a
Purdue (Krannert)	49	659	78,120	97	n/a	n/a
Queen's	72	684	57,143	90	2	600
Queensland	n/a	n/a	n/a	n/a	2	n/a
Rice (Jones)	48	625	76,745	98	n/a	n/a
Rochester (Simon)	72	647	70,824	89	n/a	n/a
Rotterdam (Erasmus)	68	630	79,545	74	n/a	n/a
Sheffield	60	600	85,188	75	3	600
Solvay	60	580	67,001	91	2	580
South Carolina (Moore)	48	630	61,500	85	2	580
Southampton	120	n/a	n/a	80	2	n/a
Southern California (Marshall)	60	689	70,979	79	n/a	n/a
Southern Methodist (Cox)	60	665	69,407	91	2	n/a
Stanford	50	716	96,000	99	n/a	n/a
Strathclyde	92	590	98,361	53	3	550
Texas at Austin (McCombs)	60	677	79,787	90	2	0
Theseus	96	620	90,909	14	3	550
Thunderbird (Garvin)	66	600	60,111	93	2	n/a
UCLA (Anderson)	54	705	85,000	100	n/a	n/a
Vanderbilt (Owen)	54	644	70,097	91	n/a	n/a
Virginia (Darden)	72	678	90,180	97	2	n/a

	Class characteristics				Programme fees	
Ratio of applicants to places	Student intake	Average age	Age range	Percentage women students	Programme fees	Comments
7:1	152	32	27-36	n/a	A$44,000 (US$28,571)	Total programme. Fee for Australian students is A$36,800
5:1	73	28	24-35	04	S$24,000 (US$13,793)	Total programme
11:1	84	30	24-36	24	S$24,000 (US$13,793)	
11:1	393	27	25-30	37	US$32,400	
15:1	27	30	24-53	48	f14,175 (US$23,238)	
3:1	42	32	26-39	39	€26,000 (US$29,545)	
8:1	264	28	25-33	27	US$31,980	Per year
10:1	519	28	n/a	28	US$34,314	Per year
5:1	28	30	26-37	11	Nkr199,400 (US$28,164)	
6:1	129	27	24-32	19	US$30,215	Per year
n/a	84	31	27-39	32	£16,500 (US$27,049)	Total programme. Fee for EU students is £15,500
3:1	39	29	25-32	33	€28,500 (US$32,386)	Total programme
6:1	125	27	23-32	25	US$24,846	Fee for Ohio students is US$13,365
2:1	17	28	25-36	n/a	US$25,500	Total programme. Fee New Zealand students is NZ$22,500
4:1	167	29	25-34	21	£23,000 (US$37,705)	
6:1	103	28	24-33	29	US$24,796	Per year. Fee for Pennsylvania students is US$14,500
9:1	892	28	26-32	33	US$35,203	
4:1	164	30	23-49	25	US$39,693	Fee for Pennsylvania students is US$24,595
7:1	160	28	24-34	21	US$24,988	Per year
4:1	74	31	24-43	20	C$51,000 (US$36,429)	Total programme
4:1	78	32	25-45	n/a	A$34,400 (US$22,338)	Total programme
4:1	166	28	25-31	31	US$31,746	
n/a	203	29	25-35	22	US$33,720	Per year
4:1	158	29	25-34	17	€34,000 (US$38,636)	
8:1	73	28	24-37	42	£12,000 (US$19,672)	Fee for EU students is £8,500
4:1	55	28	23-48	44	€16,000 (US$18,182)	
3:1	128	28	24-31	27	US$47,000	Total programme
14:1	62	33	28-45	n/a	£12,875 (US$21,107)	
8:1	262	28	26-32	31	US$32,175	Per year
4:1	79	28	25-32	24	US$31,204	
14:1	374	n/a	n/a	35	US$37,998	Per year
5:1	64	31	26-40	27	£17,300 (US$28,261)	Total programme
5:1	387	28	25-32	24	US$27,599	Per year. Fee for Texas students is US$13,063; fee for other US students is US$26,953
4:1	33	33	28-36	25	€23,500 (US$26,705)	Total programme
2:1	320	30	25-35	27	US$14,648	Per trimester
11:1	333	27	23-37	30	US$29,218	Per year. Fee for California students is US$16,973
5:1	209	28	25-33	25	US$30,345	
11:1	316	28	25-32	27	US$35,000	Per year

Comparative data, full-time programmes continues

School	Key data				Admissions requirements	
	Average number of months' work experience of students	Average GMAT score	Post-MBA salary	Percentage of faculty with a PhD	Number of years' work experience required	Minimum GMAT score required
Vlerick Leuven Gent	96	634	80,682	98	3	550
Wake Forest (Babcock)	43	642	71,000	93	n/a	n/a
Warwick	78	620	109,977	84	3	n/a
Washington in St Louis (Olin)	60	650	75,000	91	5	n/a
Western Ontario (Ivey)	60	662	55,511	90	2	600
William & Mary	72	623	64,000	n/a	2	n/a
Wisconsin-Madison	51	662	68,852	100	2	n/a
Wits	84	n/a	n/a	16	3	560
Yale	60	703	82,500	98	n/a	n/a
York (Schulich)	84	660	67,000	99	2	600

Class characteristics					Programme fees	
Ratio of applicants to places	Student intake	Average age	Age range	Percentage women students	Programme fees	Comments
6:1	33	32	26-38	21	€11,500 (US$13,068)	Total programme
5:1	105	26	23-30	27	US$28,000	Per year
4:1	98	30	26-36	22	£23,700 (US$38,852)	
7:1	134	28	24-34	24	US$33,000	
4:1	231	29	24-46	21	C$56,000 (US$40,000)	
n/a	81	28	24-32	28	US$23,362	Fee for Virginia students is US$11,860
4:1	118	28	23-32	33	US$49,004	Fee for Wisconsin students is US$18,128
3:1	60	31	24-40	n/a	R60,000 (US$7,937)	
9:1	239	n/a	n/a	31	US$35,000	
5:1	314	30	26-35	34	C$50,000 (US$35,714)	

Comparative data, part-time programmes

School	Programme	Key data		
		Average number of months' work experience of students	Average GMAT score	Percentage of faculty with a PhD
American (Kogod)	Part-time MBA	72	570	95
Arizona (Eller)	Eller Working Professionals MBA	60	557	95
Aston Business School	MBA (part time on-campus)	120	n/a	79
Bath	The Bath MBA Modular Programme	120	n/a	79
British Columbia (Sauder)	MBA Part time program	96	626	85
California at Berkeley (Haas)	Evening & Weekend MBA	91	690	98
California at Davis	MBA for Working Professionals	88	617	100
Cape Town	Part-time MBA	96	500	60
Case Western Reserve (Weatherhead)	The Evening MBA	n/a	578	96
Chicago	Evening MBA	73	n/a	97
Chicago	Weekend MBA	70	n/a	97
Chinese University of Hong Kong	MBA (Evening and Weekend Modes)	78	600	94
Curtin	Part-time MBA	132	610	80
Durham	Part-time MBA	168	n/a	89
Edinburgh	Part-time MBA	118	n/a	85
Emory (Goizueta)	Evening MBA	72	680	93
ENPC	Part-Time MBA in International Business	72	600	71
ESADE	Part-time MBA	60	n/a	71
Florida (Warrington)	Working Professional Programs	66	620	95
Glasgow	Part-time MBA	108	n/a	87
Helsinki	International Part-time MBA	120	580	80
Heriot Watt	Part-time MBA	144	n/a	n/a
Hong Kong BS	Part-time MBA	100	600	92
Hong Kong UST	Part-time MBA	84	593	100
Indiana (Kelley)	Evening MBA	60	630	76
Iowa (Tippie)	MBA for Professionals and Managers	77	565	94
Macquarie	Part-time MBA	144	n/a	87
Maryland (Smith)	Part-time MBA	68	616	95
McGill	Part-time MBA	72	635	93
Melbourne	Part-time MBA	84	616	97
Michigan	Evening MBA	72	653	100
Minnesota (Carlson)	Part-time MBA	72	600	95
Monaco	MBA - 22 Month Option	60	540	50
Monash	Part-time MBA	108	640	n/a
Nanyang	Part-time MBA	96	625	92
New York (Stern)	The Langone Program: A Part-Time MBA for Working Professionals	60	673	99
NIMBAS	Two-year Part-time and Modular MBA	96	640	100
Northwestern (Kellogg)	The Managers' Program (TMP)	84	690	99

Admissions requirements			Class characteristics				Programme fees	
Number of months' work experience required	Minimum GMAT score required	Ratio of applicants to places	Student intake	Average age	Age range	Percentage women students	Programme fees	Comments
24	n/a	3:1	40	31	25-34	43	US$930 (US$930)	Per credit hour
24	n/a	1:1	58	29	26-34	24	US$15,000	Per year
36	n/a	2:1	25	32	26-40	20	£12,860 (US$21,082)	Total programme
36	n/a	2:1	39	34	26-46	28	£20,250 (US$33,197)	Based on three year progression
36	0	69:1	45	33	28-41	36	C$36,000 (US$25,714)	Total programme
n/a	n/a	3:1	234	32	24-48	24	US$1,800 (US$1,800)	Per unit
n/a	n/a	2:1	83	31	26-38	22	US$39,840	Total programme
36	550	2:1	34	33	27-38	32	R44,000 (US$5,820)	Per year
24	n/a	1:1	99	28	23-35	28	US$3,698	Per course
n/a	n/a	n/a	384	30	25-36	25	US$3,440	Per course
n/a	n/a	n/a	112	30	25-40	19	US$3,440	Per course
36	n/a	5:1	129	30	26-36	38	US$25,730	
36	550	n/a	370	36	26-60	35	A$32,000 (US$20,779)	Fee for Australian students is A$24,000
36	n/a	2:1	45	35	28-42	29	£11,950 (US$19,590)	
48	n/a	3:1	50	32	27-41	32	£13,000 (US$21,311)	Total programme
72	n/a	2:1	66	28	25-35	8	US$20,271	Per year
36	600	1:1	2	30	29-32	50	€34,000 (US$38,636)	Fee for company-sponsored students is €42,000
36	n/a	3:1	120	29	26-35	20	€38,000 (US$43,182)	Total programme
24	n/a	2:1	171	29	26-33	27	US$25,666	Total programme
36	n/a	5:1	25	35	27-48	47	£5,000 (US$8,197)	Per year
36	500	2:1	27	35	28-46	15	€23,000 (US$26,136)	
36	n/a	3:1	34	34	24-46	24	£13,185 (US$21,615)	Total programme
36	550	8:1	65	31	25-42	38	US$24,230	
36	n/a	3:1	122	30	26-35	44	US$25,900	Total programme
24	n/a	2:1	120	29	24-35	25	US$18,870	Total programme
36	n/a	n/a	220	28	25-35	31	US$425	Per semester hour of credit
60	n/a	2:1	306	34	28-40	38	A$42,400 (US$27,532)	
n/a	n/a	2:1	370	29	25-35	29	US$803	Per credit
24	570	3:1	64	30	25-36	23	C$139 (US$99)	Per credit, Candian students; fee for Quebec students is C$56
24	550	1:1	100	30	25-36	31	A$48,000 (US$31,169)	Total programme
24	n/a	1:1	231	30	25-35	23	US$966	Per credit
24	n/a	1:1	471	28	24-36	33	US$750	Per credit
24	n/a	2:1	6	27	24-30	80	€1,150 (US$1,307)	Per course
48	n/a	7:1	152	32	27-36	42	A$36,800 (US$23,896)	Total programme
24	600	3:1	49	34	28-40	36	S$28,000 (US$16,092)	Total programme
n/a	n/a	3:1	384	28	24-32	33	US$1,190	Per credit
36	600	3:1	96	34	27-46	22	€15,750 (US$17,898)	Per year
n/a	n/a	3:1	385	29	n/a	32	US$3,204	Per credit

Comparative data, part-time programmes continued

School	Programme	Key data		
		Average number of months' work experience of students	Average GMAT score	Percentage of faculty with a PhD
Nottingham	Part-time MBA	108	600	76
Ohio (Fisher)	Part-time MBA	67	629	90
Pittsburgh (Katz)	Part-time MBA	66	570	93
Queensland	Part-time MBA	96	n/a	n/a
Rochester (Simon)	Part-time MBA	60	590	89
Singapore	Part-time MBA	84	633	96
Solvay	Part-time MBA	96	610	91
South Carolina (Moore)	Professional MBA	67	589	85
Southern California (Marshall)	MBA for Professionals & Managers	64	622	79
Southern Methodist (Cox)	Professional MBA	60	600	91
Texas at Austin (McCombs)	Evening MBA	72	664	90
UCLA (Anderson)	Fully Employed MBA	72	664	100
Wake Forest (Babcock)	Evening MBA Program - Charlotte	90	n/a	93
Wake Forest (Babcock)	Evening MBA Program - Winston-Salem	74	n/a	93
Wake Forest (Babcock)	Saturday MBA Program - Charlotte	70	n/a	93
Warwick	MBA by Evening Study	102	n/a	84
Washington in St Louis (Olin)	PMBA	60	601	91
William & Mary	Evening MBA	84	613	n/a
Wisconsin-Madison	Evening MBA	63	600	100
Wits	Part-time MBA	96	16	n/a

Comparative data, distance learning programmes

School	Programme	Key data		
		Average number of months' work experience of students	Average GMAT score	Percentage of faculty with a PhD
Aston	MBA (part time off-campus)	120	n/a	79
Bradford	Distance Learning MBA	96	n/a	70
Carnegie Mellon (Tepper)	Flex Mode MBA	48	643	97
Curtin	Distance Learning MBA	108	610	80
Durham	Distance Learning MBA	156	n/a	89
Florida (Warrington)	Internet MBA	72	610	95
Henley	Distance Learning MBA	120	n/a	61
Heriot Watt	Distance Learning MBA	144	n/a	67
IE	International Executive MBA	85	670	82
Manchester	Distance Learning MBA	120	n/a	80
Open	Master of Business Administration	144	n/a	40
Warwick Business School	Distance Learning MBA	72	n/a	84